A PHILOSOPHY
OF RELIGION

Robert Leet Patterson

A PHILOSOPHY
OF RELIGION

1970
DUKE UNIVERSITY PRESS
DURHAM, N.C.

PRINTED IN THE   UNITED STATES OF AMERICA
BY THE KINGSPORT PRESS, INC.

To My Friends and Former Colleagues in
the Department of Philosophy,
Duke University

PREFACE

An initial task confronts us at the outset of our inquiry, that of delimiting our field. It is notoriously a difficult one; so difficult that, were it possible, I would feign spare both the reader and myself the effort involved. But, for reasons which will speedily become apparent, I am convinced that this course is not feasible, that, if we seek to evade the issue, we shall but wander in the dark. Yet, if this matter is to be gone into at all, it must be done thoroughly. This I have tried to do, with what success the reader must judge. I can only hope that, if he have the patience to follow me, he will feel that the effort has been worthwhile.

In the following pages I present a systematic exposition of my own views with respect to the fundamental problems of philosophy, and, in so doing, I wish to acknowledge the manifold obligations which I have incurred in forming them. The influence of McTaggart is practically ubiquitous. I owe a vast deal to G. Dawes Hicks, and much also to J. S. Mackenzie, Samuel Alexander, G. E. Moore, J. B. Pratt, C. J. Ducasse, Wilbur M. Urban, and Arthur O. Lovejoy. Among living thinkers I owe most to my dear friend, Dr. S. V. Keeling, having profited more than I can say from our innumerable conversations. To Professors C. D. Broad, C. A. Campbell, Brand Blanshard, to Dr. A. C. Ewing, and to Lord Russell, I am also heavily indebted. I am likewise under great obligation to my friends and former colleagues, Professor Charles A. Baylis and Professor Romane L. Clark, for reading the manuscript of this book, and for their very helpful comments and criticisms.

CONTENTS

Book I. RELIGION

Book II. PHILOSOPHY

Book III. THE PROBLEM OF GOD

BOOK I

RELIGION

THE DEFINITION OF RELIGION

THE PROBLEM FORMULATED

Anyone who makes bold to treat of the philosophy of religion is immediately confronted by two crucial and inescapable questions to which he must endeavor to return satisfactory and defensible answers: What is religion? and What is philosophy? Let us take the first question first.

Shall we begin by attempting to define religion? Any definition, it may be urged, should be given at the end, and not at the beginning, of our inquiry. And this is doubtless true, if what we have in mind be a normative definition. Yet must we not start with some descriptive definition in order to make clear what we are talking about? No sooner is this question asked, however, than another question arises. Is such an undertaking feasible? The multitudinous definitions of religion which have already been advanced, none of which has yet succeeded in satisfying everybody, are like so many skeletons in the desert warning us of the perils in our path. Must we, then, venture upon so hazardous a project? Can we recoil from it without base evasion? Could we, indeed, reconcile ourselves to following the example of Clement C. J. Webb in his *Problems in the Relation of God and Man,* and to echoing his assertion that religion neither requires nor admits of definition,[1] we might well hold ourselves excused from this unwelcome task. It is to be noted, however, that, after this initial disclaimer, Webb at once proceeds to tell us a good deal about the nature of religion, which certainly suggests that he finds some sort of descriptive statement unavoidable.

We might seek, however, further to fortify ourselves in an attitude of non-commitment by appealing to G. Dawes Hicks's careful discussion of the problem in his *Philosophical Bases of Theism.*[2] He is convinced that "to attempt to reach a verbal definition which should set forth the characteristic common to all types of religious belief, is, for the purpose of philosophical treatment, at any rate, a perfectly

1. (London, 1911), pp. 3–5.
2. (London, 1937), pp. 32–36.

futile undertaking." And he gives three reasons in support of this assertion.

In the first place, it is more than doubtful whether any such common characteristic is to be found. At all events, the varieties and
conflicting formulations of it which have from time to time been
found are, to say the least, sufficient to restrain further endeavours
in that direction. In the second place, such a common characteristic, even if it could be detected, would be of so vague and so
colourless a nature as to be virtually destitute of any real significance. What can be made, for instance, of so general and
abstract an assertion as that "religion is man's total response to
his *entire* realized environment." And, in the third place, such a
common characteristic would have to be sought in religions of the
most primitive and superstitious kinds; by thus reducing religion
to its lowest terms, we should be losing its essence and grasping
its wrappings.

This is, indeed, an emphatic warning. What, then, are we to do?
"The fact is," continues Hicks,

that a procedure of this sort is, as Edward Caird and others
have convincingly shown, utterly out of place in dealing with
anything which, like religion, has been, down the ages, undergoing continuous evolution. With respect to whatsoever grows and
develops, it is the higher stages that help us to understand and
gauge aright that which is evinced in the lower. No examination,
be it ever so minute, of the seed or embryo would enable us to
predict what it will in the course of time become, unless we were
already familiar with the distinctive lineaments of the full-grown
plant or animal. Then, doubtless, when we trace back the mature
organism to the germ from which it sprang, a study of the process
of genesis throws a flood of light upon the nature of that which
has ultimately emerged. But the point is that "in the first instance,
at least, we must read development *backward* and not *forward,*
we must find the meaning of the first stage in the last." What,
therefore, we have to look for is not a characteristic common to
every type of religion, but rather a "germinative principle," as it
has been called, underlying all types, a "motive power, working in
the human mind, and essentially bound up with its structure." It
is in their relation to this underlying principle, and not in any
doctrinal or external features which they possess in common, that

religions have their basis of agreement. To a large extent the history of religious beliefs is, indeed, the exhibition of the constant conflict between the imperfections of the concrete imagery which the human mind calls to its aid in representing what it takes to be the divine reality and the demands of the fundamental principle which that imagery embodies, a conflict in and through which the full significance of the principle itself gradually comes to full recognition. The history of religions may, then, be said to be just religion progressively defining itself, and a clear discernment of its essence will be obtained, not by "peering into its cradle and seeking oracles in its infant cries," but by contemplating it in the more mature forms to which it has attained as the outcome of the entire process of its development.

And now we come to what Dawes Hicks obviously regards as the conclusion of the whole matter. "No one, I take it," he declares, "would seriously dispute the statement that the whole trend of the evolution in question has been towards a belief in God as one and not as many, manifesting Himself both in nature and to the mind of man, yet revealing Himself most completely to souls of large spiritual compass and of strenuous moral power."

If we accept this conclusion, what follows? What follows is that we are to regard the theistic religions as representing the culmination of the entire process of the evolution of religion, and then are to conceive of the "germinative principle" in the light of this evaluation. What, then, are we to do with such movements as Hīnayāna Buddhism and Jainism? Are we, in defiance of common usage, to deny them the status of religions? Are they, or are they not, developments of the same germinal principle?

It should, perhaps, be emphasized that at the present stage of our inquiry we are not concerned with the respective truth or falsity of these various systems. Conceivably they may all be false. They cannot, indeed, all be wholly true, since they disagree with one another. But they may all contain both truth and error. It is also antecedently possible that one should be altogether true, and should constitute what has been called the Absolute Religion. Again this stage may not yet have been reached; it may even be unattainable. All these questions are still *sub judice*. Whatever we may be able ultimately to determine with respect to them, they remain open. All that we now seek to know is what religion is.

Dawes Hicks has told us that we must try to discover the "germinal

principle," and he has also told us that this can be done only by
"reading backward" from the "mature organisms" into which it has
developed. But he has also informed us that it is futile to look for
any common characteristic by the possession of which they can be
identified. If the only common characteristic which they do possess
be that of having evolved from the same germ, they might be thus
identified were the source antecedently known; but it is clearly
impossible that the germ should be identified in terms of its evolutes,
unless we know what these evolutes are. In the case of any empirical
investigation, one must know something about something if the investigation is ever to begin at all.

Dawes Hicks, of course, obviously feels that he knows what the
outstanding evolutes are; they are the theistic religions. But how does
he know this? He assumes that no one would dispute his assertion.
But it certainly would be disputed by many in the Orient, and by some
even in the West. His evaluation must be based upon some definite world view. And it is fairly obvious what this world view is;
Dawes Hicks is writing as a Christian for Christians. We, however,
are beginning at the beginning, and are assuming the truth of no
particular world view. We must therefore call in question his right to
make this evaluation. And this leaves us once more in the dark as to
the identity of the evolutes which the "reading backward" process
must take as its point of departure.

We might, of course, imitate the procedure of William James in his
Varieties of Religious Experience and simply state unequivocally at
the outset what we shall take the word "religion" to mean for the
purpose of our subsequent inquiry. This would be to impose what
Professor Richard Robinson has called a stipulative definition. The
nature of the problem before us is now clear. For a stipulative definition constitutes a species of Robinson's "word-thing" [3] definition, which
in turn falls under the head of nominal definition. And the question
which now confronts us is whether we are to attempt to frame a
nominal or a real definition.

To impose a stipulative definition would be the easy course to
take. But the obvious disadvantage will be that we shall thereby lay
ourselves open to the charge of having made of our own interests
and prejudices a Procrustean bed into which the facts are to be
forced, of having made a purely arbitrary decision, dictated merely
by our own preference, which springs from an evaluation that in-

3. *Definition* (New York, 1950), pp. 18–19, 59–92.

volves an entire world view, and that we shall thus actually be framing a normative definition—a type of definition which should come not at the beginning but at the end of our study, and of which the justification should antecedently be made fully explicit.

THE NOTION OF ESSENCE

One of Professor Richard Robinson's objections—perhaps his fundamental objection—to the notion of real definition is that the formulation of it has often been equated with the search for essence.[4] And the doctrine of essence, he tells us, "is now dead among logicians." [5] It has died, one gathers, because of the impossibility of satisfactorily and consistently distinguishing between essence and property, and of accounting for borderline cases which only very imperfectly exemplify the essence.

This is a warning which we might well take to heart. And it is plain that the difficulty which confronts us is twofold. In the first place, we sometimes encounter individuals in the production of which nature seems to have fallen short of its goal, to have failed, as it were, to hit the mark. The most distressing example of such falling short is, of course, a child who is born physically or mentally defective. Such "sports" or "monsters" we are wont to consider as imperfect or faulty exemplifications of the essence of humanity. But, then, the question arises, Is there such a thing as a perfect embodiment of the essence? Is any man, for instance, as devoid of the slightest physical blemish as Absalom was thought to be, or as completely rational as we should all like to be? Is not the essence, after all, something in the nature of an ideal which is only to a greater or lesser degree actually approximated, but never fully attained? But, then, how far may an individual fall short of it and yet be said to exemplify the essence? Among all the possible degrees of failure to approximate where are we to draw the line?

The second difficulty is caused by the proliferation of species. Before the discovery of Australia all swans were thought to be white; now we know that some swans are black. When a child abnormally small is born of American or European parentage, we call it a dwarf; yet the pygmies of Africa, who have reproduced their kind since remote ages, we recognize as a distinct species of humanity, as truly human beings as the long-legged people of the same continent. Sup-

4. *Ibid.*, p. 153.
5. *Ibid.*, p. 155.

pose, however, that we were to find an Ethiopian tribe, such as Sir John Mandeville imagined, who had only one leg; should we, or should we not, classify them as men? The differentiation of species may proceed in opposite directions from a single type, and in the case of extreme types we may find it difficult to discover any significant similarity at all. At what precise point do we pass from genus to genus, or from essence to essence? Where, once more, are we to draw the line?

This twofold difficulty plainly confronts us in the case of religion. When is a particular system of beliefs and practices to be accounted religious, and when is it not? If we attempt to treat religion as a genus of which the various religions are species, we shall find that some of these species possess characteristics so dissimilar that, at first glance, they might be taken to belong to different genera. May not Dawes Hicks be right in suggesting that any common characteristic which we might discover would impress us as relatively insignificant? Let us look this difficulty fairly in the face, for it is something of a hydra, and presents us with one problem after another.

A NEST OF PROBLEMS

In the first place, there is the question as to the distinction between religion and magic. Fortunately it is a question which appears to have been quite satisfactorily answered by previous investigators. Magic, they tell us, is an attempt to dominate spiritual forces, and to subject them to the will of the practitioner; religion is an attempt to order life in accordance with the requirements of these spiritual forces. Again, magic is in general antisocial—it is the affair of the individual sorcerer and his clientele; whereas religion, despite the occasional hermit, is predominantly social. These are facts which have been so firmly established that it is needless for us to dwell upon them. It has, indeed, been pointed out that it is quite possible, at the primitive level, for the same individual to pass in a moment from the religious perspective to that of magic, at one moment to supplicate his fetish and at the next to beat it for refusing to grant his petition. Yet this psychological propinquity of the two perspectives must not blind us to their radical dissimilarity, nor to the depth of the logical abyss between them. And, as we shall see when we come to discuss the problem of origin, it is important to recognize that the view, once widely held, that magic provided the matrix out of which religion developed is now thoroughly discredited, and that if any relation of priority can be established, it will be in favor of religion.

A somewhat similar problem faces us when we seek to determine the relation between religion and superstition. "Superstition" is, indeed, something of a pejorative term; we tend to dismiss as superstitious beliefs which we deem unworthy of serious consideration, such as those which, in our opinion, are outmoded by the advance of knowledge. Thus, from the standpoint of the reductive naturalist, *all* religion is superstition; and many Protestants would doubtless brand with the same term the belief in the efficacy of relics. But although the term, like all terms, may be rightly or wrongly applied, we should, I think, agree that to call a belief superstitious implies that it is ridiculous, or at least indefensible, in the eyes of those competent to judge. Hence we cannot do better than to accept the definition given by Herbert Jennings Rose in his article on the subject in the fourteenth edition of the *Encyclopaedia Britannica*,[6] namely, "the acceptance of beliefs or practices groundless in themselves and inconsistent with the degree of enlightenment reached by the community to which one belongs."

Some beliefs, which we should now call superstitious, at a more primitive level were clearly religious. Thus the Tuatha da Danaan, who were the divinities of ancient Ireland, have sunk to the status of fairies; and the belief in them would generally be regarded as a superstition.[7] Other beliefs, which would ordinarily be included in the same classification, appear to have been suggested by religious beliefs, or derived from them by a process of illegitimate inference, but would never at any period have been ranked among them. Thus the beliefs that Friday is an unlucky day and that thirteen is an unlucky number reputedly owe their origin to the Crucifixion and to the number of persons who took part in the Last Supper; but they are very far from being articles of the Christian faith. Clearly some beliefs will stand on the borderline. We cannot simply contrast beliefs firmly established with those which are wholly groundless. For, as we are well aware, *no* religious beliefs are universally accepted; moreover, what is superstition in one man's eyes may not be so in those of his neighbor. Nor can we place the matter altogether beyond dispute by reference to "competent judges" or "sound evidence," for well-informed and

6. Vol. XXI, 577.
7. It is to be noted that W. Y. Evans-Wentz, in his *Fairy Faith in Celtic Countries* (Oxford, 1911), labored long and hard to rehabilitate it.

intelligent people may differ as to what constitutes competence in a judge or soundness of evidence. Still, if we cannot hope, in the case of every particular belief which plainly belongs in one of these two classes, to assign it to one or the other by a verdict which will be beyond question, we can distinguish satisfactorily enough between the *meanings* which we attach to the contrasted terms. Religious beliefs are those which, at the level of culture at which they are entertained, are intellectually respectable; and superstitious beliefs are those which are not.

Turning again to religion as such, we find ourselves confronted by various problems of a more difficult nature, which I shall now proceed to enumerate. In the first place, it has been reported that certain savage tribes believe both in good and benevolent spirits which, because they are benevolent, can for that very reason safely be ignored, and also in evil and malevolent spirits which, because they are malevolent, are exceedingly dangerous, and which, therefore, the tribe makes every effort to placate. Is this religion?

Professor C. A. Campbell believes that it is not. "The whole object of these cults," he writes,

> is to mollify, by gifts and sacrifices, certain supposed supernatural beings who are conceived to be inherently hostile to man; to be, in fact, "demons" rather than "gods." No doubt devotees of these cults go through elaborate rituals that are externally not easily distinguishable from those of religious worship. But the inner spirit is about as different as well could be. It is one thing to make gifts and sacrifices to a supernatural being in a mood of reverence and love that delights to do him honour. It is quite another thing to make them simply with a view to buying from him immunity from malicious visitations. Adhering to our criterion of correct usage, viz. the *duly considered* linguistic usage of competent persons, I cannot think that the term "religion" is properly applied to organised bribery on a vast scale, even if it be supernatural powers to whom the bribes are offered.[8]

Professor Campbell is certainly right in emphasizing the fact that very different, and even antithetical, psychological attitudes may find expression in very similar ritual acts. This is a very important point, and one which we must keep in mind throughout the following discussion. And he is also, surely, right in his contention that it is in the

8. See his Gifford Lectures entitled *On Selfhood and Godhood* (New York, 1957), p. 242.

light of its "inner spirit" that a claim on the part of any cult to be recognized as genuinely religious must be evaluated. It is entitled, he maintains, to be so recognized only if its object is regarded as "endued with transcendent *worth* or *value*"; and it is in accordance with this principle that he refuses to include demon-worship under the term "religion." In this decision, which is based upon the antithetical character of the attitudes involved, we cannot, I think, decline to concur.

What are we to say, however, of cults which have as their objects beings which are simply indifferent to man but which may be prevailed upon to use their power to benefit their worshippers? "In so far as this, and this alone," writes Professor Campbell,

> is the motive that inspires ritual acts, we come not a step nearer to religion proper. Currying favour with gods is no more a "religious" act than is bribery of demons. Indeed it seems to me that both of these types of ritual show a much closer approximation to magic than to religion. In them as in magic, certain ceremonies are performed whose object is to "work upon" supernatural forces in the service of natural human purposes. There are, of course, significant differences also. One main difference is that, whereas the ritual of the cults aims at making use of supernatural forces through the agency of supernatural beings who are believed to have such forces at their disposal, the ritual of magic is often designed to work *directly* upon the supernatural forces, with no thought of supernatural beings as intermediary. In that respect, since religious worship is normally, and perhaps always, directed to supernatural *beings*, the cults may be said to come a little closer to religion than magic does. But if they come a little closer to religion, they must still be accounted leagues away from it, unless we are prepared to deny a propostion that to me at least seems indubitable, viz. that religion is fundamentally a matter not of overt acts, but of the inner spirit.[9]

In this conclusion Professor Campbell is consistent with his previous decision. Without disputing the justice of his verdict I would point out, however, that it raises a number of difficulties. In the first place, the same power is often ambivalently regarded. It is conceived of as subject to moods; at one moment it is benevolent, and at another, malicious; now it inspires terror, and now hope and confidence. To this

9. *Ibid.*, pp. 242–243.

art and literature bear abundant witness. The gods and goddesses of the *Iliad* and the *Odyssey*, for instance, were motivated by their own passions and interests as well as by a regard for moral principles. If Professor Campbell be right, then, in his view that genuine religion is never found apart from the attribution of moral worth or value to some object, it is clear that religious beliefs are often included in a wider perspective into which enter beliefs which are not religious, and which we should have to describe either as non-religious or as pseudoreligious. There is nothing incredible in this, but if such be the case, it is important to take note of it, and to recognize that the transition can be made in an instant from a religious to a non-religious attitude.

In the second place, what are we to say of a man who worships the Christian God for no higher motive than a desire to escape Hell and to be assured of a happy hereafter? Can we doubt that many men, especially in the so-called age of faith, have lived, if not with unvarying consistency, at least habitually on no higher level than this? The Christian God is, indeed, believed to be "endued with a transcendent worth or value," and in this respect his cult is on a different footing from that of a hostile or ethically neutral power. Yet is worship directed to him for purely prudential reasons morally much superior to efforts to "bribe" or to "curry favour" with such a power? Consider, for instance, the attitude of Locke.

"The philosophers," writes Locke,

showed the beauty of virtue; they set her off so, as drew men's eyes and approbation to her; but leaving her unendowed, very few were willing to espouse her. The generality could not refuse her their esteem and commendation; but still turned their backs on her, and forsook her, as a match not for their turn. But now there being put into the scales on her side "an exceeding and immortal weight of glory," interest is come about to her, and virtue now is visibly the most enriching purchase, and by much the best bargain. That she is the perfection and excellency of our nature; that she is herself a reward, and will recommend our names to future ages, is not all that can now be said of her. It is not strange that the learned heathens satisfied not many with such airy commendations. It has another relish and efficacy to persuade man, that if they live well here, they shall be happy hereafter. Open their eyes upon the endless, unspeakable joys of another life, and their hearts will find something solid and powerful to move them. The view of heaven and hell will cast a slight upon the short pleasures and pains of this present state, and give attractions and encouragements to virtue, which reason and interest, and the care of ourselves, cannot but allow and prefer. Upon this foundation, and upon this only, morality stands firm, and may defy all competition. This makes it more than a name; a substantial good, worth all our aims and endeavours, and thus the Gospel of Jesus Christ has delivered it to us.[10]

One may charitably hope that Locke, in writing these cynical lines, was untrue to his highest self. But is their "inner spirit," as Professor Campbell would say, different from that of a man who believes himself to be making a profitable investment? Are we, or are we not, to dignify such an attitude by applying to it the adjective *religious?* If the answer is to be in the affirmative, we should at least agree, I presume, that it exemplifies a very inferior kind of religion.

And, in the third place, if we assent to Professor Campbell's judgment that, where worth or value is not ascribed to the object of worship, there is no religion, we may find ourselves drawing from it unexpected and rather astonishing inferences. The first step would naturally be to use it as a criterion by which to evaluate the claims of Zurvanism, a cult of considerable historical importance, which gives us a Deity who is wholly beyond good and evil. Of Zurvanism its latest investigator has written as follows: "The general impression is one of gloom. In this life Man must be content with his lot, extinguish his passions, and resign himself to fate. For the rest, he can only know that he will pass on to the 'house of eternity' the fate of whose citizens is utterly unknown; for a 'veil is drawn' over their eternal destiny, and 'Time is and shall be all.' " [11] In this case the "inner spirit" appears to be one of agnostic resignation, rather different from the anxiety to "curry favour" with the supreme power, concerning which Professor Campbell has written so disparagingly. Nonetheless, the absence of worth from the conception of this being would seem to settle the question for those who accept his criterion.

Undeniably Zurvanism does not constitute a "live option" for the average twentieth-century occidental. But the same issue arises nearer home, and its very nearness enables us to see how important it is. The attribution of moral worth to the object of worship is something in

10. *The Reasonableness of Christianity.*
11. Professor R. C. Zaehner, *Zurvan: A Zoroastrian Dilemma* (New York, 1955), p. 272.

which all exponents of the *via negativa*, insofar as they remain consistent and refuse to qualify their assertions, will not permit us to indulge. Consider, for example, the God of Hobbes and the God of Spinoza. Perhaps no one will be shocked if we question the religious character of Hobbes's philosophy, but Spinoza is frequently extolled as an outstanding example of the religious man. Yet Spinoza tells us that the divine and the human intellects have no more in common than have the constellation called "the Dog" and the dog that barks; and the same will hold true of divine and human goodness. Or consider the God of Maimonides, whose influence in orthodox Judaism is comparable to that of Aquinas in Roman Catholicism. Here we have a Deity who stands upon the same moral level as the Gods of Hobbes and Spinoza, a level which is practically identical with that of Zurvan. To this God no positive qualities can be ascribed. The only statements which in their literal sense hold true of him are negative statements. Hence, of the statement that God is good, as Hobbes points out, only three alternative interpretations are permissible. We may take the term "good" in an honorific sense; it is one which it is seemly to use in worship. Or we can take the assertion to mean that God is the cause of good things—as he is also of evil things. Or, lastly, we can ascribe to it the purely negative meaning, God is not evil. Here we have, indeed, a Deity who is "wholly other"; one who, from an axiological point of view, is as neutral as Zurvan.

The majority of Christian and Muslim theologians endeavor to escape the unwelcome consequences of the *via negativa* by introducing—whether consistently or not this is not the place to inquire—a doctrine of analogous predication according to which goodness, and other "perfections," are to be ascribed to God *secundum modum altiorem*, that is, in some higher sense than that in which they can be attributed to any finite intelligence. The believer in this doctrine is thus privileged to "have it both ways." If his opponent point to the problem of evil as a stumbling block for the theist, that opponent will be told that he is picturing God as "a big man," and that this is stupid anthropomorphism. But, let the opponent go on to draw the inference that God is neither good nor evil, and he will at once be informed that by means of the theory of analogous predication it has been shown that God is supremely good, even though this supreme goodness be inconceivable by the human mind.

I have no intention of undertaking at this point to criticize the redoubtable doctrine of analogous predication. That is a task which will confront us later. I would only point out that it is a matter of life and death for the believer in this theory to make it good against all comers, if he is to vindicate his claim to be called religious in Professor Campbell's sense of the word.

And how of Professor Campbell himself? His suprarational theism can be accounted religious only if his symbolic theology, which is professedly based upon a foundation other than the doctrine of analogous predication, prove capable of being successfully defended. For, to one who does not accept it, his suprarational Deity looks as ethically neutral as Zurvan. "To be *supra*-moral," he assures us, "is by no means to be *non*-moral." [12] Unless the soundness of this contention can be established, Professor Campbell will indeed be "hoist with his own petard."

Such are some of the difficulties which confront us as we contemplate the task of framing a definition of religion. But we are not yet at the end of our survey. To the average occidental it may well seem, as it seemed to Dawes Hicks, that the evolution of religion has culminated in the belief in a single personal God and in the immortality of the soul. When we turn our gaze backward, however, and try to place ourselves in the position of the ancient Assyrians, Babylonians, Hebrews, or Homeric Greeks, a very different perspective opens before us. Faith in divine powers, or in a divine power, is, indeed, vivid and strong; but what of the hereafter? Aralu, Sheol, and Hades are regions of gloom and darkness. Postexistence of a sort is not denied; yet the nebulous and phantasmal nature of the sepulchral existence which there awaits the dead might well seem less desirable than absolute annihilation. The efficacy of the gods is confined to this world. They are primarily gods of the tribe, of the nation, or of the πόλις; and although the individual worshipper may hope for their favors, these favors are largely of a material kind— length of days, a multitude of children, deliverance from enemies, rich harvests, wealth, and peace. Hence the outlook is extremely thisworldly, and the Roman principle of *do ut des* is generally accepted as axiomatic.

Somewhat similar, yet exemplifying a more rarified kind of thisworldliness, is the cosmological outlook of Epicurus. For him the human body and soul are composed of atoms which at death are dispersed; hence any postexistence is impossible. The gods, who inhabit the interstellar spaces, are also of atomic structure; but they are

12. *On Selfhood and Godhood*, p. 357.

so constituted as to enjoy enormously long, passionless, and blissful existences. They are utterly unconcerned with man; hence from them there is nothing either to fear or hope for. Yet in the contemplation of their carefree and happy life, so unlike his own, man can take a pure and disinterested pleasure which is the noblest feeling which he is capable of experiencing. Once again, then, with respect to a purely this-worldly outlook, we must repeat our question, Is this religion?

Contrast such a point of view with the faiths and philosophies of India. "All forms of Hinduism," wrote that profound student of comparative religion, the late James Bissett Pratt,

> lay their unfailing and their supreme emphasis upon the soul. Here, I believe, is the central point of them all, here is the fundamental *Credo* which makes Hinduism, in spite of its bewildering sects and branches, in some true sense *one* religion. In their thought of God they vary through all the phases of polytheism, theism, pantheism, and atheism; but in their insistence upon the reality and the supreme importance of the self, and its contrast to the external world of matter or illusion, in this they are at one.[13]

It is precisely this belief in the uncreated and sempiternal soul which, in the case of the great dualisms or pluralisms of India, puts the whole question of theism in a light very different from that in which it appears to the Western mind. The souls of gods (i.e., of exalted spirits existing at a superhuman level), of men, of animals, and of devils are potentially equal, and are alike capable of rising or falling within the structure of the universe. All are bound to the same wheel of birth and death from which all alike need deliverance. It is a strangely "democratic" outlook in a society in which, in the realm of politics, absolute autocracy has been the normal state of affairs.

Let us glance first for a moment at Jainism, which is habitually referred to as a religion. Here we have a system of thought which posits no supreme mind as the controller of the world. The universe is as self-existent as are the souls which it contains. The state of ultimate deliverance, however, which every Jain aspires sooner or later to attain, is one of endless bliss. Freed at last and forever from the grip of Karma, the released soul ascends to the "umbrella" at the summit of the universe where it enters into a state of omniscience. In this emphasis upon the positive character of the supreme and final

13. *Matter and Spirit* (New York, 1922), p. 220.

state the Jain is in full accord with the Christian and the Moslem, although he conceives of it very differently, since its bliss is in no way the consequence of any vision of God.

When we turn to the Nirīśvara Sāṁkhya, however, the perspective changes profoundly. Here there is no ultimate bliss to be attained; there is only a state of complete aloofness and detachment from all spatio-temporal concerns, a state of freedom from pain and sorrow, one of unbroken and negative tranquillity. And the same is the case in the Yoga system, despite its introduction of a supreme Self who is exempt from birth and death, and who disinterestedly proffers his aid to souls seeking deliverance. For fellowship with him is no part of this deliverance; the soul which has escaped from bondage passes at once into a state of tranquil isolation.

In the Nyāya and Vaiśeṣika systems we discover, indeed, a more vigorous theism, for here the supreme Self, Iśvara (the Lord), although still non-creative, functions as a principle of order in the universe; it is he who brings together souls and atoms after their periodic dispersal during the recurrent periods of *pralaya* and initiates a new world process, and it is he who enforces the law of Karma. His soteriological function, however, is identical with that of the Iśvara of the Yoga philosophy; for, although he extends his aid to souls struggling for deliverance, these souls, once delivered, enjoy no communion with him. On the contrary, the state of the soul who has escaped from the wheel of birth and death is one of oblivion so complete and so unbroken that, as Sāṁkara ironically remarked, it has no more consciousness than has a stool.

In the case of Buddhism the situation is much more complicated. As for the Mahāyāna, it may be stated with rough accuracy that here we encounter an impressive recrudescence of monism, with certain concessions to theism and polytheism, and that Nirvāṇa—insofar as it has not been supplanted in the popular mind by the notion of the Pure Land—is clearly conceived of as a positive state. When we turn to the Hīnayāna the situation is less clear. The attitude of Gotama himself seems plainly to have been as non-theistic as that of any Jain or Sāṁkhya; that he conceived of Nirvāṇa as a positive and blissful state is, I think, the view which scholars are tending in increasing numbers to adopt. Later Hīnayānists, however, appear to have been divided upon this very important issue; and it seems clear that some adherents of the Southern School, both in the past and in the present, have equated or do equate Nirvāṇa with annihilation, and that, instead of the unconscious immortality of the Naiyāyikas and the Vaiśeṣikas, these men posit a complete cessation of existence as the ultimate goal to be striven for. In the case of each of these views we encounter a pessimism even more profound than that of the Zurvanist who professes no more than a complete ignorance as to man's destiny. What the occidental materialist or reductive naturalist admits to be a regrettable, although inevitable, calamity is by these thinkers envisaged as something better than conscious existence at its best, so full of inescapable evil do they find life to be.

Nominal versus Real Definition

We have now taken what we term a bird's-eye view of the principal types of belief which have been traditionally associated under the term "religion." Do the extreme dissimilarities which we have noted inhibit us from attempting to formulate a definition? Is it not clear, I ask, that some definition we must have? For, after all, when we discuss religion there are plainly many subjects which will not constitute our primary interest, even though their influence upon religion, or the influence of religion upon them, may awaken in us a derivative and secondary interest. If we devote ourselves to investigating the religion of any people, our basic concern will certainly not be their monetary system, their form of government, their laws of marriage or of inheritance, their military organization, the origin of their language, their architecture, or their means of transport. These are emphatically some of the things which either we should not consider at all or we should touch upon only because of their relation to something else. What is this something else? Obviously there is an area which requires to be delimited and described, even if, like Maimonides' God, it can be described only by saying what it is not.

This is the more needful since the word "religion," like the word "God," is invested with a certain aura of respectability which many thinkers and writers are desperately anxious to turn to their own advantage. So long as a man consent to use the word "religion," whatever sense he may put into it, and however thoroughly he may empty it of its traditional significance, he is entitled, according to their contention, to call himself a religious man, and to hurl the charge of intolerance at anyone who questions his right to do so. Thus many reductive naturalists, in whose thought there is no place either for God or for immortality, who regard man as an accidental by-product of the cosmic process, and whose whole outlook is, in the most extreme sense of the word, this-worldly, nonetheless lay hold upon and proceed to "reinterpret" in conformity with their own views the word "religion." [14] Their conviction seems to be that the hallowed associations which cluster around it pertain to it as a vocable, and not as the bearer of any definite meaning, and hence will continue to accompany it even after the traditional meaning has been totally transformed. Of such a position Professor Roy Wood Sellars' *Religion Coming of Age* is an excellent exposition.

Again the word "religion" is frequently used with very farfetched meanings in which analogy is clearly strained to its utmost limit, and which are yet presumed to be enlightening. Thus we are often informed, and with apparent solemnity, that Bolshevism is a religion. The underlying thought seems to be that religion produces fanatics who are habitually unscrupulous about the use of means, who desire to convert the whole world, and who will impose their views by force where possible, and that, since Bolsheviki display these characteristics, Bolshevism must be accounted a religion. On such occasions the employment of the word has a subtly implied pejorative force. Sometimes, however, it is uttered with an apologetic accent. Thus an esteemed acquaintance has informed me that "music is my religion." Such usage, if taken not in a metaphorical but in a literal sense, is plainly indefensible. Yet, to demonstrate its indefensible character, we must first know what genuine religion is in order to distinguish it from counterfeits; and, unless we can succeed in describing it, we shall find ourselves talking about every subject under heaven. As Professor Campbell has well said, "In point of fact it is usually quite clear in the case of those writers on religion who insist that definition is impossible at the beginning, that they themselves tacitly assume one from the beginning. The working of an implicit definition in their mind reveals itself throughout in their selection of phenomena to be studied as phenomena of religion." [15]

The problem of definition is, then, plainly inescapable. We return, therefore, to our earlier question: Shall we essay to formulate a nominal or a real definition? If we attempt the former, we must suffer our-

14. It seems rather strange that the right to exercise this unlimited license of interpretation should be laid claim to only in the realm of ideas. Any man who undertook to repay a loan in quarters instead of dollars, and who maintained that it was intolerant to dictate in what sense he should interpret the word "dollar," would speedily find himself in trouble. The inference appears to be that the physical world is the "real" world, where definiteness is obligatory, whereas ideas are "unreal" and unimportant, and hence with respect to them complete terminological freedom is the birthright of every individual.

15. *On Selfhood and Godhood,* pp. 233–234.

selves to be guided by common usage. But how shall we distinguish between common and uncommon usage? We can, of course, appeal to the authority of admitted specialists in the field, to the students of anthropology, of ethnology, of sociology, of history, and above all, of comparative religion. But how do these, for their part, manage to distinguish religious from other phenomena? And, even supposing that we find them in complete agreement, have we any right to foist upon them the responsibility for the performance of an undertaking which we dare not attempt ourselves? Moreover, to formulate a nominal definition, we must be able to tell how the word is used. And, to tell how the word is used, we must be able to tell what it stands for, since it is used to stand for, or to mean, something. But what is this except to give a real definition? In other words, is it possible to give a nominal definition without at the same time giving a real definition? Are they not like two sides of the same shield?

Before we answer this question, we shall do well to consider an ominous warning on the part of Professor Robinson. The attempt to define religion is, he suspects, what he calls the "search for a key," [16] that is, "the attempt to find some one fact about x from which everything else that is true of x can be deduced." [17] "What is clear," he writes,

is that such definitions must include, or be preceded by, a legislative nominal element. It is no good looking for a real definition of religion from which to deduce all religious occurrences, until we have subjected the word "religion" to some stipulative redefinition. For the word "religion" as it stands is attached to reality in various ways. Some people exclude morality from religion. Some make morality the whole of religion. It is most unlikely that any definition could generate all the types of occurrence actually covered by the common use of the word, because it is most unlikely that the word covers only one homogeneous field. The definition of triangle generates all the properties of the triangle only because the word "triangle" is formally restricted to the definition given by a deliberate choice which need not coincide with actual usage; and occurrences are not envisaged or referred to except in so far as they may happen to embody the pattern defined. A definition of religion, on the other hand, professes to be about occurrences, about the actual prayer and worship of actual persons. When we are dealing with a common word of wide application, like the word "religion," no real or es-

16. *Definition,* p. 162.   17. *Ibid.,* p. 163.

sential definition of the thing meant is likely to be a true key to the area covered, until this area has been inspected piece by piece, the affinities of its parts ascertained, and the meaning of the word judiciously narrowed and explicitly announced. The physicists and chemists made systematic investigations for many years before reaching their essential definitions of the simpler parts of matter. The anthropologist does the same with religion.

The conclusion is that real definition as a search for a small key to a large area is a possible and valuable activity, but not one to be attempted lightly or hastily, and always requiring to be accompanied by nominal redefinition of the term used.[18]

If we decide, then, to begin, as Professor Robinson has told us to do, with a nominal redefinition—which is to say, with a stipulative definition—in accordance with what principle shall we formulate it? To escape the charge of arbitrariness we must, surely, do one of two things. Either we must suffer ourselves to be guided by the facts, in which case we must know what the relevant facts are, or else we must be guided by the usage of scientific authorities who have already investigated the facts; and then the question how do they know what facts are relevant arises.

Professor Robinson appears to suggest that we ought to analyze the material before us. Of this method of procedure he thinks very highly. "The great advantage of the analytic method," he tells us, "is, of course, that besides letting us know what the word means it also gives us an analysis of the thing, which is a most valuable knowledge." [19] Indeed it is. And it would seem very much like the formulating of a real definition. For it tells us what the thing is, and is not this to define the thing? Professor Robinson hesitates whether or not to qualify his anathema with respect to the use of the phrase "real definition" in this connection but finally decides not to do so, on the ground that there are other uses of the same phrase with which this usage might be confused. It is better, he concludes, simply to call it analysis.

Before we begin our analysis, however, we must get our material together. And how shall we select this material? In our preceding survey of the various types of what has been called religion we have followed the guidance of common usage. But it is possible that common usage may be misleading, and as our analysis proceeds we may find that the material falls apart and that between some of the systems of belief the differences are profound whereas the resemblances are su-

18. *Ibid.*, pp. 164–165.   19. *Ibid.*, p. 97.

perficial, so that to classify them together would be to confuse the issue. In this eventuality should we not be compelled to choose, and, in view of the facts, to restrict the application of the word "religion"? But does not this suggestion bring up again the notion of essence, concerning which Professor Robinson has said so many harsh things?

The notion of essence has, of course, been persistently employed by very many philosophers during a very long period; and this would seem to indicate that, whatever faults may be found with it, it has actually proved useful. It is useful because, as a matter of fact, we do classify things together because of certain characteristics which they have in common. Needless to say, we look for characteristics which are relevant to the purpose of our inquiry. Thus we group medicines together because of their capacity to heal, and weapons because of their capacity to inflict wounds and death. We look also for what we may call basic characteristics, characteristics the possession of which involves that of certain others. In terms of these we classify, dividing entities which possess them from those which do not. If, now, we can find some such characteristic which pertains to all, or to most, of the systems of belief which we have surveyed, we shall at least have something to build on. Such a characteristic may not of itself suffice to establish a definition, but, once found, we may be enabled to associate with it other characteristics, and all these taken together may suffice. And has not Professor Campbell given us a valuable clue by his emphasis upon the "inner spirit" which is the soul both of belief and practice?

"Inner spirit," someone might object, is a vague term. But perhaps it is not so vague as it is elastic, and this elasticity may actually render it helpful. It has reference, shall we say, both to the motivating force and to the purview wherein it operates; the former may vary in intensity and the latter in comprehensiveness. Yet this last consideration need not disquiet us if we be prepared to admit that there are degrees of religion. We must expect, however, to find borderline cases which will be difficult to classify; and, to deal with these, it would seem that we must introduce the notion of a common standard.

At once another challenge confronts us. In doing this shall we not be covertly formulating a normative, rather than a descriptive, definition? Is not this, as Professor Robinson has urged, to conceive of "real definition as the adoption and recommendation of ideals," [20] or as what Professor C. L. Stevenson has called a "persuasive" definition?

20. *Ibid.*, p. 165.

And about persuasive definitions Professor Robinson has harder things to say than he has ever said about essences. "Persuasive definitions," he writes, "aim at altering the meaning of a term without altering its emotional meaning, thus directing attention toward a new object." [21] And this, as we have seen, is precisely what reductive naturalists, such as Professor Sellars, are trying to do; which is one reason why a descriptive definition is needful.

"The habit of evaluating things," observes Professor Robinson,

> is presumably ineradicable from human nature. The habit of trying to get other persons to share our own evaluations is a desirable way of trying to change people's opinions. The argument against it is that it involves error and perhaps also deceit. The only persons who are influenced by a persuasive definition, it may be said, are those who do not realize its true nature, but take it to be what every real definition professes to be, a description of the objective nature of things. A persuasive definition, it may be urged, is at best a mistake and at worst a lie, because it consists in getting someone to alter his evaluations under the false impression that he is not altering his evaluations but correcting his knowledge of the facts.[22]

In this condemnation Professor Robinson concurs, although it is fair to observe that his attitude appears to be influenced to some extent by his conviction that "ethical language is not descriptive but evaluative." [23]

In order to avoid exposing myself to recriminations of this sort I have abstained from offering a stipulative definition, against which similar fulminations would certainly be directed. After all, if religion do constitute a genuine field of inquiry, there must be *some* way of delimiting it, no matter how variegated be the territory which it includes; otherwise we should be dealing with a mere will-o'-the-wisp. As I have already remarked, there are numerous subjects open to investigation which we should never think of including within the sphere of religion. Readers of Moses Maimonides' *Guide for the Perplexed* will recall how he suggests [24] that it is possible to arrive at a

21. *Ibid.*, p. 168. 22. *Ibid.*, pp. 169–170.
23. *Ibid.*, p. 170.
24. (New York, 1904), Part I, chap. lx. This suggestion is, of course, inconsistent with the fundamental contention of the *via negativa*, namely, that *no* positive knowledge of God is possible; for, if by following the *via negativa*, we can arrive at a positive knowledge of God, it will have refuted itself. But this consideration is here irrelevant.

positive knowledge of a particular by stating fully and explicitly what it is not. Fortunately such a roundabout course is unnecessary, for unless we had some knowledge of what the thing is, we could not tell what it is not; and if we do have some positive knowledge, we had best begin by explicating it. I have called attention to the fact that there are some subjects which lie outside the field of religion only to stress the further fact that the field has its limits and that these limits are not altogether unknown to us, however imperfect our knowledge of them may be as yet.

Now there is one characteristic which all the types of so-called religion we have surveyed do have in common, and it has been brought out by the discussion of the relation between religion and magic. They all involve an adjustment, on the part of an individual or of a group of individuals, with respect to some external reality, be that reality the universe as a whole, or some power, or powers, within or above the universe. However this external reality be conceived, there is no attempt to dictate to it or to control it. Here, as we have seen, and as is generally recognized, is the great difference between religion and magic. The magician, in his effort to impose his will upon external reality, resembles the scientist rather than the religious man. Indeed magic may properly be described as a pseudoscience; it is pseudo because it misconceives the situation, because the laws of the universe are not what it takes them to be.

In saying this I would not be understood to assert that the motive of inducing the external power to comply with one's desire is absent from religion; such a statement would be an obvious falsehood. But I would point out that petitioning is not commanding, nor conforming controlling, that there is, as Professor Campbell has said, a profound difference of "inner spirit." In religion subjective compliance comes first, whether or not it issues in a modification of the attitude of its external object. This subjective state of compliance is all-important; and, in the mauger of Professor Robinson, I venture to call it essential. At least it is in virtue of it that we distinguish between religion and magic; it is therefore a characteristic of all forms of religion. Accordingly, in recognizing it as such, we still adhere to objective fact; hence we are still genuinely concerned with a descriptive, and not with an ideal, a persuasive, or a normative, definition.

This process of compliance with, or adjustment to, the dictates of external reality is, as we have observed, compatible with three very different evaluational attitudes. In the first place, the external power may be envisaged as evil, or, to employ more technical language, as endued with negative value. In the second place, it may be regarded as morally indifferent, as axiologically neutral. And in the third place, it may be looked upon as good, as endued with positive value. By this last I do not mean that it must be thought of as personal, although it usually is so, but that it must be believed to possess intrinsic worth and to be capable of satisfying human needs.

At a certain level of culture it is quite possible for the same individual to adopt one of these points of view at one moment, and another at another. It may be thought that the same power is now benevolent, and now indifferent or malevolent. To such psychological fluctuations art and literature bear abundant witness. Yet this in no way blurs the ineradicable distinctions between these three attitudes.

I have suggested that we should follow Professor Campbell in pronouncing the first of these attitudes definitely not religious. It might, perhaps, be urged that in so doing we introduce an evaluative judgment into our definition. We might reply that the evaluation is not made but found, that it is not our work but that of the people whose cults we are inspecting. Yet this defense might be waived aside as specious. If we agree not to apply the word "religion" to these cults, it will be said, the decision is ours. And we make it because we disapprove of them. Moreover, we must remember that a tribe which undertakes to placate or to "bribe" what it takes to be a malevolent power is not animated by a desire to insure the triumph of evil as such. On the contrary, the effort is directed, not to worsening, but to bettering the situation. Even when the means resorted to, such as human sacrifice, are ethically reprehensible, must we not assume that the persons who are sacrificed, or who immolate themselves, frequently offer themselves in a spirit of public service? Perhaps, could we accept the presuppositions of the worshippers, we should pronounce the whole thing ethically commendable. Ought we not, then, to include demon-worship under the heading of religion?

I have put the argument as forcefully as I could, yet I do not think that it sways the balance. It would be absurd to suggest that when the English people paid the Danegeld to the Vikings they were engaged in a religious activity. Is the case significantly altered when the enemies bought off are not human but superhuman? Although the rites and ceremonies performed in demon-worship may frequently be very similar to, or even identical in form with, those performed in the worship of benevolent powers, the psychological attitude is absolutely antithetical. The difference is as wide as the world. Moreover, it is obvious that it is the reverence for worth or value which constitutes the starting point of the process of religious development which has culminated in the higher religions. It would be unwise, therefore, to frame a definition so broad as to blur, instead of emphasizing, a dissimilarity as profound as any in the realm of human thought. And it seems highly unlikely that even Professor Robinson would maintain that in concurring in Professor Campbell's verdict we are engaged in a pernicious effort to inveigle anyone into altering his evaluations under the impression that he is correcting his knowledge.

With respect to the second attitude—that involved in the attempt to "curry favor" with axiologically neutral powers—the situation, at first glance, is not so clear. I think that Professor Campbell is right in his judgment that the first two evaluative attitudes belong together, in contrast to the third, and that they stand closer to magic than to religion. But I have raised the question whether, if we so agree, we must not refuse to characterize all consistent exponents of the *via negativa* as religious men. Logical consistency, and not convenience, doubtless should be our goal; yet convenience is not to be ignored, and in this instance it might well carry the day, for so radical a restriction of terminology would appear to verge upon paradox. The question is too important to be dismissed in a sentence or two.

In reply to it I wish to make two points. The first is that if the principle of the *via negativa* be consistently adhered to—and if, in obedience to it, we refuse to ascribe any positive characteristics to the religious object—we shall have definitely made our own the second attitude. The logical outcome will be something like Zurvanism. We shall find ourselves confronted by an ultimate reality which is axiologically neutral.

My second point is that the method has not really been consistently applied by any of the eminent thinkers whom it would seem arbitrary and paradoxical to characterize as not religious. There is an inconsistency, if not in theory, at least between theory and practice, or between theory and emotional attitude. To make clear what I mean, let us glance at the position of Maimonides.

Maimonides' suggestion that the *via negativa*, which forbids us to predicate positive qualities of God, should yet lead us to a positive knowledge of God is clearly self-contradictory. By thus claiming at once both to know and not to know Maimonides is obviously trying to satisfy two incompatible desires. Whence comes the need to know? It springs from the desire to revere, love, and trust in God. Whence comes the need not to know? It is evidently connected with the only fundamental dogma in Judaism, that of the divine unity, which is enunciated in the Shema. And it must be envisaged in the light of the conviction which practically all medieval thinkers share that where there is multiplicity there is composition and that, accordingly, what is ontologically ultimate must be simple. Consequently, to admit that God can be characterized by a plurality of positive qualities is to deny his unity and his ontological ultimacy. But, if God have no positive qualities, he cannot be described in terms of them; thus the validity of the *via negativa* seemed to Maimonides to be implied by the affirmation of the divine unity.

Actually, of course, this position can be reconciled with the vigorous anthropomorphism of the Old Testament only by a strenuous process of allegorizing. What Maimonides is especially anxious to do is to make good his contention that God does not experience anything resembling human emotions. When God acts in a merciful manner, he informs us, it is not to satisfy his own feeling of pity but for the benefit of the pious; likewise, when God afflicts men with calamities, it is not to satiate a feeling of anger but to punish the wicked. And this, he urges, is precisely the example which a just governor should aspire to imitate.

> The governor of a country, if he is a prophet, should conform to these attributes. Acts (of punishment) must be performed by him moderately and in accordance with justice, not merely as an outlet of his passion. He must not let loose his anger, nor allow his passion to overcome him; for all passions are bad, and they must be guarded against as far as it lies in man's power. At times and towards some persons he must be merciful and gracious, not only from motives of mercy and compassion, but according to their merits; at other times and towards other persons he must evince anger, revenge, and wrath in proportion to their guilt, but not from motives of passion. He must be able to condemn a person to death by fire without anger, passion, or loathing against him, and must exclusively be guided by what he perceives to be the guilt of the person, and by a sense of the benefit which a large number will derive from such a sentence.[25]

This rather startling picture of what Maimonides would consider a just governor does, however, bring out an important point. God is the champion of the moral law; he can be the object of trust and confidence. And, although this consideration is not mentioned in the paragraph just quoted, he is the giver of revelation and the chooser of the chosen people. He is not really axiologically neutral or indifferent. There is an inconsistency here, and it is due to Maimonides'

25. *Ibid.*, p. 77.

own religious interest. Were we to examine the positions of other eminent exponents of the *via negativa* within the field of religion, we should discover, at least in the majority of cases I am convinced, similar inconsistencies. But this discovery would only render it more evident that the logical conclusion of the *via negativa* is a conception of ultimate reality which is incompatible with a genuinely religious outlook and that Professor Campbell's verdict that the second attitude "does not come a step nearer to religion than the first" is fully justified. Hence, if we make bold to identify religion with the third attitude, and to describe it in the light thereof, we may justifiably maintain that we are formulating a real, not a nominal, definition of religion and, moreover, that our definition is not "persuasive" in any pejorative sense of the word.

A normative definition, could such be given, would describe religion as it is in its perfect or ideal state, whether that state have ever actually been realized or not. It would tell us wherein a complete adjustment consists and how it is accomplished and the nature of the external reality to which adjustment is made. And the consideration of truth would enter into such a definition, for plainly the perfect religion will be the true religion. Quite obviously we are not now in a position to attempt to do any such thing, and, equally obviously, we have not attempted to do it. What we have done has been to distinguish between three possible ways of seeking adjustment and to identify one of them as genuinely religious. We have not tried to determine the nature of the object to which this adjustment is made except in the very general sense of prescribing that it must possess value. We have not attempted to decide whether it be personal or impersonal or whether the value be actual or only potential. Nor have we stipulated that the attitude of the religious man must be one of worship in the sense of adoration of any person. Thus the goal of the Jain or the Buddhist, for instance, may be his own perfected self; and it would be only in a metaphorical sense that a man could be said to worship such an ideal. I have tried to make my conception as inclusive as possible in view of the ascertained facts without broadening it unduly. We must now try to render it more definite.

DISCUSSION OF A PROPOSED REAL DEFINITION

In view of the foregoing discussion I do not propose to enter upon a lengthy analysis of all the well-known definitions of religion which have been advanced by outstanding thinkers, nor shall I at once proceed to formulate a new definition of my own. Instead I intend to examine a single definition which has already been proposed, and which appears to me to come closer than any other to doing justice to all the relevant facts as they have been disclosed to us by our preceding survey. I refer to McTaggart's definition of religion as "an emotion resting on a conviction of a harmony between ourselves and the universe at large." [26]

In the first place, let us consider what McTaggart has to say in its defense. "In the case of the early traditional religions," concedes McTaggart,

> the harmony is only rudimentary. In the early stages of these religions men had scarcely formed the conception of the universe as a whole, and did not therefore ask the question whether they were in harmony with it as a whole. But their religion was based on theories which enabled them to regard with more or less approval the part of the universe in which they were interested. The gods were regarded as having great power. They were also conceived as being, in the main, like men, as having the same ideals, sympathies, and standards as men. In so far as they differed from men they were held to be morally their superiors. (The actions reported of them would, indeed, have often been judged very wicked in men, but, when attributed to the gods, they were not thought wicked. This distinction is often required when dealing with more developed religions.) On the whole, then, the dogmas [27] of these creeds led to a belief that the world was to a large extent good, and better than it would have been judged to be by the same men if they had not held these dogmas. These religions, therefore, were accompanied by a conviction of a certain harmony between the individual and the universe.[28]

By calling attention to the fact that actions which would have been thought wicked if performed by men were not judged to be so when performed by the gods, McTaggart has brought out a very important consideration. The history of religion includes much that is revolting to the moral judgment of the modern civilized man, but we must recognize the moral judgment of primitive man was not similarly outraged. At a certain level of culture crgiastic fertility rites plainly aroused no qualms of conscience. Cannibalism, again, as Professor

---

26. *Some Dogmas of Religion* (London, 1906), sec. 3.
27. It is important to remember that McTaggart employs the word "dogma" to mean "any proposition which has a metaphysical significance" and that, accordingly, the word "creed" is to be understood in the sense of a system or assemblage of such propositions.
28. *Ibid.*, sec. 4.

Mircea Eliade has emphasized,[29] had a religious origin and, appalling as it seems to us, did not appear depraved to those who practiced it. Human sacrifice, again, was clearly regarded as an obligation which the deity had the right, and perhaps also the need, to impose.[30] Where children were looked upon as their fathers' property, as in the ancient Semitic world, the claim to the sacrifice of the first-born was deemed not unreasonable, and compliance therewith was accounted a proper acknowledgment of divine sovereignty. This is clearly revealed to us by the story of the sacrifice of Isaac, a story which is, however, itself indicative of a transition state of opinion. Abraham, although grieved, is not outraged by the command to offer up his first-born son; his willingness to do so is definitely a virtue in the eyes of the narrator; it evinces his unquestioning obedience and marks him as a genuinely pious man. And it is because of his absolute submission that God, not in recognition of any right, but as an act of free grace, announces his intention of waiving his claim then and thereafter. It was only at a more advanced stage of religious and moral development that the thought that God had ever commanded human sacrifice became no longer tolerable.

We must recognize, therefore, that an outlook is genuinely religious so long as it does not impugn but, on the contrary, definitely affirms the worth or value of the religious object, even though such an affirmation appear groundless or unjustifiable to those who have attained a higher state of moral insight. A power which commanded or condoned human sacrifice could only appear diabolical in our eyes, and we may well be thankful that such is the case, but this must not blind us to the fact that an ancient Indo-European or Semite or an Aztec of the days of Cortez would have been profoundly shocked had this judgment been enunciated in his hearing. Moreover, McTaggart's warning that "this distinction is often required in dealing with more developed religions" is very much to the point. Liberal Christianity, which acquired so great an impetus in the last century, was chiefly, although not exclusively, motivated by the conviction that the doctrines of original sin, the substitutionary atonement, election, and predestination were ethically obnoxious. With the justice of this evaluation we are not at present concerned. The point is that the defenders of these doctrines were not, and are not today, prepared to admit that they do impugn the divine goodness. Even though the orthodox

29. *The Sacred and the Profane* (New York, 1961), pp. 102–104.
30. Thus the gods of the Aztecs required human hearts for their sustenance; if deprived of these, their power would fail, and they would be unable to protect or benefit their worshippers.

be compelled to resort to the doctrine of analogous predication and to confess that God is not good in the same sense in which a man may be called good, they would still affirm that God is good *secundum modum altiorem,* even though it be in a sense which surpasses our powers of conception, even though to finite intelligences it may appear evil. Whether or not we concede the soundness of their contention, we must admit that it is advanced in sincerity; we must recognize that its proponents really do believe that God is good, and that their attitude is, therefore, genuinely religious.

Reverting now to the proposed definition, we must ask what kind or what degree of harmony between man and the universe is essential to religion. "If complete harmony were necessary," observes McTaggart, "no one could be called religious except the few mystics who deny the existence of any evil, since any evil must involve some want of harmony. We must say, I think, that religion is a matter of degree. The more complete harmony it asserts, the more completely religious will it be. Of course the complete religion is not necessarily the more true, for it may assert a harmony which does not exist." [31]

The distinction thus drawn between degrees of religion and degrees of truth, or approximation to truth, on the part of religion is one upon which we have already touched, and which is of considerable importance. At first blush, no doubt, it may appear paradoxical to suggest that the highest degree of religion may be not merely irrelevant to but incompatible with the truth of religion. Nevertheless we have seen that the process of adjustment which the religious impulse invariably and inevitably inspires does posit some sort of harmony, and we cannot therefore evade the issue of what sort of harmony there must be if we are to have any religion at all. Clearly *some* harmony must obtain if all religion is not illusory, and the religion which posits a greater or a lesser degree of harmony than actually exists will have fallen into error. But will *any* degree of harmony suffice?

"Some minimum," writes McTaggart, "there must surely be. For the conviction that the universe was not quite as bad as it could possibly have been would involve a belief in some harmony between ourselves and the universe. But this is not sufficient for religion. It would be an inadequate foundation for a religion that every man is not always hungry. And yet this shows some harmony between ourselves and the universe." [32]

The justice of these remarks should be quite obvious in view of our

31. *Some Dogmas of Religion,* sec. 2.   32. *Ibid.*

preceding discussion, for we have seen that the harmony in question, if it is to suffice for religion, must be axiologically grounded. McTaggart continues,

> It seems to me that the minimum harmony required to give us an emotion which could now be called religion, is that the universe should be judged to be good on the whole. That is to say, the harmony must be a harmony with what is judged by us to be the highest part of our own natures, and not with those of our desires which, even while we have them, we recognize as comparatively worthless or as wrong. And the harmony must be sufficiently complete to admit of the universe as a whole being approved rather than condemned.[33]

Before we proceed to criticize and evaluate this statement, we should do well to notice an important qualification which McTaggart at once subjoins.

> I have said that this is necessary for an emotion which could *now* be called religion. In the more rudimentary stages of religion, no doubt, it is different. A god is worshipped if he is believed to make things rather better, or to abstain from making them worse, for the worshipper and his neighbours. No question is raised as to the universe as a whole, or as to the balance of good and bad. And in a still more rudimentary stage the question is only as to the satisfaction of the desires of the individual, regardless of their moral quality.
>
> But religion has developed into a more exacting form. It was impossible, as the conception of objective good developed, to find sufficient harmony with our nature in anything which we condemned as evil, even if it were personally convenient to ourselves. And when the universe came to be regarded as a whole—which was inevitable for monotheists—it was impossible to find sufficient harmony in anything less than the universe as a whole. When once the objective and the universal had been realized, no subjective or partial harmony could be adequate.[34]

Several questions are at once suggested by the perusal of this passage. What is the significance of McTaggart's distinction between "What could *now* be called religion" and "the more rudimentary stages"? Does he mean that at a higher stage of development it is

33. *Ibid.*   34. *Ibid.*

necessary to redefine religion and that in view of the new definition the earlier stages are to be pronounced not religious at all? Clearly there is room for some confusion here. Moreover, it will not escape the reader's observation that in the description of "the more rudimentary stages" there is no attempt to discriminate among the three attitudes which Professor Campbell has taught us to distinguish; or, perhaps, it would be more correct to say that it is only the first two that are envisaged at all. McTaggart's viewpoint was, I think, affected by the belief he shared with Hegel, and which appears now to be thoroughly discredited, that magic constituted the matrix out of which religion developed. He distinguishes it quite legitimately from religion by pointing out that, although it does seek to establish a harmony, this harmony rests upon the inherent power of compulsion which the magician is believed to possess. But by implication he raises the question which we have already considered, whether it be possible to frame a definition which will cover both the rudimentary and the advanced stages of religion. And our answer would seem still to hold good. In consequence of having discriminated among the three possible fundamental attitudes of axiological evaluation, we have seen that the first two stand together in sharp opposition to the third, and are closely associated with the standpoint of magic; and we have thereby been enabled to pitch upon the third as constituting the basis of all genuine religion. Hence, a definition founded upon this fact should cover all stages of religious development. And it would seem that this is what McTaggart has given us. For is it not a harmony between what at every stage of the evolution of religion is judged to be the highest in our nature and the universe at large that is posited by the act of positive axiological evaluation which is expressive of this third attitude?

It may be objected, however, that McTaggart is himself of the opinion that, at the more rudimentary stages of this development, the idea of the universe had not yet been formulated, and that, accordingly, his definition—as he himself seems to be aware—does not cover these stages. But does not McTaggart, we may ask, concede too much? Was there ever a time, so far as we are able to judge, when men had not formed the notion of the universe? The answer to this question we may leave to the students of comparative religion. Certain it is that the idea of the world, or of the universe, appears very early. Should we find it necessary, however, to posit a stage at which this idea had not yet been conceived, we may venture to substitute the phrase "the total environment" for "the universe as a whole"; and this will apply equally well to all stages of development, including the highest. Nevertheless, since every religion of any importance has equated the total environment with the universe as a whole, it may be more convenient, and will not be misleading, to retain the definition in the form in which McTaggart has stated it.

It is further to be noticed that McTaggart appears to believe that gods were conceived of, and were worshipped, even at the most primitive stage. But such a suggestion would certainly be rejected by the upholders of the theory of animatism. According to this view at the earliest stage men believed in an impersonal, yet spiritual, power; the notion of soul was a later development, and posterior to this again that of deity. But this is a theory which demands a great deal of our powers of faith.

Doubtless primitive man conceived of the self as endowed with physical characteristics, as constituting a sort of double, normally inhabiting the body yet separable from it. Back of this we surely cannot go, for there is evidence that even the Neanderthal men believed in a life after death, which seems clearly to imply the existence of some sort of soul. No doubt the notion of an immaterial soul was very slow in forming. But that of impersonal spirit is even more rarified, so rarified indeed that many contemporary thinkers would pronounce it a meaningless *contradictio in adjecto*. Add to this the further consideration that the case for the antiquity of the worship of the "High Gods" has been so forcefully stated by Andrew Lang and Father Schmidt that it appears to have gained general assent, and the case for animatism will seem very shaky indeed.[35]

35. The theory of a pre-animistic animatistic stage of development and the theory that magic was the origin of religion are associated and dismissed by Professor Mircea Eliade in the following interesting passage:

> We cannot therefore really talk of *mana* as "impersonal," for such a notion would have no meaning within the mental limits of the primitive. Nowhere do we find *mana* existing of itself, standing apart from things, cosmic events, beings or men. Further still, you will find, on close analysis, that a thing, a cosmic phenomenon, in fact any being whatsoever, possesses *mana* thanks either to the intervention of some spirit, or to getting involved in the epiphany of some divine being.
>
> There seems in fact to be no justification for seeing *mana* as an impersonal magic force. To go on from this to seeing a pre-religious phase—dominated solely by magic—must therefore be equally mistaken. Such a theory is invalidated in any case by the fact that not all peoples (particularly the most primitive) have any such belief as that in *mana;* and also by the fact that magic—although it is to be found more or less everywhere—never exists apart from religion. Indeed magic does not dominate the spiritual or "primitive" societies everywhere by any means; it is, on the contrary, in the more developed societies that it comes to be so prevalent. (*Patterns in Comparative Religion* [London, 1958], p. 23)

Whether McTaggart be right or wrong on this point, however, does not affect the soundness of his definition. For, granted that there actually was a purely animatistic stage of development, even at this stage a harmony would have been posited between what was then judged to be highest in our natures and the universe, or the total environment. Again, even if McTaggart were right in his view that religion developed out of magic, his definition would still stand. For, in defining religion, we are primarily concerned, not with how it originated, but with what it is.

A further merit, and a great merit, of this definition is that it enables us, without forcing or straining it in any way, to include in the same classification not only monotheistic, polytheistic, and pantheistic systems of thought but also such atheistic faiths as Jainism and at least one form of Hīnayāna Buddhism.

"It might be objected," remarks McTaggart,

> that Buddhism does not assert any harmony between man and the universe, since it teaches that all existence is evil. But it teaches, also, that the constitution of the universe provides a way by which it is possible for each of us to escape from the tyranny of existence. With the wise and good man the universe is in harmony. For he strives towards the goal of Nirvana, and the universe is such that, if he is wise enough and good enough, he will attain it.[36]

Surely, it may be said that, in the light of our previous discussion of the subject, what McTaggart has said does not suffice. It would do well enough for Jainism, for Jainism does envisage a positive goal which can be attained by a process of harmonization. It appears highly probable, moreover, that the Buddha himself held a similar view; and it is certain that many adherents of the Hīnayāna would concur.[37] Yet it is no less certain that many others would dissent,[38] and that they would emphatically equate Nirvāṇa with the total annihilation of the self, or, at any rate, with the complete cessation of consciousness.

Here we come upon an issue, and an issue obviously of the first importance, which cuts right through the very heart of the Hīnayāna. Adherents of both views would agree that there are gods who, although themselves standing in need of deliverance, are capable of bestowing this-worldly benefits; they would agree that there are heavens and hells, and that the former are to be hoped for and the

36. *Some Dogmas of Religion*, sec. 6.
37. See J. B. Pratt, *India and Its Faiths* (Boston, 1915), p. 376.
38. *Ibid.*, p. 377.

latter to be feared; and they would further agree that life in a Heaven, although it is far happier than life on earth, does not, because of its transitory nature, constitute an ultimate goal. This transitoriness casts a darkening shadow over the life of the gods, and thus renders it more evil than good. Even from heaven one would wish to be delivered. Upon this all are agreed; nevertheless they are profoundly at variance as to whether deliverance consists in fulness of life or in the final cessation of life. In view of the fundamental character of this divergence, do not all agreements, whether in belief or in practice, impress us as relatively insignificant; and does not this issue in all its starkness sunder the two groups "as far as the east is from the west"?

In his *India and Its Faiths*,[39] J. B. Pratt recounts an experience of his own which may throw some light on this question. A young Burmese interpreter, who had assured him that Nirvāṇa is "equivalent to being totally dead," was corrected by an old monk who told the boy that he was claiming to know more than could be known on the subject, and that there might well be consciousness in Nirvāṇa, concerning which all that could be affirmed is that

> it is the end of birth, old age, and death, the end of lust, ill-will, and ignorance.
>
> The boy was obviously much impressed by this view and said this was the first time he had ever heard such a description of Nirvana. On our walk back from the monastery he returned to the subject and dwelt upon it long and thoughtfully. The possibility that Nirvana might be in any sense consciousness instead of blank non-existence came to him, he said, with unhoped-for comfort. Hitherto it had seemed to him (for so he had always been taught) that conscious existence inevitably involved suffering, and life had seemed to him necessarily melancholy. He had longed for Nirvana as complete cessation of existence and the only possible escape. But if conscious life were really possible without sorrow, he would welcome it eagerly.

Can one doubt that these words would equally well express the feelings of many other Buddhists who likewise have been taught that Nirvāṇa is nothingness? If so, it would account in large measure for the fact that in the various Hīnayāna countries, as the same writer assures us, the laity are much more interested in the prospect of life in a

39. Pp. 377–378.

Heaven after death than in the possibility of reaching Nirvāṇa. It is not only that Nirvāṇa is so difficult of attainment; it is also because they do not wish to attain it, and would rather linger in the Heavens as long as may be. Even if this attitude be evidence of no more than a very hedonistic outlook, still all those who admit that pleasure is a good must also admit that it involves a judgment of axiological evaluation, and a judgment with which the belief that Nirvāṇa is annihilation is not in harmony.

It is instructive to contrast this point of view with the outlook of Lord Russell in his "A Free Man's Worship." In this notable essay annihilation is envisaged as the in-no-sense-doubtful "doom of human kind"; far from being a goal to be striven for, it is an inescapable calamity which should be faced with courage. Unlike so many contemporary naturalists Lord Russell makes no attempt to soften the blow which he administers; on the contrary, he delivers it with all his force. It is because he finds in the structure of the universe no basis for what he clearly judges to be highest in human nature, for human aspirations and ideals, because he is convinced that man is no more than a cosmic by-product, that he enunciates in such ringing tones his contention that "only on the firm foundation of unyielding despair, can the soul's habitation henceforth be safely built." The free man's "worship at the shrine that his own hands have built" is a worship which does not presuppose, but rather explicitly rejects, every notion of harmony; hence the claims of religion, in the sense in which McTaggart has defined it, are heartily and emphatically repudiated.

Far different is the Hīnayānist outlook which we have just been considering. For it annihilation, far from being inevitable, is a most unlikely occurrence; far from being a terrible event to confront which we must summon all that is heroic in our personalities, it is something most earnestly to be hoped for and endeavored after. The release from suffering which it, and it alone, offers is to be obtained only after incredible struggles and a long series of incarnations, and is to be consummated by an act of ontological suicide.

In this perspective there is indeed *some* degree of harmony between our nature and the universe. For annihilation, although difficult to compass, is possible; and the universe is not so bad as it would be were annihilation impossible, and were all of us doomed to everlasting life and everlasting misery. McTaggart has introduced the useful notion of degrees of religion corresponding to the degrees of harmony envisaged. But he has also asserted, and the assertion seems a reasonable one, that there must be a minimum degree of harmony which is essential to *any* religion. And he has suggested that the minimum degree of harmony must be sufficient "to admit of the universe being approved rather than condemned." And this, he tells us, means that the harmony must be a harmony "with what is judged by us to be the highest part of our own natures." Doubtless the phrase "by us" must be interpreted with some caution. We must take it to mean, I presume, "by us if we adopt the standpoint of the believer in some system of dogmas." It would not be fair to condemn any system as irreligious because we personally do not agree with the evaluation made by those who accept it. If *they* consider that what they judge to be the highest part of our natures is in harmony with the universe as a whole, this surely suffices.

Now, if McTaggart's definition is to apply to those who hold the purely negative concept of deliverance of which I have just spoken, it can only be because we assume them to make such a judgment. Yet could such a judgment with any plausibility be attributed to a man who thinks that annihilation is better than life on *any* terms? The question would seem to turn upon what he judges to be the highest part of his own nature. But this requires an axiological evaluation which it is doubtful whether he be prepared to make. Desire, on his view, is infected with evil because it can never be fully satisfied, and because it involves one in sorrow. Pleasure is infected with evil because it is transitory. By saying the desire and pleasure are infected with evil I do not mean that they are morally reprehensible, but only that they are to be shunned. But, when all human nature falls under this indiscriminate condemnation, is there any sense in asking whether there be a higher and a lower within it? For the Russell of "A Free Man's Worship," annihilation is an ultimate evil because life in itself has such great potentialities for good, potentialities of which an irrational universe forbids the realization; for the view now before us, on the contrary, annihilation is not an evil but the supreme object of desire, because life as such is more evil than good.

To do justice to this latter point of view [40] we must recognize that it does not deny that there is good in life, nor yet that one life may be happier, better, or worthier than another. What it does assert is that the transitory character of every good that can be attained renders it unsatisfying, that there is more pain in the loss than pleasure in the winning or the possessing, that impermanence is incompatible with the realization of any ultimate value. And the conclusion drawn

---

40. For a sympathetic and enlightening discussion of this point of view see Sir Charles Eliot, *Hinduism and Buddhism* (London, 1921), I, 202–206.

is that, since desire invariably leads to disillusionment, the only remedy is to eradicate it, even thought the eradication involve that of life itself.

Such an evaluation, we must frankly acknowledge, presupposes a depth and breadth of perspective far surpassing that of the ancient Greek or Semite. At this stage of intellectual and axiological development the harmony which at that level had been deemed acceptable is rejected as hollow, and the praises of the psalmist would seem like the crackling of thorns under a pot. A shallow or childlike mind is apt to be fascinated by the glamor of the proximate; it requires a profounder insight to penetrate to the ultimate. And, if it be true that in our experience we find nothing of abiding value, the pessimism which characterizes this attitude is only too well founded. That in its dissatisfaction with the ephemeral and the transitory it is at one with that of genuine religion we cannot fail to recognize, yet neither can we fail to recognize that in its hopeless acquiescence in an ultimate pessimism it is worlds away from it. The pessimism is so extreme as to make Lord Russell's "unyielding despair" look like blithe optimism. What for him is an inescapable and tragic doom, for it is the only ray of hope in the cosmic landscape. For it, again, if there be a part of our nature which is higher than any other, it is so only on our own subjective estimate, which is uncorroborated and unconfirmed by objective reality. Although the disharmony between our natural aspirations and the nature of the universe is not so great as it would be if we, in such a world, were condemned to live forever without hope of escape from the wheel of birth and death, yet the degree of harmony involved in the somewhat remote possibility of successfully accomplishing an act of ontological suicide is so slight as to be barely discernible. A universe which is so repugnant to the wise man that, rather than exist within it, he would prefer not to be cannot fairly be described in any but the shallowest sense of the word as in harmony with him.

In this negative conception of Nirvāṇa we encounter one of those borderline cases the appearance of which we have anticipated. What we must now do is to recognize it as what it is. A high degree of approximation to a religious outlook is evinced by the concentration upon the need for deliverance, yet the suicidal conception of deliverance is at the opposite pole from the position of genuine religion. The slight degree of harmony posited between the self and the universe is clearly insufficient to render McTaggart's definition applicable here. But I see no ground for revising the definition. Between basic optimism and basic pessimism there is an unbridgeable gulf, and all we can do is take note of the fact.

The next question is: What of the position of Sāṁkhya-Yoga and the Nyāya-Vaiśeṣika systems? [41] We cannot dismiss these from our consideration on the plea that they are only philosophies, for they are definitely concerned with religious problems, and, moreover, they inculcate a way of life. Unlike the negative school of the Hīnayāna they do not admit the possibility of a cessation of existence; for them the indestructibility of the self is a cardinal tenet. Yet, one and all, they set forth the notion of deliverance in a very negative fashion.

We reach, indeed, what is from the religious point of view the climax of paradox in the position of the Nyāya-Vaiśeṣika. Here we find posited a supreme Being who, like Plato's Best Soul, determines the rebirths of all finite selves, and who, furthermore, extends his aid to those attempting to escape from birth and death. Though it may be possible to have religion without God, it is plainly impossible, one might urge, to have God without religion; hence the existence of Īśvara must settle the question as to the religious character of this system. But, when we have examined the conception of the nature of deliverance, we may see reason to revise this verdict. Consciousness, all exponents of the Nyāya-Vaiśeṣika agree, is a nonessential attribute, one which the self may, or may not, possess. So long as the self is involved in the realm of sense-experience, it possesses consciousness, but, with the attainment of mokṣa, it loses it. Once released, the self is without pain, pleasure, or awareness of any kind; it passes into a condition of utter detachment wherein all connections with God, and with everything else, are severed; the state of deliverance is one of absolute oblivion. So explicitly is this doctrine propounded that it appears impossible to interpret it in any other than the most literal sense. And is not a state of complete unconsciousness as purely negative a goal as annihilation? To this question only an affirmative answer can be returned. Deliverance, as Professor Mysore Hiriyanna has observed, is "a success worse than defeat." [42] So repugnant is the universe to the soul of the wise man that he chooses the only possible way of escape and buries his head forever in the sand of forgetfulness. Thus the degree of harmony between the self and the universe posited by

41. Because of their similarity the Sāṁkhya and the Yoga are often treated as a single system, and the same is true of the Nyāya and the Vaiśeṣika. It will be convenient in this connection to conform to this practice, for with respect to the nature of deliverance the Sāṁkhya and the Yoga are at one, and so are the Nyāya and the Vaiśeṣika.

42. Outlines of Indian Philosophy (Mystic, Conn., 1932), p. 266.

this system is no greater than that which obtains on the annihilationist view, and our verdict with respect to it must be the same.

In the case of the Sāṁkhya-Yoga the situation is less clear. Pain and pleasure, we are told, go together; and the elimination of one involves that of the other. On the conception of deliverance Professor Dasgupta has written, "There is no bliss or happiness in the Sāṁkhya-Yoga mukti,[43] for all feeling belongs to prakrti.[44] It is thus a state of pure intelligence." [45] Yet, by one who accepted the presuppositions of the system, might not the attainment of this state be envisaged as a positive goal? The fact that it is described largely in negative terms does not preclude this possibility, for it is clearly a state which, although conceivable, is unimaginable. It is one, Principal Jajeswar Ghose assures us, of "ineffable serenity." [46] The delivered soul, soaring aloft in absolute detachment and disinterested contemplation, bears a certain resemblance to Aristotle's God. And I think that the believer in this system might urge that the realization of such a state would satisfy all that he judged to be highest in human nature, and that the degree of harmony thus posited between the self and the universe could therefore claim to be pronounced religious. While the case may be a borderline one, I should be inclined upon the whole to concede the justice of the contention.

The only question before us, then, is whether McTaggart's definition be too narrow, whether it ought to be so expanded as to include the negative school of the Hīnayāna and the theism of the Nyāya-Vaiśeṣika. But consider what follows if we do undertake to expand it. We should recognize, I have so far been contending, that the fundamental characteristic of the genuinely religious outlook is its positing of an ultimate reality endued with value—whether that reality be the universe or a deity above, or within, the universe. If this be granted, the spirit of religion is one of optimism. True enough, it is often a severely restricted optimism; for only the universalist holds that all souls attain deliverance. Yet, however restricted, the optimism is genuine. In contrast the outlook which sees no alternative to annihilation or oblivion is one of an almost unrelieved pessimism. The two outlooks are poles apart. What lies between? What lies between is obviously a naturalism like that of Lord Russell. His despair is the annihilationist's hope. Accordingly, if we are so to expand our definition as to embrace

43. The state of emancipation.
44. The realm of matter and sense-experience—i.e., nature—in opposition to that of soul.
45. Surenda Dasgupta, *A History of Indian Philosophy* (Cambridge, 1932), I, 273.
46. *Sāṁkhya* (Calcutta, 1940), p. 137.

both poles, we must also include what lies between. But, then, all conceivable world views will be religious, and equally so, for now we shall have no criterion left for discriminating between degrees of religion. Lord Russell, despite his indignant and impassioned protests, will be a religious teacher, and one of no mean order; and the same, of course, will be true of Lenin and Hitler. Will not this be a *reductio ad absurdum?* I, at least, can think of none more flagrant. I conclude, therefore, that sanity requires that we abstain from any such attempt at emendation.

It is instructive, however, to contrast the position of the Buddhist annihilationist, or that of the Nyāya-Vaiśeṣika, with that of the Mīmāṁsaka. While the later Mīmāṁsakas gravitated to a negative point of view, the early Mīmāṁsakas apparently envisaged no possibility of any escape from the wheel of birth and death; yet this, so far from inducing pessimism, seems to have inspired them with optimism. For, if life have its depths, it has also its heights; if there be evil in it, there is also much good; if there be Hells, there are also Heavens. The perpetual turning of the wheel assured them that if no victory be final no disaster is irrevocable; that, however low one may fall, there are no heights to which one may not thereafter ascend. Here we have an optimistic evaluation of existence no whit inferior to that of the most vigorous occidental, yet coupled with a cosmic sweep of vision which is characteristic of India. The perspective thus disclosed markedly resembles that which Plato presents to us in the *Phaedrus,* in which souls whose wings have sprouted and who have flown upward to the realm of the gods are in perpetual danger of falling back into this world, and yet, having thus fallen, retain the capacity to reascend. In this perspective the degree of harmony between the self and the universe, although imperfect, is yet very pronounced; it is quite sufficient to eliminate an unqualified pessimism and to inspire a temperate optimism. Clearly, therefore, it is to be esteemed genuinely religious.

We have now to ask whether McTaggart's definition be applicable to the primitive faiths of the Homeric Greeks and the ancient Semites. In this connection our especial concern, of course, is with the faith of the primitive Hebrews, inasmuch as this is the acorn out of which grew the mighty oak of Judaism. And here we face a distinction of fundamental importance. Such fully developed theisms as Judaism, Christianity, and Islam are definitely committed to the doctrines of a resurrection and everlasting life which present the self with a goal which, once attained, is never lost. The same is true of Zoroastrianism. And the religions of India likewise provide the self with an ultimate τέλος, however it be conceived. Even annihilation, whatever else may be said of it, is certainly ultimate. But the primitive faiths of Greek and Semite are this-worldly in their outlook. An afterlife is not, indeed, denied; but it is pictured as so phantasmal that it might well be regarded as worse than annihilation. That among the Hebrews the sense of personal communion with Yahweh was vivid and intense no one will question. The psalms bear eloquent witness to it. It might be contended, however, that his relationship to God, as conceived by the early Israelite, was defective in two important respects, namely, that it was prudentially motivated and that it was thought of as purely transitory.

That the Hebrew, like the Roman, often sacrificed to his God in the spirit of *do ut des* cannot be denied, although he would probably have shrunk from describing the situation in language as thoroughly cynical as that employed by Locke. In so doing he was not peculiar, for in the case of any religion the prudential motive is that most powerfully operative among the baser spirits. There is, of course, nothing essentially ignoble in recourse to divine aid, any more than there is in a drowning man's cry for succor. Still it must be admitted that at an early period in the history of Israel the belief that God always protects and benefits the righteous and invariably punishes the wicked was treated as a basic dogma; with the consequence that personal misfortune could be regarded, as Job's friends regarded it, as indicative of personal guilt. Viewed in this light worship might seem to be no more morally elevated than a business transaction. But the fifty-first psalm is in itself a standing and sufficient refutation of the suggestion that this was all that there was to it. And there is abundant evidence that what the finer spirits desired was an ennobling fellowship with a Deity who was not only powerful but also just, benevolent, and righteous. The same motivation, be it remarked, is apparent in the Assyrian psalms; and Plato's Socrates bears witness to its presence in the more spiritual minds of Greece.

That fellowship with God was conceived as transitory cannot be doubted. It could at best persist only throughout the earthly life of the worshipper. In this respect it resembled the harmony envisaged by the Epicurean, yet it must have been susceptible of a far greater intensity; for the God of the Hebrew, unlike the interstellar Deities of Epicurus, was capable of response; the affection of the worshipper was reciprocated, and the relationship thus established was productive of a harmony which resulted in a high degree of satisfaction. "I will sing to the Lord as long as I live," exclaims the psalmist. "I will sing praise to my God while I have being. May my mediation be pleasing to him, for I rejoice in the Lord." [47] It is obvious that these words give utterance to an exalted emotion.

We must remember, moreover, that especially in the earliest period Yahweh was thought of as the God of the nation rather than of the individual, and that worship was conceived of as primarily a communal activity. So long as the nation survived and flourished under the divine administration, the harmony was accounted satisfactory. And if, in addition, the individual enjoyed divine favor and divine fellowship throughout a long life, this was all that could be expected. While the thought of Sheol could never have been other than a gloomy one, any protest on the part of the individual would have been regarded as unreasonable.[48] We are justified, therefore, in concluding that the degree of harmony posited between what was judged highest in human nature and the universe was, at this stage, deemed on the whole satisfactory, and that, accordingly, McTaggart's definition will apply to it.

It is true that at a later stage, with the growth of individualism and an increasingly spiritual conception of man's relationship to God, this degree of harmony came to be regarded as unsatisfactory and that the situation was thereupon remedied by the introduction—probably under the influence of Zoroastrianism—of the belief in a future life qualitatively superior to the present, in which personal relationship to God would continue forever unbroken. But we are not justified in attributing such an axiological evaluation to the more primitive stage.

Much the same must be said with respect to the attitude of Epicurus. The satisfaction which he, and his followers, derived from contemplating the blissful existence of the gods, although certainly not prudentially motivated, was equally certainly transitory. Yet it was clearly considered to be the expression of what was highest in man's nature; consequently the definition will apply to it also.

It would seem clear, however, that within the field of religion we have now to distinguish between religions which are primarily this-worldly and those which are primarily otherworldly in outlook. We might conveniently term the former religions of relative salvation and the latter religions of absolute salvation. It is interesting to observe that the former, insofar as we have examined them, are all polytheistic, henotheistic, or—perhaps, at a certain stage in the develop-

47. Ps. 104:33–34.   48. See Eccles. 41:1–4.

ment of the religion of Israel—monotheistic; whereas the latter are monotheistic, polytheistic, pantheistic,[49] or—in the sense of positing no supreme Mind—atheistic. The question, therefore, naturally arises whether this need be the case. Could there be an atheistic, this-worldly religion? It is not easy to see what form this could take, for a this-worldly atheism will almost inevitably be some form of naturalism; and Lord Russell has convincingly shown how complete, for a typical naturalism, is the absence of harmony between the self and the universe.

Perhaps it will be urged that a naturalism such as that of Alexander should be accounted religious. It provides, indeed, no ultimate goal for the self, its perspective includes no superhuman Intelligence with whom communion is possible, in whom one might trust, or to whose aid one might appeal; all that it offers is an impersonal, cosmic principle which carries forward the evolutionary process, a nisus toward perfection, with which one may voluntarily co-operate, even though it be unable consciously to co-operate with us. Deity is a goal which perpetually flits before us; for the next higher state, when realized, ceases to be Deity. "In the hierarchy of qualities," says Alexander, "the next higher quality to the highest attained is deity. God is the whole universe engaged in process towards the emergence of this new quality, and religion is the sentiment in us that we are drawn towards him, and caught in the movement of the world to a higher level of existence." [50] If we place ourselves at Alexander's standpoint, as we have just done at that of Epicurus, must we not concede that we find a harmony between what he judged to be highest in our nature and the universe? I think that we must, and that Alexander, like Epicurus, must be accounted a religious man.

So far we have seen no reason for revising McTaggart's definition of religion. But we have not yet settled the question whether this definition can be accepted as it stands.

A Suggested Revision

McTaggart has equated religion with an emotion, an emotion which is produced by a particular belief. That emotion is included in the religious experience is a fact so obvious that we may take it for

49. Although we have not turned our attention to them, the Advaita Vedānta and some forms of the Mahāyāna, as well as a certain form of Sufism, may surely be termed pantheistic.

50. *Space, Time, and Deity* (London, 1920), II, 429.

granted. But the question may still be asked whether emotion be all that there is to religion. If the emotion be dependent upon belief, why should the belief be excluded? We are accustomed, indeed, to speak of religious beliefs, and by so doing we seem to imply that the beliefs are part of religion. What, again, of the type of conduct which is prescribed by religious beliefs? Religion, to be genuine, must, surely, be practiced as well as believed; and the actual living of it out constitutes for most of us the principal difficulty.

As regards the last point, I believe that McTaggart was inclined to underestimate the closeness of the connection between morality and religion. "Our views on religious questions," he writes,

> may affect some of the details of morality—the observance of a particular day of rest, or the use of wine or beef, for example. But they are quite powerless either to obliterate the difference between right and wrong, or to change our views on much of the content of morality. At least, I do not know of any view maintained by anyone on any religious question which would, if I held it, alter my present belief that it is right to give water to a thirsty dog, and wrong to commit piracy or to cheat at cards.[51]

He next considers the suggestion that the acceptance of certain beliefs with respect to questions of religion might weaken one's will to live virtuously. "This view," he continues, "seems refuted by experience, which, I think, tells us that the zeal for virtue shown by various men, while it varies much, does not vary according to their views on religious matters. The men who believe, for example, in God, or immortality, or optimism, seem to be neither better nor worse morally than those who disbelieve in them."[52]

It is the latter contention, I feel sure, which is most likely to be challenged. And it would seem that McTaggart himself has provided grounds for such a challenge. For emotion is a stimulus—shall we say the only stimulus?—to action; hence, if religion be an emotion, it will provide the man who feels it with a stimulus which will be lacking to the man who does not feel it. And it is religious beliefs which direct the application of the stimulus which emotion imparts. It is true that many of the good deeds done by a religious man might equally well be done by a moral man who was not religious, such as providing food for the hungry or money for the destitute. Yet there is also good which the non-religious but moral man could not do. That

51. *Philosophical Studies*, ed. S. V. Keeling (London, 1934), p. 38.
52. *Ibid.*

Christian missions have done harm as well as good no impartial person would deny; yet the fact remains that the good which they have done could only have been done by Christians.

"We may think what we like," wrote J. B. Pratt,

> of the intelligence of those missionaries who have believed in the universal damnation of the heathen, but there can be no question about their courage or their self-devotion. It is they who have gone and who are still going to the comfortless spots, to the perilous spots, on the verges of civilization, where the more liberal type of missionary seldom ventures. "Do you really believe that all the heathen who do not hear about Christ will be eternally damned?" I asked a woman missionary whom I met a few years ago in Annam. "Do you suppose," she replied, turning on me almost with anger, "that I would have said good-bye to my children for years, and be starting up into mountainous Yunan, where any day I may be killed as so many of my colleagues have been, if I did not believe just that?" [53]

Thus even the belief in eternal damnation has been productive of good. It is true that many people who make a parade of trying to improve the characters of others impress us as presumptuous busybodies. Yet there have been persons whose lives and teachings have profoundly influenced for good the souls of many; and he who believes that the selves whose characters are thus affected will live forever, and will thus reap a permanent benefit, has a stronger motive for engaging in this subtle and difficult type of benevolence than the man who thinks that his neighbor's soul will die with his body.

Reverting now to McTaggart's first contention, we may ask whether it be not a fact that advance in ethical insight has in general been connected with progress in religious thought. Thus the recognition that moral obligations extend beyond the limits of one's own nation or one's own class seems to have been associated, in the case of the Hebrews, with the rise of prophetism, and, in that of the Greeks, with the development of Stoicism. It is also unfortunately true that certain religious beliefs have had a very pernicious influence upon men's moral judgments. The cruelties of the Inquisition, for example, would have been impossible had it not been for the generally accepted view that it is one's duty to constrain the heretic to renounce his heresy, and thereby to insure his salvation. And Christian Scientists, again, may

53. *Can We Keep the Faith?* (London, 1941), p. 162.

object on religious grounds to the inoculation of children, and thus obstruct the prevention of disease.

But if McTaggart, as I think, failed to recognize adequately the intimacy of the connection between religion and morality, his position was clearly much sounder that that of those who go to the opposite extreme. Not infrequently we hear it said that without religion we should have no ethics. And this is undoubtedly a gross exaggeration. That a decline of religion always has its repercussions in the sphere of morality is, as I have just been contending, a fact which experience brings home to us; and we may leave it to the psychologist and the historian to determine, if they can, just how far these repercussions are likely to extend. But that all bases for moral action would thereby be destroyed is an unwarranted conclusion. McTaggart's fundamental point, and it is a point well taken, is that ethics is, in a very important sense, independent of metaphysics. It is independent in the sense that ethical propositions are not directly deducible from metaphysical propositions. Indeed it is the other way around. From ethical propositions metaphysical propositions can be deduced. I cannot stay to make good this assertion, which I shall undertake to substantiate in its proper place, for this would involve an inquiry into the status of values. But it is a very important point which it is incumbent upon us to recognize. For there has been a recurrent tendency to attempt to identify religion with ethics. And this, as McTaggart truly says, would leave us with two words for the same thing, and with no word at all to take the place of the word "religion."

At once the question arises, however, whether, if ethics can live without religion, religion can live without ethics. What would become of it? We see what becomes of it in the case of the Jñāna-Yoga of India. Here we encounter another tendency, the tendency to identify religion with speculation, or perhaps I should say with intuitive insight. The adherent of this doctrine, in its unqualified form, aspires to attain deliverance through pure thought. From all forms of action, from right as well as from wrong acts, he endeavors to abstain in order to avoid the accumulation of Karma which will involve him in the temporal process and eventuate in rebirth.

Does not all this, it may be asked, show the wisdom of McTaggart's definition? Religion is not pure thought, neither is it moral action; it is emotion which is vitally connected with both but which must be distinguished from both.

I may say at once that I do not regard the issue as one of fundamental importance. So long as the intimate connection among the three factors of intellection, emotion, and volition be fully recognized it does not, perhaps, matter very much whether religion be defined in terms of any one or of all of them. Nevertheless, there is the desire for maximum precision, and there is the consideration of practical convenience. Let us look again at the situation. Religious emotion is not something that can arise of itself *in vacuo*. It is dependent upon and arises out of belief. Belief, then, is logically primary; it is the root of religion. Emotion, again, expresses itself in action. While it does not provide the basis for moral judgments, it reinforces them; it even appears to suggest them.

Go back as far as you will, you find these relations obtaining. There are always religious beliefs which generate appropriate emotions, and there are always codes of action prescribed. Even in primitive religion the gods are the guardians of social mores—of the rite of hospitality, for example—and tribal custom is sustained by divine sanctions. As we descend the stream of time these relations become more and more intensified. When we find any of these relationships severed, we at once discover that the vital unity has been destroyed. If beliefs perish, emotion evaporates. If pure thought be divorced from daily living, we may have metaphysics, but not what we should recognize as religion. If action be sundered from religious belief and emotion, we have only ethics. The line runs straight from belief through emotion to action. For, after all, as psychologists have been telling us for decades, the self is not a mere adjunction of three mutually distinct faculties; it is a thinking, feeling, willing unit.

No one has recognized this fact more explicitly than McTaggart in the later stages of his thinking. For he avowedly adopted a theory of the nature of volition advanced by G. E. Moore, and proceeded to develop a similar theory of emotion.[54] There are, he maintains, no such things as psychic states which are pure volitions or pure emotions. All psychic states are "cogitations"—i.e., states of awareness. But some of these states, in addition to having each the quality of being a cogitation, have each the further quality of being a desire, and among these there are some each of which has also the quality of being a volition. Likewise there are some states each of which, in addition to having the quality of being a cogitation, has the quality of being an emotion. And, obviously, there may be some states which possess all these qualities.

This view, which I take to be in accord with the results of psycho-

54. *The Nature of Existence* (Cambridge, 1927), Vol. II, secs. 446, 456.

logical investigation, I propose to accept; and I suggest that in the light of it we have ample justification for emending McTaggart's definition. For, if religion be anything at all like what we have seen reason to believe it to be, it is surely the orientation of the whole man with respect to his universe. I venture, therefore, in view of these considerations, to suggest the following as a descriptive definition of religion. Religion is the belief in a harmony between what is judged to be the highest in human nature and the total environment, together with the emotion to which this belief gives rise and the type of conduct motivated by this belief and this emotion.[55]

55. This is substantially the definition advanced in my *Introduction to the Philosophy of Religion* (New York, 1958), p. 36, slightly emended in the interest of clarity. I have substituted here, as there, the words "total environment" for McTaggart's phrase "the universe as a whole" in order to take into account his suggestion that there may conceivably—although I do not think probably—have been a stage in the development of primitive religion at which the conception of the universe, or the all, had not yet been formed.

CHAPTER TWO

THE NATURE OF RELIGION

If the conclusion we reached at the end of the preceding chapter be sound, if religion be a relation of harmony between the integrated personality and the universe as a whole, then any disintegrating tendency in the self is bound to affect adversely its relationship to the universe and to give rise to a more or less aberrant form of religion. To speak of integration and disintegration in connection with the self has, indeed, the disadvantage that it may suggest to a careless reader that the self is a unity composed of antecedently existing parts, and that these are capable of being subsequently separated from it. Such a view of the self, as all philosophers are aware, has actually been advanced; but it is a theory which, for reasons to be given later, appears to me to be quite indefensible. I wish, therefore, to make clear that when I speak of the integration or unification of the self, like most other people who do the same, I am employing terms which I should admit to be fundamentally metaphorical and which I use only in default of better. That the self is in some sense a unity which can never be totally disrupted is an assumption upon which psychoanalysts have been proceeding, and proceeding with considerable success; and it is one which I regard as philosophically sound.[1]

Nevertheless we know that the self can undergo such calamities as loss of memory, neurotic compulsion, and all the disorders which are subsumed under the familiar phrase "dissociation of personality"; and we know as well that these disorders are in many, if not in most, cases found to yield to psychoanalytical treatment. Our present concern, however, is not with these but with maladjustment on the part of the relatively normal self. One need not be a defender of the outmoded "faculty psychology" to recognize that cognition, emotion, and volition are the strands out of which consciousness is composed and that a harmonious blending of them is requisite to the highest degree of psychic health. An undue predominance of any one of these constitutes

1. I may add that I dissent from Professor G. F. Stout's view that the unity of the self is basically teleological. For me it is substantial, as will later become evident. See *God and Nature* (Cambridge, 1952), Book V, chap. xvi, sec. 9.

a deviation, sometimes a serious deviation, from that exact balance which is the ideal norm, yet to such deviations we are all liable.

We habitually speak of the intellectual or the emotional type of individual, and also of the hardheaded, practical type. In so doing we more or less consciously imply, I think, that persons of the first type are emotionally cold and possibly also deficient in resolution, that persons of the second type, while they may likewise be lacking in will-power, are clearly of mediocre intellect or else mentally lazy, and that persons of the third type, whatever their intellectual capacity, are pronouncedly characterized by strength of volitional drive and, more surely than those of the first type, emotionally under par. We should therefore anticipate that when any one of these three kinds of deviation is carried to an extreme the religious attitude will be so compromised that we may say with rough accuracy that religion itself has evaporated. And, as a matter of fact, this is what we do find.

I have already cited the Jñāna-Yoga as instancing the fate which befalls religion when subjected to a process of overintellectualization. I fully recognize that the goal of the Jñāna-Yoga lies beyond the sphere of discursive thought and is conceived to be attainable only by direct intuition; and I do not suppose that this ultimate insight, be its nature what it may, can be gained otherwise than as the result of prolonged concentration which involves a strenuous exercise of willpower, nor yet that the gaining of it can fail to be productive of emotional satisfaction. Nonetheless, the exclusive emphasis of the Jñāna-Yoga is upon insight; everything else is subordinated to this and is of importance only as it leads to this. The ultimate state is conceived to be one of tranquil serenity, undisturbed by any problems either intellectual or moral. Moreover, he who seeks to win it should abstain so far as is possible from all actions, from right actions as well as from wrong, for right and wrong alike subject the self to the law of Karma and involve it in the process of birth and death; the divorce between the way of salvation and ethical conduct is thus definitely established.

Here we have indeed a profound deviation from the normal course of religious development. For the connection between religion and conduct is present even at the most primitive stage and becomes ever more pronounced as the religious outlook widens. We have only to think of the ethical idealism associated with the great world religions to see how pronounced is this departure from the norm. By turning his back upon all human interests and shuffling off all moral responsibilities the follower of the Jñāna-Yoga has sought to isolate himself from his kind. He has abstracted the metaphysical interest from all other concerns save the concern for his individual destiny; hence in his attitude we find neither religion in the sense in which the saints of the world faiths have known it, nor yet philosophy in the breadth and sweep in which it presented itself to the greatest thinkers of our race, to such men as Plato, Aristotle, and Plotinus, to Spinoza and Hegel, or to Sāṁkara or Rāmānuja.

In the case of emotional aberration the situation is somewhat different. Emotion requires some fuel to feed on, and religious emotion feeds upon religious beliefs. But, when the flame rises in an all-consuming conflagration, it is apt to burn up the capacity for intellectual development and to produce a lack of interest in moral and social problems. The man who wallows in an emotional orgy may fancy that he has been raised to a level at which he can be a law to himself and that he has been absolved from the obligations which are binding upon those not thus favored. Antinomianism is a recurrent danger which religion has to dread. The Brethren of the Free Spirit are a case in point. The evil is not that emotion is too strong but that intellect and conscience are too weak. When the balance is thus impaired, emotion, lacking nobler fuel, frequently turns to feed upon the senses; hence the sexual license which sometimes disgraces religion at a level at which it can no longer plead in its defense the confused naïveté of primitive man. When moral considerations are thus cast aside it perhaps matters little whether we say that religion has been lost or that it has been perverted; at least its health and genuineness have gone. At this stage, moreover, we sometimes discover an attempt to substitute the beautiful for the good, an attempt which generates what is at once both decadent art and decadent religion.

Within the field of religion itself, moreover, emotionalism is in large measure responsible for the appearance of two sinister characters, the sentimentalist and the zealot. The sentimentalist is a familiar and a rather pathetic figure. What makes him what he is is the fact that his emotion is not genuine but forced, whipped up, and assumed. His attitude is usually the product either of timidity or of mental laziness, or of both, when confronted by the crucial problems of religion. At once arises the cry of the intellectual defeatist that speculation is hopeless, presumptuous, a sacrilegious tampering with the holy, and that the only proper attitude is one of uncritical acceptance of some external authority, more or less arbitrarily chosen, or of what the sentimentalist himself wants to believe and therefore asserts to be the fundamental truth. Although to the genuine thinker and to the genuine

religionist alike the sentimentalist is an unmitigated bore, his in
fluence may nonetheless be both powerful and pernicious upon persons
whose temperament is congenial to his own. That a vast deal of
sentimentality underlies contemporary neo-orthodoxy it requires no
very profound psychoanalyst to discover.

The zealot is usually something of a sentimentalist as well, but a
sentimentalist who has successfully repressed his doubts in the depth
of his subconscious, and who thence derives an obsessive drive to
buttress his own confidence by forcing all the world to agree with
him. No man who is willing fairly and impartially to face fundamenta
problems would desire, even were he able, to constrain the thinkin
of another. To attempt to do so, whether by physical force or by din
of numbers, is indicative of a bad conscience or of intellectual im
maturity. To debate with zealots is a waste of time, as every generatio
discovers afresh; for their opinions are based not upon reason bu
upon passion, and in many, if not in most, cases upon passion tincture
with a strong infusion of self-interest. To try to argue with a be
liever in racial equality is as futile today as it was fifty years ag
to argue with a prohibitionist or a hundred years ago with an abol
tionist. Concerning zealots of this last type, one who knew them we
has written "their narrow fury angered you." [2] In this narrow fury of th
fanatic, emotionalism sinks to its nadir.

A disproportionate emphasis upon the will involves us at once i
a preoccupation with conduct, and this expresses itself in one of tw
forms. In the case of healthier minds it is productive of a narrow
ethical outlook. An impatient desire to eradicate thinking so far a
possible from religion speedily manifests itself. Speculation abo
the nature of the universe or about the destiny of the soul aft
death is loudly decried as both useless and irrelevant. Otherworld
ness is denounced as cowardly evasiveness. All that matters, we a
told, is the obligation to live a good life, to struggle with all on
might to realize one's loftiest ideals. One's sole determination shou
be, in the words of Job, to "hold fast to righteousness and not l
it go."

What results, of course, is the substitution of ethics for religic
This is a stage through which habitually pass a relatively small nu
ber of devoted souls, and in which some permanently remain. I s
"a relatively small number," for it will scarcely be contended that t
average man is prepared to give himself wholly to the pursuit of
moral ideal in utter disregard of the claims of self-interest both in t

2. See Rebecca Harding Davis, *Bits of Gossip* (New York, 1904), p. 165.

world and the next. To do so is a purifying and strengthening experience, for thereby the self discovers its ability to live nobly without the twin stimuli of hope and fear. Locke's prudential attitude is now definitely repudiated, and with this repudiation comes a sense of moral cleanliness. A certain type of lofty Stoicism is thus cultivated which remains an abiding possession, and one who has passed through this stage can ever after treat with contempt the cynical jibe that religion is no more than an enlightened self-interest. Indeed we may say that only he is entitled to the consolations of religion who has shown himself prepared to live without them.

Nonetheless, this attitude, invigorating though it is, soon reveals itself as defective in more than one respect. In the first place it is almost certain to produce an unhealthy preoccupation with self-scrutiny which tends to defeat its own ends. Moral improvement, like happiness, is best achieved when it is not the sole object of concern. Character grows best when it is not the object of tireless examination, when the individual become absorbed in the pursuit of ends other than perfecting himself. The Stoic is too prone to make a god of his idealized image of himself.

In the second place he who devotes himself to the realization of moral ideals must inevitably ask himself upon what they are based. If, like Lord Russell, he conclude that they have no other basis than his own subjective preference, he must, again like Lord Russell, admit that those who prefer to adopt other attitudes are equally entitled to theirs, and that he is justified in condemning such characteristics as cruelty, selfishness, and deceit upon no other ground than that he personally finds them distasteful. One of two consequences is thus almost sure to follow. Either his own resolution will be weakened or, if he succeed in conserving its primal intensity, he must recognize that in opposing those whose moral attitude he condemns he can appeal to no other arbitrament than that of force; and he will thus tend to fall into the "narrow fury" of the zealot. If, on the other hand, he concludes that moral judgments are grounded in the structure of the universe, he will have opened a door to philosophical speculation which he can thereafter close only at the cost of contradicting himself. The limitations of a purely this-worldly outlook will no longer be capable of satisfying him. He will be compelled to recognize that intellect and emotion have their rights as well as volition, and that a cosmic outlook is both essential and desirable. He will thus have passed beyond the stage of a purely ethical enthusiasm, and, without losing what he has gained thereby, he will now find himself concerned with the orientation of his whole nature with respect to the universe to which it belongs; in other words, he will have arrived at the standpoint of genuine religion.

The second form in which a preoccupation with conduct may manifest itself is a concern for ritual. And it cannot be too strongly emphasized that ritual is essential to religion in any of its communal forms of expression. This is as true in the case of the atheistic Jains as in that of the theistic Christians. Whenever and wherever people come together to join in common worship or devotion the establishment of some routine is unavoidable. There is no escape from this necessity. The silence of a Quaker meeting is a ritual silence. Some persons find a relatively simple service more dignified and impressive than a highly complicated and elaborate service, while others are of the contrary opinion. Some minds, it would seem, have a native liking for symbols and revel in their multiplication, whereas others would eliminate all that are not absolutely essential as barriers between themselves and reality. To the former ornate symbolism is emotionally uplifting, to the latter it is irritating and repulsive.[3] But there can be no doubt that any form of service which has become hallowed by habitual usage throughout the centuries makes a strong emotional appeal and performs the important function of binding the generations together and enabling the participants to realize their membership in a community which extends across the ages and unites the living and the dead.

We raise an important issue, however, when we inquire whether the value of ritual consist solely in the psychological response evoked from those who practice it, or whether ritual possess an efficacy of its own. Is baptism essential to salvation? Is it, as Calvin taught, a means of grace? Do the bread and wine of the eucharist become the body and blood of Christ? Does a sacrament produce its effect *ex opere operato?* Obviously we are not yet in a position to attempt to answer such questions. Impatiently we may exclaim that those who would respond to them in the affirmative have reverted to the intellectual level of primitive men with their hunting dances and their

---

3. Thus Jalālu'ddīn Rumi exclaims:

> How long wilt thou dwell on words and superficialities?
> A burning heart is what I want; consort with burning!
> Kindle in thy heart the flame of love,
> And burn up utterly thoughts and fine expressions.
> O Moses! the lovers of fair rites are one class,
> They whose hearts and souls burn with Love another.
>
> *The Masnavi,* trans. Whinfield (London, 1898)

rites of seedtime and harvest. Yet, even if we see in extreme sacramentalism the survival or resurgence within Christianity of a pagan
outlook, we cannot deny that it is an outlook which is genuinely
religious. To apply to it, as some frequently do, the term "magical," is
both insolent and unjust. For the sacramentarian—at least the enlightened sacramentarian—makes no attempt to constrain the supernatural
nor to compel it to serve his individual and, mayhap, antisocial
interest, as the magician does. On the contrary, he supplicates it. In
the mass, which may be taken to constitute the extreme development
of sacramentalism, the miraculous is deemed to be present, but not
the magical.

The danger of ritual, especially when it is believed to exercise an
efficacy *ex opere operato*, is that it may be substituted for morality.
And a recurrent danger it is, always present whenever ritual is valued
for its own sake. To this the passionate denunciations of the Hebrew
prophets and the contemptuous repudiation of the Buddha bear eloquent witness, and with these blends the solemn voice of Plato as he
excoriates as the "worst atheism" the belief that the gods can be bribed
by the performance of any rite to overlook evil conduct. When descent
to such a level has taken place we can justly say that the soul of
religion has fled, and has left behind only its corpse.

We must also recognize, however, that orthodox belief has, with
perhaps greater frequency than ritual act, supplanted virtuous conduct
as the grand essential in the eyes of many. Here we are concerned, not—as in the case of the Jñāna-Yoga—with a claim to supernormal insight, but with the mere acceptance of dogma promulgated
by some authority. When we recollect that in the Middle Ages heretics
were frequently detected by the sanctity of their lives, when we
recall the atrocities of the Inquisition, when we survey the history of
persecution throughout the centuries, we cannot fail to be appalled by
the terrific power of this tendency. It is bound to reassert itself
whenever correctness of belief has come to be regarded as essential
to salvation. When the divorce between belief and conduct has become complete, and when belief has come to be regarded not merely
as essential but as all-sufficient, the balance will have been destroyed,
and we shall have passed, as we have already recognized, beyond the
pale of genuine religion. Needless to say, no authorized spokesman
of orthodox Christianity—the most dogmatic of religions—would
officially countenance such a repudiation of moral responsibility; yet,
at some times and places, popular thinking has actually sunk as low

as this, and when orthodox belief includes an acceptance of the aton-
ing efficacy of ritual we find a revolting parody of religion of the
type which Plato so unsparingly castigated.

That religion in the course of its evolution has been the source of
frightful evils is a truth with which we are all familiar. But such
horrors as human sacrifice and cannibalism are to be found, not indeed
at the earliest, yet at a comparatively early stage of its progress, and
were due to the remorseless logic with which early men developed the
implications of their crude presuppositions, presuppositions which
today we should not hesitate to call superstitious. Intolerance and
persecution, however, are frequently to be discovered in connection
with the most highly developed religions, and while we are justified,
I should maintain, in regarding them as perversions, yet we must
recognize that the bigot who is not indifferent to moral considerations
still stands within the boundaries of religion, deeply as we may de-
plore his presence there. And we must recognize too that his zeal,
emotionally unbalanced and extravagant as it is, has its roots in certain conceptions of authority in religion and of the nature of the
Deity which we have not yet examined, and in virtue of which he
would impugn the justice of our condemnation.[4] Considerations of this
sort, which involve such questions as the nature of faith and the seat
of authority in religion, we shall take up in the next chapter.

4. Cf., for instance, the following citation from Father R. A. Knox's *The Beliefs
of Catholics* (Garden City, N.Y., 1958):

> You cannot bind over the Catholic Church, as the price of your adhesion to
> her doctrines, to waive all right of invoking the secular arm in defense of her
> own principles. The circumstances in which such a possibility could be
> realized are indeed sufficiently remote. You have to assume, for practical
> purposes, a country with a very strong Catholic majority, the overwhelming
> body of the nation. Probably (though not certainly) you would have to
> assume that the non-Catholic majority are innovators, newly in revolt
> against the Catholic system, with no ancestral traditions, no vested interests
> to be respected. Given such circumstances, is it certain that the Catholic
> Government of the nation would have no right to insist on Catholic education
> being universal (which is a form of coercion), and even to deport or imprison
> those who unsettled the minds of its subjects with new doctrines?
> It is certain that the Church would claim that right for the Catholic
> Government, even if considerations of prudence forbade its exercise in fact.
> The Catholic Church will not be one amongst the philosophies. Her children
> believe, not that her doctrines may be true, but that they *are* true, and con-
> sequently part of the normal make-up of a man's mind; not even a parent
> can legitimately refuse such education to his child. They recognize, however,
> that such truths (unlike the mathematical axioms) can be argued against;
> that simple minds can easily be seduced by the sophistries of plausible
> error; they recognize, further, that the divorce between speculative belief and
> practical conduct is a divorce in thought, not in fact; that the unchecked

Enough has been said, I think, to confirm the contention that, whenever we find religion in a healthy condition, we can see that it consists in an orientation of the whole self with respect to the universe and that such an orientation involves a balance between intellect, emotion, and volition. This assertion holds good of religion in all stages of its development from the most primitive to the highest. Its unifying tendency extends to all aspects of human life, individual and communal. Whenever and wherever religion is present it constitutes the central interest and acts as a focus of all subordinate interests: hence any attempt to treat it as a separate factor, on an equal footing with all others, springs from a misconception of the situation, and is productive of consequences injurious both to religion itself and to all other interests. In primitive society religion blends with custom and consecrates every phase of tribal life. Art and government fall within its orbit; peace and war alike are its concern. Nor did the rise of the early civilizations alter this state of affairs. The nation succeeded the tribe as a religious unit. The sacral character of kingship is a phenomenon of outstanding importance. The first scientists were priests. Even the city-states of Greece were—if I may so put it—at once ecclesiastical and political units. It was only at a relatively late stage in the history of civilization that religious organizations began to distinguish themselves from the political.

In the case of the Jews this was due to the development of a national cult lofty enough and strong enough to survive the loss of independence. The evolution of henotheism into monotheism, the emphasis upon the doctrine of a chosen people, and the rise of an intense religious legalism constituted peculiar advantages which enabled the Jews to establish their corporate life upon a purely religious basis. Elsewhere the situation was transformed by the appearance of great religious teachers each of whom professed to have a message for

---

development of false theories results in ethical aberrations—Anabaptism yesterday, Bolshevism to-day—which are a menace even to the social order. And for these reasons a body of Catholic patriots, entrusted with the Government of a Catholic State, will not shrink even from repressive measures in order to perpetuate the domination of Catholic principles among their fellow-countrymen. (pp. 241–242)

This passage, I feel sure, requires no elucidation. Readers will observe that the imaginary country described corresponds very closely to present-day Spain, where even now Carlists are demanding the revival of the Inquisition.

(Since the lines above were written the declaration of the Vatican Council affirming the right of every man to religious liberty has officially repudiated such a position as that of Father Knox and has given to all non-Roman Catholics a most welcome assurance, even though some may still feel inclined to ejaculate "Timeo Danaos et dona ferentes.")

all mankind—Zarathustra in Iran, and the Mahāvīra and the Buddha in India. As a result communities were formed upon a purely religious foundation. In due course Judaism gave rise to Christianity, and Judaism and Christianity together to Islam; each of the new religions claimed the whole world as its province and attempted to extend its sway over men of all nations and races.

Where any of these faiths established itself, however, it at once attempted to mold the entire socio-political structure in accordance with its own ideals. But religion now spoke to society *de haut en bas*. It was at once in the world yet not of the world. The formation of the Roman Catholic Church provided Western Christianity with an organization which was definitely supernational and which to a great extent did succeed in dominating the national life of medieval Europe; and a somewhat similar dominance within its own sphere of influence was attained by the Caliphate.

The Reformation, by establishing national churches, to a certain extent reversed the course of history. An established church, in theory at least, is the embodiment of the spiritual life of the nation; and the union thus achieved in some degree resembles the city-state of ancient Greece. Nevertheless the regression—if such it be—is not complete. Although a national church constitutes a distinct ecclesiastical entity, yet it is in communion with other national churches founded upon the same doctrinal basis. Thus the various established Calvinist and Lutheran churches stand with respect to the Calvinist and Lutheran movements much as species stand in relation to their genera. And the same must be said of other Calvinist and Lutheran denominations which are not established churches—such as those which exist in the United States.

This brings us to the consideration of the role of sects in the life of religion. Sectarianism is a phenomenon of tremendous importance in the history of Christianity, Buddhism, and Islam, and of somewhat lesser importance in the histories of Judaism and Jainism. And it is, of course, closely connected with the notions of orthodoxy and heterodoxy. Where thought is free, differences of opinion are bound to arise. How important these are deemed to be will depend upon the perspective within which they are viewed, and upon the presuppositions which are entertained. However tolerant a man may be, one cannot expect him to stand by without protest while a teaching which he regards as both true and of the highest importance is, to his mind, being misinterpreted or transformed. When controversies occur over points which are considered to be of vital significance, parties are formed, and the old organization is frequently sundered into two or more new organizations. Each of these will naturally claim to be the genuine representative of the original and will seek to discredit the claims of its fellows.

In the Christian world there are several denominations, each of which denies that it is a sect and insists that it is identical with the original church and that all other bodies are in "schism"; and to these it applies the word "sect" in a pejorative sense. Other Christians, adopting a more genial point of view, would identify the church with the entire group of denominations, all of which without exception they would regard as sects. In general, however, throughout the Christian world, the existence of sects is considered undesirable, as a rending of the "seamless robe of Christ"; and perpetual efforts are made to restore the unity of the church by persuading the various sects to coalesce. So far as such efforts have been successful, the success has usually been achieved by prevailing upon the denominations involved to waive their divergent views as relatively unimportant.

In the Buddhist world, however, the multiplication of sects is generally looked upon rather as an asset than as a liability, and as indicative rather of the strength than of the weakness of the religion. It reveals, we are told, the capacity of Buddhism to satisfy different types of mentality. This is a point of view which, in its broadmindedness, can scarcely fail to appeal to the philosopher. If it be asked why persons who hold divergent opinion cannot join together for the practice of the spiritual life, the answer must be that there is a connection between theory and practice and that differences with respect to the one may have an important bearing upon the other. Thus it is clear that in a group of people who have united with the purpose of endeavoring to enter into communion with a personal God, there will be no logical place for an atheistic Jain or a Hīnayāna Buddhist intent only upon the attainment of Nirvāṇa.[5] And it is equally obvious that a strict monotheist and an avowed polytheist would

5. The disparateness of viewpoints is well brought by an anecdote recounted by J. B. Pratt in *The Pilgrimage of Buddhism* (New York, 1928), p. 135: "It is said that when in 1877, Bishop Titcomb, the first British bishop of Burma, went out to take up his duties in that land, he visited a Buddhist temple soon after his arrival and seeing a monk at his devotions asked him, with typically British directness, 'To whom are you praying and for what?' To which the monk replied with equal promptness, 'I am praying to nobody and for nothing.' " (The story was originally told by John Nisbet in *Burma under British Rule* [Westminster, 1901], p. 89.)

have difficulties in performing their devotions together. In these instances, of course, the gap is wider than between individuals professing the same religion. Yet often between Christian and Christian or Muslim and Muslim the disagreement is sufficient to render joint devotion as habitual practice difficult, or even impossible. Consequently the division into sects, and into sects within sects, is not without its advantages. For it is, surely, a good thing that differing points of view should be definitely and clearly stated, and their logical implications worked out; for this elaborate development of rival theories the better enables the inquiring mind to choose between them.

To admit so much, it may be objected, is a base concession to pragmatism; it implies that an organization is to be valued for its utility, and not for the truth to which it bears witness. The function of religion, we shall be informed, is to proclaim truth; it is not to speak smooth words to the spiritually lazy, or to comfort the mentally immature by the prescription of intellectual patent medicines. Error is always bad, and the thing to do with unsound presuppositions is not to deduce their consequences but to blast them at the root.

Let me hasten to assure the objector that I repudiate pragmatism and all its works. To defend doctrines in which one does not oneself believe on the ground that they may benefit one's mental inferiors is, I admit, a disgusting manifestation of an intellectual snobbery which has too often disgraced "modernism." A powerful infusion of the Zoroastrian horror of lying into Christianity, and perhaps into other religions as well, would doubtless be conducive to moral health. But in the formation of sects sincerity is not the issue. One is entitled to assume that the founder of any school of thought takes the position that he does because he believes it to be sound, and when people divide into groups upon the basis of theoretical differences we are justified in inferring that they consider these differences to be important. Where freedom of thought prevails such divisions and groupings are almost inevitable. It is stimulating, moreover, to the impartial inquirer to find that the various possible points of view have already been distinguished and developed, so that he can begin by comparing and contrasting them. And, while the shallow mind is apt easily to be satisfied with a superficial theory, the profounder mind is likely to think its way from one position to another until it finds its own level.

We are prone to assume that the true religion must be the one best fitted to fill the needs of the "average man," and frequently we hear it said that the profoundest view is sure to be the simplest.[6] We may well hope that such is the case, and it may even be the case; yet are we justified in assuming at the outset of our inquiry that it must be the case? Were it the case, should we not discover a far greater degree of general agreement than actually obtains? Is the proliferation of rival religions and rival philosophies due solely to an innate perversity in the human mind which leads it to turn away from obvious truth and to burrow into ever deeper levels of obscurity? This does not seem a very plausible suggestion. It was, we may recall, the considered opinion of Plato, who cannot, I think, fairly be accused of intellectual snobbery, that the Father and Maker of the universe is not easily to be known, nor yet made known to others, and that the worship of local gods and heros is that best adapted to the needs of the average man. We must, surely, beware of the easy conviction that truth in these matters is to be attained with the minimum of intellectual effort, and also of the easy despair which concludes with such facility that truth can never be attained at all. We must therefore conclude, I believe, with the Buddhist, that the rise of sects is a healthy manifestation of religious vitality.

As a culmination of this tendency we find individual thinkers developing what we may term private or personal religions, that is to say, metaphysical systems which are the product of their own reflection and which are undoubtedly religious in spirit and content but which yet cannot be regarded as falling within the compass of any of the great world faiths. We have but to think of such men as Plotinus, Bruno, Spinoza, Bradley, and McTaggart to realize that such is the case. And we must frankly acknowledge that their efforts have contributed to the advancement of human thought.

It is in thought, as we have seen, that religion is rooted, and it is

6. A notable instance of the expression of this conviction is to be found in Channing's sermon entitled "Unitarian Christianity Most Favorable to Piety." "Unitarianism," declares William Ellery Channing,

> is the system most favorable to piety, because it presents a distinct and intelligible object of worship,—a Being whose nature, whilst inexpressibly sublime, is yet simple and suited to human apprehension. An Infinite Father is the most exalted of all conceptions, and yet the least perplexing. It involves no incongruous ideas. It is illustrated by analogies from our own nature. It coincides with that fundamental law of the intellect through which we demand a cause proportioned to its effects. It is also as interesting as it is rational; so that it is peculiarly congenial with the improved mind. The sublime simplicity of God, as He is taught in Unitarianism, by relieving the understanding from perplexity, and by placing him within the reach of thought and affection, gives him peculiar power over the soul. (*Works of William E Channing* [Boston, 1886], p. 390, col. 1)

belief which integrates the emotional and volitional manifestations of the religious life. This is true of religion at every stage of its development. The religious thinking of primitive man, together with that of the early civilizations, we are wont to term "mythology." What do we mean when we employ this word, and how is it to be defined? The answer would seem to be that when we use it we intend to designate a stage of human thought at which it had not yet become fully conscious of its own principles, and of the methods which are proper to it. Early men reasoned much as we do, but their presuppositions frequently impress us as bizarre to the last degree. The influences of tradition, authoritative pronouncements, sense-experience, ethical insight, intuition, and logical inference must have mingled in their minds in well nigh inextricable confusion. Mythology, we may fairly say, stands to metaphysics much as superstition stands to religion.

Readers of Professor Mircea Eliade's *Patterns in Comparative Religion* will realize how inevitably the heaven, the sun, the moon, rocks, mountains, trees, and waters furnished men with their religious symbols, and why the primitive agriculturalists naturally devoted more attention than did the food-gatherers to the sequence of the seasons and the movements of the heavenly bodies. We can understand why the fact of sex seemed to offer man a principle of explanation, and why he was so prone to think in terms of theogonies. It was only very gradually, and at the cost of vast effort, that civilized man succeeded in rising above the mythological stage of thought.

In India, indeed, philosophy developed directly out of mythology. In Ionia a speculative movement which was to give birth both to science and to metaphysics managed to cut itself loose from mythology, although—as Professor Werner Jaeger has shown [7]—by no means from the religious interest. In Palestine mythology passed imperceptibly into genuine theology, and the growth of ethical insight was rooted in the notion of inspiration. It was only at a comparatively late stage in the development of civilization that philosophy was given recognition as a distinct type of intellectual activity and that the problems of its relation to religious authority and to religious experience coincidentally arose, problems which we shall presently examine.

Throughout its entire history the connection of religion with art has been an intimate one. That it should have been so was, indeed, inevitable; for, as we have seen, religion by its very nature seeks to dominate the whole of human life. Since the aesthetic impulse must

7. *Theology of the Early Greek Philosophers* (New York, 1947).

needs express itself through some sensuous medium it was unavoidable that religion, with its emphasis upon the spiritual, should now and again have reacted, and reacted excessively, against its own manifestations upon the aesthetic level which at times seemed to suffocate it. Thus iconoclasm has burst forth at recurrent intervals with devastating force, and puritanic asceticism has looked upon art with suspicion, and even with hostility. The moral and the beautiful, instead of manifesting themselves in conjunction, have thereupon found themselves standing in a relation of temporary opposition. And the artist, impatient of censure and control, has torn off the shackles of religion and vociferously enunciated a demand for "art for art's sake." It requires no very great degree of penetration to discern that when the outward trappings of religion have become drab and uninspiring, and when art has sunk to the level which it has reached today, the life of the spirit is in an unhealthy condition. Religion and art have need of each other. For religion must express itself in the aesthetic, as well as in the moral and intellectual realms; and art requires the stimulus of religion to attain the vision of the beautiful and the divine.

As we survey the history of religion we cannot fail to become aware of two more or less antithetical tendencies both of which are of the first importance. One of these we may call traditionalism. It is to this that the life of religion owes its continuity throughout the successive generations. Without tradition communal manifestations of religion would be impossible; we should be left in a state of spiritual anarchy. Even the most radical of theorists is dependent upon tradition, at times seemingly unconsciously so; yet often the radical aspires only to be a more loyal traditionalist than his fellows and directs his efforts to discriminating between genuine and counterfeit tradition. Thus the Protestant reformers desired nothing more than a return to primitive Christianity. Every fresh advance in the development of religion in its turn becomes enshrined in, and perpetuated by, a fresh tradition. It is tradition which conserves the achievements of the past; hence its importance can scarcely be overestimated; hence the anxious care with which it is guarded; hence the unwisdom of disturbing or challenging it without adequate cause.

Yet, left to itself, tradition would choke all progress. Indeed, the pure traditionalist is wont to deny that any progress is possible, and to denounce any suggested change as sacrilegious. Yet progress there has been; the religious outlook has altered, the religious perspective has widened, higher points of view have been successively attained,

We may call this tendency progressivism; and we can see that it is equally essential to the healthy life of religion. This tendency has, of course, manifested itself most spectacularly and dramatically in the emergence of the towering figures of great religious teachers who have dominated subsequent centuries. It is, perhaps, too much to hope for that these two vital tendencies will ever function in perfect harmony, that they will never clash and generate opposing movements. And it is not our present business to endeavor to adjudicate between them in any particular instance; we have only to recognize them and to acknowledge the vital services which they both render.

This leads us naturally enough to observe the ambivalent attitude which religion at its advanced stages has assumed toward historic events, and the relative degrees of importance which it has attached to them. Where there is no history, where established custom of immemorial antiquity is the sole basis of authority, no such ambivalence of outlook is possible. But, when great personalities have appeared and are remembered, and when their teachings have been conserved by tradition, the relation of religion to historic events becomes one of deep significance; and this relation has been differently conceived and evaluated by various faiths. Zoroastrianism, for instance, is based upon the teachings of one of the most galvanic personalities ever to have appeared upon this planet, and during the centuries which separate us from him no teachers even remotely comparable to him have arisen within its tradition. Whatever material later Zoroastrianism has assimilated from external sources, it is largely to the abiding stimulus imparted by its great prophet that it owes its continued life. Thus Zoroastrianism may justly be classified as a historical religion par excellence. Hinduism, on the other hand, looks back to no individual founder. Like a great stream it flows from a source so ancient as to be only imperfectly descried. It has had its great saints, its great teachers, and its great thinkers; all of these are important figures, yet none of them dominates it; they fall within it, and the subordinate traditions to which they gave rise are conserved within the whole. Thus Hinduism "sits loose" with respect to history; accordingly it may fairly be classified as fundamentally a metaphysical, and not a historical, religion.

Again, while the impartation of any great religious teaching, whether it profess to be derived from revelation or—as in the case of Jainism or of Buddhism—to be due to the attainment of supernormal, although not supernatural, insight, is obviously an event of historical importance, yet the content of that teaching may, or may not, embrace historical, or reputedly historical, events. Thus Mahāyāna Buddhism, in some of its manifestations—in Amidism, for instance— is almost completely devoid of any concern with history; whereas orthodox Christianity, with its fundamental doctrine of a unique Incarnation which occurred at a definite time and place, and with its dogma of *extra ecclesiam nulla salus,* is definitely wedded to the historic, or to what it takes to be such. And the issue raised by these conflicting points of view is clearly one of the first importance for the philosopher of religion.

In this chapter we have been concerned with the phenomenology of religion, that is to say, with its multifarious and characteristic modes of manifestation, and not with the question of its validity. This question, needless to add, constitutes our fundamental problem; and with it we shall wrestle throughout the following chapters. Before embarking upon it, however, a bird's-eye viewing of the entire field has been a necessary preliminary. This having been accomplished, our next step must be to consider the question, which may turn out to be a blind alley, whether an investigation of the origin of religion can shed any light upon its validity.

CHAPTER THREE

THE ORIGIN OF RELIGION

The question with which we closed the last chapter is no sooner asked than two further problems force themselves upon our attention: (1) Is it possible to discover the origin of religion? and (2) Does this question lie within the purview of the philosopher of religion? To take the latter question first, it may be maintained that the philosopher is concerned solely with the validity of religion, and that to this issue the problem of its origin is irrelevant. However it originated, religion is here, expressing itself in thought, emotion, and conduct, integrating and dominating the lives of those who profess it. And it is in view of what it is and of what it does, and not of how it arose, that religion is to be evaluated. What we wish to discover is whether religion can be explained in purely subjective terms, or whether it requires us to posit something objective in the structure or nature of ultimate reality. What we must ask, then, is whether the study of religious experience contributes significantly to our conception of the universe as a whole, and whether, on the other hand, what metaphysics can tell us about the universe as a whole tends to substantiate the claims of religion. In other words, do the two, as it were, play into each other's hands, or do they not? Clearly both these lines of inquiry must be pursued *pari passu,* and, equally clearly, the question of origin is irrelevant to both of them.

To this contention it may plausibly be replied that the question of how a belief has arisen cannot fail to bear upon the truth of the belief. The belief has arisen as the result of some experience or was drawn from some inference. Could we, then, determine the experience, or identify the inference, we should be in a position to evaluate the soundness of the belief. Plainly, therefore, the question of origin cannot be irrelevant.

This brings us back to the first question. Is it possible to discover the origin of religion? Numerous theories have been advanced which professed to solve this problem, and some of them at least have been pretty thoroughly discredited. No one today would take seriously, for instance, the view so popular three centuries ago that religion sprang from the doctrines promulgated by designing priests, for it fails to account for the existence of the priests or to explain how they succeeded in evoking general credence in their teachings. Again the theory, recently so widely held, that religion developed out of a primitive animatism has lost ground, both because of lack of evidence that any such condition ever existed, and because the notion of "impersonal spirit" is one which cannot plausibly be attributed to primitive man. The attempts to derive religion from totemism or shamanism have likewise been pronounced failures, and, again, for two reasons: because neither totemistic nor shamanistic beliefs are universally prevalent, and because they are found in conjunction with the beliefs in the soul and in spirits or gods, which beliefs are obviously not derivable from them but which they rather presuppose. It likewise appears hopeless to seek the origin of religion in the distinction between the sacred and the profane, inasmuch as this distinction itself clearly presupposes a religious outlook.

Is it permissible, however, to posit a stage of human thought at which communal rites were believed to function *ex opere operato,* a stage which constituted the common matrix out of which genuinely religious, philosophic, and scientific theorizings were later to develop? In the caverns of Europe we find clay representations of the cave bear which retain the marks of spear thrusts. Do not these provide evidence of a rite which was believed to exert its efficacy in subsequent combat with the bear? And was not the hunting dance a similar rite? Were not the splendid pictures which portray the hunt on the cavern walls painted with a practical purpose in view? Granted, however, the close association between primitive religion and sympathetic magic, the speculative attempt to derive them both from a prereligious and premagical—or magical—intellectual matrix is plainly hazardous—if, for no other reason, because the beliefs in the soul and in an afterlife are found at the most primitive level, and these are obviously of religious significance.

In view of this may we not revert with some degree of confidence to Tyler's theory—which, in consequence of the discrediting of the animatistic hypothesis, may fairly demand reconsideration—that the notion of the soul was the germ of religion? Clearly it was a conception of tremendous significance, and its formulation was perhaps the greatest intellectual achievement of primitive man. Moreover it seems natural to assume that it was his first, for what was nearer to man than himself? We must not, of course, suppose that primitive man was capable of forming the notion of a purely spiritual substance. This was a conception which, in the Western world, awaited the appearance of

Plato and Aristotle. Doubtless early man thought of the soul as a sort of double of his body, as animating yet capable of leaving this body, as having extension, shape, and color, and as visible upon occasion, as in dreams. Without such a conception the belief in spirits, demons, and gods would appear to be inexplicable. Hence, to postulate a gradual advance from animism through polydemonism to polytheism, and thence to henotheism, and so to monotheism or pantheism, seems plausible enough.

Are we entitled, however, to posit a purely animistic stage of thought preceding the development of polydemonism or polytheism? In so doing, would we not be building upon insufficient evidence? And is any such hypothesis requisite? Once the conception of the soul had been formed, must not man have thought of many, if not most, objects, of animals, trees, and plants, of rivers and thunderstorms, of all that lived or moved, even, perhaps, of mountains and rocks, as besouled; and must he not thus at once have found himself a member of a society which contained beings superior, as well as beings inferior, to himself? Was not, then, polytheism born together with the soul?

The issue thus raised, it may be said, is of subordinate importance. Whether the belief in non-human spirits arose coincidentally with or subsequently to the belief in the soul matters little. In either case, the belief in the soul is clearly fundamental. It constitutes the germ of religion, as Tyler held. But perhaps it is only the germ. It seems probable enough that man could not conceive of a harmony between himself and the universe as a whole before he had formed the conception of superhuman intelligences upon whom he could rely. Go back as far as we may, everywhere we find prevalent the belief in spirits; hence we can with some degree of assurance aver that polydemonism or polytheism was the primitive religion of mankind. Has not the discerning Hume with his habitual clarity given us a convincing statement of the situation? He writes,

> We may as reasonably imagine that men inhabited palaces before huts and cottages, or studied geometry before agriculture; as assert that the Deity appeared to them a pure spirit, omniscient, omnipotent, and omnipresent, before he was apprehended to be a powerful, though limited being, with human passions and appetites, limbs and organs. The mind rises gradually, from inferior to superior; By abstracting from what is imperfect, it forms an idea of perfection: And slowly distinguishing the nobler parts of its own frame from the grosser, it learns to transfer the former, much

elevated and refined, to its divinity. Nothing could disturb this natural progress of thought, but some obvious and invincible argument, which might immediately lead the mind into the pure principles of theism, and make it overleap, at one bound, the vast interval which is interposed between the human and the divine nature. But though I allow, that the order and frame of the universe, when accurately examined, affords such an argument; yet I can never think, that this consideration could have an influence on mankind, when they formed their first rude notions of religion.[1]

Here we have an outstanding instance of the argument from probability, from εἰκός, as Athenians of the classic period would have termed it, that type of argument of which the ancient λογογράφοι thought so highly. Yet it behooves us to bear in mind the Greek proverb, "Count it probable that the improbable will occur." In the face of reflections of so general a character, would not a little evidence go a long way? Now, it may be contended, such evidence is before us. For the investigations of recent researchers have made it plain that the belief in the "High Gods" and "Sky Gods" is more ancient than was formerly supposed, and very widely prevalent; moreover they have established that the worship of these beings once occupied a much more prominent place than that which was subsequently accorded it. What more plausible, then, in view of these well-ascertained facts, than to conclude that once the worship of a single heavenly Being constituted the only form of religion, and, accordingly, that monotheism was the primitive religion of mankind? Such is the contention we find stated and defended upon anthropological grounds in the extensive works of that eminent scientist, Father Wilhelm Schmidt.

Here, once more, we must beware of leaping to a conclusion. Granted that the worship of a High God is of great antiquity, and that it once played a far more prominent part in communal life than it has done for centuries, are we justified in inferring that at a remote period the worship of a single Deity obtained over the whole earth and among all peoples? Can we be sure that he had neither consort nor offspring, nor representatives nor subordinates of any kind, and that no other being was worshipped along with him? Any such inference would seem clearly to carry us far beyond the available evidence. The following statement of Professor Eliade depicts with admi-

1. "The Natural History of Religion," sec. 1, in *Essays: Moral, Political, and Literary*, ed. T. H. Green and T. H. Grose (London, 1912), II, 311.

rable caution the situation as it stands in the light of our present knowledge:

> We cannot say for certain that devotion to sky beings was the first and only belief that primitive man had, and that all other religious forms appear later and represent corruptions. Though belief in a supreme sky being is generally to be found among the most archaic of primitive societies (Pygmies, Australians, Fuegians, and so on), it is not found amongst them all (there is none, for instance, among the Tasmanians, the Veddas, the Kubu). And it seems to me, in any case, that such a belief would not necessarily exclude all other religious forms. Undoubtedly, from the earliest times man realized the transcendence and omnipotence of the sacred from what he experienced of the sky. The sky needs no aid from mythological imagination or conceptual elaboration to be seen as *the* divine sphere. But innumerable other hierophanies could coexist with this hierophany of the sky.[2]

It is, of course, obvious that the evidence provided by the worship of the Sky Gods, so far as it goes, will be welcome to orthodox theologians who are committed, in view of their dogmatic presuppositions, to the belief in the impartation of a divine revelation to the first ancestors of the human race. As we have not yet examined these presuppositions, we are not now in a position to pronounce upon them. All that we can at present say is that, should we ultimately be led to concede the soundness of these presuppositions, we, in company with the theologians just referred to, will hail such evidence as is provided by the cult to the Sky Gods as tending empirically to corroborate our view. But should we, on the other hand, find ourselves unable to make this concession, we shall be compelled to acknowledge that the case stands as it has been stated by Professor Eliade.

In light of the foregoing discussion we cannot refuse to acquiesce in the conclusion reached by Professor Georges Dumezil that the science of religion must renounce the quest for origins.[3] Search as we will among the beliefs of the most primitive peoples with whom we are acquainted in the effort to identify, through comparison and contrast, a common "deposit of faith," we must face the unwelcome fact

2. *Patterns in Comparative Religion,* p. 54. See also E. O. James, *Comparative Religion* (New York, 1961), pp. 212–214.

3. See his preface to Mircea Eliade's *Traité d'histoire des religions* (Paris, 1949), p. 6. This work has been translated into English under the title *Patterns in Comparative Religion,* but the preface to the French edition remains untranslated.

that we cannot say definitely of any belief, or any system of beliefs, that it had no predecessor but that it is as old as our race. How man became man is still shrouded in mystery, and so also is his becoming religious. All we dare assert is that so far as we can tell Homo sapiens has always been religious. As of the Levites it was said, "The Lord is their inheritance," [4] so of man we may say that religion is his most ancient and most precious heritage. We may, indeed, conjecture that religion, in its initial stage, cannot have been very different from that of the most primitive peoples known to us, yet this remains conjecture only.

Professor Dumezil has announced, not perhaps without a certain irony, that the science of religion surrenders to philosophy the quest for origins. But the philosopher, before he accept the responsibility for pursuing this quest, must make it plain that he envisages it otherwise than does the scientist. It is not with the temporal origin but with the metaphysical basis of religion that he is primarily concerned, that is, with its validity. The problem which confronts him, and which he hopes will not prove insoluble, is whether religion be no more than a vain imagining on the part of a being who is himself no more than an ontological accident in a universe which is indifferent to him or whether it be an appropriate response on the part of rational selves to a rational universe in which they possess *droit de cité*.

4. Deut. 10:9.

CHAPTER FOUR

PHILOSOPHY AND RELIGION

We must now face the second of the two questions posed at the beginning of our investigation: What is philosophy? And at first glance it might seem a question which admits of no satisfactory answer. In the case of religion we found it possible, by penetrating behind discordant doctrines, to detect an underlying unity of purpose; but in the case of philosophy it seems painfully apparent that no corresponding unity of purpose is to be discovered. As to how philosophy is to be defined, how its field is to be delimited, what its fundamental problems are, and what method is to be employed in dealing with them, upon these questions, as upon all others, philosophers are in disagreement, and, when philosophers disagree, who shall adjudicate between them? Is any other course open to us, therefore, than to settle the question by a fiat of our own, and to lay it down that for the purpose of our present inquiry the word "philosophy" is to mean what we decide it shall mean? Unattractive as we shall doubtless find this cutting of the Gordian knot, it may be urged that no alternative presents itself.

Nonetheless, the fact remains that however much philosophers disagree we do associate them all together and regard them as a class clearly distinguishable from that of scientists, for instance, or that of politicians. Something in common, then, they must have, be it only a common point of departure or a common ground upon which to differ. And what this common something is the history of philosophy clearly reveals to us. For it will scarcely be contested that the task which throughout the centuries philosophers have set before themselves has been to determine the nature of ultimate reality. Some philosophers, indeed, have renounced the task as an impossible one. Yet the appraisal of it has always been the initial effort of every thinker, and whatever attitude he may assume with respect to it, precisely because he does assume *some* attitude toward it do we account him a philosopher. His metaphysical assertions may be positive or negative in character; he may affirm, doubt, or deny; but he cannot shirk taking up some definite position with respect to this basic question if he wish to be regarded as a serious thinker. This is true, not only of the skeptic and the agnostic, but equally of him who subscribes to the dogma, so fashionable today, that all metaphysical propositions are meaningless. Whether a man turn his face or his back to the fundamental problems of metaphysics, he cannot avoid making some pronouncement upon them. In the light of history, therefore, we may affirm without fear of contradiction that philosophy can be defined as the effort to determine the nature of ultimate reality or, to put the same point in other words, of the universe as a whole.

We pass now to a problem which to the philosopher of religion is one of crucial importance. Religion, as we have seen, is rooted in belief. Upon what authority are religious beliefs to be accepted? Upon the authority of reason? Or upon some authority other than reason? What are the credentials of this authority, and how does reason stand with respect to it? Does this authority itself appeal to reason to vindicate it? Then is not reason ultimately the sole authority? Or are the two authorities co-ordinate? What, then, if they differ, or appear to differ? Where shall we find an umpire to arbitrate between them? Or, again, does reason possess no authority whatever in matters of religion? Is its function merely to argue on behalf of dogmas which it is deputed to defend? If so, will not any attempt to develop a philosophy of religion be a fatuous and presumptuous undertaking? And must not philosophy, as gracefully as possible, abdicate in favor of a theology which is founded solely upon faith? Such are the questions we must now consider.

As a point of departure let us take the view, often enunciated with as much apparent confidence as though it were merely the statement of an obvious truth, that philosophy is concerned with judgments of fact and religion with judgments of value, that since they thus operate in different spheres they may both proceed in complete independence of one another, and that, accordingly, no conflict can arise between them. Such was the position taken by Albrecht Ritschl, whose views enjoyed so great a popularity a generation ago. The obvious objection, which critics were quick to raise, is that value and fact cannot thus be completely and permanently sundered. However long and far the axiological arrow may fly in the clouds, sooner or later it must drop to earth; and there we shall find it fixed in some hard-bitten fact. And such, in truth, was the notorious fate of Ritschl's arrow. Value and fact for him came together in Christ, and the basic proposition of his system, all the more dogmatic in sound for the skeptical accompaniment against which it contrasts, is that Christ has the value of God. And this evaluative judgment is asserted to have been formed, not by Ritschl *in propria persona,* nor by any other private individual, but by the Christian community as such.

Like Kant, Ritschl was prepared, in default of proof, to postulate the existence of God; but for Ritschl it was not so much a moral as a religious postulate. Man, he held, is driven by his own spiritual needs to assume the existence of a God whose purpose it is to establish a world-kingdom founded upon the principle of love; and Christ owes his position in the religious consciousness to the fact that he is the outstanding personality in history who made this purpose his own, and who lived and died in an effort to realize it. In magnificent independence of all extraneous considerations the religious consciousness thus proceeds to formulate its own demands and to make whatever assumptions will satisfy them. If Ritschl be right, all that remains for the philosopher of religion to do is to burn his books and to repeat Ritschl's formula after him.

It is quite clear, I submit, that we are here confronted by a theoretical tour de force. The divorce between judgments of value and judgments of fact which Ritschl presupposes can be accounted valid only if values can successfully be subjectified. For if values possess objective reality they will certainly fall within the realm of the factual. If love, for instance, be the supreme value, this is itself a fact and must be recognized as such.

Moreover, the unlimited freedom to postulate which Ritschl demands for the religious consciousness is plainly motivated by an intellectual desperation which springs from a rooted distrust of the powers of reason. For no sensible man will be content with mere postulation so long as proof remains possible. Before Ritschl can appear upon the stage the metaphysician must be induced to commit intellectual *hara-kiri,* and it is possible that the metaphysician may succeed in resisting this demand. We must be sure of his demise before the curtain be raised for Ritschl's performance.

Again the claim that Christ has the value of God is one of those resounding yet hopelessly vague assertions which set the philosopher's teeth on edge. What is meant by "the value of God"? Is God to be valued for what he can do for us? But, then, surely, it is relevant to ask if anyone can possess this value but God himself. If Christ possess this value, must not Christ be God? And if the answer be in the affirmative, how can it be made good except in terms of one of the traditional dogmas—the orthodox, the Nestorian, or the Monophysite —all of which Ritschl, with a lordly gesture, has pushed into the background as not worth considering? For if the appeal be made to history alone, while we may concede that Christianity has been the grandest and the most successful of the movements which aspired to establish the reign of brotherly love, we must also recognize that other religious teachers—the Buddha and Zarathustra, for instance— also initiated movements aimed in the same general direction and attended with considerable success, which would seem to indicate that these teachers also instantiated divine value, and that the difference between them and the prophet of Galilee was one of degree and not of kind.

The force of Ritschlianism appears largely to have spent itself, yet it is instructive to glance thus briefly at this movement because of the profoundly pragmatic spirit which inspired it. Though the impetus of pragmatism, like that of Ritschlianism, is on the wane, nevertheless it has not yet been completely driven from the field; and its influence occasionally manifests itself in the most unexpected quarters, as in Bradley's famous definition of metaphysics as "the finding of bad reasons for what we believe upon instinct" or in Martineau's declaration that "we do not believe in immortality because we can prove it, but we try to prove it because we cannot help believing in it." The philosopher of religion must expect to be told repeatedly that religion is an affair, not of the head, but of the heart, and that, this being the case, the honest thing and the wise thing to do is to acknowledge the fact, to give over all the vain head work which gets nowhere, and boldly to let the heart speak for itself. The pragmatic identification of truth with workability has been widely hailed as a master stroke which lays open a new approach to metaphysics and thereby enables life to triumph over logic and feeling over intellect. Concerning this contention a few words must be said.

In the first place the so-called identification of truth with workability in no way resembles a Hegelian synthesis of two notions which, although incompatible at a lower level, when raised to a higher level of intelligibility are found to have been purged of their discrepancies and to be capable of fusing in a single coherent idea. On the contrary it means that, of two concepts which we already possess, one is to be retained and the other ruthlessly discarded. That workability is in a certain sense and to a certain degree a test of truth is an affirmation which need disconcert no one. If I believe that I have the key to a crytogram, the way to find out whether I be right is to proceed to decipher it. *That* the cryptogram has been deciphered is not itself a workable theory; it is something of which I have perceptual assurance. Here, as in every case, the ultimate test is self-evidence. But, with this qualification, the usefulness in some cases of workability as a test of truth would be generally conceded.

I have said "in some cases" and not "in all," for it is obvious that there are some cases in which as a criterion it is inapplicable. That Julius Caesar, on the morning of the day before that upon which he was assassinated, was planning a dinner party for the following week is a proposition which is quite understandable; yet in what intelligible sense could it be pronounced workable? It is noteworthy that it is beliefs, rather than propositions, which the pragmatist is in the habit of pronouncing workable; yet, if he recognize this, he gives away his whole case. For, to be workable, a belief must assert that something or other is a fact, that some state of affairs actually obtains or will obtain; it cannot merely be a belief that some other belief is workable, for this would launch us upon an infinite regress. Indeed, the notion of workability is one which is adapted primarily to the prediction of sensible occurrences and to the manipulation of sensible objects. When extended to a wider field it become hopelessly vague and nebulous.

The pragmatist sometimes tells us that a belief "works" if it makes life more "meaningful," but in so doing he attempts by one cloudy term to clarify another. Should I believe that if I work hard I will pass an examination, the belief may encourage me to work hard and I may in fact pass. The pragmatist will doubtless say that the belief has "worked." Yet, while A's belief that he can beat B in a tennis tournament may induce A to put forth his best efforts, and may "work" for him, B's belief that A can beat him may have the reverse effect and lead to B's defeat. The belief "works" for A but not for B. Is it, then, true for A but false for B? It is clear that as soon as we talk about a belief being "true for" someone we are no longer talking about what anyone but a pragmatist means by the word "truth," but about something else; and what this something is seems indefinite to the last degree. Let us suppose that a general, on the eve of a battle, raises the lowered morale of his troops by spreading the report that reinforcements are about to arrive, that his men's confidence is thereby restored, and that as a consequence he does win the battle. The belief "works" both for the general who does not accept it and for the men who do. Will the pragmatist, then, say that it was a true belief? Yet it is not true in the sense that reinforcements were actually approaching. Here it is plain that we are only juggling with words.

The pragmatist frequently attempts to evade such problems by falling back upon the assertion that it is only beliefs which serve society as a whole during a period of considerable duration which can be pronounced true in his sense of the word. Yet the individual remains, together with his private beliefs. Are these beliefs neither true nor false? And how long must a belief serve a society, and how inclusive must the society be, for the belief to be true? It is obvious that a belief which may prove useful to one society may prove harmful to another, if we are to judge only by worldly gain and loss. Thus the belief in predestination inspired Calvinists of the period of the Reformation with titanic energy, whereas it has sapped the vitality of the Muslim world. Hence the same difficulty which we encountered in the case of individuals breaks out again in that of societies.

With respect to religion, as everyone knows, the attitude assumed by pragmatists is far from uniform. Under the influence of Dewey, pragmatism, having adopted a thoroughly this-worldly outlook and having aligned itself on the side of naturalism, was henceforth concerned with the notion of workability as this applied to problems of everyday living, of scientific investigation, and of socio-political activity. Doubtless this form of pragmatism had much to do with fostering the growth of logical positivism and linguistic analysis. William James, however (at least James in a certain mood), ardently desired to apply the pragmatic criterion to religious experience, and in this desire Peirce to some extent concurred. But it is precisely in this field that the pragmatic criterion develops its maximum of vagueness. In what sense can religious beliefs be said to "work" except in the sense that they make us happy? Yet, if this be what is meant by "workability," it would seem that we are entitled to believe whatever we want to believe. It is true that James would insist upon qualifying this conclusion; our religious beliefs, he would decree, must not be incompatible with other empirically well-grounded beliefs, above all with our scientific beliefs. Nevertheless, the genuine pragmatist habitually betrays an unwillingness to put his desires on one side and honestly to ask himself what is the nature of objective fact, or yet to concede that anyone else is capable of initiating a disinterested inquiry of this sort. Moreover, he frequently displays a further tendency perpetually to revert to the implicit assumption that some beliefs, such as scientific beliefs, really are true in the sense that they do correspond to the actual facts, whereas religious beliefs are true in some other sense.

All this bears so close a resemblance to a coolly conceived process of self-deception that it can scarcely fail to revolt the honest mind. For it is precisely in the field of religion, where the issues arise which concern us most, and where, if anywhere, we are face to face with ultimate reality, that disinterested contemplation of objective fact is most requisite. If we permit our desires to control our thinking and volition to determine our conclusions, we thereby render it impossible for us ever to know that our hopes are well grounded and that our desires are destined to be realized. Self-delusion springs from an insincerity which ultimately plays into the hands of pessimism. Unless we face the possibility that the worst *may* be true, we can never hope to attain to the knowledge that the *best* is true.

The foregoing discussion of pragmatism has been undertaken, not merely for its own sake, but because it has an important bearing upon the notion of faith. Faith is a term which is used in very different senses by the Roman Catholic and by the Calvinist.[1] The standing definition in Roman Catholic theology is "the assent of the intellect at the command of the will." This does not mean that it may not be accompanied by religious experience of an intuitive sort, but it does mean that faith is basically volitional. It is a virtue infused into the soul by divine grace, and given to some but not to all. It must be directed upon a worthy object. One must not "believe lightly," as St. Thomas accuses the Muslim of doing. There must be justifiable grounds for so doing. On the other hand, were there absolute certainty, the exercise of volition would be impossible; we should then have knowledge, not faith, and the merit acquired by faith would be lost.[2]

1. I say the Calvinist rather than the Protestant, for it is the Calvinist who has emphasized, and who has worked out in detail, a conception of faith opposed to that of the Roman Catholic; and his theory has exercised a tremendous influence upon Protestant thinkers. This is not to say that a view akin to that of the Roman Catholic is not also widely prevalent in the Protestant world (see, for instance, George Galloway, *The Philosophy of Religion* [New York, 1914], pp. 329–333; also F. R. Tennant's article entitled "Faith" in the fourteenth edition of the *Encyclopaedia Britannica*, IX, 40–41), but it is in Roman Catholic theology that we find it most fully treated; hence the two points of view are best brought out by contrasting the Romanist and the Calvinist.

2. Merit plays as great a part in Roman Catholicism as it does in Buddhism. In Hīnayāna Buddhism it is acquired by good deeds, in Amidism by faith alone, and in some forms of the Mahāyāna both by deeds and by faith.

It may be remarked that the notion that merit can be gained by volitional assent renders intolerance peculiarly unjustifiable in the case of the Roman Catholic. For insofar as he attempts to compel others to accept such doctrines as those of transubstantiation, the supremacy of the Church of Rome, or the intercession of

Thus the pragmatic spirit is no stranger to the realm of Christian thought. On the contrary, it has been present in the church from a very early period—precisely how early does not particularly concern us. But it is noteworthy that for St. Anselm, in whose thought scholasticism began to flower, faith in the sense of volitional assent is a necessary preliminary both of theological and of philosophical speculation. There is, in fact, no sharp distinction between the two. The Christian thinker must begin by accepting all the doctrines of the Church. He is thereafter free to try to prove any of them. If he succeed, well and good; if not, he must, St. Anselm tells us, bow his head and accept them all the same. The view that merit can thus be acquired by assent to doctrines the truth of which has not been demonstrated, and which may even seem to violate the principles of rational thought, carries with it consequences for the believer of a very serious nature and implications as to the divine character which will certainly impress some minds as truly extraordinary. These last have been forcefully stated by William Ellery Channing:

> He who is compelled to defend his faith, in any particular, by the plea that human reason is so depraved through the fall as to be an inadequate judge of religion, and that God is honored by our reception of what shocks the intellect, seems to have no defense left against accumulated absurdities. According to these principles, the fanatic who exclaimed, "I believe, because it is impossible," had a fair title to canonization. Reason is too godlike a faculty to be insulted with impunity.[3]

In regard to the general position it is to be observed that insofar as its doctrines rest upon divine revelation Christianity is a supernatural religion and that, insofar as they are demonstrable, it is also a rational religion. Should all its doctrines turn out to be demonstrable—and antecedently we have no ground for dismissing this as a possibility—Christianity will be at once wholly supernatural and wholly rational.

To the judgment of St. Thomas Aquinas the position of St. Anselm did not commend itself *in toto*. In the first place St. Thomas points out that faith in the content of revelation involves trust in a revealing

---

saints, he is trying to foist upon them doctrines which he does not *know* to be true but which he is individually prepared to accept by an act of will. Whether or not such an act be justified on his own part, it is clearly presumptuous to demand that others make a similar choice.

3. *Works*, p. 339, col. 1.

God and that trust in a non-existent being would be fatuous.[4] Hence the existence of God, he maintains, cannot be one of the articles of faith; it is a truth which must be known and, therefore, must be demonstrable.

Pursuing this line of thought St. Thomas distinguishes sharply between those doctrines which fall within the field of human reason, and consequently are susceptible of demonstration, and those which fall within the sphere of revelation and so are proper objects of faith. A doctrine such as that of the immortality of the human soul which falls within both spheres is at once an article of faith and susceptible of demonstration, but, in general, doctrines which are revealed cannot be proved, and those which can be proved are not revealed. In philosophy one proceeds by relying upon reason, and appeals to faith are illegitimate; in theology, on the other hand, faith is a prerequisite, and reason, although it may be employed to some extent to clarify the content of faith, cannot aspire to demonstration. It would be fair to say then that St. Thomas' philosophy is rationalistic whereas his theology is pragmatic.

Although this dichotomy between faith and reason is once more subscribed to by contemporary Thomism, it found less and less favor with the scholastics immediately posterior to Aquinas, who tended more and more to assign an increasing number of doctrines to the sphere of revelation. Indeed, William of Ockham, in his enthusiasm for a purely empirical approach, thus dealt with all Christian doctrines—with the possible exception of the existence of God—and so practically made of Christianity a completely supernatural religion. This outlook, which constituted the intellectual heritage of Luther, accounts for the latter's vehemently expressed contempt for the powers of human reason as contrasted with the authority of revelation.

It rapidly became clear, however, that if the Reformation was to base everything upon faith, the notion of faith itself required to be revised; for the distrust of reason inspired by the decay of scholasticism was so great that a return to the position of St. Anselm appeared definitely impracticable. This revision, as carried out by Calvin, amounted to a veritable transformation. Although the volitional element was not altogether eliminated, it was accorded no more than

4. This is an important consideration, and although St. Thomas did not emphasize it by a terminological distinction it would seem nonetheless convenient for us to do so. *Trust*, let us say, is felt toward a person; *faith* is accorded to a doctrine or a proposition. Our habitual English usage to some degree bears out this distinction. Thus it would be natural to say that a man has *faith* in the doctrine of transubstantiation, but not that he *trusts* it.

a subordinate place. Fundamentally faith, as now conceived of, is insight evoked by divine illumination. Calvin tells us that the same spirit that spoke through the prophets and by their agency transmitted the revelation incorporated in the Scriptures must also speak to our hearts and authenticate the message thus delivered. This it does by imparting an ineffaceable impression of the glory and divinity of the Gospel. And Jonathan Edwards, who is especially interested in stressing this aspect of Calvin's teaching, assures us that divine illumination does not bestow a knowledge of propositions; it is aesthetic, rather than intellectual, in character; what it does is to awaken the mind to the apprehension of divine beauty. This experience is one of spiritual elevation which raises the soul to a supernatural level and restores the capacities injured by the Fall. And upon this experience all else depends, for it constitutes the divine attestation to the authority of the Scriptures; no doctrine, therefore, is to be accepted which is not found set forth in the sacred writings or is not logically deducible from statements contained therein.

It can scarcely be denied, I think, that the Calvinistic view of faith is more impressive than any of the other theories which we have just examined, and that, from the point of view of those attached to a traditional conception of Christianity, it possesses certain peculiar advantages. In the first place the notion of faith is purged from all taint of pragmatism. There is no question of choosing, or not choosing, to see. In the second place a frank appeal is made to religious experience as the ultimate source of authority, and, furthermore, this experience is clearly conceived of as mystical in nature. It is intuitive, not inferential.[5] As Jonathan Edwards says, it can "be represented as opening the blind eyes, raising the dead, and bringing a person into a new world." [6] In other words, it is an extremely vital experience. There is a breath-taking quality about it, a transforming power, and a sense of contact with ultimate reality. It is at once cognitive and emotional. And, in the third place, it is an experience which is called forth by, and is directed upon, the objective revelation contained in the Scriptures. Inner and outer authorities are thus mutually confirmatory, and the mystical impetus is thereby inhibited—at least a formidable effort is made to inhibit it—from deviating into unorthodox channels.

5. "He that truly sees the divine, transcendent, supreme glory of those things which are divine, does as it were know their divinity intuitively; he not only *argues*, but *sees* that they are divine" (Edwards, *A Treatise Concerning Religious Affections* [London, 1801], Part III, sec. 5).
6. *Ibid.*, sec. 4.

Again, it must in fairness be added that the Calvinistic position is stronger than it may appear at first sight to the eye of one accustomed to associate orthodoxy with a naïve fundamentalism. For it does not commit one to an assertion of the verbal infallibility of the Scriptures nor compel one to champion the scientific or historical accuracy of the biblical text. All that the "witness of the Spirit" is understood to validate is the inerrancy of the Scriptures as the source of *religious* knowledge.

Nonetheless, the Calvinistic position lies open to serious attack from three different directions. In contrast to the Thomist the Calvinist not only does not profess to demonstrate the existence of God but inveighs against every attempt to do so. In his eyes it is both useless and presumptuous. It is useless because God is "sensible to the heart," and it is presumptuous because, having revealed Himself, He has a right to be believed.[7] Does this mean that the Calvinist, like the ontologist, claims to possess a direct awareness of God? He often speaks as though he did; yet, if pressed, his answer would seem to be in the negative. For Calvin himself has declared that God is known "non pas quel il est en soymesme, mais tel qu'il est envers nous." [8] The Calvinist professes, accordingly, to be aware, not of the divine beauty in itself, but as it is reflected in the Scriptures and in the Gospel therein contained. Such knowledge, however, is surely not direct but inferential. Despite his unwillingness to recognize the fact, the situation is the reverse of what the Calvinist asserts it to be. Instead of accepting the Scriptures because of the attestation of God, actually he believes in God because of the Scriptures and the excellence which he ascribes to them. His position, indeed, is very similar to that of the Advaitin who believes in Brahma because of the testimony of the Vedas. And, like the Advaitin, the Calvinist is compelled to expatiate upon the superhuman glories of his own sacred writings in justification of his belief.[9]

This leads us naturally to the consideration of a second line of attack upon the Calvinistic position. Once the theistic hypothesis is taken seriously—as it certainly deserves to be taken—the notion of a divine illumination becomes both plausible and inspiring. But how do we know that Calvin's insistence upon the complete coincidence between an objective revelation embodied in the Scriptures and a sub-

7. See August Lecerf, *Introduction à la dogmatique reformée* (Paris, 1931), I, 51–52.
8. *Institution de la religion chrestienne* (Paris, 1936), I, 77.
9. A Calvinistic ontologism would obviously constitute a far stronger position, but so far as I am aware it remains yet to be developed.

jective revelation in the form of an illumined heart is justifiable? What is the evidence for it? And what, in this connection, do we mean by evidence? How do we know when we are illumined and when we are not illumined? We are driven, apparently, to judge as well as we can by the response of our own intellect, emotion, and conscience to what is presented to us. There is much in the Vedas, and even more in the Upaniṣads and the Bhagavadgītā, that is noble and beautiful. How do we know that the Spirit does not fall on the Hindu as he peruses his sacred writings, even as upon the Christian when he reads the Bible? Once we ask this question, all the evidence provided by the study of comparative religion becomes relevant and requires to be sifted and evaluated. Are we told that in the sacred literatures of non-Christian religions there is much that is uninspiring and even unedifying? But the same is true of our own Scriptures.[10] If a line of demarcation is to be drawn, we must have some justification for drawing it, and a better justification than the unsupported asseveration that one type of religious experience is valid and that all others are illusory.

Finally, we must observe that the Calvinistic doctrine of individual illumination is one that is charged with a potential menace to the orthodoxy which it is designed to support. For now the decisions of councils and synods, and the dogmas therein set forth, derive all their authority from the biblical texts whereon they repose. The Church has no authority of its own; the only authority is the Spirit, and the Spirit speaks to individuals. The witness of the Spirit does, indeed, establish the divine origin and character of the Scriptures, but in the interpretation thereof it would seem plain that no man has a right to dictate to his neighbor. In spite of repressive measures the assertion of the right of individual interpretation was speedily advanced under the aegis of the Reformation and proved impossible to silence. This led to a decreasing emphasis upon the doctrine of illumination, which was seen to contain the seed of intellectual anarchy, and to the laying of an ever greater stress upon the authority of the Scriptures. Yet this authority, deprived of the divine attestation accorded it by illumination, now seemed to be baseless. Clearly a new foundation needed to be laid.

This was the task to which Locke addressed himself, and it is in his thought that we find worked out a new, and extremely important, theory of the relationship between reason and revelation. To put it succinctly, the theory may be said to posit a relationship precisely the

10. Cf., for instance, the tale of Yahweh's attack upon Moses in the lodging house (Exod. 4:24–26).

reverse of that previously believed to hold between these two authorities; in other words, what it proclaims is the primacy of reason. Reason, Locke tells us, is "natural revelation." [11] And this is a point the significance of which can scarcely be exaggerated. For it is obvious that revelation can never be in conflict with itself; hence, if reason be a form of revelation, it is clear that any other form of revelation must be in accord with reason.

In all this, it may be objected, there is nothing original, but only good scholastic doctrine. Truth is one, say St. Thomas and the other great doctors of the Church; therefore, since truth can never contradict itself, reason and revelation must always be in harmony. Yes, but what do they infer from this? What they infer is that whenever any process of reasoning leads him in the direction of conclusions incompatible with revelation the philosopher must take this as a sure indication that he has committed some error. The central doctrines of orthodoxy can neither be demonstrated nor yet fully grasped by human reason; they exceed its scope and must be accepted by an act of faith which, as we have seen, is basically an act of volition. Thus in scholasticism the pragmatic spirit triumphs over the rational.

For Locke, on the contrary,

> revelation is *natural reason enlarged* by a new set of discoveries communicated by God immediately; which reason vouches the truth of, by the testimony and proofs it gives that they come from God. So that he that takes away reason to make way for revelation, puts out the light of both, and does muchwhat the same as if he would persuade a man to put out his eyes, the better to receive the remote light of an invisible star by a telescope.[12]

It is one of the functions of reason, then, to vindicate the claims of genuine revelation and to discredit those of spurious revelation.

That there is such a thing as genuine revelation Locke is thoroughly convinced. But he had lived through the Commonwealth period when strange sects proliferated and while he wrote doubtless had in mind the Muggletonians, the Fifth Monarchy men, and the extravagances of the early Quakers. As we read his chapter on enthusiasm, we shall probably not be far wrong if we conjecture that, in his opinion, for one truly illumined man it was easy to find a hundred ranters. Firm-

11. *Essay Concerning Human Understanding* (New York, 1924), Book IV, chap. xix, sec. 4.
12. *Ibid.*

ness of persuasion, as he takes pains to point out, is in itself no evidence of the truth of any doctrine. "If they believe it," he remarks, because it is a revelation, and have no basis for its being a revelation, but because they are fully persuaded, without any other reason, that it is true, then they believe it to be a revelation only because they strongly believe it to be a revelation; which is a very unsafe ground to proceed on, either in our tenets or actions." [13]

What follows? What follows has been stated by Locke with admirable force and clarity:

> He, therefore, that will not give himself up to all extravagances of delusion and error must bring this guide of his *light within* to the trial. God when he makes the prophet does not unmake the man. He leaves all his faculties in the natural state, to enable him to judge of his inspirations, whether they be of *divine* original or no. When he illuminates the mind with supernatural light, he does not extinguish that which is natural. If he would have us assent to the truth of any proposition, he either evidences that truth by the usual methods of natural reason, or else makes it known to be a truth which he would have us assent to that it is from him, by some marks which reason cannot be mistaken in. *Reason must be our last judge and guide in everything.* I do not mean that we must consult reason, and examine whether a proposition revealed from God can be made out by natural principles, and if it cannot, that we may reject it: but consult it we must, and by it examine whether it be a revelation from God or no: and if reason finds it to be revealed from God, reason then declares for it as much as for any other truth, and makes it one of her dictates.[14]

That there are truths which are "above reason" in the sense that a knowledge of them could not be obtained by a mere process of rational inquiry Locke is quite prepared to admit. As examples of such he refers to the revolt of the angels or to the resurrection of the dead at the Last Day. There is nothing repugnant to reason in these conceptions, yet it is clear that any knowledge that they refer to actual events must be communicated to us by revelation.

"Reason, therefore, as contradistinguished to faith," writes Locke,

> I take to be the discovery of the certainty or probability of such propositions or truths, which the mind arrives at by deduction

13. *Ibid.*, sec. 11.   14. *Ibid.*, sec. 14.

made from such ideas, which it has got by the use of its natural faculties; viz. by sensation or reflection.

Faith, on the other side, is the assent to any proposition, not thus made out by the deductions of reason, but upon the credit of the proposer, as coming from God, in some extraordinary way of communication.[15]

Faith, then, is something eminently rational; it reposes "on the credit of the proposer," and it is only after scrutinizing both the proposer and his credentials that we repose our confidence in him. What are these credentials? Locke is looking for something quite objective and open to the apprehension of all men however much they may differ in background, in experience, or in psychological constitution. And he finds it in *miracle*. Both Moses and Christ, he is assured, performed miracles; moreover Christ delegated the power to do likewise to his immediate disciples as evidence of the genuineness of their mission.

Here, to the eyes of our contemporaries, Locke's doctrine is at its weakest; in fact it may be said to be on the point of collapsing. We must remember, however, that at the time when Locke wrote, it was generally believed that the miracles referred to had been recorded by eyewitnesses whose written testimony had been preserved, and that, the record having been faithfully transmitted to us, the historicity of these events was satisfactorily established. Today the progress of textual criticism has forced us to acknowledge that the evidence which we possess is of a quality very inferior to what Locke believed it to be; furthermore the study of comparative religion has caused us to become aware of the extraordinary facility with which the belief in miracles can originate and propagate itself. To make this acknowledgment is not equivalent to denying the possibility of the occurrence of miracles. Indeed that possibility can be said to follow logically from the acceptance of the theistic hypothesis. But the *actual* occurrence of miracles is a very different question. And, in view of the nature of the evidence, it is not too much to conclude that any doctrine of revelation which is based upon the miraculous is at its last gasp.

Is there anything which we could put in its place? We could still consider the character of the teacher, the content of his message, and the historic effects of his mission. Yet into such a process of evaluation the subjective element, which it was Locke's desire and intention to eliminate, would certainly enter, and the unanimity which he sought

15. *Ibid.*, Book III, chap. viii, sec. 2.

to secure by an appeal to well-authenticated sensible occurrences would have vanished.

Is there, then, nothing left of Locke's theory? Yes, there is something left of great significance, and that is the place which he accords to reason. By saying this I do not intend merely to call attention to the fact that Locke, in agreement with the Thomists and in opposition to the Calvinists, held that it is both feasible and necessary, before developing a doctrine of revelation, to demonstrate the existence of God. I mean that for Locke, and even more for such a man as Channing upon whom this aspect of Locke's teaching exercised an extremely profound influence, reason was accorded a higher evaluation than ever before as the characteristic through the possession of which man most nearly resembled God, and as constituting within him the presence of a potential divinity. It is not too much to assert that human reason was now looked upon as a mystical faculty through the exercise of which man communed with God. The soundness of this contention will, I believe, be borne out by the following extract from the first of Channing's two sermons on self-denial.

Human reason, imperfect though it be, is still the offspring of God, allied to him intimately, and worthy of its divine Parent. There is no extravagance in calling it, as is sometimes done, "a beam of the infinite light;" for it involves in its very essence those immutable and everlasting principles of truth and rectitude which constitute the glory of the Divine Mind. It ascends to the sublime idea of God by possessing kindred attributes, and knows him only through its affinity with him. It carries within itself the germ of that spiritual perfection which is the great end of the creation. Is it not, then, truly a "partaker of a divine nature"? Can we think or speak of it too gratefully or with too much respect? The infinity of God, so far from calling on me to prostrate and annihilate reason, exalts my conception of it. It is my faith in this perfection of the Divine Mind that inspires me with reverence for the human, for they are intimately connected, the latter being a derivation from the former, and endued with the power of approaching its original more and more through eternity. Severed from God, reason would lose its grandeur. In his infinity it has at once a source and a pledge of endless and unbounded improvement. God delights to communicate himself; and therefore his greatness, far from inspiring contempt for human reason, gives it a sacredness, and opens before it the most elevating hopes. The error of men is not that they exaggerate, but that they do not know or suspect the worth and dignity of their rational nature.[16]

Of course it may be said, and it often is said, that confidence in reason is itself an act of faith, inasmuch as reason cannot, without arguing in a circle, proffer a vindication of itself. To this it may justly be replied that confidence in reason is something very different from the Thomist's "assent of the intellect at the command of the will," that it is in no sense a volitional act which can either be performed or abstained from, but rather an experience of illumination which arises with an utter inevitability and which more nearly resembles faith as the Calvinist conceives of it. That only admits of and requires a vindication which is not ultimate and self-sufficient. Needless to say, should rational thinking fail to enlighten us as to the nature of reality or terminate in self-contradiction, the claims of reason would have to be pronounced fraudulent. If, however, it can be shown, on the one hand, that rational processes ultimately depend upon direct insights which carry with them the assurance of self-evidence, and, on the other hand, that reason is capable of developing a world view which is intelligible and coherent and does adequate justice to all relevant facts, the challenge of the irrationalist will be met.

If we thus find ourselves driven to adopt the position of the rationalist, does it follow that reason, instead of being, as Locke called it, "our last judge and guide in everything," becomes our only guide? If reason be not founded upon faith, is there no place for faith founded upon and justified by reason? Does the repudiation of Locke's appeal to the miraculous put the quietus upon any attempt to vindicate the claims of any suprarational authority? Is reason not only the primary source but the sole source of religious knowledge? Before presuming to answer these questions we must first scrutinize more closely the notion of revelation, and together with it certain kindred notions— those of inspiration, illumination, and mystical intuition.

Of revelation in the religious sense of the word it may at once be said that it is a thoroughly rational notion. There is assuredly nothing mysterious in the conception of the impartation of information by one intelligence to another, nor does the situation lose its intelligibility if one of these intelligences be divine. Indeed it may be affirmed that a doctrine of self-communication on the part of the divine is an almost inevitable correlate of the theistic hypothesis. It is true that Aristotle's

16. *Works*, p. 338, col. 1.

God is represented as engaged in perpetual self-contemplation, indifferent to, and seemingly ignorant of, the world of whose motion he is the final cause. And it is equally true that the gods of the Epicureans display a similar indifference to human affairs. In general, however, it may be asserted—and the contention will scarcely be contested—that where the belief in a personal God is entertained he is credited with a providential interest in human kind and that for most men a *deus* who was thoroughly *absconditus* would not be a *deus* at all. For Locke and for Channing, as we have seen, God has revealed himself to all men by endowing them with rational intellects whereby they are enabled to enter into communion with him. This is, indeed, a view the truth of which is contested by those theologians who hold that by the Fall the human mind has been rendered no longer *capax Dei* and therefore the need for some other form of self-disclosure on the part of Deity has become imperative. Yet both Locke and Channing, on the one hand, and the neosupernaturalists, on the other hand, would agree about the reality of divine self-disclosure.

Such self-disclosure might take the form of a constant and unvarying afflatus extended to all men in all places and at all times, imparting to them an assurance of the reality of the divine presence, "the light that lighteth every man that cometh into the world." This is termed, in the language of Calvinistic theology, the activity of common grace. It is also conceivable that the divine should disclose itself to the individual in a manner relevant to the circumstances in which he is placed. So it was thought to do by the American Indian who went alone to forest or mountain to dream a dream which should impart to him an awareness of his guardian divinity and, perhaps, in addition, some foreknowledge of his own destiny.

Obviously self-disclosure of the former type could appropriately be termed "universal" or "general" revelation, and that of the latter type "individual" revelation. In the case of the former, however, inasmuch as the experience is one of communion rather than of the reception of a definite message with dogmatic content, the term "illumination" would be equally applicable. And the latter might fittingly be called "special" revelation, were it not for the fact that usage seems to have pre-empted this term for the promulgation of a teaching directed to a people, a race, or an organization—such as the Church.

Special revelation, in this sense of the word, requires as its vehicle a man with a sense of social mission and the conviction that he functions as the mouthpiece of Deity. Thus arises the notion of inspiration. The prophet is conscious of being appointed, of being used; he speaks, not in his own name, but in the name of God. To dare to do this is no light thing. Yet, doubtless, many madmen and fanatics—such as Te Ua among the Maoris—have so dared. We are not at present concerned, however, with the problem of distinguishing between genuine and false claims to inspiration; we have simply to observe the rôle which prophecy, or what has been taken to be such, has played in the history of the great religions. In the case of the Vedas we have to do with compositions of prehistoric antiquity whose authors are unknown to us. But when within the range of human memory a great prophetic figure has arisen this has always constituted a historic event of the first importance, as in the case of Zarathustra, of the prophets of Israel, of Jesus, of Mani, or Muhammad. Thus, where the belief in revelation prevails, religion tends to become closely tied to the historic.

It might, then, appear that the religious experience of the average individual sinks into insignificance as contrasted with the weighty testimony of revelation. And undoubtedly a preoccupation with revelation has at times affected adversely the mystical impetus which is so essential to vital religion. Hence Calvin's doctrine that the same Spirit which revealed itself through the prophets also bears witness to the authenticity of its own message by illuminating the mind of the individual was, from the ecclesiastical point of view, a tactical master stroke. For it at once stressed the importance of living religious experience and prevented it from getting out of hand by directing it upon the Scriptures as its proper source of nutriment, and thereby forestalled the occurrence of a new revelation which would supersede the old.

The balance which Calvin had thus established between subjective illumination and objective revelation was to a certain extent upset by his own disciple, the most famous of American theologians, Jonathan Edwards. Edwards brought this about by laying increasing emphasis upon the aesthetic element in religious experience. And it will be worth our while to examine Edwards' view, for it is unconsciously anticipatory of a new doctrine of revelation which we must shortly consider. But it must not be supposed that Edwards' own position differed essentially from that of Calvin, or from that of the medieval scholastics before him. For all these men the process of revelation, so far at least as religious issues were concerned, was inerrant. The inspired man functioned as God's mouthpiece or amanuensis—as we should say today, as his stenographer. God spoke, man recorded. Active the prophet must be in proclaiming his message, yet he had no part in formulating it. His own personality went for nothing. Hence inspiration was not dependent, Edwards assures us, upon the character of the inspired man. God could use whom he pleased and as he pleased as his spokesman. Inspiration, therefore, is an "extraordinary" gift of grace.

Illumination, however, is something very different. It is not, indeed, an effect of common grace which is imparted to men in general; on the contrary it is a special grace reserved for the elect. And, as already stated, it is aesthetic in character. Upon the soul it exercises an uplifting and transforming power which raises the recipient, while yet in this life, to a supernatural level. Hence it is a serious error, in Edwards' opinion, not to recognize that "the ordinary sanctifying influences of the spirit of God are the *end* of all extraordinary gifts." He writes,

> Salvation and the eternal enjoyment of God is promised to divine grace, but not to inspiration. A man may have those extraordinary gifts, and yet be abominable to God, and go to hell. The spiritual and eternal life of the soul consists in the grace of the spirit, which God bestows only on his favourites and dear children. He has sometimes thrown out the other, as it were to dogs and swine, as he did to Balaam, Saul, and Judas; and to some who in the primitive times of the Christian church committed the unpardonable sin. (Heb. VI.) Many wicked men at the day of judgment will plead, "Have we not prophesied in thy name, and in thy name cast out devils, and in thy name done many wonderful works." The greatest privilege of the prophets and apostles, was not their being inspired and working miracles, but their eminent holiness. The grace that was in their hearts, was a thousand times more their dignity and honour, than their miraculous gifts. The things in which we find David comforting himself, are not his being a king, or a prophet, but the holy influences of the spirit of God in his heart, communicating to him divine light, love and joy. The apostle Paul abounded in visions, revelations, and miraculous gifts, above all the apostles; but yet he esteems all things but loss for the excellency of the spiritual knowledge of Christ. It was not the gifts but the grace of the apostles, that was the proper evidence of their names being written in heaven; in which Christ directs them to rejoice, much more than in the devils being subject to them. To have grace in the heart, is a

higher privilege than the blessed virgin herself had, in having the
body of the second person in the Trinity conceived in her womb,
by the power of the highest overshadowing her. Luke, XI. 27, 28.[17]

Here we have an estimate of the value of individual religious experience so exalted that it seems on the point of rendering revelation
itself otiose. Why, we may ask, does it not pass this point? The answer
clearly is that orthodoxy is par excellence a historic religion and that
it is revelation which weds it to history by presenting a "scheme of
salvation" which involves the acceptance of the Incarnation and the
Atonement as historic events. If God have entered into history, through
the historic must he be known. Not only in Christianity, but in all the
revealed religions, the belief in revelation acts as a brake upon the
mystical impetus.

Suppose, however, that mysticism were to spread its wings and
fly away from the historic and the temporal. Beyond the limits of
space and time might it discover an "eternal gospel" which, like the
truths of mathematics, would be unaffected by whatever arises and
passes away? This is a suggestion which seems strange to one brought
up in the Judeo-Christian tradition, to whom it seems natural to attribute whatever insight the contemplative may attain to divine grace.
In India, however, we find a very different point of view, and it is conditioned by a conception of the self quite unlike that which prevails
in the West. Whether the self be regarded as a *dravya*, or substance,
as among the Hindus, or it be thought of as a succession of psychic
states, as by the Buddhists, in either case it is believed to be without
beginning, and also to be unending—or at least to have no end short
of deliverance from the wheel of birth and death. Furthermore, the
general opinon is that selves are fundamentally equal [18] and that such
inequalities as prevail among them are transitory and are due to their
respective Karma and to the nature of their embodiment. Thus the
self which is now a gnat may in future become a god, and the self
which is now a god may in future become a gnat. Gods, men, animals,
plants, and demons are thus essentially akin, and all without exception
stand in need of deliverance. For the yogi, therefore, to seek to ad-
vance to a superhuman level is no manifestation of $\ddot{v}\beta\rho\iota\varsigma$ but only a
sane attempt to actualize his own native potentialities.

Now the Jains and the Buddhists alike believe that their respective

17. *The Distinguishing Marks of a Work of the Spirit of God* (London, 1755),
sec. III, iii.
18. It is true that some schools believe in a supreme God who is exempt from
the process of birth and death, but this is irrelevant to our present interest.

founders, in the one case Vardhamāna, and in the other Gotama, have attained the state of ultimate deliverance while yet in this life and have thereby reached a level of synoptic insight which embraces the universe as a whole, so that their teachings can be taken as infallibly authoritative by their followers. At first glance such claims are likely to impress the occidental as absurdly extravagant, but this is in part due to the fact that they are unfamiliar and that he does not share the world view with reference to which such claims are made. It is true that we can point out that, inasmuch as they are not in complete agreement, both the Buddha and the Mahāvīra cannot be infallible, and thus score a point. Yet this does not obviate the fact that in each case the world view is one which has been carefully thought out and cannot simply be brushed aside and that in the notion of supernormal enlightenment there is nothing self-contradictory.

It behooves us who are at the ordinary level of consciousness to refrain from dogmatizing about the degrees of insight to which the contemplative may conceivably rise; and doubtless we cannot be sure to what extent the present limitations of our knowledge are due to the essential nature of our intellects, or to blocks or stoppages which may be removable. I do not think, therefore, that the authoritarian claims of these religions can safely be dismissed with a smile. Yet it is difficult to see how they could be substantiated in any other way than by developing a coherent and satisfactory world view of such a nature as to render them plausible, which brings us back to Locke's contention that "reason must be our last judge and guide in everything." No doubt to anyone who is inclined to accept the theistic hypothesis it will seem far more probable that truths of a cosmic scope should be imparted by a divine Intelligence than that they should be grasped as the result of unaided, although intense and concentrated, effort of the human mind. Should we find it impossible to accept the theistic hypothesis, however, our outlook might change. Yet it is perhaps more probable that the very notion of infallibility would become increasingly difficult to take seriously.

It may be urged that when we find a claim to unique intuitive insight in conjunction with a conviction of being the bearer of a message "to gods and men," as in the cases of the Buddha and the Mahāvīra, we have passed beyond the realm of mysticism proper, as truly as in the case of the prophet, and I should certainly concur in this judgment. What I wish to emphasize, however, is the fact that the notion of intuitive insight is not only logically separable but has actually been separated from the doctrines of revelation and of divine illumination and, in its extreme form, is capable of providing a basis for claims of the type in question.

In this connection we may take notice of a somewhat similar claim to ultimate and infallible authority in matters of religion which to the Western mind may appear even more extraordinary, namely, the contention of the Mīmāṁsakas that the Vedas are uncreated, eternal, and inerrant. This doctrine is sharply to be distinguished from the position of the orthodox Muslim, who holds that the Koran is uncreated. For what Muslim thought has done has been to identify the content of a book with the Logos and thus to make it the external expression of the divine consciousness. But for the atheistic Mīmāṁsā there is no divine consciousness in the sense in which the Muslim conceives of it, and the Vedas have being in their own right. When the Vedas are recited or written down, every pronunciation or writing down of a word is a particular occurrence, yet the word itself is not an occurrence but an eternal entity, and the order in which these entities stand is also eternal.

To the occidental believer in the realistic theory of universals this doctrine will appear quite congenial, and the only strange thing about it will be the inerrancy ascribed to the content of the Vedas, for which he will see no justification, for he will contend that what is true of the Vedas is true of every literary composition. The speaking or writing of a word is a particular event, but the meaning of the word is not an event, nor, except in the case of proper names, is it a particular. Yet this fact in no way guarantees the truth of what is spoken or written, and with this reflection he will doubtless consider himself entitled without more ado to dismiss the claim advanced by the Mīmāṁsakas.

We have now before us various theories of authority other than human reason which in the field of religion have been developed at various times and in various places. The most impressive of these would seem clearly to be the doctrine of revelation, whether or not it be taken in conjunction with that of divine illumination, for, as we have seen, the notion of self-disclosure is plainly involved in the full-fledged concept of Deity. Yet the doctrine will be worth discussing only if a satisfactory case for theism can be made out. This is a problem the investigation of which we shall postpone; but it is to be observed that, if inerrancy be an essential characteristic of revelation, there can be only one genuine revelation. All other claimants, inasmuch as they differ from it, will be infected with error and must either be dismissed as fraudulent or regarded as so contaminated as to be without authority.

It is now time to take into consideration a relatively new theory of revelation—usually termed the "liberal" view—which has arisen within the last two centuries, and which half a century ago seemed likely to carry all before it, but which contemporary theological reaction has put upon the defensive. According to this view the traditional conception of the relationship obtaining between the divine and the human intelligence is an erroneous one and is definitely to be rejected. The inspired man is not a merely passive instrument of the Deity, as a telephone is the passive instrument of the man who speaks over it. Revelation is a process in which God and man are both active, and both endeavoring to enter into communication with each other. Locke's saying that "God when he makes the prophet does not unmake the man" conveys a profound truth. The intelligence of the inspired man, with all its capacities and its limitations, has its contribution to make, and the total result is a joint message in which the divine and the human are blended. We must therefore assume that the teaching of any religious teacher will be affected by the outlook of his own time, race, and country, as well as by his peculiar psychological constitution and his own individual point of view. The mind which is enlightened by the Spirit of God, like Shelley's "dome of many-coloured glass," at once transmits and colors the radiance of revelation; consequently it is futile to look for infallible authority anywhere. What is of God is, of course, inerrant, but when what is of God is fused with what is of man the problem is precisely to determine what is of God, and to this no easy answer can be given. For the divine and the human in the prophet's message do not remain distinct, as do oil and water; rather are they blended like water and wine.

Inspiration is now conceived as having a far wider range than it has on the traditional view. It is an influence constantly playing upon all men everywhere, ever seeking to elicit a response. Not only the religious teacher but the poet, the artist, the thinker, and the man of action as well consciously or unconsciously may be stimulated by it. There is no such thing as an unrevealed religion; all religions are revealed religions. Yet it does not follow that they are all equally true; for revelation admits of degrees of purity, clarity, and definiteness and is always conditioned by the capacities of its recipients. As St. Paul said, "we know in part, and we prophesy in part." [19]

19. I Cor. 13:9.

There is a breadth and sweep about this doctrine which commends it to many. It appears to do justice to all forms of religious life without disregarding significant differences; it is neither equalitarian, undiscriminating, nor exclusive. Moreover, it frees the believer in it from the uncongenial task of attempting to explain away errors, discrepancies, and contradictions in the written records of revelation, since these can always, in accordance with the theory, be ascribed to human agency. It is also to be observed that the distinctions which, on the traditional view, are so hard and fast between revelation, inspiration, illumination, intuition, common grace and special grace, general and special revelation, now tend to become obscured; the notion of degrees of revelation absorbs and confounds them all.

The conservative will of course protest that unless it be possible to discriminate satisfactorily between what is of God and what is of man and to isolate a divine residuum the whole purpose of revelation will have been frustrated. But is not this to assume, asks the liberal, that the purpose of revelation is to eliminate all intellectual effort upon our part and to liberate us from the responsibility of moral judgment; and is this a rational assumption? Doubtless revelation *could* have taken this form, yet, continues the liberal, do not the facts show that this is not the form in which it *has* actually been imparted? And do we not have a nobler conception of revelation if we assume that it requires us to develop our own capacities for understanding and evaluation?

Leaving the issue there for the moment I would call attention to the fact that this controversy has given rise to yet a third theory of revelation which has been introduced with considerable fanfare.[20] According to this new doctrine revelation consists primarily of divine acts, not of divine pronouncements; and the sacred Scriptures are the record of these acts. The motivation which inspired the formulation of this theory appears to have been twofold. In the first place, all difficulties which arise in connection with textual criticism are thereby brushed aside, inasmuch as the Scriptures, on this view, are not themselves revelation but only the records of revelation. And in the second place, it now becomes feasible practically to identify revelation with a unique act, namely, the Incarnation, all that precedes being in the nature of mere preliminary, and all that follows being in the nature of anticlimax. Obviously a full discussion of this view would require an examination of the doctrine of the Incarnation, which in

20. The theory has been set forth in detail in Archbishop Temple's *Nature, Man and God* (New York, 1934).

turn would entail that of the theistic hypothesis, and into these fields we are not yet ready to enter. But even at this point we can see, I think, that the theory constitutes a tactical readjustment of the conservative line of defense, and that it raises no genuinely new issues for the philosopher.

We are now in a position to raise the fundamental question what should be the attitude of the philosopher of religion toward the problem of the seat of authority in religion. He is confronted by numerous claimants of his intellectual allegiance. If he reject them all and acknowledge the sole sovereignty of reason, does not this mean that in the last resort he is relying entirely upon his own reasoning powers, of the limitations of which he cannot but be all too conscious? And does he not thereby cut himself off from the right to participate in the riches of any tradition, and so become, as it were, a "lone wolf" in his chosen field? Would it not be wiser and more modest to attach himself with some degree of definiteness to one of these great traditions and, employing this as a standard, to endeavor with reference to it to assess the relative merits of other positions? But how is he to choose? Straightway to adopt the tradition with which he is most familiar, which will be that of his own time, race, and country, would clearly be an arbitrary decision. There is, indeed, nothing to prevent his making such a decision, but thereby he will abdicate as a genuine philosopher and will of necessity become an apologist. There have been great apologists whose work contains philosophic material of high value. But will any fair-minded man wish to attach himself to their company?

The situation can be to some extent simplified, however, if we distinguish between those claimants to authority who are prepared to buttress their claims by reason and those who are not. As for the latter it would appear preposterous to ask us to assent to them, for must not any decision in such a matter be reached on rational grounds, and to these they scorn to appeal. The scholastic conception of faith as "the assent of the intellect at the command of the will" at once comes to mind and, by so doing, brings the issue to a head. Can such a psychological feat actually be performed? How can the intellect, being what it is, assent to anything except to sufficient evidence? To command it to assent would be as futile as Canute's command to the tide to turn. What really happens, obviously, is that the intellect ceases to function, and the will, taking over, proceeds to act *as if* the intellect had accepted what was propounded to it. It is true that St. Thomas warns us that we must not "believe lightly," that we must have *some* grounds for our decision; yet the evidence cannot be constraining, or we could not withhold assent. And it is precisely because we could thus withhold assent that, on his theory, we acquire merit by assenting.

How extraordinary a view of what can make an act meritorious is here involved! And what a conception of the Deity does it imply! To the genuine philosopher this dangling before his eyes of the hope of obtaining merit through intellectual self-stultification is nothing less than revolting.

The pragmatist may, perhaps, object that while the repudiation of the conception of merit is doubtless justifiable, there is yet a good deal of truth in what St. Thomas says. In situations where deductive knowledge is not obtainable but where nevertheless we *must* act—inasmuch as the decision to remain quiescent is itself an act—the only sensible thing to do is to act in accordance with what we take to be the most probable view. Now such is the situation in which we stand when confronted by any of the great religions, say, by Roman Catholicism. We must either accept it or reject it. There is no middle ground. Will not our decision, then, inevitably be dictated by our estimate of the probable? Yes, but this estimate will be arrived at by a weighing of the evidence. Reason, after all, will furnish the grounds for our decision; our decision, therefore, will be a rational decision, at least as rational a decision as we are capable of making. But what of the prudential motive? What of Pascal's wager? If we accept, we may at last obtain everlasting bliss; if we refuse, we may incur damnation. Does not prudence, therefore, enjoin us to accept, however fragile the evidence, since the consequences of rejection may be so terrible?

Yes, but why should we not think that it would be more prudent to accept, and more imprudent to reject, Islam? How are we to choose between these theological rivals otherwise than by a rational decision, even though it be based only upon an estimate of relative probability? And if we bring ourselves to act in accordance with a purely prudential motive, must it not be because we really think it credible that Omnipotence should confront us with so fearful a choice which will decide our eternal destiny? Twist and struggle, then, as we will, is it not obvious that we cannot avoid the truth of Locke's pronouncement, and recognize that reason is, in the last resort, our only guide?

If this conclusion be sound, it is clear that any authoritarian claims must be based upon rational grounds. And Locke has shown us that there is nothing incredible in the notion of such an authority. For if there be a divine Intelligence, it is surely quite conceivable that this

Intelligence might have occasion to acquaint us with certain truths respecting its nature, its will, or its purposes, to a knowledge of which our human minds are incapable of attaining by the exercise of their natural powers. There is certainly nothing self-contradictory or absurd in the idea. *Why* God should see fit to act in this way is a different question, and one which we might well be unable to answer, inasmuch as we cannot view all things from the standpoint of Omniscience. On the assumption that we have adopted the position of the theist, the problem of revelation, like that of miracle, would appear to be, not so much a theoretical, as a factual problem. The notion of revelation is intelligible enough. The question at issue is what evidence have we that revelation has actually taken place.

The most impressive argument in defense of the doctrine of revelation is that based upon an analogy drawn between religious and artistic experience. We should all admit without hesitation that a great musician, a great painter, a great sculptor, or a great poet has a clearer and more vivid vision of beauty than do the rest of us. We regard such persons as possessed of a certain authority in their respective fields, and we listen with profound respect to what they tell us, even if we do not always understand it. Now the same holds true, so runs the argument, in the case of religion. Here the mystic and the prophet are the experts. They know at first hand what they are talking about, and their reports, accordingly, ought to be received as authoritative.

It is true that artists have their critics, and as the critic stands in relation to the artist, so stands the philosopher in relation to the mystic and the prophet. It is the philosopher's business, and a very difficult business it is, to evaluate their testimony and to try to develop a coherent theory with respect to it. To discuss what his conclusion should be would carry us at once into the realm of metaphysics. What I wish to point out now is that it is pretty clear whither this line of reflection is leading us. It is leading us toward the conclusion that if any view of revelation be acceptable, it is the liberal view.

For if we take the conservative point of view, two courses lie open to us, and whichever of these we adopt will get us into trouble. On the one hand we can assert that the only genuine revelation is special revelation and that special revelation has been confined to a single line of development. The orthodox Jew need acknowledge no revelation but his own. The orthodox Christian must recognize the Judaic revelation, and will regard his own as constituting its culmination. The orthodox Muslim will take the same attitude with respect to the Christian revelation. The Hindu will proclaim the unique authority of the Vedas. But all these individuals, if they subscribe to the theory we are now discussing, will hold that apart from the tradition in which each happens to stand, there has been no revelation at all. But, then, the amount of evidence in support of the notion of revelation will be vastly reduced. And if all the great thoughts, noble teachings, and inspiring passages to be found in the writings of other religions are to be regarded as the product of the unaided and uninspired human intellect, the probability that the same is true of those in one's own scriptures is very considerably increased. A man will need to have an extreme confidence in the incomparable excellence and unique superiority of the sacred books of his own religion to take such an attitude. In opposition to him the liberal will protest that it is precisely where the scriptures of the various religions most resemble one another, and where the general agreement is most obvious, that the evidence for revelation is the strongest. It is not likely that his words will have much effect upon the typically orthodox mind; yet many persons will agree with his judgment that what the orthodox has to say sounds very like special pleading.

On the other hand we may maintain that in addition to, or as a preparation for, our own special revelation, there has also been granted a general revelation to all mankind. Our own inerrant and special revelation, accordingly, will constitute a standard; and insofar as the teachings contained in the scriptures of other religions differ from it, these will be in error. What the liberal has affirmed with regard to all revelation will therefore hold good of general revelation; that is to say, it will result from an interaction between Deity and humanity, and in the joint product divine and human elements will be mingled. Why should we assume that our own revelation has been exempt from this process of blending? Because we are convinced that our scriptures are inerrant? But this is a tremendous claim, and how are we to make it good?

Again two alternatives lie before us. We may insist, if we choose, that our revelation as it was imparted—the "original" revelation, as Locke would call it—was inerrant, and that all the errors in our scriptures have arisen in the process of transmission. But this is to give our whole case away to the liberal. For our revelation as it now stands—our "traditional" revelation, to employ the Lockian terminology—will, on our own showing be infected with error, and so will constitute an amalgam of the divine and the human, precisely as the liberal has asserted. And as for our claim that the original revelation was inerrant, it is easy to make but impossible to substantiate.

The other alternative will be boldly to affirm that our sacred writings, as we now possess them, are inerrant; and this will be a preposterous claim to make on behalf of the scriptures of any religion. Let us assume that we are adherents of the Judeo-Christian tradition. If we are to interpret the term "inerrancy" in the strict and literal sense, as is done by popular Fundamentalism, no errors of any kind whatsoever can be admitted; and the presence of a single one will suffice to demolish our position. Yet the presence of errors in the form of discrepancies and contradictions is a fact so notorious and indisputable that it does not require to be enlarged upon.[21]

It would appear, therefore, that the only possible course will be to concede the presence of what we might term purely factual errors, while simultaneously affirming the infallibility of the Scriptures in matter of "faith and doctrine." Yet it seems plain that the latter assertion is incapable of being sustained even by the most ingenious employment of allegory. The line of argument which leads to this conclusion has been so frequently, fully, and lucidly presented by liberals that it would be superfluous to do more than refer to it, were it not for the contemporary conservative reaction which, too often, affects to disregard it.

How is the theory in question to be reconciled with the theological development which is clearly portrayed in the literature of the Old Testament? We begin with a crudely limited and anthropomorphic conception of a national God who is one among a group of deities, even if he be supreme among them, a God who walks in the garden in the cool of the day, who descends from heaven to observe what is going on upon earth, who precedes the migrating Israelites in a column of cloud and fire, who talks with Moses "as a man speaketh with his friend," who comes and stands and calls for Samuel, a God who cannot even overcome the opposition of the Canaanites in their chariots of iron;[22] and we end with an unmistakably monotheistic Deity, the Lord of heaven and earth, beside whom there is no god.

21. We should have to account, for instance, for the two irreconcilable stories of the creation in the first and second chapters of Genesis, and for the contradictory instructions with regard to the number of animals to be brought into the ark which are given to Noah in the sixth and seventh chapters of the same book. We should have to deal with the two distinct and incompatible genealogies with which Jesus is provided in the Gospels of Matthew and Luke, and with the story of the Virgin Birth, which is in conflict with both of them. And we must also account for the fact that the resurrection appearances are located by Matthew in Galilee and by Luke in Jerusalem. I mention these only as prominent instances of the type of discrepancies which are familiar to every student of textual criticism.
22. Judg. 1:19.

This metaphysical expansion of the idea of God is accompanied by a change of moral outlook. In early times God was thought of as capable of "breaking out" in waves of tempestuous anger, a notion which passed away together with the primitive anthropomorphism which had inspired it.[23]

It is true that what the liberal would regard as progress is by no means uniform, nor always victorious. To the tremendous emphasis laid upon sacrificial religion we can oppose utterances of the prophets[24] and psalmists,[25] and in contrast to the doctrine of the uniquely chosen people—a belief which obviously had its origin in the period when each nation was thought to have its own national God—we can point to pronouncements indicative of an incipient universalism.[26] Yet we must recognize that these "progressive" tendencies were modified, and to some extent counteracted, by the Deuteronomic reform and by the postexilic reaction headed by Ezra and Nehemiah. Some such compromise was, perhaps, inevitable if the Jews, unlike their kinsmen of the northern kingdom, were to survive as a people; all that is relevant to our present consideration is the reflection that tides of action and reaction, achievement upon one line conflicting with achievement upon another, are quite compatible with the liberal's theory of revelation. Everywhere he sees the divine and the human joined together, sometimes in co-operation and sometimes in conflict, the divine ever seeking to elicit the potentialities of the human.

If, therefore, we are to adopt any theory of revelation, it seems quite clear that it must be the liberal theory; and it is also quite clear that if we do adopt it, the rational character of our position will not thereby be impugned. For revelation, as we have fully recognized, is a thoroughly rational conception. It is also clear, however, that we have no right to make use of it until we have examined the position of the theist and unless we have found ourselves able to accept it.

What, then, shall we say in conclusion about the relation between philosophy and religion? Between certain types of philosophy and

23. Can we really believe, for instance, that God in his anger would have destroyed the Israelites had it not been for the intervention of Moses (Exod. 32:9–14), that he actually commanded the total extermination of the Canaanites, that he sent a lying spirit into the mouths of Ahab's prophets to lure him to his death (I Kings 22:19–23; II Chron. 18:18–22), or that he took the life of Uzzah for laying his hand upon the ark in an effort to keep it from falling (II Sam. 6:6–7; I Chron. 13:9–10)? Again in Exod. 34:7 and Deut. 5:9 we are told that God visits the iniquities of the fathers upon the children to the third and fourth generation, a belief which is passionately repudiated by Ezekiel (18:19–20).

24. Cf. Amos 5:21–25; Isa. 1:11–17.   25. Cf. Ps. 50:8–14; Ps. 51:16–17.
26. Cf. Amos 9:7; Mal. 1:11.

certain types of religion the chasm is, indeed, as profound as could well be imagined. On the one side we have logical positivists and linguistic analysts who shelter themselves behind a barrier of epistemological and ontological dogmas from every breath of religion. And on the other, we have religionists of the type of Tertullian, Kierkegaard, Barth, and Brunner who effect to pour unmitigated scorn upon human reason.[27] Yet the main current of philosophy and the main current of religion have tended throughout the centuries to flow together and mingle in a single stream. And this is both natural and inevitable, for each is nothing less than the concentrated activity of the human intelligence and personality seeking to understand, and to adapt itself to what it understands, to find a way of knowledge which shall also be a way of life. What, then, is the difference between them? If the surmise which is common both to the metaphysician and to the religionist, the surmise that reality is in the fullest sense of the word intelligible, and therefore capable of satisfying the needs of the human spirit, be sound, there is at bottom no difference between them. To be rational is to be religious, and to be religious is to be rational. The great saying of Erigena is, then, the conclusion of the whole matter, "the true philosophy is the true religion, and conversely the true religion is the true philosophy." [28]

We have as yet, however, no right to acquiesce in this tremendous dictum. As genuine philosophers we must "follow the argument whithersoever it may lead," and we cannot tell in advance whither it may lead. It may end in pure disillusionment. Intellectually we must put all to the hazard in the same spirit as that which animated the Marquis of Montrose.[29] Without impartial investigation no conclusion can be reached which is worth the having. In the words of Professor S. Radhakrishnan we must "let our desires set, but not solve, our problem." But unless our desires had set the problem, we should not be interested in religion at all—nor yet, we may add, in philosophy as the greatest philosophers have understood it. Erigena's saying, therefore, will constitute the epitome of our hope.

The task which lies before us is, in a sense, twofold. We must seek

27. Thinkers of these two schools are, of course, equally opposed to rationalism. It is natural, therefore, that they should seek to establish a concordat. I have long anticipated that efforts would be made in this direction, and now I observe with some amusement that my expectation is being fulfilled.

28. *Liber de Praedestinatione*, chap. 1.

29. He either fears his fate too much
Or his deserts are small
Who dares not put it to the touch
To win or lose it all.

to discover whether religious phenomena shed any light upon the nature of the universe in which they occur. And we must also try to find out all that we can from other sources as to the nature of the universe in order to learn whether the knowledge thus acquired tends to substantiate, or to discredit, the claims of religion. Yet these two activities constitute only two aspects of a single undertaking, the effort to learn all that we can from all sources about the nature of ultimate reality so as to discover whether that nature be in harmony with all that is highest in our own.

There is no royal road to this end. Before us lies the steep and rocky path of metaphysics. Only intellectual fainthearts have sought to bypass it, and we have seen that their efforts at evasion have got them nowhere. Let us therefore, without more ado, set our feet upon it.

BOOK II

PHILOSOPHY

CHAPTER ONE

STARTING POINT AND METHOD

At the opening of our metaphysical inquiry we are confronted by a twofold question: Where shall we begin, and what method shall we employ? And these twin queries give rise to a third: Will not the answer to one inevitably determine our answer to the other? System and method, it may be said, should develop *pari passu;* yet will not the selection of a definite ποῦ στῶ fix the direction of the subsequent development both of the system and of the method which grows out of it? If, on the other hand, we decide in advance what our method is to be, may it not prove to be a Procrustean bed into which we shall find ourselves violently forcing reality and thereby distorting its essential features? Our difficulty presents a certain analogy to that of the scientist who is unable simultaneously to determine both the position and the speed of a particle. A presuppositionless philosophy is what we desire, but is the thing feasible? Are we driven at the outset to make a choice the grounds of which we cannot ourselves adequately evaluate, and which may deflect the entire course of metaphysical speculation?

Reflections such as these have driven certain thinkers up the blind alley which today bears the name of psychologism. It seemed to them that what was called for was a preliminary critique of the mind's powers of knowing, and that, until this had been satisfactorily accomplished, a moratorium should be declared upon philosophic speculation. But it soon became apparent that the notion which had inspired the enterprise was a self-contradictory one. The mind's capacity to know can be investigated only if it have actually succeeded in knowing, only if there be genuine instances of knowledge before us. Thus the projected critique itself presupposed the knowledge which it was designed to validate. Psychologism is an old error which is now one of the commonplaces of the history of philosophy, and which need detain us no longer.

From our predicament, however, a way of escape offers itself, one associated with the names of St. Augustine and Descartes; yet one the soundness of which many philosophers have failed to recognize. Our task, therefore, shall be, not only to tread it again, but also to endeavor to remove those misunderstandings which have prevented others from joining us. We shall be primarily concerned, however, not with the exposition and interpretation of what previous thinkers have written, but with the problem before us. Grateful for whatever light they may throw upon it, we shall wrestle with it as best we may.

It is the famous method of doubt to which we now appeal, a method which will cause the dilemma which confronts us to dissolve before our eyes, one which will provide the Ariadne's thread to conduct us out of the labyrinth wherein we seem to be imprisoned, and one which will turn the skeptic's weapons with fatal consequences against himself. Yet, strange as it may appear, it is a method which has been so frequently misunderstood that we cannot devote too great pains to the business of clarifying it.

Cartesian doubt, we are told time and again, is not genuine doubt; the doubter's attitude, it is alleged, is assumed merely as a tactical device. It is psychologically impossible to doubt everything, and to profess so to do is a mere pretense the latent insincerity of which robs it of all effectiveness. To refuse to be content with the probability which is within one's grasp, to disparage it in comparison with an unattainable certainty, to repudiate belief and to lay claim to a knowledge which is not for mortals, is to commit the ancient Hellenic sin of ύρβις, and thereby to render oneself liable to the penalty of ultimate disillusionment and frustrated hopes.

Comments in this vein upon the Augustino-Cartesian method of doubt have been so frequent and so vociferous as to fill any sober hearer with amazement, for never in the history of philosophy has there been a more glaring missing of the point. The recognition that it is psychologically impossible to doubt everything, so far from being inconsistent with the practice of the method proposed to us, is the very insight that inspires it. We are not urged to *doubt* everything, but to *try* to doubt everything. Were it possible to doubt everything, we should only become enveloped by a fog which never lifted. But, if there be things which cannot be doubted, we can determine what these things are only by attempting to doubt them and finding that our attempt is vain. We must attempt, therefore, to "shake everything in heaven and earth that the things that are unshaken may remain."

Nor is there any pretense or insincerity in this attempt. On the contrary, it is a grimly honest business. For, unless we be already bitter pessimists, complete cynics, or self-centered egoists, among the things that we must try to doubt are some that will be precious to us. Yet they must be tried as by fire, for only so can their genuineness be established beyond question. In all this inexorable thoroughness is required. Whatever collapses when struck is thereby demolished, but whatever does no more than vibrate must be struck again. We must not be put off by "natural propensities" or "instinctive tendencies" to believe, or by the claims of "animal faith," such as realists often invoke to support their acceptance of a physical world, or theologians to buttress their faith in God. It is precisely these demands to be exempted from the ordeal which are most to be suspected, and which cry loudest for examination.

The method of doubt, be it understood, does not require that one make the mind a blank, that one empty it of all the ideas with which experience has filled it; for where there are no ideas neither are there any doubts. Nor does it involve an attempt to relive in retrospect the process whereby the mind of the infant grew into that of the mature man. Could such an undertaking be successfully accomplished it would none the less be fruitless, for it would leave us precisely where we already are. It is not the infantile but the adult mind, and not the adult mind of the "plain man" but that of the reflective and critical philosopher who has learned how to bring unconscious assumptions into the light and how to make implicit judgments explicit, that has most fully developed the ability to doubt, and it is the doubts of such a mind that must be laid to rest.

The way upon which we have entered is a familiar path, and everyone is aware where it terminates. It terminates, of course, with the self—the one thing whose existence cannot be doubted. For of everything else of whose existence I am sure my assurance rests upon the fact that, directly or indirectly, I am aware of it. Could I doubt my awareness of it, I could doubt its existence. But, if I do not exist, I can be aware of nothing. Upon my certitude of my own existence, therefore, reposes my certitude of the existence of any other thing. The second certitude is not, indeed, inferred from the first; but it is involved in the first. Although it would not be true to say that my own existence is the only thing that I cannot doubt, it would be true to say that the certitude of my own existence is my primal certitude upon which rest all other certitudes. To be certain of anything is to be aware that I am aware of it; that is, to know myself as knowing it. If I can doubt that I exist I can also doubt that I am aware of it, and, if I doubt, I do not have certitude.

Thus, if anyone profess to be uncertain of his own existence, we may point out to him that there is nothing else of which he can be certain. For only an existent self can be certain of anything; hence, if the existence of that self be a matter of doubt, its certitudes are no longer certitudes. Such a man cannot even consistently affirm that he thinks it probable that he exists; for if he can doubt that he exists, he can also doubt that he deems his existence probable.

To impugn the existence of the self, therefore, is to fall into a skepticism so profound as to be suicidal. If it be said that what I am certain of is not the existence of myself but the existence of a doubting, the answer is that I can be certain of nothing of the sort unless I be aware of myself as doubting. Doubt and belief alike are known only through awareness of the doubting or believing self. "Si fallor sum," wrote St. Augustine, and in so writing he expressed that fundamental awareness which it is meaningless to question. The same truth has been stated with equal clarity and greater adequacy by Spinoza: "Qui absolute nescit se existere, simul nescit se affirmantem aut negantem, hoc est, certo se affirmare aut negare.

Notandum autem hic, quod, quamvis multa magna certitudine affirmemus et negemus, ad hoc, quod existamus, non attendentes; tamen, nisi pro indubito hoc praesupponatur, omnia in dubium revocari possent." [1]

In these words Spinoza has answered in advance the objection which has sometimes been urged to the effect that the existence of the self is known, not directly, but by inference. Upon whatever grounds such an inference might be based, and however indubitable they were, our certitude that they were indubitable would depend upon our awareness of them as being so, and upon the further awareness of ourselves as thus aware of them. But this, it may be urged, involves us in an infinite regress which is vicious. If my certitude with respect to anything depend upon my certitude that I am certain of it, this certitude again will depend upon my certitude that I am certain that I am certain of it, and so ad infinitum. The threat conveyed by this objection is, however, a hollow one. Certitude with respect to anything involves the knowing of it, and knowing involves a knower. To be certain of the knowing is to be certain of the knower as knowing. If I can doubt the knower, *eo ipso* I doubt the knowing, and with the knowing that which is known. My certitude that I know, however, involves nothing more than my awareness of myself as knowing. Since this awareness conveys certitude, it is immune to doubt, and is not

1. *Principia Philosophiae Cartesianae,* Pars I, Propositio I (The Hague, 1914).

susceptible of implementation. To be certain that I am certain that I am certain would not make me more certain.

Since my certitude that I exist is the basis of my certitude of the validity of any inference, it is clear that it cannot itself be the conclusion of any inference. Descartes' observations on this point are very just.

> When we become aware that we are thinking beings, this is a primitive act of knowledge derived from no syllogistic reasoning. He who says, *I think, hence I am, or exist,* does not deduce existence from thought by a syllogism, but, by a simple act of mental vision, recognises it as if it were a thing that is known *per se.* This is evident from the fact that, if it were syllogistically deduced, the major premise, *that everything that thinks is, or exists,* would have to be known previously; but yet that has rather been learned from the experience of the individual—that unless he exists he cannot think.[2]

Moreover, it is surely legitimate to ask how any process of inference could disclose to us the existence of the self unless we were already in possession of the idea of the self, and how this idea could have been acquired otherwise than through direct acquaintance with the self. The object in asking this question is to support the claim to direct acquaintance with the self in the only way that the claim to direct acquaintance with anything can be supported—by showing the untenability of any alternative view.

At this point, however, another objection may be advanced. Self-consciousness, or self-awareness, it may be said, is not something that we are born with, but something that we achieve. Can it seriously be contended that a newborn child is aware of itself? Can a similar supposition with any plausibility be advanced in the case of the lower animals? It is only through a psychological process extending over a period of years that the human being attains to self-awareness. Is it not plain, therefore, that self-awareness is not immediate but mediate, and consequently inferential?

To this objection we may reply as follows. We have not asked you, we may say to our hypothetical disputant, *how* you became aware of yourself. What we asked you is whether or not you are now aware of yourself. Do you really and honestly doubt that you exist? If you

2. *Reply to Objection II,* trans. E. S. Haldane and G. R. T. Ross (Cambridge, 1931), II, p. 38.

can doubt that you are a self, you can doubt that you are aware of anything. And, thus doubting, you will doubt the basis for any inference whereby the existence of your self might conceivably be established. You will have enveloped yourself in a skepticism so complete that affirmation and denial have become equally meaningless. Yet do you, and can you, actually thus doubt bona fide? Genuinely to get rid of explicit self-awareness you would, surely, have to retreat through all the stages of the psychological process through which you have passed and return to infancy. But this is an impossible achievement. If all that you are concerned to do is to emphasize that it is through such a process that you have arrived at explicit self-awareness, your concern is legitimate. You have learned to discriminate between what is within you and what is without you, and to make explicit judgments that were once merely implicit. And without memory, without retentiveness and recognition, without the ability to compare and contrast, you would not have arrived at the stage where you are. All this we willingly concede to you. And, if you wish to distinguish between "psychical" and "psychological" immediacy, we shall not haggle over words. What we desire to point out is that the awareness which you now have of yourself is not inferential or indirect but direct and indubitable. If you like to assert that your memory may be fallacious and your past illusory, that you may conceivably have come into being with the present moment, we shall not at this instant quarrel with you. All that we ask you to acknowledge is that you are certain that you are now a self.

To concede this, it may be said, is not to concede very much. To admit that one is a self in the psychologist's sense is not to admit that one is a self in some metaphysical sense. It is not to assert that self is other than the body, or that it is other than a succession of conscious states or events. It is only to affirm what every sane man would also affirm, namely, that there *is* a self; it is not to assert anything as to *what* the self is.

Yet let us not be impatient. "Link by link is chain mail made." We are now certain of something. That is much. We have our ποῦ στῶ. But we cannot be certain of the *that* and yet be wholly ignorant of the *what*. What, then, do we encounter when we introspect? Descartes was very certain as to what he encountered. "I know," he said, "that I am a thing that thinks." Perhaps the use of the word *thing* is unfortunate. Inanimate objects are called *things*. We might replace *thing* by the vague word *entity*. Descartes' meaning, however, is quite clear.

He is discriminating between the thinker and the thinking. He is conscious of both. In introspection, he tells us, we are simultaneously aware both of the ego that thinks and of the thinking in which it is engaged. Whether or not this be an accurate report every man must test for himself.

Some have contended that it is an inaccurate report; in this connection Hume is usually cited. Let us, then, bow in reverence to custom and turn to the famous passage. "For my part," writes Hume, "when I enter most intimately into what I call *myself*, I always stumble on some particular perception or other, of heat or cold, light or shade, love or hatred, pain or pleasure. I never catch *myself* at any time without a perception, and never can observe anything but the perception." [3]

Thinkers who believe in the existence of a genuine and abiding ego, and who maintain that this ego can be known, not directly by introspection, but only inferentially from the data supplied by introspection, have frequently asserted that Hume has been guilty of a fatal omission in his account in that he is oblivious of the fact that it is Hume who is entering into himself, and is stumbling over the perceptions which he discovers there. What Hume ought to have done, we are told, was to have realized that he could never make himself his own object, but that what he was aware of was the contents of his own mind, and that from the existence of these data he should have inferred that of his own introspecting self.

Why, we may ask, should he have chosen this course in preference to developing his own "bundle theory" of the self? Presumably because the bundle theory will not stand up. But why will it not stand up? What happens in introspection according to the bundle theory? What happens is that one perception is inspecting other perceptions. It cannot identify itself with any one of them, or with all of them together, without violating the law of identity. All of these perceptions exist, or occur, as it were, "on their own." All that the introspecting—or, to put it more accurately, the inspecting—perception can do is to recognize that it and all these other perceptions are members of the same bundle. Yet how can it know that all the other perceptions do belong to one and the same bundle? And how can it possibly know that it itself belongs to this bundle, or to any bundle at all, unless it can become aware of itself? But then, on Hume's own showing, what can this mean except that it has split into two perceptions, one of which now

3. *Treatise*, Book I, Part IV, sec. 6.

inspects the other? And now a similar difficulty arises in the case of the new inspecting perception, which will again require to introspect itself; and thus it will find itself confronted by a process of fission which will continue ad infinitum.

Such considerations do, I think, suffice to show that the bundle theory cannot give a satisfactory account of what happens in introspection. But we may still ask on what grounds Hume should have based the inference which he ought to have made with respect to the existence of an introspecting ego which can never become its own object, and can never be directly known. Shall we say that he should have recognized that all the perceptions, volitions, feelings, all the mental states or occurrences which he encountered, possessed the common characteristic—to use a term of Professor Broad's—of being owned? Yet how could Hume know this, if he had never encountered the owner? If the owner be an *ego absconditus,* why should not Hume regard them, as he does, as the property of no one?

This question naturally leads on to the consideration of Professor C. D. Broad's own theory, which he advances with a great deal of confidence.

Neither the characteristic of selfhood nor that of material thinghood is simple; and the concept of each of them is in part *a priori* and in part empirical. Selfhood and material thinghood are two different specifications of the more abstract characteristic of being a continuant. The concept of this is *a priori;* but the concepts of its two different determinate specifications involve notions which are empirical. In the concept of material thinghood the empirical notions of being contained within a closed spatial boundary and occupying the same spatial position or a continuous series of such positions throughout a period of time are important constituents. In the concept of selfhood it is much harder to name the empirical notions. One empirically conceived factor is the peculiar kind of unity which ties together various simultaneous experiences in a single specious present; another is the fact that some experiences in one specious present are ostensibly memories of certain experiences in earlier specious presents; another is the fact that some experiences in one specious present are ostensibly fulfilments or frustrations of certain expectations in earlier specious presents; and so on. When people say that the characteristic of selfhood is simple and that the concept of it is empirical I suspect that what they mean is often no more than that the empirical factors in it are quite unique and peculiar and cannot be defined in terms of the empirical factors in the notion of material thinghood. This seems to me to be plainly true.[4]

Professor Broad goes on to insist that it is only by repeated experiences accompanied by comparison, recollection, and reflection that "the characteristics which differentiate selfhood from material thinghood and both from the generic characteristic of being a continuant" can be grasped. The concept of a continuant is clearly closely related to the Kantian concept of substance; like it, it is a priori, and, like it, is imposed upon the raw data furnished by experience. Professor Broad appears to be primarily interested in the notion of a continuant as opposed to that of an occurrent. This is an issue which will in due course concern us also; but at present our concern is, not so much with the duration, as with the structure of the self. The crucial question is whether Descartes be justified in his claim that he can discriminate in introspection between the ego, or subject, on the one hand, and the states, or acts, of the ego, on the other.

Have you not already asserted, I may be asked, that the question is one which the individual must decide for himself? If you have introspected, and if your introspection have revealed to you an ego which functions as the subject of mental states, this should suffice for you; and you are an intellectual milksop indeed if you hesitate or equivocate in the face of adverse declarations, however thunderous be the tones in which they are delivered. There is much truth in these observations. I, for one, believe firmly that I can and do discriminate in introspection between my ego and its states or acts, and on this I am prepared to stand. Yet, when one finds eminent philosophers in disagreement—as we find Descartes and Hume opposed—however convinced one may be of the rightness of one's own view, one must recognize that one's own declaration has no authority for anyone else. The philosopher of religion may well feel the need for a substantival ego, and may be accused of a wilful determination at all costs to find one. Nor are those who adopt the opposite view above all suspicion. The fact that Kant frowned upon the notion of a "pure ego" is in itself enough to make many a philosopher cringe at the suggestion that he is veering toward a theory so devoid of intellectual respectibility. It is not a waste of time, therefore, to try indirectly to support one's own claim to direct awareness by showing, if one can, that one's opponent's views are untenable, or at least lacking in plausibility.

4. *Examination of McTaggart's Philosophy* (Cambridge, 1933), II, Part I, 168.

Professor Broad's view possesses, at any rate, the advantage that it does not require us to *infer* the existence of the self. An a priori concept is obviously closely akin to, if it be not identical with, an innate idea—*pace* certain Kantian enthusiasts—and Professor Broad has defended in brilliant fashion the doctrine of innate ideas, and has triumphantly shown how weak are many of the objections which have been advanced against it.[5] On his theory the difficulty which I previously raised as to how it could be possible to infer from any data whatsoever the existence of a self unless we were already in possession of an idea of the self, and as to how this idea could ever have been acquired if the self were never actually intuited, no longer perplexes us; for if the concept of the self be innate, there is no question of acquiring it. All that is requisite is the appropriate occasion, which experience supplies, to call it forth and to insure its application.

I should have thought, however, that the theory would have gained in plausibility if it had presupposed the existence of an abiding ego which could serve as the permanent repository of innate ideas. Even so, it would suffer from the serious disadvantage, which Professor Broad frankly acknowledges, that the innate ideas or a priori concepts constitute a screen between the apprehending mind and the reality apprehended. Thus, even if we were genuine selves, we could never know ourselves to be such; we could know only—if I may so put it— that we were constrained to think of ourselves as selves.

Professor Broad seems to hold, however, that there is no abiding ego but only a succession of mental states. It is with some diffidence that I attribute this view to him, for I do not see how, on his showing, he could know this much; nevertheless such appears to me to be the conclusion which his language implies. The situation now becomes far more complicated. For the a priori concept or innate idea will be perpetually perishing and perpetually being reborn as mental states succeed one another. This seems a very strange state of affairs. Will it help us to make use of Professor Broad's own illustration of a scar in the human body which persists despite the fact that the material of the body is constantly being renewed? The illustration does not seem to be a happy one, for the body has a persisting structure and the material which it incorporates originally existed outside it; whereas, if there be no abiding self but only a succession of mental states, there will be no persisting structure and no external stuff to be assimilated. What guarantee have we that each successive state will be the bearer of a concept similar to that borne by its predecessor? It might, of

5. *Ibid.*, I, 47–51.

course, be asked what guarantee we have that it will not. I confess that it is difficult to determine what follows from the hypothesis that there is no ego other than a succession of psychic states, for it seems to me that one who can accept this theory can believe almost anything. There is, however, a further difficulty confronting us.

Granted that a mental state emerges endowed with an a priori concept of the self which it proceeds to impose upon the data presented to it, what will these data consist of? Presumably they will include past states of the same series, probably also data of present experience such as kinesthetic feelings. Yet how can this state include itself under its own concept unless it be able to introspect itself, which, on the present theory, it cannot do? The extraordinary conclusion appears to follow that although we can know *that* there are selves, we cannot know that *we* are selves! The difficulty which confronts us is similar to that which wrecked the bundle theory. In the face of it Professor Broad's theory seems to collapse, and I do not see how it can once more be set afoot.

Nor do we fare much better, I believe, if we assume that there is an abiding ego, which, on the theory before us, we have no right to do. All that we know is that we have an a priori concept which functions as a kind of psychic lens through which we contemplate the data provided by introspection, and we cannot tell whether this lens distorts or correctly conveys these data. If one try to think of what could be meant by an a priori concept, one finds oneself invoking analogies such as the above, which are not really analogies, and do not make the situation appreciably clearer. A concept through, or by means of which, we think—what could such an entity be? In his ingenious defense of the doctrine of innate ideas Professor Broad propounds the hypothesis that all normal human beings are endowed with dispositions to form certain concepts which, it would seem, are suggested by but yet not directly derived from experience. The concept, then, is a mental product of some sort, an entity in itself, something in the nature of a *tertium quid.* This is the position of the conceptualist. Conceptualism is a doctrine which we shall have to examine at a later stage of our inquiry in connection with our theory of knowledge, and it would be premature to undertake such an examination here. We may content ourselves, however, for the present with a fourfold observation.

In the first place, unless the conceptualist doctrine can be sustained, Professor Broad's theory falls. In the second place, even if conceptualism be a defensible theory and be applicable in other connections, it does not seem to fit the facts before us. For a concept, presumably, is something in terms of which I think *about* reality, whereas, in perceiving myself, I do not necessarily think *about* myself, I *think myself* in all my concrete individuality. In Professor Broad's view, however, what I think is not myself but the concept of *self*.[6] Third, if I be not directly aware of myself, I cannot be sure that I have any concepts, or that I am aware of anything at all. And fourth and last, even if the thinking subject be an abiding ego which subsumes the data given in introspection under the concept of *self*, it will not only be unable to determine whether the concept corresponds to anything actually existing *in re* but will also have no ground for identifying itself with that existent entity even if it be actual. In view of these considerations we are justified, I conclude, in dismissing Broad's theory as unsatisfactory.

It may be urged, however, that we have been too easily discouraged in the attempt to infer the existence of an abiding ego. For what do we encounter when we introspect? We encounter feelings, awarenesses, volitions, emotions. Now, whether we regard these as acts or states or occurrences, it is clear that they cannot be ultimate. An act involves an actor, a state must be a state of something, an occurrence does not happen *in vacuo*—there is something to which, or in which, it occurs. You cannot have feeling without a conscious being that feels it, knowing without a knower, willing without a willer, an emotion which is not entertained by someone. The truth of this contention is self-evident, so why not build upon it?

Now I think that the truth of this contention is self-evident; nevertheless, to the suggestion taken as a whole I have two objections. The first is that it falsifies the actual state of affairs. When Hume said that he never caught himself without a perception, he was right—if one be allowed to interpret the term "perception" somewhat largely—

---

6. If it be objected that on Broad's view we do not "think the concept of the self" but rather "think the self," I should reply as follows. The concept of a continuant is distinctly stated by Professor Broad to be a priori. It becomes enlarged, or absorbed, I take it, into the concept of the self when it is applied to the "empirical factors" discovered by introspection. The application of the concept would seem to involve the setting of these factors in a certain perspective. What are these "empirical factors" apart from this perspective? If they be characteristics of, or events in the history of, an abiding subject, a pure ego, which cannot be directly intuited, then it seems clear that we think *about* the self by thinking *of* the concept which we have formed, to which it corresponds in the sense that the concept enables us to give a correct description of it. If, on the other hand, there be no pure ego, if the psychic continuant be only a succession of occurrents, then the concept which we have formed will be a logical—or psychological—construct, a practical device which proves its utility by providing a sort of symbol of the flow of psychic states, but to which no objective reality actually corresponds.

but when he added that he never observed anything but a perception, he was misstating fact in the interest of theory. We do not, when we introspect, observe a bare act of will or of awareness, or a bare feeling; we observe a willing, knowing, or feeling ego.

My second objection is that, although the propositions that a state cannot exist without that of which it is the state, or an act without an actor, are self-evident, the question can still be asked why we can not doubt them. And the answer is because we are aware of ourselves as aware of their self-evidence. Could we doubt the existence of ourselves, we could also doubt the self-evidence of that of which we are aware. Our awareness, therefore, rests upon a prior self-awareness, and so is circular.

At this point, however, yet another objection may be raised. A subject, it may be said, can never be its own object. There is a fatal duality in self-awareness, for a relation requires at least two terms. If this objection were sound, not only awareness of the self but all knowledge and all certainty would be impossible. Since our awareness of our existence is indubitable, and is the root of all knowledge and all certainty, it is clear that not all relations do require two terms, and that self-awareness is a relation which has only one term. That in self-awareness the knower and the known are one is the primal intuition upon which all knowledge reposes. I have reiterated this assertion, perhaps ad nauseam, yet not, I think, unwarrantably, for its blatant obviousness has been strangely overlooked. Yet what can be more inescapably evident than the fact that if I do not exist, I know nothing; and the twin fact that if I can doubt my own existence, in *that* doubt I also doubt the existence of all other things, since my assurance of their existence involves my being directly or indirectly aware of them. That we are directly aware of ourselves is a fact of which no direct proof is possible, inasmuch as any such argument must presuppose it. To every man's own consciousness, however, we may appeal. Let any man candidly ask himself whether he cannot and do not use the word "I" meaningfully, whether, when he uses it, he is not quite certain of its referent, whether he is not conscious of himself as standing in manifold relations to other beings, as suffering pain or enjoying pleasure, as making plans for his own future and forming resolutions which he intends to carry out, and I feel confident that unless he shut his eyes to obvious fact in the interest of dogmatic preconceptions, he will answer yes. He must, at any rate, refrain from denying that he is aware of himself, since, in making such a denial, he contradicts himself.

Where direct proof is impossible, however, an indirect proof will frequently provide support by furnishing a *reductio ad absurdum* of the opposing view. In the present case, if it can be shown that the self cannot be known inferentially and by description in such a way as to distinguish it from everything else, it will follow that the self is known directly, since, as I have just pointed out, the denial that it is known at all lands us in self-contradiction. Such an argument has been developed by McTaggart in *The Nature of Existence*.[7] Briefly recapitulated, the argument proceeds as follows:

I can be aware that I am aware of something, it matters not what, be it a particular or a universal. Let us take McTaggart's example, "I am aware that I am aware of equality." Here the act of awareness of equality is conjoined with a second act of awareness of which it becomes the object. The judgment is formed, "I am aware of this awareness." "This is not merely a judgment that a particular person is aware of this awareness. It also asserts that the person who is aware of the awareness is the person who is making the judgment." But unless the identity of the subject who is aware of the awareness and the subject who makes the judgment be intuitively recognized, what justification is there for this assertion? It seems clear that there is none. If there be no direct apprehension of their identity, the subject of the awareness of the awareness and the subject of the judgment may, for all that anyone can tell, be numerically distinct. As McTaggart truly says, "If 'I' can only be known by description, it seems impossible that I can know that I am aware, either of this awareness of equality, or of anything else, since the judgment 'I am aware of X' always means that the person who is aware of X is also the person who is making the judgment."

It is evident, I submit, that the argument is conclusive. Yet it may perhaps be objected that so finespun an argument concerns only the philosopher in his study, and that in daily life we possess a "practical certainty" of the existence of a substantival self strong enough to enable us to brush aside with a rough hand all cobwebs of theory. We are in possession, I should reply, of something better than a practical certainty—whatever that may be—we are in possession of absolute certainty; but this is only because the self is known directly. Without such direct awareness we should possess no certainty of any kind.

7. (Cambridge, 1927), Vol. II, secs. 382–387. McTaggart records that the argument was suggested to him by a passage in Lord Russell's article "Knowledge by Acquaintance and Knowledge by Description," *Mysticism and Logic* (New York, 1954), p. 211.

Let us, however, consider F. R. Tennant's objection, which appears to be directed against the earlier Russell as much as against McTaggart. The point is put somewhat differently, yet the issue is at bottom the same.

> The I describable as "now aware of red," and the I describable as "aware of the awareness of red" cannot logically be identified; yet their identification is necessary, if the I is to know itself by description. But the bridge which abstract logic cannot throw, actuality does throw. For the second I could not be described as it has been, were it not identical with the first. Unless the "awareness of red" were *erlebt* by it, the second I could have no inkling of red having been sensed, or of sensatio having occurred.[8]

Here we have a blatant prejudging of the issue involved. Unless the two *I*'s be identical, the description of the one will not apply to the other; so much is painfully obvious. But unless we be aware of this identity, we cannot know that the two descriptions do apply to the same *I*. And the question remains: How are we aware of it? If intuitively and directly, the case is clear. If not, what process of inference will avail?

We are sure, it may be urged, that all awareness connected with the same body pertains to the same self. Are we indeed? How do we know that more than one self may not be connected with the same body? And how do we know that the awareness of red may not be connected with another body than that with which the awareness of this awareness is connected, or with no body at all? At the present stage of our inquiry, surely, so confident an assertion, for which no grounds are yet given, is out of place. What is in fact proposed to us is a devious detour through the region of probability, and out of probability certainty cannot issue. Yet certainty of our own existence we have, and must be accounted for. Direct apprehension does account for it, and it should now be plain that nothing else can. We are thus driven back to the position which we had already reached, that the *Cogito*, as Descartes claimed, constitutes the only sure foundation upon which we can build, and that self-awareness is the root of all certainty.

8. *Philosophical Theology* (Cambridge, 1928), I, 76.

CHAPTER TWO

THE CONTENTS OF THE *COGITO*

The path we have hitherto followed has been that trodden by Descartes, and I believe that I have shown that the objections which have been brought against his procedure are groundless. We have now to consider whether we can continue to avail ourselves of his guidance. In the *Cogito,* Descartes maintained, certain "common notions" emerge which fall into two classes, those which are "things or the affections of things" and the formal principles of their interconnection which he nominates the "vincula of knowledge." [1] Instead of entering upon a detailed defense or criticism of Descartes I propose to go into the question afresh in my own way. It is obviously a question well worth raising, since whatever is known in the knowing of the self will partake of the same certainty.

Now it is unquestionably the case that when we introspect we are aware of the self, not as an indescribable and characterless somewhat, a mere featureless monad, but as a concrete existent, possessed of qualities, standing in relations, the subject of states, acting and being acted upon. All this is revealed to us in the *Cogito,* and is apprehended with indubitable certainty. Adequately to elucidate and render explicit the knowledge thus acquired will carry us, however, beyond the limits of the *Cogito.* Nor is there any reason why it should not do so. That the self is not alone in the universe, that it has an environment, has never been seriously doubted. In introspection we are aware of the self as the subject of sense experience. It is not yet apparent how that experience is to be interpreted, but of its reality there can be no question. Moreover, it is a fact worth remarking, and one which might give pause to those philosophers who maintain that the existence of the physical is more certain and more easily known than that of the self, that, while there have been many thinkers who were subjectivists in the matter of sense experience, there is none on record who has actually doubted the reality of other selves. *How* we are aware of it has occasioned some dispute, but *that* we are aware of it all are agreed. Solipsism is not a view which has ever been seriously

1. *Reg.* xii, *Prins.* I, xiii, xlviii; cf. Dr. S. V. Keeling, *Descartes* (London, 1968), pp. 111–112.

defended by anybody. That the self has an environment, that it is confronted by sense data (whatever be their genuine status), and that it is connected with other selves we shall therefore presuppose. The notions of quality, substance, relation, state, act, and causality are all exemplified by or in the self; yet some, at least, of these are also exemplified in its environment, to which we shall take leave to refer whenever it may seem desirable.

QUALITY

It will be convenient to begin with quality, for the sum of the qualities of a thing can be said to constitute its nature, and it is in terms of its nature that a thing is most adequately described. Quality, as McTaggart has rightly observed,[2] must be taken as indefinable. It is, nonetheless, something which can be distinguished. In introspection we can become aware of the self as anxious or hopeful or miserable or happy, and these characteristics provide examples of what we mean by quality. We are quite certain, moreover, in the case of the self, that what we are aware of is a real entity and not mere appearance, and that it really does possess these characteristics. Thus, without going beyond the limits of the *Cogito*, we have established the status of quality. In sense experience, however, we become aware of what are at least seemingly external entities, and with them of a host of qualities, such as shapes, colors, sounds, and smells.

Some qualities, it is clear, admit of degrees and some do not. The self, for instance, may be more or less happy; hence happiness obviously admits of degrees. Circularity, on the other hand, whether or not it actually characterize anything, plainly does not admit of degrees, although there may be degrees of approximation to it.

By saying that quality is indefinable I mean, as McTaggart meant, that it cannot be analyzed in terms of what is not quality. The question, nevertheless, may still be raised whether some qualities can be analyzed in terms of other qualities, and are, in this sense, definable. Are there, in the first place, compound qualities, that is, qualities which are formed by the conjunction of other qualities which may in their turn be either compound or simple. McTaggart believes that there are, and he gives us two illustrations of what he has in mind—red-and-sweet and square-and-triangular. The last obviously can qualify nothing; nonetheless it constitutes, in McTaggart's judgment, a compound quality. This linking together of incompatibles may well im-

2. *The Nature of Existence,* Vol. I, sec. 60.

press us as extremely odd; yet if we could admit the first example, we might, perhaps, seriously consider the pretensions of the second. But can we? The issue seems clearly to be an ultimate one and, therefore, not susceptible of argument or proof. I can only acknowledge that when I have stated that a thing is red and that it is sweet, it seems to me that I have said all there is to say about it in this connection, and that I detect no third quality compounded of the other two.

Are there, however, complex qualities? A complex quality, according to McTaggart, is a quality "which does not consist of an aggregate of other qualities, but which can be analyzed and defined by means of other characteristics, whether qualities or relations or both." [3] He gives us but one example, "conceit," which he defines as "the possession of a higher opinion of oneself than is justified by the facts." But opinion is of the nature of judgment. The proposition which is the content of the judgment is a complex, but does it thereby infect the mind which entertains it with complexity? By the possession of an opinion is meant, I presume, the formation of and assent to a judgment. Does this constitute a complex quality of the apprehending mind? Or does it rather fall under the head of state or act? These are questions which cannot be answered offhand. Is triangularity a complex quality? It would seem so. Yet the notion of complex quality is an elusive one, and frequently one finds it hard to be sure whether what one is contemplating is not an aggregation of qualities or a simple quality plus a relation or relations. I think, however, that we are probably justified in admitting the notion of complex quality.

McTaggart has confronted us with two further issues of considerable importance, and these are the questions whether there are negative qualities and relational qualities. A negative quality, on McTaggart's view, is the not having a corresponding positive quality. To use his own illustrations, since a man is not a phoenix, he possesses the negative quality of not-phoenix, and whatever is not square possesses the negative quality not-square.[4]

I can see no more justification for this assertion than I can for the assertion that there are compound qualities. It seems clear that it is because a man possesses the qualities of a human being that he is not a phoenix, not because he possesses the quality not-phoenix. I cannot but suspect that McTaggart, clear thinker as he was, had here become confused in the use of his own terminology. "True," he tells us, is a

3. *Ibid.*, sec. 63. "Characteristic" is a term used by McTaggart to designate either qualities or relations. The usage is a convenient one, and I shall hereafter avail myself of it.
4. *Ibid.*, secs. 31, 61–62.

term applicable to beliefs and assumptions, whereas "true of" is applicable to qualities.[5] Since, then, we can say that it is true of a man that he is not a phoenix, it appears to follow that what is true of him is the quality not-phoenix. I would not contest the contention that the phrase "true of" is often used in the way McTaggart indicates. "It is true of a man that he is not a phoenix" is a perfectly intelligible sentence. But it has precisely the same meaning, I maintain, as the sentence, "It is true that a man is not a phoenix." And in the latter case, there is no suggestion of his possession of a negative quality. Far be it from me to imply that linguistic usage can ever provide an ultimate ground for the settlement of a philosophical issue. Nonetheless a psychological confusion may be engendered, strengthened, and seemingly confirmed by a familiar mode of speech. And I am inclined to believe that in the present instance, this is what happened in the case of McTaggart. I think also that the same confusion may have vitiated his treatment of relational qualities. In concluding the present discussion I would urge that to say that it is true of something that it does not possess a certain characteristic is only another way of asserting that the judgment or proposition that it is devoid of this characteristic holds good with respect to it. I propose, therefore, to reject the notion of negative qualities.

Relations, according to McTaggart, generate qualities in the related terms. A relational quality must be sharply distinguished from any other quality which a particular may acquire as a result of standing in some relation. If I move my hand close to the fire it will get hot; but the heat is not a relational quality, although it is a consequence of the establishment of that relation. The relational quality is merely the quality of being close to the fire.

"A relation in which a substance stands," writes McTaggart,

> may generate in this manner not only one quality but many qualities. If A admires B, C and D, this places A in only one relation—the relation of admiration. But there will be three derivative qualities generated in A. He will possess the qualities "admirer of B," "admirer of C," and "admirer of D." It may be convenient to say that, while admiration and equality are relations, the admiration of A for B, and the equality of A and B, are Relationships. We can then say that each relationship generates a quality of each substance which is a term of that relationship. A has the quality "admirer of B," and B has the quality "object of A's admiration." [6]

5. *Ibid.*, sec. 60.   6. *Ibid.*, sec. 85.

A's admiration for B clearly arises out of what A knows, or thinks he knows, about B's nature; and if A were not related to B, he could know nothing about B's nature. But this relation is not identical with A's admiration for B; it merely makes it possible, or, perhaps, inevitable. If there be a relation of admiration connecting A with B, it seems clear that it is generated by a feeling produced in A in consequence of his knowledge of B, and this feeling I take to be a quality of A. It is obvious that some relations are generated by qualities. If B, for instance, be a better man than A, this is a relation—or, to use McTaggart's terminology, a relationship—and it is plainly generated by the degree of virtue possessed by B and that possessed by A. It is, to employ the usual phrase, "grounded in the nature of the terms." I see no difficulty, therefore, in the view that qualities can generate relations; and I am, accordingly, prepared to concede, although with some hesitancy,[7] that A's quality of admiring B may generate a relation of admiration between A and B. But it is not apparent to me that this relation in turn proceeds to generate further qualities.

Take any relation you please. If the entities thereby related did not possess some of the qualities which they do possess, they could not be so related; if, for instance, they were not extended, they could not be spatially related to each other. Call the entities in question A and B. It is true that A is related to B, and it is true that B is related to A. McTaggart would insist that it is, then, "true of" A that it is related to B, and "true of" B that it is related to A; and that this is equivalent to saying that A is not only related to B but has also the quality of being related to B, and that B is not only related to A but has also the quality of being related to A. I have already discussed a similar contention in connection with negative qualities, and what I have said there with regard to McTaggart's use of the phrase "true of" is equally applicable here. I conclude, therefore, that we are justified in refusing to recognize relational qualities.

If we concede that there are compound, negative and relational qualities, we shall also be compelled to admit that every particular possesses an infinite number of qualities. For everything will possess not only a certain number of positive qualities but in addition all the negative qualities which correspond to the positive qualities which it does not possess. And these qualities, both positive and negative, can be compounded and recompounded ad infinitum. Again, everything will be related to all the positive and negative qualities which it does possess, and it will then have the qualities of having these

7. I say "with some hesitancy" because I am not sure that there is a relation of admiration.

qualities; moreover, it will likewise be related to these relational qualities, and these relations will generate in it new relational qualities to which it will also be related, and this process of qualitative generation will be endless. Whether or not the conclusion that the nature of every particular contains an infinite number of qualities might turn out to be of importance for metaphysics, it is one which, as I have indicated, I see no ground for accepting. So far as I can make out, introspection acquaints me neither with compound, nor with negative, nor with relational qualities; and the only reason advanced for admitting them is that it is "true of" everything that it has them.

SUBSTANCE

In introspection we become aware both of certain qualities of the self and of the self which has them. We can be aware of neither without the other. What confronts us is the concrete actuality self-having-qualities. It is this experience, according to some psychologists and philosophers, which gives rise to the notion of substance; indeed, this notion fits the self as the key does the lock. Let us, however, proceed to examine it.

Qualities are, in scholastic terminology, *entia entis;* they do not exist "on their own" but in something which is not quality. To use another scholastic term, they *inhere;* and the ultimate subject of inherence is substance. True enough, one quality may qualify another; we can speak of a color, for example, as bright or dull. Yet the process is one which cannot go on indefinitely; we must come at last to a quality which qualifies a substance. A quality, again, may qualify a relation; some relations, for instance, are transitive, and some reflexive. Yet these relations hold between entities which are not relations, but which stand in relations and which have qualities. A quality, moreover, may qualify an event, even as relations may relate events to one another. The battle of Gettysburg was an event; it was a three-day battle, a hard-fought battle, a Federal victory. It took place after the battle of Antietam and before the battle of the Wilderness. Yet events themselves cannot be ultimate, and so, once more, we are led on to substances.

The truth of this last statement I should of course expect to be challenged. The attempt to treat events as ultimate, to substitute them for substances, has frequently been made in recent philosophy, aided by the prejudice against substance which undoubtedly obtains. Here history in an impressive manner has repeated itself, for, over two thousand years ago, Buddhist philosophers developed their doctrine of momentariness in opposition to the Hindu notion of *dravya;* and the reader of ancient debates between representatives of the various schools of Indian thought will encounter there many of the arguments which are current today. Pertinacious as this effort at substitution has been, it has never succeeded in instilling universal conviction. However disparaged, the notion of substance has always provided a rallying point for those unconvinced by the iconoclasts.

Since substances and events both possess qualities and stand in relations, what, we may ask, is the difference between them? Substance, it may be answered, is that which *sub specie temporis* endures; whereas an event is a happening. The former is a continuant; the latter an occurrent. But this does not appear to be a satisfactory reply, for some processes outlast some substances. If we take a house as an example of what we mean by substance, it is quite possible that as soon as the last shingle has been put on the roof or the last nail driven, the building may be consumed by fire, bombed, or destroyed by an earthquake; yet, during its momentary existence as a completed structure, it was as truly a substance as if it had stood for a thousand years. The cascading of a waterfall, on the other hand, may have gone on for thousands of years; yet these millennia do not make it more of a substance than it was sixty seconds after the first drops fell.

In this connection it might be worth while to inquire whether it would be convenient to distinguish between an event and a process. An event we might define as a single happening, a process as a succession of similar happenings. The fall of an individual drop of water might be taken to constitute an event, the cascading of a waterfall to be a process. Yet it is doubtful whether our distinction will stand. If we could be sure that there is a genuine minimum of duration, we could think of this as embracing a single world-wide event, which we might then proceed to subdivide spatially into a multiplicity of concurrent events. But if time be infinitely divisible, each event will constitute a process, and our distinction will not stand. One drop of water will pass through successive portions of space in successive moments of time, and if the number of spaces and moments be infinite, so will the number of events be.

Yet our distinction may not be entirely useless if we decide to apply the term "process" to a succession of events which are in a qualitative aspect repetitive. At first glance a mountain, for example, seems to be a very different sort of thing from an explosion; but if the partisans of the theory of events are to be believed, the difference is much less than the plain man would suppose. The mountain is a process which has much longer duration than the explosion. Again the included events will all occur in the same *locus*. And most of these events will greatly resemble each other. There will be, perhaps, an initial event in the form of a cataclysm which heaves the mountain up. As the centuries pass the elevation of the mountain may diminish, and its sides become less rugged. Yet, to the neighboring farmer who observes it off and on throughout the years of his life, the mountain will appear to exhibit an unbroken continuity and such persisting uniformity of nature as inevitably to suggest—unless the farmer be also a philosopher of a certain school—that it is a perduring *thing*. This impressive similarity between its successive states cannot, surely, be due to the states themselves; for these are transient occurrences each of which happens and is gone. If we say that these occurrences are ultimate, we do not account for their qualitative continuity. And yet this requires to be accounted for. We can imagine, by way of contrast, a series of occurrences in which there would be no such quantitative continuity—a sound, for instance, followed by an odor, followed by a flash of light. A mountain is nothing like this. Its qualitative continuity is most impressive; and if the occurrences which are supposed to constitute the mountain cannot account for it, this can be done only by recognizing some other factor which is not an occurrence, and then the occurrences will no longer be ultimate.

When we look more narrowly at the notion of an event we see how fatuous it is to propose to treat events as ultimate. For the occurrence of an event always involves an entity which is not an event, or entities which are not events. Thus the occurrence of the battle of Gettysburg involved the *terrain* upon which it was fought, the men who fought it, and the weapons they used. Again, a flash of light or a noise is not something which happens "on its own"; there are physical particles or waves involved in the propagation of light, there is a sonorous body which emits the sound. A "pure" event would be like a "pure" act which is the act of no one or nothing. The notion of an event is plainly a relative notion; it is futile to try to substitute it for that of substance which is not relative but absolute.

The inveterate prejudice against substance appears to be due to a tenacious misunderstanding. For the question is repeatedly raised, If there be substances, what kind of things are they? Seemingly the answer desired would be one which gave a description of substance apart from its characteristics. But this is an impossibility. The kind of thing a substance is depends upon the qualities which it has and the relations in which it stands. Apart from these it is nothing. It is that which has them. To demand that we describe substance apart from its characteristics is equivalent to asking what characteristics a substance possesses in addition to the characteristics which it has. The question is absurd, and therefore admits of no answer.

Our difficulties, however, are not yet at an end. What are we to say of images, such as the reflection of the sun in a lake, or of a man in a mirror? These clearly have qualities and stand in relations. Yet each is dependent upon a continuous process of reflection; let a cloud obscure the sun or the man move away from the mirror, and the image is gone. The traditional notion of substance carries with it the characteristic of *aseity,* of having its being in itself; and this an image does not possess, for its being is in something other than itself, in the lake or the mirror. We shall be well advised, then, to adhere to the traditional terminology for the sake of clearness, and to exclude images from the class of substances. We shall later inquire what their precise status is.

What shall we say, however, of such an entity as a waterfall? The cliff over which the water pours is no more a process than the mountain is, but the falling of the water is a process in the sense that it is a sequence of events. The water itself is not a process any more than the cliff. What we have here is a conjunction of two different kinds of substance plus process; and while we may properly call a waterfall a particular, we should not, I think, term it a substance.

But what of an oak or a man? Do these possess *aseity?* The oak is dependent upon soil and moisture for its nutriment; the man will continue to live only if he eat his meals at reasonable intervals, and will die unless he continue to breathe. Is there after all such a gap between event or process, on the one hand, and substance, on the other, as our previous reasoning had led us to suppose?

We may at once concede that if we look for *aseity* in a sense which involves complete independence of everything else, we shall find it nowhere short of the universe as a whole—and not even there if we accept the doctrine of creation, or the theory of emergence put forth by Alexander and certain other naturalists. Nevertheless, as we have seen, there are important differences between the various kinds of entities the universe contains. A quality is *in* something in a sense different from that in which the something is *in* anything. Brown is *in* the table in the sense that it qualifies the table; the table, again, is *in* the universe in the sense that the universe contains it, but not in the sense that it qualifies the universe. A relation would not in ordinary usage be said to be *in* the things which it relates; it connects them but does not qualify them. An event might be said to occur *in* a substance, or a group of substances; yet it is not *in* them in the sense in which a quality is *in* a substance—it does not, so to speak, *inhere*—although it will involve qualitative or relational change, or both. A stone or a tree is not *in* the universe in the sense in which the image of the sun is *in* the lake. The stone and the tree have a relatively independent structure, and neither can be simply obliterated *in toto* as the image can. The stone can be broken into bits, and the tree can be cut down, but the stone will leave behind its fragments, and the tree its trunk and stump.

By substance, then, we mean that which is qualified but which does not qualify, that which is related but does not relate, that which is involved in occurrences but is not an occurrence, that which has being in itself and not in another. Throughout the preceding paragraphs in which we have been concerned with the meaning and applicability of the term "substance" I have been assuming, for the purposes of discussion, the existence of physical objects. But to assert their existence, at the present stage of our inquiry, would obviously be unjustifiable. All that we have before us is the self and its experience. That the self is endowed with sense experience is, of course, undeniable; but we have not yet entered upon the investigation of the nature of that which is experienced. We are still engaged in plumbing the depths of the *Cogito*. And it is to the self par excellence that the notion of substance is applicable. Physical objects, if there be physical objects, are composite; they can perish by being taken apart, and only so. In the self, however, we find a substance which has no parts in the sense of separable entities, but which is, on the contrary, indivisible. It is, I submit, self-evident that the occurrence of an act of awareness, a feeling, or a volition involves a self which knows, feels, or wills. States of consciousness cannot be isolated from the whole with which they are inextricably conjoined. The self is the subject of qualities, states, and acts; in it events occur and processes go on; it is the basis and support of them all.

But what of the body with which the self is so intimately connected? We are not yet in a position to affirm or deny the existence of matter; let us, however, assume for the moment that the body is a material entity. Are the self and the body, then, two substances, or do they constitute a single substance? Could a single substance possess the extraordinarily heterogeneous characteristics which pertain to self and to body? Surely there must be *some* unity in the nature of a thing, some fundamental characteristic, or group of characteristics, which constitutes it an instance of its kind. Though the traditional doctrine of essence has suffered rough treatment at the hands of recent logicians, still there is clearly some basis for it. Any specimen of a particular type will possess certain salient characteristics indicative of its status. When, however, we compare the self with its body what we observe is extreme dissimilarity.

The body is made up of *partes extra partes,* whereas consciousness is unextended and indivisible. The parts of the body are continually being replaced as matter passes out of and into it; but there are no external bits of thought which are laid hold of by the self and incorporated into its structure, nor are there any which are extruded from it. When Descartes declared the essence of soul to be thought and that of body to be extension, he was only stating in his own way a very obvious fact. A single substance consisting of soul [8] and body would be a sort of ontological iceberg, half of its being submerged in the sea of materiality and half soaring aloft in the air of pure spirituality.

Moreover, there is truth in Plato's dictum that the soul is the ruler of the body. There are, indeed, cases in which the reverse is true, when the self is overwhelmed by bodily weakness or bodily passion; yet these conditions, as we fully recognize, are exceptional. Normally mind is master. Even when a depraved will leads the body into courses which subject it to disease or calamity, it would seem that the self is ruining the body rather than the body the self. And when a good will leads the body to encounter danger and death on behalf of principle, as has happened upon countless occasions, we cannot but acknowledge that here the self has a purpose of its own incompatible with the interests of the body. I do not assert that Plato's argument—as I have here developed it—is a conclusive one, but I do say that the theory that self and body are two interacting substances does seem to fit the facts better than the view that they constitute a single substance.

A better argument, however, in support of the same conclusion has been advanced by Descartes. Whatever can be conceived without reference to a second thing can also exist apart from it, otherwise it could not be conceived without reference to that second thing. Now we can conceive of the self as the subject of mental states without reference to the body. Were this impossible, I may remark, there could be no immaterialists and no spiritual monists. Hence it follows that the

8. The good old English word "ghost" is perhaps ruined beyond all saving, since popular usage has equated it with "apparition." But the word "soul" may possibly yet be rescued, and it is well worth saving. I propose, therefore, to employ it as a synonym for "self."

self can exist apart from the body. This argument impresses me as conclusive.

Do you not see, an objector might perhaps interject, that by thus insisting upon the disparateness of self and body you have rendered any union of the two inconceivable? And yet they are united. Something, then, is wrong with your argument.

The objection seems to be based upon the conviction that interaction can take place only between entities which resemble each other in certain very definite respects, and that, since interaction does take place, self and body cannot be two distinct substances. Now we have not yet discussed the theory of interaction; although it may not be amiss to observe that it is the view which everyone accepts in practice and applies in daily living, and that to doubt it requires a faith so robust that only philosophers are capable of attaining it, and this only while philosophizing. But the difficulty just raised is not removed by the assumption that self and body constitute a single substance; rather, as I have pointed out, it is accentuated. The disparateness remains, and I have not overstated it. Despite the assumption, consciousness remains unextended and body extended; we can still conceive of self without body and body without self; and the connection between them remains no less mysterious upon this assumption than upon the view that they are two distinct substances. The force of Descartes' argument, therefore, is unimpaired by the objection.

We are justified, then, in regarding the self as a substance in its own right. It is a simple substance in the sense that it is not made up of parts and is, therefore, uncompounded. Whatever complexity we discover in its nature is not incompatible with, and in no way impugns, its indivisibility. Thus it is precisely in the self that we find the fullest exemplification of *aseity*.

Have we, however, been too hasty in concluding that because it is spatially indivisible, the self is in every sense indivisible? In what other sense could it be divisible? Clearly it is not qualitatively divisible. The nature of the self is, indeed, logically divisible into the qualities which compose it; yet the self cannot be identified with its nature. To affirm that the self is a complex of qualities would involve us in insuperable difficulties. For what would the qualities qualify? Obviously they could not all qualify each other. It would be absurd to say, for example, that wisdom is happy or that happiness is wise, that dishonesty is miserable or that misery is dishonest. As we have seen, there must be that which is qualified but which does not qualify. Qualities are universals; the self is a particular. The self is not its nature; it is that which has the nature.

Suppose that we assert, however, that the self is temporally divisible, that its successive states constitute its parts? That they are parts of its history is obvious; but the self is not to be identified with its history any more than with its nature. So to identify it would be to revert to the view that process can be taken as ultimate, a view which we have already pronounced untenable. Moreover, this would involve us in further difficulties. For then the whole self would never be an existent. At any instant we should be confronted by only a part of the self. If the whole self be its history, we should have paradoxically to assert that the self has come into being only when it has ceased to exist.

Again, each of these successive states will have a subject of which it is the state; and, if these subjects be numerically distinct, we shall have not one self but a series of selves. And if each state be infinitely divisible in the temporal dimension, we shall have an infinite series of selves. Moreover, if we attempt to regard these selves as parts of an inclusive and perduring self, we shall have to hold that more than one self can be the subject of the same awareness, the same emotion, and the same volition; and this, I submit, is self-evidently impossible. Furthermore, it is clear that McTaggart's argument for a common and intuitively known subject of coincident awarenesses—an argument which we have accepted as conclusive—will apply equally well in the case of successive awarenesses. I conclude, therefore, that the view that the self is a simple and uncompound entity can be taken as established.

What follows? What follows is of the highest importance, both theoretical and practical. Since the self is simple it can neither be put together nor taken apart. In what way, then, can it begin to be, and in what way can it cease to be? If it were a process it might both begin to be and cease to be; although we could not say that it will necessarily both begin and cease to be, for the duration of a process is determined by something beyond itself, by that which produces it. But the self is not a process. Neither is it a quality. Were it a quality, and were it a quality which admits of degrees, there would be some point in Kant's suggestion that it might perish through elanguescence, that is, by progressive diminution of intensity. But since the self is not a quality but a substance, the suggestion is pointless. It follows, therefore, that the self is without beginning or end, a permanent constituent of the universe. We may emphasize the point by a further recourse to scholastic terminology. The self, we may say, possesses not only *inseity* but also *aseity;* in other words, that it exists not only *in* itself but also *of* or *through* itself.

In developing this argument stress has been laid upon the structure, not upon the duration, of the self; for as I have already remarked, some processes last longer than some substances. The endless duration of the self follows from its being a simple substance; its substantiality does not follow from its duration. Empirical corroboration of the view that the self is a perduring substance is, however, furnished us by the experience of memory. If the self were a succession of mental states, it would follow that there was also a succession of subjects of these states, for a state without a subject would be a contradiction in terms. There would, then, be a stream of momentary egos successively born and dying. Accordingly, when after a lapse of, say, fifty years an experience is recalled which during that interval had been forgotten, what happens? Between the momentary ego which underwent the original experience and the momentary ego which recalls it a vast number of momentary egos must be intercalated, none of which knew anything about the original experience at all. How, then, is the memory transmitted? Are we to assume that an awareness of what occurred is passed on from the subconscious dimension of each momentary ego to that of its successor until, after fifty years, it emerges at the conscious level? This would be to make of William James's metaphor of inheritance a metaphysical doctrine. Or shall we assume the persistence of a "trace" in the brain, leaving it to the ingenuity of psychologists to explain how a physical state of the brain could record an event and serve as the basis of memory? In either case the momentary ego which, in recalling the past, affirms, "I remember that I had such and such an experience," is misstating the situation. What it should say is, "I am a member of a series of momentary egos one of which, fifty years ago, had such and such an experience." Now it is quite obvious that nothing like this happens in the case of memory. The recalling ego identifies itself with the ego which underwent the experience, and this is possible only because the ego is directly and intuitively aware of its own identity throughout the temporal sequence.

The recognition of an abiding self-identical subject of consciousness —which is to say, of a substantial self—at once commits us to the assertion that the existence of the self is both beginningless and endless. This a theory which is so widely accepted among Hindu philosophers as almost to pass as axiomatic; whereas in the West it has found few defenders since the decline of Hellenistic philosophy. This, doubtless, is largely due to the dominance of the Judeo-Christian tradition, on the one hand, and of materialism on the other. Our argument, however, has led us directly to it; and it appears inescapable without resort to some intellectual *tour de force*. It carries with it, of course, as an inevitable corollary, the doctrine of a plurality of lives; of which we can be certain of three at least, namely, this present life, one before birth, and one after death.

[*Note*] In the above discussion I have made no mention of McTaggart's definition of substance for the reason that I regard it as inadequate. As originally formulated it ran as follows: substance "is that which exists and has qualities and is related without being itself either a quality or a relation." [9] In order to exclude facts it was later amended to read, substance "is that which has qualities and is related, without being itself either a quality or a relation, or having qualities or relations among its parts." [10] While I am in accord with Professor Broad in viewing this as a satisfactory definition of a particular, I also agree with him in rejecting McTaggart's claim that it does justice to the traditional notion of substance. The definition, as McTaggart points out, is so framed as to include events. Now the distinction between substance and event, I have contended, is fundamental. Professor Broad has stressed rather the fact that McTaggart has disregarded the distinction between continuants and occurrents, and has suggested that this is due to his doctrine of the unreality of time. I am not happy with this terminology, for the use of the terms "continuant" and "occurrent" suggests that the difference is one of duration. Such, I have urged, is not the case; the basic difference is one of structure. A substance is something which exists of itself; an event is a happening which occurs to or in something, or somethings, other than happenings, which it presupposes and only in terms of which is it conceivable. A substance has *aseity* whereas an event has only *abaliety*.

Moreover, even if time be unreal, the eternal correlate of a temporal event will be other than the eternal correlate of a temporal substance. The eternal correlate of the latter will be an eternal substance, but it would be self-contradictory to talk of an eternal event. For an event involves alteration in the qualities or relations of some pre-existing substance or substances, whereas in the eternal nothing can be other

9. *The Nature of Existence*, Vol. I, sec. 67.
10. This formulation is taken from "An Ontological Idealism" (see *Philosophical Studies*, ed. S. V. Keeling [London, 1934], p. 275, also McTaggart, *Contemporary British Philosophy*, ed. J. H. Muirhead [London, 1924], I, 252).

than it is. The reality which lies behind an event, therefore, will be a complex entity the constituents of which will be quality, relation, and substance.

Again McTaggart has asserted that it is self-evident that no substance can be simple but that every substance must have parts. This assertion he seems to regard as equivalent to the affirmation that every substance must have content. It is conceivable that a substance should be divisible into more than one set of parts, and by content McTaggart means "that plurality which is identical in the different sets of parts of a group." [11] The statement that every substance must have content does not, then, prove very enlightening, since it presupposes that every substance is a group, or, in other words, that it is compound. It is precisely this presupposition which I see no reason to accept. To me, as to Professor C. D. Broad, it does not seem self-evident. When the claim is made that a certain proposition is self-evident, direct argument is, of course, impossible. Nevertheless an indirect argument can frequently be advanced. If, for instance, it can be shown that the proposition thus asserted contradicts some other proposition to which the assertor is committed, it is clear that something is wrong somewhere. Now I believe that this can be done in the case before us.

If McTaggart be right every self is made up of a set of parts each of which is a perception, and each of which is infinitely divisible into other perceptions. Professor Broad is surely right in maintaining that this doctrine bears a close resemblance to Hume's bundle theory of the self; and it is obviously inconsistent with McTaggart's own argument, which he has so brilliantly elaborated, to the effect that the various perceptions have a common subject. If two or more perceptions have a common subject, that subject must be indivisible; for were it divisible, there would be no common subject, but each perception would have its own subject. The conclusion to which his argument plainly leads is that the subject of all the awarenesses of the self is an indivisible unity, as I have contended in the preceding section of this chapter.

The issue is of an importance which can scarcely be overestimated; for were the self divisible into separable parts which were capable of existing in isolation from the whole, the argument I have developed for the indestructibility of the self, which is based upon its simplicity, would collapse. Were the parts, on the contrary, inseparable, and incapable of existence apart from the whole which they compose, the

11. *The Nature of Existence*, Vol. I, sec. 125.

argument would, indeed, require to be reformulated. It would now have to be founded, not upon the indivisible, but upon the inseparable, nature of the unity; but it would still stand. If, however, the self be a substance, and a simple substance, its indestructibility at once follows.

In this connection it is worth pointing out that if by the nature of a substance we mean the sum total of the qualities it possesses, and if it be the case that the nature of every substance is composed of a plurality of qualities, this will not of itself impugn the simplicity of the substance. For an individual quality is not part of the substance, it is part of its nature. The substance is that which has the nature. Hence, even if the qualities which make up its nature were infinite in number, the substance itself might nonetheless be simple.

STATE

In introspection we never perceive the self as a featureless monad; we are always aware of it as the subject of experiences, as standing in relations and possessing various qualities. We frequently speak of "a state of anxiety," "a state of happiness," "a state of doubt," or "a state of confidence." It seems clear that when we use the word "state," we always have in mind some span of time during which the self is characterized by some definite characteristic or characteristics, whether qualities or relations, or both. This temporal span may be relatively short, as when we speak of "a state of transition," "a state of flight," or "a state of sneezing." On the other hand, it may be relatively long. A state of animation, for instance, endures thoughout the entire life of a physical organism.

In this connection it will be instructive to recall McTaggart's definition of a fact. A fact, he tells us, is "either the possession by anything of a quality, or the connection of anything with anything by a relation." [12] If what has been said in the preceding paragraph be sound, this definition would apply equally well to a state. What, then, is the distinction between states and facts?

Although the contention that linguistic usage can settle any philosophical problem for us is, in my opinion, preposterous, I do believe that attention to usage may at times enlighten us as to our habitual ways of thinking. Now it is to be observed that we may, for example, with equal propriety speak of the self being in a state of anxiety, of the fact of its being in a state of anxiety, or of the fact that it is in a state of anxiety. In the last two expressions we make use of both

12. *Ibid.*, sec. 10.

terms. Yet this is not needful. We can perfectly well speak of the fact of the self being anxious, or of the fact that the self is anxious. What does this freedom of usage indicate? Our ability to employ *both* terms suggests that *some* distinction between them is envisaged, however obscurely.

Carrying our inquiry further we may remark that, when we refer to the past, we are far more likely to talk of facts than of states. It would be quite natural, for example, to say that it is a fact that Mr. A was very ill a year ago. But it would not seem natural to say that Mr. A is in a state of having been ill a year ago. Were we to hear someone thus express himself, we should, I think, infer that Mr. A's illness has left behind it traces which have not yet been wholly obliterated, or, in other words, that he has not yet entirely recovered. Were his recovery complete, nobody other than a philosopher who wished to stress identity and temporal continuity would be likely to resort to such usage.

Moreover, it seems clear that one state can fall within another state. A state of sickness may include a state of crisis and a state of convalescence. But I believe that most of us would hesitate to say that the fact that Mr. A is critically ill is included within the fact that he is ill.

In view of these considerations I would suggest that the use of the word "fact" always involves an implicit reference to truth. When we speak of a fact we have in mind a state of affairs concerning which a true judgment can be made, or a true proposition affirmed. With judgments and propositions, and with truth and falsity, we shall concern ourselves in due course. At present I wish merely to point out that in introspection we become acquainted with states of the self, and I would add that McTaggart's definition of fact applies equally well to state.

Whatever mystery attaches to the notion of state is due to its association with time and change, and the problems presented by these will engage our attention later. At this point, however, it is important to observe that the word "state" is sometimes given a meaning which disqualifies it for application to the self. "A state," writes H. W. B. Joseph, "is something which characterizes a whole through the condition of its parts; thus we call a man shod, because he has shoes on his feet; or healthy, because each part of his body is functioning rightly; the healthiness of his body does not mean that each part of it is qualified alike, nor his being shod that every part of him has shoes on." [13] Since

13. *An Introduction to Logic* (New York, 1916), p. 51.

the self is without parts, it is also without states in such a sense as this.

RELATION

Relation, like quality, is indefinable in the sense that it neither admits of analysis nor is describable in terms of entities more fundamental than itself. To know what relation is we must experience it. Hence, if any man deny its reality, all that we can do is point to an instance of it. If we can find instances of relation within the realm of the *Cogito* its reality will be indisputable. And that we do find relations within the self is perfectly obvious. Thus one state of the self is earlier or later than another, one throb of pain follows another and is succeeded by a third. If it be objected that this assertion presupposes the validity of memory, we may bow to the objector and reply that it suffices if we confine ourselves to the specious present; for even within this we find before and after, and therewith relation. Again, of two simultaneously felt emotions, one may be more intense than another, as when fear overmasters curiosity. And two conjointly experienced desires may be in conflict. The reality of relation, therefore, can be accepted as indubitable.

In our discussion of relations, however, we shall not confine ourselves to the sphere of the self, but, assuming that whatever the character of the self's environment, relations will be found there also, we shall proceed to investigate their nature. In the first place we may observe that relation may be one-one, as when A is equal to B, one-many, as when A is aware of B, C, and D, and many-one, as when B, C, and D are contemplated by A. We may also note that the third of these relations is the converse of the second, so there clearly are converse relations. And we may, without more ado, accept the customary classifications of relations into transitive, non-transitive, and intransitive,[14] and into symmetrical, non-symmetrical, and asymmetrical,[15] since the recognition of these involves no special problem.

Next we may consider McTaggart's classification of relations as reflexive, not reflexive, and unreflexive. An unreflexive relation is one which cannot hold between a term and itself. Fatherhood is such a

14. To employ McTaggart's illustrations, ancestorship is clearly a transitive relation, whereas fatherhood is intransitive, and cousinship is simply non-transitive—or, as McTaggart prefers to write it, not transitive, since the fact that A is the cousin of B does not determine whether he is, or is not, the cousin of C.

15. Equality is obviously a symmetrical relation, and fatherhood, equally obviously, is asymmetrical; whereas admiration is merely non-symmetrical, inasmuch as A's admiration for B does not determine whether B does, or does not, admire A.

relation, since no man can be his own father. A not reflexive relation is one which may, or may not, hold between a term and itself. Admiration is proffered as an example, inasmuch as a man may admire either himself or someone else. It is with respect to reflexive relations that the issue becomes crucial, for some would deny the possibility of a relation with only one term. Obviously, if this contention can be sustained, the classification with which we are now dealing will collapse.

The example of reflexive relations which McTaggart offers us is the relation of identity. The issue thus raised is clearly stated by Professor Broad,[16] who is prepared to deny not only that there is any such relation as that of identity but also that a term is ever related to itself by a symmetrical reflexive relation. Let us begin by considering the first denial. Professor Broad writes

> Take, for example, "Tully is the same as Cicero" and "$1 + 1 = \sqrt{4}$" The first means: "There was a man who had the property of being called *Tully* and the property of being called *Cicero*, and neither property belonged to more than one man." The second means: "There is a number which has the relation of sum to 1 and 1 and and has the relation of square root to 4, and neither property belongs to more than one number." If this kind of analysis be right, identity is not a relation between a term and itself; in fact there is no relation of which the word "identity" is the name. What is meant by sentences that contain the word "identity" can be expressed by sentences which do not contain it or any synonym for it, but do contain some symbol for the coinherence of different attributes in a single term.

Is not this, one might ask, solution by evasion? Can the refusal to mention seriously be considered as indicative of the unreality of that to which the term is commonly taken to refer? Could not every issue under heaven be in like manner bypassed by a sufficiently ingenious linguistic device? A highly developed skill in this kind of verbal agility constitutes, indeed, the supreme merit of a philosopher in the eyes of a majority of our contemporaries, but it has the disadvantage that it leaves everything precisely as it was before.

Coming now to the case before us, we may ask, if the man called Tully is not really identical with the man called Cicero, is it not plain that the same man will not possess the two properties of being called *Tully* and being called *Cicero?* Is it not, then, the case that identity is a real relation? And is it not true that to say that "neither property belonged to more than one man" is merely to put the point in another

16. *Examination of McTaggart's Philosophy*, I, 90–91.

and evasive fashion, since, if the properties in question do not belong to more than one man, it is clear that they belong to the *same* man? An affirmative answer to each of these questions does seem plainly to be called for.

Professor Broad raises a further consideration when he calls attention to the fact that McTaggart concedes that a term which stands in a reflexive relation "has a certain aspect of duality." [17] Professor Broad goes on to deny the possibility of such a duality. Can we concur in this denial? If self-awareness, for instance, be a reflexive relation,[18] the self will simultaneously be the subject and the object of this awareness. Of course on McTaggart's view that relations generate relational qualities, the self will have the quality of being aware of itself and also the quality of being known by itself, and thus the "aspect of duality"—or the duality of aspects—will be more pronounced for him than it is for us who have seen no sufficient justification for admitting relational qualities. Even for us, however, the duality will not be wholly eliminated, yet I do not see that it constitutes a problem or gives rise to any mystery. A reflexive relation is, so to speak, doubled back upon itself; it departs from and returns to the same term.

Although he denies that a term can ever be symmetrically related to itself, Professor Broad concedes that a term may be non-symmetrically related to itself; yet here a qualification, he believes, is necessitated. The distinction between direct and indirect relations is, as he truly says, an important one. Take now the case of self-contempt. For McTaggart, for whom perceptions are parts of the self, "the feeling of contempt would be a particular which is part of the more inclusive particular which is the self A. . . . Thus the relation of A to itself is the indirect relation which is the relational product of the two relations of 'having a part' and 'being a perception of.' " [19] Indirect non-symmetrical relations such as this between a term and itself Professor Broad appears willing to accept, whereas he remains skeptical of direct relation between a term and itself.

His argument may be a telling one against McTaggart, but how does it affect us? I have urged that to admit that perceptions are parts of the self involves the admission of a plurality of subjects of these perceptions, and that this plurality of subjects will constitute a plurality of selves, with the consequence that many subordinate selves will be included within a single self—an admission which McTaggart himself

17. *The Nature of Existence*, Vol. I, sec. 79.
18. It might, indeed, be maintained that awareness is not a relation but a quality, although it will certainly involve *some* relation.
19. Broad, *Examination of McTaggart's Philosophy*, I, 92.

definitely rejected. Agreeing with him that it is self-evident that one self cannot include another, I have maintained that perceptions are not parts but states or acts of the self, and that they have all a common subject, namely, the self whose states or acts they are. If I be right in this contention, the relation involved in self-awareness will be direct, although non-symmetrical. Such a relation as remorse, however, which can be felt only by a man for himself, will be both indirect and non-symmetrical. It will follow, of course, that the self as a unitary whole will be the subject in self-awareness, and also that it will be the object, since whatever is known in introspection, be it a quality, relation, state, or act of the self, cannot be known in isolation from the self which has it. But it does not follow that all these features of the self can be simultaneously known, or even that all of them can ever be known, for the range of introspection is unfortunately limited—otherwise psychoanalysts would have no function.

The discussion of identity naturally leads us to the consideration of the question whether or not we shall accept the scholastic distinction between "real relations" and "relations of reason." [20] A "real" relation is one whose terms—in scholastic language, whose "extremes" —exist *in rerum natura* and is itself a connection holding between those terms *extra mentem.* Of this sort are quantitative relations, as well as those resulting from action and passion. A "relation of reason" is one which is due to the mind alone, and of this type identity is a stock example. "Reason," says St. Thomas, "apprehending some one thing twice considers it as two; and so it apprehends a certain habitude of the thing to itself." Other examples given by the same thinker are the relation of being to non-being, and of genus to species. Sometimes, however, one term pertains to nature and the other to the mind. Such a relation is "real" only in one term and "rational" in the other. "Right," declares St. Thomas, "is not predicated of a column except in so far as it is placed to the right of an animal; whence a relation of this kind is not really in the column but in the animal."

If two or more entities be contemplated by the same mind an indirect relation between them is thereby established. But a relation of reason, in St. Thomas' sense, is something other than this; it is an actual product of the mind which is foisted upon external reality. Indeed, it might with some justification be termed a fabrication, inasmuch as it has no existence *in rerum natura.* On this view the mind

---

20. For Aquinas' view of the problem see *De Pot.*, q. 7: a. 9. c., a. 10. c.; *Phys.*, Book V, chap. ii, lect. 3.; *Comm.* on Peter Lombard's *Sentences*, I, dist. 26. q. 2. a. I. sol.; I dist. 30. q. I. a. I. sol. and ad. 3[m]. See also my *Conception of God in the Philosophy of Aquinas* (London, 1933), pp. 378–380.

is to be credited with a productive power which deserves to be called creative; and by mingling its own products with external reality, it distorts the situation, and its knowledge is thereby infected with what can only be called error. Between being and non-being, for instance, it is clear that there can be no relation whatever, for relations can hold only between realities; to think of non-being as related to anything we must first posit it as being, and so contradict ourselves.

But what about relations between imaginary entities—between the king of Lilliput and the king of Blefescu, let us say. Are these real relations? Indeed they are. The only relations and qualities which we can imagine are those with which we are empirically acquainted. The characteristics of imaginary entities are thoroughly familiar to us, and thoroughly real. It is because the descriptions of the king of Lilliput and the king of Blefescu do not apply to anything that we call these two kings imaginary and unreal. The relations are real relations, but in this case they have no instances, there is nothing for them to relate.

The notion of relations of reason is, perhaps, a not unplausible one in the perspective of that conceptualism which lurks behind the so-called moderate realism of Aquinas and the later scholastics. Conceptualism is a theory which we shall shortly have occasion to examine, and about which it would be premature to say more at present. But I shall make bold to affirm that the theory of relations of reason is a philosophical "monster," as Bradley would say. To hold it is to attribute to the mind a capacity—unpleasantly reminiscent of magic—to produce what it contemplates, and to concede that in the very act of knowledge, it distorts what it knows.

It is surely far preferable to deny with Professor Broad that identity is a genuine relation at all than to pronounce it a relation of reason. If there be such a relation, it is certainly real, for by affirming the contrary, we should commit ourselves to the assertion that it can be without being real.

As to whether identity be a relation it is not easy to make up one's mind. In the first place we must distinguish between qualitative and numerical identity. If, *pace* Leibniz, we may suppose that two entities could be exactly similar, we should say that they are qualitatively identical. By this we should mean that both possess the same nature. And if we be realists in our view of universals, we should say that any characteristic, wherever and in connection with whatever particular it be found, is always itself and not something else.

By saying that a thing is numerically identical with itself we mean that it is always the same *thing* and not some other thing. Since nothing, as we shall see, can have a nature which is wholly simple, numerical identity is always found in connection with some diversity. The four corners of a house are all corners of the same house, although each corner is not identical with any other corner. Two successive awarenesses, the awareness of a lion and the awareness of an elephant for example, are different awarenesses; yet they may have a common subject. Two mutually distinct qualities may be qualities of the same man. But when we say that the house or the subject or the man is the same, we say what is true. It is true because the entity in question is identical with itself. And this does seem to me to constitute a real relation of the entity to itself; otherwise, of what does our statement hold true?

Let us now take up the consideration of another problem analogous to one we encountered in the case of qualities. We find, as we should have anticipated, that McTaggart classifies relations, as he did qualities, as simple, compound, and complex. "A Simple Relation," he writes, "is one which is incapable of analysis, and therefore indefinable. A Compound Relation is one which can be analyzed into an aggregate of simple relations. A Complex Relation is one which does not consist of an aggregate of other relations, but which can be analyzed and defined by means of other characteristics, whether qualities or relations, or both." [21]

When McTaggart talks of analysis in connection with relations he does not mean to suggest, any more than he did in the case of qualities, that a relation can be analyzed in the sense of being reduced to entities which are not relations but out of which it is composed. A simple relation, like a simple quality, is unanalyzable and, in this sense, indefinable. The reality of such relations cannot be proved; we believe in them because we encounter them. It may be disputed whether knowledge be a relation, a quality, a state, or an act; but at any rate, it involves a relation of subject to object, and it is clear, I think, that this is a simple relation. *Before* and *after* are also relations which fall into this class. *Between,* again, although it is not a dyadic but a triadic or polyadic relation, must be regarded as simple.

Is it evident that the reality of complex relations must also be acknowledged? All indirect relations, such as the relation of uncle and nephew, are in a sense complex. And if we care to describe such a relation—after the prevailing mode—as the product of two other relations, no harm is done, although I for one fail to see that such a

21. *The Nature of Existence,* Vol. I, sec. 84.

procedure is especially enlightening. Similarity, again, in the case of particulars is a complex relation, since, if one particular resemble another, it will be in respect of some common characteristic.[22] Again, two determinates of the same determinable will be indirectly related through this determinable, and this will be a complex relation. Two determinates of different determinables, however, will resemble each other only inasmuch as they are both determinates; here similarity is a simple relation. And the same holds true in the case of two determinables.[23]

Qualitative dissimilarity in the case of two particulars will be a complex relation; for these particulars will be dissimilar either because they possess incompatible qualities or because one possesses some quality which the other lacks. In the case of universals, however, dissimilarity is a simple relation. Red differs from blue, not because one possesses a further characteristic which the other does not, but because red is red and blue is blue. Hence it may be convenient to follow the usage of Aquinas, and to speak of simple difference as diversity.

With regard to compound relations the same difficulty arises as in the case of compound qualities. A relation does not seem to be the kind of thing which can be an aggregate. A king, for instance, is the sovereign not only of his nation but also of each individual member of the nation. Yet his relation of sovereignty to the nation is clearly not compounded of his relations to all the individual citizens, for if it were, it would lapse if any one of these individuals were to transfer his allegiance to another sovereign. It is unfortunate that McTaggart has given no illustration of what he had in mind. Since I can think of no relation which could plausibly be called compound, I am driven to conclude that there is none such.

We have now to face a further issue, one which bulks as large in the perspective of contemporary thinkers as that of real relations and relations of reason did in the eyes of the medievals. It is the problem of internal and external relations. The most clarifying treatment of the subject with which I am acquainted is to be found in Dr. A. C. Ewing's *Idealism*[24]—a treatment so adequate and enlightening that it deserves to become classic. As I find myself in general agreement with Dr. Ewing, I shall do little more than recapitulate the more important and relevant of his conclusions.

22. For the nominalist, indeed, for whom all characteristics are particulars, similarity will be a simple and unanalyzable relation.
23. Is it worth while, however, to identify indirectness with complexity, and so be saddled with two terms for the same thing?
24. (London, 1961), chap. iv.

An external relation, of course, is a relation which is not internal. We must therefore seek to learn in the first place what is meant by "internal"; having done so, we shall then be in a position to determine whether we think that all relations are internal, that none of them is, or that some are and some are not. Dr. Ewing's analysis, however, reveals the fact that relations have been held to be internal in at least ten different senses of the word. It is in the last five of these that our special interest lies, since these alone have vital relevance to our present problem.

The first sense, however, is one which we cannot afford entirely to disregard, for its meaning is to be found in the doctrine of relational qualities which I have ventured to reject. If it be true that every relation generates in each of the terms which it connects the quality of standing in that relation, it follows that were the relation absent, each of these would lack the quality thus generated, and would to that extent be different from what it is. But it does not necessarily follow that any of their other qualities would be different from what they are. If there be relational qualities, all relations are in this sense internal; if not, none is.

Turning next to Ewing's sixth sense, we find that relations are internal if they be "grounded in the nature of the related terms." The phrase is Bosanquet's, and Ewing understands it to mean that the presence of such relations "depends on, and is determined, *either causally or logically,* by characteristics of their terms." [25] This holds true unrestrictedly, he points out, of mathematical relations and of the relations of similarity and difference. But in the case of many relations, the statement must be severely qualified. If a thing did not have some at least of the qualities it has, it could not stand in the relations in which it does. It must, for instance, be spatial if it is to have spatial relations. Thus its qualities will always be "relevant to the relations in which it can stand"; its nature will be a "necessary," although not always a "sufficient," condition of these relations.[26] It will not be sufficient when the relation is also determined by some external agency, as when a man arranges his books in a certain order. Usually, if not invariably, relations presuppose the presence in the related terms of a common determinable. Thus similarity presupposes a common determinable of which the related terms possess determinate values,[27] arithmetical relations presuppose number, and spatial relations extendedness. Sometimes the common determinable is not easy to discover. A mind and a sensible object certainly have little in

25. *Ibid.,* p. 126.　　　　26. *Ibid.,* p. 128.
27. Ewing obviously has in mind the relation of similarity between particulars.

common, yet the successive states of the one may be correlated with those of the other, and this involves a common temporality—or, at least, apparent temporality. It is clear that internality in this sense admits of degrees; it will be complete if the nature of the terms be the sufficient condition of the relation, partial if it be only necessary but not sufficient. And it is also clear that all relations will be wholly or partially internal in this sense.

A relation is internal in the seventh sense if, were it absent, the natures of both or all the connected terms could not remain unaltered in respect not only of their relational but of their original qualities. Plainly similarity, difference, and quantitative relations are of this sort. To employ an excellent illustration of Dr. Ewing's, if the relation half-of did not hold between two entities, these entities could not both be of the size that they now are. It is clear, however, that many relations are not of this kind. Spatial relations, for example, are constantly changing between entities whose natures remain unaltered. If a cat, for example, wander through a room, the relations between its body and the furniture will be different at successive instants, yet both body and furniture will be unaffected by its passage. Furthermore, it is to be observed that a relation may be in this sense internal in one term and external in another. Thus one entity may depend for its existence upon a second entity, whereas the second is not so dependent upon the first. A man is independent of his photograph in a way in which the photograph is not independent of the man.

A relation is internal in the eighth sense when, from a knowledge of the relation and of some definite characteristic of one term, we can infer the presence of some definite characteristic in the other term. Thus, if we know the size of one entity, and if we know that it is half the size of another entity, we can infer the size of the second entity.

Causal dependence constitutes the ninth sense of internality. "A is internally related to B by the relation r when A could not exist unless B existed and was related to it by r." [28] And when the dependence is logical, as well as causal, we have internality in the tenth sense. It may, indeed, be maintained that causality involves logical connection; and in fact such is Dr. Ewing's position. This is a contention which we shall shortly attempt to evaluate. But at present we may note that similarity is a relation which is internal in the tenth sense. And it is equally obvious that many, indeed most, relations are not internal in this tenth sense. Thus there is nothing in the

28. *Idealism,* pp. 135–136.

nature of the Washington Monument nor in that of a banana which entails that one should be half a mile distant from the other. It is plain, in fact, that in the seventh, eighth, ninth, and tenth senses, some relations are internal and some are not.

ACT

In introspection we are often conscious that we are setting ourselves to do something. Volition is, of course, involved; yet there is more than volition, for we may well determine to do in the future something for which the time is not yet ripe. Action is the fulfilment of volition; decision is followed by deed. Sometimes decision is preceded by a process of deliberation, at other times it is spontaneous. In sudden danger, for instance, there may be no time for deliberation. At the unexpected approach of an automobile we leap at once to safety. In the case of instinctive action there is no place even for decision; we act like automata. The function of habit is to serve as a sort of acquired instinct, and so to render decision easier, or, perhaps, to render it unnecessary. Decision in the past has led us to form the habit which now translates that decision into act without reviewing it. Thus a well-drilled soldier will spring to attention as though by instinct at the word of command.

Attention itself is an activity, and one from which we cannot always free ourselves, even if we set ourselves to do so, as every victim of sleeplessness knows. In a state of relaxation when thoughts chase one another through the mind, activity is still going on, not only in the form of conscious attention, but also in those subconscious processes which bring fleeting ideas before us. We are never completely passive unless in state of total unconsciousness.

Readers of the scholastics will have noticed how the Latin *actus* stands both for "act" and for "actuality." The distinction, however, is an inevitable and an important one. Not all the capacities of the self can be exercised together; most of them lie latent until they are called for. Yet the self possesses them nonetheless. They are powers or potentialities, and as such they are real. A capacity is real, even though it be unexercised. As Sir W. David Ross has so well put it, "there is no such thing as potentiality that is not rooted in actuality." [29] Whatever mystery there may be about this has to do with time and change.

Leaving the problems which these present for future consideration,

29. *Foundations of Ethics* (New York, 1939), p. 292.

may we say that attention, *sub specie temporis,* is an activity? Attention is clearly selective; and it seems equally clearly to admit of degrees. There is a vast difference, as everyone is aware, between wrestling with a difficult problem and allowing one's thought to float from topic to topic or image to image as association may conduct it. But how are we to distinguish attention from consciousness? Are they one and the same thing? Clearly we cannot be conscious without being conscious of something; not to be conscious of anything is not to be conscious at all. Perhaps we should do well not to distinguish between them. Yet what of the self which is active in attending? Some characteristic it must have. And, surely, to be conscious is the fundamental characteristic which all selves have in common. Descartes seems to have been obviously right in pitching upon this as the essential quality of selfhood. Does not, therefore, saying that consciousness or attention is a quality of the self bring us nearer the truth? It is the conscious self which acts. But what is an act? "Acts of attention," writes James Ward, "are changes in the distribution of this attention." [30] An act, then, involves change. This seems incontestable. But shall we not, in consequence, need to distinguish between "act" and "activity"? For activity can be unvarying. To arrest the flow of thought, to fix the mind upon some definite object and keep it there, is a well-known practice of the mystics, and one which, they tell us, involves activity in its most strenuous form. But how if, remembering that some philosophers have regarded motion as a quality, we assert that consciousness is at once an activity and a quality of the self? We can then keep the word "act" to designate change in the direction of attention. Can we not also claim that this solution is not merely verbal, but one which does justice to the facts as we find them? It would seem so.

In what we may call a full-fledged mental act, however, as distinct from spontaneous and instinctive reaction, volition enters in and the prevision of the end. The putting forth of energy at the behest of the will and for the realization of a purpose is something that appears quite understandable and intelligible in the sense that we can give a reason for it. Even instinctive reactions are intelligible in this sense, although the reasons for them are not consciously entertained by the subject nor is volition any longer involved; what was once, we may suppose, the result of decision having now become a kind of psychic mechanism. Habit is thus seen to be an intermediate stage between conscious choice and instinct.

When we turn to sense experience, however, and to the realm which

30. *Psychological Principles* (Cambridge, 1920), p. 72.

it reveals, intelligibility disappears. That events of various kinds are accustomed to follow one another in definite sequences we are well aware, yet we can detect neither logical determination nor constraining force. *That* water boils at a certain degree of temperature at a certain altitude is a familiar fact, but *why* it does so—in any ultimate sense of the word "why"—is hidden from us. It was the seemingly transparent efficacy of consciousness in initiating change, contrasted with the absense of such efficacy in the physical world, that led Plato to affirm in the *Phaedrus* (245) that the ultimate source of motion is to be found in soul. These considerations bring us naturally to the threshold of the problem of causality.

CAUSALITY

The distinction I have drawn between act and activity is not without relevance when we turn to causality. One can be active in the sense of being attentive without initiating change in one's environment. And one can also be emotionally active in the sense of feeling an emotion without being productive of change; although it is true that if the emotion be sufficiently intense, bodily repercussions normally follow. Again one may be volitionally active in the sense of entertaining a resolution, and yet remain otherwise quiescent. To act, on the other hand, is to "set oneself" to accomplish something, to realize a desired end by initiating whatever changes are necessary thereto. Even when we act without reflection, instinctively, or by irresistible impulse, we are conscious of the ensuing changes as due to a mental reaction on our own part. And this reaction seems to be clearly in the nature of volition, even if that volition be completely determined, inevitable, and subconscious.

Awareness of the self as acting thus seems plainly to be at the root of the notion of causality. Obviously one can never be aware of the self as unconscious; we are always conscious of ourselves as conscious of something, and, therefore, as active. True enough, we are not always conscious of ourselves as acting, as doing something; we find ourselves at times in a relatively passive and quiescent state. Yet we know that we *could* act, if only upon ourselves. Even a man in chains is conscious that he could direct his attention in this way or that.

Out of the experience of self-awareness thus spring the two notions of substance and cause. So intimate, indeed, is the connection between them that it has led some thinkers to assert that they are not genuinely distinct, that in reality we find but a single notion, that of the self.

Yet this appears plainly to be an exaggeration; unless, indeed, we admit the further contention that to be is to act. But this is a contention to which, surely, we cannot accede. For if being is an act, of what is it the act? Of non-being? Act requires an actor—so much is self-evident—and only that which is can act. Substantiality and causal activity, it seems clear, are two aspects of selfhood, neither of which is reducible to the other.

We are aware of the self as an indivisible unity, possessed at once of *aseity* and of the power of initiating change. In these respects it is unique. It is, to say the least, difficult to conceive, and certainly impossible to imagine, any entity as thus capable of exerting or putting forth power without regarding it as a self. And the reason seems clearly to be that the notion of power is inextricably intertwined in our minds with that of volition. Here we find, in all probability, the basis of the widespread tendency of primitive man to personify natural objects. It was doubtless the realization of this fact that led Plato to affirm that soul is self-moving, and thus the ultimate source of motion. And here we find the origin of the activity view of causality which has aroused such intense opposition.

The theory rests, we are often told, upon a confusion of bodily with psychical states. The strain and stress of which we are conscious in wrestling with obstacles, pertain not to the self as distinct from its body but to the body, or at least to the body-mind composite. Although frequently advanced as absolutely conclusive,[31] this objection does seem to admit of a convincing answer. In the first place, the physical strain and stress are clearly accompanied by states of mental resolution, and these seem to increase in intensity in proportion to the increase of physical effort. We struggle harder, and with more and more determination. And sometimes the alternative of success or failure depends upon the willingness to "go on." Any man who has striven to improve his golf shot, or to master the intricacies of the Sanskrit verb, will scarcely feel impelled to deny that a good deal of what, for want of a better term, we may call "mental energy" has obviously been involved.

In the second place, we constantly observe mental acts of volition to be followed by appropriate and frequently efficacious bodily movements, and to believe that these sequences are purely fortuitous passes most men's power of faith. When I decide to go out for walk, and thereupon do go, it seems perfectly obvious that I went because I

31. See, for example, G. Dawes Hicks, *The Philosophical Bases of Theism* (London, 1937), pp. 172–174.

had decided to do so; and if I be told that my decision had no efficacy at all, I feel at once incredulous and amazed. Would anyone, I ask myself, make so utterly fantastic an assertion except in the interest of a theory which he is committed to defend come what may? I concede, of course, that what seems in the highest degree improbable may nevertheless be true; but the burden of proof is upon the affirmer, and in this case the burden is a very heavy one.

And in the third place, when my volition is directed upon myself, when I will to produce some alteration of my own mental state, the presence of an intrinsic connection between the act of will and its consequence appears to be indubitable. I will to resist a certain temptation, and I resist it. How I make my body move I have not the least idea. But when cause and effect are both in the mental realm, and embraced within the limits of a single self, the shadow of mystery seems to be entirely dissipated.

All these considerations tend strongly to support the activity theory of causality. It is not a theory, however, which has won general acceptance; and one reason for this state of affairs we have already touched upon. It is inevitable that the notion of *act* should prove applicable in the mental realm, since it is in the experience of self-awareness that it has originated; but when we undertake to apply it in the non-mental world, we find it difficult to free ourselves from anthropomorphism. As Dr. Ewing has pointed out,[32] if act be interpreted in terms of "conscious rational volition," we are on the highroad to theism; whereas, if we understand by it "some kind of semi-conscious striving," we may need to go no further than panpsychism; but if we purge the notion of every trace of vitality, and say that "what is involved in causation is a quality which we experience consciously but which can exist without being experienced in any way," we escape such definite metaphysical commitments. The question is whether for the privilege of utilizing the last of these interpretations we should not have to pay too high a price. With "conscious rational volition" we are all familiar; and if by "semi-conscious striving" be meant effort which is not the outcome of rational deliberation and which is instinctive in character, perhaps even inaccessible to introspection, we may well agree that there is no difficulty here. But when we are asked to separate act from psyche, to precipitate it, as it were, into the external world, we find ourselves at the vanishing point of intelligibility. Imagination fails us, and conception, to say the least, falters. As Dr. Ewing remarks, "we are apt to think of cause as a

32. *The Fundamental Questions of Philosophy* (New York, 1951), p. 170.

kind of depersonalized will";[33] but this is clearly a hybrid conception which concedes either too much or too little to the personalist. The exorcism of anthropomorphism has thus landed us in obscurity.

Now anthropomorphism is a word which on the lips of many, if not most, contemporary philosophers has a pejorative ring. And we may well ask ourselves why. The humanistic naturalist shrinks from anthropomorphism in horror, and well he may, for any concessions in this quarter will prove fatal to his system. Let us hasten to acknowledge that there is, however, legitimate ground for hesitancy. The issue may, I think, be fairly stated as follows. If the activity theory of causality be capable of standing by itself, and if, when thus established, it prove to be the basis upon which some particular metaphysical system, be it theistic or panpsychic, can be erected, well and good. But if the activity theory presuppose the soundness of one or other of these metaphysical doctrines, it cannot stand alone; and the doctrine in question must first be vindicated before the activity theory can claim our acceptance. We must therefore proceed to scrutinize the rival theories of causality in order to estimate their relative strength, and to discover what metaphysical commitments they will involve us in.

The regularity theory of causality is one which has enjoyed great popularity, and which has been accorded wide acceptance. On this view any notion of power, efficacy, constraint, or determination is to be rejected. There is no intrinsic relation between cause and effect. There are only types of habitual sequence which experience discovers. The senses do not acquaint us with any transmission of force or energy. All that experience reveals to us is regularity of succession, and this is all that we are entitled to posit. An event of type A is always followed by an event of type B, and this is all that there is to it. To assume that there is any ground of the orderly succession which we find is to objectify what is a mere figment of the imagination, and in the light of it to distort the pure data of experience.

This view has, of course, always possessed a special attraction for empiricists of the school which maintains that all knowledge is derived from sense experience. And from the point of view of the philosophy of religion we may observe that the issue thus raised is one of very great importance. With the exception of the ontological argument, all the arguments for the existence of God, so far as I am aware, are causal arguments; and the regularity theory, if sound, will cut the

33. *Ibid.*, p. 169.

nerve of every one of them. For if there be nothing more in causality than what the senses disclose, there will be no ground for any inference to the existence of a supreme spirit.

In recent years the regularity theory has been subjected to searching criticism by a number of eminent philosophers,[34] and with somewhat shattering results. So conclusive do I find this criticism that I shall, in the first place, merely enumerate what I take to be the principal arguments advanced against the regularity theory and in the second place, subjoin various comments of my own.

1. If there be no intrinsic relation between cause and affect, it is senseless to talk of the motivation of any action.

2. It will also be futile to make plans for future action, since no volition will in any way necessitate or constrain the motions of our bodies or the occurrence of any subsequent events in our own minds.

3. All argumentation will be futile, however logically the argument be presented, for if no event ever necessitate the occurrence of any other, the mind of the hearer will never be constrained to accept the proof offered him.

4. If present states of consciousness be undetermined by past events, it will be impossible to account for memory.

5. Rational inference will be impossible, since the mental state which apprehends the premises of an argument will in no way determine a subsequent mental state to accept the conclusion.

6. In scientific investigation one constantly argues from cause to effect. But if the cause do not really necessitate the effect, such arguments will have no validity.[35]

7. Scientific laws with regard to the sequence of events—such as the boiling of water at a certain altitude at a certain degree of temperature—rest upon generalizations which presuppose some connection between events other than temporal succession. On the regularity view such laws would be reducible to mere runs of luck.

34. See W. P. Montague, *The Ways of Things* (New York, 1940), Part II, sec. 2.; Ewing, *Idealism*, pp. 151–187, also *The Fundamental Questions of Philosophy*, pp. 160–162; Brand Blanshard, *The Nature of Thought* (London, 1939), Vol. II, chap. viii; G. F. Stout, *Mind and Matter* (Cambridge, 1931), Book 1, chaps. ii–iv, also *Proceedings of the Aristotelian Society*, Supplementary Vol. XIV (1935); A. N. Whitehead, *Process and Reality* (New York, 1967), pp. 255–274.

35. "A premiss," remarks Ewing, "is a proposition or a set of propositions, and a cause an event; but how can there be a valid argument from a proposition or set of propositions to another proposition or set of propositions unless the content of the fact referred to in one is really entailed by the content of the fact referred to in the other? If it is not, the argument is simply a *non sequitur*" (*Idealism*, p. 167).

8. If such laws rest upon nothing more than past experience of regular succession there is no reason to believe that they will hold good in the future, for no one has experienced the future.

9. On the regularity view the notion of necessitation itself cannot be accounted for.

10. The experiences of being passive in perception, of being acted upon, and of encountering obstacles to our own action, involve a consciousness of necessitation which is incompatible with the regularity view.

11. The notion of a physical object which endures through successive states implies that these are grounded in the nature of a substance, and are thus connected by some relation other than that of temporal sequence.

12. On the regularity view it will be difficult, if not impossible, to account for the occurrence of single events.[36]

13. There are temporal sequences which no one would regard as causal.[37]

14. Although the regularity theory is correct in its assertion that sense experience does not reveal to us the presence of necessitation, yet in the mental realm we do sometimes perceive such necessitation— as in the case of grief following upon the news of the death of a loved one.[38]

As we review this array of arguments we observe that the first five are concerned with mental states as necessitating or necessitated. Taken together they support very strongly Dr. Ewing's contention that the regularity theory would make nonsense of our everyday life. Such a consequence is, surely, intolerable; hence any theory which involves it should be regarded with the deepest suspicion, and ought not to be accepted if any more plausible alternative can be found. Dr. Ewing's contention receives further support from the fourteenth argument—if argument it may be called, for it is rather an appeal to direct ex-

36. "Nobody has succeeded in discovering a really satisfactory formulation of statements about the causes of these in terms of the regularity view. If we say that Hitler's invasion of Poland caused the second world war to break out when it did, we no doubt mean that the war followed it, but the rest of what we mean is not that wars always or usually follow invasions of Poland, it is something much more specific" (Ewing, *The Fundamental Questions of Philosophy*, p. 161).

37. "For instance, the sounding of a hooter at 8 A.M. in London is regularly followed not only by men going to work at that factory in London but by men going to work in a factory in Manchester which also opens at 8 A.M. Yet everybody would say that, while arrivals at the factory in London were caused by the hooter in that factory, the arrivals in Manchester were not" (*ibid.*).

38. Practically all these arguments may be found in the works of Dr. A. C. Ewing, who has treated the subject with exemplary thoroughness.

perience. But, as presented in his *Idealism*,[39] this appeal is complicated, if not confused, by his doctrine of degrees of self-evidence. This doctrine, accordingly, we must briefly examine.

It is possible, Dr. Ewing maintains, "that some degree of *a priori* insight may occur without certainty and without yielding definite clear-cut judgments."[40] It may be "something vague, not stateable, at least by us, in a definite form of words and only capable of being understood progressively if we add to the original non-inferential cognition inference, analysis and testing by its applications."[41] "Non-inferential cognition," he tells us, "is not a ready-made knowledge of propositions complete once for all, but a developing faculty and one which can only work in conjunction with inference."[42]

I think that Dr. Ewing has described very well the psychological process one goes through in the grasping of a priori propositions. But it seems to me that a certain amount of confusion, and very lamentable confusion, is caused by a misinterpretation of the English rendering of the Latin phrase *per se notum*. A proposition which is *per se notum* is one which, when understood aright, is at once seen to be necessarily true. To say that it is self-evident means that it is evident *in* itself, not that it is evident *to* a self. Whether it be so or not is dependent upon the capacity of the intelligence which contemplates it. It is quite possible, as Dr. Ewing insists, to be pretty sure that something certain is presented to us, and yet to be deplorably vague as to just what it is that is certain. We seek to isolate it, to assure ourselves that we have not confused one proposition with another, to render definite what it is upon which our attention is riveted, to see what follows from it, and so to envisage it in its proper locus. We may well suspect that we are confronted with certainty before we are sure of it, and suspicion fades with the increase of clarity. A consciousness of our own fallibility will continue to haunt us even then; often we recognize that the seeming clarity may be illusory, and due to our having overlooked some important factor. It is in relatively few cases that subjective certitude rises to the level of unshakable assurance. The wise man will generally be content to say, "this seems self-evident to me," and will leave it so. Dr. Ewing would have done better, I submit, if instead of speaking of degrees of self-evidence, he had spoken of degrees of intuitive or non-inferential insight. This, I think, is what he actually has in mind, and with regard to it I am in full agreement with him.

39. Pp. 176–181; cf. *The Fundamental Questions of Philosophy*, pp. 166–167.
40. *Idealism*, p. 179.   41. *Ibid.*, p. 260.   42. *Ibid.*

It will be observed that no proposition the truth of which is arrived at by deductive inference will be *per se notum,* since it is known to be true, not in itself, but through the premises of which it is the conclusion. Now it is clear that the proposition that one mental state necessitates the occurrence of another in the way that Dr. Ewing suggests will, if true, be *per se notum,* inasmuch as it is not established by inference. Of the truth of it we will be directly aware. Our knowledge that it is true will be empirically acquired, yet the proposition itself will be not empirical but a priori. When Dr. Ewing says that he believes that in this instance we have "faint glimmerings" of a priori insight, what he appears to mean is that the proposition that bereavement causes grief looks very like a proposition that is *per se notum,* but that we cannot be sure that it is so.

I think that we can heartily agree with him that it looks very like it. Of course that statement of the proposition might require to be modified to meet conceivable objections. Were the loved one suffering from an incurable and painful illness, the grief might well be outweighed by a feeling of relief; yet grief there would be both for the death and for the sickness which caused it. Again, if a man were himself at the point of death, and if he believed firmly in a future life and in the certainty of reunion, the feeling of bereavement might not even be present. "Beautiful and pleasant were they in their lives," sang David of Saul and Jonathan, "and in death they were not divided," and who could desire a lovelier epitaph? The feeling of bereavement is the result of separation, and therefore affects most powerfully those who are young and in full health, and should be found in the highest degree in him for whom, as Whittier says, "no stars shine through his cypress trees." Thus we may fully acquiesce in Dr. Ewing's statement that "it is *universally* true both, (*a*) that the love of a person makes the occurrence of grief at his death *more* probable than would otherwise be the case, and (*b*) that, *other things being equal,* the person who loves him would always feel grief. When he does not this is due to other counteracting factors." [43] What we have every right to affirm is that the occurrence of a state of grief after hearing of a loved one's death is not purely fortuitous, and that the connection between the two events is not merely one of temporal sequence. I do not see how we can deny this without talking nonsense. Yet this denial the regularity theory requires us to make; hence the regularity theory, at least when the attempt is made to apply it in the mental realm, cannot stand.

43. *Ibid.,* p. 180.

In the case we have just been considering the self is first acted upon by the external world, and the resultant knowledge in its turn brings about the occurrence of a state of grief. But there are plenty of instances in which we act upon ourselves with the same inevitability of sequence. I will to turn my mind to the conjugation of a Greek verb, and I do. Now in all cases of either kind do we actually detect the presence of necessary connection, or do we merely infer it from uniformity of sequence, from the fact the volitions are followed by the desiderated states and events? If we only infer it, then causation in the mental world will stand upon precisely the same footing as in the physical. Yet, as Dr. Ewing has so strongly urged, such does not appear to be the actual state of affairs; we are surer of necessitation in the mental realm than we are in the physical, and this greater assurance must be accounted for.

Perhaps in this connection we ought to take cognizance of Professor C. D. Broad's suggestion [44] that we detect the presence of causality— presumably in the sense of logical entailment—even in the physical world by "non-perceptual intuition," that while the senses reveal only the impact of a stone and the breaking of a window, we are nonetheless non-sensuously aware that the occurrence of the prior event neces- sitates the occurrence of its successor. Were this suggestion a sound one, the regularity theory would receive its complete quietus. But can we accept it as such? I do not believe so. It does not seem to me that I see *why* the impact of the stone breaks the window in the way that I see *why* bereavement is productive of grief. It may be that other people see this, yet I know of no one who does. The point is an important one, for if a necessary connection between events in the physical world cannot be intuited, we have still to account for our greater confidence as to its presence in the mental world. And I do not see how this can be done unless we be prepared to admit that we are directly aware of it there, that we actually do intuit a necessary connection between certain mental events. And why should we not be willing to do so? After all, what would it be like to detect a necessary connection? What would it be other than what happens when we observe one mental event giving rise to another? Knowledge produces emotion and volition produces action in a way that appears wholly transparent and devoid of all the mystery that envelops succession in the external world. If such connections be necessary, and can be seen to be so, then certain propositions concerning them will be *per se nota*. I strongly suspect, to use my own phraseology, that such is the case.

44. *Examination of McTaggart's Philosophy*, I, 45–46.

The sixth, seventh, and eighth arguments also form a group. They are concerned with the orderly and habitual succession observed in the external world, and they are directed to showing that this succession cannot be due to chance. Now, if the regularity view be right in ruling out necessitation of any and every kind, nothing is left but chance. And this, surely, is incredible. Some basis there must be for regularity, and what can it be but necessitation?

Taking these arguments in conjunction with those that went before, we might contend that since we have discovered the presence of necessary connection in the mental realm, and are therefore assured of its reality, and since we have seen that it *must* be present in the non-mental realm, we are justified in asserting that it *is* present. But on the other hand, one might urge that if necessary connection be not only present in the mental realm but also discoverable there, it would in all likelihood also be discoverable in the non-mental realm were it present there; and, accordingly, that the fact that it cannot be detected there is a good reason for believing that it is absent. The situation is further complicated by the fact that we are not yet in a position to make up our minds as to the nature of the external world. We cannot yet determine whether what we ordinarily call the material world be reality or appearance. Dr. Ewing, of course, holds that there is a material world, but that we are indirectly aware of it through the instrumentality of sense data. In this view, since we are never directly aware of material objects, nor of events which occur in the material world, it is obvious that we could not be directly aware of necessary relations between such events. It would be premature to pursue this line of speculation at present. But we are entitled to register our dissatisfaction with the notion of an orderly and uniform succession of fortuitous occurrences, which is all that the regularity theory offers us.

We come now to the ninth argument, and it is a very strong one. If there be no such thing as necessary connection between events, how did anyone ever come to think that there was? The question is certainly apropos; for practically everyone who does not belong to a certain school of philosophy thinks that there are such connections. If we attempt to answer the question as to how the idea arose, we give a reason for it. We show, in other words, that the idea must have arisen in the circumstances in which it did arise; but this is necessitation, which we are purporting to explain away. We thus refute ourselves. If, on the other hand, we say that the idea arose spontaneously, unnecessitated and without any reason for its coming into being, we merely invoke one incredibility to exorcise another.

The tenth argument appeals to everyday experience. In perception we are stimulated through our sense organs which are acted upon by some external agency. Every time we try to open locked doors or to move heavy objects or to force our way against the wind we encounter external opposition of some sort which affects our bodies and indirectly ourselves. It is true that in dreams we seem to encounter similar opposition, and a subjective idealist would try to explain our waking experience on the basis of such an analogy; yet even he, were he to attempt an adequate explanation, would have to bring in God or other finite selves as agents. So far as it goes, then, this argument lends some support to the activity theory.

The eleventh argument is one which we are not yet entitled to make use of, inasmuch as we have not yet sought to vindicate the notion of a physical object. But we can see, even at this point, that the argument may turn out to be a cogent one. For we have already dismissed as untenable the view that events can be treated as ultimate. If there be physical objects they will be substances, and their successive states must be grounded in their natures.

The twelfth, thirteenth, and fourteenth arguments fall together in their turn, for they are all designed to show how hopeless it is to try to apply the regularity theory in practice, to determine what is or is not a causal sequence, or to discriminate between a cause and what is not a cause.

The great claim of the regularity theory is of course that it sticks close to the facts; and this it certainly does. Indeed it sticks so close to them that it leaves them practically as it found them. But it is not enough for a theory merely to point to a set of brute facts; its *raison d'être* is to enable us to understand those facts, to show us how to interpret them so as to render them intelligible. This the regularity theory does not do. To treat the laws of nature as only runs of luck, and this is what in effect it does do, amounts to a confession of intellectual bankruptcy. Be it granted that these laws are merely descriptive; what they describe is orderly sequence. If a die kept on turning up six time after time, no amount of insistence that this succession of events was purely fortuitous would avail to banish our conviction that the die was loaded. The law that water will boil at a certain altitude at a certain degree of temperature has been found to hold good times without number, and with each fresh verification it becomes more and more wildly improbable that this regularity of sequence can be due to chance. Almost any other theory would be better than this.

The question, then, is what to put in the place of the regularity theory. What Dr. Ewing and many others among its critics are inclined to do is to have recourse to the entailment or rationalist theory. What this is has already been made pretty apparent by some of the arguments against the regularity view. Causality involves, it is maintained, an intrinsic and necessary relation between cause and effect. The presence of a certain characteristic in event A involves the presence of a certain other characteristic in event B. It is agreed, of course, that there must be more to causality than this. For there is temporal sequence; the cause comes first and the effect after. But just what is this "more"? Here we encounter the vagueness concerning which adherents of the regularity view are so fond of declaiming. And it is no good trying to blink the fact that vagueness there is. The general opinion of the advocates of the entailment theory seems to be that causality is a complex relation which no one has yet been able satisfactorily to analyze, but of which ontological implication is certainly one of the strands. The situation might be described by saying that while the regularity theory is incredible, the entailment theory is only partially intelligible.

It is obvious where the difficulty lies. It is to be found in the temporal aspect of causality. The problem of time, perhaps the most fundamental and perplexing of all philosophical problems, has a way of obtruding itself into the discussion of many other issues, and it has done so here. Could we see our way, as some thinkers have believed themselves to see their way, to regard time as illusory, the notion of ontological entailment would emerge from the penumbra of mystery which envelops it. To say, for instance, that shape entails extension is clear enough. Our trouble arises with the interconnection of events. The difficulty has been forcibly stated by Professor C. D. Broad.

> The suggested analogy between admitted cases of non-formal entailment, in geometry, e.g., and the alleged cases of causal entailment breaks down almost completely for laws of sequence. All the admitted instances of non-formal entailment are instances of what I call "conveyance" of one characteristic by another. They are all concerned with the *co-existence* of attributes in *substances*. Laws of sequence, on the entailment view, would all involve

instantial propositions. For they would all assert, *inter alia*, that the occurrence of an event of one kind entails the occurrence of another event of a certain other kind. There is not the least analogy between such entailment and the conveyance of one characteristic by another.[45]

Professor Broad has put the point very strongly, perhaps even too strongly. For is it fair to say that there is *no* analogy between conveyance and the type of ontological necessitation envisaged by proponents of the entailment theory? Might we not urge that the two relations are similar in that they both involve necessitation but that they differ in that the former holds between co-existent states of the same substance and the latter between successive events? And might we not suggest that the latter must find its explanation in the systemic character of the whole, and that this may require us to regard the universe as one tremendous substance; a suggestion that would seem to carry us some way toward a world view like that of Lotze? It is certainly the case, as Dr. Ewing insists, that acceptance of the entailment theory will have an important effect upon metaphysical speculation. For causality will constitute a relation which is internal in his tenth and strongest sense. And unless we be prepared to deny its universality, we must agree that causality will directly or indirectly interrelate by a necessary connection all the entities in the universe. As Dr. Ewing has well said, "One of the most fundamental differences there are in philosophy is between those who think of the world as a rationally connected system and those who regard it as a mere collection of brute facts externally related, and which side we take in this controversy will depend chiefly on whether we, consciously or unconsciously, assume the entailment view of causation or not." [46]

It will be obvious that if I have argued correctly in Book I concerning the relation between religion and rationalism, it is the first of these contrasted points of view which will be congenial to the philosopher of religion. For this reason we should scrutinize it very carefully to make sure that our especial interest do not lead us to accept it without sufficient justification. As we have seen, it is not entirely satisfactory in that it does not profess to offer a complete and final analysis of causality. It does not possess what we may call the pseudoclarity of the regularity view. Yet it does offer us something positive and some-

45. *Proceedings of the Aristotelian Society,* Supplementary Vol. XIV (1935), pp. 95–96.
46. *The Fundamental Questions of Philosophy,* p. 169.

thing important. It has laid hold upon one of the strands of the causal relation—logical entailment. That we must acknowledge this as a genuine strand is, I think, inevitable, for the following reasons:

1. If there be no necessary relation between cause and effect, then the effect might just as well not follow as follow. Regular sequences of events in accordance with natural laws render the hypothesis that these laws are nothing but generalizations based upon runs of luck so vastly improbable that it can be dismissed as absurd.

2. Since necessary connection between mental events is actually observable, the hypothesis that it is present, although unobservable, in the non-mental world can be regarded as probable. Had we, indeed, sufficient reason to suppose that if present there it must be observable, the hypothesis would be inadmissible; but no such reason has been given.

There is a further point in favor of the entailment theory which we ought not to overlook, namely, that it would seem to provide a better means than does the regularity theory for handling counter-factual conditionals. This point has been well brought out by Professor Broad.[47] Take the statement, "Every determinate under ϕ is invariably accompanied by a certain one determinate under ψ." "If it is interpreted instantially," he adds,

it implies that there are in nature instances of *every* determinate under ϕ. Now in many cases the number of determinates under ϕ is enormous, and perhaps even infinite. It is extremely doubtful whether every possible pressure or temperature or volume has had or will have an instance in nature. Yet no one would think that this was any reason for doubting a well-established formula connecting the pressure, the volume, and the temperature of gases. If, on the other hand, it is interpreted non-instantially and yet in accord with the regularity view, it becomes trivial as regards any determinate under $\phi\gamma$ which has no instances in nature. If there are no particulars in nature which have the determinate ϕ, it follows of course that there are no particulars in nature which have $\phi\gamma$, and lack a certain determinate $\psi\gamma$ under ψ. But this is entirely trivial. We want to be able to say: "If there *were* a particular which had ϕ in the form of $\phi\gamma$ (which there is not), it would have ψ in the form of $\psi\gamma$ (though no particular in fact does)." The entailment view can give a meaning to such statements which does not reduce them to trivialities. So far as I can see at present the regularity view cannot.

47. *Proceedings of the Aristotelian Society*, p. 101.

But now how stands the entailment theory when compared and contrasted with the activity theory? The attraction of the activity theory is that at first glance it does seem to illumine the notion of activity by connecting it with volition, or, at least, with conation. We are experientially acquainted with volition, and we observe anticipated and desired events to follow upon it. And even unwilled, instinctive reaction seems intelligible when we think of it as issuing from a living, conscious being. In the case of classical materialism, however, motion was an awkward problem. To ascribe to atoms the capacity for self-movement—and such was the materialist's answer—seemed a mere verbal solution, like the famous attribution to laudanum of a dormative power; for all the other characteristics ascribed to atoms appeared compatible rather with inertia than with motion. And even when scientists had accepted the Cartesian pronouncement that a particle, once put in motion, will continue to move until its motion is arrested by some other body, it still seemed to many philosophers that such motion was merely derivative, and that an ultimate source of motion was still required.

Now, however, scientists talk of matter and energy as mutually transformable into each other. With energy as a term of measurement we are well acquainted, but when we seek to transform it into a physical or metaphysical reality, clarity begins to fade. Even though we submissively acquiesce when the scientist undertakes to distinguish between force and energy—the former being conceived of in terms of rate of transmission, or acceleration, of energy—we still ask, What is energy? What intelligible answer can be given to this question, asks the adherent of the activity theory, except in terms of volition or conation? Yet, when we revert, as we can so easily do, to the outlook of the unenlightened man in the street, do we not find that we think of energy in terms of *push* or *impact?* But is it possible to think in this way of volition? I have every confidence that by willing I can move my limbs, yet it would seem absurd to suggest that my will pushes or pulls the particles of my body. And it would seem equally ridiculous to suggest that when I will to turn my attention to a certain topic, my volition impels my attention as the swing of a hammer drives a nail into a wall.

Yet the defendant of the activity theory is not yet silenced. "You acknowledge," he may say, "that you are sure *that* your willing does affect your bodily movements, even though you do not know *how* it does it. *That* there is efficacy in the non-mental world you are also aware, even though you do not know *how* it exerts itself. Yet does not the hypothesis that will is also present there to some degree clarify the situation by showing that all the phenomena are susceptible of a common explanation?"

We have so far viewed the two theories as standing in mutual opposition. It may be possible, however, to combine them if, following the lead of G. F. Stout, [48] we concede that causality does involve ontological entailment but yet maintain that such entailment in turn involves volition or conation—that is, conscious striving for the realization of ends—if not in what we ordinarily take to be the proximate cause at least in nature as a whole. At first sight this view is undeniably attractive in that it would seem to enable us to confront the regularity theory with a clear-cut and far more intelligible alternative.

To the careful scrutiny of Dr. Ewing, however, it appears highly doubtful whether this proposed harmonization of the two theories will stand. He calls attention to the fact that the occurrence of the mental state which accepts the conclusion of an argument, not only follows upon, but is determined by the occurrence of the mental state which grasps the premises, that it is because I believe that X is true that I believe that Y is true, and that here volition does not enter in.[49] Of course it is true that if I did not will to think, I would not arrive at any beliefs at all. Yet it is plain that if I be actually engaged in reasoning, I do not will to believe this or that. I allowed my thinking to be constrained by the evidence. It is purely in respect of its cognitive and not its volitional character that the prior mental state determines the nature of its successor.

It is true that Dr. Ewing subjoins the following generous concession: "I must grant that in all the cases of alleged insight into causality in the psychological sphere, with this one solitary exception of the connexion between belief in premises and belief in a conclusion, conation is not only an accompaniment, but an essential factor in the causal connexion, and this suggests that it might be possible to produce a further analysis of this one anomaly that would square it with the other cases. But how this could be done I have not the faintest idea." [50]

This admission, however, appears to be quite gratuitous. For Dr. Ewing has himself given another instance of ontological entailment in which volition plays no part, namely, the feeling of grief arising from the knowledge of the death of a loved one. In such a case one does not will to feel grief, one cannot help it. In view of these facts we have no alternative, I submit, but to pronounce Stout's theory inadmissible.

If we now elect to adopt the entailment theory we may say that

48. *Ibid.*, pp. 46–65.   49. *Ibid.*, pp. 69–70.
50. *Ibid.*, p. 70.

the connection between volition and subsequent willed action is just one instance of that relation of ontological entailment which always holds between cause and effect. Yet, before we so decide, we shall do well to reflect. For by so doing, we commit ourselves to taking a definite stand with respect to an issue which we have not so far even considered—that between determinism and libertarianism. If the occurrence of every mental state be necessitated by, and in turn necessitate, the occurrence of some other mental state, none of these occurrences could fail to take place. These psychic events entail each other and constitute an unbroken chain of happenings; the self is the locus wherein they occur, and it stands toward them in a relation of relative passivity. Such is the situation as viewed through the eyes of the determinist.

To the indeterminist, however, the description appears a complete travesty of actual fact. There are volitions, he contends, which are not necessitated and which need not have occurred. They do not happen *in* the self or *to* the self; they issue *from* the self, which acts as an indivisible unit. It is essential to the libertarian's case to maintain that the self might have acted otherwise. The utmost that he will concede is that the self may have been under the necessity of performing some one of two or more alternative acts, of choosing, say, between acts A, B, and C. But while it is constrained to choose one of them, it is not constrained to choose any particular one; it *may* choose B, but it *might* equally well have chosen A or C.

If the indeterminist be right, such an act on the part of the self will not be ontologically entailed by any previous event; for if it were, it would not be a free act, and the self could not have abstained from so acting. It will, of course, have consequences; and the indeterminist can afford to admit that these consequences are entailed by it. Ontological entailment can then be understood to link every effect to its cause, and if that cause be also an effect, to link it in turn to a prior cause. But the chain will have a first link which fastens it to a free act of will which is linked to nothing. The self is thus capable of functioning as an ultimate cause, as Plato contended; it can initiate a sequence of events of which it is the origin.

It is plain, therefore, that the indeterminist cannot, without stultifying himself, renounce the activity theory. The entailment theory may be applicable to derivative causes and their effects, but it will not hold with respect to ultimate causes which are unnecessitated volitions. Hence, if the indeterminist be right, the self will be rooted in the fundamental stratum of reality. It will possess a unique power of initiating change which, so far as we know, it shares with nothing else in the universe. And it is worth pointing out that this is a view which is quite compatible with the doctrine of the underived being of the self which we have already seen to follow from the recognition of the self as a simple substance.

This is not the place to debate the issue of determinism versus indeterminism. For we are now concerned with the contents of the *Cogito*, and although the consideration of these contents has carried us far afield, we have been concerned with notions which arise directly from the contemplation of the self, even though they may also be applicable to external reality. In introspection we are aware of the self as a causal agent, and the psychologist is no doubt right in finding here the origin of the notion of causality. But it is, to say the least, very doubtful and highly disputable whether introspection can enable us to decide in favor either of determinism or of indeterminism. The determinist, so far as I am aware, has made no such claim. Some indeterminists, on the other hand, have made such a claim; but their right to do so has been vehemently contested. There are, moreover, other important problems which are closely connected with this vital issue and which we are not yet in a position to discuss. It will be convenient, therefore, to postpone further consideration of it till we can view it in a larger perspective.

In summing up the more or less tentative conclusions of our inquiry, we may say, in the first place, that we have found considerable justification for rejecting the regularity theory. One of our chief reasons for so doing was the enormous improbability of an unbroken regularity of succession being ungrounded and unnecessitated. In fairness we must add, however, that our confidence in this conclusion will be strengthened or weakened according as we shall hereafter be confirmed or disillusioned in our conviction that the universe is rational. It is significant that the regularity theory has been especially favored by philosophers of a naturalistic persuasion who view reality as ultimate process, and reject as illegitimate the demand for a rational explanation thereof. It is true, as Dr. Ewing has emphasized, that acceptance of the entailment theory does definitely commit us to the view that the universe does constitute a rational system. Furthermore, as I have argued in Book I, it is a view which is clearly included in the religious outlook. Nonetheless, further considerations may conceivably lead us to reject it or revise it or, perhaps, more emphatically affirm it.

Another chief reason for rejecting the regularity theory was the conviction that in the mental realm we are directly aware of instances of ontological entailment. This is a very important consideration, and one which goes far toward substantiating the entailment theory.

A third main reason for rejecting the regularity theory was its inability to account for the genesis of the notion of necessitation without refuting itself. And, in addition, there were the two further reasons that the regularity theory would invalidate all processes of inference and would make nonsense of our everyday existence.

The entailment theory, as has been freely admitted, does not profess to offer a complete analysis of causality, but it does profess to make an important contribution toward the hoped-for consummation of such an analysis. So far as it goes it appears to be the most satisfactory of the theories before us, if by satisfactory be meant intelligible.

The activity theory probably stands or falls with the doctrine of free will. It might be contended, however, that, like the regularity theory, it is incompatible with the view that the universe is rational. But as we shall see, there is more than one sense in which the universe might be deemed rational; and we may discover that the activity theory is not incompatible with one of these.

If the believer in the activity theory refuse to concede anything to the entailment theory, he will be driven either to commit himself to panpsychism or to deny that there are any genuine secondary causes, and to regard every occurrence in the external world as the immediate effect of divine volition.[51] Either of these views *may* conceivably be the true view, yet we should rightly demand further reasons for conceding that it *is* the true view. But it would seem quite possible for him to admit that the entailment theory does hold for secondary causes and their effects, and to limit the application of the activity theory to ultimate causes. He might, then, be likened to one of the Iranian horsemen employed by Alexander, each of whom rode one horse into battle and led a second by the rein, shifting from one steed to another in accordance with the exigencies of combat; whereas the champion of the entailment theory will resemble the normal cavalier who manages a single horse.

The "Laws of Thought"

Under this traditional caption it has been customary to subsume the "laws" of identity, of non-contradiction, and of the excluded middle.

---

51. He will not escape this consequence by resorting to a subjective idealism, since, unless he introduce divine agency, he will land in solipsism.

They do, indeed, rule our thinking, for if we attempt to disregard them, rationality is obliterated and we are left with futile nonsense. Yet it is clear that they dominate our thinking because our thinking is of reality. They are primarily ontological, and they provide our logic with a metaphysical foundation. The point has been made with such force and clarity by H. W. B. Joseph that I cannot do better than to quote his words:

> Though these are called laws of thought, and in fact we cannot think except in accordance with them, yet they are really statements which cannot but hold true about things. *We cannot think* contradictory propositions because we see that *a thing cannot have* at once and not have the same character; the so-called necessity of thought is really the apprehension of a necessity in the being of things. This we may see if we ask what would follow, were it a necessity of thought only; for then, while e.g. I could not think at once that this page is white and not white, the page itself might at once be white and not be white. But to admit this is to admit that I can think the page to have and not have the same character, in the very act of saying that I cannot think it; and this is self-contradictory. The Law of Contradiction then is metaphysical or ontological. So also is the Law of Identity. It is because what is must *be determinately* what it is, that I must so think. That is why we find a difficulty in admitting the reality of absolute change, change when nothing remains the same; for then we cannot say what it is that changes; "only the permanent," said Kant, "can change." The Law of Excluded Middle is so far different as a disjunctive proposition expresses doubt, and doubt belongs to the mind, not to things. But to deny that this page need either be or not be white is to deny that it need be anything definite; determinateness involves the mutual exclusiveness of determinate characters, which is the ground of negation; and this is a statement about things. In other words, unless the primary Laws of Thought were Laws of Things, our thought would be doomed by its very nature to misapprehend the nature of things.[52]

This being the case, the question arises why these laws should be included among the contents of the *Cogito*, since they hold true without exception of whatever is. Following the lead of Father Gabriel Picard [53] we may answer, because our primal assurance is of the being

52. *An Introduction to Logic,* p. 13.
53. *Le Problème critique fondamental* (Paris, 1923), chap. iii.

of the self, because we see that these laws do apply to the self, and, further, because we see that they apply to it, not in consequence of its specific characteristics, but because it *is,* and, therefore, that they apply equally to all things that *are.*

One who adopted the Kantian position might perhaps contend that the laws in question hold true only of appearances, and not of things in themselves. It would seem feasible, indeed, to meet the objector on his own ground. An appearance enjoys only a derivative being, yet, we might urge, it is not nothing, it is a real appearance, otherwise we could not be aware of it. This statement will hold true not only of sense but also of the objects of dream and hallucination; had they no being at all, they could not be taken for other than they are. A mirage, again, could not mislead us unless it really were a mirage. And we can see that the so-called laws of thought hold true of all such entities because they *are,* not because of *what* they are.

This reply, I believe, suffices to quell the objector. Nonetheless there is a tactical advantage, if nothing more, in beginning with the sole reality of which we have at present absolute assurance—namely, the self—inasmuch as we are not yet in a position to discriminate between reality and appearance in the external world, or even to be sure that there is any reality other than selves and their states and characteristics. Now we can see that the self is what it is, and cannot be other than it is. Its being is a determinate being; and we can see, as we contemplate it, that this must be so, that being is not something which can be exemplified by a particular which has no determinate nature at all. Being, as Joseph has said, must be determinate; and we can see that determinates must either determine or not determine, and that if an entity is determined by any one of them, it cannot also be determined by another incompatible with it. And since we cannot without contradicting ourselves deny that the laws of thought are laws of being, it is clear that the mind is capable of knowing reality. This is not a truth which we can prove, for every proof presupposes it; but it is a truth which we cannot doubt, and which is *per se notum.* The position of the agnostic who holds that our knowledge is only of appearances is, therefore, untenable.

CHAPTER THREE

THE PROBLEM OF METHOD

Dialectic has also taught me that there ought to be no dispute regarding mere words whenever there is agreement on the matter which they are intended to signify, since words are used merely for the sake of signifying; that whoever disputes on mere words in such a contingency, is to be shunned if he does it through malice; that he is to be taught, if he does it through ignorance; that if he cannot be taught, he ought to be admonished to do something else, rather than waste time and effort on needless matters; and that if he does not comply, he is to be entirely disregarded.*

From the contemplation of the self we now turn to the investigation of the nature of the universe to which it belongs, and of its own place therein. As we saw at the conclusion of the previous chapter, we have nothing to fear from the agnostic; although it may not be amiss to reinforce our position by bringing forward the familiar argument to the effect that appearances can be recognized as such only in contradistinction to the reality whose appearances they are; from which it follows that if reality cannot be known, appearances cannot be known to be appearances. Hence, even if the agnostic's theory were true, it could never be known to be so; inasmuch as he would inevitably take appearances to be reality.

As yet, however, we have not considered the position of the skeptic. Is there any reason, we might ask ourselves, why we should do so? In its extreme form, which denies that any propositions can be known to be true, or in its modified form, which denies that any general propositions can be known to be true, has it ever been maintained by anyone other than a philosopher in his study for his own delectation and for the annoyance of his fellows? In other words, has it ever honestly and seriously been held by anybody? When the philosopher leaves his study does he not, as Hume confessed in his own case, think as other men? Does not skepticism, therefore, reek with intellectual insincerity?

---

* St. Augustine's *Contra Academicos*, trans. as *Answer to Skeptics* by Rudolph Arbesmann (New York, 1943), p. 193.

Can we not, accordingly, afford to disregard it, even as one disregards solipsism which is generally admitted to be logically irrefutable?

The answer must be, I think, that we cannot. The motives of the skeptic are nothing to us, but we cannot afford to leave behind us an enemy whose utterances are unevaluated. What he says, therefore, must be listened to. Yet have we not already convinced ourselves that no one who is not hopelessly muddled can fail to acknowledge the existence of his own self; and cannot the skeptic, therefore, be silenced by St. Augustine's *Si fallor, sum?* But what if we meet a skeptic who is prepared to affirm that he does not know whether contradictory propositions may not both be true, or what propositions are contradictory, or whether he may not both exist and not exist, or neither exist nor not exist, or whether there be any subject of his thoughts, or whether he have any thoughts, or whether there be any objects of thought or anything at all? So long as the skeptic make no assertion he cannot be refuted; let him retreat into silence and he cannot be pursued. But this is what in all likelihood he has no intention of doing; most skeptics are extremely vociferous. Let the skeptic make a single affirmation, however, be it what it may, and therewith he lays claim to knowledge. If he claim that he knows that he knows nothing, he claims to know something. Any claim to knowledge, however restricted, constitutes a breach in the wall of skepticism; for if one truth be known, another conceivably may become known; and so the skeptic is driven back from his outworks to some inner fortress of restricted skepticism which will be surrounded by the terrain of the knowable. Nor does it avail the skeptic to concede under pressure that probability may be attained, although certainty may not; for any judgment that a particular proposition is true is itself a claim to knowledge, and, if it be infected by probability, this can be known only in virtue of a second judgment, and so the skeptic will be launched upon an endless regress.

The Greek skeptics were keenly alive to the paradoxical nature of their position, and exercised considerable ingenuity in the effort to obviate it; hence the perennial interest which attaches to the writings of Sextus Empiricus. They did not assert, so they kept repeating, that no knowledge is possible, but only that none had been attained; and they attempted to buttress their contention by their doctrine of contradictory equipollent propositions—by which they meant propositions of equal weight—which they professed always to find in the investigation of any issue. Thus for them every problem constituted an antinomy.

Ingenious though it be, the defense is clearly hopeless. That all problems constitute antinomies is a universal proposition which obviously could not be known a priori; it would have to rest upon an enumerative induction which plainly would not be feasible; and in either case the judgment that it was certainly or probably true would constitute a claim to knowledge incompatible with the denial that any knowledge has been gained. Likewise, in the case of any two propositions, the judgment that they were equipollent would constitute a similar claim. Let the skeptic open his mouth, and he refutes himself.

To say this, we shall probably be told, is to claim too much; for the doctrine that no proposition is applicable to itself saves the skeptic from self-refutation. The proposition that no propositions are true applies to all other propositions but not to itself; hence the skeptic can safely affirm it. He can profess to know that it is true, and to know nothing else.

McTaggart has shown us [1] how to deal with this line of defense in the light of his twofold distinction between propositions which are applicable to propositions and propositions which are about propositions, and between propositions which are about propositions and propositions which are about characteristics. The argument proceeds as follows. If the proposition "all propositions are false" were about propositions, clearly it would be about all propositions other than itself and could therefore be known to be true only as the result of an enumerative induction which could be made only by a mind practically omniscient. No such incredible affirmation would be made by a skeptic who expected us to take him seriously. If he assert the proposition in question, he must profess to know it a priori. But then the proposition will not be about other propositions but about characteristics. What the skeptic must assert is that nothing can have the characteristic of being a proposition and not have the characteristic of being false, that the possession of the first characteristic implies that of the second. But although the proposition is about the characteristics of being a proposition and of being false, it nevertheless applies to itself, for it is a proposition; hence its truth "implies its falsity."

"In the same way," continues McTaggart, "the words 'all propositions which are believed are false' have a meaning, and are the statement of a proposition. Here the proposition is not strictly speaking *self*-contradictory, but its truth, together with the truth of the assertion that the sceptic believes it, implies its falsity." [2]

1. See his article, "Propositions Applicable to Themselves" in *Philosophical Studies*, ed. S. V. Keeling (London, 1934).   2. *Ibid.*, p. 182.

The skeptic's last line of defense has thus been pierced, and his position has clearly been rendered untenable. Some propositions, then, can be known to be true. Among these, as St. Augustine has rightly observed, are certain hypothetical propositions. "Certum enim habeo," he writes, "aut unum esse mundum, aut non unum; et si non unum, aut finiti numeri, aut infiniti." [3] Of mathematical propositions we can have definite knowledge. It avails nothing to urge that they are mere conventions; for, were they so, they would be susceptible to change; nor yet that they are "mind-made," for were such the case we might have abstained from making them or, conceivably, have made them otherwise. If we take the position that we find it difficult to doubt these propositions because upbringing and the influence of authority have rendered belief in them habitual, we implicitly commit ourselves to one of two assertions, either (1) that by making a sufficient effort we could free ourselves from prejudice, and could then see that two plus two, for instance, need not equal four, but might just as well equal three or five; or (2) that although we cannot *conceive* that the addition of two and two could yield any other sum than four, yet it might nonetheless be true that it could yield some other sum, in which case we are asserting that we could conceive of reality as we cannot conceive of it, and so contradict ourselves.

Furthermore, when we undergo such experiences as those of pleasure or pain, we cannot really doubt that we are having these experiences. It has, indeed, been contended that introspection is always retrospection, that the mental states of which we are aware have all receded into the past, and that, accordingly, what purports to be knowledge of them may conceivably be erroneous. To test this theory try to persuade yourself when next you have a violent toothache that your experience is not of the present but of the immediate past, and that your interpretation and evaluation thereof may quite well be erroneous, and see whether you can thereby raise in your mind any actual doubt as to the presentness and painfulness of your experience. I have every confidence as to what your answer will be.

The data of sense, memory, dream, and imagination are directly presented to us, and however we may account for them, and whatever opinion we may form about their nature, of their reality there can be no question. We are aware of ourselves as being directly aware of them, and this places them beyond the reach of doubt.

Is there anything else of which we are certain? Of good and evil, of right and wrong, of beauty and ugliness we can become cognizant

3. *Contra Academicos*, p. 23.

only through direct acquaintance. By no process of inference can any-one be led to grasp the meaning of these words who has not ex-perienced the realities for which they stand. The realm of values, like that of colors, must be known by direct inspection if it is to be known at all. So general is the agreement upon this point that it is superfluous to dwell upon it. And the reality of that of which we are directly conscious is indubitable.

Of the reality of ourselves and of our states and acts, of qualities and relations, of the varied data of immediate experience, and of the truth of the laws of being and of the propositions of mathematics, we can, then, claim to have certain knowledge. And this is much. We have now a foundation whereon to stand as we survey the uni-verse. What we seek to discover, of course, is truth. And what is truth? At once we are confronted by the discordant answers which philoso-phers have given to this question.

Let us begin by recalling one of the most ancient of these, one suggested by St. Augustine in his *Soliloquies:* [4] *verum mihi videtur esse id quod est*—"the true seems to me to be that which is." Un-satisfactory as this definition is, and as it was at once seen to be by St. Augustine, the confusion of the notion of truth with that of being which it reveals is not without interest for the psychologist, if not for the philosopher. Our English word *sooth,* derived from an older *sonthus,* is connected with the root of a verb meaning *to be,* as also are the Gothic *sunjis,* the Greek ἐτεός, and the Sanskrit *satya.* St. Augus-tine's attempt at definition thus brings to light an extremely wide-spread confusion into which it is not astonishing that he should have fallen, and which is indicative of the intimate connection of the two ideas; nonetheless, it leaves us with two words for the same thing. Commenting upon it St. Thomas succinctly observes, "useless repeti-tion of the same thing is meaningless; so, if the true were the same as being, it would be meaningless to say, 'Being is true.'" [5] Recogniz-ing that he has gone astray, St. Augustine at once remarks, "nihil ergo erit falsum; quia quidquid est, est verum." Accordingly he is inclined to revert to his own earlier suggestion that what is true is that which is as it appears to be, and to buttress it by the assertion that what is false is that which is not as it appears to be.

This, again, is of interest to us, for our English word *true* often

4. Book II, chap. v.

5. *De Veritate,* q. 1. a: ad I^m; trans. the Rev. Richard W. Mulligan. It is perhaps worth noting that according to the *Fonolexica Langenscheidt,* the Hebrew תָּמִים means, not only truth, but also firmness, duration, security, faithfulness, and אֱמֶת that means also whole, complete, perfect, innocent, upright.

has the meaning of genuine, and at other times that of trustworthy or loyal. Readers of Chaucer will recall the lines:

> My maister Bukton, whan of Crist our kyng
> Was axed what is trouthe or sothfastnesse,
> He nat a word answerde to that axing,
> As who saith, "No man is al trewe," I gesse.[6]

This brief excursion into etymology reveals how easy it is to confuse the distinction between truth and falsity with that between reality and appearance. Clear thinking obviously requires that their disparateness be recognized. Things are real, but things are not true. A particular man is real; it is permissible, if we wish to assert that he is loyal or that he can be relied upon, to say that he is true, even as, should we consider him disloyal or unreliable, it is to say that he is false; yet he is neither true nor false in the sense in which a statement is true or false. A true statement, indeed, is one which can be relied on, but its trustworthiness is not identical with its truth but is derivative from it.

What, we ask once more, is truth? Of one thing, at least, we can be sure. When, not only the proverbial "man in the street," but any human being who is not philosophizing, says that some assertion is true, what he means is that the fact is as stated. This is a consideration of the greatest importance. It does not, indeed, follow that the popular view ought to be accepted without scrutiny or criticism; yet the fact that to most people this notion of truth seems quite clear and satisfactory is certainly an impressive one. And it is also an impressive fact that we find people who profess to reject this view displaying a persistent tendency in unguarded moments to fall back upon it, as though it were after all inescapable.

It may be urged, however, that a judgment or belief is a state or act of the apprehending mind, and that, while as such it is undoubtedly real, it is no more true than a stone or a tree. To answer this objection we must distinguish between a state of consciousness and that of which it is conscious, between the act of judging and the content of the judgment. It is the content or meaning of an assertion, and not the mental state which asserts it, that is true or false. And it is this meaning which is apprehended in common by all minds which direct their attention toward it, which is either affirmed, presupposed, doubted, or denied by them all, and which remains identical in all verbal expressions of it. It is this meaning which is called a proposi-

6. *Lenvoy de Chaucer a Bukton.*

tion. If what is meant be the case, if the fact be as stated, the proposition, we say, is true.

What, then, is the relation between a proposition and a fact which renders the proposition true? The answer seems obvious; it is one of conformity to the fact. This relation of conformity is generally called correspondence. And often as the point has been made, it is probably expedient to re-emphasize that the proposition does not copy or imitate the fact. Such misapprehensions have been so frequently entertained that Dr. A. C. Ewing has been moved to suggest the substitution [7] of the term "accordance" for the term "correspondence," in an effort to escape them. The choice of words, however, is not a matter of great importance. What is desirable is that it should be grasped at the outset that the relation between a true proposition and a fact is ultimate and unanalyzable, and therefore incapable of definition *per species et differentiam.* Yet it is not inapprehensible, for we can point to as many instances of it as we may desire. The correspondence theory of truth, as I have said, would seem to be justified in its claim to present the point of view of the plain man; and of all the various theories, it is the least occult and, superficially at any rate, the most plausible.

Let us now turn to the systematic investigation of its rivals. In the first place, let us take up the consideration of pragmatism, inasmuch as it is the putative ancestor of the verification theory which is still popular.

The pragmatist proposes to identify truth with utility or "workability." In so doing does he deny that there is such a relation as that of correspondence between a proposition and a fact? If not, the issue is a purely verbal one; he merely takes it upon himself to substitute the word "truth" for the word "utility" or for the word "workability." It is clear, however, that the pragmatist means something more than this. He is prepared definitely to reject the notion of correspondence. F. C. S. Schiller, for one, was quite explicit upon this point. Truth, he insisted, "cannot be defined as the agreement or correspondence of thought with 'reality,' for how can thought determine whether it correctly 'copies' what transcends it?" [8] Here, we may observe, Schiller reveals that like so many pragmatists, he has misunderstood the correspondence theory, otherwise he would not talk of copying; but for the moment, we are concerned with the soundness of his own view.

7. See *Idealism,* pp. 207–208.
8. *Encyclopaedia Britannica,* 14th ed., XVII, 413.

And his view is that the meaning of phrases "is really defined by their use."

A defender of the correspondence view may readily concede that in some cases, the usefulness or workability of a belief will provide a test of its truth. If, for example, you believe that you can swim a river, the belief will be useful if you desire to swim the river, and if you really are able to do so. And if you actually swim it, you will have put your belief to the test and found it justified. Be it observed, however, that the belief was useful because it was true in the sense of corresponding with the fact that you were able to swim it; had it not been so, you could not have swum the river, and you might have drowned. The utility of the belief was not, then, identical with its truth, but was dependent upon it. Truth is clearly one thing, and utility another.

Moreover the adherent of the correspondence view will point out that false beliefs can on some occasions prove extremely useful for the purpose in hand, otherwise propagandists would find their function a very restricted one.

It may also be remarked that some beliefs which are obviously and unquestionably true to everyone but a pragmatist are of no use at all. Bradley's illustration of the starving man who descries fruit growing at the top of an unscalable cliff comes at once to the mind. Will the pragmatist say that no fruit is there?

Furthermore, a belief that is useful to one man may be the reverse for his neighbor. You, as a physical scientist, find the belief in the absolute uniformity of nature of extreme utility; to me, as a fundamentalist for whom the occurrence of miracles is an article of faith, it is anathema.

It is vain for the pragmatist to protest that his concern is not with individual and relatively transient but with social and abiding utility. For every society is made up of individuals with their beliefs, and the pragmatist's definition of truth must be applicable to these individual beliefs. But, even if we consider only beliefs which are shared by practically all the individuals in a society, difficulties will arise. The belief that the Koran was dictated to Muhammad by the archangel Gabriel will prove useful to orthodox Muslims concerned with the propagation of Islam, whereas it will appear highly detrimental to Christian missionaries. In terms of which evaluation is it to be pronounced true or false? Shall we be told that it is simultaneously true from one point of view and false from another? Are we, again, to take seriously the pragmatist's contention that truth itself can change, that a belief—such as the belief in the Ptolemaic astronomy—which was once true is now false? To most minds it will surely appear that we are approaching, if we have not already reached, a *reductio ad absurdum*. And if the pragmatist, in the effort to make his doctrine seem less paradoxical, take refuge in the theory of degrees of truth, he will fall into the hands of the advocates of the coherence theory.

On all these counts the pragmatic theory of truth must be pronounced highly unsatisfactory. What has become increasingly evident as we have proceeded is that the pragmatist, far from being desirous to free from what he takes to be confusions and misapprehensions the common notion of truth, has definitely rejected it, and is concerned with something quite distinct from it, namely, utility. In other words, his boasted theory of truth is nothing of the sort. What he really advocates is merely a change of terminology. His position would be much less obscure and more disingenuous were he boldly to repeat the assertion of Protagoras that while no beliefs are true, some beliefs are more useful than others.

Doubtless many persons have rallied to the banner of pragmatism because of the extraordinary misconception of the correspondence theory which we have just seen illustrated in the case of Schiller. We can never get outside of our own consciousness, it is contended, to see whether our beliefs do correspond with external reality. The objection presupposes that the product of our own thinking stands as a screen between us and reality. But there is no justification whatever for this assumption. The reality judged about is the reality directly or indirectly apprehended. This is a proposition to which a Berkeleyan could agree as readily as anyone else. In the sense that we are always cognizant of an external world we are always outside ourselves. There is no screen to be broken through or barrier to be surmounted. Knowledge, as has frequently been said, is transcendent; otherwise we could know nothing and think of nothing but our own mental states, and, consequently, should all be solipsists.[9]

Let us turn next to the verification theory of truth which, although its prestige now appears to be distinctly on the wane, has played so great a part in recent controversy. To know what a proposition means, declare the advocates of this view, we must know how it could be verified. As first enunciated the theory was understood to assert that an unverified proposition has no meaning; but the consequences of such an affirmation would involve one in absurdities which even the

9. The point is well discussed by Dr. Ewing in *Idealism*, pp. 204–205.

hardiest dared not face. For it would follow that before the Russians had photographed the other side of the moon, it was meaningless to assert that it had another side, and that when scientists are debating whether the center of the earth be gaseous, molten, or metal, none of the disputants means anything at all. In order to save the theory, therefore, from becoming utterly ridiculous, it became necessary sharply to distinguish between imagined and actual verification. A proposition, it was agreed, has meaning if it be possible to imagine how it might be verified; actual verification constitutes its truth.

A further delimitation of the notion of verification was at once seen, however, to be imperative. Protestant theologians, for whom religious experience is the ultimate seat of authority, showed an alarming tendency to adopt the theory. But were they to be permitted to do so, the door to metaphysics would still be left open. And it was in order to shut and permanently seal this door that the theory was devised. To say this is, I realize, to impugn the impartiality and dis-interestedness of those who concocted it. But I think that there can be no doubt that the hope of its authors was to deliver a mortal blow to metaphysics, and thereby to religion, and that to attain this end they were prepared to incur a serious risk of trespassing upon the territory of the fantastic and the incredible. Accordingly it was dogmat-ically decreed that verification must be in terms of sense experience, a proviso which definitely ruled out all propositions of metaphysical import. From it ensues, indeed, the somewhat awkward consequence that all objective theories of ethics were included in this anathema; hence the proliferation of subjective theories which we have recently witnessed.

I have, indeed, just yielded to the temptation to write with a tinge of irony of a theory which has been ushered upon the stage of con-temporary philosophy with such a blast of trumpets. But can it be denied that there is a presumptive insolence in a doctrine which asserts that the vast majority of the outstanding thinkers of history from Plato to Whitehead were habitually engaged in talking nonsense, and that only within the present century has anyone spoken sensibly? Yet irony, I agree, is not refutation. Let us therefore proceed to scrutinize it.

In the first place it is to be observed that there is no imaginable way in which the verification theory itself could be verified in terms either of sense experience or of any experience at all, and that on its own showing, therefore, it is devoid of meaning. What more damning accusation could be brought against any theory than that its fundamental principle is unintelligible? What more need be said? Yet there is more to say.

At first glance one is impressed by the dogmatism with which verification is restricted to the realm of sense experience. Is there any justification, one asks, for so arbitrary a procedure? The world of sense experience, it may be replied, is a common world, whereas ethical and religious—and, incidentally, aesthetic—experiences are private. Does the case stand so, indeed? We have heard much from philosophers, generally regarded as of outstanding competence, of the privacy of sense data, and of the private spaces wherein they appear. These thinkers, we may be told, do no more than illustrate the ease with which one may yield to the unfortunate tendency to talk metaphysical nonsense; for what they say cannot possibly be verified in terms of sense experience, and is, therefore, meaningless. Yet equally meaningless by the same token must be the opposing doctrine; for how can the theory that the world of sense experience is a common world be verified in terms of sense experience? How can I conceivably know that you sense what I sense? On the theory before us the assertion that the sense world is a common world is as meaningless as its denial. Hence the condemnation pronounced upon the theologians ought in fairness to be repealed.

The identification of meaning with imagined verification seems plainly to be a putting of the cart before the horse. For how are we to imagine what the verification of a proposition would be like unless we already know what the proposition means? If it be stated in a language of which we are ignorant its meaning is not conveyed to us, and it is impossible for us to imagine how it could be verified. The ability to imagine depends upon a prior understanding of the meaning. This consideration, obvious as it is, deserves to be emphasized; for once we have seen that meaning is one thing and verification, actual or imagined, another, the verification theory of meaning and truth becomes "but an empty noise."

Furthermore, is it not clear that some propositions which have a perfectly explicit meaning could, from the nature of the case, never be verified? Take, for instance, the proposition that the last thought of a man who has died alone in a wilderness, and whose body has been consumed by a forest fire, was one of satisfaction at having done his duty. How could such a proposition conceivably be verified? There is no evidence, not even the expression of the dead man's face, upon which to found an assertion. Nonetheless, we are quite clear beyond all cavil as to what such an assertion would mean; for its content is a proposition which we can all contemplate and which is completely intelligible.

That verification, in certain circumstances, furnishes a *test* of truth we may frankly concede. You tell me that there is a horse in the grounds, I look out the window and see one, and I know that you have spoken truly. But I look out the window only because I am aware that in this way I can find out whether you have spoken truly, and I am so aware only because I have already understood the meaning of your words. I know that you are talking about a horse, and not about an elephant or about the next presidential election. And while my seeing the horse verifies the proposition, it is not identical with the truth of the proposition; for the proposition would have been true had I never tested it, had no one seen the horse, and had it left no traces of its passage.

It may, perhaps, he objected that in the foregoing discussion I have been too much concerned with the crude identification of truth with verification in terms of sense experience, and too little with the later subtleties of Wittgenstein and his followers. For these last, as G. R. G. Mure has well said, "the nature of truth, at all events as a specific problem, drops away, and the dominant theme is the constantly reiterated assertion that the meaning of words is only to be discovered in their actual use." [10] They have thus, as he puts it, "abandoned truth for meaning." [11]

We certainly need not shrink from admitting what is obvious beyond all question, that the meaning of words is frequently modified—or, shall we say, enhanced—by the context in which they are used or the circumstances in which they are uttered. Much depends upon intonation, gesture, and facial expression; much upon the assumed powers of inference of our hearers. We often fail to complete our sentences when we have made clear to our interlocutors what we "are driving at." The North American Indians, we may recall, developed a system of communication by gesture in lieu of speech, so that men who could not comprehend each other's spoken languages could nevertheless converse with each other with the utmost facility; and in this they have been to some extent imitated by our own deaf-mutes. And for all of us a single word can at times take the place of a sentence, as when one cries out "Fire!" in a crowded theater or when Wittgenstein's mason shouts "Slab!" Moreover, we recognize that in the idioms peculiar to any language—such as *secundissimus*

10. *Retreat from Truth* (New York, 1958), p. 157.
11. *Ibid.*, p. 165.

ventus or *avoir beau dire*—words are employed in what is other than their normal sense.

Incontestable as these facts are, they are clearly of minimal importance for the philosopher. To say that the meaning of a word is to be found in its use is to enunciate a tautology; for a word is a sign, it is used to stand for something else, and this use is its meaning. To note that it is not invariably made to stand for the same thing is merely to recognize that its use can vary. Nonetheless there is a normal or basic usage which it is necessary to comprehend if we are to understand the variations from the normal which constitute a secondary usage with which linguistic analysts are concerned, and which is intelligible only in the light of the primary. This is why to learn a foreign tongue one must grasp the standard meaning of the words. One can know a good deal about the inflections, the sentence structure, and even, as we say, about the genius of a language and yet find it difficult to understand, to speak, to read, and to write it because of a wretched memory for vocabulary—as I, for one, know full well. But once the vocabulary, inflections, and sentence structure are mastered, the variations of contextual usage rapidly become clear.

To contend, as analysts are prone to do, that we are all helpless and hopeless victims of habitual usage which functions as a linguistic tyrant, controlling our thinking with a despotic power against which we struggle in vain, and that the seeming problems of philosophy are mere intellectual confusions which it generates, is to make a claim which is woefully exaggerated. For, after all, there is nothing demonic about usage. It may at times mislead us, as cautious philosophers have always recognized, but it is not inherently evil. The function of language is to symbolize reality, and thus to render possible the communication of meaning. Not only physical objects but also emotions, cognitions, and volitions are thus symbolized, for they too are real. The reference to reality is always primary. Usage consists of conventional rules for the employment of these symbols. Convenience has much to do with it, so has psychology; and behind usage lies a history. It is the task of philologists to investigate the role of this last factor; and much of what they tell us reveals the presence of what we can only call accident—as, for instance, the use of a singular verb with a neuter plural noun in classical Greek.[12] Convenience is doubtless responsible for the disappearance of grammatical gender in English. And the psychological influence, never to be discounted, is sometimes plainly ap-

12. The neuter plural, we are informed, was once an abstract noun; hence the singular verb.

parent. The presence of alienable and inalienable possessive adjectives in American Indian languages, and of verbal forms which signify whether the statement made is based upon observation, hearsay, or inference, are clearly indicative of the interests of the aboriginal mind. And Dr. B. F. C. Atkinson assures us that the formation in Greek of masculine nouns of the first declension with the termination *ās* "shows a logical clearness of grammatical conception, behind which lies an orderly neatness of mind and a linguistic suppleness proving a capable instrument for these qualities." "The Greek language," he adds, "is full of such illustrations; indeed it is the expression of such qualities." [13]

All this, however, is of no concern to the philosopher as a philosopher. It is only when he suspects that familiar and habitual usage may be leading his thinking astray that he need direct his attention toward it. Obviously usage, upon the whole, must work pretty well; otherwise language, instead of being applicable to reality, would constitute a barrier between us and the real, and would be a complete failure as an instrument for the communication of meaning. Thus in English we lack a synthetic future tense; yet we manage well enough by employing the present with a future meaning in the protasis of a future conditional sentence, and by inserting in the apodosis a periphrastic future with *shall* or *will*, the former originally signifying constraint, the latter volition. In Hebrew, where the verbal forms indicate only complete and incomplete action, one employs the former to signify the past, and the latter the future; whereas for the present one can use the participle—with or without the verb *to be*—or may even dispense with any verb at all.[14] The absence of inflections in English and Chinese is compensated for by a rigidity of sentence structure. In short the human mind seems to be resolved, like Humpty-Dumpty, to be master of its words and not their servant.

If any man definitely assert that the structure of logic is arbitrary and might quite well be other than it is, that it is conditioned by and

13. *The Greek Language* (London, 1933), p. 69.

14. This usage has the disadvantage of involving at times an ambiguity. Thus the brief statement which constitutes the only creed of Judaism, "Yahweh elohenu Yahweh ehad," may be taken to mean, "Yahweh our God Yahweh is one," "Yahweh our God is one Yahweh," or "Yahweh is our God, Yahweh alone." In Arabic, where the same usage obtains, "Allah Akbar" (literally, "God great") is ordinarily understood to mean "God is great." But when the Mogul emperor, Akbar, on planning the erection of a temple to the one God, proposed to inscribe over the entrance "Allah Akbar," one of his ministers pointed out that this could be read "Akbar is God." The Semites, however, enjoy the advantage, for what it is worth, of being able to employ sentences expressive of propositions as proper names; as, for example, Elijah (Eliyahu) "Yahweh is God"—cf. the feminine names Abigail ("My father is joy") and Hephzibah ("My delight is in her").

dependent upon our habitual modes of expression, and that from these there is no appeal to any objective standard, he cannot be refuted, for he has placed himself at a level where no argument can reach him; but he may, as St. Augustine has remarked, with propriety be disregarded. For to take him seriously would be to concede that we are living in a world of intellectual chaos in which no genuine knowledge is possible—even, of course, the knowledge that we have no knowledge. One can talk in this way, but one cannot think in this way; for intelligibility and coherence are essential to all genuine ratiocination.

To assert that all genuine problems fall within the fields of the various sciences, and that for philosophy there are no such problems at all, is to deny to philosophy at once a field and a *raison d'être*. In reply it is legitimate to point out what has been so often emphasized already, that science raises no ultimate problems but begins with uncriticized assumptions—or at least with assumptions which are not thoroughly criticized—and is concerned largely with the practical task of prediction. It is for this reason that it is so dangerous to take over concepts or theories which have proved useful in scientific investigation and to attempt to utilize them in philosophy without preliminary examination and evaluation. But it certainly does not follow that the philosopher is wrong in trying to pursue these problems to the ultimate, working in his own way and by his own methods. How true this is we can easily see by glancing at the field of epistemology. Whether what we ordinarily take to be the same object which appears different from different standpoints and at different times to the same observer, and to different observers from their respective standpoints at the same time, can consistently and successfully be treated as a single entity, or must be dissolved into a plurality of entities, is quite obviously not a verbal question, but a problem which arises directly out of our experience of the external world; and to represent it as anything else is an insult to the intelligence.[15] The only universe in which there could be no problems for a finite intelligence would be a wholly irrational universe in which there were no laws and no universal characteristics, in which no reason could be given for any occurrence, and in which, therefore, no questions could be asked.

In light of these various considerations we are justified in dismissing the verification theory as quite preposterous. The removal of the

15. Of course, if we like, we can agree to understand by "physical object" a "family of sense data," but this will constitute a change of meaning, not the solution of a problem.

limitation of verification to the realm of sense experience, while it would frustrate the motivation behind the theory, avails nothing to save it, since meaning and verification refuse to be identified. Once this fact is grasped, the view is clearly seen to be untenable. To some other doctrine, therefore, we must turn.

What, then, of the coherence theory? An array of famous names can be cited in support of it. So much has been written both in defense of, and in attack upon, this theory that I shall touch only on those points which appear to me to be of fundamental importance.[16]

That coherence is *a* test of truth practically everyone, including the pragmatist, will agree; for when statements conflict with each other, it is obvious that something is wrong. But can it justifiably be claimed that coherence is *the* test of truth? In his *Idealism* [17] Dr. Ewing seems inclined to admit as much, but in his later work he appears to have reconsidered his concession. "It is clear in any case," he writes, "that we cannot do with just one criterion of truth." [18] What are the other criteria he proposes for our acceptance? They are sense perception, memory, and intuition.[19] After considering the pragmatic test, for reasons which are not altogether clear to me he rejects it as an ultimate criterion. It is, of course, as he remarks, perfectly obvious that in the case of a false belief, the anticipated consequences do not follow. "The point which shows the belief false," he observes, "is not its practical bearing, i.e. that it injures somebody, but the fact that it conflicts with experience." [20] Quite so, but in virtue of what criterion do we pronounce it false? Is it because of the absence of sensuous or intuitive corroboration, or because the belief in question and the judgment that the expected consequences have not followed are mutually incoherent?

It has frequently been contended that a belief can never be refuted by a bare fact. As James Bissett Pratt succinctly put it, "the only thing that can conflict with a belief or a proposition is another belief

16. The best recent defense of it with which I am acquainted is to be found in Professor Blanshard's *The Nature of Thought*, chaps. xxv–xxvi, and the best criticism of it in Dr. Ewing's *Idealism*, chap. v, and *The Fundamental Questions of Philosophy*, chap. iii.

17. P. 250.

18. See *The Fundamental Questions of Philosophy*, p. 65.

19. By intuition Dr. Ewing seems clearly to mean awareness of truths of a non-sensuous order, such as logical and ethical propositions—although he does not say so, it would appear that truths of an aesthetic nature should also be included—as well as the awareness of the coherence of coherent propositions.

20. *Ibid.*, p. 66.

or proposition." [21] The belief or proposition which conflicts will be *about* a fact, but it will not *be* a fact. Let us take an historical instance of a false belief. An engineer in the train of Cortez persuaded him that the siege engine which he proposed to construct would be of use in destroying the fortifications and buildings of Tenochtitlán. The first stone discharged from the machine fell back upon it and smashed it to pieces. If a pragmatic test was ever worth anything it was this one. Certainly no theorist of any school would affirm that the test was useless. The belief that the engine would work was indubitably not borne out by the fact. But was it the mere visual and auditory awareness of the falling stone and the destruction of the engine that sufficed to disillusion Cortez, or was it a judgment thereby engendered which was seen to be inconsistent with the previous judgment?

Before answering this question we should do well to remember that it is possible to be mistaken about corroborative events—or at least about the judgments which they do, or do not, corroborate. For example, the airplane designed by Samuel P. Langley of Pittsburgh, when put to the trial, failed to fly, and was preserved in a museum as a curiosity. Its failure was taken to prove its incapacity to fly. This was a judgment, and a false judgment; for after Orville Wright had flown his plane, Langley's plane was taken out and successfully flown. Some trifling maladjustment accounted for the preliminary failure.

It seems, then, that we must acquiesce in the contention that while beliefs, judgments, or propositions can be inconsistent, facts cannot be inconsistent with anything; and we shall therefore be justified in concluding that the pragmatic test is not an ultimate criterion of truth. The same will hold good for sense perception, intuition (in Dr. Ewing's sense of the word), and memory. Coherence between propositions will furnish the only ultimate test of truth, although the propositions themselves may be grounded in empirically ascertained fact.

Believers in the coherence theory, however, press us to concede more than this. They wish us to acknowledge coherence not only as the test but also as the definition of truth. And once this acknowledgment is made, we shall be told that inasmuch as there are degrees of coherence, it follows that there are degrees of truth. Absolute truth is to be identified with the all-inclusive system of propositions which directly or indirectly imply each other. And from this admission it is a short step to the assertion that reality also admits of degrees.

21. *Can We Keep the Faith?* (London, 1941), pp. 78–79.

In the last paragraph I have roughly outlined the position which has been that of the majority of absolute idealists.[22] As one contemplates it, one is likely to feel simultaneously repelled and attracted. One is repelled by the golden opportunity which the theory affords, an opportunity often exploited to the full, to "have it both ways" in the matter of almost any issue. Is time real? we ask. Is space? Is the self? The answer will be that all these possess some degree of reality, but that none is ultimately or absolutely real. Perhaps the self, as Bradley conceded, may be accorded a higher degree of reality than time or space, yet its absolute reality is nonetheless denied. All this is inevitably productive of a feeling of impatience in the mind of him who is skeptical with regard to the entire position. Possibly he may be reminded of the man who rowed Benedict Arnold down the Hudson to the British fleet, and who, when urged by the deserter to follow his example and revert to the British allegiance, replied that "he would be damned if he fought on both sides."

Yet it must be freely admitted that on their own principles, supporters of the doctrine cannot answer otherwise. Since any intelligible proposition cannot, in this view, be wholly false, it will possess *some* degree of truth and will put us in touch, as it were, with *some* degree of reality. This consideration is almost certain to encourage in the mind of him who subscribes to the theory a breadth of outlook which we cannot but regard as admirable, and which can scarcely fail to appeal to us. It is true that the desire to find some truth in every view may, if not counterbalanced by a demand for clarity and definiteness, be productive of reprehensible wishy-washiness, but when one casts a backward glance over the history of philosophy and observes how lack of sympathy with, and understanding of, opposing doctrines have often resulted in narrowness of outlook and commitment to extreme positions, one may conclude that the coherence theory provides a valuable safeguard against the tendency to rush up blind alleys. I, for one, am prepared to admit frankly that if the correspondence view were to prove untenable, it would be the coherence theory which would command my allegiance.

The difficulties in the way of accepting it, however, appear to be insuperable. In the first place, if the theory be sound, no finite mind will be capable of embracing in its grasp the system of all mutually implicatory propositions which constitutes absolute truth. Any theory, therefore, which a finite mind can excogitate will be infected to some

22. McTaggart is, of course, an outstanding exception.

extent with error. And this statement applies to the coherence theory of truth itself.[23] The theory, therefore, is partly true and partly false. The best that could be said for it would be that it approximates to absolute truth more closely than does any other theory. Yet how far this approximation exceeds that of any other view we could never know. This leaves us in a state of uncertainty not very far from that of complete nescience. One sees how easily the theory could absorb the doctrine of the pragmatists, as Bradley himself pointed out, yet this would involve its taking upon its shoulders all the difficulties which have already become apparent in connection therewith.

In the second place not all propositions are about other propositions; some of them are about facts.[24] A proposition which is about a fact professes, as one may put it, to state the fact as it is. So to state the fact is to correspond or accord with the fact. To deny this would make nonsense of such propositions; yet to admit so much is, surely, equivalent to conceding that the correspondence theory is true. In other words, coherence is plainly one thing and correspondence another; and correspondence is what is normally meant by *truth*.

In the third place, since the theory asserts that a proposition is true insofar as it is eligible for membership in the all-inclusive system of mutually implicatory propositions, it requires us to deny that the truth of any proposition is self-evident. Yet how is such a denial to be sustained? Those who so glibly deny the validity of the notion of self-evidence fail to see that, as Dr. Ewing has pointed out,[25] when we accept the conclusion of an inference, we do so because it appears to us self-evident that it follows from the premises. Were this not the case, every argument would go on forever. This is not to say that we

23. On this very issue I find Professor Brand Blanshard's able defense of the doctrine unsatisfactory. "When I assert that this is true," he writes, "I am asserting that the theory, as I now understand it, is true according to the evidence now available; I am not asserting that omniscience itself must subscribe to it in exactly this present sense" (*The Nature of Thought*, II, 290). But, surely, if omniscience cannot subscribe to the theory as it stands, it is because it is partly false. Indeed the quotation from Joachim's *The Nature of Truth* (Oxford, 1906, p. 175), which Professor Blanshard subjoins in a footnote (p. 291), I cannot but regard as letting the cat completely out of the bag. "Assuming that the coherence-notion of truth is sound, no theory of truth as coherence can itself be completely true, but is at most possessed of a 'truth' which we may believe, but have not proved, to be 'symptomatic' of perfect truth." Could the severest critic desire a more explicit admission?
24. I do not, of course, intend to deny that the mutual consistency or implication of two propositions is a fact. What I have in mind is facts the constituents of which are not propositions—such facts, for example, as "this room is too hot," "I am unhappy," "kindliness is a greater virtue than prudence."
25. See *Idealism*, p. 260, n. 3; also *The Fundamental Questions of Philosophy*, p. 64.

are never mistaken in regard to self-evidence. Plainly we sometimes are, otherwise none of our inferences would ever be erroneous. No criterion of knowledge could endue a finite mind with infallibility. But it does show that the notion cannot be dispensed with, for then no inference would be possible.

Again, how do we know that two propositions are mutually coherent? If the proposition that they are so be not self-evident, the test of coherence must be applied; but this will involve a fourth proposition to the effect that the third proposition coheres with the first two; and if this fourth proposition be not self-evident, the same test must once more be applied, which will involve the introduction of a fifth proposition, and so ad infinitum.

Moreover, how do we know that if two propositions be both true they are coherent? Consistently with the coherence theory this proposition cannot be pronounced self-evident. Unless awareness of its truth be imparted to us by the *intellectus agens,* as some of the scholastics believed, it would seem that it must be regarded as an assumption which is validated by the pragmatic test. But how is it validated? By enabling us to avoid contradiction? But why should we seek to avoid contradiction? Some of the neosupernaturalists have shown themselves undeterred thereby.[26] Are we lesser men than they? Why not boldly affirm that the two conflicting theories of the nature of light are mutually inconsistent, yet are both true? Why not assert that man is at once free and determined, or that three personal Gods can constitute a single personal God? How many difficulties would be banished by this potent solvent! Why not, then, apply it? Because we see that we should be talking nonsense? Yea, verily; but how do we see it? The answer is that we see it as self-evident.

And, in the fourth place, there is a further consideration which bears upon the notion of degrees of truth. Take Professor Blanshard's illustration [27] of the schoolboy and the historian, each of whom makes a judgment which can be expressed by the sentence, "Napoleon was defeated at Waterloo." It is Professor Blanshard's contention that the two judgments differ in their degrees of truth, the latter far exceeding the former in amplitude, embracing as it does a multiplicity of characteristics, causes, and consequences of which the schoolboy is ignorant. Neither judgment, according to Professor Blanshard, is a mosaic

26. See Pratt, *Can We Keep the Faith?*, pp. 62–63.
27. I freely admit that one proposition can be more false than another, in that it may misstate the facts more than another. To say that Napoleon won the battle, for instance, would be more false than to misstate the number of Frenchmen killed, wounded, and missing.

of beliefs each of which is, or may be, wholly true. Each judgment, if I understand him, constitutes in itself a unity not made of parts, unanalyzable into simple and included judgments.

Now it is precisely this contention which I feel compelled to question. The historian's perspective, I would urge, does include a whole mosaic of propositions with regard to the events of the battle, the causes which brought it about, and the effects which followed from it. If these propositions correspond with the facts they are all equally true, and none of them is any truer than the simple proposition, "Napoleon was defeated at Waterloo," entertained by the schoolboy. There is more truth in the historian's perspective in that it embraces more true propositions; in other words, it is a numerical preponderance, and not a matter of degree. The coherence theory apparently requires us to conceive of a judgment as including within itself all its own implications, and as thus constituting not a compound but a complex unity which, as such, cannot be divided into parts. That an *act* of judging constitutes an indivisible unity is an assertion with the truth of which I am not at present concerned, but it does seem to me as clear as day that the *content* of the judgment made by the historian does constitute a compound proposition composed of a host of simple propositions. I do not think that anything more that I could say would make my position clearer and therefore submit it, as I have stated it, to the reader's judgment.

In the face of all these objections, however, I think that it is plain that the doctrine that truth is to be identified with coherence, and that it admits of degrees, will not stand. But there is a fourth view which demands our notice. It is the so-called identity theory; and its fundamental contention can be most succinctly expressed by saying that it maintains that truth and fact are two words for the same thing. One's first comment might well be that if this be so, it is indeed unfortunate that we have these two words, since, had we only one word, we should have been spared any problem. It may be observed, nevertheless, that the theory constitutes something of a regression toward the position of St. Augustine, "the true is that which is." On this view, if I say, "the car is at the door," the truth of the statement is to be identified with the actual situation, car-at-the-door. If, however, there be no car at the door, there is no fact wherewith the truth of the statement can be identified, and it is therefore false.

The theory is confronted by a difficulty which, as the French say, "leaps to the eyes," and which is of so serious a nature as to appear fatal. A statement, whether it be true or false, so long as it be not mere gibberish, has meaning. And as we have seen, it is quite possible that the meaning of a statement should be definite and clear, and yet that the statement should be incapable of verification, so that we can never know whether it be true or false. What, for example, was the last conscious state experienced by Sir William Wallace? If I affirm that it was one of confidence in the eventual triumph of the cause for which he died, that it was one of despair, that it was one of hatred, or that it was a wish to be freed from pain, what I say is perfectly intelligible; yet which of these it was, or whether it was none of them, no man can tell. We know the meaning of these statements, but we have no knowledge of the fact. Fact and meaning, therefore, cannot be identified. In the case of a true proposition the *fact* is what is *meant* in the sense that it is what the statement refers to, but the *meaning* is plainly other than the fact. In the case of a false proposition there is meaning without a requisite fact. And even if we proceed to the extreme measure of introducing "false facts," we shall not have got rid of the relation of correspondence. All that we are now asserting is that true propositions correspond to genuine facts and false propositions to false facts.

Moreover, it is obvious that the notion of a "false fact" is self-contradictory. We do indeed speak of a "false window" or a "false door"; yet it is quite clear that when we do so we are using *false* in the sense of *apparent* as opposed to *real,* a meaning which is irrelevant to our present discussion. One would not speak of a false window as a "false fact," nor even of a real window as a fact. The notion of *fact* involves a certain plurality, a state of characterization of some entity or entities. And it is to such a state of affairs that a true proposition corresponds. A "false fact," then, would be a state of affairs which both obtained and did not obtain—which is nonsense. We cannot escape, therefore, from the notion of correspondence; and it is to the correspondence theory of truth that, having vainly scrutinized the rival views, we must at last revert.

Truth we shall accordingly define as the relation of correspondence between proposition and fact. With this taken as established, and convinced that all the prohibitions pronounced by contemporary philosophers against metaphysical speculation are no more than "sounding brass and a tinkling cymbal," we set ourselves definitely to the task of trying to learn something about the nature of the universe as a whole. But how to go about it? We must proceed experientially, says the empiricist. But are we to take all aspects of human experience at their face value, or shall we pick and choose? Among empiricists themselves we discover an important difference of opinion on how this question should be answered. There is a narrow, or restricted, empiricism which is founded upon the conviction that all knowledge is derived from sense experience. Plainly it is impossible for us to take this position; for knowledge of the self, as we have seen, is the basis and presupposition of all other knowledge, and such knowledge is attained, not through sense experience, but through introspection. But what if we take introspection and sensation as the twin sources of knowledge? This would involve our treating ethical, aesthetic, and religious experience as subjective in character; in which case these forms of experience are not what they appear to be, for they seem to tell us something about the external world whereas we must now hold that they tell us only about ourselves. We have not yet examined the question of the objectivity of values; but even at this stage of our inquiry, we are entitled to remark that if we thus discriminate and pick and choose among the different forms of experience we are not proceeding empirically but dogmatically, and that we are doing so in accordance with an evaluative assumption which is not itself based upon experience but is unfounded and arbitrary. It is the broader empiricism, which treats all forms of human experience as on the same footing, which is more genuinely empirical. These remarks, be it understood, apply only to the choice immediately proposed to us. If, after having examined in detail the theory of the objectivity of values, we find ourselves compelled to reject it, we may then make bold to renounce the broader and revert to the narrower form of empiricism—that is, if we find the empirical position on the whole satisfactory.

But is it satisfactory? There is one thing, certainly, of which we can be sure: the beings the existence of which is revealed to us by experience are contained within the universe, and consequently the universe is the kind of universe which can include them. Still it does not follow that the universe is, as it were, all of a piece, and that the portion of it with which we are acquainted is a fair sample of the whole, any more than it follows from the fact that the United States contains the Mojave Desert that the entire area of the United States is desert.

McTaggart's observations upon this head [28] are very much to the point. They have not, indeed, been generally attended to; but one may not unjustifiably suspect that this is because it is easier to ignore

28. See *The Nature of Existence*, Vol. I, secs. 42–43, 264–271; cf. *Some Dogmas of Religion* (London, 1906), sec. 15.

than to answer them. If we are to proceed empirically in our effort to determine the nature of the universe as a whole, we shall be compelled to resort to generalizations based upon induction. And there are two reasons why this is not feasible.

In the first place, we shall have to provide a philosophic justification of the principle of induction, and no such justification appears to be forthcoming. It is obvious that we cannot argue that since induction has been successfully employed by scientists, the philosopher can safely rely upon it; for this would be employing the principle to prove itself. It is also clear that we have no ground for believing that the instantiation of any quality will always be accompanied by the instantiation of another quality unless we have ground for believing that the first intrinsically determines the second. In some cases, indeed, we know a priori that intrinsic determination is involved. Thus we know that whatever is colored must be extended. Here we have no need of induction. "We only know *a priori* that there are intrinsic determinations because we know *a priori* what the intrinsic determinations are." [29] But we cannot argue that because there are intrinsic determinations that are known, there are probably others that are unknown, for this argument would itself be an induction.

Even if it be granted that there are intrinsic determinations among events, can induction enable us to discover what they are? Might it not still be the case that the regularity of sequence observed by us was entirely fortuitous? Even if we could know beyond question that a certain event was an intrinsic determinant and that a certain other event was intrinsically determined, and even if in our experience events of these types occurred in constant conjunction, it would still be possible that the one determined, and that the other was determined by, events of which we were ignorant, and that the conjunction of the two was contingent.

In the second place, at the beginning of a metaphysical investigation the probability of any induction will depend upon the relation of the field of observation to the field of inference; in other words, induction will be purely enumerative. At a later stage of inquiry it is conceivable that the field of inference might have become so delimited that we would have some notion of the proportion obtaining between the observed and the unobserved instances, but at the outset such is not the case. When the entire universe constitutes the field of inference we have absolutely no notion of the proportion obtaining between observed and unobserved instances. Were we therefore to resort to in-

29. *The Nature of Existence*, Vol. 1, sec. 267.

duction, we should, to use an illustration of McTaggart's, be like a man who, having encountered a Chinese of evil character, inferred that all Chinese in this respect resembled him.[30]

These considerations are obviously weighty. What are we to say to them? The difficulty of the problem of induction is sufficiently notorious. It is plain that Dr. Ewing hopes to find in the entailment theory of causality a basis for a philosophic justification of induction. And it might be contended that he has committed one of the errors enumerated by McTaggart in arguing for the presence of intrinsic determinations in the physical world where, as he admits, we cannot perceive them. But as a matter of fact Dr. Ewing does not argue directly from the presence of perceived intrinsic determinations in the mental realm to the presence of unperceived intrinsic determinations in the physical realm. His argument is rather that it is more plausible to assume that the regular sequences of events in the physical world with which we are familiar are due to intrinsic determinations than that they are purely fortuitous. He glances at the mental realm merely to assure himself and us that there actually are causal connections in which intrinsic determination is involved, and thus to give his hypothesis greater plausibility. And he adds further support to his position by pointing out that very many of the judgments which we habitually make with the greatest confidence would be denuded of all probability if we accepted the regularity view of causality. These considerations, too, are weighty.

McTaggart would in all likelihood have replied that we have not sufficient ground for preferring Dr. Ewing's hypothesis to the view that the occurrences in question, among which no intrinsic determinations are perceptible, are all due to chance. Can we really be sure, have we even sufficient justification for dismissing as improbable, the suggestion that the so-called natural laws are in the nature of runs of luck? As he puts it, "If I cast a die ten times and throw a six each time, I should have little doubt that it had been loaded. But if I cast it sixty million times, and got only one run of ten sixes, I should find no difficulty in supposing that it came by chance." [31]

Dr. Ewing might well reply that for this alternative hypothesis to acquire any plausibility we should have to be in a position to know that the laws of nature had begun to function only at a definite moment in the past, and that for a very long period before this moment

30. See *Some Dogmas of Religion,* sec. 15.
31. *Ibid.,* sec. 201.

they had not functioned at all.[32] It seems quite possible that the world as we know it came into existence through something in the nature of a primal explosion such as certain scientists have posited, and even if we feel compelled to assume that this was not an ultimate beginning, and that before it there must have been a world of some sort, it is conceivable that the laws of such a universe were different from those of ours. But the assumption that the natural laws with which we are familiar have not always functioned within this present world is, I think, much less plausible than Dr. Ewing's hypothesis. While it is true that we cannot by inspection discover in nature the presence of intrinsic determinations, nevertheless, if we are obliged to choose between positing unperceived intrinsic determinations or ascribing all regularity of sequence to chance, the former alternative will clearly put less strain upon our credulity.

With regard to enumerative induction, however, and to our igno-

32. It may be remarked that there is a similarity between Dr. Ewing's argument and the argument advanced by McTaggart in *Some Dogmas of Religion* (sec. 200) to show that, on the supposition that matter exists, it is reasonable to posit the existence of a divine intelligence to account for "the traces of order directed towards good" which are discoverable in the universe, for such a cause will at once explain the order, whereas the undirected motions of material particles might just as well have been productive of an indefinite number of other arrangements incompatible with it. It is also true, McTaggart points out, that various other arrangements of matter could have been equally productive of an order directed toward good, and so

the greater improbability of the hypothesis which excludes a directing mind is not to be expressed, as is sometimes maintained, by the proportion of a large number to unity, but of one large number to another. But the number of arrangements which would show some traces of such an order is very small as compared with the total number of arrangements of which undirected matter is capable. And thus the argument, if not as strong as has been sometimes supposed, retains considerable strength.

McTaggart next brings in the illustration of the die cited above, and observes that "it is possible that all the traces of order in the universe are in the position of the run of ten sixes among sixty million throws." He concedes, however, that "the improbability that the traces of order should be due to chance is thus lessened, but it is not removed. For the existence of vast areas of reality in which no trace of order is to be observed, while certainly possible, is not more than possible." His conclusion, then, is, as already stated, that the argument has some force, and does show that for one who believes in matter the hypothesis of the existence of a divine mind is to be preferred to the alternative hypothesis that all traces of order are due to chance. That he does not himself accept it is due to the fact that he sees no justification for the belief in matter. But the interesting fact is that we find McTaggart, like Dr. Ewing, arguing on the basis of such an assumption from the existence of an observed order to a cause of such a nature as to account for it. And we must concede, I think, that each argument has weight.

rance of the proportion obtaining between the field of inference and the field of observation, the truth of what McTaggart urges must surely be conceded. How the portion of the universe known to us stands to the portion which is unknown is something of which we have no knowledge. With what face, then, can we pretend to make any inferences a posteriori from the nature of the one to that of the other? Before the discovery of Australia all swans were presumed to be white. That they should be so seemed a law of nature, yet experience itself has given the lie to the generalization based upon it. The fundamental laws of nature, it may be said, must hold good everywhere. Were they the product of a priori knowledge with its characteristics of universality and necessity, yes; but this is precisely what they are not. If we take seriously the theistic hypothesis—and it is plainly one which, pending future examination, deserves to be taken seriously—we must hold that natural laws are what they are because the divine intelligence has so decreed. But how can we venture to assume that it has decreed that they shall be the same everywhere? How do we know that the Deity has not seen fit to establish various and very dissimilar systems of legislation in different parts of the universe, much as the Code Napoleon, which is in force in Louisiana, differs from the Anglo-Saxon law of Alabama? In view of these considerations we must, I think, concede the soundness of McTaggart's contention that if we are to know anything definite with regard to the structure of the universe as a whole, we must proceed by the a priori method—at least until we have succeeded in so delimiting the field of inference that we can form some notion of how it stands with respect to the field of observation.

The objection, however, will at once be raised that this will involve the admission of synthetic a priori propositions, and that the admission is under the ban of popular disapproval. With this objection we can deal as McTaggart dealt with the affirmation of the skeptic. That there are no synthetic a priori propositions is not itself an a posteriori proposition; for if it were, it could be based only upon an enumerative induction founded upon an examination of all propositions affirmed, doubted, denied, thought of, or unthought of. Obviously no finite mind could conceivably complete such an induction. The proposition in question is not about propositions but about characteristics; it asserts that nothing can have the characteristic of being a proposition and also the characteristics of being synthetic and a priori. But, although it is not about itself, it applies to itself; for it is a proposition, and it clearly claims to be synthetic and a priori. It is therefore self-contradictory, and can be dismissed as such.

The a priori method has traditionally been associated with the great rationalistic systems of the past. To what extent and in what respect are we justified in regarding the universe as rational? What do we mean by a rational universe? These are questions which demand a preliminary investigation before we proceed further.

Chapter Four

THE NOTION OF A
RATIONAL UNIVERSE

What do we mean by a "rational universe"? We must answer this question before we raise the question whether the universe may be irrational, for the negative can be defined only in terms of the positive. Rationality, we may say, involves law and order, yet it clearly involves more than this; for we may encounter order which we must recognize but cannot account for, and law which seems to us as arbitrary as decrees imposed by the whim of an irresponsible sultan. Rationality, we may further suggest, involves intelligibility; yet, in saying this, have we done more than substitute one synonym for another? Perhaps we have; for we might urge that the two words are not completely synonymous, and that "intelligibility" emphasizes more forcefully the intellectual transparency of that which is apprehended. Thus in the realm of the a priori we encounter universality and necessity. An a priori principle holds good always and everywhere; its application is not restricted by the limitations of our experience; we see that it must be what it is, and that it could not be otherwise. Yet this is not the only sense in which we may meaningfully speak of intellectual transparency; we may fittingly use the same phrase when we contemplate an action motivated by conscious volition which is directed toward an end worthy of approval, and which employs the most efficient means for the realization thereof.

Could a universe in which we discovered regularity of sequence be pronounced rational? Before assenting to this suggestion we should require to be assured that the regularity of sequence was grounded in, and expressive of, the nature of the universe; for, clearly, a regularity that was fortuitous would be in the nature of a run of luck and would be the offspring of chance, than which nothing could be more completely devoid of rationality.

Are we to think of the rational, then, as expressive of the nature of mind? Would a rational universe be a universe which derived from mind, if not its being, at least its order and structure? As soon as this question is asked we think of Kant and his Copernican step. And we remember that he was driven to taking this step by the difficulties he encountered, and by the contradictions into which he believed himself to have been led, as a result of proceeding upon the assumption that the external world possesses in itself a rational structure which the apprehending mind is able, as it were, to "read off." This subjectification of rationality, as we may well call it, is therefore in a sense a counsel of despair. It is plainly something in which we ought not to acquiesce until we have become as assured as was Kant that no other course is possible. And at the present stage of our inquiry, we have attained to no such assurance. We have merely to recognize that Kant's position is one to which we may conceivably be driven hereafter.

On Kant's view every mind makes its own world in the sense that it orders the data provided for it by sense experience in accordance with the forms of space and time under which it perceives them and which are subjective in character, and imposes upon them the categories which are psychologically rooted in its own nature and in terms of which it is compelled to think them. The similarity of our worlds is due to the common nature which all human minds possess. It is true that for Kant this world-making is also in part due to a common stimulus imparted by the things-in-themselves which we cannot directly apprehend. But this feature of Kant's system, which aroused such widespread dissatisfaction, does not seem to be logically required. Since the similarity of our worlds is due to the common human nature which we all share, the stimulus to form these worlds might be attributed exclusively to the same source; and the subjectification of reason would thus reach its culmination in a subjective, pluralistic, personalistic idealism. As a matter of fact such a view appears to have been developed without reference to Kant by the Hosso sect of Japanese Buddhism. All that was needed was to individuate the *Ālaya vijñāna* or repository consciousness of the Yogācāra school of idealism which derives from Asaṅga and Vasubandhu. According to the Hosso doctrine each mind thinks or dreams its own world, and these worlds are in some respects similar and in other respects dissimilar, the similarity being due to the common nature of the thinkers or dreamers, and the dissimilarities to their respective individualities. This doctrine, which might be termed an atheistic Berkeleyanism, wild as it doubtless appears to those temperamentally unsympathetic with its fundamental outlook, cannot be dismissed by the fair-minded thinker as obviously absurd, and ought to be recognized by us as a view deserving of serious consideration.

Reverting for a moment to a scrutiny of Kant's position, we may observe that it is confronted by what appears, at first sight at least, to be a very serious difficulty, and one which would seem to be very hard to deal with upon his own principles. If the individual mind order its own experience by imposing upon it the forms of space and time and the categories, it is certainly possessed of a terrific potency. Yet this potency is rooted in what we can only call its own sub-conscious nature, and it expresses itself with entire disregard of the desires and volitions of the conscious mind. If we make our own worlds, we cannot make them as we wish them to be. If a man so order his experience as to shut himself up in a dungeon, he cannot get out of it by altering his spatio-temporal forms of perception, or by rearranging his imposition of the categories. Nor could we deliver him by sending a psychoanalyst to help him to put his mental house in order. The only way to get him out is to unlock the door. If we can so influence other persons' experiences as to enchain and imprison them, causal efficacy must relate self to self, and not merely interrelate the data of the individual self.

Turning now to a different and yet related topic we note that Kant maintains that we are justified, on the basis of moral postulates which we find ourselves impelled to make, in believing, or at least in assuming, that there is an order in the external world which is imposed by a divine Mind. In his almost gleeful remark that he has "removed knowlege to make room for faith" we should probably be right in recognizing the persistent influence of the pietism in which Kant was reared. In this emphasis upon "the primacy of faith" [1] as opposed to reason, not only in the moral and religious life, but also in the realm of constructive speculation, we have found the most fundamental of all the differences which sunder a Protestant of the traditional type from the Roman Catholic. Yet the Kantian faith has lost an element of intuitive and mystical insight which is characteristic of the Protestant conception. There is no hint of the *testimonium Spiritus Sancti internum*. Rather does it tend to approximate to the volitional attitude, "the assent of the intellect at the command of the will," which constitutes the act of faith for the Roman Catholic. Enough has been said on this topic in our previous discussion of faith and reason, but it is important to recognize that upon this very shaky foundation rests all justification for holding that the Kantian universe is rational *in se*.

The great post-Kantian systems of objective idealism sought to vindicate the rationality of the universe by positing an Absolute Mind

1. I quote the title of one of Professor Richard Kroner's recent books.

as the only ultimate reality. Rejecting the notion of the thing-in-itself, they envisaged a universe the categorial structure of which is imposed upon it by this Absolute Mind, of which the world is only the manifestation, and in which our finite minds are included. The objectivity of the rational is thus reasserted with resounding emphasis; the external world is intelligible because it is the expression of Intelligence. And yet, in a sense, the subjectivity of the rational is also sustained, for it is its own nature which the finite mind finds reflected in the world it beholds. But the finite mind is not the fashioner of this world; it is merely its beholder. The Absolute, which is beyond the distinction between subject and object, and which manifests itself in both, is at once within and without.

Still, the objective idealist must acknowledge that even if the universe be wholly rational *in se,* it is not so *quoad nos.* No one has affirmed this more explicitly and emphatically than that convinced rationalist, McTaggart, who writes,

> It is certain that the universe is not completely rational for us. We are not able to see everything around us as a manifestation of the Absolute Idea. Even those students of philosophy who believe on general grounds that the Absolute Idea must be manifested in everything are as unable as the rest of us to see *how* it is manifested in a table or a thunder-storm. We can only explain these things—at present, at any rate—by much lower categories, and we cannot, therefore, explain them completely. Nor are we by any means able, at present, to eliminate completely the contingency of the *data* of sense, which are an essential element in reality, and a universe which contains an ultimately contingent element cannot be held to be completely rational. It would seem, too, that if we are perfectly rational in a perfectly rational universe, there must always be a complete harmony between our desires and our environment. And this is not invariably the case.[2]

The absolute idealist will of course maintain that by a process of pure thought he is able to lay bare in its broad outlines the general structure of reality, but must confess that he is unable to show in detail how the data of experience are subsumed under this general structure. This is by no means a damning confession. It would, indeed, be marvellous were he able to accomplish more than this. That he has serious difficulties to surmount if he is to make his contention good is obvious. But we need not follow him further in his endeavor, for

2. *Studies in Hegelian Dialectic* (New York, 1922), sec. 150.

we are now engaged only in a preliminary survey of the various answers which have been given to our question, What is meant by the assertion that the universe is rational?

It is worth while remarking, however, that whereas for Kant it is the rational structure of the finite mind which is the source of the rationality which is present in the world of its experience, for absolute idealism the rational structure of the universe is derivative from the Absolute Mind. And it is the finitude and imperfection of our individual minds that are responsible for the seeming irrationality of our quotidian experience.

Let us turn to a different philosophical tradition, that which has its origin in Plato. Doubtless we should seek there in vain for a single answer to our question, and such replies as are given are qualified answers which would not completely satisfy the thoroughgoing rationalist, at least not without further elaboration. For in Plato's universe the irrational is always present to some extent and in some degree, and this presence is left unresolved, nor is there any hint that it can be dealt with as mere appearance.

In Plato's middle period the rational world is the changeless world of the Forms. Below it lies the realm of soul, where we find both permanence and change, and below this again the world of sense where we have only becoming. These three worlds appear to be irreducibly distinct from one another, although interconnected, and soul occupies a rather awkward position between the world above and the world below. It is capable of ascending to a vision of the intelligible structure of the realm of Forms, and is thus potentially rational; yet it may also become drunken [3] and immerse itself in the world of sense. These two lower worlds are made up of particulars, and the characteristics of these particulars are due to their participation in the Forms—whether such participation be conceived of as imitative, or as constituting a unique and unanalyzable type of relation. Such rationality as the two lower worlds possess is thus owing to this participation in the Forms.

In the *Phaedo* and the *Phaedrus* souls are clearly conceived of as sempiternal; there can be no question, therefore, of their being derived from the Forms. Moreover their number is said to be finite, and no reason is given why the number should not be greater or less. Each soul, therefore, in a sense is to be regarded as a "brute fact." Its nature

---

3. According to the *Phaedrus* the souls of the gods are, indeed, secure from the danger of falling, and enjoy a constant, or constantly recurring vision of the Forms, and it is this clear vision which renders them divine.

is, indeed, derived from the Forms in which it participates, and without a nature it could not exist; yet the principle of individuation which makes it a particular does not appear to be supplied by the Forms, and the same holds true of sensible particulars. Whether Plato would have subscribed to the view that the particular is individuated by its nature, or would have welcomed Leibniz' theory of the identity of indiscernibles, we cannot tell; but, however this may be, he bequeathed to subsequent philosophers a knotty problem—that of the individuation of particulars.

In his later period Plato suggests, or at least seems to suggest, that the plurality of sensible particulars is the result of the reflection of the Forms into space. And he also ascribes the origin of souls to their direct or indirect derivation from the Deity. It is, indeed, difficult to determine whether Plato intends the language of the *Timaeus* to be taken literally. The opinion of the majority of scholars appears to be that he did not so intend, and that we find in Plato no genuine doctrine of creation, although perhaps we do find the basis of a theory of emanation.

In the *Timaeus* the irrational principle is the spontaneous and undirected motion pervading space; in the *Laws* it is identified with evil soul, but whether this means that Plato was prepared to adopt from Zoroastrianism the notion of a demonic being engaged in perpetual warfare with the "best soul" (i.e., God), or that he referred to the freedom of all individual and finite souls to choose evil rather than good, is a question upon which commentators have disagreed.

Plato, however, has presented us with two distinct and fruitful ideas which have been developed by subsequent thinkers. On the one hand, by bringing the Forms down from heaven and giving them the function of inhering in and characterizing particulars, it might be possible to show that the universe constitutes an ordered system of which the parts are interconnected by internal relations, a system existing in its own right and which can therefore be equated with ultimate reality. Could this be accomplished, rationality would once more be objectified; far from being the source of this rational structure, mind would be rational through its possession of the capacity to apprehend this structure. And this idea is susceptible of further development. We are sometimes told that the basic contention of absolute idealism is that values occupy a dominant position in the universe. To establish this it is clearly not enough to show that values are objectively real; for they might be so and yet not be dominant, as in the philosophy of Nicolai Hartmann, for whom the *existent* world of values and the *real* world of particulars are mutually independent although over-lapping. What would be requisite would be to show that values occupy, as it were, the central position in the universe, that it is ordered with respect to them, or, to employ a somewhat pompous phrase, that it is axiologically oriented. Could this be done, the universe could be pronounced both "rational and righteous," to use one of the idealistic watchwords. And since rationality and righteousness can be shown to imply each other, the rationality of the universe would be vindicated as fully as one could reasonably desire.

On the other hand we may take seriously the notion of a supreme and ordering Mind which Plato has offered us, and which had been developed before him by Zoroaster and the prophets of Israel. The universe will, then, be rational in the sense that it is expressive of purpose, and of a wise and good purpose. This view requires carefully to be distinguished from the second of the positions outlined above, namely, that of a typical absolute idealism. In the idealist view the universe is not something external to the Absolute Mind; it evolves within it, and all finite beings are contained within the divine consciousness. According to the theory we are now considering, the universe is distinct from the divine Mind which controls its development, and is relatively passive with respect thereto. It stands to the design imposed upon it as Aristotelian matter stands in relation to form.

This gives rise to the question, Has the universe a rational structure of its own distinct from that imposed upon it by the Deity? If not, all the laws to which it is subject are dependent upon the divine volition, and may conceivably be annulled thereby. But we have seen that we cannot, without contradicting ourselves, deny that the "laws of thought" are laws of being; these laws therefore must be independent of all volition, and have being in their own right. Hence, on the theistic hypothesis, the universe must be rational in a twofold sense; it must be rational partly *in se,* and partly *ab alio.* It will possess in itself a structure which is logically rational, and in addition there will be imposed upon it an order which is axiologically rational; for we may, surely, assume that the purpose of the divine Mind will be the instantiation of values. This leaves us with a fundamental and rather awkward dualism—that between the Deity and the world upon which he acts; and unless this dualism can be resolved, and some intrinsic relation between God and the world be discovered, the demands of rationalism will not be satisfied.

It has been suggested that the Deity should be viewed as standing to the world in a relation similar to that in which the human soul stands to its body; but if this be taken as ultimate, it will be in the nature of a "brute fact" which, although ultimate, is unintelligible; and so the universe will not be fundamentally rational. If, on the other hand, the relation be derivative, we must seek the source whence it is derived.

The doctrine of creation is sometimes advanced as a stopgap to fill this ontological breach. If all finite entities, it is urged, be produced by a divine fiat, the universe and its entire structure will be the result of divine volition, and its rationality will thereby be established. Having just recognized the inconceivability of all cosmic laws being the product of volition, we must pronounce this claim exaggerated. Yet it might be contended that the doctrine of creation will fully account for the existence of particulars, and that the acceptance of it will therefore give us a universe which, while only partly rational *in se* and only partly rational *ab alio,* is nevertheless *wholly* rational.

In commenting upon this suggestion I would first point out that if we have been right in concluding that the sempiternity of all selves has been fully established, there will be a vast number of particulars which the doctrine of creation will not be required to account for. And in the second place, I would ask if the notion of creation be itself intelligible. The answer usually given is that while it is not, and could not be expected to be, rational *quoad nos,* inasmuch as we are creatures and therefore capable of viewing it only from the standpoint of the created, it is, nonetheless, perfectly rational *in se,* and in the divine perspective. But does this help us very much? If the notion of creation be unintelligible to us, it is not, so far as we are concerned, a bona fide notion at all. What justification have we, then, for introducing it into philosophy where clarity and intelligibility are the primary requirements? It is plain that our only justification for so doing must be the authority of revelation.

To embark upon an examination of the authority of revelation before we have even considered the question of divine existence would obviously be a putting of the cart before the horse. Our present concern is solely with the notion of rationality. We have already seen, however, that the concept of revelation is in itself thoroughly rational. And it might be maintained that, were revelation once admitted to be a fact, there would be nothing incredible in the supposition that we might be certified by revelation *that* a certain doctrine is true, even though we are unable to understand *how* it is true. And by way of illustration it might be added that we often have to tell children *that* a certain state of affairs obtains, although we know that they cannot understand *how* this can be so. In comparison with the divine Mind, it might be urged, all finite minds are intellectual infants, and are entitled to ask nothing better than to be treated as such.

We cannot, I believe, usefully carry this discussion further at this point, for it would raise various problems which we are not yet in a position to examine. Doubtless it would be some satisfaction could we find justification for *believing* that the universe is rational, even were we unable to *see* that it is so. Nevertheless, a heavy burden of proof lies upon the champion of the doctrine of creation, and with this reflection we may temporarily dismiss the topic.

For the moment we may well be content to terminate our discussion at this point, inasmuch as our present business is not to prove or disprove any particular theory but only to review the various conceptions of a rational universe which have been advanced, and to estimate their degree of self-consistency and coherence. We may, however, observe that the notion of purpose, which is of course a perfectly rational one, is the cornerstone of theism; and this may suggest to us that, although the theistic hypothesis does not of itself suffice to provide a rational explanation of the entire structure of the cosmos, it may nevertheless conceivably be included within, and furnish a valuable contribution to, a more comprehensive world view.

Having thus surveyed the various senses in which the universe has been thought to be rational, we are now in a position to discuss the question how we are to understand the assertion that the universe is irrational. In view of what has been said it is clear that the universe will be irrational *in se* if it be an utter chaos, if it do not constitute a system of which the parts are subtended by internal relations, or if it fail to be axiologically oriented. To talk of the universe being irrational *ab alio* would sound absurd, since it would seem to imply that the universe was prevented from being rational by some external agency. But we may say that it is *not* rational *ab alio* if it be not ordered by a supreme Mind external to it, and in accordance with a wise and good purpose.

It also seems clear that there are degrees of conceivable irrationality. Thus a universe which included within itself various ordered systems, even were these not integrated in a single, all-inclusive system, would be less irrational than a universe devoid of every systemic feature, and which was nothing but chaos. Again, a universe which was expressive of no cosmic design would be less irrational than one which was ordered in terms of some diabolic purpose. And a universe which contained no values would be less irrational than one in which dis-values occupied a predominant position, and which was oriented with respect to them.

With these various meanings of the terms "rationalism" and "irrationalism" clearly in mind, let us now proceed to a detailed examination of the claims of rationalism.

Chapter Five

THE CLAIMS OF RATIONALISM

Is there any ground for assuming at the outset of our inquiry that the universe is rational in one or more of the senses which we have distinguished in the previous chapter? In raising this question we should be quite clear about what we are doing. Heretofore we have endeavored carefully to avoid all presuppositions, all premature and ungrounded commitments whatever. We have accepted nothing which did not pass the test of the Cartesian method of doubt; we have recognized as indubitable only the immediate data of introspection and sensation, self-evident propositions, and conclusions deduced therefrom. Upon all other issues which we have considered we have abstained from definite commitment. As we have begun, it may be urged, so we should continue. Any assumption of whatever kind is to be rejected as a base concession to wishful thinking. However much we may desire the universe to be rational, we must not even hint that it is so until we can prove it.

With a rigorism such as this every honest man must sympathize. But we must also allow for the possibility that a preliminary scrutiny of the characteristics of rationalism and those of opposing views may constitute the first step in the development of a proof. Any conclusion reached from so general a comparison will of necessity be tentative; yet it need not be groundless. If it be the result of an impartial weighing of antithetic opinions, it has every right to a respectful considera- tion. And further investigation may either confirm or discredit it. If, however, preliminary inspection prove suggestive of a view which subsequent argument supports, and which better than any other can stand the test of doubt, our thinking will have developed in a coherent manner, each link of the chain being sustained alike by its predecessor and by its successor. In all this there will have been no trifling with baseless suppositions nor any compromise with wishful thinking.

We have accepted a definition of religion in terms of a harmony between what is highest in human nature and the universe as a whole; surely we need not argue in defense of the judgment that what is highest in our nature is the rational element, if this be understood in the broad sense as inclusive of emotion and volition. A universe which was rational both *in se* and *quoad nos* would be one the general structure of which we could, to some extent at least, understand, which satisfied our highest emotions, and in the nature of which we could acquiesce. Now harmony, as we have seen, admits of degrees. It might seem, then, that a universe which was through and through transparent to our intellects, in which our highest emotions were always completely satisfied, in which no unworthy desires were ever entertained, and in which no worthy desires were ever frustrated, would be one with which we were in perfect harmony and which was indisputably rational. But it is quite indisputable that such is not the kind of universe we inhabit. That there is evil in our universe is a fact of which we are repeatedly and frequently assured, and that often in a manner which is unpleasantly emphatic. It may, of course, be the case, as certain idealistic philosophers have contended, that the evil which is present is essential to the realization of a greater good, and that it is somehow counterbalanced, overcome, or negated in the Absolute; but obviously we have no right, at the very threshold of our inquiry, to make any such assumption.

It may be, then, that the whole religious enterprise which posits and seeks to establish a fundamental harmony is in the nature of a wild goose chase or the search for the pot of gold at the rainbow's end, that the disharmony may prove to be more fundamental than the harmony, and that we may have to abandon our undertaking in a state of disillusionment. But, once more, it would be absurd to begin by making such a supposition. What we must do is to examine more closely the rival views. Experience assures that there are not only disorder and evil but also order and goodness in the universe. It is clear, therefore, that if the universe be basically irrational, it is so in such a way as to include rationality in some of its parts; and that if it be basically rational, it is so in such a way as to include irrationality in some of its parts. Is there any way of determining whether one of these alternative views is more acceptable than the other?

So far as I am aware, the philosopher who has dealt most thoroughly with this subject is McTaggart. In the fifth chapter of his *Studies in Hegelian Dialectic* (secs. 160–167) he examines three hypotheses: (1) that the universe is fundamentally irrational, (2) that it is "the product of two independent principles of rationality and irrationality," and (3) that it is "the work of some principle to which rationality and irrationality are equally indifferent—some blind fate, or mechanical chance." And he informs us that he will "use 'irrational' here to

signify anything whose nature and operation are not merely devoid
of reason but opposed to it, so that its influence is always in the opposite direction to that exercised by reason." [1]

As we might anticipate, McTaggart has little difficulty with the
first hypothesis. Pointing to the indubitable evidences of the presence
of some rationality in the universe, he observes that it is as inconceivable that what is fundamentally irrational should manifest itself as
rationality as that the fundamentally rational should manifest itself as
irrationality. And he also remarks that "the completely irrational cannot be real, for even to say that a thing is real implies its determination by at least one predicate, and therefore its comparative
rationality." [2] This last statement implies that reality is a predicate—a
view which, whether sound or not, would certainly be rejected by many
thinkers. Without going into this moot question, however, we may
bring out what is the substance of his contention in another way. We
have only to revert once more to Joseph's dictum that we cannot
without self-contradiction deny that the laws of thought are laws of
being to grasp the fact that whatever is real is rational in the sense
that these laws apply to it.

That the universe is to some extent and to some degree rational is,
then, an inescapable conclusion. The crucial question is whether it be
wholly so, or whether it be also to some extent and in some degree
irrational. Is it possible to permit the rationalistic camel to put his
nose under the edge of the cosmic tent and yet to prevent him from
at last walking away with the entire tent? There does seem to be
something rather strange, we may admit, in asking the intellect to
show us that the universe is not completely rational. By so doing we
implicitly assume that the standards to which the intellect appeals
are to some extent subjective, and as such alien to the external world;
that the mind fashions its own ideals and then blames the universe
for refusing to acknowledge them. If we thus posit an axiological gap
between mind and nature, do we not degrade mind from the status of
being a mirror of reality, and regard it rather as a sort of cosmic fungus?
And in denying to mind a cosmic grounding, do we not thereby in-
sinuate that reason is itself irrational?

It is clear, at least, that the opponent of rationalism must not concede too much to the principle of irrationality, lest he make it
fundamental and so fall back upon the first hypothesis and become
confronted with all its incredibilities; neither dare he concede too

1. *Studies in Hegelian Dialectic*, sec. 160.
2. *Ibid.*, sec. 161.

much to the principle of rationality, for fear of acknowledging its pre-dominance and thus subscribing to the very doctrine he wishes to contest. He must balance himself, as it were, upon an intellectual tight-rope, inclining neither to one side nor to the other, but maintaining an attitude of rigid perpendicularity under threat of immediate and ir-redeemable disaster. Thus he must not assume that the universe con-tains certain restricted areas in which the rational principle holds sway—islands of rationality, so to speak—yet that these are sundered from one another by a sea of irrationality; for, on this supposition, the universe as a whole would be irrational, and the rationality of certain of its parts would be in the nature of an inexplicable freak—thus he would have reverted to the first hypothesis. Nor may he concede, on the other hand, that the universe as a whole is rational without giving away his entire case. He may contend, if he please, for the irrationality of some of the parts, or constituents, of the universe, but in so doing he will "fight as one that beateth the air"; for who will venture, or even desire, to take the field against him? Any rationalist who should make bold to assert that evil and irrationality are purely illusory would have to explain away the fact that the illusion itself was evil and irrational. In acknowledging the presence of evil and irra-tionality in the universe the majority of philosophers would certainly concur. All that the sober rationalist maintains is that such evil and irrationality are not incompatible with the goodness and rationality of the whole; and if his opponent be prepared to concede so much, the controversy is at an end.

The notion, therefore, of restricted areas in which either rationality or irrationality is dominant, clearly will not stand. We see, then, why McTaggart considers that if the second hypothesis is to be defended, the principles of rationality and irrationality must be assumed to be not only mutually independent but everywhere operative. As he puts it, "both forces are regarded as all-pervading. neither can exist by itself anywhere. every fact in the universe is due to the interaction of the two." [3] Moreover, one of these principles, that of irrationality, can be defined and described only in relation to its opposite; for it is essentially negative, whereas rationality is essentially positive. [4] The

---

3. *Ibid.*, sec. 162.

4. McTaggart momentarily obscures the development of his argument by assert-ing that the two principles "can only be described and defined in relation to one another." It is clear that we cannot define A in terms of B and then define B in terms of A. But he at once proceeds to assume that we know what rationality is, and that the irrational must be defined in relation to it.

clear implication, then, is that rationality is the more fundamental of the two.

"We cannot, besides," continues McTaggart,

> describe anything as irrational, or as indifferent to reason, without ascribing to it certain predicates—Being, Substance, Limitation, for example. Nor can we refer to a principle as an explanation of the universe without attributing to it Causality. These determinations may be transcended by higher ones, but they must be there, at least as moments. Yet anything to which all these predicates can be ascribed cannot be said to be entirely hostile or indifferent to reason, for it has some determinations common to it and to reason, and must be, therefore, in more or less harmony with the latter. But if this is so, our complete dualism has been surrendered.[5]

In other words, the difficulties which impressed us as insuperable in connection with the first hypothesis are now seen to be reasserting themselves as we endeavor to sustain the independence of the second principle involved in the second hypothesis. Even if we disregard these, however, it appears very doubtful, contends McTaggart, whether the hypothesis will stand. For the two antagonistic principles will either be in a state of equilibrium or else they will not. If one of the two principles be gaining upon the other, the universe, he submits, is "fundamentally a process." Should this be thought too strong an assertion, it must, surely, be agreed that the universe is involved in process. "The process," continues McTaggart,

> must be finite in length, since we can attach no meaning to an actual infinite process. And, since it is still continuing, we shall have to suppose that the two principles came into operation at a given moment and not before. And, since these principles are, on the hypothesis, ultimate, there can be nothing to determine them to begin to act at that point rather than any other. In this way we shall be reduced to suppose an event to happen in time without antecedents and without cause—a solution which cannot be accepted as satisfactory.[6]

Even should we demur to the notion of an absolute beginning, and insist upon positing a beginningless process, we still shall not escape from our predicament. For in this case, one of the two opposing forces should long ago have established its absolute supremacy and should

5. *Studies in Hegelian Dialectic*, sec. 162.   6. *Ibid.*, sec. 163.

have eliminated its rival. If the struggle have always been going on, this can only be because the two powers are fundamentally equal, so that the gain of either can be but transitory. We are thus led to the second alternative—that of basic equilibrium. This is, however, an extremely hazardous hypothesis, as McTaggart proceeds to point out. "In the first place," he observes,

> we should have to admit that the odds against this occurring were infinity to one. For the two forces are, by the hypothesis, absolutely independent of one another. And, therefore, we cannot suppose any common influence acting on both of them, which should tend to make their forces equal, nor any relationship between them, which should bring about this result. The equilibrium could only be the result of mere chance, and the probability of this producing infinitely exact equilibrium would be infinitely small. And the absence of any *a priori* reason for believing in such an equilibrium could not, of course, be supplied by empirical observation. For the equilibrium would have to extend over the whole universe, and we cannot carry our observations so far.[7]

In the second place, the hypothesis, far from being confirmed by the course of events, appears rather to be incompatible with it. What we observe is not a constant balance of good and evil but progress and regress; we see a worse state followed by a better, or a better by a worse. "Of course we cannot prove," concedes McTaggart,

> that the balance between the two forces does not remain the same, if we consider the whole universe. Every movement in the one direction, in one part of the whole, *may* be balanced by a corresponding move in the other direction somewhere else. As we do not know the entire universe in detail it is impossible for us to refute this supposition. But even this supposition will not remove the difficulty. We have two principles whose relations to one another are constant. Yet the facts around us, which are manifestations of these two principles, and of these two principles only, manifest them in proportions which constantly change. How is this change to be accounted for?[8]

We turn, then, to the remaining hypothesis, "that the world is exclusively the product of a principle which regards neither rationality nor irrationality, but is directed to some aim outside them, or to no aim at all." "Such a theory," McTaggart remarks,

7. *Ibid.*, sec. 164.   8. *Ibid.*

might account, no doubt, for the fact that the world is not a complete and perfect manifestation either of rationality or irrationality. But it is hardly exaggerated to say that this is the only fact about the world which it would account for. The idea of such a principle is contradictory. We can have no conception of its operation, of its nature, or even of its existence, without bringing it under some predicate of the reason. And, if this is valid, the principle is, to some extent at least, rational.[9]

However great, then, may be the difficulties which confront us when we attempt to conceive of the universe as rational, we find ourselves faced with others which are, at the very least, equally serious when we try to think of it as irrational. Yet these considerations, although weighty, are of general import. It may help us, therefore, if we envisage a hypothesis of a more definite and concrete character. If the universe be in part rational and in part irrational, it is plain that the only defensible philosophical position will be some sort of absolute dualism. And the type of dualism which a retrospective glance at the history of philosophy will most forcefully suggest to us will be that of mind and matter. It is not easy, indeed, to formulate such a theory in view of recent developments of physical science; for matter shows an alarming tendency to transform itself into energy, and the notion of energy is certainly an enigmatical one. To give it definiteness we seem forced to interpret it in terms of spirit, and any such interpretation will be fatal to absolute dualism. Let us assume, however, that there are non-mental entities having extension and shape, and that the two kinds of reality—mental and non-mental—are underived, mutually independent, and everlasting. The coexistence of these two kinds of entities will, then, be in the nature of a "brute fact," of which, in view of its ultimacy, no explanation can be given. The universe, accordingly, will be to this extent irrational. Our present concern is not to work out the hypothesis in detail but to ask the fundamental question, Is it tenable?

Are we, or are we not, to admit interaction between these two very disparate kinds of entities? Conscious beings certainly appear to be perpetually stimulated by, and constantly engaged in ordering, sensible objects. Hence, if we admit interaction, and if, in addition, we accept the entailment theory of causality, we shall have to hold that between entities belonging to the two realms there are intrinsic relations, relations which are internal in the fullest sense of the word; and this will

9. *Ibid.*, sec. 165.

clearly involve the admission that the two realms are not mutually independent but included within a larger and systematically ordered whole. And this admission will be fatal to our absolute dualism. We shall be compelled, therefore, to resort to the activity theory of causality in its extreme and uncompromising form.

We have seen, however, that the activity theory will commit us either to theism or to panpsychism. But might we not opt for panpsychism and yet succeed in holding to an absolute dualism? We should have to concede that all activity is psychic in nature and origin, but could we not still maintain that sense data are underived, self-existent, everlasting entities, inactive and impassible? Could we not also assert with some plausibility that cognition is non-causal, and so maintain the complete mutual independence of the mental and the non-mental?

Even could we accomplish all this successfully, our difficulties would not have been entirely eliminated. For we should have to deal with the question of values, and to inquire whether their objective reality is to be recognized. Could we demolish the theory of the objectivity of values, they would, indeed, give us no further trouble; but it is highly doubtful whether this be feasible. And should we decide that it is not feasible, we should be faced with the fact that value is present in both realms. Beauty, for instance, is undeniably present in the sense world; and moral goodness is certainly to be found in the mental world. Value thus leaps the chasm between our two realms; can they, then, be mutually and wholly independent? Must we not, on the contrary, assume that they fall within a single, all-inclusive system? Since we shall have to return to this issue later I shall not pursue it further, but merely indicate that it raises a serious difficulty for the absolute dualist.

There is, moreover, another fact, one to which we have already so often had occasion to call attention, namely, that the laws of thought are laws of being both for the mental and the non-mental worlds. It is equally true of a self and of a stone that it cannot both have a characteristic and not have it. Furthermore, such categories as Quality and Relation are predicable both of the mental and the non-mental. Clearly, therefore, the universe possesses a basic ontological constitution to which both realms owe allegiance; and the recognition of this fact is incompatible with adherence to absolute dualism.

Is there any other ground upon which the claims of rationalism could be contested? In connection with the theistic hypothesis we found it necessary to distinguish between the view that the universe is rational *in se* and the view that it is rational *ab alio*. Is it possible that this distinction might offer a last refuge to the opponent of rationalism? What if he were to concede that the universe does possess *in se* an ontological structure, but nevertheless to maintain that such axiological and teleological order as it displays is *ab alio*? And what if he were to say the same of axiological and teleological disorder? What if he were to have recourse to the notion of an evil soul, a conscious yet diabolic cosmic Mind, engaged in ceaseless conflict with the Good? What if he were to posit a supreme, but morally evil, Intelligence?

Such a suggestion, it may be objected, is too wild to be taken seriously. Perhaps it is. Yet we have the right to ask upon what grounds it is to be so indicted. May it not be that the native optimism which is so characteristic of the human outlook, and which provides so powerful an impetus to the struggle for survival, together with our natural unwillingness to entertain so gloomy a hypothesis, blinds us to its plausibility? If we can show that it is in truth fantastically improbable, we shall have made it plain that the last refuge of the opponent of rationalism is one to which no reasonable man would resort. But inasmuch as our object is to give a fair hearing to the anti-rationalist, we must consider it impartially.

His hypothesis can be presented in two forms, a weaker and a stronger. The weaker form envisages two opposing powers, one good and one evil; the stronger envisages only a supreme evil power. And of the two the stronger is, I think, the more plausible. For if we posit a cosmic conflict, although we may not unreasonably suppose that the fortunes of battle might fluctuate throughout a considerable period, it seems hardly conceivable that victory would not ultimately incline toward one power or the other. A beginningless and endless conflict would involve the participation of two contestants who were exactly equal in power; and as McTaggart has pointed out, such a hypothesis is in the highest degree improbable. Moreover, evil is essentially chaotic and disruptive, whereas goodness is essentially coherent and constructive. The good power would thus command resources access to which would be denied to the evil power and should therefore be in a better position to wage war successfully. But if the evil power be without a cosmic rival, and in full control of the universe, the situation will be very different.

The absurdity of such a hypothesis, the objector may urge, is rendered immediately apparent by the presence of great and incontestable good in the universe. But stay a moment. Incontestable as is the presence of good, is it not equally incontestable that it is a fleeting presence? The great tragedy of life is that we barely taste of values which are snatched away from us, if not by the vicissitudes of our mortal lot, yet surely and ruthlessly by death. But this cannot be the end, it may be said. Have we not established by what we considered a conclusive argument the sempiternity of the self? And if we are to live forever, can there be any justification for pessimism? I am inclined to believe that, skilfully played, the belief in immortality might prove to be the best card in the pessimist's hand. What could be a worse lot than that of an immortal self in a universe in which evil was predominant? Even the door of annihilation would be closed. The greatest evil consists in the frustration or elimination of goodness, and how do we know that a cosmic evil purpose may not be directed to this very end? May there not be truth in Channing's memorable words: "the future may show that the very laws and works of the Creator, from which we now infer his kindness, are consistent with the most determined purpose to spread infinite misery and guilt, and were intended, by raising hope, to add the agony of disappointment to our other woes"? [10]

It is true that if we survey the course of human history we discover there a notable intellectual and moral progress which, during the last few thousand years, has been proceeding at an accelerated rate. And it is also true that, although this process has been subject to periodic retrogressions, yet the lowest level of any backwash—as Gordon Childe and Arnold Toynbee have so emphatically indicated—has never been as low as that of its predecessor. But how do we know that this long and impressive advance may not reach a terminus, and be succeeded by an equally impressive retreat? In view of the enormous increase of human powers of destruction, this is certainly not an unthinkable possibility. And may it not have been foreseen and counted upon by an evil cosmic Mind?

I have dealt so fully with a hypothesis which few will seriously entertain for the following reason. I believe that the investigation into the nature and status of values which we are shortly to undertake will show us that the view that the universe as a whole is indifferent to human desires and aspirations is quite untenable, and that it will become apparent that the universe is either so ordered as to provide for their fulfilment or so ordered as to provide for their frustration;

10. *Works of William E. Channing* (Boston, 1886), p. 466, col. 1. Needless to add, this is not Channing's own view. But he urges that it is a genuine possibility, if it be denied that divine and human goodness are essentially univocal.

in other words, that it is fundamentally either a good or a bad universe, but certainly not neither good nor bad. Accordingly, it is to some such hypothesis as the one before us that, in my judgment, the opponent of rationalism will in the long run be driven; and as I have already remarked, if it be fantastic, there is no better way of discrediting his position than to show it to be so. To accomplish this, we must first consider what can be said in its favor.

I must therefore repeat my previous question. If it be indeed fantastic, upon what grounds are we to pronounce it so? A wholly evil intelligence, it may be said, could not even exist. I wish that we could be sure of that. One thinks of Plato's argument for immortality in the tenth book of the *Republic*—everything has its own evil, vice is the evil of the soul, yet vice cannot destroy the soul. Plato would thus seem to have contemplated the possibility of the existence of an absolutely evil self. It has, of course, frequently been asserted that vice can no more completely corrupt than it can completely destroy the soul. Always, it is maintained, there is some good left. Yet this seems to be the affirmation of faith rather than the verdict of experience. Are there not plenty of men in the world today who, if they have not reached a stage of total moral corruption, have at least approximated it? Yet the normal evil man, it may be urged, does not pursue evil for its own sake but because of genuine good which it will bring him, his own happiness or that of a minority in whom he has a disproportionate interest. If he be antisocial, it is because of a conditioning to which, as a finite mind, he has been subjected, and which has warped his character; and no such fate could befall a cosmic Intelligence. The desire for evil as evil carries us beyond the limits of the normal. It is a mark of criminal insanity; and whatever else we may believe of a cosmic Mind, we cannot doubt its sanity.

That there is some force in this contention I gladly admit; yet it is difficult to evaluate, and as it stands it does not impress me as conclusive. What I wish to point out, however, is that everything assumes a different aspect once we assume that the universe is axiologically oriented. If values be, as some philosophers have thought, an expression of, or emanation from, the supreme Mind, there can be no question as to that Mind's goodness—or perhaps I should say its super-goodness. At any rate, it seems quite clear that it cannot be evil. And the same would, surely, hold true of a supreme Mind which did not produce, but was merely contemplative of, objective values. For although it is true that extreme cleverness is perfectly compatible with extreme wickedness, it is difficult to conceive of a supreme Mind as merely clever. It could hardly avoid the just appreciation of values which goes with wisdom, and it could scarcely appreciate them without desiring to actualize them. And even if there were no supreme Mind, in a universe which was axiologically oriented, the role of evil would plainly be a very restricted one—indeed, the principal problem will be to account for its being present at all. If we can deal with this problem with some degree of success, we shall have gone a long way toward vindicating the rationalistic outlook.

If the previous discussion have brought out anything it is that the crucial problem for rationalism is the status of values in the universe. And we can see that the rationalist is faced with a twofold problem. In the first place, he must show conclusively that the universe is axiologically oriented. And in the second place, he must make it appear credible that the axiological orientation of the whole is compatible with the presence of irrationality and evil in some of the parts. This is obviously a formidable task; yet if he is to make good his case, the rationalist must accomplish it. But before we turn to the consideration of values, we must first take up the problem of universals.

[Note] Needless to say, a conclusive case could be made out against rationalism if it could be shown that reason cannot avoid violating its own rules and thereby disqualifying itself. The antinomy is therefore the favorite weapon of many opponents of rationalism. In India it was wielded with great effect by Nāgārjuna, the founder of the Mādhyamika school of Buddhism; and in the Hellenic world it constituted the chief reliance of the skeptics, recurring as it does ad nauseam in the writings of Sextus Empiricus. In the history of philosophy, as in that of warfare, the opportune revival of the seemingly obsolete has often proved extraordinarily successful. It was by bringing the antinomy out of the philosophical arsenal that Kant scored his greatest victory, and the lesson has not been lost upon his successors. All the world knows the major role which it plays in the metaphysics of Bradley. The antinomy is there used to establish conclusions avowedly incompatible with Christian orthodoxy; yet it is also being exploited, if less persuasively with no less enthusiasm, by various theologians of a neosupernaturalist or existentialist persuasion in defense of this very orthodoxy.[11]

11. Cf., for instance, Professor Richard Kroner's *Culture and Faith* (Chicago, 1951) and his trilogy entitled *Speculation and Revelation in the History of Philosophy* (Philadelphia, 1956–61). With respect to many of the neosupernaturalists, J. B. Pratt has remarked that "ever more extreme and snappy paradoxes" are "the firecrackers with which they celebrate their Declaration of Independence from the restrictions of reason" (*Can We Keep the Faith?*, p. 63).

For us to attempt to deal in advance with all the purported antinomies which have heretofore been propounded would obviously be an undertaking which would carry us too far afield and divert us from our proper task. Anyone who has turned his attention to the subject will be aware that in their enthusiasm the opponents of rationalism have found antinomies lurking behind every bush. All that we can legitimately be expected to do is to deal with any which we find in our path, if and when they occur.

Something more ought to be said with respect to the role which the irrational plays in the philosophy of Nicolai Hartmann. For Hartmann the individual subject is surrounded by a "court of objects" which are reflected in its own subjective representations. Each of the entities, some of whose aspects have thus been objectified, possesses other aspects which have not yet been objectified, but which may or may not be objectifiable; hence there is a realm of the "transobjective" which requires to be recognized. However far the process of objectification may proceed, it can never reach its terminus, which is at an infinite remove. There is, accordingly, a territory into which reason can never penetrate, and which constitutes the realm of the irrational. By calling it "irrational" Hartmann does not mean that it is chaotic, or devoid of law or structure; he means only that its laws or structure can never be grasped by the human mind, owing to the limitations of a finite intelligence. "Rational" is a term which is used by Hartmann in a very restricted sense; it is applicable only to the realm of entities which are subtended by intelligible relations. At bottom, therefore, there is an arbitrary element in everything. Thus the laws of logic constitute a system; yet the system itself is not intelligibly grounded in some super-system, and so is basically and ultimately irrational. So reason itself is fundamentally irrational. The rational is relatively superficial, and everywhere the irrational underlies it.

What are we to say to Hartmann's contentions? Obviously there is much truth in them; yet one can honestly urge that he has overplayed his hand. It requires no excessive degree of modesty to admit that one does not expect to attain to omniscience. Perhaps we ought not arbitrarily to dismiss as preposterous the view we find advanced in Hindu philosophy that the greatest sages, at the very apex of spiritual development, attain to a degree of insight which is at once intuitive, synoptic, and cosmic in its purview. But at least we may confidently affirm that even granting that such a claim were sound, its soundness could be made manifest only to one who had himself arrived at such a state of illumination. For the rest of us it remains only an unsupported dogma. No rationalist today would for a moment contemplate imitating the extravagance of Hegel, who in the flood tide of enthusiasm professed to demonstrate a priori that there could be only seven planets, and thereby made a laughingstock of himself, as no rationalist is ever permitted to forget. We must frankly acknowledge that every entity of which we are aware possesses characteristics which will never be known by us. Since all the particulars in the universe are interconnected—they are all, for instance, mutually similar or dissimilar in various respects—it follows that all the entities with which we are acquainted, our own selves included, stand in manifold relations to entities unknown to us, and that these relations are likewise unknown.

There are, however, two points upon which the rationalist may justifiably lay emphasis. The first is that his aim is to become acquainted, not with each and every particular in the universe, and with the totality of its characteristics, but with the general characteristics, structure, and nature of the whole; and that nothing that Hartmann has said suffices to discredit this undertaking in advance. Its feasibility can be judged only in the light of his own efforts. We cannot tell how successful he will be until he has tried. And his second point will be that it is both illegitimate and misleading to apply the term "irrational" to the ultimate because the ultimate is not grounded in, necessitated by, dependent upon, or relative to, anything beyond itself. We have every right to inquire into the relation of a part to the whole, of one element to other elements within the same general structure, to discriminate between the contingent and the necessary, between the transient and the permanent, between appearance and reality; but to ask reality why it is real, and why it is as it is and not otherwise, is to raise meaningless questions which, because of their meaninglessness, admit of no answer.

Moreover, to presume to set limits to the progress of human knowledge and to pronounce various problems insoluble, as Hartmann has done, is to give hostages to fortune. In this connection we shall do well to recall Bergson's words: "Auguste Comte declared the chemical composition of the heavenly bodies to be forever unknowable by us. A few years later the spectroscope was invented, and to-day we know, better than if we had gone there, what the stars are made of." [12]

12. *Mind-Energy*, trans. Wildon Carr (New York, 1920), p. 36.

CHAPTER SIX

UNIVERSALS

It is clear that human experience is largely—some would say wholly—made up of acquaintance with particulars. Of the existence of one particular, himself, each of us, as we have seen, is directly and indubitably aware. And each of us believes with invincible assurance in the existence of other selves, who are also particulars, resemble us in the possession of certain qualities and differ from us in the possession of certain others, to whom we are related and who are related to each other in manifold ways. And in sense experience each of us becomes aware of a plurality of sensible particulars which are also qualified and interrelated. It is true that certain philosophers have questioned whether some, at least, of the characteristics which appear to characterize actually do characterize these particulars; but at the level of common sense no such doubt is, in general, entertained (although common sense is frequently perplexed by instances of what we are wont to call erroneous perception), and yet it is precisely at this level that the notions of "thing," "quality," and "relation" have been rendered explicit. Philosophy has expanded the notion of "thing" into that of "substance," and has retained—on good grounds, as we have seen—the notions of "quality" and "relation." When we rise to the level of philosophic speculation, however, we are confronted by a crucial problem.

Some entities resemble each other in various respects, and differ from each other in various other respects. How is this to be accounted for? Are characteristics as particular as the entities they characterize? Or is a characteristic something which a plurality of entities can possess in common? To this question a number of conflicting answers have been given.

1. One answer, and at some periods in the history of philosophy a very popular answer, has been that of nominalism. The qualities of an entity, it has been affirmed, are as particular as the entity which they qualify; and each of the relations in which the entity stands is a particular relation. Are we to say, then, that only the words which name the entities, qualities, and relations are universals? Clearly this

suggestion must prove inadmissible, for every utterance of a word, every writing down of a word, and every thought of a word is a particular event. We cannot without inconsistency say that all utterances of a word have something in common, and that this is a universal; for with equal propriety we might affirm that all apples have something in common, and that this is the universal apple. A consistent nominalism, it is clear, must refuse to recognize a universal anywhere.

How, then, are we to account for similarity? If two entities have nothing in common how can they be similar? The answer frequently given by the nominalist is that similarity is an ultimate and unanalyzable relation.[1] Two apples can be pronounced similar because

1. In this connection it is perhaps worth while to advert to the rejoinder given by Professor Roy Wood Sellars in *The Philosophy of Physical Realism* (New York, 1932):

I would reply that resemblance is a fact about things which is discoverable *under the condition that a mind thinks them together.* This togetherness, when achieved, is external and expressive of an operation of the mind. Mind is a kind of spectator capable of a ghostly supervenience. Thinking together is not a real relation between the things. It is a mental kind of relating which is unique and must be so regarded. And things can be said to be similar *if* they would be judged similar were they to be thought together. This is an important point, for it shows that similarity is not a relation but a fact about the things due to their natures. (p. 174)

But is not a fact inherently relational? Professor Sellars has his answer ready. He has subjectified the notion of "fact." "A fact is what is known," it is "a bit of knowledge about" (p. 224). But what is it about? "I have set *fact*," he writes, "in contrast with *what is the case*" (p. 227). And in an explanatory paragraph, he adds: "Since I do not wish to build upon popular usage alone, I shall substitute such terms as things, events, state of affairs for the term, what is the case. As I see it, then, facts have a *logical structure,* while what the facts are about have an *ontological structure*" (pp. 227–228).

Yet this does not remove the difficulty. What Sellars has done is to leap the barrier between nominalism and conceptualism (see pp. 145, 343). But his mental agility, however much it may confuse us, does not free him from inconsistency. Nominalism is one position, and conceptualism is another. Moreover, if resemblance be the work of mind, things do not resemble one another *in re;* if, on the other hand, things do resemble one another *in re,* resemblance is not the work of mind, although the recognition of it is an act of mind.

If the relation of resemblance can be thus subjectified, so with even greater plausibility can all relations be. There seems to be in nominalism an inherent tendency to gravitate toward such a position, which is of course characteristic of certain forms of idealism. For this tendency it is not easy to account. It would seem that relations tend to impress the mind as being somehow more diaphanous, so to speak, than qualities. And this may explain the persistent urge, which the history of philosophy reveals, to reduce relations to qualities. But it is an urge which must be resisted, for it is obvious to reflection that in experience relations are given to us with the same objectivity as qualities.

they have similar qualities, but of the qualities nothing more can be said than that they are similar. Again, if two apples rest upon a table, the relation of above and below which holds between one apple and the table will be similar to the relation which holds between the other apple and the table, and, once more, this is all that can be said about it.

Is not similarity, however, a universal the recognition of which is inevitable? So thought Lord Russell when he wrote *An Inquiry into Meaning and Truth*.[2] And honesty compelled him to add that if this be the case, "it seems hardly worth while to adopt elaborate devices for the exclusion of other universals."[3] This is a concession, however, which the nominalist cannot afford to make, for it involves giving up his whole case. He must therefore assert that there is no such universal as similarity, but that there are only particular similarities between which hold other particular relations of similarity, and so ad infinitum. We must concede, I think, that such an infinite would not be vicious; yet the admission of it will have the unfortunate consequence that we can never twice use the same word, but only similar words, not twice with the same meaning, but only with similar meanings, and this will severely limit our capacity for communicating with one another.

2. Of the remaining theories, that closest to nominalism is, of course, conceptualism. The conceptualist agrees with the nominalist in his assertion that in the external world there are only particular things with particular qualities standing in particular relations; and he further agrees that the minds which apprehend them are also particulars. Where he differs from the nominalist is in his contention that the human mind possesses the capacity to form general ideas. It is capable of thinking of one characteristic of an object apart from that object's other characteristics, and of thinking at the same time of other objects possessing similar characteristics. It can think, for instance, of the red in an apple, of the red in a rose, and of the red in a flag. It can dismiss the thoughts of apple, rose, and flag and think only of the reds. Next, by some mysterious mental alchemy, it can form the general idea of redness which extends, and is applicable to, all red things. This, the theory maintains, is the only genuine universal, and it is mind-made. It stands in a one-many relation to the particulars existing *extra mentem* of which it can be predicated. It can be thought of in itself apart from, and without reference to, these particulars. Since

2. (London, 1940) see pp. 434–437.
3. *Ibid.*, pp. 436–437.

it is a mental product, it is frequently called a *concept.* Not all concepts are universals, for there are also concepts of particulars; but
the concepts connoted by so-called abstract nouns are universals, and
there are no other universals.[4]

3. A third view regards universals as objectively real, quite as much
so as particulars. The mind does not make them, it discovers them.
They have their being in the particulars they characterize. The same
quality may be possessed by any number of particulars; the same
relation may have any number of instances. The red of the apple,
the rose, and the flag is qualitatively identical; the relation of above
and below between a bird and a roof and a man and a chair is the
same relation. Yet, so the theory asserts, universals have no being
apart from particulars; we cannot posit them *ante rem,* nor yet *post
rem* as mind-dependent, although they can of course be thought of
without reference to their instances. This theory, which might be
termed one of "restricted realism," is, rightly or wrongly, frequently
associated with the name of Aristotle; accordingly, without troubling
ourselves to determine whether the attribution be just, we may in
deference to general opinion nominate it Aristotelianism.

4. A closely related doctrine of universals differs from the previous
theory by going further and positing the being or reality of universals
ante rem and apart from particulars.[5] Particulars are characterized
by universals, and are dependent upon them in the sense that a particular cannot exist as a bare and characterless entity. It must have a
nature, and this nature is composed of characterizing universals. Universals, however, are not in the same way dependent upon particulars;
although it is a legitimate question to ask whether there may be
universals which at no time characterize anything, and thus constitute
what Professor C. D. Broad has called "non-characterising characteristics." [6] It has frequently been asserted by defenders of the theory that
universals "subsist" whereas particulars "exist." A further question
then arises as to whether a characterizing universal can properly be

4. As employed by Thomist writers the term "conceptualism" is habitually given
a more limited significance, and is practically identified with the Kantian view that
the objects of knowledge are mental constructs, and that things-in-themselves are
unknowable. The "moderate realism" of the Thomist corresponds in a general way
to the conceptualism of non-scholastic thinkers. The universal, so Thomistic
philosophers maintain, exists *in re* only in the sense that it can be abstracted from
the particulars found there, and its abstraction is the work of mind.

5. A typical exposition of this view will be found in Lord Russell's *The Problems
of Philosophy* (New York, 1912), chaps. ix–x.

6. *Examination of McTaggart's Philosophy,* I, 25.

said to exist in the particular which it characterizes.[7] Whether or not this be a purely verbal question can be decided only after further inquiry. As contrasted with the preceding view the theory may be termed "unrestricted realism."

5. Lastly we come to the position of Plato. As usually interpreted the Platonic Ideas or Forms are entities closely resembling the universals of modern thinkers, but with this difference: they abide in a changeless realm of their own from which they never descend into the flux of time and space to characterize particulars. The relation of particulars to the Forms is sometimes described by Plato as one of resemblance, whereas at other times he employs the noncommittal term "participation" ($\mu\acute{\epsilon}\theta\epsilon\xi\iota\varsigma$). Since Forms are never to be found in the realm of particulars, there can be no question of abstracting them thence. The philosopher is compelled to posit them in order to account for instances of resemblance upon this plane, and he is the more able to do this because he has himself been directly aware of them in a prenatal and unembodied state, and still retains a genuine, if somewhat vague, recollection of such an experience. Such is the famous doctrine of reminiscence which has impressed many modern thinkers as so fantastic that they have been loath to admit that Plato could ever have seriously advanced it, and have sought to relegate it to the realm of myth; yet the incredulity of such scholars does not provide sufficient reason for doubting that, in his middle period at least, Plato did definitely commit himself to this view. And this conclusion is borne out by the fact that Plato expressly stresses the possibility that by turning away from the world of sense experience and by developing the potentialities of his intellectual soul the philosopher may, even in this life, ascend to a state of direct awareness of the Forms.

It seems pretty clear that these five theories exhaust the possibilities of the situation. One or other of them is the true view. The question is which. In order to find a satisfactory answer our best course will be to submit them to the test of the survival of the fittest. In other words, let us try to "shake" them, that we may discover which, if any, will resist our efforts.

A preliminary inspection, it seems to me, at once suggests that the weakest of all these theories is that of the conceptualist. For conceptualism is reared, as it were, upon a substructure of nominalism. What-

7. Cf. McTaggart, "An Ontological Idealism," in *Contemporary British Philosophy*, I, 252; see also *Philosophical Studies*, p. 274. Cf. Professor Broad, *Examination of McTaggart's Philosophy*, I, 25–31.

ever weaknesses infect nominalism may well extend to it also, whereas whatever strength nominalism possesses may well suffice to render it superfluous. And it also seems fairly evident that conceptualism is involved in difficulties peculiar to itself which it does not share with nominalism. What are these difficulties?

In the first place conceptualism is committed to a doctrine of abstraction. The word "abstraction" is frequently employed with as much confidence as if its meaning were clear and definite; yet when we try to discover this meaning, we at once become involved in obscurity. The genuine universal, we are told, is a concept; and a concept is a mental product which is formed by the mind as it contemplates two or more particulars possessed of similar characteristics. By what mysterious fusion, or by what process of creativity, does the mind accomplish this? Granted that we can fix our attention upon the red of an apple, the red of a rose, and the red of a flag, and disregard to some extent the other characteristic of these entities—I say, "to some extent," for it is scarcely possible that we should be entirely oblivious of them—what then? The three reds, on the theory before us, will be three particular entities *in re;* and the apprehension of them, even if it be a single apprehension, will be a particular awareness. Still we have not reached the universal. How do we reach it? Though we reiterate this question till doomsday we shall receive no intelligible answer. Does the general idea appear *ex nihilo* like some psychological Melchisedec? It would seem so. For a general idea is not an idea of the general or the universal. *Extra mentem* there are only particulars. The general idea *is* the universal itself. Its function is to stand for the particulars to which it is related by a one-many relation. It can be thought of, and the thought of it is a particular thought. It constitutes universality extruded, as it were, from the mind, and dependent thereon. The particular has given rise to the universal, and this involves a transition from kind to kind. The whole process is as mysterious and inexplicable as the conjuring up of a palace by the waving of an enchanter's wand.

Even if we grant, however, that a particular mind can produce an idea which is not an idea of the universal but is itself a universal, our difficulties are not at an end. For the mind has other things to do than perpetually to contemplate this universal concept which it has itself produced. What happens when the mind turns its attention to something else? Does the universal concept relapse into nothingness? If the mind again have need of it, what is it to do? Must the creative process once more be gone through? But, surely, what is produced

will not be the same concept, but only one similar to it. For how can
they be the same if they be numerically distinct products of numerically distinct acts? Yet, obviously, we cannot have two universal red-
nesses or squarenesses which succeed one another in time. We seem
compelled, therefore, to assume that the universal concept, once produced, remains in being. Our only recourse, then, will be to relegate
it to the realm of the subconscious, there to abide until the conscious
mind again call it forth. Whether psychoanalysis can proffer any evidence for the presence of such entities—as distinct from particular
thoughts of them—appears, to say the least, highly doubtful. Let us
suppose, however, that it can. What happens at death? As the concept
came into being must it not also pass out of being? On conceptualist
principles it would appear so. Yet the ideas of beginning and ending
seem incongruous when associated with that of a universal, the very
notion of which might be taken to involve supratemporal or trans-
temporal being.[8]

Let me now ask the conceptualist another question. How is your
individual concept related to mine? If you can form a general idea of
redness, so can I. Yet you form yours, and I mine. You form yours at
one moment, and I at another. When I die, mine passes into nothingness, whereas yours persists in all its strength and vividness. What
have they in common? As a good conceptualist you cannot say that
both concepts possess a common nature, for by so doing you will posit
a universal which both exemplify but which is produced neither by
your mind nor by mine; in other words, you will give away your case
to the believer in objective universals which are independent of mind
and subsist *in re*. Nor can you well say that there is an unanalyzable
relation of similarity which holds between them, for this is the basic
contention of the nominalist with respect to particulars which are
alike; and if you appeal to it, you must show cause for bringing in
general ideas at all. You must reply to his assertion that he needs
no general ideas to have general knowledge, since he can always
let some one particular stand for those which resemble it in certain
respects. Is it not plain, then, I would ask, that the general idea
or universal concept of the conceptualist is a metaphysical monster possessed of incompatible attributes, at once common and individual, universal and particular, temporal and eternal? In the light

8. It might be urged that a conceptualist who believed in the sempiternity of the
self would have permanent *locus* for his universal concepts. This is of course true;
but inasmuch as most conceptualists certainly do not believe in it, I can still press
the *argumentum ad hominem*.

of the foregoing discussion I submit that we must pronounce it to be so; and that, consequently, we are justified in rejecting conceptualism as an untenable view.

Let us next turn to the Platonic doctrine, although, in so doing, our emotions may well rival, and even surpass, those of Plato himself as he contemplated doing violence to Father Parmenides. For in the eyes of a believer in the objectivity of universals this famous doctrine shines like a beacon. Nevertheless, as we survey it, we become conscious of a difficulty of which Plato himself was undoubtedly aware. The difficulty is that the notion of resemblance will not stand, whereas the notion of participation is too enigmatical to be of use.

The first half of this assertion may, of course, be challenged by those who are prepared to maintain that by this very notion of resemblance Plato has solved his problem. Two photographs of the same man, we shall be told by way of illustration, resemble each other because they both resemble the same man; and we shall be further assured that while it is quite correct to say that his photograph resembles the man, it would be incorrect to say that the man resembles his photograph. In the same way, we are informed, two particulars resemble each other because both resemble the same Form, and while it is correct to say that the particular resembles the Form, it would be incorrect to say that the Form resembles the particular. Hence the Forms, it is claimed, provide a metaphysical basis for the occurrence of similarity, and thus suffice to account for it.[9]

It is quite obvious why it would be fatal to admit that the Form resembles the particular. For then Form and particular would be, as it were, on the same footing, even as the photographs are; the proponents of the view would therefore be compelled, in accordance with their own underlying assumption, to posit a second Form which the first Form and the particular both resemble, and thus we should be involved in a viciously infinite regress. This is, of course, the famous argument from the "Third Man."

As to the underlying assumption, it flies in the face of the fact that resemblance is a symmetrical relation. If A resemble B, B must

9. This contention may well remind us of the famous story of Hideyoshi and his courtier. In a sportively tyrannical mood Hideyoshi asked the courtier if it were true that he resembled a monkey. The terrified nobleman was allowed a period of reflection before answering. When at last called upon to give his considered opinion the courtier answered, "May it please your Excellency, you do not resemble a monkey, but the monkey resembles you." The reply saved the courtier from punishment, but then neither Hideyoshi nor the courtier was a Platonist (see James A. B. Scherer, *The Romance of Japan through the Ages* [New York, 1928], p. 143).

resemble A. If the photograph look like the man, the man must look like the photograph. If the particular resemble the Form, the Form must resemble the particular. The proposition that similarity is a symmetrical relation is, I think, self-evident. From the nature of the case, then, it cannot be sustained by further argument; and to anyone who professes to doubt it, nothing more can be said.

That Plato felt the force of this objection appears probable in view of his introduction of the vague term "participation." The supposition that he never succeeded in satisfying himself that he had grasped the precise relation of particular to Form seems a likely one; and his remark to the effect that, while it is difficult to believe in the Forms, it is even more difficult to do without them, may well be taken as expressive of his final attitude. Yet we may still ask why Plato considered it necessary to insist that the Forms remain aloof in an empyrean of their own.

We may plausibly conjecture that he was impelled to do so by the conviction that, were the Forms actually to characterize particulars, they would thereby be involved in becoming and change, and that the very basis of genuine knowledge, as distinct from opinion, would thereby be destroyed. Such an admission would inflict a severe blow upon his philosophy of religion, for it seems clear that for Plato ultimate beatitude consisted in the contemplation of the immutable and eternal. These reflections, however, do not avail to remove the obscurity attaching to the notion of participation; hence the Platonic theory, highly important and profoundly suggestive as it is, cannot be deemed satisfactory.

Let us therefore revert to the opposite extreme, and proceed to examine and evaluate the position of the nominalist. Nominalism is a view which possesses for many—and above all, perhaps, for the student who is being introduced to philosophy—an attractiveness because of the initial impression of intellectual hardheadedness which it produces. It seems to express the outlook of stern, uncompromising, and unemotional common sense, and to be devoid of all "metaphysical nonsense." The pure empiricist feels immediately drawn to it, and rightly so; for in the long run his case stands or falls with it. The consequences of accepting or rejecting it are indeed momentous; for they cannot fail to affect profoundly one's whole philosophic outlook.

Can nominalism, we may then ask in the first place, satisfactorily account for general knowledge while rejecting general ideas or concepts? The nominalist will in all likelihood reply that Berkeley has shown how this can be done. We can always let some one particular stand as the representative of all particulars which in some respect resemble it; and what holds true of it will therefore hold true of them. The phrase, "in some respect," will of course need to be modified, since there is no characteristic which characterizes more than one entity. But entities are similar if they have similar characteristics, and what holds true for one will hold true for those like it. Thus, if it be true that the angles of a particular triangle equal two right angles, the same will be true of anything which possesses a similar shape.

Yet the phrase, "what holds true," will require to be analyzed; for as it stands, it at once suggests a proposition which can be thought of by more than one mind. But the nominalist can no more admit the reality of such entities than he can that of universals; for in his view propositions, no less than universals, are particulars. For the nominalist there can only be particular judgments made by particular minds. No two minds can form the same judgment, but only similar judgments. You make yours, and I make mine. Again, if every characteristic be a particular, the characteristic of having three angles equal to two right angles which is possessed by *this* triangle can be possessed by no other triangle, which must resign itself to possessing a similar characteristic—whatever that may be. Triangularity itself, however, can characterize no more than one entity; inasmuch as no two entities can have the same shape, but only similar shapes. Both language and thought, then, lose all their definiteness. There is no common meaning which can be communicated from mind to mind; there are only similar meanings entertained by similar minds, or by the same mind at different moments. But what of "the same mind"? Here there can be no difficulty, the nominalist may exclaim, for minds are particulars; and we are concerned, not with numerical, but only with qualitative identity. But what of the successive states or acts of the same mind? That consciousness is not immutable, that there are such successive states or acts—from the temporal point of view at least—cannot, surely, be denied; yet each of these states or acts will be related to its subject, not by the same relation as any other, but only by a similar relation. The whole universe appears to be dissolving away into similar similarities. No common content of thought, let alone of science, is left for us. We shall be driven, like the ancient Greek skeptic, to confine ourselves to pointing.

Here at last the opponent of nominalism may be permitted to raise his voice. The fault of nominalism, he would urge, is not that it contradicts itself, but that it contradicts experience. For there are common characteristics, and there is common knowledge. Resemblance is not unanalyzable; it holds whenever things have a common characteristic, and the presence of this common characteristic is the ground of the relation. Here, once more, the appeal is to self-evidence; but this need not disconcert us, for this is where every valid argument leads if pursued to the ultimate. It is worth no more than the basic premises upon which it is reared, and which cannot be argued, but only accepted or rejected; and if accepted, accepted not by an arbitrary act of volition but in consequence of an insight which permits no doubt. That qualitative identity is empirically discoverable in things, and relational identity in their connection, the antinominalist holds to be indubitable.

Were the nominalist right, he continues, our experience would exhibit a bewildering complexity which we simply do not discover there. Take an extended and colored surface, such as that of the petal of a flower or of a piece of note paper. Scissors will divide either into a multiplicity of tiny particulars. The nominalist must maintain that each of these particulars will then be characterized by a color which is not qualitatively identical with, but only similar to, the color of any other part. Any surface which appears uniformly colored is not really so; every part thereof in reality possesses its own particular color which is unshared by any other. And the similarity which holds between the colors of any two of these microscopically differentiable parts will not be identical with but only similar to the similarity which holds between either of these parts and any other part, or between any two parts in the entire collection. Moreover, the same will hold true of all data of sensation, memory, fantasy, illusion, or introspection. No man ever saw, remembered, or imagined two instances of the same color, no two bits of food ever tasted precisely the same, no two notes ever sounded with just the same resonance or pitch, no two experiences of pleasure or throbs of pain were ever exactly alike, no two feelings of guilt or self-satisfaction, not even any two conceptions of nominalism; no two conscious beings in the universe have at any time or anywhere enjoyed experiences qualitatively identical. "Credat Judeaus Apella!"

If, in the effort to avoid so sweeping, indemonstrable, and dogmatic an assertion, the desperate resolution be taken to deny that relations have instances, still this offers no way of escape. There will now be no similar relations of similarity, but only one relation of similarity which holds between all similar things. Yet what is this but the universal of the realist which the nominalist seeks to rebaptize. Nominalism is retained in words but surrendered in thought. And the case becomes clearer when we turn to qualities, for here the nominalist obviously can concede nothing without conceding everything. If the same quality can ever characterize two entities, the nominalist's faith is vain and he is yet in his sins. Thus, upon close inspection, the very position which at first glance seemed the most down-to-earth and coldly business-like of all becomes so nebulous and fantastic that we turn from it in despair.

Clearly, therefore, the attempt to dispense with universals has failed. This is a conclusion of the first importance, but one which seems plainly inescapable. How, then, if we turn to the restricted realism of the Aristotelian? Here we find a point of view for which universals are as objective as particulars, and for which they actually do characterize particulars. There is no question of bringing them down from an eternal heaven. They are down to start with. They belong to the spatio-temporal world as truly as do the particulars in which they have their being. Is not such a view, while it condemns the claims both of the Platonist and of the nominalist, fully capable of satisfying all rational demands?

There is, of course, the stock argument urged against it by the Thomists. If it be admitted that there is *in re* such an entity as a universal, and that it actually characterizes any particular, one of two inadmissible consequences is bound to follow: either all the universal will inhere in that one particular so that nothing will be left of it to characterize any other particular, or only a part of the universal will inhere in that particular, in which case the particular will be characterized not by the universal but only by a part of it. Thus, if the universal in question be, for instance, redness, either all of redness will be absorbed by some one particular—a particular apple, for example—and then nothing else in the universe can be red, or else only a part of redness will characterize any one particular, and another part another particular, and so on indefinitely—with the result that redness as such will never characterize anything.

The objection is based upon the assumption that a universal is a whole made up of parts. And there is clearly the further assumption that each of the parts can characterize only one substance, or, in other words, that it is a particular characteristic of a particular thing. But a whole made up of particulars would itself be a particular, and not a universal. Thus the argument begins with the assumption that a universal is not a universal, but a particular. It would be better, therefore, to make the assumption explicit, and to claim that whatever exists—or, if one prefer, whatever has being—is a particular.

I can but report that this proposition does not appear self-evident to me. Experience, indeed, does not bear it out; for it acquaints us not only with particulars but also with characteristics which they possess in common; and these characteristics are obviously not wholes made up of parts. If nominalism be rejected, we must admit that universals are entities which are capable, without disruption, of characterizing indefinite numbers of particulars. The realist claims that this notion is not self-contradictory, and that experience acquaints us with such entities. The reality of universals is not something which can be deduced from any premise; it is something of which we are directly aware. The only way in which such an assertion can be supported is by the indirect method of *reductio ad absurdum,* by showing—as I have just tried to show—that nominalism is incredible, that we cannot deny the reality of universals without making nonsense of our experience. That universals are objectively real is therefore a proposition which I am prepared to accept as self-evident.

It does not follow, however, that we are committed to the Aristotelian doctrine of restricted realism. Indeed, there are good reasons for regarding it as unsatisfactory. In the first place, if universals have being only *in re,* they will have being only in the particulars which they characterize. But the same universal may have characterized a greater or a lesser number of particulars yesterday than it characterizes today, and tomorrow it may characterize a greater or a lesser number than today or yesterday. Yet should we be prepared to say that the universal has more being at one time than at another? If not, can it be wholly dependent for its being upon the particulars which it characterizes? Moreover, while it is practically impossible to eliminate all the instances of any universal—or, at least, to have any ground for supposing that we have succeeded in so doing—there is no logical impossibility in conceiving of their entire elimination. In such a case, if the universal have being only in the particulars, it would perish with them, and would be permanently lost to the universe. Is this credible? And if so, must we also admit that a new universal, a genuine stranger to the universe, may at any moment come into being *ex nihilo?* This is a concession which some thinkers would certainly find it hard to make.

In the second place, are we compelled to hold that every universal at every moment characterizes something? Again, what of Professor

Broad's "non-characterising characteristics"—i.e., universals which never characterize anything? Is this an impossible notion? The situation is complicated by the fact that there clearly are characteristics which admit of degrees. Each of these degrees will, then, constitute a subuniversal. Must we hold that all of these are instantiated? This will mean not only that every degree of heat and that every degree of loudness, for instance, must have its instance, but also that every degree of pain or pleasure, of vice or virtue, must actually characterize some self. This is a rather appalling consequence; one which plainly ought not to be accepted without ample reflection, and one the truth of which we might well, on purely empirical grounds, feel inclined to doubt.

And in the third place, it seems possible to contemplate some of these subuniversals without presupposing the existence of any instances. Can I not, for example, think of a degree of metaphysical profundity surpassing that of Plato, or of a degree of intellectual obscurity exceeding that of Hegel, without assuming that either has ever characterized anybody? And if we concede the reality of complex characteristics, the soundness of this contention becomes even more obvious. I can think of the characteristic of having a million equal sides. Am I, then, compelled to conclude that somewhere in the universe there must be a body which possesses it?

These reflections lead naturally to the consideration of the fourth point of view, which we have called that of unrestricted realism— the view that universals have being *ante rem,* apart from particulars, as well as *in re,* in particulars. There seems no difficulty in such a view. Once we have admitted the objective reality of universals, what ground have we for holding that their reality is dependent upon that of particulars?

This question, it may be contended, reveals a fundamental misapprehension of the situation. The being of particulars and that of universals, it may be urged, are mutually implicatory. As a particular cannot exist without a nature, and its nature is the complex of universals characterizing it, so a universal cannot have being or subsist in abstraction from its instances. Particular and universal belong to each other; they are, so to speak, enmeshed, and cannot be sundered without disrupting the entire structure of the universe. But how is this contention to be made good? It overlooks the fact that the particular is one kind of entity and a universal another, and that what holds true of the former need not hold true of the latter. It is clearly one thing to affirm that there could not be a universe which contained no particulars whatever, and a very different thing to assert that every universal must be perpetually instantiated. Even if we interpret the Aristotelian doctrine to mean that the particulars in which the universal has its being need not exist simultaneously, but are to be identified with all those past, present, or future which ever instantiate it, the possibility remains that there may occur a temporal interval during which it characterizes nothing at all. What, then, of the being of the universal? Does the universal lapse into nothingness, only to emerge therefrom at a later date? And, upon this reappearing, is it the same universal, despite the temporal gap in its being, or only a similar universal? I do not see how, on the Aristotelian theory, any intelligible answer can be given to these questions. If we concede, however, that universals have being, not only *in re*, but also *ante rem*, no difficulty arises. To this theory, accordingly, we seem driven; although we must now recognize that the question whether there be "non-characterising characteristics" becomes a legitimate one.

Under the head of universals it is customary to include both qualities and relations; and our only excuse for not doing so would have to be either that we had found it possible to reduce one to the other or that, like Bradley, we were prepared to deny the ultimate reality of both. In the history of philosophy the attempt has frequently been made to eliminate relations and to substitute qualities in their stead.[10] The most formidable argument in favor of rejecting relations has been made famous by Bradley. If a relation, he contended, is to connect two or more terms, it must be related to them. This will involve, in the case of two connected terms, two more relations, one relating the original relation to one of the terms, and the second relating it to the other term. Each of these relations, however, will in turn require to be related to the original relation, on the one hand, and on the other, to the apposite term. Thus at each step the relations multiply, yet the connection is never established; and so we find ourselves involved in an infinite regress which is vicious, inasmuch as it requires to be

10. For McTaggart's reflections upon this curious fact see *The Nature of Existence*, Vol. I, sec. 82. I would add that qualities seem to impress the mind with greater facility and force than do relations. One cannot observe a particular without becoming to some extent aware of its nature. I cannot contemplate a rose, for instance, without noticing that it has shape and color, but I can very well fail to notice that it is to the east of my garage. To many philosophers, again, it has seemed that a characteristic which connects two or more entities somehow falls between them, that it has, so to speak, no proper *locus*, and that this is a scandalous admission. In other words, they have demanded of a relation that it behave like a quality—an unreasonable demand which is the outcome of antecedent prejudice.

completed if anything is to be related to anything; hence the very notion of relation, maintains Bradley, is self-contradictory.

The obvious answer would seem to be that this argument derives its plausibility from treating a relation as though it were not a relation but a third term [11] which requires to be connected with the other two. Recognize a relation for what it is, and the plausibility disappears. So St. Thomas Aquinas, who in his day was familiar with the same argument, saw fit to reply to it. Thus he wrote: "Dicendum quod relationes ipsae non referuntur ad aliud per aliam relationem, sed per seipsas, quia essentialiter relationes sunt." [12] Succinct as this rejoinder is, it does seem to go to the root of the matter.

G. E. Moore's response, although more lengthy than that of St. Thomas, appears to make the same point.

It has, I think, been suggested that *whenever* we say of one thing A that it *has* the relation R to another B, part of what is meant by saying that it *has* this relation to B, is that it has some relation *to* this relation. And what I want to point out is that this is quite impossible. It cannot possibly be the case that part of what is meant by *having* a relation R to so-and-so is merely the *having* another relation *to* R. For obviously, if we say this, we are trying to explain the notion of *having* a relation by means of the very notion we set out to explain. If we cannot understand, to begin with, what is meant by *having* the relation R, we cannot possibly understand any better what is meant by *having* another relation *to* R. Our proposed explanation is no explanation at all. We must, therefore, insist that the notion of *having* a relation is an ultimate notion; and that it cannot possibly include as a part the *having* of another relation *to* that relation.[13]

In the passage above there is, I think, some degree of obscurity, if not of confusion. Moore is talking of relations, of the notion of a relation, and of this notion as having parts. One might suppose that a part of a notion would itself be a notion, yet it turns out to be a relation. Some of the obscurity may be removed if we assume that by "notion" Moore intends us to understand, not a psychic state, nor a concept in the sense of a mental product, but what is meant, namely, the relation itself. Even so, I must protest that Bradley, whom Moore surely here has in mind, does not require us to think of one relation

11. See *Examination of McTaggart's Philosophy*, I, 85.
12. *De Pot.*, q. 7: a. 9. ad. 2^{m}.
13. *Some Main Problems of Philosophy* (New York, 1953), p. 346.

as part of another relation. What Bradley says is that we cannot posit a relation without positing with it a whole viciously infinite series of relations, but this is not the same thing as asserting that all these relations are included one within another like a Chinese box. Moore's fundamental point is to be discerned when he insists that "the notion of *having* a relation is an ultimate notion." Whatever here be meant by "notion," he surely intends us to understand that standing in a relation is not susceptible of further analysis. The point becomes clearer in Moore's further observation:

> Why I am insisting on this point is because it follows that where a *property* consists in the having of a relation to something or other, then this property *belongs* to the thing which has it, in some sense which does not mean that it is *related* to that thing. It is, I think, worth while insisting on this point, because, if we say, "Such and such a property *belongs* to A," it is very natural to think that what we mean by the word "belongs" must be some relation which the property has to A. But, you see, where the property itself consists in the having of a relation to something or other, this certainly cannot be the case. The property of being a member of A and B is a property which *belongs* to A in some sense which does *not* mean that it is related to A. This follows because to say that A has this property is merely equivalent to saying that A *has* the relation of membership to A and B; and we saw that no part of what is meant by *having* a relation can possibly be the *having* a relation *to* that relation. It is quite clear, then, that properties which consist in the having of a relation to something or other, *belong* to the things of which they are properties in some sense which does *not* consist in being related to them.[14]

Relations, therefore, for Moore, are not related to their terms; they "belong" to them. The term "belong" is not a particularly fortunate one, for when it occurs in ordinary usage, it certainly does denote a relation. We say that a house or a pocketbook belongs to a man, and this clearly means that it stands to him in the relation of a thing owned to its owner. What, then, are we to understand by "belonging"? It would seem to be equivalent to the "property" of having a relation; and this property, again, is identical with the having of the relation. And the notion of having a relation is, as we have seen, an ultimate notion. Two points of importance emerge from this discussion. The

14. *Ibid.*, p. 347.

first is that for Moore, as for Aquinas, a relation is not related to its terms; and the second is that for Moore the property of having a relation is nothing other than the having of it, it is not a relational quality generated by the relation.

Let us now examine McTaggart's treatment of the same topic. He is prepared to maintain that any relation generates an infinite series of relations and relational qualities, but he insists that such infinite series

> are not vicious, because it is not necessary to complete them in order to determine the meaning of the earlier terms. The meaning of an earlier member in this series does not depend on a later, but, on the contrary, the meaning of any later term depends on that of an earlier term. The fact that A is good starts an infinite series of qualities and relationships. But the meaning of "A is good" does not depend on the meaning of the propositions asserting these qualities and relations. Such an infinite series, therefore, is not a sign of error.[15]

And he adds in a footnote, "I venture to think that this consideration removes the force of Mr. Bradley's argument for rejecting the validity of the conceptions of quality and relation."

The proliferation of relational qualities thus envisaged carries with it the consequence that the nature of everything will include an infinite number of qualities. If we be ready, however, to reject the notion of a relational quality, this conclusion will not follow. Must we concede, nevertheless, that every relation generates an infinite number of relations; that if A stand in a relation to R, it is related to R, and related to its relation to R, and again to this relation, and so on ad infinitum?

Before we attempt to answer this question, let us turn our attention for a moment to qualities. It is generally agreed, I take it, that when Bradley objects to the notion of quality on the ground that when you say "sugar is white" you are violating the law of identity, since sugar can only be itself and not something else, he is confusing the *is* of predication with the *is* of identity. But what is involved in predication? When we say that a lump of sugar is white, do we mean that the universal *whiteness* stands in some relation to the lump? Is qualification a relation? The question is indeed important for one who believes in the reality of universals *ante rem*. The leaf that is green in summer turns red in autumn. Red begins to qualify an entity

15. *The Nature of Existence*, Vol. I, sec. 88.

which it did not qualify before. What is this but to enter into relation with it? But, it may be asked, was not the universal related to the leaf before it began to qualify it? Is not everything in the universe related to everything else? I do not see how one can avoid admitting that such is the case; yet there are indirect, as well as direct, relations. Must we assume that there is a direct, yet purely negative, relation of non-qualification between a quality and a particular which it does not qualify? I do not see that we must. Yet it does seem very plausible, on the other hand, to assert that qualification is a genuine, and a direct, relation.

With this admission does not Bradley's argument appear to return upon us with greater force than before? [16] If qualities cannot characterize particulars without being related to them, must not the same be said of relations? After all, both are universals. How can a universal descend into the realm of particulars except by establishing some connection therewith, and will not this connection constitute a relation which, as such, in its turn requires to be related to its terms by other relations which repeat the same demand, and so on forever? Was not Bradley then right, as against Moore and McTaggart, in maintaining that a viciously infinite series of relations sunders our original relation from the particulars which it aspires to connect as completely as Dives is sundered from Lazarus?

Are we, then, in despair to reconsider our previous decision, and to deny that qualification is a relation? Will this help us in our present predicament? What is qualification? Is it nothing at all? Is it a mere *flatus vocis?* There is certainly a great difference between having a quality and not having it. Wherein does this difference consist? Somehow or other a universal must pass from the state of being *ante rem* to the state of being *in re,* but how does it accomplish this feat? Should this reflection lead us to a further reconsideration? Can we escape from our difficulty by reverting to the Aristotelian position? Is it the distinction between *ante rem* and *in re* that makes the trouble, and, if we repudiate it, will all be well? Clearly our problem will reappear under another form. Instead of asking how a relation which already is can begin to function, we shall now ask how it can be at all. For if it can *be* only in particulars, and if it be sundered from particulars by a viciously infinite series of its own kind, it is plain that by falling into self-contradiction it will have committed metaphysical suicide.

The issue which confronts us is a very serious one. If the notion of

16. I owe this suggestion to my friend and former colleague, Professor Romane L. Clark.

relation will not stand, we face the following dilemma: either we must pronounce qualification a relation, and thereupon proceed to repudiate it, and with it the notion of quality, or else we must deny that qualification is a relation in the effort to save qualities from the wreckage. In either case, whatever system of metaphysics we may construct will differ widely from one which admits the notion of relation; how widely we cannot tell till we have tried.

Is the second alternative, however, really open to us? Experience acquaints us with relations as directly—although, perhaps, not so obviously—as with qualities; and on empirical grounds we have no more right to repudiate one than the other. With regard to the notion of relation McTaggart has observed: "It might be admitted to be valid, and yet denied to be ultimate and indefinable. It might be said that it really was true that substances were in relations, but that the fact expressed in this way could be expressed in terms of qualities only, without bringing in relations. But this also is false. No fact which can be stated in terms of relations between substances can ever be stated in terms which omit the conception of relation." [17] The soundness of this observation must, I think, be conceded. If so, qualities and relations stand or fall together. And if qualities fall, substances fall with them, for the notion of an unqualified substance will not stand for a moment. Consequently either qualities and relations must both be saved, or we must reconcile ourselves to following the guidance of Bradley. In the latter case we shall be compelled to posit an Absolute which may perhaps be directly experienced in a state of mystic illumination, but which cannot be conceived in terms of any categories which the philosopher employs, inasmuch as all these will be infected with self-contradiction. Such an Absolute may perhaps with propriety be called "suprarational," but it will certainly not be rational in any human sense of the term. The notion of a rational universe must therefore be renounced, and with it the conception of religion to which we have tentatively, yet hopefully, committed ourselves. Needless to say, we ought not to shrink from following the argument whithersoever it may lead, provided we are sure that the argument is sound; yet we have every right first to question whether it be sound.

In all honesty I affirm that I regard the argument with deep suspicion. I am convinced that there is something wrong with it somewhere. One way out, of course, would be to deny that qualification is a relation, and to say the same of characterization in general. We

17. *The Nature of Existence*, Vol. I, sec. 81.

should thus, by a single fiat, save qualities; as for relations, we could deal with them as Aquinas and Moore and McTaggart have done. My difficulty is that when we speak of qualification, we mean something; the question is *what*. It seems to me that our trouble has arisen from our allowing ourselves to be enticed by the same assumption which has beguiled Bradley and other thinkers before him—the assumption that relations must behave like qualities. After all, a quality is not a relation, and there is surely nothing monstrous in the requirement that if it is to characterize a particular it must be related to it. But relations are not qualities. To talk of a relation "qualifying" would be absurd, as everyone would recognize; and it would be absurd because we should be treating a relation as though it were not a relation but a quality. May we not, then, justifiably assert that relations connect particulars not by being related to them but by relating them? A relation, we may say, begins to hold between particulars; but this beginning to hold is not the establishment of new relations but merely the linking of particulars. I do not think that this is a merely verbal solution; it seems to me a fair account of what actually happens. And if I be right, our difficulty is at an end.

St. Thomas' brief statement of the case we now see to have been justified. Does it follow, as McTaggart thought, that a relation which begins to hold between terms does, in virtue of this holding, proceed to generate further relations between itself and its terms? Were it to do so, we need not be disquieted by the infinite series of relations thus generated, inasmuch as this would not be vicious—unless, indeed, the notion of a coexistent infinite should disconcert us. But what sort of relations would these be? Let us take a concrete case. Boston is north of New York, and New York is south of Boston. But Boston is not north of the relation *north of*, nor is New York south of the relation *south of*. There are certainly no spatial relations between either of these terms and either of these relations. Need we assume that there are any others? If neither relation must be related to its terms *in order* to characterize them, is there any reason to suppose that *by* characterizing them it generates an infinity—although not a vicious infinity—of further relations? I must report that I do not see that it does.

Some qualities, such as heat, admit of degrees; whereas others, such as circularity, do not. Any degree of a quality will itself constitute a universal, for it is obvious that it may characterize a plurality of entities. Some relations, likewise, admit of degrees. One thing may be more distant from some object than is some other thing. There are relations of superiority and inferiority; and relations of this sort will be grounded in the respective degrees of some quality which the related entities possess. There are other relations, however, which do not admit of degrees—such a relation, for instance, as fatherhood. Relations, again, possess qualities.[18] A relation may be symmetrical, reflexive, or transitive.

Are qualities and relations the only universals? What shall we say of acts? In positing Forms of sitting and flying was not Plato on the right track? Definite and recognizable ways of acting, or modes of action, there plainly seem to be. Shall we regard these as constituting a third type of universal, or shall we attempt to subsume them under the head of qualities? But precisely what is an act? Must it issue from a conscious volition? Is a sneeze an act, or a reflex motion of a knee when tapped by a physician's hammer? We speak of the action of water or of fire; we speak of a volcano as being active, or as being in a state of activity. Linguistic usage suggests that common notions on this subject are deplorably vague. Again, what of that which is acted upon? Can the stone which blunts the edge of an ax, the tree which splinters under its stroke, and the fog which remains serenely indifferent to its swing, be said to react in accordance with their respective natures? Action and reaction, in the case of what we call physical objects, seem plainly to be relative terms.

Should we decide to treat acts as qualities we might appeal to precedent, for motion has frequently been included among the primary qualities. Lord Russell, however, would insist upon analyzing motion into a series of states. Like the Buddhists he cannot abide the notion of a persisting substance which can exist at different places at different times and yet remain self-identical. For it he proposes to substitute a succession of entities each of which exists for a single instant at a particular point in space, there is nothing, on this hypothesis, which passes from one position to another. Such a ruthless elimination of substance, however, involves the substitution for it of process as ultimate reality; and this, as we have seen, lands us in utter unintelligibility. Are we therefore driven to hold, with Bergson, that each motion is a unity which cannot be analyzed into a succession of motions, and is, in a sense, a simple unity? The swing of a golf club, we should then have to say, passes through a succession of states, but it is not itself a succession of states, nor is it composed of motions which are its parts. But the golfer's body is in motion as well

18. I have to thank my friend, Stephen A. Emery, for having pointed out to me this obvious fact.

as the club. Are there, then, two motions, one imparted and one derived? Or is there only one motion, imparted by the golfer and derived in the club? As Joseph puts it: "To be acted on implies something acting; indeed, if action and reaction are equal and opposite, for a thing to be acted on implies that it acts itself; and it is often difficult to say to which of these categories a predicate is to be referred. A ship travels: are we to attribute the motion to the ship, and say that she acts, or to the engines and say that she is acted on? Or shall we say that the engines in turn are acted on by steam?" [19]

Yet a further difficulty now confronts us. Actions and motions of differing types fall into definite patterns, if I may so call them. To hit a golf ball one takes a back swing as well as a forward swing. In running, one lifts one's feet and puts them down again. "The archer hitteth the target partly by pulling partly by letting go; the boatman reacheth the landing partly by pulling partly by letting go." A seed grows into a rose bush, and an acorn into an oak, through a complicated succession of motions which are imitated by every other member of its species. Here we seem to encounter a type of complex universal which we cannot afford to ignore. [20]

What, then, shall we say to these things? We must distinguish, I think, between acts which originate motions and the motions which follow. A mental decision would, in ordinary usage, surely be accorded the title of "act"; yet it is not a motion, although motion may issue from it. Again, the notion of act is closely connected with that of responsibility. We shall do well, therefore, to restrict the application of "act" to considered volitions and the motions which they originate, and to refrain from applying it to derived motions. Acts, motions, and complex patterns of motions seem clearly to constitute distinct types of universals,[21] and I doubt whether anything is gained by attempting to reduce them to qualities.

Numbers, again, clearly claim a status within the realm of universals, for they are entities which can have instances and which yet can be thought of apart from their instances. Any pair is an instance of twoness, any trinity an instance of threeness. There seems no reason why integers and rational fractions should not be treated as quali-

19. *An Introduction to Logic,* p. 60.
20. S. V. Keeling has directed my attention to the way in which the Aristotelian doctrine of "essence" takes such facts into account. The essence of an oak, although potentially present in its matter, does not actualize itself all at once, but by degrees. Viewed in this perspective the Aristotelian essence might be said to constitute a "longitudinal universal."
21. These we might well term "processes."

ties. And it is tempting to analyze negative numbers into qualities which are coupled in the mathematician's thought with the notion of subtraction—in other words, as *res fictae* constructed *ad hoc* for practical purposes. A discussion of irrational and imaginary numbers would involve us more deeply in the philosophy of mathematics than this writer dares to venture; he presumes no further than to claim for genuine numbers *droit de cité* in the realm of universals.

It requires no more than a relatively superficial inspection to convince us that not every universal can be instantiated in conjunction with any other. It is obvious that the presence of one is incompatible with that of certain others—a box, for instance, cannot simultaneously be black and white all over, nor can a volition be triangular. And it is also clear that the presence of one characteristic frequently necessitates that of another. As Professor Broad has suggested, such characteristics may conveniently be called *inseparable*. As an example of what he means he gives us extension and shape. "I think that inseparable characteristics," he writes,

> are always determinables. We find things that have different determinate values of C_2 and the same determinate value of C_1; and we find things that have different determinate values of C_1, and the same determinate value of C_2. Although neither determinable can occur without the other, any determinate value of the one can be accompanied by any determinate value of the other. It is this fact which enables us to recognise that we are dealing with two characteristics, although the two are inseparable.[22]

What are we to say, however, of different shapes as related to shape as such, or of different colors as related to color as such? With this question, genera and species confront us. Are we to think of species as determinates, and of the genus as the common determinable? But what of genera? Are they ultimate determinables, or are they determinates of a determinable yet more ultimate? Are all qualities determinates of the determinable *quality*, and all relations determinates of the determinable *relation?* And how of these? Are they in turn determinates of the determinable *universality?* And now what of universality? Is it a determinate of the determinable *being?* But, on this hypothesis, being is neither a quality nor a relation. How, then, can it be a determinable? And are we to say that a particular is characterized by being, by universality, by quality, and by redness, instead of merely saying that it is red?

22. *Examination of McTaggart's Philosophy*, I, 116–117.

So far as being is concerned we know, of course, the stock answer. A wave of the Kantian wand, we shall be told, has exorcised being from the array of predicates. What, then, is being? Is it nothing at all? The coin which I imagine has the sheen and the shape of one that comes fresh from the bank, yet its non-existence may seriously inconvenience me. To say that "lions exist" means "there are instances of lionhood" is both tautologous and unenlightening, for what is the meaning of "are"?

But perhaps we have gone the wrong way about in viewing the problem through Aristotelian, rather than through Platonic, spectacles. To use a crude illustration, we might say that for Aristotle the species are like the planks of a boat and the genus is like the keel, whereas for Plato the genus is the boat. In other words, the genus, as Plato conceives it, does not exclude, but includes, the species. The species, in his terminology, are its "parts"; that is, they are constituents of it. This is, of course, to make of genus a distributive unity; yet in so doing, we shall not have fallen back into the position of Stout, whose distributive unity is composed of particulars. We are required, however, to envisage the species as a kind, or mode, of the genus; and this necessitates our taking the notion of *kind* as ultimate, which we may not find it easy to do. Yet if the position can be sustained, it bestows upon us certain advantages. The genus will not be above, or apart from, the species; it will be *in* them. We shall not now have to put quality as a characteristic alongside of redness. It suffices to say that a thing is red. Quality will not be *a* quality; it will be the whole system or complex of qualities, as relation will be of relations. And what of universality? How if we make bold to identify universality with being? Being will then be the sum total of universals.

It is often said that a universal is "real" or "subsistent" whereas a particular "exists." The usage is convenient, and our present view enables us to justify it. A universal *is* being, whereas a particular *has* being in the sense that it is characterized by some *kind* of being. And, continuing to follow the guidance of Plato, we may admit that some universals are capable of "blending" with one another. Pink, for instance, is produced by a mixture of white with red. It is not composite in the sense that it is a mixture of white and red spots; yet we are wont to say, and in some sense we say truly, that we can "see" the white and the red in the pink. There is no difficulty, surely, in holding that a new universal is constituted by a blend of the two.[23]

23. In calling it "new" I do not, of course, mean that it begins to be, but only that it actually is blended of the other two.

One reason why so many thinkers have been unwilling to speak of universals as "existing" is that by so doing they might be understood to imply that universals are involved in time and change. To say that they are "real" or "subsistent" is quite consonant, on the other hand, with the contention that they are eternal entities. Here we find operative the same motivation which led Plato to refrain from conceding that the Forms actually do characterize particulars. On the theory now before us, however, this admission has been made. Is such a concession, we may ask, consistent with the assertion that universals are non-temporal entities? And we may further inquire whether our theory necessitate such an assertion. Our present concern is not with the problem of time but with the status of universals; nonetheless, even at this stage of our inquiry, there are several relevant observations which can be made.

It is evident, in the first place, that any difficulty which confronts us is due to the assumption that time is real. The question will then arise whether only particulars—or possibly only some particulars—be in time, or whether universals be in time also. Yet if universals be in time, must they not change? But it is utterly incredible, it may be urged, that a universal could change; a universal can never be other than it is, hence it is plain that it cannot be in time. The question we face is closely connected, however, with another—whether characterization be a relation. If the conclusions reached in our previous discussion of this topic are sound, it is clear that the difficulty will press upon us in connection with qualities, inasmuch as we have seen that it is plausible to regard qualification as a relation. Now a quality may qualify at one time a certain number of particulars, and at another time a different number. And if relations generate relational qualities, the universal will at one time have a relational quality other than the relational quality which it possesses at another time. What we may call its essential nature will not change. The universal will never be other than it is. But it will change in respect of its relational qualities. And it may plausibly be urged that there is nothing objectionable in such an admission. It is an admission, however, which we are not compelled to make, inasmuch as we have not recognized relational qualities.

Nevertheless, if qualification be a relation, the relation of qualities to particulars will change. Now a particular cannot exist without being qualified. A substance is, indeed, more than the sum of its qualities; it is that which has a certain nature, but it must have a nature; it cannot exist with no nature at all. Clearly, therefore, the relation of a substance to its qualities will be a relation which is internal in one term—i.e., in the substance. Yet it is no less clear that in the quality, the relation will be external; for the quality is not dependent for its being upon the substance. It can subsist *ante rem* whether or not it exist *in re*. One wonders whether, had the situation been thus presented to him, Plato would not have conceded that this is all the aloofness his Forms require. It is, at least, all the aloofness which we are justified in admitting.

Still, it may be objected, this is not enough to preserve the eternity of universals. Change takes place in time. Hence, if the relations of qualities to particulars can change—even though these relations be external in the qualities—are not the qualities clearly involved in time? And is not the same true of relations, which at one moment may hold and at another moment cease to hold between particulars? Indeed, if anything be in time, is not everything in time? So phrased, the question seems to dictate its own answer. Perhaps we ought rather to ask, Is not the temporal rooted in the eternal, as the changing in the changeless? But for the moment let us postpone further discussion of this problem.

The conclusion of our inquiry, then, is that the case for the fourth position with respect to universals—that of unrestricted realism—is overwhelmingly strong. In any event, if our criticism of nominalism and of conceptualism be sound, we are justified in feeling absolutely convinced of the objective reality of universals. On one of the most important issues in metaphysics, therefore, we shall have made up our minds. The full significance of this conclusion will only gradually become apparent. But one aspect of the situation is already clear.

If universals be objectively real, awareness of their interconnections will be productive of a knowledge which extends beyond the limits of experience, and which holds good always and everywhere. As Lord Russell has emphasized in *Problems of Philosophy*, such knowledge is arrived at empirically—it is acquired, and not something with which we are endowed at birth—yet its content is a priori, which is to say that it has the characteristics of universality and necessity. Pure empiricism, therefore, is an untenable doctrine. The realm of universals is the realm of a priori knowledge to which access cannot be denied. The balance has thus swung in favor of rationalism and against empiricism.

Chapter Seven

THE REALM OF VALUES

That values [1] constitute a subclass of universals is a view of fundamental importance for epistemology, metaphysics, axiology, and the
philosophy of religion. It behooves us, therefore, to scrutinize it closely.
We can see at first glance that it is congenial to the theory of universals which we have already developed; for once the objective reality
of universals be admitted, it would appear arbitrary indeed to deny
values a place among them. By so doing we should introduce an axiological conceptualism or nominalism into the very heart of a realistic
doctrine. It has been objected, however, that we do not become aware
of values, as we do of other universals, through sense experience; and
that consequently we have not the same justification for believing in
their objectivity.

In reply to this objection there are three things which may be said.
In the first place it may be pointed out that so far as aesthetic value
is concerned, the objection does not hold, inasmuch as we become
aware of aesthetic value through sense experience. In the second
place, attention may be called to the fact that the objection rests
upon one of two presuppositions—i.e., either that sense experience is
the only form of consciousness, or that there is more than one kind of
consciousness but that sense experience is the only kind of consciousness through which we become directly aware of anything. And
either supposition is a mistake. It is clear that we are not limited to
sense experience. Nor does there appear to be any justification for
assuming that there are different kinds of consciousness, only one of
which is capable of making direct contact with reality. Feeling and
volition do, indeed, qualify certain cognitive states, but they are not
themselves distinct and separate modes of cognition. To be conscious
is to be aware of something. In introspection we are aware of ourselves. In sense experience we are dependent upon the functioning
of our sense organs for the stimulation of our attention by sensible
objects; yet it is not evident that we are aware of these in any other

1. In this discussion I shall be concerned with intrinsic values. Anything which
is instrumental to the realization of an intrinsic value is, of course, an extrinsic
value.

way than we are aware of ourselves. The difference is in what is presented and in the mode of presentation. Thus the fact that moral value is not apprehended in sense experience is no ground for questioning the veridical character of our cognition. Were we required to postulate some special and mysterious faculty in the case of such cognition, then, indeed, our position would be much more open to question. But such an assumption would be plainly gratuitous.

And in the third place, we must recognize that there are universals of the instantiation of which we become non-sensuously aware. Thus the coherence of proposition with proposition, the implication of one proposition by another, the convergence of two or more arguments to a common conclusion are relations which are not detected in sense experience; yet we are nonetheless directly acquainted with them. Hence it is no derogation from the status of moral value that the same should hold true of it.

I believe, therefore, that we become acquainted with values, as we become acquainted with other universals, by encountering instances of them. And by an instance I mean—as I hope that I have already made clear—not some *tertium quid* interposed between a universal and a particular but a particular which actually possesses value. Value I take to be a genus whereof the two species most easily distinguished are virtue and beauty. By virtue I mean moral goodness. But I do not intend the term to apply only to those qualities which are dependent for their actualization upon conscious volition, such as benevolence, prudence, impartiality, justice, modesty, patience, resolution, or courage. I mean it to apply also to love and to kindred emotions. McTaggart was in my judgment profoundly right in distinguishing love as an emotion felt for persons from another emotion felt for groups of persons or institutions, such as one's nation, one's family, one's church, or one's college. And he was equally right, I believe, in distinguishing love from another emotion felt toward persons loved by those we love. From what has been said it will, then, be obvious that virtue itself constitutes a subgenus falling under the genus "value."

Is the same true of beauty? Is the beauty of a mountain or a river different in kind from that of great prose, a song, a painting, or a woman? Or is beauty a simple quality, although the things it qualifies are of very different kinds? Is beauty, again, found only in sense experience? Mathematics has been described as "music without sound"; and if this be more than a merely metaphorical description, must we not conclude that those capable of penetrating this supernal region discover beauty there? We sometimes speak, moreover, of a "beautiful character" or a "beautiful soul." What do we mean when we talk in this way? Clearly we mean something positive, but do we mean only that the character or the soul is good? There have been individuals whose characters, I suspect, we should not hesitate to pronounce good, but which we should never think of calling beautiful —such persons, for example, as John Adams or John Calvin. Is this because we consider that, although the character of the individual in question exemplifies certain virtues in a very high degree, it is yet deficient in other important respects, that it lacks, as we say, "well roundedness"? Perhaps it is. Frequently we say that a certain person possesses charm, and sometimes we add that it is present in an individual who is not possessed of physical beauty. Yet we may suspect that much of what contributes to charm is such characteristics as wit and intense vitality, which we should not consider moral qualities. The situation is further complicated by the undoubted fact that personality can affect not only the bearing and carriage but also the facial expression of an individual, and that so powerfully as almost to transform the features and to give them what we might call an imparted beauty. And what are we to say of the apprehension of divine beauty which plays so great a part in religious experience of an exalted type? To what does all this point? Are we to concede that there are kinds of beauty? I am inclined to answer this question in the affirmative, although it is difficult to form a definite opinion when we run so much danger of being imposed on by metaphor. Fortunately, however we decide the point, our conclusion will not affect the subsequent development of our argument.

What, now, of pleasure? Of this I have so far said nothing, yet it is to pleasure that many philosophers would point as to one quality which is an undoubted value. Antisthenes, who declared that he had rather go mad than experience pleasure, has been notably lacking in followers. Are we entitled, however, to affirm that pleasure, whenever and wherever experienced, and in any connections whatever, is always good? Many thinkers would say so, and they would say so even when the total situation in which pleasure occurs they would unhesitatingly pronounce bad. Thus the pleasure I get from turning on my television is, in this view, a genuine good; and it remains so even if I seriously disturb and discompose a very sick person by turning on the television. The suffering which I thereby cause and my own hardness of heart, I shall be told, are bad, and are sufficient in themselves to render my action wrong; yet they do not impugn the goodness of the pleasure as such. This is not an implausible view, and it is one of an appealing simplicity. Should we adopt it, we could then affirm that pleasure is a simple quality, and that whenever and wherever it occurs it is good.

The case for this theory has been clearly and emphatically stated by Professor Charles A. Baylis:

> There is nothing intrinsically bad in the pleasure felt by a sadist in making another person suffer. There is something very bad about the sadist's character, about the condition of his mind, and so on, but these things are evil because they have such bad consequences both for the sadist himself and for his victims. But we should avoid the error of guilt by association. The sadist is a wicked person but this does not make the satisfaction the poor devil derives from his vice wicked or bad. Pleasant experiences are always good in themselves but some of them have very bad consequences, so bad that a person would be a fool to seek them. For in such cases the relatively small amount of intrinsically good pleasure must be paid for by a tremendously large amount of intrinsically bad suffering.[2]

Having at one time held this view myself, I can quite understand how it can be defended even by as thoroughly kindhearted a person as Professor Baylis. Yet there are occasions on which it seems to lose all its plausibility. Thus the favorite summer evening entertainment of the Iroquois, we are informed, consisted in torturing slowly to death a prisoner at the stake. Now, if the Iroquois had at any time enough prisoners to provide such entertainment on every evening, they must have had a very pleasant summer. And if pleasure of whatever kind be always good, the pleasure which the Iroquois derived from this sort of thing actually lessened the evil involved in it. But can the pleasure really be separated from the suffering they inflicted, and from the hellish feelings of cruelty by which their characters were degraded, and be pronounced good in itself? Was not the pleasure rendered abominable by what it was pleasure in? If the Iroquois had tortured their prisoners merely to inspire terror in unsubdued and actually threatening enemies, and yet had themselves taken no delight in it, would the situation have been so bad? It would have certainly been very evil. But would it have been *so* evil as it really was? Did not the pleasure enhance the evil of the whole proceeding? Was it not a bad pleasure?

Let us now take an instance of the opposite type. Consider the

2. *Ethics* (New York, 1958), pp. 264–265.

statement of Nathan Hale on going to execution: "I regret that I have only one life to give for my country." Must we not infer that Nathan Hale experienced an exalted pleasure in his act of self-sacrifice, and that the pleasure was of this exalted kind precisely because it was blended with his feeling of self-dedication? And did it not better the whole situation? I think that we must answer both these questions in the affirmative. Consequently I believe that the theory before us must be modified, although we thereby detract from its engaging simplicity.

The view which I now advocate is that there is both pure pleasure and blended pleasure. By "pure pleasure" I mean pleasure which is felt in the performance of an act which ethically is relatively indifferent [3]—such pleasure as I may derive, for example, from playing chess or taking a walk. Pure pleasure seems to me always good; and I should agree with McTaggart that it is wrong not to enjoy it when we can, since thereby we augment the total amount of good in the universe. By "blended pleasure" I mean pleasure which derives its peculiar "tone"—which is "perfumed," as the Buddhists would say— by the right or wrong act which I am now performing and which I like doing. If the act be right the pleasure, I should say, is good, and is better than a pure pleasure; if the act be wrong it is a bad pleasure.

It will be observed that I have so far said nothing about what are commonly taken to be two types of intrinsic value—truth and religious value. I shall now proceed to discuss both these topics in turn. To anyone sympathetic with the Platonic and Neo-Platonic tradition it will very likely appear nothing less than scandalous that I have not included truth in a triad with goodness and beauty as the highest, if not the only, intrinsic values.[4] I acknowledge that I have not done so because it is not evident to me that truth is an intrinsic value. Truth I take to be the correspondence of a proposition to a fact, and this does not seem to me to constitute an intrinsic value. The knowledge of truth is often of high instrumental value, not only in giving us guidance in action, but also by sometimes giving rise to lofty and intense emotion. Holding, as I do, that emotion always qualifies some state or act of cognition, I do not deny that such cognitive states have

3. I say "relatively indifferent" because I do not wish to become involved in the disputed question whether there be any acts which ethically are wholly indifferent.

4. "Goodness" is a term which may be used either in a wider or in a more restricted sense. Used in a wider sense, it may be equated with value; when employed in the restricted sense, it connotes moral goodness. I shall make bold to use it in either sense, relying upon the context to make my meaning clear.

value, but it is the emotion which seems to me to impart it. And sometimes such emotion is wholly absent. I once heard G. E. Moore say that if we could know some truth about an atom which was not of the least use to anyone, such a truth would be worth knowing. Yet, presumably, such knowledge would acquaint us with some general principle or universal law; and therewith it would acquire an emotional coloring. It is noteworthy that it is to the apprehension of immutable laws or general principles that those who maintain the intrinsic value of truth are forever pointing. Yet there are also many truths which impress us as trivial, and which no sane man would have the faintest wish to know. By the expenditure of the requisite time and energy I could ascertain how many times the definite article has been used in the ten volumes of Professor Toynbee's *Study of History*, and I could compare it with the number of times the same word occurs in Gibbon's *Decline and Fall of the Roman Empire*. Would this be worth doing? Why not? The result would be knowledge as genuine as knowledge can be. Would it be worth having? No, because it is inherently worthless. In fact it would probably arouse a feeling of disgust with its triviality which would be a genuine disvalue. It is not in pure cognition, I maintain, but in cognition characterized by enjoyable or exalted emotion that inherent value is to be found; and it is to be found there precisely because of the emotional element.

Having now defended myself against the charge of displaying an incredible baseness in my estimate of the value of truth, I must next undertake to furnish a defense of my attitude toward the question of religious value. I confess that I do not find in religion any values which I do not also find elsewhere. It may be that in religion we find them all intensified, yet this is not the same thing as discovering that which is a value *sui generis*. Take worship, which is often regarded as *the* religious value par excellence. In worship, at its highest, we find trust, adoration, love, and joy. All these, however, are experienced in human relationships. Perhaps it will be urged that this is not true of adoration, that it is an emotion differing in kind from the most intense admiration which can be felt for human beings, however noble, wise, and saintly these may be. Yet this assertion can be questioned, and it is not easy to see upon what grounds it could be sustained. Surely it is plausible to affirm that adoration of the Deity is the same emotion as admiration for human virtue but experienced in a more intense degree? If this be denied, may we not suspect that what our opponent has in mind is the "creature-consciousness" or "creature-feeling" which Rudolf Otto so emphasized, and which he regarded as *sui generis?* [5] This is a topic I have already discussed in connection with religious epistemology; and I have nothing further to add except to observe that I see no value in the excessive self-depreciation therein involved.

It is, of course, true that in the sacred literature of every great religion, whether theistic or non-theistic, we encounter passages of noble serenity and peace of mind, of the satisfaction of seeing through illusion, of deliverance, of the attainment of a final goal; [6] yet in all this, I submit, we encounter nothing *sui generis.* Be it granted that the feelings and emotions thus recorded were of an intensity unequalled in human experience, and possessed of a very high degree of value, still they are not utterly foreign to experience of a non-religious type, nor does the skeptic who reads of them find them so strange as to render descriptions of them unintelligible. The intrinsic values which I am prepared to recognize are, therefore, virtue, beauty, pure pleasures, and blended pleasures which derive their coloring from their association with right acts and good ends.

Our knowledge of values is empirically acquired, but its content—inasmuch as it is composed of universals and their interconnections—is a priori. Our reason for believing in the objective reality of values, then, is that we are acquainted with them. Any argument in support of this contention, accordingly, must be a *reductio ad absurdum* of some opposing view; for were a direct argument possible, our knowledge of values would itself have to be indirect. It is worth while, however, to consider some of these opposing views, since, if they can be shown to be untenable, or even implausible, our own position will thereby be indirectly strengthened.

In the first place I shall consider the view that values are subjective. In this view it is the interest we take in, or the liking we have for, anything that constitutes its value. In other words, "value" becomes identical with "valuing" or with "valuation." Accordingly, on the assumption that every man knows what he cares for, no man can ever be wrong. The assumption is not an altogether safe one, for psychoanalysts tell us that individuals are frequently mistaken as to the nature of their desires. The subjectivist will assure us that such mistakes are usually due to confused thinking on the subject of ethics. A man feels that he ought to desire, and tries to persuade himself that he does de-

5. See *The Idea of the Holy* (Oxford, 1925), p. 10.
6. Even the atheistic Jain can speak of "the nectar-juice of Highest Bliss" or of "the bridal day of the Glory of Deliverance" (see Barend Faddegon's trans. of the *Pravacana-sāra* of Kunda-kunda Ācārya, together with Amṛtacanda's commentary thereon entitled *Tattva-dīpikā* [Cambridge, 1935], pp. 2–3).

sire, something which in fact he does not desire. Were he a clear-thinking and convinced subjectivist, however, he would realize that his own genuine desires determine what are values for him, and he would have no further hesitation in acknowledging them, whatever they may be. Thus Lord Russell informs us that he personally dislikes oppression and cruelty, and would eliminate them if he could; yet he is prepared to acknowledge frankly that this is indicative only of his own psychological constitution, and that there is no reason why a Bolshevist or a Nazi who delights in oppression and cruelty should not try to satisfy his desires. There is nothing, he believes, in the nature of the universe which favors one outlook rather than the other. Argument therefore becomes impossible, for both parties to any ethical dispute are equally in the right. Hence it is plain that the only way to settle such a disagreement is by resort to force.

To escape from this ethically chaotic situation some thinkers have laid it down as a maxim that the individual is bound to accept the standards of the group, milieu, or society to which he belongs.[7] But this is plainly inconsistent with the theory. If it be the psychological constitution of the individual which determines his values, with what face can we ask him to renounce his own set of values and accept those of other selves? Unless we adopt the hypothesis of a group mind—a hypothesis which requires us to concede that one mind can include others—and unless we further assume that this group mind has desires of its own which fix the values for all individuals belonging to the group, the demand will obviously be an unreasonable one. The individual might justly reply, in the words of Paul, "Why is my liberty judged by another's conscience?" [8] If the desires of A, B, and C conflict with those of D, why should D give way to them unless he be forced to do so? If we once agree, moreover, that the ethical standards of the society to which we belong are to be regarded as ultimately authoritative and sacrosanct, the untoward consequence will follow that any individual who refuses to conform to these standards is, *ipso facto*, in the wrong, and may justifiably be treated as a criminal. The very notion of a social reformer will become self-contradictory. The ethical standards of the community will be frozen as long as this view remains the dominant one. Furthermore, unless our community embrace the entire world, there will be other societies with different sets of standards which will be equally authoritative

7. Thus I once heard an instructor tell an assemblage of students that if a student belonged to a group accustomed to cheat in examinations, he ought to do likewise.
8. I Cor. 10:29.

for their citizens. Thus we may conclude that at present polygamy is permissible in Arabia, and polyandry in Tibet, whereas in America only monogamy may be practiced. But suppose that an individual transfer his residence from the domain of one society to that of another. Is he to carry his old morality with him, or shall he adopt that of his new environment? On the former alternative he remains an outsider. Shall he, then, take the other course? May an American who settles in Arabia proceed to practice polygamy with a clear conscience? Is it rational to suppose that a man can alter his code of ethics with the same facility that he takes off a suit of clothes? Is it merely prejudice that inhibits him? Then he upon whom ethical obligations sit the lightest will be not only the most unprejudiced but the most moral man!

In the face of these considerations it is, I think, sufficiently obvious that if the subjective theory of values be accepted, there can be no appeal to the standards of the group. Each individual's likes and dislikes will determine his set of values, and the standards which are authoritative for him. Social conditions will then depend upon the likes and dislikes of the majority; the individual will be under no moral obligation to accept them; his conformity must be secured by constraint. The domination of the community over the individual will thus be *de facto* and not *de jure*. And by the same token, the individual will have no rights which the majority will be bound to respect. Unlimited democracy, oligarchy, and despotism can with equal facility be justified by this theory. Every man is justified in struggling for what he wants, and in trying to eliminate his opponents; but one thing he cannot ever truthfully say of these opponents, so long as they know their own minds, is that they are unethical. The situation will be reminiscent of that in which the ancient Hebrews found themselves: "In those days there was no king in Israel; every man did that which was right in his own eyes." [9] It does not follow that such a society will be disorderly, but it does follow that there can never be any appeal to right as against force. One may well recall Luther's remark when he heard of the burning of Servetus: "With fire they settle everything." The utmost that can be hoped for is that the majority of individuals will find that their desires are sufficiently in accord to enable them to accept roughly the same set of values.

What is especially striking about this theory is its inability to vindicate the notion of obligation. One determines one's own set of values, and this will doubtless influence one's conduct to some extent;

9. Judg. 21:25.

yet there can be no obligation to seek to actualize these values. For obligation involves a relation of self to other. To say that one is under obligation to oneself is, in the highest degree, misleading; it is to treat the self as though it were two selves, and this it is not. To say that A is under obligation to B, when A and B are two selves mutually distinct, is intelligible; but to say that A is under obligation to A is meaningless. But on the subjectivist theory, the only self involved is the self which, in psychological isolation as it were, determines its own values.

I have been speaking of moral values; but on the theory which we are discussing, aesthetic value is equally subjective. If I say that a thing is beautiful, I mean that I admire it, or that I enjoy contemplating it. Here, again, assuming that I introspect aright, I cannot be mistaken, for I am merely correctly reporting the condition of my own individual psyche. As one man likes cereal for breakfast and another prefers bacon and eggs, so one man likes rock and roll and another prefers Beethoven. There can be no question of one man's taste being better than another. This does not mean that one man's appreciation may not be more cultivated than another's. The study of painting or music will lead to a familiarity with either subject, and may result in a change of taste; and this change may well be productive of greater pleasure. If a man think that a musical education will be likely to enhance his capacity for pleasure, there is no reason why he should not subject himself to it; but if he dislike the effort involved, there is no reason why he should. A changed taste is no better than that which it supplants except insofar as it is more pleasurable, and as to this every man is his own judge. The Chinese Roman Catholic considers the explosion of firecrackers a fitting accompaniment to the celebration of the mass, and the Abyssinian Christian the beating of drums; bizarre as either custom appears to the Westerner, his own judgment is indicative only of his personal prejudice, and provides no more ground for condemnation than one man's dislike for strawberries gives him a sufficient reason for condemning his neighbor's fondness for them.

It will be obvious, from what I have said, that I do not claim to have refuted the theory of the subjectivity of values; but it is plain that it is quite incompatible with the truth of the widespread conviction, which I think that most people untrained in philosophy entertain, that some ethical judgments are true and others false, that the views of aesthetes are as a rule better grounded than those of tyros, and that there are moral obligations which we may, or may not, fulfil yet cannot honestly refuse to acknowledge. This conviction is quite explicable if we be, as I contend, empirically acquainted with values; and the implications of the subjective theory, which seem so incredible, follow from its refusal to recognize this fact. Moreover, it is important to observe that the believer in the objectivity of values is not logically compelled to assert that his own evaluations are all ultimate and infallible; it is precisely because he believes that values are objective that he is prepared to revise his evaluations, and thinks that there may be something to learn from outlooks dissimilar to his own.

Dissatisfaction with the subjective theory, coupled with an unwillingness to recognize the objectivity of values, has led to the development of the subjective-objectivist view. This doctrine, if I understand it correctly, is in the nature of an axiological adaptation of the objective-relativist theory of sense perception. By this I do not mean that it is not possible to be a subjective-objectivist without accepting the objective-relativist view of sense perception, or vice versa; what I do mean is that both theories rest upon the same fundamental conception, and that the former may fairly be said to complete the latter.

According to objective relativism it is a mistake to suppose that the relation of a thing to its qualities is dyadic; on the contrary, the relation is triadic. A thing has such and such qualities in a certain perspective, whereas in another perspective it may possess other qualities; and each perspective is relative to an apprehending consciousness.[10] Thus a mountain, surveyed from five miles away, actually is blue; as seen from five hundred yards away, it really is green. A contradiction, we are told, would arise only were the mountain simultaneously blue and green in the same perspective. And if we ask what the mountain is in itself, the answer is that the question is meaningless. The mountain is nothing outside of, or apart from, the various perspectives in which it is apprehended; it *is* the congeries of these perspectives, or perhaps I should say, their common focus.

It is clear that on this view, the notions of substance or thing, if retained at all, become secondary, whereas that of perspective becomes primary. And it is also clear that if the theory is to be saved from collapsing into idealism, the objective and subjective poles of the perspective must stand on the same footing and be in the same sense

10. Lord Russell, in his *Analysis of Mind* (New York, 1921), has sought to eliminate this dangerous emphasis upon the function of mind by substituting for consciousness spatial location. Both theories have been criticized with devastating thoroughness by Arthur O. Lovejoy in *The Revolt against Dualism* (La Salle, Ill., 1930).

equally real. Even so, it is obvious that the conception is not far removed from the notion of a perception in the idealistic philosophy
of Asaṅga and Vasubandhu. This is not the place, however, to subject
the doctrine to further criticism; our present concern is with the theory
of subjective-objectivism.

In this view the mountain is not beautiful in itself, apart from any
perspective. If, when looking at it, I see it as beautiful, it *is* beautiful
in that perspective; which is to say that it is beautiful as-apprehended-
by-me. The universal "beauty" actually does characterize the complex
mountain-apprehended-by-me. If I shut my eyes, does beauty vanish,
to reappear when I open them? It would seem so. But what of my
neighbor who apprehends the mountain as ugly? [11] Must not the
subjective-objectivist assert that in this other perspective the mountain
is ugly? It is difficult to see how he can avoid doing so; but then the
axiological chaos which we found to be involved in the subjectivist
theory will recur. And how are we to deal with the change of taste
resulting from growth in aesthetic appreciation? Does the perspective
change with the enhancement of the capacity for such appreciation?
Can my mental development of itself bring about the instantiation of
a universal which before was not instantiated? The theory would seem
to require an affirmative answer. Even so, the new perspective will
be no more real, and no more objective, than was the old. The mountain which now *is* beautiful then *was* ugly. It is evident, I submit, that
the ingenious theory of the subjective-objectivist leaves us in practically the same situation as did the simpler subjectivism.

And how of moral values? These become instantiated when men
deal with men. They characterize complexes consisting of interpersonal
relationships. In society certain ends become good and certain actions
right. But here the doctrine appears if anything less plausible. Take
the individual apart from society. Is his conduct devoid of all moral
worth? In the lonely, primeval wilderness of Kentucky, Daniel Boone
daily displayed wisdom, resolution, and courage. Were not these virtues? Or do they become such only when contemplated by others like
ourselves? Again, what of the relation of the individual to society? Shall
we postulate a communal perspective, which seems plainly to involve
the incredible hypothesis of a group mind? Or is there only a congeries

11. When traveling through a famous gap in the southern mountains my father
remarked to an old man who obligingly opened a gate, "This must be beautiful in
the fall." The old man responded, "You would think so, sir, but the sap all runs
down into the ground, and the leaves all turn red and yellow." To the old man
the autumnal mountains were ugly.

of individual perspectives? Will not, then, the individual's outlook be ultimate for him? Will not Paul's dictum, "Let every man be fully assured in his own mind," [12] be as apposite in cases of ethical or aesthetic disagreement as he believed it to be to the question of keeping holy days? If, however, we assume that the concurrence of the majority suffices to bring about the instantiation of values, what shall we say about the possibility of moral progress? Is the reformer justified in disturbing the equilibrium of society only to bring about the re-instantiation of values which were instantiated before? The new axiological perspective which is the result of his activity, if successful, will be different from the old, but in what sense will it be better? The new moral standards are no more objective, and no more authoritative, than were the old in their day. Like the old, they are as objective and as authoritative as the community, or rather the majority, esteems them to be. They may, indeed, be productive of more pleasure. But unless pleasure be a good in itself, and not merely in some perspective or other, what criterion can it furnish of moral progress?

The new theory, it seems clear, leaves us much where we were before. Subjective-objectivism, in my opinion, is related to pure subjectivism much as conceptualism is related to nominalism. Whatever difficulties arise in connection with the simpler view are also involved in the more complicated theory, while in each case the latter introduces fresh difficulties of its own. As conceptualism brings forward the strange notion of an entity produced *ex nihilo* by an individual mind and thereafter dependent upon it, which yet is a universal, so does subjective-objectivism astonish us by its doctrine that values characterize not entities in themselves but entities as related to minds, or in other words, mind-object relationships. Clearly this closely resembles, if it be not at bottom identical with, the objective-relativist view that qualification is a triadic relation. Each theory is obviously formulated *ad hoc*, in order to steer a middle course between two unwelcome extremes. Each is a running with the hare and a hunting with the hounds. Each is ingenious and each is, I believe, untenable. The notion of the ontological primacy of the perspective as more ultimately real is more obvious in the case of objective relativism, yet nevertheless seems to hover in the background in the case of subjective-objectivism. On the latter view it is neither mind nor object, but the complex mind-aware-of-object, which values characterize; it would seem natural, therefore, to treat this complex as ultimate, and

12. Rom. 14:5.

to regard subject and object as abstractions from it. By so doing, we should find ourselves well on the way to an absolute idealism resembling that of the Mahāyāna. And such a view would of course be incompatible with the acknowledgment of the simplicity and sempiternity of the self.

Even should we refrain from proceeding along this way, however, the view is plainly unsatisfactory. Take even the aesthetic situation where I have admitted it to be more plausible than in the ethical. If you see the mountain as beautiful, and I as ugly, is it a mere matter of inexplicable contingency that beauty characterizes one mind-object relationship and ugliness the other? Is there nothing in the nature of the mountain, on the one hand, or in your and my psychological constitutions, on the other, which accounts for the fact? This seems highly improbable. But if we take the former alternative, there is something objective, something in the nature of the mountain, although it is not beauty, which accounts for your seeing it as beautiful; and something else, equally objective, although it must not be called ugliness, which accounts for my seeing it as ugly. Whatever these two mysterious characteristics be, they must be compatible, for the mountain has them both. This is, indeed, objectivism with a vengeance. If, on the other hand, we take the second alternative, we shall have practically reverted to simple subjectivism, and might as well candidly acknowledge the fact.

While I do not claim to have refuted subjective-objectivism, I think that I have shown that it is a very improbable theory, and that there is no reason whatever to believe that it is true. And I venture to make the same claim with respect to the subjectivist theory. Many recent thinkers appear to concur in my estimate of these two doctrines, for they have found it necessary to develop even more radical views. They have seen that the whole question of the subjectivity or objectivity of values can be evaded, if it can be shown that there are no values at all. This is an undertaking which might well appall the stoutest heart; but the history of thought makes it abundantly clear that no doctrine is too extreme to be held if there be a sufficiently strong psychological urge in support of it. In the present instance the urge has given rise to several different theories.

One of these theories contends that what purport to be moral judgments are in reality commands; that they do not tell us what to believe, but what to do. At once we ask, who issues the commands, and why should we obey them? We can scarcely be expected to do what anyone orders us to do. *Some* authority, surely, must invest the commander. If he speak merely in his own name, we shall laugh him to scorn. Does he speak in the name of society? This implies a deification of power, and enough has been said on this topic in connection with subjectivism and subjective-objectivism. Will it be said that the individual issues commands to himself? But to say this, as I have already pointed out, is to substitute misleading metaphor for significant assertion. To "command" oneself, if we can attach any intelligible meaning to the phrase, is nothing else than to resolve. And why should I so resolve? Is my resolution groundless? Then it is purely irrational; it is an inexplicable, and wholly contingent, event. Is there a reason for it? This must be found in the situation with which I am confronted; and with this admission, we return to the position of the objectivist. Does he who utters the command speak in the name of God? How do I know that he is empowered to do so? Or does God himself speak through revelation? Neither view would be in the least likely to commend itself to the thinkers of whom I have spoken. Nevertheless such views have been held, and it may be well to glance at some of the difficulties they involve.

In the first place, it is clear that either view derives ethics from theology. I must know that God exists and, in addition, either that he has delegated his authority or that he has given a definite revelation of his will. I must therefore develop a metaphysic and a theology before I am entitled to form any ethical judgments. Such judgments, accordingly, will follow from an extremely long, and possibly hazardous, chain of inferences. If this be the actual situation, it is certainly a very unfortunate one; and before we acquiesce in this conclusion, we ought clearly to explore every other possibility. There are, moreover, further difficulties which ensue. The commands issue either from the divine will or from the divine intelligence. In the former case, they are wholly arbitrary. We ought not to steal simply because God has forbidden us to do so; had he commanded us to do so, we should have been bound to obey. This is an admission from which many, if not most, theists would shrink; for by it the notion of power is obviously given the primacy, as compared with the notions of the right and the good. Or do the commands issue from the divine intelligence? Even so, they will appear arbitrary to the human being unless, through his possession of reason which enables him to commune with God, he can become cognizant of the rationality of these commands. Will not this imply, however, that the divine and the human intelligence share common standards which are valid for both, which the Deity is prepared to enforce but which he does not himself create? [13]

Enough has been said, I think, of this theory, in its various forms, to show that it is thoroughly unsatisfactory. Let us therefore pass to another view, according to which ethical statements are indicative of approval or disapproval. This in turn divides into two subordinate theories. According to one of these, ethical statements are judgments as to the attitudes of approval or disapproval which most men would take; according to the other, they are expressive of the attitude of the individual who utters them. As to the first form of theory, its weakness is immediately apparent. What if most men approve or disapprove? What relevance have such facts for the individual? Does he concur, or does he not? If he himself approve, this should suffice for him, whatever the opinion of others; if he do not concur, surely it is his duty to defy the majority, as many of those whom we revere as the noblest of human beings have dared to do. Has the majority never been wrong? If it be always right, what we proudly call the history of human progress needs to be rewritten. Let us, then, turn to the second form of the theory. At once we ask, Why do I approve? Is approval groundless? Is it something that arises, as it were, out of thin air? If so, moral approval is reduced to the level of a liking for strawberries. It is a mere quirk of the individual's psychology. Approval is, surely, a considered response to the objective characteristics of the situation, to an end that one sees to be worthy or to an act that one sees to be right.

Reflections of this sort have perhaps been responsible for the formulation of yet another theory according to which ethical statements are merely expressions of emotion, and are no more true or false than

13. Perhaps the clearest and most emphatic statement of this point of view is to be found in the writings of Channing. Speaking for himself, and for his coreligionists, he declares:

We conceive that Christians have generally leaned towards a very injurious view of the Supreme Being. They have too often felt as if He were raised, by his greatness and sovereignty, above the principles of morality, above those eternal laws of equity and rectitude to which all other beings are subjected. We believe that in no being is the sense of right so strong, so omnipotent, as in God. We believe that his almighty power is entirely submitted to his perceptions of rectitude; and this is the ground of our piety. It is not because He is our Creator merely, but because He created us for good and holy purposes; it is not because his will is irresistible, but because his will is the perfection of virtue, that we pay him allegiance. We cannot bow before a being, however great and powerful, who governs tyrannically. We respect nothing but excellence, whether on earth or in heaven. We venerate not the loftiness of God's throne, but the equity and goodness in which it is established. (Works, p. 376, cols. 1–2) are laughs or sighs.[14] But why the emotion? Does it arise in utter spontaneity? Is it not felt *for* anything or *because* of anything? Professor Baylis has put the case against the theory in a nutshell. "It is a falsification of the facts to say that we first have a pro emotion toward anything and then express that emotion by saying that this action is right. It is rather the case that we first discover grounds for believing it right and then approve of it because we have come to believe that it is worthy of approval." [15] Nothing more remains to be said, and with this damning observation the theory may be dismissed.

It is worth while, however, to inquire what could induce men to develop such farfetched theories, which crumble at the first touch of criticism, rather than assent to the doctrine of the objectivity of values. Is there any difficulty, which we have not hitherto noticed, about the theory? Or is there some unacknowledged *arrière pensée* which makes these men loath to subscribe to it, some cherished interest which is threatened by it? I think that both questions must be answered in the affirmative, but I shall at present touch only upon the former.[16]

The objection is constantly reiterated that were values in truth objective every normal person must be aware of them, and that, consequently, disagreement, both in ethics and in aesthetics, would be impossible; whereas, as we all know, the contrary is emphatically the case. Disagreements are manifold and profound. It has been said that no code of ethics has ever been accepted which does not enjoin some action which some other ethical code forbids. And is not such disagreement the consequence of invoking a supposed capacity for intuitive apprehension which the human mind does not in fact possess? Have we any choice, then, but to renounce the hope of obtaining a priori knowledge of an axiological nature and to resign ourselves to a purely empirical approach?

Let us take the last point first. I have already called attention to

14. With this theory the cat has at last fully emerged from the bag. And what an emaciated feline it is! The effort to reduce ethics to utter irrationality, and to discredit completely all grounds of moral obligation, can hardly conceivably be carried further. If the study of history reveal anything to us it is that every great civilization has been based not only upon a religious outlook which inspired conviction but also upon ethical standards which were taken to be objective. It is characteristic of a time of transition, like our own, with its inevitable, and indeed, in many respects, its healthy, questioning of authority, that purely destructive theories, such as the above, should become current. The rats are obviously leaving the ship which they judge to be in the process of sinking.

15. *Ethics*, p. 129.

16. I should have a suggestion to make about the latter were we to come to consider the relation between the philosophy of religion and the philosophy of politics.

the fact that the upholder of the objectivity of values has no need to posit any suprarational or infrarational faculty of cognition, or to rest his case upon a mere appeal to feeling. There is direct, as well as indirect, knowledge. Were we not aware of colors and shapes, we should never suppose that such things existed; no argument would ever lead us to them. And the same is true of self-awareness. If we did not have direct experience of the self, we should not know that it existed. And by the same token, if we were not directly acquainted with values, we should be incapable of conceiving of them or of theorizing about them. As a matter of fact, every theory of ethics that has ever been devised somewhere appeals to direct insight.[17] How do we know that pleasure is good? Because we perceive it to be so. How do we know that ethical statements evince emotion? By observation, and in no other way. For the advocate of any other theory, then, to reproach the doctrine of the objectivity of values for involving the notion of direct awareness is a flagrant instance of the pot calling the kettle black. But if we concede that the knowledge thus acquired is a priori, must we not also admit that there are synthetic a priori propositions? Certainly we must; yet we need not hesitate, for as we have already seen, the proposition that there are no a priori propositions is itself an a priori proposition. Any objection to our theory on this ground, therefore, is inadmissible.

Can the theory, however, be made to square with the facts? What of the notorious discrepancies in moral and aesthetic judgments with which the historian and the anthropologist threaten to overwhelm us? We may reply, in the first place, that the possession of direct insight does not endow us with infallibility. Yet can we be mistaken, it will be asked, in regard to that which we are directly aware? Undoubtedly

17. Professor C. D. Broad notes:
Sidgwick points out, what most Egoists and Utilitarians seem to have failed to notice, that Egoism and Utilitarianism cannot do without self-evident ethical propositions altogether. Both would hold it to be self-evident that nothing is ultimately worth aiming at but pleasure and absence of pain. The Egoist finds it self-evident that an individual ought to aim at a maximum balance of happiness for himself, and that, if necessary, he ought to be ready to sacrifice any amount of other men's happiness in order to produce the slightest net increase in his own. The Utilitarian, on the other hand, finds it self-evident that each individual ought to aim at the maximum balance of happiness for all sentient beings present and future, and that, if necessary, he ought to be ready to sacrifice any amount of his own happiness provided that he will thereby produce the slightest increase in the general happiness. And there might be other very general principles, mainly about the proper distribution of a given amount of happiness, which either Egoists or Utilitarians or both would accept as self-evident. (*Five Types of Ethical Theory* [London, 1930], pp. 148–149)

we can, and often are. In sense perception are we not directly aware of something? Yet the presence of error in connection with sense perception is beyond question, as the proliferation of epistemological theories bears witness. But these errors are errors of judgment based upon sense experience. Quite so, and the disagreements with which we are concerned are indicative of erroneous judgments based upon axiological experience.

Be it granted that sense experience is something in which the meanest intelligence participates as fully as the subtlest or the wisest, whereas the capacity for axiological experience is something which is susceptible of cultivation, and is not possessed by all to an equal degree. Yet, as we survey the field of human life and human history, we encounter everywhere a general agreement as to the reality of good and evil, of beauty and ugliness. The disagreements we discover are about *what* is good and *what* is evil, *what* is beautiful or *what* is ugly, or about relative goodness or evil, or relative beauty or ugliness. All that our theory requires us to admit is that erroneous judgment is possible—and this every other theory must also admit.

Acquaintance with the circumstances and actual environment in which such a judgment is formed often enables us to see how ignorance, failure to observe and discriminate, a lack of sense of proportion, or intellectual confusion could have given rise to it.[18] To the twentieth-century Anglo-Saxon pity is a manly emotion, and cruelty a cowardly vice; to the eighteenth-century Iroquois pity was a cowardly weakness and cruelty a manly virtue. Here we have two ethical judgments which are directly antithetical. Of the falsity of the second judgment it is, I presume, safe to say that we are all assured. Yet we can see something of the way in which it was formed. It is true that pity cannot be allowed in all circumstances to dictate one's course of action. It is true that in battle a man must steel himself to inflict wounds and death; yet it is also true that when the conflict is ended, he who was foremost in the fight may be the first to succor the wounded and dying. What the Iroquois did was to exaggerate sternness to such a degree that it became a revolting ferocity, and to disparge pity as such.

"It should be noticed, in justice to the Iroquois," writes Francis Parkman,

> that, ferocious and cruel as past all denial they were, they were not so bereft of the instincts of humanity as at first sight might appear. An inexorable severity towards enemies was a very es-

18. Cf. A. C. Ewing, *The Definition of Good* (New York, 1948), pp. 18–30.

sential element, in their conception, of the character of the warrior. Pity was a cowardly weakness, at which their pride revolted. This, joined to their thirst for applause and their dread of ridicule, made them smother every movement of compassion, and conspired with their native fierceness to form a character of unrelenting cruelty rarely equalled.[19]

And in a revealing footnote to the above passage Parkman adds, "When Bressani (one of the Jesuits who had fallen into the hands of the Iroquois), tortured by the tightness of the cords that bound him, asked an Indian to loosen them, he would reply by mockery, if others were present; but if no one saw him, he usually complied." The Indian possessed the instincts common to humanity; it was his effort to realize his perverted ideal of the warrior which led him to suppress the element of kindness, a task in which the sadistic pleasure which plays so sinister a part in human motivation undoubtedly aided him. His conception of the warrior is not merely revolting; its utter lack of proportion is indicative of intellectual immaturity. Moreover, it is based upon a fundamental misapprehension of the facts of psychology, for we know very well from experience that cruelty is by no means productive of courage, but is compatible with the extremity of cowardice; and that mercy, so far from being indicative of weakness, is rather a mark of magnanimity. Nonetheless we can see, to some extent at any rate, how such a conception was formed. And we must also allow for the effect upon children subjected to the inculcation of such a notion from their earliest years, who grew up in an environment in which ideas of this sort constituted the recognized standards. How ghastly were the consequences of such training of generation by generation is forcefully brought out by the following observation of Theodore Roosevelt

Any one who has ever been in an encampment of wild Indians, and has had the misfortune to witness the delight the children take in torturing little animals, will admit that the Indian's love of cruelty for cruelty's sake cannot be exaggerated. The young are so trained that when old they shall find their keenest pleasure in inflicting pain in its most appalling form. Among the most brutal white borderers a man would be instantly lynched if he practised on any creature the fiendish torture which in an Indian

19. *The Jesuits in North America* (Boston, 1867), pp. 256–257.

camp either attracts no notice at all, or else excites merely laughter.[20]

I have no intention of trying to exonerate the Indian by pleading that he was true to his own standards. They were perverted standards, and it was he who perverted them. Nor do I envy the subjectivist or subjective-objectivist who must make his theory square with the ghastly facts. I have mentioned them only to show that we can form some idea of how, under the conditions of intertribal warfare, such perversion could take place. And I would point to the fact that certain individuals, such as Tecumseh, were capable of rejecting such standards; this, it seems to me, is indicative of a native capacity for objectivity which is quite in accord with the view that the human mind is endowed with direct insight into axiological reality.

Turning from so extreme an opposition of outlooks to perplexities and disagreements such as beset us in daily life, I would stress the great difficulty which often attaches to the formation of what we consider sound judgments. It is one thing, for instance, to affirm that kindliness is a greater virtue than thriftiness—a proposition which would, I assume, receive general assent—and quite another thing to estimate the relative value of such virtues as loyalty, integrity, impartiality, and resolution. Disagreement here is, surely, quite understandable; yet it does not follow that because some judgments will be wrong no judgment can be right. In the case of aesthetics disagreement would seem to be even more pronounced; and this may be taken to indicate that the capacity for the appreciation of beauty is more rudimentary in most of us, and requires greater effort for its cultivation. Nevertheless, the view that beauty is objective can alone account for the need for such cultivation of taste, and for the greater degree of agreement which prevails among those who have devoted themselves to it than among the masses. Complete agreement as to the end which is to be striven for is quite compatible with profound disagreement as to the means whereby it is to be realized, and a vast number of controversies and dissensions are of this sort. In other words, disagreement is very frequently not about what is good and what is evil but about what is right and what is wrong.

An act is right, I maintain, if the performance of it will actualize the maximum amount of good. If there be two or more acts either

20. *The Winning of the West*, Knickerbocker edition (New York, 1917), I, 68, n. 1. This is, perhaps, the most damning condemnation ever passed upon any people.

or any of which will be productive of this result, then either or any of these is or are right. If an act be productive not of the greatest but of a lesser amount of good, then such an act is partly right and partly wrong. The act which ought to be done is the act which will result in the greatest amount of good, yet it is better to perform an act which will produce a lesser amount than to abstain from producing any good at all. An act which is productive of less than the maximum amount of evil is not wholly wrong; it ought not to be done, yet it is better to perform it than to perform an act which will be productive of the greatest amount of evil. Such an act is wholly wrong; and if there be two or more acts which will produce the greatest amount of evil, each or all of these acts is or are equally wrong. I see no difficulty in admitting that an act can be partly right and partly wrong; and I consider this usage preferable to saying that an act can be good, but not right, or bad, but not wrong. The rightness or wrongness of an act, I maintain, is derivative from the goodness or evil of the end toward which it is directed. As to right and wrong, then, it is quite obvious that the opinions of honest and well-meaning men may easily differ, and that to decide which act is right may often be a matter of extreme difficulty.

In this connection I would urge that it is important to distinguish between what is right and what is one's duty. It is one's duty to do what one believes to be right. One is responsible for doing one's best to form a true opinion, to abstain from ill-considered decisions, to be on the alert for lurking prejudice, and so forth; but it cannot be expected of anyone that he will be infallible. Take the case of a surgeon who, in the light of all his knowledge and past experience, believes that by performing a certain operation he can save a patient's life. If, as a matter of fact, the operation prove unsuccessful and the patient die, it is plain that to operate was not the right act, since it did not produce the result aimed at, which in itself would have been good. Yet is it not clear that it was the surgeon's duty to do what he believed would save the patient's life, that he ought to have done this? On this point there would, I am sure, be general agreement. An act may be wrong and yet be thought to be right, so that it is one's duty to do it. And in like manner, an act may be right and yet be thought to be wrong, and so be done from an evil motive. We may say, then, that it is one's duty to do acts which are *ostensibly right* and to refrain from acts which are *ostensibly wrong*.

Were we adherents of the Neo-Platonic tradition we should be content to recognize objective values, and should refuse to acknowledge objective disvalues. There can be absence of good, we should hold, but not positive evil; and there can be absence of beauty, but not positive ugliness. Consistently, then, we ought also to maintain that there can be absence of pleasure, but not positive pain. I doubt, however, whether there be any philosopher so hardy as to make this assertion. If there be I suggest that he insert his finger into the flame of a candle and report his subsequent experience. I have every confidence that he will experience something other than mere lack of pleasure. But if pain be something positive, why should we hesitate to admit that evil and ugliness are also positive, a conclusion in which experience will plainly bear us out? We must concede that there are disvalues because we are empirically acquainted with them, as directly as we are with values. As there is pleasure so there is pain, as there is beauty so there is ugliness, as there are virtues so there are vices.

It follows, therefore, that the realm of universals is subdivided by a threefold classification. There are values, there are disvalues, and there are universals which belong to neither group, and which I propose to call the "neutrals." Into the interconnections of these three groups, and into the mutual relations of universals and selves, it is now our business to inquire.

CHAPTER EIGHT

THE AXIOLOGICAL ORIENTATION
OF THE UNIVERSE

If death be a departing hence of the soul to another place, and if it be a true statement that all the dead are there, what greater good could there be than this?[*]

That values and disvalues are alike objectively real is, I have contended, the only tenable position. But now we face another question. If it be granted that such is the case, why should we concern ourselves, why should we "set ourselves," as Sir David Ross would say, to actualize values, that is to bring instances of these into being? And why should we set ourselves to eliminate instances of disvalues? That we are obligated to do both is, I submit, beyond question. Let any man ask himself whether there be not certain courses of action which he is assured are admirable, and which it is incumbent upon him to follow, and certain others which are unworthy or despicable, and from which it is incumbent upon him to abstain, and whether this assurance be not so absolute that no conceivable theory could explain it away, and I have no doubt as to what his honest answer will be. While a man may habituate himself to act in disregard of such insight, and, giving himself a willing victim to the lust for power or wealth, pursue courses directed toward the realization of evil ends, it is psychologically impossible for the normal human being to be wholly unaware of what he is doing.

We stand, then, to values in a relation of obligation. It is clearly a simple relation in the sense that it cannot be analyzed into an aggregate of other relations. And it is grounded in the nature of the self, on the one hand, and of values on the other; it is what it is because they are what they are. In other words, it is a relation which is internal in Dr. Ewing's tenth sense. It could not fail to hold unless the self were not a rational self, or unless values were not values. And a similar relation, internal in the same sense, holds between the rational self and disvalues. The self is equally obligated to preserve so

[*]*The Apology of Socrates.*

far as it can such instances of value as it finds in being, and to bring into being as many fresh instances of value as it can, and also to eliminate as many of the instances of disvalue which it finds in being as it can, and to abstain from bringing others into being. Accordingly we may sum up the situation by saying that the self stands to values in a relation of obligation-to-actualize and to disvalues in a relation of obligation-to-negate, and that both these relations are internal in the tenth sense.

It is also clear that there are counterrelations holding between values and disvalues, on the one hand, and the self on the other hand. The effort is sometimes made to express the status of values by saying that a value is "something which ought to be." Yet it is plain that this phrase cannot be taken literally. Only of that which is not, or which might not be, do we say that it ought to be. Of the being of values there can be no question; like all universals, they *are*. It is the instance of value, the characterization by it of a particular, which may, or may not, be. We might, then, say that a value is something which ought to be instantiated. Yet even this statement is in the nature of an anthropomorphism. For if we say that a value ought to be instantiated, and that someone ought to cause it to be so, it is obvious that we are not using the word "ought" in a univocal sense. Only an intelligent being can acknowledge responsibility. And the same is true if we say that a value "demands" to be instantiated, for only intelligent beings can make demands. Yet it is equally plain that a value does stand to the self in a relation different from that in which any other universal stands, that it does present itself as a goal or as an end, as a τέλος, that it does in some sense require to be actualized. It is doubtless true that we have no name for this relation, which is the converse of that of obligation-to-actualize; yet this fact does not excuse us from recognizing it. Disvalues, again, stand to the self in a relation which is equally unique, one which is the converse of obligation-to-negate. And this also is nameless. We may try to state it by saying that disvalues are "negative ends." They are "there," if I may put it so, to be shunned and detested; reverting to anthropomorphic language we may say that a disvalue is something which "ought not to be." It will be convenient, I think, to call the relation of obligation-to-actualize a relation of "positive obligation," and the relation of obligation-to-negate a relation of "negative obligation"; the converse relations may fittingly be termed those of "positively obliging" and "negatively obliging."

Let us now look more closely at these relations. It is obvious that a dyadic symmetrical relation which is internal in the tenth sense [1] is so in both terms. And the same is true of a dyadic asymmetrical relation. If A be the cause of C, and C the effect of A, the relation of cause and effect could not hold between them unless both terms were what they are. A dyadic non-symmetrical relation, on the other hand, may well be internal in only one term. My admiration of a forested mountain, for example, is conditioned by the mountain in a way that the mountain is not conditioned by my admiration of it.

Now it is clear that the relations of positive and negative obligation, and the relations of positively and negatively obliging, are all internal in both terms. They could not be what they are unless the self were what it is, and unless values and disvalues were what they are. A self which acknowledged no standards and recognized no values would not be a rational self. It could not even consciously pursue pleasure. That it must have ends to live for, if it is to be human, is as indisputable as anything can well be. Abolish values, and the self as we know it disappears with them. Values and disvalues, again, could not present themselves as positive and negative ends unless there were selves to present themselves to. That such is the situation is strikingly obvious in the case of virtues and in the case of pleasure. For there is nothing which these universals can characterize other than conscious beings. And while we might be ready to admit that a universal *may* have no instances, we cannot fail to realize that a universal which *could* have no instances would be a contradiction in terms; for a universal is precisely the kind of thing which *can* have instances. It is clear, therefore, that in a mindless universe there could be neither virtue nor pleasure; and by the same reasoning, there could be neither vice nor pain.

At first glance, however, it might appear that beauty stands in a different position. Beauty, it may be urged, can be instantiated wherever there are sensible objects, and surely these do not require the presence of mind for their existence. With the truth of this last affirmation we need not at present concern ourselves, nor speculate as to what would become of sense data were there no minds to contemplate them. Let us grant, for the nonce, that sensible objects can exist, even if unapprehended; and let us grant, in addition, that they may be beautiful. Yet these will be only instances of beauty; and it is not with them but with the universal beauty that we have to do. Were beauty a primary quality, such as circularity, or a secondary

1. It is with this sense of internality that I shall be concerned throughout the following discussion.

quality, such as redness, it might seem that there would be no difficulty in positing its existence—or, if one prefer, its subsistence—in a
mindless world. But beauty is a value, and can there be a value
with no one to evaluate it? A value, as we have seen, offers itself
as an end to be realized, as a goal to be striven for; and this it can
do only if there be conscious beings who can make it their end and
endeavor after it. Beauty in a mindless world would therefore be as
much a contradiction as a shield with only one side. And what is
true of beauty is likewise true of ugliness.

I trust that from what I have said it will be quite clear that I am
not arguing that values are mental products. What I do contend is
that the reality of rational selves involves that of values and disvalues,
and that the reality of values and disvalues involves that of rational
selves; that in the structure of the universe they are mutually interrelated, and that neither mind, on the one hand, nor values and disvalues, on the other, could be expunged without subverting that
structure.

Turning next to the neutral universals, we observe that selves do not
stand in direct and internal relations of positive or negative obligation
to any of these. We feel under no obligation, for example, to conserve
or to bring into existence as many instances as possible of redness or
squareness, nor yet to eliminate as many instances as possible of these,
nor to abstain from producing more of them. We may speak, if we
like, of values as constituting a system, and of disvalues as constituting
another system. These two antithetical systems may be said to stand
to each other like two opposing mountains, whereas the neutrals compose the plain between them and are, as it were, indifferent to the
opposition which obtains above them.

Yet it is plain that neither good nor evil ends can be realized to
any extent without the co-operation of the neutrals, and this is as
true in the realms of ethics and aesthetics as in that of pleasure. I
may make a good resolution, and this will no doubt to some extent
strengthen my character. But to resolve means to seek to *carry out,*
and I cannot carry out my resolution *in abstracto.* Let us suppose that
I determine to contribute money toward the erection of a hospital.
My contribution will take a physical form. And the building of the
hospital will involve the utilization of stones, bricks, concrete blocks,
beams, and girders, the natures of all of which are composed of neutral
universals. Again, if I be a painter, I may resolve to paint a picture,
and this once more is excellent so far as it goes. But it does not go
very far until I begin to work, and then I shall need paint and canvas,

and the production of the picture will involve the instantiation of shape and color. And in the case of pleasure, of course, the contribution of sensible objects is too obvious to require more than a mere mention. What is true of the realization of good ends is equally true of the realization of evil ends. The neutrals are, so to speak, the *terrain* upon which the combat between good and evil is waged; they are like the turf which lends itself with equal facility to the construction of entrenchments by either of the two opposing forces.

Moreover, good and evil do not supervene upon any entity regardless of whatever characteristics it may possess. Moral goodness has its basis in very definite qualities which we call the virtues because they participate in goodness; and moral evil is rooted in equally definite vices. A physical object, again, is beautiful because of its outline, texture, color, etc.; and in the same way an ugly object is ugly. Pleasure and pain, moreover, do not arise without mental and physical concomitants. By saying this I certainly do not mean to suggest that values are susceptible of being analyzed without remainder into collections of "natural" qualities; for I have already contended that value is *sui generis*. What I wish to point out is that values are internally related to various other qualities, so that the possession of these entails the possession of value. And I wish further to call attention to the fact that, whereas selves are *directly* connected by internal relations of positive and negative obligation only to values and disvalues, they are also *indirectly* connected through values and disvalues to the neutrals, so that selves and universals, taken together, are comprised within an intelligible system all the components of which are subtended by internal relations. And in this system the particulars which the neutrals characterize must also be included, so that this intelligible system will be identical with the universe.

That the universe constitutes an intelligible system follows, as we have seen, from the adoption of the entailment theory of causality, either in its pure form or in combination with the activity view. Which of these alternatives we should embrace was a question we shelved pending a discussion of the issue of free will versus determinism. Nevertheless, in view of the fact that the regularity view appeared quite unsatisfactory, it seemed clear that the entailment view, in one form or another, had strong claims upon our acceptance. And the conclusion to which this led us has now been powerfully reinforced by the independent chain of reasoning we have just completed. Not only does this line of reasoning support our previous conclusion, however, it also expands our ontological perspective. For now we see that the universe possesses, as it were, a positive and a negative pole, the former being constituted by the system of values and the latter by the system of disvalues.

This enlargement of our perspective is of the highest importance. We had, indeed, already been led to admit that the universe is, to some degree and in a certain sense, rational. Our recognition that the "laws of thought" are laws of being, and that the causal connection is internal in the tenth sense, had assured us of so much. Yet this does not of itself suffice to vindicate the outlook of religion. A universe which was rational only in this sense might still be utterly indifferent to human aspirations, desires, and hopes. But once we take as established the objective reality of values and disvalues, and once we recognize that these must be included in the integrated structure of the universe, the situation is changed. A valueless universe would be a universe which was wholly indifferent to us in the sense that there would be nothing in its structure which was relevant to human ideals and to human destiny. But a universe which includes in its structure values and disvalues cannot be thus indifferent. This is what I had in mind in making my previous assertion that the universe may be either a good or a bad universe, but that it must be one or the other.

Permitting myself for a moment to employ anthropomorphic language, I may describe the situation by stating that, whereas the neutral universals make no direct claims upon particulars, values demand to be actualized and disvalues to be negated. It seems clear, therefore, that values constitute the zenith, and disvalues the nadir, of the realm of universals. But the realm of universals is not a separate universe. The world is made up of universals and particulars, and the nature of every particular is composed of universals. However the realm of particulars be ordered, it must be so integrated with that of universals that the two compose a single universe, and it is difficult to see how this can be accomplished unless the position in the universe occupied by values be a predominant one.

Perhaps it will be urged that this going too fast, that the argument as I have so far presented it proves too much. If values attract and disvalues repel, would it not follow that the universe as a whole must be so oriented with respect to values that these alone will be instantiated, so that there will be no room in it for evil at all, so that disvalues will be mere toothless dragons which can never bite, like the evil in a child's fairy story which amuses by its very impotence? But there is evil, and great evil, in the universe. And does not the recognition of this undoubted fact require us to revise our entire position?

I quite agree that we are by no means entitled to rush to an optimistic conclusion, that we must proceed slowly, step by step, making sure as we go of the ground upon which we tread. Many problems of a highly crucial nature lie before us, upon which we have not even touched. Of these the most prominent at the moment is the problem of evil. I can only plead the inability to discuss all topics at once from which all philosophers suffer. What we have done was to pass from the consideration of the self to that of universals, and next to that of values and disvalues. I propose now to continue further upon the line which we have so far followed. We have seen that selves, values, and disvalues, taken together, constitute a subsystem within the system of the universe; and we have seen that the self and values and disvalues are so interconnected that the reality of one involves the reality of all. Disvalues are the obverse of values, and the self is, if I may so put it, suspended between the two, being connected by relations of positive obligation to the former and by relations of negative obligation to the latter.

The self cannot fail to recognize the reality of these relations, yet it can fail to act in accordance with such recognition. It can, and frequently does, pursue evil rather than good. How is it possible, we ask, that a rational self should act irrationally? It is easy to answer that rationality is an ideal which the self is capable to some extent, but never completely, of realizing. Yet this does not settle the matter. Is it psychologically possible for the self to say "evil be thou my good"? In other words, is it possible for the self consciously and avowedly to make the actualization of disvalues its goal? Many thinkers have denied this. They have maintained that when the self seeks to actualize evil, it does so because it mistakenly envisages it as good; as when cruelty, for example, is erroneously conceived to be a virtue. Clear vision, they have insisted, always issues in right action. This is the famous Socratic contention, that no man knowingly does wrong, that vicious conduct invariably springs from ignorance. Yet other thinkers, following the lead of Aristotle, have conceded that the self may through weakness fail in its moral resolution, that it may give way to the pull of a lesser but more immediate good, that it may, for example, surrender to the powerful attraction of sensuous pleasure in disregard of the call of duty. Some thinkers, however, have not shrunk from the more pessimistic conclusion that the self is capable of taking a perverted delight in the conscious actualization of evil as such, and in this they have been supported by psychoanalysts who have explained to us the processes of conditioning whereby such pathological perversion comes about.

In general estimation the Socratic view appears to be regarded as untenable. Whichever of the two remaining views be correct—and I find it difficult, myself, to reject the latter—it is clear that the self can consciously pursue courses which it recognizes to be unworthy and harmful, as both determinists and indeterminists acknowledge. In so doing the self acts *as if* the relations of positive and negative obligation had been transposed; but inasmuch as such transposition has not actually taken place, it is in so far "acting a lie," as we say; it is in so far acting against nature. And insofar as the self acts in accordance with its obligations, it is acting in accordance with its nature and with the nature of the universe. Insofar as the self makes values its ends, they function as final causes; insofar as it makes disvalues its ends, they too function as final causes. And in either case, the self is, of course, the efficient cause.

The process of instantiating values does not leave the self unchanged. The truth of this assertion is most obvious in cases where the good aimed at is the self's own moral improvement; nevertheless, the change may be even greater when the end in view is the material or moral benefit of other selves. A persistent effort to make oneself a better person, and to instantiate in oneself one's own ideal, is doubtless an excellent thing. The world would be a better place were more people seriously concerned about their own moral progress. Too exclusive concentration upon it, however, is apt to result in a self-absorption which tends to defeat one's own efforts; too much feeling of his moral pulse may make a man something of a spiritual hypochondriac. Character often grows best when one is not looking at it, and devotion to others is the mightiest agency in such growth. Yet, however it comes about, moral development involves the progressive instantiation of higher degrees of value. But one does not thus instantiate values as one dons a suit of clothes in the morning to doff it again in the evening. Instantiated values enter into the nature of the self, which thereby becomes other than it was.

What is the goal of this process? Or has it an ultimate goal? Or is there only an infinite series of proximate goals, each stage being the proximate goal of its predecessor? Shall we, then, state the situation with sufficient accuracy if we say that the goal is at an infinite remove from us, and would require for its realization an endless time? And are we, accordingly, justified in adopting in Kantian fashion the hypothesis of an unending future life as a moral postulate?

I would point out, in the first place, that we have something very much better than a moral postulate; for we have already accepted as absolutely conclusive a metaphysical argument for the sempiternity of the self. And I would urge, in the second place, that in order to have a sufficient motive for leading a moral life, the acceptance of such a postulate is unnecessary. If values be objectively real, and if we stand to them in a relation of obligation, it is clear that we ought to fulfil these obligations whether we be immortal or not. Even if we cannot progress forever, we ought to progress as far as we can. I acknowledge, indeed, that if we be not immortal, the obligation will be lessened; and this is a fact which is often overlooked. Yet it is clear that if our greatest efforts can be productive only of transient effects, either in ourselves or in others, the obligation to put forth these efforts is less than it would be were the effects enduring. The possibility of the greater good entails the greater obligation to realize it. Nevertheless, if we be not immortal, the obligation, although lessened, remains; and many have found in it sufficient motivation for leading a good life. Moreover, the appeal to a belief in immortality as a motive for good conduct is unpleasantly like demanding a reward.[2] There is a stern grandeur in doing right for its own sake regardless of consequences; and many will agree, I think, that only the man who can rise to this level is morally entitled to the further satisfaction of a cosmic optimism.

In the third place I would suggest that, upon surveying the entire situation, we may find what is better than a mere moral postulate, and that is sound reason for believing in an afterlife, and this quite distinct from the argument which previously led us to acknowledge the sempiternity of the self, and, therefore, providing powerful reinforcement of our general position. I should not, indeed, be prepared to accept without question the notion of endless progress, for there is a vagueness about it which inspires mistrust. Is it possible, I would ask, actually to conceive of the self as increasing in qualitative excellence ad infinitum? Doubtless it would be a serious mistake to pitch our hopes too low. What above all distinguishes the religious from the this-worldly outlook is the splendid optimism of the former. Not only for the Christian but also for the believer in many another re-

2. To see how low a philosopher can fall who yields to this temptation one need only consult Locke, *Reasonableness of Christianity*.

ligion is it true that "it is not yet made manifest what we shall be." [3] Paul's hope of being transformed "from glory to glory" [4] is a precious heritage. Nevertheless, it does not follow that there is no ultimate τέλος, no beatific vision which constitutes a final attainment, no state in which every capacity for good obtains its maximal actualization and every capacity for evil is utterly eradicated. Perfection, rather than endless progress, seems clearly the goal we should posit; for the notion of endless progress requires us to think of the self as a sort of psychic balloon capable of limitless inflation.

Perfection is plainly too lofty a goal to be attained *secundum statum praesentis vitae*. The scope and clarity of insight, the completeness of emotional satisfaction, and the fulness of joy unmixed with pain which it involves are not be had while we are joined to these mortal bodies and subjected to the evils of this present state. How far we can rationally hope that moral evil is susceptible of being eliminated from this earthly sphere is no doubt a debatable question, but we can hardly expect that it will ever be completely eradicated. Even were this feasible, however, pain and suffering would certainly remain. Moreover, the greatest of all values, love, dooms us to experience anguish in the death of loved ones. With extraordinary callousness Plato declared that the good man experiences such anguish to a lesser degree than the evil man.[5] But if experience teach us anything, it is that this assertion is profoundly untrue. Far truer is Froude's observation that "if happiness means absence of care and inexperience of painful emotion, the best securities for it are a hard heart and a good digestion." [6] It is precisely the man who is most capable of love who is most capable of sorrow, and it is the self-centered man who suffers least.

All this is true, it may be said, yet all this is irrelevant. Suffering is evil, and it is bad that the good should suffer most; yet how do we know that the universe is not very bad? But let us look once more at the situation in which we have found the self to be placed. We have seen that selves, values, and disvalues constitute a subsystem the components of which are linked by internal relations, and that the reality of any one of these three groups of constituents involves the reality of

3. I John 3:2.   4. II Cor. 3:18.
5. Possibly Plato meant that the good man, if he be a philosopher, will be consoled by the conviction that the separation caused by death is but transitory. This is true; yet the consolation, while it does indeed mitigate, does not abolish sorrow; and it is the good man, in the sense of the true lover, who will feel sorrow most.
6. See his essay, "Calvinism," in *Short Studies in Great Subjects* (New York, 1964).

all. We have seen that values which could not be instantiated would not be values, that disvalues which could not be negated would not be disvalues, and that the self which did not adopt values as its final causes would not be rational, and would be without an end to live for. Granted, the opponent may concede; still, so long as there are selves in the universe the requirements are fulfilled. A succession of transitory selves would do as well as a company of immortal selves. The data before us provide no ground for the conclusion that the individual self must live forever.

In reply to this objection there are four points which I would stress. The first is the obvious one that there can be no obligation where there is no possibility of performance. If the self stand in relations of positive and negative obligation, this means that it is capable of fulfilling them. It cannot be obligated to strive for perfection unless perfection be attainable. And yet the religious man actually does strive *as if* it were attainable. My second point is that we must take into consideration, not only the bringing into being of an instance of value, but also the subsequent state of exemplification thereof. Thus the end of right action is twofold, production and conservation. Instances of value are brought into being in order that they may be. This leads us to the third point. In any particular case of the instantiation of value, we have to consider not only the kind and degree of value exemplified but also the duration of its instantiation. And while in an individual case it may be difficult to determine whether length of duration will compensate for inferiority in kind or degree—whether, for example, a state of moderate physical pleasure which lasted for a thousand years would or would not be preferable to a state of pure and exalted emotion which lasted for half an hour—it is clear that, other things being equal, the longer an instance of value endures the better. The more instances of value there are, and the longer they last, the better the universe which contains them. My fourth point is that the eradication of any instance of value involves the instantiation of a corresponding instance of disvalue; the greater the value destroyed, the greater the disvalue actualized. Thus the destruction of the statue of Zeus at Olympia, which the ancients accounted it a misfortune to die without having seen, left the world poorer in that it was permanently deprived of an object of surpassing beauty.

When a thing lacks something which normally belongs to it, it is commonly said to be in a state of privation. Thus a one-armed man may be said to be in a state of privation with respect to the missing arm. But now it will be convenient to make a distinction. If the man were born with only one arm, he may properly be said to be in a state of privation, inasmuch as the normal human has two arms whereas he never had but one. If, however, he once had two arms and subsequently suffered the amputation of one arm, it would better fit the case to say that he is in a state of deprivation with respect to the lost arm. We may now extend the notion of privation to apply to any unrealized possibility. Thus we are told that Shah Jahan intended to erect a building which would reproduce in black marble the design of the Taj Mahal. This was not done, and with respect to the unerected building, the universe is in a state of privation. But with respect to the statue of Zeus, which once actually existed and was at a definite moment destroyed, the universe is in a state of deprivation.

Is it not plain, one might ask, that some states of privation or deprivation will leave the world better rather than worse? If what was not actualized, or if what was destroyed, were an instance of vice or ugliness or pain [7] or evil pleasure, the world will be the better; if it were an instance of virtue or beauty or good or pure pleasure, the world will be the worse. For whereas privation or deprivation are negative states, the good or evil they carry with them are not negative but positive; there is no such thing as negative goodness or negative evil. [8]

Has the Universe Value?

Before we answer this question, as I think that we ultimately must do, in the affirmative, let us examine it carefully. Were the universe a mere aggregation of entities, or a mere conjunction of processes, devoid of any systemic and intelligible structure, and were the presence of any good or evil particular purely fortuitous, the only sense in which we could speak of the universe as being either good or bad would be in respect of the preponderance of good or evil particulars it contained. [9] But were this the case, would it not be more correct to

7. Are there states of good pain as well as of evil pleasure? I think that we must say that there are. Sympathetic pain is pain that is well felt, that a good man feels because he is a good man. The situation is better because of it, although the situation is bad as a whole.

8. It is for this reason that it is preferable to speak of "disvalues" rather than of "negative values," for a disvalue is as positive as a value.

9. "There is," writes McTaggart,
a sense in which a predicate may be used of a whole which is really applicable only to the parts, and to use it in this sense is quite legitimate, if only the distinction is clearly made. It is quite legitimate to say that one town is more drunken than another, although it is impossible for a town to get drunk at all.

acquiesce in McTaggart's contention that the universe *has* no value, although there is value *in* it?

"Even if, as I believe to be the case," McTaggart declares,

> all existent reality forms a single unity, in which the unity is as real and important as its differentiations—even in that case the goodness or badness to be found in the whole would not be a unity. It would be a multiplicity of separate values—positive or negative—which would indeed be added together as respects their quantity, but which, when added, would only be a mere aggregate, not a unity like the unity of existence. In other words, again, the universe as a whole is neither good nor bad. I do not mean by this that it is equally good and bad, but that the terms, in their strict sense, have no application to the universe as a whole.[10]

In order to clarify his statement McTaggart has made use of the following illustration:

> To say that the universe has value is as incorrect as to say that a town is drunken. A town cannot be drunken, since the inhabitants, as a single substance, cannot drink at all, and therefore cannot drink to excess. But we can speak of the total, or average, drunkenness in a town by adding together the drunkenness of the drunken inhabitants to get the first, and by comparing this with the total number of inhabitants to get the second. And either of these would often be spoken of as the drunkenness of the town, though, as we have seen, this would be incorrect. In the same way, people often speak loosely of the value of the universe, even when they hold that only selves have value. But they should then speak of the value in the universe.[11]

What is meant is either that the aggregate drunkenness, or the average drunkenness, of the inhabitants is greater in one town than in another. In the same way, if we came to the conclusion that the average conscious being in the world was in a good state, or was becoming better, we could say that the universe as a whole was in a good state or was becoming better. But we should not be speaking of any value as belonging to the universe as a whole, but of the average value of its conscious parts. ("The Individualism of Value," in *Philisophical Studies*, pp. 102–103)

It is, presumably, in this sense that McTaggart has permitted himself to speak of the "ultimate nature" of the Hegelian universe as "rational and righteousness" ("The Further Determination of the Absolute," in *Philosophical Studies*, p. 212).

10. "The Individualism of Value," in *Philosophical Studies*, p. 97.

11. *The Nature of Existence*, Vol. II, sec. 790.

It might be objected, however, that in all probability the drunkenness of the drunken inhabitants of a town is not unconnected with the fact that they live in this particular town. In this respect they differ from the members of a mere fortuitous aggregation of individuals, such as the crowd in the waiting room of a railroad station. Let us suppose that there are three hundred people in the waiting room, and that twenty of them are drunk. Clearly the drunkenness of the twenty is not due to their being members of this haphazard and transient collection of persons. The habitual drunkenness of a certain percentage of the inhabitants of a particular town, on the other hand, in all likelihood has a very intimate connection with the system of legislation in force and with the character of the authorities who enforce it.

The truth of this assertion McTaggart would not contest, yet he would stoutly maintain that it is irrelevant as an objection. "The doctrine that value cannot belong to the universe or to societies, while it does belong to their parts," he states,

> has often been condemned as unduly atomistic. This, I think, has been due to the mistaken supposition that the doctrine involves that the value of a self is independent of the other selves with which he stands in relation, or of the relation in which he stands to them. This, of course, would not be true, but it does not follow from the doctrine. Drunkenness can only be a quality of a man. It cannot be a quality of a town. But the drunkenness of a man may be largely determined, positively or negatively, by the character of his neighbours and the institutions of his town. In the same way, the value in each self does very largely depend on his relation to other selves. But this is not inconsistent with the fact that all value must be in a particular self.[12]

Briefly stated, then, McTaggart's view is that only conscious beings can possess intrinsic value, and that, since the universe is not a conscious being, it can possess no intrinsic value. Yet it can, and does, he insists, possess extrinsic value.

"Now the universe as a whole," he writes,

> can be of value as a means. The fact that the universe is a unity, and that it is this particular sort of unity, may be known to conscious beings, and this knowledge of it may increase their happiness, or stimulate their virtue, or may in some other way

12. *Ibid.*, sec. 791.

change their conscious states so as to affect the value of those states. Then their knowledge and virtue may have ultimate value. And so the universe as a whole may have value as a means of providing this knowledge or virtue.

. . . .

Again, the unity of the universe, and the fact that it is a particular sort of unity, will certainly influence all conscious beings, whether it is known to them or not. They would be different from what they are if the unity of the universe were different, or if they themselves were not parts of the universe. (In the latter case, indeed, it might be maintained that they would not exist at all.) And so it will affect their natures, and therefore their values, and will itself have value as a means.[13]

What of McTaggart's contention that only conscious beings can possess intrinsic value? It seems clear to me that we must reject it. For beauty is an intrinsic value, and it is certain that beauty can characterize sensible objects. Moreover, as we have already noted, we sometimes find the adjective *beautiful* applied to realities of a different order, as when it is applied by mathematicians to the realm of mathematics. Whether or not it be then employed in a univocal sense is, perhaps, a moot question; but in any case, we must concede that the integration of a plurality in the unity of a system can inspire the mind qualified to contemplate it with a feeling of delight, and that this delight is called forth by some characteristic of the system as a whole which, if it be not purely aesthetic in nature, is at least closely akin thereto. Necessary connections, relations of implication, form a structure characterized by a rationality, an intelligibility, which is as objective a value as the beauty of autumn leaves.

Now, if this be true of any system, is it not plainly true of the all-inclusive system which we call the universe? For unless the course of reasoning we have so far pursued have led us completely astray, we have found that the universe is no mere aggregation of entities, but a system, teleological in its structure, and axiologically oriented. We have seen, in the first place, that all the particulars whereof we have any knowledge—and presumably all the particulars that exist—are directly or indirectly interconnected in a causal *nexus* of internal relations. We have seen, in the second place, that selves, values, and disvalues, taken together, constitute a subsystem the constituents of which are directly interconnected. And we have seen, in the third

13. "The Individualism of Value," in *Philosophical Studies*, p. 102.

place, that both these subsystems are included in a vaster system wherein selves are directly connected with values and disvalues by relations of positive and negative obligation, and through values and disvalues are indirectly connected with the neutral universals whose co-operation is essential to the actualization of values and disvalues. And what holds true of neutral universals holds true also of sensible objects, whatever their ultimate nature. It is this systemic character of the universe, I submit, which gives it value.

McTaggart, as we have observed, insists that the universe as a whole has value only as a means. In ordinary usage to speak of something as having value as a means is equivalent to speaking of it as having instrumental value. And the use of the term "instrumental" is suggestive of design. Thus an ax is designed to cut, and a dagger to stab. Obviously the universe does not have instrumental value in this sense. A political constitution, again, is frequently termed an "instrument" of government. Had we reason to believe that the general scheme of the universe has been designed by a supreme Mind, we could concede that it is instrumental in some such sense. But inasmuch as we have seen reason to hold that the fundamental axiological structure of the universe is composed of eternal selves and eternal universals, we are not in a position to make such a concession. The term "instrumental," however, may also be used to refer to a relation of accidental dependence. Thus the laws of logic and of mathematics were not designed to help us think. Even St. Thomas would not assert that God had created, or could alter or destroy, these. Yet acquaintance with them can greatly facilitate the process of thinking. But the laws of logic and of mathematics constitute a very different kind of reality from conscious processes. There is nothing, however, beyond the universe, nothing which is other than and accidentally related to it.

What we are concerned with is the relation of the universe as a whole to those "parts" or members of it which are conscious beings. McTaggart certainly did not hold that this relation is accidental, yet he did hold that the universe as a whole is productive in its conscious "parts" of intrinsic values of which it is itself devoid. Now I should, of course, admit that since it is not a conscious being the universe cannot be wise or honest or resolute or courageous. And I should further admit, and have already admitted, that were it the kind of universe which pure empiricists and naturalists have often declared it to be, a universe wherein causality obtains only in the regularity sense of the term, wherein there are no objective values or disvalues, wherein life and mind simply "emerge" *ex nihilo,* a universe of pure becoming wherein there is no final and rational explanation of anything, such a universe is as a whole neither good nor bad. But such a universe seems to me to be the figment of an imagination divorced from contact with reality. When I inspect the universe as well as I am able I find it, as I have repeatedly said, axiologically oriented. It leans, so to speak, in one direction. Its structure is fundamentally teleological. To say, then, that it has value only as a means would to my understanding be implicitly to affirm that this structure is actually fortuitous, and to deny its necessity and its eternality. This structure is not only logically but axiologically integrated. It is rational and intelligible in the fullest sense of these words. I affirm, therefore, that as a whole it has value.

Perhaps it will be urged, however, that I have no justification for ascribing any qualities to the universe as a whole. Substances, events, acts can have qualities; but the universe falls in none of these categories, for it does not fall under any category. It includes both universals and particulars; hence it is itself neither a universal nor a particular. It does not occur, it is not a process, although events occur and processes go on within it. And so we might continue, much in the strain of an adherent of the *via negativa* when speaking of his God.

Now I fully admit, as I cannot fail to do, that the universe is *sui generis.* It is not only numerically one; it is unique. There is no other universe. Although not a particular in the sense of being one constituent of a real or possible many, it is, like the God of the scholastics, an individual. Yet the fact that it is an individual, and the fact that it is *sui generis,* do not prevent it from having characteristics. For we can make true statements about it, and these statements are true because of its nature. It is not an amorphous, unqualified, and indescribable something. It has a systemic unity. It is rational and intelligible. Clearly, then, it has characteristics, and among these is value.

It may, nevertheless, be objected that if the universe be rational, not merely in the sense of exemplifying the laws of logic, but in the wider sense of possessing value and excellence, it is inconceivable that all its constituents should not likewise be completely rational in the same sense, and that, accordingly, every particular in the universe must be possessed of value and must be devoid of disvalue. Now this we know not to be a fact. For if we be certain of anything at all, it is that many conscious beings are morally evil or foolish, or both, and that many sensible objects are ugly.

The problem thus presented, be it noted, presses more forcefully upon the determinist than upon the indeterminist. If nothing could fail to be as it is, if whatever occurs or has occurred could not have happened otherwise, then indeed the determinist who is also a rationalist will find the presence of evil in the universe difficult to account for.[14] His usual assumption is that evil states must be passed through on the way to the attainment of an ultimate good. But if we ask why the attainment of the ultimate entails the antecedent occurrence of evil states, we must be prepared to be told that we must not expect to understand in detail how or why this statement holds true, and that we must simply accept the general principle that we cannot have the greater good without the lesser evil. This leaves us precisely where we were; and there, as determinists, we seem fated to remain.

To the indeterminist, however, the situation appears in a very different light. If genuine freedom of choice be essential to the development of moral character, and if it be obvious—as I think it is—that a free act is an act which *need not* have occurred, it will be evident that it is abundantly possible for selves possessed only of finite capacities to act wrongly instead of rightly. Freedom to do good implies freedom to do evil. The presence of this twofold possibility is essential to a universe which is axiologically oriented. Thus the rationality of the whole involves the potential presence of evil in the parts.[15]

This last consideration is one of fundamental importance for the axiological idealist, and from it follow two corollaries which are likewise of great importance. The first is that the presence of intrinsic value in the whole is quite compatible with the presence in the parts of any amount of evil which results from free choice; for that evil results from the misuse of a capacity the proper use of which would have produced a corresponding amount of good, and without which the production of either moral good or moral evil would have been impossible. The second corollary is that the greater the sum total of moral good in the universe the more the parts conform to the

14. For the determinist who is not a rationalist the presence of evil in the universe is, of course, an ultimate fact which, like all ultimate facts, must simply be accepted as such, and neither requires to be, nor admits of being, explained.

15. Viewed from this angle it is the distribution of beauty and ugliness which constitutes the knottiest problem for the rationalist. It is true that the indeterminist can point to the fact that a vast amount of ugliness is the result of the activity of conscious beings, and that, in so far, he is in a better position than is the determinist. But, aside from this, both alike can do no more than call attention to general considerations, such as the limitations of our powers of aesthetic appreciation (Has not Ruskin emphasized how recently mountain scenery has been thought beautiful?) or the need for contrast to produce a total effect (e.g., the hackneyed illustration of the dark and the light in a picture); yet both must concede that it is impossible thus to explain in detail the presence of concrete instances of beauty and of ugliness.

structure of the whole. For the axiological set or orientation of the universe is toward the actualization of value and the elimination of disvalue. There is thus an essential connection between the intrinsic value of the whole and the sum total of intrinsic value in the parts, the former providing for the production of the latter in the only way that is possible—through the free choice of conscious beings.

The "bearer," as Professor C. D. Broad would say, of any instance of value or disvalue is, of course, the particular in which it is found— that is, if it can be found. But suppose that it cannot be found? This question brings us back to the topic of privation and deprivation.

PRIVATION AND DEPRIVATION

When what is lacking is a part of some existing entity—such as an arm—or a quality—such as rationality—we should say that the subject in the former case is a one-armed man, and in the latter case, an idiot. We might appropriately speak of such cases as instances of partitive or qualitative deprivation. But in the case of the unerected building or the destroyed statue, to what shall we ascribe privation or deprivation? Such cases are instances of what we may describe as *substantial* privation or deprivation. Each is a state of disvalue; and in each case we may ask of what it is a state. All states are particular states, and every state is the state of some subject. But it is clear that neither the statue which has ceased to exist nor the building which has never existed can function as the subject of anything. Yet, in the former case, the sum total of value in the universe has been diminished, and in the latter case, the augmentation of the sum total of value in the universe has been restricted.

It is true that both the states which we are now considering have been produced by the action of conscious beings. The barbarians who destroyed the statue produced the state of deprivation, and the ruler who might have erected, but did not erect, the replica of the Taj Mahal produced the state of privation. These conscious beings were *responsible* for the occurrence of these states; yet it is clear, surely, that they cannot be the subjects of these states nor the bearers of their value. In each instance, however, there obviously must be a subject, and what can that subject be but the universe? Does this mean that the universe as a whole is a worse universe than it would otherwise have been?

In answering this last question there are two points to be kept in mind. In the first place we may remind ourselves that coincidental actualizations of certain good or of certain evil states are frequently incompatible. Thus the occurrence of a state of privation or deprivation may be involved in the foregoing of a lesser good for the sake of a greater good. In such a case the sum total of good in the universe will be increased, not diminished. We have no assurance, however, that in every occurrence of a state of privation or deprivation the disvalue thus actualized will be outweighed by the actualization of some instance of greater value. Indeed, in the two cases to which I have called attention, such a supposition would appear highly improbable. In the second place, however, we have seen that the intrinsic value of the universe as a whole cannot be attained by the occurrence of any state of disvalue resulting from the free choice of conscious beings; and this consideration we can assume to be relevant in these two cases

Let us now proceed to examine the situation in the light of a different assumption. Leaving aside the argument for immortality which we have accepted as conclusive—namely, that from the simplicity of the self—let us inquire how our whole axiological perspective would be affected by the supposition that the self ceases to exist after the death of its body. No one would maintain that such an event could result from the volition of any finite self. Whether we be mortal or immortal, we have no choice in the matter. And if we can will only that which is possible of performance, it is plain that we can will neither to be annihilated nor to live forever. What will eventuate is wholly beyond us; it is the affair of the universe.

THE INTRINSIC VALUE OF THE UNIVERSE AND IMMORTALITY

If our previous conclusion that the universe as a whole is the subject of any and every state of substantial privation or deprivation be correct, and if it be the case that at death every self is annihilated, it follows that when a self which is struggling to perfect itself, or which *mirabile dictu* has attained a state of perfection, is thus destroyed, the resultant evil will be borne by the universe. And since all selves are thus annihilated, the amount of evil borne by the universe as a whole will be immense. The evil will, of course, endure throughout the entire subsequent temporal process; inasmuch as a self, once annihilated, will be annihilated forever. Moreover, if the temporal process be endless, the duration of the evil thus instantiated by the annihilation of any individual self which was advancing toward perfection will be infinite *a parte post*. And if the amount of instantiated evil must be reckoned in terms not only of its intensity but also of its duration, the outlook thus presented to us is pretty appalling. This vast amount of evil, be it observed, does not arise fortuitously; it is necessitated by the very structure of the universe.

It may be worth while to observe that in the case of the annihilation of a self which is advancing toward, but has not yet attained, perfection—and we are empirically acquainted with no selves which have attained it—there would result both a state of deprivation and one of privation, or perhaps we should say, a mixed state. The universe would be deprived of the virtue already instantiated by the self in question, and the virtue which it might subsequently have instantiated would never be instantiated at all. This is serious enough in the case of moral virtues such as integrity and loyalty. But it is even more serious in the case of love, if it be true—as I believe we should agree— that love is the highest of all values. If the personal relations of devotion which constitute the chief values of our lives endure forever, the value thus actualized will not only be infinite in duration but will qualitatively surpass all other goods; if they perish with our bodies the ensuing evil will be proportionately great.

Were the universe so constituted as to be the bearer of so great an amount of evil, we should be fully justified, I believe, in calling it a hellish universe. For the evil would not be fortuitous, but would spring from, and be involved in, its very nature. Is there any reason to hold that the universe is so ordered? Certainly we have found none so far. Our examination of the status of values and disvalues, and of the relations in which the self stands to them, indicates rather that the position of values is a predominant one, that the universe is ordered with respect to them, and that the temporal process is directed toward their progressive instantiation. And it is now clear that this process involves the presence of the self as a permanent constituent of the universe.

It may be objected, however, that by concentrating our attention upon the subsystem composed of selves, values, and disvalues we have abstracted it from the system of the universe wherein it falls, that we have treated the self as though it were a disembodied spirit soaring in a realm of universals, and that our optimistic conclusion is therefore premature. But I would urge that the considerations which I have brought forward cannot simply be brushed aside. After all, selves, values, and disvalues, I contend, do constitute a subsystem, and they are interconnected in the manner in which I have represented them to be. They are included within the structure of the universe, but as a subsystem within a more inclusive system. Had we reason to assume that the universe as a whole is nothing more than a heterogeneous aggregation of entities fortuitously interconnected, we should be compelled to conclude that what we have taken to be a subsystem is, as it were, an island of rationality in an ocean of the irrational. But we have seen that the systemic character of the whole is evident beyond reasonable doubt. Our hypothetical objector, accordingly, will have to urge that the subsystem is not really integrated with the all-inclusive system, that between the two there is an ontological fissure, that while the universe as a whole constitutes a system the parts of which are interconnected by various internal relations, such as similarity and causality, the axiologically oriented subsystem has its own characteristic principle of organization which sharply differs from the whole which contains it. And the self, it might then be contended, belongs to both systems; as embodied and united by causal relations to other entities it is a member of the inclusive system, as axiologically oriented it is a member of the included system.

Even were we to concede all this, we should have admitted nothing which would invalidate the argument I have just developed, for it is from the membership of the self in the axiologically oriented subsystem that its immortality has been inferred. Recognizing the presence of the ontological fissure, we might proceed to develop a metaphysic which would bear some resemblance to the dualisms of the Jains, the Sāṁkhyas, or the Mīmāṁsakas. But the fissure itself would be in the nature of a "brute fact" which would impugn the rationality of the universe; hence the suggestion of it may justifiably arouse our suspicion. And there are several considerations which tend to reinforce this suspicion.

In the first place, if I be right in my view that the universe as a whole is a bearer of values and disvalues, the axiological orientation of the whole is a conclusion which would appear to be inescapable. Moreover, we found that those universals which I have ventured to call the neutrals are neutral, not in the sense that they hold themselves apart from values and disvalues, but in the sense that they are equally ready to be assimilated and included within axiological structures of either of the opposing types. Their position with respect to values and disvalues, then, is intermediate, but in no sense disruptive of the structure of the whole. Furthermore we have seen that in the sense-world value and disvalue are undeniably and impressively present in the forms beauty and ugliness. Seldom, if ever, do we find a sensible object which is characterized solely by neutrals, and which is devoid of any degree of beauty or ugliness. And as a matter of fact, we find that in nature beauty is present in a vastly greater number of instances than is ugliness.[16] Whatever we are to make of this, it at least assures us that throughout the universe, so far as we know it, value and disvalue are both present, and that they are present in such a way as to be not only compatible with but actually suggestive of the truth of, our view that the universe as a whole is axiologically oriented. We cannot, indeed, regard our view as fully established until we have looked the problem of evil fully in the face; but at this stage of our inquiry, we are, I claim, quite justified in considering it as the most satisfactory hypothesis.

[*Note 1*] Throughout this chapter I have contended that the τέλος of the self is the instantiation of value. The presupposition is that the value actualized by free volition becomes an abiding characteristic of the self. The legitimacy of the presupposition may, however, be contested. Thus McTaggart has written as follows:

> There is, perhaps, no difficulty on any theory in saying that a man is good or bad at the moment when he is willing well or badly. But this is not all that we do say. Half an hour after ordering a murder, Nero may be eating his dinner, and thinking about nothing else. In the intervals of his labours, St. Francis, too, must eat, and may be too fatigued even to plan fresh labours. Yet we should call the one wicked, on account of his past crimes, and the other good, on account of his past services. The whole fabric of morality would be upset, if our approval or condemnation of a man for his volition had no right to last longer than the volition itself. Nor would any indeterminist, I imagine, be prepared to deny its right to last longer.[17]

The determinist, according to McTaggart, is justified in thinking and speaking in this way, since, on his view, a man's volitions issue from his nature. But the indeterminist, so McTaggart maintains, is not justified in so doing, since, on his view, a free volition, although not unmotivated, is undetermined.

"According to him," writes McTaggart,

> the volition in each case is a perfectly undetermined choice between two motives. When the volition is over, it has ceased to

16. The most hideous objects the eye ever encounters are the product of the activity of "civilized" man.
17. *Some Dogmas of Religion,* sec. 146.

exist, and it has not, on the indeterminist theory, left a permanent cause behind it. For, according to that theory, it has no permanent cause at all. Directly Nero has ceased to think of a murder, nothing at all connected with it remains in his moral nature, except the mere abstract power of undetermined choice, which is just as likely to be exercised on the next occasion in an utterly different way. How then can the indeterminist venture to call Nero a wicked man between his crimes? And yet he certainly would call him so.[18]

The assumption here clearly is that, for the indeterminist, the action is fortuitous inasmuch as, although it is not performed without a motive, nothing determines what the choice between conflicting motives will be. The "permanent cause," in McTaggart's eyes, is the abiding nature of the self which determines its volitions. This the indeterminist cannot admit. Yet for him also, *pace* McTaggart, there is a permanent cause; it is the self. For here the entailment theory of causality will not help us, since, insofar as a volition is entailed, and its occurrence thereby necessitated, by a previous state, the volition is not free. With free choice the activity theory of causality comes into its own.

For a detailed defense of the indeterminist's position I cannot do better than refer the reader to Professor C. A. Campbell's discussion of the subject in the ninth chapter of his Gifford Lectures entitled *On Selfhood and Godhood*. With his view I find myself in complete agreement. As he has well written,

A man's strongest desire at any moment may in fact be regarded as a function of his character in relation to a given situation. But if that is so, moral decision cannot be experienced by the agent *as flowing from his character*. For it is of the very essence of the moral decision as experienced that it is a decision whether or not to combat his strongest desire, and hence to *oppose* his formed character; and presumably strongest desire or formed character cannot find expression in the decision whether or not to fight against itself.[19]

Professor Campbell has laid emphasis upon the fact that in the vast majority of cases, there is no conflict between desire and duty. Such conflict arises only in the relatively small number of instances

18. *Ibid.*, sec. 147.
19. (New York, 1957), p. 150.

where desire points in one direction and duty in another. In such cases, moreover, the limitations of free choice are narrowly circumscribed. "By the very nature of the case," writes Professor Campbell,

> the range of the agent's possible choices is bounded by what he thinks he ought to do on the one hand, and by what he most strongly desires on the other. The freedom claimed for him is a freedom of decision to make or withhold the effort required to do what he thinks he ought to do. There is no question of freedom to act in some "wild" fashion, out of all relation to his characteristic beliefs and desires. This so-called "freedom of caprice," so often charged against the Libertarian, is, to put it bluntly, a sheer figment of the critic's imagination, with no *habitat* in serious Libertarian theory.[20]

Thus a free act is not purely fortuitous.

The point I wish to emphasize, however, in the present connection is this. Although a free volition is not determined by the character of the self, it yet *makes* character. And the character thus made becomes the self's abiding possession. And as the possessor of such a character, it can quite justly be called good; and as justly when it is eating its dinner as when it is willing to perform right actions. As the process of moral growth continues, the possibility of conflict between desire and duty will become ever more restricted; and if the process ultimately terminate in a perfected character, it will vanish. Because of previous free choices the condition in which temptation presents a "live option" and in which moral tension can occur will have been transcended, and right action will have become spontaneous.

[*Note II*] From his doctrine that all value is to be found in individuals McTaggart has drawn a conclusion which I believe to be both true and very important, and the truth of which I believe to be consistent with the falsity of the premise. This conclusion will be found in the last paragraph of his essay, "The Individualism of Value."

"If what I have said is true," declares McTaggart,

> it will follow that, whatever activity it is desirable for the State to have, it will only be desirable as a means, and that the activity, and the State itself, can have no value but as a means. And a religion which fastens itself on a means has not risen above fetish-

20. *Ibid.*, pp. 173-174.

worship. Compared with worship of the State, zoolatry is rational and dignified. A bull or a crocodile may not have great intrinsic value, but it has some, for it is a conscious being. The State has none. It would be as reasonable to worship a sewage pipe, which also possesses considerable value as a means.[21]

These are sentences which emphatically deserve to be remembered, particularly at the present day and in the light of contemporary events and tendencies. They are, in my judgment, profoundly true. Not only every organized state, but every tribe, every family, every church, every society of any kind whatsoever, has come into existence in time; whereas, if our view be correct, the individuals who are members of these institutions have not come into existence and will not pass out of existence. Temporal societies, therefore, are of value only as they minister to the welfare of eternal selves; so McTaggart maintained, and so much I gladly concede.

It does not follow, however, that the eternal society of selves which constitutes the universe has no intrinsic value. I do not propose here to restate the argument I have already advanced in support of this contention. What I wish to do is to show that it is quite consistent with McTaggart's own view of the nature of Heaven, which he envisages as a unity which is composed of selves, a unity which is not only *in* the parts but also *for* the parts (see his *Studies in Hegelian Cosmology*, chaps. 1–2). To do this it will suffice, I think, to cite the following passage from the *Hegelian Cosmology:*

I have endeavoured to prove that there is nothing in Hegel's metaphysical conclusions which entitles us to believe that our present society is, or ought to be, an end for its individual citizens. But we can go further, and say that the true lesson to be derived from the philosophy of Hegel is that earthly society can never be an adequate end for man. For Hegel has defined for us an absolute and ultimate ideal, and this not as a vain aspiration, but as an end to which all reality is moving. This ideal we can un-derstand—dimly and imperfectly, no doubt, but still understand. And to any one who has entertained such an ideal, society, as it is, or as it can be made under conditions of time and imperfection, can only be external and mechanical. Each of us is more than the society which unites us, because there is in each of us the long-ing for a perfection which that society can never realise. The

21. See *Philosophical Studies*, p. 109.

parts of a living body can find their end in that body, though it is imperfect and transitory. But a man can dream of perfection, and, having once done so, he will find no end short of perfection. Here he has no abiding city.[22]

"Under conditions of time and imperfection!" But what if those conditions no longer obtain? In this magnificent passage McTaggart has given us one of the noblest expressions of the spirit of other-worldliness that has ever been penned. Of course no society can be an end for man other than the society of Heaven, that eternal, un-originated, imperishable society, the uncreated church. That society can truly be an end for man; it is as essential for him as he is for it. It has intrinsic value as he has intrinsic value. Well may the meta-physician who has risen to the contemplation thereof exclaim, "Let me die the death of the righteous, and let my last end be like his."

22. (Cambridge, 1918), sec. 202.

Chapter Nine

AWARENESS OF OTHER MINDS

The object of our concern in the preceding chapters has been the self and its relations to the realm of universals. We turn now to the consideration of the self in its relations to the realm of particulars. Common sense would assure us that these particulars are of two kinds—living beings and lifeless beings. Yet what right have we to make such an assumption? The authority of common sense has often proved a broken reed. And the position of the solipsist has generally been conceded to be logically irrefutable. But no sane man has ever seriously adopted solipsism, and the obvious reason is that it turns out to be a practical impossibility. It involves, as it were, a voluntary submission to solitary confinement, and the strain proves to be greater than the hardiest speculative intellect can endure. The state of Robinson Crusoe on his island would be as nothing in comparison with it. Moreover, even if the solipsist's position be logically irrefutable, it is also indemonstrable; and this consideration has acted as a potent lure in the direction of sanity. Thinkers who have tried the experiment of "going into the silence" have always come out of it again with vociferous enthusiasm.

Shall we, accordingly, do as the majority are wont to do, and accept the existence of an external world as an assumption alike beyond proof or doubt? Before we answer we shall do well to reflect that, although all agree that there is an external world, there is considerable difference of opinion as to the types of entities which compose it. The objective reality of universals, as we are thoroughly aware is widely called in question; indeed many contemporary British philosophers repudiate it with a dogmatic brusqueness so emphatic that its very vehemence is suggestive of a basic lack of confidence. Panpsychists and Berkeleyans again—and representatives of both schools are still in existence—refuse to admit the reality of physical objects; independence of mind, they contend, is only apparent and illusory. It is solely upon the existence of other minds that all are agreed; and yet there is no general agreement as to why we should make this admission, nor as to whether our knowledge of other minds be direct or inferential.

Such being the case, let us briefly review the situation for ourselves. In the first place let us be quite clear as to the fact that no one maintains that solipsism is a position which is ever held by the unreflective mind, and from which it requires to be converted. All men naturally believe in an external world; and the only question is whether its existence be merely a practical, or also a theoretical, certainty. How can I be sure beyond the faintest shadow of a doubt that I do not produce my own world by thinking of it? Do not I remember, it may be asked, that I was a child, totally dependent upon others for protection and sustenance without which I could not have survived? Yes, this is what I do remember. But how do I *know*, and not merely account it highly probable, that my memory is veridical; how do I know that I have a real past beyond the present moment, and that I am not simply dreaming it?

Again, I habitually distinguish between what I call the imaginary figments of dream and the sense data experienced in what I call my waking life; the latter I find to be more vivid and more coherently and intelligibly arranged than the former, and this I account for by the supposition that I am, at most, only a part cause thereof. But does not this distinction depend once more upon the work of memory, and upon acts of recollection and comparison, the veridical character of which I have no right to take for granted; and what do I know of causality except as I experience myself as active and productive?

That my world is solely the product of my own conscious will is, indeed, a hypothesis which cannot stand for a moment, since so much that I experience occurs unsolicited by, and often in flat opposition to, any conscious volition of mine. It is true that the images of fantasy come before my mind when summoned, and the same is frequently true of those of memory—although not invariably, for these sometimes arise unbidden. I do not, however, consciously will to dream when I am dreaming, however pleasant the dream may be; and it is beyond all question that the adventures of a terrifying nightmare are something which I would not undergo could I escape them.

Psychoanalysts tell us, nonetheless, that our dreaming is the offspring of unconscious volition. Why, then, may I not extend the hypothesis to my waking life? Or is it inconceivable that my waking experiences should occur in complete independence of my conscious or unconscious volition, and that they should yet be necessitated by other psychic states of my own—by my emotions, for instance?

It is doubtless desirable to show the solipsist, if we can, that even on his own principles his hypothesis will not stand. And to do this we had best revert, in my judgment, to our awareness of universals. I realize, as I have already stated, how widely the objective reality of universals is called in question. But I have also stated why such skepticism impresses me as utterly groundless, and why I hold that the awareness of universals is, not inferential, but direct. Having done my best, I can do no more, and as Bradley would say, "I fear I must leave it so." I make bold, therefore, to take for granted the objectivity of universals; and I now proceed to point out that even for the solipsist it will be the case that his images will possess common characteristics. Even though there be no particulars other than himself and the figments of his thought, it will still be true that if he image two centaurs, the two images will be characterized by common qualities. Will it be said that as he produces the two instances, so he produces the common characteristics? But what intelligible meaning are we to ascribe to such an assertion? Is it contended that he images two centaurs together with an identical shape pertaining to both, that the two particulars and the universal alike depend upon his act of imaging? With the cessation or passing away of the act, therefore, the particulars will pass away, and presumably the universal also. Suppose, now, that he once again image two centaurs. The images will be two fresh particulars, but what of the universal? Is it a fresh universal? But this, surely, is nonsense. If it arise and pass away with the particulars to which it pertains, is it not plainly itself a particular? Yet if, *per impossibile*, we are seriously to regard it as a universal, we must admit that it will have something in common with the universal previously produced; and this something will constitute a third universal. And this third universal will participate with the other two in a characteristic common to them all—a fourth universal, and so ad infinitum. Will anyone contend that this endless array of entities is the product of the solipsist's mind? Surely we are sinking into a bottomless abyss of absurdity!

Further difficulties, however, confront the solipsist. Not only must he account for universals in terms of his own causal activity, he must also do the same for the laws of arithmetic, of mathematics, and of logic. Yet to these laws his thinking is absolutely subjected. While he can imagine two pairs of fairies whenever he likes, he can never

Solip.

make the sum of the two pairs either greater or less than four, be his efforts what they may.

Lastly, there is the consciousness of obligation. This the solipsist may, indeed, attempt to disavow. For there is no other mind, human or divine, in his universe whom his actions may conceivably affect; nor can he be under obligation to himself, for obligation is not a reflexive relation. Granted, yet does it follow that it is a matter of complete indifference to the solipsist himself how he conducts himself, whether he be clean or filthy, whether he endure the nightmare through which he passes with courage, resolution, and self-possession or give way to terror, repinings, and lamentations? Surely it will be plain to him that one course is better than another, more commendable—even though there be no one to commend—more compatible with his own self-respect. There must, then, be objective values which the solipsist did not originate, which he can neither alter nor destroy, which are other than himself, and to which he stands in a relation of obligation.

Can it in similar fashion be shown that the individual's knowledge of particulars existing apart from and in independence of himself cannot meaningfully be questioned? Here the situation is more complicated. For the child, and for the adult who is still at the pre-philosophical stage of intellectual development, there are no problems; and this, not because of a clarity of vision which excludes "category mistakes," but because the level of rational reflection has not yet been attained. The distinction between appearance and reality receives only a perfunctory and inadequate recognition. The submerged stick is "really" straight, it only "looks" bent; the flower is "really" red, although to the jaundiced man it "looks" yellow. Common sense is content with a verbal, rather than with a genuine, explanation because of a dawning consciousness of its own incapacity to furnish more.

It is inaccurate to say that in this state the existence of physical objects and of other minds is grasped by an "implicit inference"; the realization of any need for such inference has not yet arisen. For common-sense physical objects are directly sensed, and the same is true of other people. They *are* their bodies, which are seen and touched, which move and gesture, and from which issue sounds that are heard. This is not to say that common sense is materialistic, any more than that it is idealistic; it is below the intellectual level at which such distinctions can be formulated. It vaguely grasps, but shrinks from rendering definite, the contrasts between beings which are indubitably alive and those in which the presence of life cannot be detected.

It is by reflecting upon, and endeavoring to explain away, the incompatibilities and contradictions generated by these half-formed notions that we ascend to the level of philosophic inquiry. We gradually learn that we may be mistaken in our classifications, that what we take to be a rock on the hillside, for instance, may turn out to be a cow. We learn that the movements of living beings are, to a certain extent at least, unpredictable; that, although we may with some assurance foresee, we cannot be absolutely certain in advance when the horse will shy or the cat will scratch. And thus we discover that the thoughts of other people are not directly accessible to us; that, while we can see what they do and hear what they say, we cannot know, but only with some probability infer, what they think; and we also come to realize that we ourselves enjoy the same inviolable privacy. We have here reached the point at which it becomes possible, and inevitable, that we should distinguish between the self and its body. And now perforce the question arises, Is the existence of other selves known only inferentially? Is there, indeed, any other way in which it could be known?

Without claiming any unique acquaintance with the thought of the average educated man, I would venture the opinion that he would answer that such knowledge is inferential, but that it is an inference so inescapable, so indubitably valid, that it need give rise to no uneasiness, and that any suspicion on the part of any individual that he may be alone in the universe would be as absurd and neurotic in actuality as it would be horrible if taken seriously. And I think it quite probable that this is as good an answer as anyone could give. Philosophers, however, appear to be increasingly dissatisfied with it. Some of this dissatisfaction may be due to a confusion between the assertion that the belief in the existence of other minds *originated* as the result of inference, and the assertion that it can be *justified* only by inference. Nevertheless there seems to be a growing unwillingness to entertain the view that a belief of so great importance to us, and one which appears so unquestionably true, requires to be substantiated by any process of reasoning, and that its truth is not immediately evident. Human reason, it may be urged, is fallible, wherefore the abstract possibility of error is always present; whereas the belief in the existence of other minds is absolutely certain, and must therefore be the product of an infallible intuition.

The question, then, presents itself: How is this intuition to be conceived? Surely it is not an intuition of the proposition, "There are other minds," as a self-evident truth. It is not the proposition, we may take it, but the minds themselves that are intuited. Yet, presumably, it cannot be *all* minds, nor even all minds presently existing or embodied, which are the objects of this direct consciousness. But which minds? The most plausible view would seem to be that they are the minds conjoined to the bodies which are sensuously apprehended by us. Upon sense awareness, accordingly, there will supervene a non-sensuous, yet direct, awareness of another mind. But will not such an awareness involve a consciousness of the thoughts, feelings, and volitions of that other mind which notoriously we do not possess? Can one be directly aware of another mind and yet be unaware of any of its characteristics? Possibly the Leibnizian notion of a "clear-confused" perception may help us here. Such a perception will be definite with respect to its object, yet muddled with respect to the nature of that object. Is it not conceivable that I may be conscious that I am in contact with, or that I am contemplating, an entity which is one, alive, and conscious, and yet have no definite awareness of the states or acts of that consciousness? May not the experience be analogous to the sight of a crowd of persons in which no single individual is identified?

If the analogy really held, we should be directly aware of a multiplicity of mental states even though we were able to identify none of them. As a matter of fact, however, we do not seem to be directly aware of *any* mental states but only of the face and form, the words and gestures from which we infer both their presence and their character.

We ought not, moreover, to be forgetful of the tendency which over and over again has manifested itself in the history of thought to posit direct awareness of something the existence of which we cannot prove, but of which we are supremely confident. It is so satisfying to throw off the whole burden of proof, and to point out that demonstration is both impossible and needless. I do not by any means intend to assert that such a course is never justified. I should be the last person in the world to say so, for it is the course which I have myself adopted with respect to universals. Various theologians have done likewise with regard to the existence of God, and enthusiastic ontological realists have done the same with respect to physical objects. And it is quite conceivable, for all that we can tell in advance, that in each instance such a claim is justified; and equally conceivable that in no instance is it justified. What we have to do in each instance is to make clear to ourselves precisely what the claim involves, to inquire whether experience seems to bear it out, and to see whether the denial of it lands us in hopeless difficulties.

Now the difficulty in the present instances is that the *that*—as Bradley would say—is completely divorced from the *what*. To claim that we can be directly aware of a mind and yet not be aware of what that mind is thinking, feeling, willing, or doing would appear to involve us in flat self-contradiction. I have done the best I could for the claim by invoking the notion of a "clear-confused" perception, yet I must admit that it seems to be incompatible with the recognition of the data of experience.

Perhaps it will be contended, however, that in this connection we ought to take into consideration the evidence for telepathy; evidence which is impressive and which continues to accumulate. And is not Bergson's suggestion, it may be asked, a plausible one, namely, that here we have the vestige of a capacity once enjoyed by all, but of which the sphere of application has gradually been restricted by the progressive emergence of reason? While it survives to a noticeable degree only in the case of favored individuals, may we not posit a modicum of it in everyone; and will not this account for the absolute assurance which we enjoy as to the existence of our fellows?

I do not see that this suggestion will help us in the slightest. In the first place, whatever may be true of the gifted individual, experience makes it quite clear that such capacity for extrasensory perception of other minds as is possessed by most of us is pretty attenuated. The history of warfare, for instance, shows that scouts have to rely upon sense experience to detect the presence of foes waiting in ambush, and that it is frequently possible to surprise an enemy. And it would seem that diplomats and politicians often conceal their thoughts from one another quite successfully. In the second place—and this is the more important consideration—we should know nothing about telepathy, mind reading, or extrasensory perception but for the reports of the experiences of other minds; and upon our assurance of the existence of these depends our confidence in their reports—in other words, we have assumed the conclusion which we are trying to prove.

In view of the foregoing considerations it seems plain that we must concede that even though direct awareness of mind by mind be a genuine possibility, and even though there may be grounds for the assumption that it occurs more frequently than we might antecedently have supposed, and often when those who experience it do not recognize it for what it is, yet the only solid basis for our confidence in the existence of other minds is inference from sense experience.

CHAPTER TEN

AWARENESS OF THE
EXTERNAL WORLD

There is a vagueness about the term "perception," and well there may be; for conflicting theories of knowledge interpret it in various ways. Is it, after all, a form or kind of knowledge? Or is it a species of awareness so rudimentary as not to deserve to be so called? If we can properly be said to perceive something, must we realize that it is what it is? If, to take one of Moore's examples, we encounter a sheep and take it for a goat, have we, or have we not, perceived a sheep? If we perceive a part of something, have we also perceived the whole of which it is a part? If we stand before a house, do we perceive the house or only the front of the house; if we perceive a man's hand, do we also perceive the man; if we perceive the tip of a cat's tail, do we perceive the cat; if we perceive a platoon, do we perceive the army to which it belongs? [1] Is it possible, again, to perceive a thing indirectly, by means of, or *through,* something else? If I hear a ring, have I perceived the bell that rings or have I only perceived what I was immediately aware of—the ringing sound? Is perception as such infallible, or is misperception possible? How stands perception, moreover, in relation to sensing, on the one hand, and to judging on the other?

1. Among the considerations which affect our use of the word "perception" the size and significance of the part or aspect sensed, and the degree of assurance we have as to the nature of that to which it belongs, appear to be determinative. Thus, while it is obviously impossible for me to be at once aware of the interior and exterior—including all the sides—of a house, if I see one side, I should feel justified in saying that I perceive the house. But should I discover that what is before me is a wall built to resemble the front of a house as part of the setting for a movie, I should no longer claim to have perceived a house, but only what looked like a house. Again, if I saw a face peering out of a window, I should not hesitate to say that I had perceived a person, even were I uncertain whether it was man or woman; but if all I was aware of was a hand raised above the top of a wall, I should say only that I had perceived a hand. If a man were standing ankle-deep in sand, I should not hesitate, once more, to say that I had perceived him; but were his feet alone visible, I should say that I had perceived only these. And if I saw a platoon, I should no more think of saying that I had seen the army of which it was a part, than I should think of saying, after it had marched past, that the army had marched by. But whether our usage upon all such occasions be consistent or not has little or nothing to do with the problem immediately before us.

Is sensing one specific kind of awareness, and is judging another; and, if so, where does perception fall? How true sound the words of Dawes Hicks, "Perceiving appears to be a sort of mongrel, in which thought loses part of its pure nature as concerned with universals and relations, and sense is raised above its crudeness in merely accepting the given." [2]

Confronted by this host of questions it behooves us to remember that our present concern is with our apprehension of physical objects, or of what we take to be such. Let us, then, begin with the last question. Shall we follow Plato's guidance, and for every kind of reality posit a unique faculty or mental capacity or power whereby it is apprehended? Is sense experience one kind of awareness, is the awareness of supersensible particulars—if such there be—another kind, and is the awareness of universals a third? Is inference the manifestation of a capacity other than that whereby the first principles of knowledge are grasped? Is the supreme vision of the Form of the Good, or of the One, the function of yet another capacity? And at the lower end of the scale, are memory, imagination, fantasy, and dreaming all to be classified as distinct and separate powers?

It seems clear that we ought not to acquiesce in such a proliferation and hypostatization of faculties or capacities unless a careful inspection of our own experience force us to do so. So far as I can discover from introspection it seems to me that conscious awareness, if I may put it so, is "all of a kind." [3] By this I mean that I am aware of an "image" of fantasy, of an object in my dream, of a sensible object, and of a universal in precisely the same way; that so far as my consciousness is concerned, there is no difference of mode or kind or manner of operation. The differences are all to be found in the nature of that which is presented, and in how it is presented. In saying this I do not intend to imply that any awareness ever occurs in stark isolation. Possibly in dream or fantasy I may be cognizant of a single "image" with only the vaguest of backgrounds; although even then recognition, which doubtless springs from some sort of retentiveness, always enters in. But in sense perception we are habitually confronted by a "presentational continuum," as James Ward called it, of the fringes of which we are only vaguely aware; and within this

2. *The Bases of Critical Realism* (London, 1938), p. 18. It should be added, however, that Dawes Hicks would never have acquiesced in such a dichotomy between thought and sense.

3. For a defense of the notion of "faculty" which is quite compatible with my contention here see Professor C. A. Campbell, *On Selfhood and Godhood*, pp. 118–121.

continuum, as interest and attention vary, we concentrate now upon this particular and now upon that, and proceed to discriminate the salient features of what we thus discover. Yet in discriminating the parts of any object presented to us, we do not necessarily lose consciousness of the whole; nor in discriminating the qualities of anything, do we cease to be aware of that which they qualify; nor, again, in discriminating the relations between entities, do we become oblivious of the relata. Thus consciousness, as we are so often told, proves to be a unity in diversity; a unified awareness which can expand its purview without becoming oblivious of the features already distinguished, and which can include the data of memory with those now presented in one synthetic state of awareness. In saying this I do not, of course, mean to imply that one awareness is inserted into another as one box is placed inside another, but rather that one awareness can blend with another in somewhat the same fashion as one drop of water blends with another.

That there is in sense experience an element of direct or immediate awareness is quite obvious, for without its presence indirect or mediate awareness would be impossible. Yet we must beware of assuming that the line between the two can be so painlessly and so clearly delineated that sensation and thought can be distinguished and contrasted as easily as if they constituted two separate, although co-ordinated, faculties which co-operate with each other much as artillery might co-operate with infantry or airplanes with tanks. On the contrary, we must realize that recognition, comparison, and contrast are processes which are involved in the very beginning of our sense experience, which without their aid would lose all coherence, and would be reduced to psychical chaos.

Let us suppose, for instance, that I apprehended what I take to be a yellow orange. Had I been born blind and had I just obtained the power of vision, not only should I be unaware that what was presented to me was an orange, I should not even realize that it was round or colored. By the use of touch I might, indeed, succeed in identifying the characteristic "roundness," and so in establishing a correlation between touch and sight; and by reflection I might arrive at the conclusion that what qualified the surface before my eyes must be what my fellow men call color. But I certainly would not be in a position to affirm that the color was yellow. Indeed, for those who all their lives have enjoyed normal vision it is possible to be mistaken in the finer processes of classification—to mistake a certain shade of green, for instance, for one of blue.

So quickly do we pass from sensation to a fairly complex state of apprehension. As J. B. Pratt has well written, "A pure sensation is something that few of us who have passed infancy any longer experience. Our simplest forms of perceptual activity are drenched with meaning. The immediately given is already significant; it is never a mere sense datum, but a sense datum that means more than it is." [4]

Perception, then, is a very complex affair; and there is as yet no general agreement as to just what it involves. It is the contention of the majority of idealists that with the passage from immediate sense awareness to apprehension, judgment enters in. To discriminate, to recognize, to compare, or to contrast, we are told, is to judge. It is admitted that introspection frequently does not acquaint us with explicit judgments of these various kinds; but it is maintained that such judgments can be implicit, yet nonetheless real, and that they can be formulated practically instantaneously. In proof of this assertion it is pointed out that what at the first glance of reflection appears to be immediate apprehension sometimes turns out to be mistaken. That occurrences of this sort do take place is indubitably the case. How easy it is to mistake an artificial flower for a real one! We have all had experiences of this type. The waxen policeman in Madame Tussaud's is a standard example of this kind of thing. Now where error is possible, judgment, it is affirmed, must be present; and undoubtedly the contention is extremely plausible.

Many realistic epistemologists, however, will not have it so. The idealist, they tell us, overlooks the fact that there can be an awareness which is no more than a mere "taking for granted," a state which is one of mere "perceptual acceptance." [5] We have no right, they urge, to posit in defense of a doctrine the formation of judgments which introspection does not reveal to us. Introspection does not reveal them for

4. *Eternal Values in Religion* (New York, 1950), p. 103. Compare the following from Cook Wilson:
Consider a sensation and our knowledge of it. The mere having a sensation, though it is consciousness, is not knowledge and must be distinguished from apprehension. To know what a sensation is I must recognize in it a definite characteristic which distinguishes it, e.g., from other sensations. I recognize, let us say, that it is a pain, and then again a burning, or a pricking, pain, as the case may be. But this implies comparison of pain with other sensations and other pains; and thus by the activity of comparing we go beyond the mere passive state of being pained, and this activity, we are sure, *ex hypothesi*, is thinking. Thus though the sensation is not originated by us we require an originative act of consciousness to apprehend it. (*Statement and Inference* [Oxford, 1926], I, 46)
5. For a defense of "perceptual acceptance" see Professor H. H. Price, *Perception* (New York, 1950), chap. vi.

the simple reason that they do not occur. Doubt must arise before judgments can be formed, and in taking for granted or perceptually accepting there is no doubt. That is why we are genuinely astonished when we discover ourselves to be in error.

That this is also a very plausible view must, I think, be admitted. And yet, on this theory, recognition constitutes something of a problem. If, on seeing a flower, I at once identify it as a rose without comparing it with any flower or flowers which I remember having seen, how is this to be explained? Past experience must have generated a retentiveness which functions, as it were, automatically and instantaneously. Whether this be accounted for by physical traces left in the brain or by dispositions retained in the subconscious, the question inevitably arises to what extent hypothetical agencies are now being appealed to in defense of a preconceived theory.

There is, however, another question which forces itself upon our attention. What is the difference between perceptual acceptance, on the one hand, and an implicit judgment on the other? Without venturing to deny dogmatically that there is a difference, I make bold to affirm that it seems pretty shadowy. Is it, indeed, necessary for us to commit ourselves on this matter? We may, surely, agree on two points: (1) that introspection does not disclose any inferential process and (2) that the apprehension in question may or may not be erroneous.

The unsettled question, however, suggests a further query. Is there not something in the nature of acceptance—perceptual or conceptual —in the assent to any judgment? In the case of a self-evident proposition—that is, a proposition which is immediately seen to be true as soon as its meaning is understood, and so is *per se notum*—acceptance on the part of him who apprehends it correctly is wholly justified. Yet, as the history of philosophy makes all too painfully clear, it is possible to be mistaken in regard to what is self-evident. I may regard as self-evident a proposition which is not so, or I may not regard as self-evident a proposition which is so. In the former case I do not realize that doubt is legitimate, in the latter case I do not realize that it is illegitimate; in the former case my acceptance is unjustified, in the latter case it is qualified when it should be absolute. In the case of all other judgments legitimate doubt must be removed, and this removal will involve an ultimate acceptance. Were it not so, we should be involved in an infinite regress. For if, to judge that proposition A corresponds to a fact, we must first assent to proposition B which asserts that proposition A does correspond to a fact, plainly we can assent to proposition B only by first assenting to proposition C which asserts that proposition B corresponds to the fact that proposition A corresponds to a fact. And this will in turn involve our prior assent to proposition D—and so on ad infinitum. Clearly, therefore, every judgment must ultimately repose upon an apprehension which is not another judgment.

Error, as Stout has insisted,[6] is due either to ignorance or inadvertence, on the one hand, or to confusion on the other. We take something to be what it is not. Reaching into Plato's aviary,[7] we put our hand on the wrong bird. To elaborate Moore's example, let us suppose that I see in the distance an animal. Were I a Polynesian from a remote Pacific island where the largest animal that can be found is a rat, possibly I might not even realize that what I see is an animal. As it is, however, I discern body, head, and legs, and without explicit reference to past experience yet clearly as a consequence thereof, I recognize it as an animal. I also observe that it is white. Had I been born blind and just attained vision, or had my experience been limited to objects possessing only other colors, I should not have been able thus effortlessly to classify it as I do. Let us now further suppose that I take it to be a sheep but that as I approach it I find that it is a goat. Why did I take it to be a sheep? Possibly because I had heard that there were sheep in this field but not that there were any goats, and was thus psychologically conditioned to assume that it would be a sheep; possibly because I was more familiar with sheep than with goats, and was therefore less likely to recognize the characteristics of a goat; possibly because of some peculiarity of the individual animal's physiognomy which was suggestive of goathood. I dwell on these possibilities because they serve to bring out the plausibility of Descartes' contention that error involves volition in the form of premature assent.

COMMON-SENSE REALISM

The object of these reflections has been to stress the fact that there is a kind of apprehension which, whether or not it fall under the head of judgment, does not—so far as introspection can tell us—involve any process of inference, but which nonetheless may be true or false. The point is of importance, for it is frequently contended by extreme realists that, since the belief in physical objects is not

6. See his essay entitled "Error" in his *Studies in Philosophy and Psychology* (London, 1930).
7. *Theaetetus,* 196B–199D.

arrived at by inference, it must be immediate and cannot be mistaken. In opposition to the representationalist theory of perception it is asserted that it is quite obvious that we do not first become aware of sense data and then proceed to argue from their existence to that of physical objects. This is a contention the truth of which would not, so far as I am aware, be questioned by the most convinced representationalist or idealist. They would not question it, in the first place, because they are themselves convinced of its truth, and in the second place, because it is totally irrelevant to the issue with which they are concerned.

The "average man" or the "man in the street"—in other words, the man who has never seriously reflected upon the nature of sense experience—has never doubted the existence of physical objects because, in a confused way, he thinks that he is immediately aware of them. It seems to him that he looks out of his eyes as he might look out of a window, that he hears through his ears as a man might listen at a loophole, and that the world of physical nature lies directly open to his inspection.

It is thought at this level which is productive of "the world of common sense"; that world which, many contemporary philosophers insist, must be taken to be what it claims to be—that is, as ultimately real, not an appearance or manifestation of something else, but absolutely genuine in itself. All theories which question or deny this claim, and which would substitute some other interpretation of our experience, according to them are to be rejected out of hand, and in advance of any critical examination, as certainly wrong, and as the offspring of "category mistakes," wishful thinking, or some other mental vagary.

In the face of this widespread tendency it is worth while to point out that the world of common sense is not unchanging, and that what the man in the street today regards as falling within its purview would have seemed to an ancient Greek of Anaxogoras' time a product of vicious abstraction, a purely theoretical construction remote from actual experience. For the man in the street of the twentieth century is throughly familiar with the word "matter," and although he has only a vague notion of what it stands for—perhaps no vaguer than that of many a scientist—yet he is quite sure that it stands for something non-mental and devoid of life, and that of it are composed the physical objects which surround him. Again he is likewise familiar with such words as "spirit," "soul," and "mind," and while he finds it difficult to conceive and impossible to imagine what they stand for, he yet assumes that they are supposed to refer to some kind of reality which is in itself wholly immaterial and not dependent for its existence upon matter, which has life not derivatively but in itself, and which somehow partakes of the nature of thought.

Now a Greek who had conversed with the Milesian philosphers or who had talked with Pythagoreans or who had attended the lectures of Leucippus would find such an intellectual outlook foreign and strange; it would seem as remote from his world of common sense as the universe of the theoretical physicist does from ours. To the Greek it would appear obvious that not only men and animals but also gods and demons had bodies; and that mountains and rivers were alive as truly as were plants and flowers. Possibly he never went so far as to formulate such generalizations as "all souls are embodied," or "all bodies are besouled"; yet in a general way he thought of the living and the physical as coextensive. The accepted view appears to have been that soul was breathed in and expelled with air—for air was soul and soul was air—and that death resulted from an inhibition of respiration which prevented fresh soul from entering the body. And in like manner the universe was believed to breathe in soul from the circumambient mass of air and mist.

Were our ancient Greek revived and among us today he would in all likelihood insist that his common-sense world is the real world, and that our common-sense world is the product of abstraction. Fanciful as this supposition may be, it is difficult to treat with more respect the assertion so frequently reiterated by numerous contemporary philosophers that no sane man can honestly doubt the reality of physical objects since he directly perceives them, or at least is absolutely certain that they *must* exist.[8] In reply it suffices to point out that the non-inferential character of the plain man's belief shows only that it is a

---

8. It is equally farfetched to contend, as Professor Martin E. Lean does not disdain to do (see the introduction to his *Sense-Perception and Matter* [London, 1953]), that the whole issue can be settled by an appeal to linguistic usage; for language was developed at the level of common sense, that is to say, before philosophic questions were even raised. To treat usage, therefore, as an oracle is equivalent to acting on the absurd assumption that the popular mind at a remote epoch had not only considered such questions but had also answered them, and that with a unanimous verdict. Moreover, if I understand Professor Lean rightly, he would claim that popular usage admits of a purely phenomenological interpretation; and such a claim, I would submit, is utterly groundless. Can anyone for a moment seriously entertain the idea that the "average man" of this era or of any other has or had any doubt whatsoever as to the existence of his house, his implements, or of any other objects when he was not sensing them? We have all been plain men before we were philosophers, and frequently become such again at unreflective moments, and I confidently appeal to the reader for his ingenuous answer to such a question.

childlike belief, and that when a question has not yet been raised, it cannot have been answered. The awkward facts which give rise to the problem of sense perception are only dimly recognized by the plain man. They are brushed aside by common sense because, no sooner do they become obvious, than it becomes conscious of its inability to deal with them, and conscious also that for practical purposes it is unnecessary to deal with them. The stick which in the water appears to be bent is straight enough when you pull it out; and you learn by practice to allow for distortion in spearing your fish.

Discrepancies in sense perception are of two general types; dissimilar appearances to different people at the same time of what we take to be the same thing, and dissimilar appearances of the same thing to the same person at different times. All these are subsumed by the plain man under the head of "seeming." The house in the distance really is of the same size as we find it when we stand in front of it, but it "seems" or "appears" or "looks" to be much smaller. The jaundiced man really sees the green of the leaf, yet the leaf "seems" yellow to him. There is only one real candle flame, although there "seem" to be two flames when you press your eye, and so on. Ask the plain man wherein seeming consists, and how a thing can appear to be other than it is, and you will get no intelligible answer. Probably he will lose his temper, an example which some realistic philosophers are inclined to follow. Yet the difficulties which confront us are real difficulties. It is futile to try to deal with them by assuming an attitude of scornful superiority; and it is equally futile to pretend that we gratuitously make them ourselves, and that they will vanish if we revert to an attitude of primal and unsophisticated innocence. Wittgenstein with all his horses and all his men cannot make our sense experience other than it is, nor resolve all our difficulties by a magnificent gesture.

This brings us to another point which must be emphasized, one which Dawes Hicks was never tired of stressing, and rightly so.[9] If we adopt the position of extreme or naïve realism, a view which seems again to be becoming popular, and if we be prepared to deal with the theory ingenuously, we must recognize that its fundamental tenet is that our awareness of physical objects is unmediated and direct. This means that consciousness does not follow the track of the incoming stimulus. In perception we are aware, not of waves nor of the inverted image on the retina nor of the inside of our heads where all is dark, we are aware of the physical object before us. Hence

9. See *Critical Realism,* pp. 64–65.

nothing that occurs during the transmission of the stimulus from the object where it originates to the sense organ, no distortion on the part of the medium through which the stimulus passes, no refraction nor diffraction, can account for our ascription to the object of characteristics which it does not possess. To assert that it can is tantamount to conceding either that our awareness is mediate and not direct or that a physical object is not what common sense takes it to be. It is therefore preposterous to invoke the laws of perspective to account for errors in perception. (Professor Lean's book furnishes an outstanding instance of such an illegitimate appeal.)

Perhaps it will be urged that this is too extreme a statement; that while the process of stimulation cannot evoke a perception of what is not, it may nonetheless restrict our perception of that which is. Thus Alexander has endeavored to account for the fact that a physical object, such as a plate, appears to be smaller when it is further removed from us on the ground that "the same plate when near or far excites different extents of the retinal tract and is seen in different size." [10] From this it follows that as the plate is removed from us we see less of it. "The size which we see is a portion of the real geometrical size of the plate and the varying sizes are real appearances and are contained within the real size." [11] Thus the thing is "the totality of its perspectives." [12]

There is, moreover, yet another difficulty. If the size of the plate, as we see it at a distance, be only a portion of the "real geometrical size," what becomes of the portion of the size which we do not see? Presumably it is still there, although unseen. Do we, then, see right through it as though it were transparent glass? Let us suppose that the plate is white with a purple band around its edge. Which portion of it do we continue to see, and which do we fail to see, when we view it from a distance? Something, surely, ought to be missing, the purple rim or the white center. But what we observe is that the plate retains its general design; it is still white with a purple rim. Only there is less of it. It seems to have shrunk all over, as it were. The process resembles the deflation of a balloon rather than the breaking up of a solid. Yet that such shrinking should occur as an actual event *in rerum natura* is quite incredible.

Alexander has, however, a further explanation which, if I understand it aright, seems to be incompatible with that already given, and to introduce yet another difficulty. "What we see," he writes,

10. See *Space, Time and Deity* (London, 1920), I, 193–194.
11. *Ibid.*, p. 194.   12. *Ibid.*, p. 196.

is an illumined disc, whose various parts are at different dates because of the conditions of vision. The ends of the diameter are later than the centre. When the disc is moved off, its geometrical shape and size are unaltered, but its points as *illumined* alter their times with the distance. Simple geometry shows that at a greater distance the time-interval between the end and the centre is reduced, because the distance of the ends from the eye, the path which the light has to travel from them, is increased relatively less than the distance from the centre is. Consequently the ends are later than the centre by so much less when the disc is far off than when it is near. Thus while it is still the whole disc which is seen in its full geometrical extent, the extent looks smaller because it is filled with the qualitied events of illumination and is only apprehended through them. We see a smaller disc because the disc occupies less time under the conditions of vision. Were it not for these conditions there would be no such appearance.[13]

This theory presupposes the soundness of Alexander's doctrine that every point-instant in the brain is accompanied by its own act of awareness, that consciousness is thus "spread out" so that the center of the eye may discern what the periphery of the same eye fails to observe. This view, I make bold to confess, appears to me absolutely incredible in itself as well as totally devoid of any empirical confirmation. To speak of consciousness as extended is surely as meaningless as to speak of "purple quadratic equations"—to borrow an appropriate illustration from McTaggart. And it is equally difficult to attach any meaning to the assertion that distinct, individual acts or states of consciousness associated with a multiplicity of point-instants are somehow capable of being amalgamated in a unified state of awareness. The issue involved has already been considered in our treatment of the self, and we need not here return to it.

Many contemporary thinkers have shared with Alexander and Dawes Hicks the conviction that between direct realism and some form of idealism there is no tenable intermediate position; and this conviction, coupled with a strong antipathy to idealism, accounts for their willingness to accept almost any hypothesis, however extreme, rather than "deny the faith." Professor D. M. Armstrong, for example, clearly inclines—although, to his credit, with evident hesitation—to identify "sense-impressions" with "acquirings of beliefs."[14] At first

13. *Ibid.*, pp. 196–197.
14. *Perception of the Physical World* (London, 1961), p. 131. For his defense of this conclusion see pp. 87–93, 127–132.

glance this seems quite preposterous; a belief, it will be said, is one thing, and a sense impression is clearly another. To identify what are plainly two distinct entities or experiences is to talk nonsense. A belief, to be intellectually respectable, requires a ground; but the ground of the belief is not the belief itself. It is interesting, however, to observe that what we have here is an appeal, in defense of realism, to a view commonly thought of as characteristic of a certain form of idealism— the view that all perception is of the nature of judgment. Even so, it is clear that a judgment must be about something other than itself, and that the awareness of that something, although it constitute an element in the judgment, is not to be identified with the judgment as a whole. Plainly, therefore, it is a mistake to say that a sense impression is to be equated with a belief about the nature of a physical object, even though it provide the basis for that belief.

We find another move, executed in the interest of realism yet in the direction of idealism, in the case of those philosophers who make great play with the so-called internal accusative, as opposed to the "act-object" or "act-objects," analysis of sensations.[15] On this view *some* sensations at least are to be understood on the analogy of such an experience as that of feeling a pain. In a case of this kind we do not for a moment suppose that the pain is an external object of which one is simply aware; on the contrary, we do not distinguish between "feeling a pain" and a "painful feeling." The pain is not something we feel, but the "way" we feel. It is not a thing, but a characteristic of the self or of a state of the self. Similarly, it is argued, to sense blue is merely to sense "in a blue way" or to sense "bluely."

With respect to this hypothesis there are two things to be said. It may be urged, in the first place, that an obvious pitfall lies directly in front of its defender, for he is sliding down an inclined plane upon which there is no stopping. If to sense blue be merely to sense "bluely," then to sense a chair should be merely to sense "chairily," or in a "chairy" manner. Logically there is no place to draw a line; hence we find ourselves involved in a subjective idealism of the most extreme type. Personally I have no emotional antipathy to such a conclusion, nor any concern as to what common sense will say about it. My sole concern is whether it is true. And this brings me to my second point.

When I feel pain, I am not only aware that I do so; I seem to myself

15. See Professor H. H. Price's article, "The Nature and Status of Sense-Data in Broad's Epistemology," and Professor Broad's reply in *The Philosophy of C. D. Broad*, ed. Paul A. Schilpp (New York, 1960).

to be fully conscious that the pain is a characteristic of the awareness. It is a painful awareness; not an awareness of something other than, or external to, myself. And it seems quite absurd to suggest that the pain might be there when I am not conscious of it. On the other hand, when I am aware of a blue patch, my awareness is not associated— unless accidentally—with any physical pain or pleasure; it is not a state of feeling but a state, or an act, of cognition; it has an object, and that object seems quite clearly to be an entity in the external world. I realize, of course, that the last statement may be disputed; yet it is difficult to see how this can be done with any plausibility. For a patch is extended and shaped; hence, if it be somehow included within the self, the self will be extended and shaped; and as I have already urged, to attribute these characteristics to the self is to talk nonsense.

In the feeling of pain we have something that is obviously subjective, and in the patch something that is obviously objective. Extension and shape are primary qualities, and the non-mental status of that which they characterize will unhesitatingly be conceded by most. Blue, however, is a secondary quality; and with respect to secondary qualities can one, without becoming dogmatic, be so definite? Their status has been very fully discussed by Professor Broad, and I find myself in general agreement with what he says. We should like to lump all secondary qualities together and to assign them either to the objective or the subjective realm. Yet this is not easy to do. Color seems clearly to stand at one extreme, and taste at the other, with the remaining secondary qualities falling somewhere in between. I find it myself almost, if not quite, as hard to conceive of taste apart from consciousness as to conceive of pain apart from consciousness. To say that sugar is sweet when no one is tasting it seems almost as ridiculous as to say that iron feels hot to itself. And it seems quite clear, on the other hand, that color can characterize only what is extended; and that what is extended is *extra mentem*.

To save the theory which we are now considering it is essential, however, to show that all the secondary qualities can be classified as subjective, and that what we may aptly call the "adverbial analysis" is applicable to them all; in other words, that to see blue is to sense "bluely," to hear a sound is to sense "noisily," to smell is to sense "smellily," and so on. But then we face a further difficulty. For now we must admit that entities characterized only by primary qualities can exist *in rerum natura*, and is this conceivable? Can there be extension, for instance, without something that is extended, or shape which bounds and limits nothing at all? Perhaps we may escape the difficulty raised by these questions if we be prepared to treat space as a sort of quasi-matter, as Samuel Alexander seemed willing to do. Yet the problem generated by the plurality of spatial appearances in different perspectives will still confront us, and to deal with it must not the adverbial analysis be extended to them also? Thus, to say that we see a sphere must be interpreted to mean that we sense spherically. But is not this to describe inaccurately what we directly experience?

I have devoted more attention to this theory than I consider that it really deserves because it is the product of an evident desire to develop some sort of compromise view which will fall between common-sense realism and representationalism. Another manifestation of the same tendency can be seen in the effort to reconcile the claims of direct realism with those of the sensum theory by employing the former to validate the notion of veridical cognition and by utilizing the latter to account for error. Thus it is maintained that from the optimal point of view—as when, for instance, we stand directly over a penny and, in this position, discover that the findings of sight and touch are mutually corroborative, so that we both see and feel it to be circular—we directly cognize the object exactly as it is, namely, as possessing both primary and secondary qualities which really do characterize it. When, however, we seem to see the penny as it really is not—as when we see it as elliptical—what we actually are directly aware of is not the penny itself but a sensum which represents it with some degree of inaccuracy.

We have not yet discussed the sensum theory, but when we do so, should we find it convincing, we may well ask ourselves why we should not accept it *in toto*, what justification we have for restricting its application in the way proposed, and why we should introduce a different theory to account for the awareness experienced at the optimal point of view. Thus we find Professor Broad advancing against Professor Marc-Wogau the following considerations:

> I think that *all* the arguments for the non-corporeality of visual sensibilia rest on considerations of continuity. In view of the continuity in the external conditions of our visual sensations, I find it very hard to believe that *some* of the visual sensibilia which we sense *are* parts of the surfaces of the bodies which we see, and that others are not parts of the surface of *any* body, if to be a "body" and to be "a part of the surface of a body" be understood in the simple literal way which I have tried to state and illustrate.

Now I also find it very hard to believe that *all* the visual sensibilia which we sense *are* parts of the surfaces of the bodies which we see, if "body" and "part of the surface of a body" are understood in that way. Therefore I am strongly inclined to think that *none* of them are. I admit that neither severally nor collectively are the arguments conclusive. What I may call Professor Marc-Wogau's "half-and-half" theory *is* logically possible; but it is the kind of theory of which I can only say: "If it should be true, I'll eat my hat." [16]

With these remarks I am in general sympathy. It is possible but improbable, I should agree, that the "half-and-half" theory is true. Can even so much be said, however, for the common-sense theory of direct realism? By a common-sense theory I mean one which holds the ordinary view of a physical object entertained by the plain man; the view, namely, that a thing is a continuant, made up of contiguous parts, and occupying a definite and limited spatial area. Here sight and touch raise the principal difficulties, for they purport to bring us into immediate contact with the object.[17] This hearing and smell do not; for it would seem quite natural to say that sounds travel or that a smell pervades a certain locality. And it will be generally acknowledged, I presume, that our crucial problems are visual in character. For if an object be directly presented to us, must it not be seen as it is, and how can it be seen as it is not? Surely a thing either has a characteristic or does not have it, and surely it cannot be simultaneously characterized by incompatible characteristics. The stick is either straight or bent, the penny is either circular or elliptical, the railroad tracks are either parallel or convergent, the leaf is either green or not green, or part green and part not green, either there is one candle flame or there are two candle flames. If the jaundiced man see as yellow an apple which the rest of us see as green, how can he and we both be right? And yet, according to the theory of common-sense realism, can anyone be wrong? For as thing is seen, so must it be.

It is futile to say that the green apple only "seems" green to the jaundiced man. For there is no magical efficacy to be extracted from such words as "seem," "look," or "appear." No mere repetition of them will suffice to exorcise our difficulties. Real difficulties require real

16. See *The Philosophy of C. D. Broad*, pp. 807–808.
17. If taste cannot be subjectified, it will cause similar difficulties; for how can the same thing taste different to different people at the same time, or to the same person at different times?

explanations. No verbal legerdemain can avail. Now it is plain that, for seeming to occur, there must be confusion of one entity with another, or failure to discriminate between one entity and another. And what we are entitled to ask for is some intelligible explanation of how this can come about.[18]

From what has been said it is clear, I think, that direct realism of the common-sense type can provide no such explanation. Hence it must either be abandoned or else modified in such a way as to account for the seeming possession by the object of incompatible characteristics. If the latter alternative be chosen, and if the project can successfully be carried out, the form of direct realism thus developed may well turn out to be as far removed from the standpoint of common sense as are some types of idealism.

MODIFIED FORMS OF DIRECT REALISM

One course which we might elect to follow would be to transform— to explode, so to speak—the physical object into a plurality of "appearances." Thus at every point from which, to use everyday language, a certain star is actually or potentially visible, there is an "appearance" of the star. And if we follow Lord Russell, who was a pioneer in this particular line of speculation, we shall maintain that all these

18. Dr. A. C. Ewing has well written,
It has been suggested that what we perceive immediately is not that the immediate object of sense has a certain quality but only that it seems or appears to have such a quality. On that view, when we look at a straight stick immersed in water, what we perceive directly is not really bent but only looks or seems bent. This would no doubt be the best solution if it could be reconciled with our immediate experience, but can it? Clearly what we think we are immediately aware of is not merely something that looks bent but something that is bent; the physical object itself may be straight, but surely whatever it is that we directly perceive in that case, one fact about it at least is clear from immediate experience, namely, that it is something bent. Therefore to say that there is nothing really bent but that it only looks or appears bent is not merely to deny that we perceive physical objects as they are but to take the much more serious step of asserting that our immediate experience is itself illusory, that we have been quite wrong in the majority of the judgments which we have made as to the data immediately given us, for we have held that they were coloured or shaped in a certain way when they were not coloured or shaped in that way but in another way quite different. Further, this error is not due to bad inference which we had confused with immediate experience, bad inference is certainly not the cause of sensory illusions; it is not due to an over-hasty and superficial analysis of our experience, for however carefully and long we look at the stick we see something that is bent; it is not an extraordinary and occasional illusion but an illusion present in some form in, at any rate, most of our experiences. (*Idealism*, pp. 280–281)

"appearances" are objectively real, whether or not they be perceived by any mind. The star will thus no longer be a particular, but a class of particulars, of which class every "appearance" will be a member. It is of course clear that in this context the word "appearance" is employed in an unusual sense, namely, in the sense of membership in a class. There is nothing illusory about an individual "appearance" of the star; it is precisely what it purports to be. Its relationship to the star is comparable to that of an individual man to humanity. Any hint of the familiar contrast between "appearance" and "reality" would be quite out of place; for the class is no more real than its members, and the individual member appears only in the sense that it is actually or potentially visible.

As originally developed by Lord Russell the theory was obviously designed to deal only with visual data. Doubtless sounds and smells could be treated in the same manner with equal plausibility; but the data discriminated by touch and taste would certainly be more recalcitrant, for these are found only where, in ordinary language, "the thing is." To accommodate all these data the theory will plainly need to be developed; and the "thing," from being a "family of appearances," will have to be expanded into a "clan," of which the constituents will be the "families"—or "septs"—comprising respectively the data pertaining to the various senses. Even so, it is hard to see how what common sense would regard as things adjacent to one another—the bushes in a hedge, for instance, or the flowers in a flower bed—could be transformed into classes of "appearances" without space becoming crammed with these entities, which must be supposed neither to mask nor to displace one another. How, for example, could the collision of two stars be explained in accordance with this theory? Or the explosion of a bomb? Such events must take place wherever the appearances are; yet such entities, surely, must be incapable of annihilating one another. Our bodies and brains, moreover, must be subjected to the same treatment as all other physical objects; they must therefore be dissolved into classes of appearances the members of which are to be found everywhere except *where we are.*

Despite the acute difficulties into which it leads us, Lord Russell's drastic effort to deal with the object by thus exploding it is extremely instructive,[19] for it is clearly indicative of the lengths to which we

19. Lord Russell's theory is further complicated by his contention that some of the spatio-temporal appearances of the object are events occurring in our brains. No one, I think, would advocate so paradoxical a view who was not determined to eliminate at all costs any fundamental distinction between mind and matter. His view has been subjected to a devastating criticism by Lovejoy (see *The Revolt against Dualism,* chap. vii).

must be prepared to go if direct realism in any form is to be retained. And it is to be observed that Lord Russell's most crucial difficulty results from his uncompromising determination to keep mind out of the picture, and to insist that sense data are relative only to location in space. Other thinkers, however, of a less intransigent temperament, have believed it possible to compromise on this issue without surrendering *in toto* the claims of direct realism. Two general types of theory have in consequence been developed which Professor Broad has distinguished and nominated respectively the "Theory of Multiple Inherence" and the "Multiple Relation Theory of Appearing." [20] After careful and detailed criticism he has concluded that each theory presupposes an absolute space, and is therefore less plausible than the representationalist theory which makes no such assumption.

I do not propose to recapitulate Professor Broad's criticisms but rather to ask the following questions: (1) Can either theory be so stated as to be clearly distinguishable from any form of epistemological idealism? (2) Can either theory be shown not to involve conclusions which are compatible with an ontological idealism? True enough, we have not yet discussed any idealistic theory, so our conclusions at this stage of our inquiry may be no more than tentative. But we cannot discuss all subjects at once, and when we come to examine the idealistic point of view, we shall have opportunity to reconsider our conclusions, and, if need be, to revise any which appear to be premature.

Let us look, then, at the multiple inherence theory, which I take to be identical with that which Lovejoy has entitled "Objective Relativism." It is based upon the contention that characterization—so far, at least, as sensible qualities are concerned—is not a dyadic but a triadic relation. Thus it is not permissible to say of any entity that it is red or round *simpliciter;* rather we must say that it is red or round in a certain perspective or from a certain point of view. Yet, in that perspective and from that point of view, it actually is red or round. No contradiction will arise, however, if in another perspective and from another point of view, it be actually green or square. For if characterization be a triadic relation, a contradiction would arise only if the same entity were to possess incompatible characteristics in the same perspective and from the same point of view.

This theory brings with it a plethora of questions. Does not the view that characterization is a triadic relation abolish the distinction between appearance and reality? Is the presence of an apprehending mind, or of a human or animal organism, at a definite position essential to the projection thence of the characteristics envisaged in any one per-

20. *The Mind and Its Place in Nature* (London, 1925), sec. B, chap. iv.

spective, or are these dependent solely upon the structure of space? (With the latter hypothesis we are back again in Russell's theory, with all its difficulties; with the former, fresh questions arise of which we must take cognizance.) Are there physical events which occur, although unperceived by us, at the focus of converging perspectives, and if so, do whatever characteristics pertain to the invisible entities therein participating likewise involve triadic relationships? If such be the case, what is the objective constituent in any perspective? Or is there none at all, and must we resign ourselves to subjectivism?

Let us take the first question first. As Professor Broad has stated the theory, there is an "emitting region" where physical events take place and whence light rays proceed, and there is also a "pervaded region" which is the *locus* of the projected characteristics; when the two coincide we have veridical perception, but when they are distinct—as in the case of a reflection or a mirage—error can occur through confusion of the two. In the former instance we have reality, in the latter, appearance. This would seem to be as satisfactory an answer as could be given in terms of the theory; yet we may ask whether the "veridical" *perceptum* be anything other than a *phenomenon bene fundatum?*

If it be assumed that the presence of an animated organism at the point of projection is essential, we must ask whether all the sensible characteristics be thus projected, or only the secondary qualities. It seems clear what the answer must be. For if only the secondary qualities be projected, all the problems connected with the simultaneous possession of incompatible shapes will again confront us; we shall have accomplished nothing except practically to have reinstated Locke's theory. Plainly, if the doctrine is to have any originality, it must assert that *all* sensible qualities without exception are thus projected.

Is such projection, then, the function only of the physical organism, or is an apprehending mind necessarily involved? Here the realist may cautiously reflect that if he once permit the mind to take an inch, it may not improbably also take an ell; accordingly he may prudently conclude that it is better to point to the physical organism as the sole agent. But then we may pertinently inquire why a corpse will not do as well. Why need the organism actually be animated for the process of projection to occur? This is, I think, a fair question, and one which demands a straight answer. Let us waive it, however, and ask another question. If the physical organism be the sole agent, are we not entitled to assume that the products or effects of its agency will also be physical? Yet can we, with any plausibility, make such an assumption?

"To be physical," Lovejoy has written,

means to be, at the least, a factor in the executive order of nature apart from being perceived; to be potentially common to the experiences of many percipients, as an external cause of their sensations if not as an actual datum; and to conform to the laws of physics. But the putative offspring of the brain have none of these accepted marks of physicality. They are destitute of causal efficacy, at all events unless they are perceived; they give no evidence of continuing to exist and to undergo regular changes when unperceived; they are strictly private affairs, accessible only to the consciousness connected with the brains that severally beget them; so far as we have any knowledge of them, they do not conform to physical laws. They are much more like "ideas" than they are like anything that has ever previously been called a physical object.[21]

Do not these statements give us a fair summary of the situation? Of anyone who is prepared to affirm that sense data are physical entities produced by the physical organism we are amply justified in demanding more cogent arguments in support of the assertion than have so far been given us. What, then, if we make bold to assume that mind is an essential, if not the sole, agent? This, at least, can be urged in defense of such an assumption, that the majority of philosophers and psychologists are agreed that the images of dream, memory, fantasy, illusion, and hallucination are mental products. If this be granted, the argument will continue, is it not vastly more probable that sense data, which so closely resemble entities of all these various kinds, are also the product of mind than that they are the product of any other agency? (We shall later inquire whether this view can be accepted.)

Suppose, for the moment, that we grant the force of this argument. What follows? What follows, it seems, is that the view now before us is undergoing a profound alteration. What the objective relativist—the advocate of the multiple inherence theory—appears clearly to desiderate is a doctrine which will treat each perception as an ultimate unit, of which subject and object are, so to speak, the positive and negative poles, and apart from which they become mere abstractions. But now the negative pole seems to be slipping away from us. If all sense data be the work of mind, what is left of the object?

Before attempting to reply to this question we must take account of Professor Broad's distinction between geometrical and sensible

21. *The Revolt against Dualism*, pp. 106–107.

shape and size.[22] The former are intrinsic properties; if I understand Professor Broad correctly, they are properties of an area where certain physical changes unperceived by us are actually occurring. Sensible shape and size, on the other hand, can be said to "inform" a region; and the relation of "informing" may be "irreducibly triadic."

On this supposition the relation of characterization between geometrical properties and the region which they characterize will, I presume, be dyadic; it is only in the case of sensible properties that the relation will be triadic. Now this seems a rather astonishing state of affairs. To common sense it appears quite obvious that a thing will either have a characteristic or will not have it; the notion that the relation of characterization can be triadic comes as something of a shock. It is a question, I think, whether it be an intelligible notion; we accept it, if at all, only because we are assured that by so doing we shall be able to reconcile the rival claims of appearance and reality, of subjectivity and objectivity. But if we be told that there is nothing in the nature of characterization which renders it always and everywhere triadic, and that we are to assume that it is so only in the case of sensible characteristics, the notion can scarcely fail to impress us as a device employed to produce an *ad hoc* theory, and we shall become suspicious of it.

A more serious objection, from the point of view at which we have tentatively placed ourselves, develops out of the consideration that the physical changes which occur in this particular region, and from which comes the stimulus which causes the subject to project the sensible characteristics which pervade that region, are not directly perceived by us. Either they are postulated, again *ad hoc,* or their occurrence must be shown to be probable in consequence of a process of inference from the sense data which we do perceive. But such an admission will sound the death knell of direct realism. Sense data will be projected upon an object not directly apprehended, even as the representationalist contends that they are; they will depend upon the perceiving subject, and no amount of talk about triadic relationship will obviate this fact. And only by accepting the representationalist's doctrine does it seem that we can avoid falling into idealism. (I may also observe that a similar calamity will occur if we extend the notion of triadic relationship to apply to geometrical properties. For then nothing that is not relative to something else will be left except location in absolute space.)

Let us now glance at the multiple relation theory of appearing. Here

22. *The Mind and Its Place in Nature,* pp. 163–174.

we have a doctrine founded upon an explicit recognition that characterization can be either dyadic or triadic. We are required to assume that whatever characteristics the object actually possesses inhere in it dyadically. Appearance, however, is a triadic relation. It follows that from most points of view we are aware of the object, not as it is, but as it appears to be. Accordingly, unless we be prepared to evacuate the position of direct realism, we shall be forced to maintain that there is at least one position—presumably that from which visual and tactual data are observed mutually to corroborate each other—from which the object can be perceived, not as it appears to be, but as it is. No arguments, so far as I am aware, are available in support of such a hypothesis.[23] It is true, of course, that there seems to be no argument against it other than that based upon the breach of continuity involved; and this, although not without weight, cannot be pronounced conclusive. Yet we can scarcely be expected to embrace such a hypothesis merely because we wish to remain direct realists. Should we refuse, however, to accept it, we must frankly admit that nothing can be known from direct perception as to the nature of the object, and that whatever can be known will be known as the result of inference from sense data. Once again, therefore, the conclusion would seem to be that unless we be ready to accept some form of idealism, we must seek refuge in representationalism.

Epistemological Dualism

Let us turn, therefore, to the representationalist theory of perception or epistemological dualism—the sensum theory, as it is also called. This was the view regarded by the founders of modern philosophy, Descartes and Hobbes, as the only tenable one. After passing through a century-long eclipse during the reign of idealism, epistemological dualism entered upon its brief heyday of popularity with the publication of *Essays in Critical Realism* in 1920. Today it has fallen into seeming neglect, a neglect so ostentatious, however, as to impugn its own sincerity. By enthusiatic realists of the extreme type epistemological dualism is regarded as a halfway house on the road to idealism; consequently, in company with the latter view, it is an object of obloquy. Nevertheless no fair-minded man will deny that the representationalist theory of perception is the product of an exceedingly

23. "We are asked," Professor Broad writes, "to believe that in one special position the physical, physiological, and psychic mechanism produes an utterly different result from that which it produces in all other positions, no matter how close to this specially favoured one" (*ibid.*, p. 192).

thorough and careful examination of the problems arising out of sense perception, and that the principal efforts of its framers were directed to providing a satisfactory explanation of the various kinds of error encountered therein.

As frequently presented, the theory is based upon the conviction that physical objects, while they can be known to exist, cannot be directly apprehended. The term "sense data," which by new realists and neorealists had been applied to surfaces, parts, or aspects of physical objects—such as the front of a house—is now used to designate a class of entities distinct from, and representative of, physical objects; and it is these entities, it is contended, and not the physical objects themselves, which are directly apprehended.

The great merit of the theory is that if its presuppositions be accepted, it does admirably what it was designed to do—account for errors in sense perception. Adherents of the theory of direct realism had always tended to depreciate the importance of this problem; nonetheless they had never shown themselves able to deal with it in a satisfactory and convincing manner. According to the view which we are now considering, when, as we say, I "see" a penny as elliptical, what I am directly aware of is an elliptical and colored entity which is distinct from and other than the actual penny but which, from the point of view at which I am placed, appears to occupy the place where the penny is. When I look toward a candle flame with my eyes out of focus, what I am directly acquainted with is two red images which simultaneously represent to me the flame. When I behold a curved shape in the water, what I am aware of is other than the submerged straight stick which emitted the rays which reached my eyes, and it is owing to the refraction of these rays as they passed through the water that the curved image has the shape it does have. When my eyes are stimulated by rays emitted centuries ago by a distant star what I see is a sense datum which seems to occupy the place where the star was, not the place where the star is now—if, indeed, it continue to exist, as may or may not be the case.

The objection to this theory so often advanced by contemporary writers, to the effect that, were we directly acquainted only with sense data, we could never have come to believe in the existence of physical objects, is a veritable putting of the cart before the horse. For no one contends that men first believed in the existence, or in the reality, of sense data and then by a process of inference arrived subsequently at a belief in the existence of physical objects. The belief in physical objects, as I have already had occasion to emphasize, arose inevitably and spontaneously without any conscious inference. Men at the common-sense level are, indeed, conscious of errors in sense perception; yet it is as easy for them to adjust themselves to them practically as it is for them to ignore the problems which they occasion. That a thing can *seem* to be what it is not is, of course, accepted as a fact; but it is only at a reflective level where philosophical inquiry begins that it is realized that *seeming* requires to be accounted for, and that men ask themselves how this is to be accomplished. What inference is required for is not to explain how men come to believe in the existence of physical objects but to justify that belief once the problem raised by the inevitable distinction between appearance and reality begins to press for a solution.

It is here that the representative theory of perception is generally agreed to be at its weakest. On its own principles it explains errors in perception very well, but can it vindicate veridical perception? Can we argue from the existence of sense data whereof we are directly aware to the existence of physical objects whereof we are not directly aware? Or need we argue? If we resort to argument, it is to remove antecedent doubt. Is it possible, however, that we are in some way non-sensuously and non-inferentially aware of the existence of physical objects?

The situation in which we now find ourselves bears marked similarities to that which confronts the theologian. One of the first questions which he must ask himself is whether man's awareness of God be direct or inferential. And here we find a divergence of opinion. On the one hand the Thomists assure us that the existence of God must, and can, be demonstrated by philosophical arguments. In saying this they do not mean to depreciate the value of religious experience; but it is their contention that such experience can be evaluated aright only in the light of the knowledge, antecedently acquired by the activity of the reason, that God does exist. Calvinists, on the other hand, repudiate as illegitimate every effort to prove the divine existence and affirm that a direct awareness thereof is imparted to man by grace. The theologian who can sincerely adopt the latter position is freed from the toilsome task of argumentation, and from the fear that, should he be unable to carry it through successfully, his entire theology will collapse; hence the perennial attraction of this point of view.

Among adherents of the representationalist theory of sense perception we discover a similar divergence of outlook. And it would be futile to pretend that philosophers, unlike theologians, are always deaf to emotional appeals, although their presence may be less evident in the case of the former than in that of the latter. There are obvious reasons why men should wish to believe in God. But why, one may well ask, should anyone be particularly desirous of believing in physical objects? Yet we cannot avoid detecting in the utterances of some philosophers a tone approximating to that of moral indignation at the very suggestion that the belief may be unfounded. This is not so astonishing, indeed, in the case of naturalists, for whom the existence of matter is practically an article of faith, as it is in the case of theists where we also at times encounter it. "Physical objects must be real," such thinkers seem to be on the point of saying, "because we want them to be real." And if we ask why, the answer would seem to be that there is a very widespread and deep-seated tendency to regard common sense as somehow sacrosanct, as if there were something positively indecent in exploding any of its pretensions. Clearly a prejudice of this sort, like any prejudice, is unbecoming a philosopher. As Professor Broad has well written, "One likes to do as much as one honestly can for poor dear Commonsense, but one should not allow charity to degenerate into imbecility." [24]

It is, of course, quite true that there is a pull in the opposite direction of which many are conscious who are interested in the philosophy of religion; for idealism has consistently claimed to be the friend of religion. And to those who have studied the history of thought, and have pondered over the powers of the human intellect, the suggestion that mind is the fundamental, perhaps the only, reality may well come with the force of a conviction. But all such emotional appeals must be recognized for what they are, and must not be permitted to dictate our conclusions. Our duty as thinkers is quite clear. It is, as Plato would say, to follow the argument whithersoever it may lead.

Our first inquiry, therefore, must be whether the notion of a direct, non-sensuous, non-inferential cognition of physical objects be intelligible and plausible. Both G. F. Stout [25] and Dr. A. C. Ewing [26] place

24. *Lectures on Psychical Research* (New York, 1962), p. 248.
25. *Mind and Matter,* pp. 219–223.
26. *The Fundamental Questions of Philosophy,* pp. 91–92. "We do not need the philosopher," asserts Dr. Ewing,

> to tell us that we have bodies, that the earth exists, and that iron is heavier than feathers. And if a philosopher asserts that according to his philosophy these statements must be false, it is a condemnation of his philosophy rather than of the statements which he criticizes. Any philosophical arguments he can use are surely less certain than is the truth of the statements just mentioned by me. Therefore, if these statements have to be analysed in a realist and not a phenomenalist way, this is a strong argument for the philosophical truth of realism. (*Ibid.,* p. 92)

great reliance upon it, although they concede that such intuition is fallible, and that it may profess to acquaint us with objects which are in fact non-existent. Both of them, moreover, assimilate it to memory. Yet a satisfactory theory of memory is still a desideratum. A direct realist, such as Alexander, for whose doctrine it was a matter of life and death to avoid admitting the reality of images, would tell us that memory involves direct awareness of a past event which is perceived as it occurred with the characteristics which it actually had, any error being due to confusion with other objective entities, whether particulars or universals.[27] But such a theory will not be of help to the epistemological dualist, for it offers no analogy to what, on his view, occurs in sense perception. For other thinkers the memory image is subjective and present, and pictures for him who has it an event which is objective and past. If this be the case, there is in truth some analogy between perception and memory. Yet, as Professor Broad has shown,[28] the analogy is far from complete. He has called our attention to two important facts: (1) that in memory words may take the place of visual images, and (2) that there are "negative memory-situations" in which we remember not what the thing was but what it was not. "I believe," he writes, "that what is primarily known by memory is propositions like 'This was green,' 'This was long and thin,' etc.; and that this is true both in positive and negative memory-situations." [29]

However plausible this conclusion may be, I am quite sure that an advocate of the representationalist theory would be loath to see in it anything analogous to what he believes occurs in connection with sense perception. For the suggestion obviously to be drawn is that what is non-sensuously intuited in the latter case consists also of propositions—such propositions, for instance, as the following: "I see an elliptical sense-datum which I take to be that of a penny, and, if I were to move forward till I could look straight downward upon the place where I should judge the penny to be, I would see a circular sense-datum," or, "If I stretch forth my hand to the place where I judge the penny to be, I shall feel a circular sense datum." Thus the

27. More can be said in support of this doctrine than may be evident at first glance. For if the immediate data of memory be images which presently exist, how can we know that these correctly picture for us the past unless we be in some way directly aware of the past which they image? How, indeed, could we form them unless we knew at first hand the reality which they represent? But if we possess such direct awareness of the past, what need have we of images?

28. *The Mind and Its Place in Nature,* chap. v.

29. *Ibid.,* p. 248.

physical object will be transformed into a theoretical construct formed in accordance with laws of prediction derived from sense experience. This does not prove that the object, in the original sense of the word, does not exist. We could even argue that if we can know propositions about physical objects, there must be physical objects for the propositions to be about. But this will be inference, not direct, non-sensuous intuition of the object itself.[30]

What we should expect non-sensuous and non-inferential intuition to do would be to acquaint us directly with certain characteristics of the object which sense experience does not itself reveal. Thus I ought to be able to say, "Although I see this penny as elliptical, yet I non-sensuously and non-inferentially cognize it as circular." Now it is clear to me that I do nothing of the sort. At a prephilosophical level of reflection, and on the basis of a vast deal of experience from which I have learned quite a lot about what it is possible to predict, I know in general what to expect in the way of future experience of a physical object, and I uncritically assume that the object is a continuant which exists when I am not experiencing it, and that it is quite like what I normally apprehend it to be. But once I have learned to distinguish between sense data and physical objects, the latter seem to me to be purely hypothetical, and whatever reason I have to hold that they are actual must be derived from subsequent inference. Thus, while I do not claim to have shown that the notion of a non-senuous, non-inferential awareness of physical objects is absolutely unintelligible, I believe that I have shown that if we are to take it seriously, it requires to be made far clearer and far more convincing than either Stout or Dr. Ewing have made it.

If this reasoning be sound, it follows that to establish the existence of physical objects we must resort to argument. But what sort of argument? A causal argument, it may be replied. But the situation demands that we be more explicit. Anyone but a solipsist will admit that sense experience does not arise spontaneously but is due to stimulation by something external; it seems clearly to involve interaction between subject and object, each functioning as a part cause. But have I the right to assume that sense data as such are the effects of any cause or causes? That they are caused is, indeed, believed by the majority of epistemological dualists. And there is much in our experi-

---

30. I may add that when we examine the manner in which, Stout tells us, we fit together the different perspectival appearances in order to grasp the physical object, we find that a good deal of inference seems to be involved in this intuitive awareness.

ence to suggest that such is the case. Yet the theory is not without its difficulties, as we shall see.

No doubt the view that sense data are the product of causal activity is due to the belief that they are transitory; and this, again, is due to the belief that they exist only when perceived. Yet can we be sure that the latter belief is well founded? Is there anything incredible in the assertion that a sense datum could exist unperceived? To this query it is difficult to return a straightforward answer. For sense data are not, so to speak, all of a piece. Taste, it is generally agreed, seems more like a feeling than does any other sensible quality. And the notion of an unfelt feeling would, indeed, be self-contradictory. How of an untasted taste? To say that untasted sugar is sweet seems almost as fantastic as to say that fire feels hot to itself. Yet can we be sure that we are not misled by a superficial analogy? Some extreme realists assure us that they can conceive of an untasted taste. At the other extreme among secondary qualities we find color. To say that nothing can be red when no one is looking at it would to very many persons certainly fail to carry conviction. And when we come to the primary qualities, it seems quite preposterous to affirm that these require to be perceived in order to be.

Why, then, are epistemological dualists so emphatic in their insistence that sense data depend for their existence upon the apprehending subject? The answer would appear to be that by this assumption they escape the difficulties which would otherwise beset them. The elliptical penny seems to occupy the same place as does the circular penny. Yet the same object cannot at the same time be both elliptical and circular. Must we not therefore conclude that the elliptical penny is an appearance of the real, round penny, that its being consists in appearing, and that, to appear, it must appear to someone? And if visual data can thus best be treated as subjective, is it not plausible to conclude that all sense data can successfully be dealt in the same way?

If sense data be thus dependent upon the perceiver, it seems clear, as we have seen,[31] that they must be mind dependent. For the more we examine the opposing hypothesis, the more incredible it appears.[32] That

31. See p. 332 above.
32. Lovejoy has put the point so forcefully that I cannot forbear quoting him once more:
  The theory that particulars "relative to brain-events" do exist unperceived would surely be a very queer one. It would be a gratuitous and extremely inconvenient addition to physics and physiology to assume that a process in the brain can not only produce, e.g., an elliptical copper-colored entity without mass, and can (as seems to be further implied) project this instantaneously out to some more or less distant region of space, but also that this

physical changes which take place within the skull should by some strange transmission of causal efficacy produce a penumbra of entities external to the organism—entities, moreover, which do not interact with any others, and which can be observed only by the mind which animates that organism, but which to everyone else are indiscernible—is, surely, a very remarkable theory. And we are certainly justified in demanding very cogent arguments before accepting such a hypothesis.

The suggestion that sense data are mental products, or that the mind has at least a share in their production, is welcomed by many people because on the strength of it they feel entitled to classify sense data with the images of dream and fantasy and memory. Venturesome as it is to presume to speak for the "plain man," I think that it is safe to say that, whereas in the case of sense perception he is an extreme, if uncritical, realist, when it comes to dream and fantasy he is as sure that what he is aware of in these fields originates in his own mind as is any subjective idealist. Why is he so confident? In the first place because the objects of dream or fantasy do not interact with the objects he encounters in waking life, nor yet with his own body. Tigers of which he dreams, or which he pictures to himself when reading a story, do not devour him, guns which are fired do not kill anything, and so forth. And in the second place, because these images are not public but private, no one else sees the tiger of his nightmare or fantasy. Now sense data are likewise private. And they represent the external world with sufficient accuracy to make adjustment easy for all practical purposes, and yet with sufficient inaccuracy to account for all the errors in sense experience. Thus, once the individual has ceased to be a "plain man" and has begun to philosophize, representationalism is the view which will shock him least, and which will do less than any other to undermine his feeling that he is still in contact with common sense.

In any case, whether sense data be produced by the human mind or by the physical organism or by the two acting in conjunction, they

imponderable brain-begotten particular can and does exist when nobody is aware of it. For, it will be observed, if characters "relative only to (physiological) percipient events in individual organisms" are assumed to be present (although unperceived) at the places (whatever precisely these may be) assigned to them outside the organism, nothing results elsewhere in the physical world from their being there. The unsensed sensa would be otiose members of the physical universe. Unless our physics is *all* wrong, they could not be supposed to play any part in the dynamic processes of nature; and they would thus be entirely useless for the theoretical explanation of the phenomena which we actually experience. (*The Revolt against Dualism*, pp. 104–105) are not produced spontaneously and in an utterly haphazard manner. On the contrary, they are produced in consequence of the stimulation of the sense organs, and they are what they are because the stimulation is what it is. The nature of the source whence the stimulus proceeds, and the nature of the medium through which it passes, are conceived profoundly to affect their character. Nor is it possible for us, once the stimulation has occurred, to inhibit the production of the sense data. The process of stimulation, therefore, is a part cause of their coming into existence; and their function is to image for us the external world with sufficient verisimilitude to facilitate adjustment thereto.

According to this doctrine, at least in its original form and as it was taken over by physical scientists, the so-called secondary qualities— i.e., those discerned by means of a single sense—are subjective in the sense that they image nothing in the external world. But the so-called primary qualities—i.e., those jointly observed by sight and touch— are mirrored by our sense data, although not always with complete accuracy. Thus, when we look at a straight stick which is not submerged in water, the sense datum generated by this process of perception is also straight, with the result that we are aware of the stick as it is, namely, as straight; but when we look at it submerged in water, the sense datum is bent because of the refraction of the rays as they pass through the water, so that the curved image which we behold is the result of a distorted process of stimulation.

This account raises for us a number of difficulties. The process of stimulation is an enormously complicated affair. In the case of sight and in that of hearing—and sometimes in that of smell—there is an intervening medium through which the stimulus must pass after its emission by the physical object; and in the case of each of the senses, there is the transmission of the stimulus from the sense organ to the brain, together with subsequent changes in the state of the brain which duly follow. Now it is to be observed that according to this doctrine, when the sense data come into existence they do not mirror, picture, or in any way represent the proximate cause of their production—that is, the alteration in the state of the brain—but rather the ultimate cause whence the stimulus proceeded. We are quite unconscious of what goes on in our brains, or in the nerves leading thereto from our sense organs. In the case of sight, be it remarked, although we may be conscious of moving our eyes, we are not all aware of the two inverted images thrown upon their retinas; what we seem, at least, to be aware of is something in the external world. But is it not amazing that the

ultimate cause should thus be able, despite the manifold changes occurring in the intervening process, to exert so powerful an influence
upon the ultimate effect? Yet that it should do so is an essential presupposition of the assertion that primary qualities characterize the
ultimate cause.

It does not suffice to urge, in support of this doctrine, that inasmuch
as a sense datum has come into existence, it must be the effect of
some cause. For to this contention the idealist can wholeheartedly
assent. It is the *nature* of that cause which is in question. With what
right do we ascribe to the cause any characteristics of the effect?
Clearly, if we are to do so, we shall have to assert that the ultimate
effect must resemble the ultimate cause.[33] But if we are to apply this
principle, we must apply it uniformly, and not capriciously. This
means that we must apply it in the case of secondary, as well as
primary, qualities. Colored sense data must be caused by colored objects as truly as extended sense data by extended objects. The yellow sense datum which is presented to the jaundiced man must have
a cause which is likewise yellow. In the case of the primary qualities,
moreover, the same principle must be uniformly applied. The elliptical
sense datum must be caused by an elliptical penny, even as the
circular sense datum is caused by a circular penny. Thus the external
world will become filled with entities which have no place there. Our
theory, which was definitely designed to account for error, and which—
so long as its presuppositions were tacitly accepted—seemed so well
to do so, now that its presuppositions are questioned is seen to have
eliminated our errors only by objectifying them.

Shall we, then, deny that an effect must resemble its cause? Consistency will require that this denial hold good with respect to primary, as well as secondary, qualities. We shall have no ground,
accordingly, for the assumption that sense data which are extended
and shaped are caused by entities which are also extended and
shaped.

It is true that the view that primary qualities could constitute the
whole nature of a thing has recently been repudiated by more than
one philosopher.[34] It has been argued that we cannot have extension
without something that is extended, shape without something that is
shaped, or motion without qualities which "change their position."

33. For a thorough discussion of this hypothesis, of which discussion the present
treatment is merely a restatement, see McTaggart, *Some Dogmas of Religion*, secs.
65–73.
34. See Dr. Ewing, *The Fundamental Questions of Philosophy*, pp. 78, 184. Cf.
Stout, *Mind and Matter*, p. 130, and *God and Nature* (Cambridge, 1952), p. 194.

Primary qualities, we are informed, are really relational characteristics; hence whatever has them must possess secondary qualities, whether or not these be identical with any sense qualities known to us.

But this does not get us out of our difficulty. Either sense data must resemble their causes or they need not resemble them.[35] On the first hypothesis they will be caused by entities which are precisely like them, having identical shapes and colors. On the second hypothesis their causes need bear them no particular resemblance; we can no more infer, because the effect is extended, that the cause is also extended than we can infer, because the effect is red, that the cause is red.

There is, moreover, a further difficulty which confronts epistemological dualism. We have seen that on the assumption that sense data are produced by the physical organism, they also must be accounted physical, despite the fact that they do not interact with other physical objects, nor do they obey the laws of physics. As an alternative to this hypothesis, which appears quite incredible, it seems preferable to assume that sense data are the product of mind; hence they will not be physical, nor will they interact with physical entities. The mind, then, we must suppose, produces them in response to the physical stimulation of the brain. Such stimulation, therefore, may appropriately be termed the *occasional* cause of their production; the primary agent, the truly efficient cause, being the mind. Here the maxim that effect must resemble cause is obviously inapplicable; for what can be more diverse than an unextended mind, on the one hand, and an extended and shaped thing on the other? The sense datum, accordingly, cannot be produced through the manipulation or transformation of any antecedently existing reality; it is brought into being *in toto* and *de novo*. In other words, it is *created*. This is indeed a momentous conclusion; one which, if well grounded, is bound to have repercussions in metaphysics and in theology. Dr. Ewing, who seems to be quite alone in looking this issue squarely in the face, has expressed his opinion so forcefully that I shall let him state it in his own words.

It has been commonly regarded, according to the point of view taken, as one of the most incomprehensible mysteries or as one of the most absurd superstitions of theology that it asserted the

35. Of course every particular resembles every other particular in being an existent and a particular, in having qualities, in standing in relations, and in being a member of the universe. But the principle invoked demands explicit and complete resemblance of effect to cause.

creation of matter *ex nihilo,* but it seems quite clear in any case that something is created *ex nihilo* not or not only by a God but by mere human beings. So much must be admitted by any theory which allows any sensa or images at all that neither belong to the physical world nor are states of our mind. For our actually sensed sensa and images have thus been created; they come into being without ever having existed before and are not merely *changed* but brought into existence by causal action. The fact that images are new creations is obscured by the circumstance that there is a sense in which we can only form them by reproducing or combining what has been previously given in sense-experience. But the actual image itself is still created *ex nihilo,* for the identity with previous images is qualitative, not numerical. If I make an image of a centaur by combining that of a man and that of a horse, which have both been given in previous experience, this does not mean that the actual images or sensa produced when I last saw a man and a horse respectively have persisted since then continuously and are now put together by me, as I might put together bricks to make a physical wall. All it means is that I make a new image in certain respects like both of them. I must literally create the images of the man's head and the horse's body themselves anew and cannot use numerically the same images as I had, say, an hour ago or just after the time when I saw the objects on which they are modelled for these images have ceased to exist altogether. Similarly, even if the existence of sensa actually sensed by us is due partly to sensa like them existing as constituent parts of physical things, the actual sensa sensed themselves are still *created* through the interaction of ourselves with our environment and are not identical numerically with these pre-existing (unsensed) sensa external to us.[36]

Dr. Ewing has powerfully reinforced his contention that sensa are created by the apprehending subject by stressing the similarity of their status to that of images. And the same course has been followed by Stout. "Consider fully," wrote the latter,

> the status of what are called mental images, and their connexion with the original sense-impressions. Such images are themselves sensory presentations, though derivative and dependent. On the other hand no one, I presume, would assert, unless in the interests of a preconceived theory, that images can exist without being

36. *Idealism,* pp. 380–381.

experienced by some mind. But we cannot consistently hold this to be true of images and deny it to be true of the impressions of which they are revivals.[37]

"Except in the interests of a preconceived theory"—these words certainly apply to me, and to the general theory which I have been laboring to elaborate. For I have advanced what I judge to be excellent reasons for holding that the universe as a whole is rational; and as the reader will recall, my acceptance of Dr. Ewing's conclusions from his discussion of causality has been one of the chief supports of my position. If, however, we accept the notion of creation this position must be profoundly modified. For if man can create *ex nihilo*, it would be absurd to suggest that God cannot do the same. Consequently, should we see reason to adopt the theistic position, the notion of creation must be conceded to be applicable to the entire universe. This would not, indeed, involve the conclusion that the universe is fundamentally irrational. We might still be able to explain it in terms of divine purpose. Yet it would not be rational *in se* but only *ab alio*. At the core of it there will remain an impenetrable mystery, the mystery of a creative act. Nor will the mystery vanish if we refuse to adopt the theistic position. For there will still be a vast number of finite minds in the universe, all of whom will be continually creative. And what deepens the mystery is the undoubted fact that none of us has the least idea of how we accomplish so extraordinary a feat. Sometimes we do it willingly, as in fantasy; sometimes without any conscious volition, as in dreams; sometimes in opposition to our conscious desires, as in nightmare or hallucination. To bridge the gap between non-being and being is possible, the scholastics tell us, only for omnipotence. How wrong they are! For we ourselves, with all our limitations, and presumably the higher animals also, can do the same!

There is another aspect of Dr. Ewing's doctrine to which I would call attention. If I can genuinely create, why is the product of my creative activity imperceptible to anyone other than myself? Why can I not create an image that you can see? Why, once more, can I not create something that will interact with physical objects, and that will continue to exist when I am not thinking of it? Our inability to do such things surely requires *some* explanation. Yet no such explanation appears to be forthcoming; and its absence leads me, I confess, to be extremely suspicious of the whole doctrine.

Furthermore, once we submit the notion of creation to critical

37. *God and Nature*, p. 208.

analysis, it is seen to be unintelligible. The notion of making, on the other hand, is intelligible enough from the standpoint of common sense.[38] There is the efficient cause (the maker), there is the material cause which gives him something to work upon, there is the formal cause (the design which he has in mind and which he imposes upon matter), and there is the final cause (the end which the maker has in mind and which motivates his activity). Subtract now the material cause, and you subtract intelligibility along with it. Nothing is left upon which the efficient cause can act. Now you have creation. Subtract next the efficient cause, and you have *emergence,* the much vaunted principle of explanation of the naturalist, of which it can only be said that it is, if possible, at least one degree more unintelligible than creation.

Should we be willing, however, to waive these objections, the question remains whether the position of the epistemological dualist be preferable to that of the idealist. For as we have seen, whatever be the view as to the similarity of effect to cause which the dualist may adopt, it will prove for him either too much or too little. He will require a great deal of ingenuity to save himself from falling into the abyss of direct realism, on the one hand, or idealism on the other.

Now the idealist can point out that it is more economical to get along with minds and sense data than with minds, sense data, and matter. And he can ask the dualist to explain why, upon the reception of a particular physical stimulus, the mind reacts by producing *this* sense datum rather than *that;* why, for instance, green is connected with a certain wave length and red with another. It is true enough that, on his own principles, the idealist cannot hope to give a complete answer to the same question. Yet, if he be a theist, whether a Berkeleyan subjectivist or a panpsychist, he will contend that sense data come into existence in accordance with a divine purpose, that they constitute a sort of signaling system, or as Berkeley would say, a divine "language," whereby God co-ordinates the thoughts and actions of the individual mind with those of other finite minds. Needless to say, he must make good his theism if he is to make out his case, and the question of divine existence is one which we are not yet ready to take up. Still we must acknowledge that if his presuppositions be justified, his conception of the origin and function of sense data becomes very plausible. The same considerations, it may be observed, would apply as well in the case of a theist who adhered to the representation-

38. It presupposes, of course, the reality of time and of matter; but of neither is common sense skeptical.

alist theory. But in opposition thereto the subjective idealist can appeal to Berkeley's maxim that God does nothing in vain. And if sense data be mind-dependent, if they be produced by the finite mind in consequence of, and in accordance with, divine stimulation, would not our experience be precisely what it is were there no physical world at all? Would not such a world be entirely otiose? Why, then, assume that there is such a world? Why not treat it as a purely theoretical construct? As on Lord Russell's theory a "thing" will now become a system or "family" of sense data; and it is relevant to point out that the difficulties which arise for Lord Russell from the proliferation of sense data will not confront the Berkeleyan.

For the objective idealist who holds that the divine Mind itself is productive of sense data which constitute common objects for finite minds, and so make up a common world, the situation is somewhat more complicated.[39] If he be a singularist—to employ the terminology of James Ward—for whom all finite minds are differentiations within the divine Mind, the sum total of sense data will constitute a vast sense continuum which will be the object of divine awareness, in which awareness finite minds will be permitted, according to their capacity, to participate. If, on the other hand, he be a pluralistic idealist, for whom finite minds are separate entities apart from the divine Mind, he may still hold that all sense data are produced by the divine Mind. God will, then, be aware of the converging as well as of the straight railroad tracks, of the bent as well as of the straight stick, of the elliptical as well as of the circular penny, of the double as well as of the single candle flame, of the house in all its perspectives with their relative sizes, and so forth. It is clear that such a position will closely approximate that of the adherent of the multiple inherence theory; the fundamental difference will be ontological rather than epistemological.

Let us now contrast the general position of objective idealism with that of Dr. Ewing. As we have seen, Dr. Ewing holds that the individual mind creates its own sense data. And he further holds that physical objects can be reduced to combinations of sense data unsensed by us—not necessarily qualitatively the same as those which we produce and sense, but of the same *genus*—which are created and conserved by the divine Mind. He is therefore undoubtedly justified in calling himself an epistemological dualist and a representationalist. But he goes further than this. He is prepared to classify himself as an ontological dualist. "My metaphysic," he writes, "in so far as I have one,

39. Of objective idealists Stout was one of the most recent and most eminent.

is dualistic in that it recognizes two kinds of entities, minds and sensa, the difference between which is, for us at least, irreducible." [40] It is undoubtedly a relative dualism, inasmuch as all sense data—and also, as I understand, all finite minds—are created, whereas the divine Mind is uncreated. But it is clear that any thinker who does not believe that sense data are actually states of the apprehending mind, and who yet regards them as mind-dependent particulars, is in this sense a relative dualist.

Throughout the previous discussion we have assumed that sense data are mind-dependent particulars. If we could account for them on the supposition that they are states of the apprehending mind, this would be a very satisfactory solution. But we have seen that it simply will not do in the case of all particulars. Granted that when I say, "I taste something sweet," I am having a sweet feeling, it is absolutely incredible that when I seem to sense a square object, I am merely feeling "squarely." For in the latter case, I am presented with a definite object which I contemplate; and if I cannot be sure that it is distinct from me, and from my awareness of it, there are very few things of which I can be sure. Yet we have also seen that there is much in our experience to suggest that sense data are mind-dependent. Hence, if they obviously are not mental states, what can they be except created entities?

How, then, if we resort to the hypothesis that sense data are uncaused? By this I do not mean to suggest that they simply "emerge" spontaneously and sporadically, for we have seen that the notion of emergence is quite as unintelligible as is that of creation. Moreover, there are habitual sequences in our experience of sense data; there is an orderliness in such occurrences which requires to be accounted for, but is it obviously nonsense to suggest that sense data may be eternal entities which exist when unsensed? Lord Russell's theory, indeed, appears to involve such an assumption. It is true that we have seen reason to reject it. Suppose, however, that we modify it. Suppose that we assume that there are physical objects which are never directly perceived by us, and that there are also sense data which we do directly perceive and which are capable of representing physical objects to us, but which do not depend for their existence upon being perceived.

With respect to the self-existence of the sense data there would appear to be no difficulty. Unless we accept emergence as an intelligible notion, and then proceed to extend it to the entire universe,

40. *Idealism*, p. 360.

some ultimate and underived reality there must be. And why are not sense data as good candidates for this status as any other entities? Yet, if we assent to this suggestion, a crowd of awkward questions will press in upon us. The entities of whose objective existence we are the surest are those which have extension and shape. But these, surely, should be in common space, and should be perceptible by more than one apprehending mind. And yet the privacy of sense data is one of their most awkward characteristics. Shall we account for this by assigning them to private spaces, one for each observer? But shall we not thereby make them relative to the observer, and so impugn their independent existence? And this relativity, surely, can be preserved only on the assumption that private spaces are not parts of common space. Are we not thus drifting, however, toward a position uncomfortably reminiscent of that of subjective idealism—only now, instead of a host of pure spirits, we shall have a host of individual minds, each with its private *entourage* of sensible particulars, some of which it perceives at one moment, some at another, and some, perhaps, never; and in addition, there will be a vast host of unperceived physical objects. The function of sense data will be to represent these physical objects; they will appear when they are wanted, and disappear when they are not needed. Press your eye as you look in the direction of an ontologically real yet unperceived candle flame, and two colored and shaped images will immediately obligingly appear before you; bang your head, and a group of little starlike appearances will rush before your mind's eye. All the sounds that we hear are eternal entities waiting ever in attendance to come before us when summoned. When one views the penny in a certain perspective, in pops an elliptically shaped particular, only to vanish when one moves one's head, to be replaced by its appropriate successor. I do not say that this is an utterly impossible theory, for it is conceivable; but I do venture to assert that it is so complicated, and so thoroughly unsusceptible of empirical corroboration, as to be quite improbable. Furthermore, unless we be prepared to deal with images in the same fashion, we should in all likelihood do better to reverse our attitude, and to treat sense data as mind-dependent.

We are now in a position to understand better how such thinkers as Dawes Hicks and Alexander could be so firmly convinced that the admission of the reality of images would prove fatal to a realistic epistemology. According to Alexander, whose view, in my judgment, is the simpler and more impressive, the selective theory explains all errors. In sense perception, if we see an object as it is not, this is because we view it in part or confuse it with something else. In dream or in fantasy, in illusion or delusion, the mind is always in touch with the physical world, and this without being dependent for its contact upon the normal processes of physical stimulation; hence the amazing mosaic in which entities thus simultaneously cognized seem to fit together. Thus, for example, when I should ordinarily be said to be picturing to myself a centaur, what actually happens is that I am simultaneously aware of the body of a horse and of the torso of a man. This extraordinary view has been subjected by W. T. Stace to the following severe criticism.

> Other ingenious hypotheses were invented by Alexander to evade the fatal defect of the selective hypothesis, namely that it attributes incompatible qualities to the object. Thus the smaller size of an object when seen at a distance is said by him to be a *part* of the larger size of it when it is seen near at hand; and this part is selected by the mind out of the larger size. This sort of theory will not work at all in the case of different *shapes* of the object as seen from different angles, since there is no sense in which one shape can be said to be part of another. Of course, the area of an oval can be part of the area of a circle. But the shapiness of the oval is not part of the shapiness of the circle. Illusion, as when we see a grey surface as green, owing to juxtaposition of red, is explained by Alexander on the hypothesis that the green which we see is a green which is actually somewhere in the physical world, though not in the place in which we see it. This is due to the fact that the mind squints! This green which I see here on a piece of paper in Princeton is really the green of a patch of grass in Philadelphia which got transferred here by my squinting mind. The best one can say of such theorizing is that its ingenuity is only exceeded by its implausibility.[41]

So far as Professor Stace's first point is concerned, we may well hesitate to give our assent. It is true that one "shapiness" cannot be part of another; but it is also true, as he admits, that one area can be part of another; hence, if only a part of the whole be visible, it is, surely, quite possible that the shape of that part should be other than the shape of the whole. It is the hypothesis of the "squinting mind" that it is hard to accept. The phrase, indeed, is only a metaphor; but what lies behind it is the notion of a selectivity untrammeled by

41. *The Nature of the World* (London, 1940), p. 120.

physical limitations. Yet is this credible? When in normal, waking perception we are dependent for our awareness of physical objects upon the stimulation of our sense organs, can we suppose that in dream or fantasy our mind ranges freely over an indefinitely extended expanse, that when we dream of the great pyramid we are directly aware of it, or that when in reading a fairy tale we picture to ourselves a dragon, we are actually aware of a boa constrictor in South America and of a blast issuing from a furnace in a North American manufacturing town? The strain upon our credulity is too great.

Yet Alexander's attempt to dispense with images, fantastic or courageous as we may esteem it, merits our sympathetic interest. For the issue—as I shall shortly try to show—is of greater importance than many realists would appear to realize. Let us therefore consider it in the light of Alexander's theory of memory. Here, it seems to me, the case for direct realism can be presented with its maximum plausibility. For as we have seen, even he who holds that memory images are present realities must yet concede that they are accompanied by direct awareness either of the past or of propositions referring to the past. But for those who are prepared to admit that the past is no less real than the present, is it not simpler to agree with Alexander that in memory one is directly aware of events which, although no longer occurrent, are still real? [42] Images and propositions can thus be dispensed with. That portion of the past which we once experienced as present is in principle open to our inspection. If so much be granted, is it not permissible to surmise that dream, fantasy, illusion, and delusion are all ultimately explicable in terms of memory? For even those who do believe in images are forced to admit that the constituent parts of these images are made up of copies of entities previously experienced, and that such novelty as they possess is due to fresh combinations of familiar material. When the sense organs are quiescent —as in dream or fantasy, no less than in memory—may not the mind range freely as it will, and may not its "squinting"—that is to say, its seemingly haphazard selectivity—be due to its own conscious, or subconscious, needs and desires?

I advance the above suggestion with some diffidence, but it does seem to me conceivable that in this way we might succeed in disembarrassing ourselves of images. I do not for a moment suppose that of itself it will enable us to deal with all errors in sense perception.

---

42. For him who denies the reality of the past, this suggestion will be devoid of plausibility. But he must be prepared to face serious troubles of his own. We may postpone raising this question, however, till we come to discuss the problem of time.

But I would point out that if it once be conceded that there are images, and that images are mental products, the case for dealing with sense data in like manner will become overwhelmingly strong. And then the logic of the situation will carry us either toward some form of idealism, or toward a compromise theory such as that of Dr. Ewing.

SENSE DATA AND UNIVERSALS

Heretofore we have been exclusively concerned with theories which regard sense data as particulars. But we must now take notice of the contention that sense data are "essences" or universals. That they are so has been affirmed by certain critical realists—who are, of course, avowedly epistemological dualists—and also by various champions of the multiple inherence theory, and it is plain that it might equally well be affirmed by exponents of the multiple relation theory of appearing.[43]

As I understand it, the doctrine, if taken in the widest sense, does not deny that there are particulars, nor does it necessarily refuse to admit that these particulars possess characteristics which inhere in them dyadically, nor yet that these particulars together with certain of these dyadically inherent characteristics are at times perceived by us; rather its fundamental contention is that errors in sense perception can be accounted for in terms of universals which do not inhere dyadically in the said particulars. Either such universals inhere in the particulars triadically, or they do not inhere in them at all, but only appear to do so. Although it may be rather difficult to distinguish between these two alternatives, it is worth while to make the effort. Let us therefore begin with the first of these assumptions.

By the phrase "triadic inherence" we are to understand the characterization of a particular by a universal in a certain perspective. This assertion is intended to be taken in a thoroughly literal sense. There really is a particular, and it really does stand in such and such a perspective, which is to say that it is observable from some definite location. And there really is a universal, no mind-made concept, but a genuine, underived, eternal entity; and *this* universal in *this* perspective actually does *inhere in, characterize,* or *form part of the nature of,* that particular as cognized from this point of view.

43. The clearest exposition of this theory with which I am acquainted is that of Professor Broad (*The Mind and Its Place in Nature,* pp. 178–180). From this I gather that the assumption in question has been made by members of this school.

Immediately we are faced by serious questions. In the first place, is the notion of triadic inherence an intelligible one? Is it not rather one manufactured *ad hoc,* in the interest of a preconceived theory? To say that a thing, viewed from a certain angle and from a certain distance, displays, manifests, or exhibits a certain characteristic—is not this equivalent to saying that it *appears* in this perspective to possess such and such a characteristic? And when we speak of appearance, do we not implicitly contrast *appearance* with *reality,* that is, with characteristics which it genuinely does possess, regardless of perspectives, and whether it be perceived or unperceived? I believe that when we think or speak as "plain men," this is just what we do. If we refuse, however, to admit that characterization does, or can, involve a triadic relationship, the theory in question at once collapses. What if we waive the objection for the moment in order to see what follows from the supposition?

At once another question comes to the front. If we concede that characterization can *ever* be a triadic relation, must we not be prepared to assert that it is *always* so? Can there be more than one kind of characterization? If our answer be in the negative, does it not follow that the "thing" is reduced to a mere "family" of perspectives, that all its characteristics are *ab alio,* and that in itself it is nothing at all? In other words, have we not, by pursuing this circuitous route, at last arrived at the portal of idealism?

Certainly the advocates of the multiple inherence theory will not agree. Characterization, they will urge, though it be triadic, is yet characterization. And if all characterization be triadic in character, so much the better! This admission only makes their case the stronger. For it is altogether an error, they will assure us, to confuse triadic characterization with appearance. On the contrary, it is genuine reality; it is the only physical reality there is. The "thing" actually is characterized in *this* perspective by *this* characteristic. In another perspective it may just as truly be characterized by some other characteristic. If the two characteristics be, as we say, incompatible, no difficulty arises from the admission that such is the case. In one perspective the penny really is round, in another it really is elliptical. The law of contradiction would be violated only if the "thing" were possessed of incompatible characteristics in the same perspective, and this it never is. But is not error, then, completely eliminated? Indeed it is, so far as sense perception is concerned; and this is one of the beauties of the theory. We are never mistaken in what we see, but only in the inferences which we may too precipitately draw. The penny really is elliptical in the perspective in which we see it as elliptical; should we, however, infer that it is elliptical in all perspectives, we should be in error. So far as sense experience is concerned, therefore, the distinction between appearance and reality is obliterated; as a thing *appears*, so it *is*.

The theory thus briefly sketched presupposes the soundness of the realistic doctrine of universals. This is a view which has already been discussed, and which, I have urged, has the strongest claims upon our acceptance. Nonetheless some thinkers who are inclined to agree may yet be impressed by the objection which has been so forcefully urged by Lovejoy,[44] namely, that a universal which characterizes a particular is thereby itself individuated or particularized. It is the old notion of an *instance* which hovers between a universal and a particular. We know universals, it is contended, only by conceiving them; never do we sense them. What, then, do we sense? What is an *instance* of a universal? Is it a *tertium quid* which is neither a universal nor a particular? Is this an intelligible notion? Is it any more intelligible than that of a round square? I should certainly answer the last two questions in the negative. The point I take to be an ultimate one, and therefore not susceptible to argument. I can only ask any who may differ from me to try to make clear to me what they do mean; for to me what they say is meaningless, and I can do no less than avow it. But what if we say that the instance is a particular characteristic which characterizes a particular thing? What, then, will the universal be? A whole made up of particulars? Such is Stout's view, and I can only urge once more, as I urged when discussing his theory, that a whole composed of particulars can be nothing other than a particular. Once admit that there are instances in this sense of the word, and the realistic doctrine of universals is to all intents and purposes surrendered; and I, for one, had much rather surrender it explicitly than by implication. The contention of the realist who clearly envisages his own position is surely that the entity characterized is a particular substance, and that its characteristic is a universal.[45] Between universal and particular, as between heaven and hell for the Muslim, "there is no middle station." I have already argued in defense of this view as well as I am able in a preceding chapter, and I shall not now recapitulate what I

44. See *The Revolt against Dualism*, pp. 108–114.

45. We can, of course, if we like, talk of universals as being instantiated, but this can only mean for us that they are "characterizing characteristics," as Professor Broad would say; that is, that there are particulars which they characterize.

have said there. But I venture to think that the theory which we are now examining is proof against Lovejoy's criticism.

In the view before us neither the particular characterized nor the characterizing characteristic will be mind-dependent. It is impossible that the characteristic should be mind-dependent, if it be an eternal universal; and it is impossible for us to concede that the characterized particular is so, without falling into epistemological idealism—that abyss which ever yawns before us. But what of the triadic relation of characterization? Does this involve an apprehending mind? If so, once again we are tottering on the verge of idealism; for were there no minds, there would be no characterization at all. A perspective, therefore, we must hold to be an objective reality, whether or not there be a mind to apprehend at the location from which it can be envisaged. Our view, accordingly, will closely resemble Lord Russell's, with the difference that our data will be not particulars alone but universals as well. But what is the particular "thing" apart from its perspectives? The perspective now shows signs of becoming the ultimate reality; the perspective with its positive and negative poles, we might say— the subjective pole of potential apprehension and the objective pole of the potentially apprehensible. And these focus upon—what? Upon a point in space? But to admit this, Professor Broad would urge,[46] is to commit ourselves by implications to a doctrine of absolute space-time, an admission which may not suffice to damn the theory but which certainly does compromise it. At this point the epistemological realist might well feel inclined to retrace his steps. But there is another aspect of his theory which it behooves us to consider before we permit him to do so. For, like Lord Russell's view, it appears to have been developed with visual data almost exclusively in mind. Now, even if we grant that the notion of triadic characterization can successfully be applied to visual data, and perhaps to others as well, what are we to do with touch? You cannot touch a thing except where it is. Can any sense be made in this connection of the doctrine of perspective? Perhaps in the case of an object too large to be felt all over at once, we may find analogy. One thinks of the Buddhist parable of the blind men who touched the elephant, one grasping its trunk, another its leg, another its ear, and another its tail; and of the discordant impressions thus acquired. To the touch one part of an object may seem broad and another narrow, one curved and another straight. Still we do not ordinarily suppose that characteristics depend upon touch for being what they are. And in the case of a

46. See *The Mind and Its Place in Nature*, pp. 186–187.

small object, such as a coin which I can hold in my closed hand, it seems difficult to believe that the shape has anything to do with me, and that it does not inhere in the coin.

Let us therefore revise our initial hypothesis; let us assume that characterization can be either dyadic or triadic. There is plainly something to be said for this supposition, for the notion of triadic characterization is peculiarly difficult to apply in the case of mental entities. The late Franklin Delano Roosevelt appeared to some observers to be a patriotic, wise, and brave leader; to others a more composite character, at times wise, at times foolish, at times disinterested, at times personally ambitious; to others a base and self-centered demagogue. But was he nothing at all in himself, regardless of how men viewed him? He could not have been *all* appearance, there was *some* reality in him; and surely it was what it was, however the rest of us thought of him. And may not the same hold true of entities experienced in sense perception? May they not possess certain characteristics which inhere in them dyadically, as well as others which inhere triadically or perspectivally? This is, of course, the multiple relations theory of appearing. And it would seem at the outset to have this great advantage, that it enables us to discriminate between appearance and reality. Whereas the former hypothesis provided no basis for such discrimination, we can now say, "Triadic relations give us appearance; dyadic relations give us reality."

Another advantage which, at first glance at least, would seem to follow from the adoption of this theory is that it provides an excellent basis upon which to defend the claim that from the optimal point of view a thing can be perceived as it actually is. Thus, when we see the penny as elliptical, we see it as it is not; but when we see it as round, we see it as it is. Professor Broad, however, will not have it so.

"It is open to the supporter of the Theory of a Multiple Relation of Appearing," he writes,

> to assert that there may be one specially favourable position in which the qualities which a physical object *has*, and not merely those which it *seems* to have, are revealed directly to the percipient. On such assertions I have the following comments to make. (i) They are in the highest degree unlikely. We are asked to believe that in one special position the physical, physiological and psychical mechanism produces an utterly different result from that which it produces in all other positions, no matter how close to this favoured one. (ii) There is nothing in the nature of

any perceptual situation, taken by itself, to reveal to us that it differs in this remarkable way from all the rest. The unique perceptual situation, if such there be, does not come visibly "trailing clouds of glory behind it!" It would have to be discovered to have this property by comparing it and its objective constituent with other perceptual situations and theirs.[47]

Let us take the second of these comments first. Professor Broad objects that we cannot from direct inspection assure ourselves that in one particular perspective we perceive the object as it is, and not as it appears to be. Of course we cannot. He then insists that any such claim must be founded upon the results of a comparison of the perspective in question with other perspectives. Now it is clear, I think, that so long as we concern ourselves with only a single sense, such a comparison is bound to be fruitless. It is the corroboration of the data furnished by sight by that furnished by touch that provides the basis for the claim. And the claim appears to be a strong one. I see the penny as round, and I feel it as round. What more could I ask?

Turning now to Professor Broad's first objection we must admit, I think, that it possesses some force; yet not as much as if we were proceeding upon the assumption that the characteristics distinguished in sense perception were not universals but particulars. Were it indeed the case that in every perspective other than the favored one the entity directly sensed was a particular generated, or created, either by the apprehending mind, or by its physical organism, or by both together, then it would be strange, exceedingly strange, that all this "physical, physiological and psychic mechanism" should cease to function. The prima facie improbability would be so great that in my judgment we should be justified in setting aside the hypothesis which involved it. But our present concern is with the hypothesis that the characteristics distinguished are, not particulars, but universals. On the assumption that I see a round penny, it is the penny that is round, and not the roundness. If the penny actually be round, I see it as it is. If, from another standpoint, I see it as elliptical, I still see the penny. And I do not see ellipticality as elliptical. I see the penny as it is not, namely, as elliptical. In the former case I perceive the penny together with a characteristic which inheres in it dyadically; a characteristic, in other words, which it really has. In the latter case I

47. *Ibid.*, pp. 192–193. Professor Broad adds a third comment to the effect that it is open to the advocate of the sensum theory also to make "this preposterous claim," but with this issue we are not at present concerned.

perceive the penny together with a characteristic which inheres in it triadically, a characteristic which it really has not, but only seems to have. Appearance and triadic characterization are thus one and the same thing.

All this, Professor Broad would doubtless reply, is true but irrelevant. For he is not concerned to deny that characteristics are universals. His objection is the one previously mentioned—that the theory presupposes an absolute space-time. The example he gives is that of a finger reflected in a mirror.[48] Here we are dealing, of course, with a physical, and not with a mental, image. But it is an image which seems to occupy a space behind the mirror. Wherein lies the difficulty? Let Professor Broad answer.

> Now one may admit that a certain particular might seem to have a certain characteristic which differs from and is incompatible with the characteristic which it does have. But I find it almost incredible that one particular extended patch should seem to be two particular extended patches at a distance apart from each other. There is of course no difficulty in holding that the same shade of colour and the same sensible form may appear to inhere in two places at once, and that one of these places is physically filled whilst the other is physically empty; provided that you hold that colours and sensible forms seem to inhere, not in *physical objects,* but in *regions of Space.* The appearance of two particulars is then accounted for by the fact that there really are two particulars, viz., the two distinct regions of Space in which the same colour and sensible form appear to inhere at the same time. But this presupposes Absolute Space-Time as a substantial matrix whose regions are ready to appear to have such and such characteristics from other regions which are suitably filled.[49]

Why need we assume, one might ask, that the space which the reflection occupies is empty? May we not legitimately conjecture that physical occurrences are taking place everywhere, even if they are imperceptible to us? Although Professor Broad does not explicitly say so, I take the answer to be that characteristics can appear to inhere only in a perceptible particular. On his own view the difficulty does not arise, for what confronts him is a sensum which is individuated coincidentally with its production, and which is literally or apparently

48. *Ibid.,* pp. 187–188. (I should have thought that a double candle flame would have served his purpose even better, inasmuch as no mirror would be involved.)
49. *Ibid.,* p. 188.

projected to the place where we take it to be. But if he be right, the view which we are considering presupposes a theory of space similar to that of Alexander.

Whether or not we be prepared to accept Professor Broad's criticism, we can, I think, agree that the notion of triadic characterization requires further clarification. In the multiple relation theory, as I have already pointed out, it is to be equated with appearance. Would it not, then, be more just to call it a doctrine of triadic non-characterization? We have indeed three entities—the particular apprehended, the apprehending mind, and the eternal universal. Yet the eternal universal does not in dyadic fashion inhere in the particular. What, I ask, is the difference between saying that the universal characterizes in a triadic manner and saying that the universal does not characterize at all? Is the use of the phrase "triadic characterization" designed to suggest that some measure of objectivity is preserved, that appearance is not pure error?

That the word "appearance" can be used in more than one sense is, of course, a truism. By saying that a thing appears we may mean no more than that it is presented—i.e., that it is actually perceived. On the other hand, when we say that a thing appears *as* so and so, we frequently mean to contrast what the unwary might take it to be with what it really is. Now the multiple inherence theory may at least claim to employ the word "appearance" in the first sense, inasmuch as it does not explicitly distinguish between appearance and reality. But the multiple relation theory of appearing can make no such claim, for it is explicitly based upon this distinction. Perhaps it will be urged, however, that there must be some special sort of relationship between a universal and the particular which it appears to characterize. For the vast majority of universals do not even appear to characterize our particular. Granted that when I perceive the penny as elliptical, it is not really elliptical; still the fact remains that I do so perceive it, whereas I never perceive it as square or as triangular or as hexagonal. Does not appearing, therefore, involve a distinct and peculiar relation between the universal which seems to characterize and the particular? And if the phrase "triadic characterization" be intended and understood to mean no more than this, is not the use of it quite harmless? I think that we must answer in the affirmative.

There is one last point with regard to the multiple relation theory which I wish to stress. I have urged that it does provide *some* justification for the contention that there is a special or optimal point of view from which a sensible object can be seen as it is. And insofar as our interest is confined to purely epistemological considerations, I believe that the statement is true. Yet we must recognize that we cannot hope ultimately and completely to separate epistemological from ontological investigations, and that we may conceivably be led to question upon ontological grounds our epistemological conclusions. Thus the area which appears to be occupied by a solid, round, colored penny is actually, so scientists tell us, a region wherein imperceptible events of a physical nature are constantly occurring, and wherein electrons, protons, charges of energy, and whatnot, habitually disport themselves in accordance with laws peculiar to themselves. Certainly we cannot assume that these ultimate constituents of physical reality possess shape and location in the sense in which the penny does. We may even question whether they be more than "logical constructs." And we may thus be forced to extend the notion of appearance to embrace all the sensible characteristics of the penny.

I have touched upon this point in order to lead up to the consideration of a theory which, although distinct from, yet in some respects resembles the multiple relation theory of appearing. It is the view McTaggart elaborates in *The Nature of Existence*, which it will repay us briefly to examine. According to McTaggart, when we perceive a particular we are always aware of *some* of the characteristics which it actually possesses. We perceive it as existing, and as being a substance.[50] But we also perceive it as having characteristics which it does not actually possess; in other words, we are aware of appearance as distinct from genuine reality. The appearance as such is a real appearance, otherwise it would not deceive or perplex us; but that of which we are aware is not what we take it to be. Thus it is clear that McTaggart's doctrine of "misperception," as he terms it, is closely related to the multiple relation theory of appearing.

The reason why this theory plays so important a role in McTaggart's system is that he believes that he has definitely proved that whatever is real must be infinitely divisible, and that whereas spirit fulfils this requirement, neither matter nor sensa [51] can do so. From this it follows that both the primary and the secondary qualities with which sense experience acquaints us do not really qualify anything. They are, as Professor Broad would say, "non-characterizing characteristics." Here we have an epistemological consequence drawn from a

---

50. For McTaggart existence is a quality, and so is substantiality.
51. In denying the reality of sensa McTaggart is concerned to repudiate the doctrine that there are particulars and substances which are neither material nor mental.

metaphysical theory. As I have just observed, this does not necessarily imply that it is illegitimately drawn. We must expect that the lines of epistemological and metaphysical inquiry will intersect. It is both inevitable and desirable that they should do so, and our own effort must be to develop a coherent world view in the light of both. Nevertheless, our own view that spirit is simple and without parts will, if correct, disqualify this particular hypothesis.

It is interesting to observe that some philosophers who are prepared to admit the possibility of misperception have nonetheless criticized McTaggart for making use of it so extensively, and for employing it as a sort of universal solvent of all difficulties. Yet it may be questioned whether, if the notion be a defensible one, the right thing to do is not to make it do all the work it can. It may be, then, that we shall ultimately find McTaggart's theory suggestive, and perhaps utilizable in some modified form.

As developed by McTaggart, however, there are two features of his doctrine which demand attention. In the first place McTaggart rejects Moore's suggestion that when A is perceived as being X, while A must exist, it might be the case that it is not X. To McTaggart it seems self-evident—with a certain limitation—that when A is perceived as being X, it must not only exist but must also be X.[52] The limitation has to do with the specious present. "At any moment p," writes McTaggart,

I perceive not only what is happening at that moment, but also what happens at the earlier moments between m and p. Thus if A existed and was X at the moment o, I may perceive it at the moment p, when perhaps it has ceased to exist or to be X. And thus A need not be X at the moment at which I perceive it. What is meant is that, if at the moment p I perceive A as

52. "I may, of course, be mistaken in this view," remarks McTaggart, but I do not think that I am. And my contention may be indirectly supported by considering what would happen if perceptions had not this self-evident correctness. For the correctness of a perception can certainly not be proved, and if it is not self-evident we have no right to believe that any perception of anything as having any particular quality is correct at all. We should therefore know nothing about the percepta. Nor could we say that, although we were not entitled to say that A was X, we were at any rate sure that our perception of A was a perception of it as being X. For if the perception of A gives knowledge at all, it can only be about A. It cannot give knowledge of itself —the perception of A. That could only be given by another perception—the perception of the perception of A, which would have the perception of A as its perceptum. And we could know no more about this perceptum than about any other. (*The Nature of Existence*, Vol. II, sec. 513)

X, then it is self-evidently certain that X exists and is A at some moment or moments which I am then perceiving as present.[53]

All this sounds very like direct realism, and goes to bear out Mc-Taggart's claim that he was an epistemological realist. But the argument is given an unexpected turn by McTaggart's further assertion that since time is unreal, for a completely correct temporal perception we must substitute a partially erroneous eternal perception.[54] Thus McTaggart's theory of misperception is linked, not only to his doctrine of the infinite divisibility of substances, but also to his doctrine of the unreality of time.

In the second place McTaggart definitely and emphatically asserts that the seat of all error is in the "observing subject." [55] In the case of errors to which men are uniformly and inescapably prone, such as those involved in sense experience, there has been a tendency on the part of many philosophers to refer to the beliefs to which these give rise as phenomenally true. But we must remember, McTaggart cautions us, that "what is phenomenally true is really false." [56] "If nothing really exists in space," he declares, "then no tables exist, and any perception or judgment which perceives anything as a table, or asserts that a table exists, is erroneous—however inevitable or however useful the error may be. There are no tables, but only erroneous perceptions of tables, and erroneous judgments that tables exist. And these perceptions and judgments, like all other perceptions and judgments, are only within the observing self." [57]

Something, therefore, in the nature of our minds involves us in errors which are both inevitable and incorrigible. Even if I do not believe in the existence of tables, I cannot help perceiving what is before me as a table. I may correctly believe that what I am aware of is a group of souls, yet the correctness of my belief will not save me from perceiving the group as an extended object possessed of shape and color. Volition, accordingly, has nothing to do with misperception. Hence the latter must be the product of some ineradicable feature of the human mind. Can any light be thrown upon its origin, or must we reconcile ourselves to regarding it as an ultimate mystery? This is a question which we might ask of the believer of the multiple relation theory as well as of McTaggart. The former, so far as I can discover, has no suggestion to make; but McTaggart has at least a partial answer, whether or not we may agree with it.

53. *Ibid.*, sec. 514.   54. *Ibid.*, secs. 515, 591.
55. *Ibid.*, sec. 520.   56. *Ibid.*
57. *Ibid.*

Characteristics—i.e., qualities and relations—in themselves, McTaggart tells us, are real, whereas qualities and relations of existent substances are themselves existent.[58] Reality and existence are, for McTaggart, two distinct and indefinable qualities.[59] As I have stated, I am very suspicious of this distinction which, I fear, harks back to the scholastic notion of being as a kind of act. This, however, is not the main point of my criticism. I am concerned with the fact that McTaggart holds that there are negative, as well as positive, characteristics. "For every positive quality *x*," he asserts, "there is a negative quality, not-*x*, and one member of this pair can be predicated of everything that exists." [60] These negative characteristics, he holds, are as truly existent as the positive characteristics. Furthermore a positive characteristic thus negated exists as an element in the corresponding negative characteristic. "If a man cannot be a phoenix, then every man will have the negative characteristic of not-phoenix. This characteristic will be existent, and since 'phoenix' is an element of 'not-phoenix,' it will also be existent. For it seems clear that the parts of what exist must themselves exist, whether they are or are not characteristics of existent things." [61]

From this it is clear that although nothing, according to McTaggart, is really extended or square or red or sonorous or colored or hard or smelly or sweet, yet extendedness and squareness and redness and sound and coldness and hardness and smell and sweetness exist; they exist as "parts" of the corresponding negative characteristics. Thus a group of souls will not be extended, yet extendedness will exist as a "part" of the characteristic of unextendedness which really does characterize the group; and so of shape and color. Does it not, then, seem highly probable that McTaggart, holding such a view, should have believed that in sense experience we are directly aware of the positive "parts" of negative "whole" characteristics without being aware of negative "wholes," and that we should thus confuse positive "parts" with positive "wholes"? The suggestion seems to me very plausible. It does not, of course, provide a complete explanation of misperception; for it does not account for the uniformity with which we perceive "parts" instead of "wholes." Perhaps some further light might be thrown upon the matter were we to investigate McTaggart's doctrine of the fragmentary series of misperceptions which constitutes

58. See "An Ontological Idealism," in *Philosophical Studies*, p. 274.
59. *Ibid.*, p. 273.
60. *Ibid.*, p. 274.
61. *The Nature of Existence*, Vol. I, sec. 31.

the eternal counterpart of temporal appearance, but such an investigation lies beyond the purview of this chapter.

With regard to McTaggart's doctrine of negative characteristics I must say that it does not impress me as at all plausible, *mais bien contraire*. I admit, of course, that it is true that a man is not a phoenix, and that it is true because the universals which would constitute the nature of a phoenix do not characterize a man. But I do not see that it follows that there must be corresponding negative characteristics—which, as McTaggart would hold, make up one compound negative characteristic negating the nature of a phoenix—which do characterize the man. McTaggart habitually used the phrase "true of" in lieu of "true that"; he asserted, moreover, that "true of" is "a term which is applicable to qualities." [62] I cannot but suspect, therefore, that he was thereby unwittingly led to assume that whatever can be said to be "true of" anything is a quality of that thing; and that thence arose his belief in negative characteristics. And if I be right in thinking that McTaggart did conceive of misperception in the way I have described, I can see no alternative to the conclusion that his theory will not stand.

Nonetheless we cannot fail to recognize that what McTaggart was trying to do was something very constructive, namely, to give a definite account of how misperception can occur. If we be unable, however, to accept this account, we are thrown back upon the notion of triadic characterization; consequently we must ask ourselves whether it be in fact an intelligible notion, or whether the words constitute merely a meaningless phrase.

I would suggest, in the first place, that when we speak of dyadic and triadic characterization, we are not using the term "characterization" in a univocal sense. In the light of our previous discussion it is, I think, fair to say that when we assert that a universal dyadically characterizes some particular, what we mean is that it actually does inhere in that particular, and that when we assert that a universal characterizes triadically a particular, what we mean is that actually it does not inhere at all, but only *seems* to do so. It is this *seeming* that involves the *threefoldness* of the relationship.

Let us, accordingly, look at this relationship a little more closely in the effort to find out something more about it. And let us begin by contrasting it with dyadic inherence or genuine characterization. As we have already seen, where intrinsic values are involved, we are driven to the conclusion that characterization is a relation which is

62. *Ibid.*, sec. 60.

internal in both terms, so that the reality of the one involves that of the other; and this conclusion is of the greatest importance for us, inasmuch as it constitutes the basis of our axiological idealism. Where universals which are not intrinsic values are concerned, on the other hand, it seems clear that characterization is a relation which is internal in only one term, namely, the particular. For the particular is what it is because of the nature which it has, and its nature is composed of the universals which characterize it. Without this characterization it is nothing. The universals concerned, however, are in no way dependent upon the particular which they characterize; whether instantiated or no, they are what they are. Toward the realm of particulars their attitude is one of serene indifference. Now triadic characterization, or the relation of appearing, is pretty obviously a relation which is external in both terms. For the particular is what it is —which is to say that it has the characteristics which dyadically inhere in it—regardless of how it appears, or whether or not it appear.

If so much be granted, there is a further consideration which is relevant. If a universal do not characterize a certain particular, there is no need—so I have contended—to posit a purely negative relation of non-characterization. Of necessity there will be other relations between the two—such as comembership in the same universe—but, so far as characterization is concerned, it suffices to say that the relation is absent. But in the case of appearing, some genuine relationship, other than characterization, must surely be involved. And the natural conclusion is that what is involved is an indirect relation through the apprehending mind. The mind is aware both of the particular and of the universal, and it "conceives" or "perceives" or "perceptually accepts" a relation of characterization as holding between them when it does not in fact obtain. How does this come about? So far as sense experience is concerned, and this is our present interest, it seems clear that it comes about through external stimulation. And it would not seem hazardous to conclude that the complexity of the process is somehow responsible for the presence of error.

All this, it may be said, is pretty vague. Indeed it is. But the same is true of each of the rival views which we have examined. Everywhere we are left with concepts which are ultimate yet intellectually opaque. What we are trying to do is to admit enough light to generate at least some degree of plausibility. Now it may be objected that I have just said that in appearance the apprehending mind is aware of a non-characterizing universal, and that such direct awareness is impossible. But let us see. As I have already observed, it is frequently maintained that in sense experience we are never aware of universals, but only of instances thereof; and that only by some purely intellectual process of conception or abstraction do we attain to the knowledge of universals. And I have replied that to make such an admission is completely to subvert the realistic position. For the whole notion of "abstraction" is vitiated by physical analogies; it is as though instances could be plastered together much as a child plasters together blobs of mud to make a mud pie. Unless we can become directly aware of universals, by no process of inference could we ever attain to them, nor should we have any motive for endeavoring to do so.

Even so, the objector may continue, we never perceive universals in isolation, or apart from particulars. To see red one must see a red patch. Perhaps we must concede that it is possible to think of the *universal "red"* without contemplating the red patch, if one substitutes for the patch the *word "red."* Yet this involves no more than the mental trick of letting one particular stand for another, and is possible only because of a long process of association.

I am not disposed to contest much of what my hypothetical critic has here urged, although I would observe that I am not so sure that it holds true of what we may term intelligible, as opposed to *sensible,* universals. Doubtless I could not think of gentleness or kindness or courtesy or courage if I had not met gentle, kind, courteous, or brave people, or at least have heard about them; yet it does seem to me that in thinking of these universals I am less dependent upon associating them with particulars, and at least a shade nearer to contemplating them in themselves.[63] But this is not the issue before us. I frankly concede that, whether or not it be absolutely impossible, it is at least exceedingly difficult to contemplate sensible universals except insofar as they are perceived to characterize, or are remembered to have characterized, particulars. My contention, however, is that in the case of appearance, a universal is apprehended *through* or *by means of* a particular, which particular it is apprehended as characterizing. The apprehension of the universal is veridical; the apprehension of it as characterizing is erroneous.

Such error, however, cannot be purely haphazard. Were it the case that from the same point of view upon successive occasions I apprehended a penny which was really round first as elliptical, secondly as triangular, thirdly as quadrangular, and fourthly as again elliptical,

63. According to Plato, of course, this is a capacity which philosophers should be concerned to exploit.

we might well conclude that all these occurrences were purely fortu- itous. Yet such is emphatically not the case. There is, then, regularity even in appearance. And some basis for it there must be. Yet some basis there must also be for the regularity with which a certain color is associated in perception with a certain wave length; but what de- termines this conjunction is a mystery. I do not think, therefore, that in an area where so much is uncertain, the multiple relation theory of appearing is at any appreciable disadvantage in comparison with its rivals; moreover, I consider that it enjoys two distinct advantages as compared with the sensum theory and with the multiple inherence theory, in that it has no need to try to make use of the doctrine of creation, and that it does provide a basis for distinguishing between appearance and reality.

Let me assure the reader that I have not forgotten Professor Broad's objection that the multiple relation theory presupposes an absolute space-time. What if we concede both the correctness of the observation and the unwisdom of committing ourselves to a position which ap- pears to be so questionable? How if we revert to the theory of private spaces, and dismiss common space as a logical construct? Would this be a step toward idealism? Toward metaphysical idealism no doubt, yet not necessarily a step away from epistemological realism. Consider the difficulty of treating as ultimate the objects revealed by sense experience. How do they stand in relation to the electrons, protons, ions, charges of energy, and so forth which pervade the areas which they appear to occupy? Are these physical ultimates, if indeed they be ultimates, themselves colored or shaped?

What I wish to urge is that there is nothing obviously absurd in the attempt of the immaterialist to be a personalist or a panpsychist, to treat life, volition, and conation as ultimates, and to reduce what we call the physical world to mere appearance. For as Dr. Ewing has justly affirmed, we know that there are minds and that there are sense data, whereas the existence of matter is inferential. Hence to get along without it, should this be possible, would be at once more economical and more rational. To say this is not to admit that we are about to commit the same mistake as that with which we have charged the adherents of the multiple inherence theory, namely, to eliminate the distinction between appearance and reality. Behind ap- pearance must lie reality, wherein dyadically inhere whatever charac- teristics it possesses. Yet we cannot assume that all, or any, of these are sensible characteristics. It is conceivable that the realm of appear- ance and that of sense experience should coincide, in which case whatever characteristics inhere dyadically would be non-sensible. The reality which underlies appearance would, then, be spiritual in character; and the realm of sense experience would be the reflection of the interrelations and interactions of selves.

Our momentary concern, however, is merely to discover whether the multiple relation theory be capable of development to a point where it offers advantages superior to those possessed by any other theory. And we have been driven to this inquiry by the following considerations: (1) It is clear that a simple direct realism of the common-sense type is unable to account satisfactorily for errors in sense perception, and is compelled to fall back upon mere dogmatic assertions; (2) the sensum theory is forced to appeal to the notion of creation, which it fails to render intelligible; (3) an idealism of the Berkeleyan type is compelled to choose between committing itself to the notion of creation or treating sense data as mental states, neither of which alternatives can be successfully defended; and (4) the multiple inherence theory cannot satisfactorily distinguish between appearance and reality, and finally leaves the notion of triadic inherence hopelessly vague. Now it does seem possible that the multiple relation theory may succeed in extricating itself from all these various difficulties.

Perhaps the objection will be raised at this point that the theory in question clearly involves in some form the notion of misperception, and that, aside from trying to show that McTaggart's concept thereof is unsatisfactory, I have so far done little or nothing to outline any theory of misperception which will stand. I have, indeed, suggested that unless we be prepared to defend the doctrine of absolute space, we seem driven to adopt some form of immaterialism. This does not mean, however, that our epistemology will cease to be realistic. For the characteristics which appear to characterize will all be universals, genuinely and objectively real. Moreover, it seems clear that if these be apprehended as characterizing, the particular which they appear to characterize must also be apprehended. From this it follows that McTaggart was right in maintaining that some characteristics which the particular really has—i.e., which inhere in it dyadically—such as existence and causal efficacy, for instance, must also be apprehended.

All this, it may be said, does not take us very far. Why should misperception occur? I have suggested that it may be due to complexity of stimulation. But is not this to revive the Leibnizian notion of "confused perception," a notion which has found scant favor with thinkers in general? In reply I should ask to be permitted to distinguish between *perception* and *perceptum*. It is, I think, quite hopeless to maintain that the *perceptum*—i.e., that which is perceived —is a particular formed by the conjunction of hosts of little *percepta*, out of which amalgamation is generated a *tertium quid* which constitutes an appearance. But it does not seem to me absurd to suggest that an *act* of apprehension may itself be confused. For confusion, as we have seen, is a form of error which indubitably occurs, and which is all the more likely to occur when the sources of stimulation are coincidental and manifold. But what of the regularity which, as we have noted, is present even in appearance? Why should not appearance be utterly chaotic? The only conceivable answer would seem to be that there are degrees of complexity in the process of stimulation which recur in orderly fashion. Talk of vagueness, the critic may interject, what theory could be vaguer than this! I would remind the critic, however, that on the immaterialist hypothesis, we cannot hope to see through appearance in such a way as to dispell it. *Any* hypothesis as to the nature of what lies behind it must unavoidably be highly general in character. We have been forced in this direction because of the greater vagueness, sometimes even complete unintelligibility, in which we have found all other theories involved. The theory now before us we have found freer than any from such disadvantages, and it is possible that ontological considerations may contribute something further in the way of reinforcement. The notions of the self and of universals, I would remind the reader, have been shown to be clear and definite and the reality of sense data—however they are to be accounted for—is unquestionable, whereas the notion of matter is becoming progressively ever more elusive. Some sort of immaterialism therefore would seem to offer the best hope of a satisfactory world view, and the multiple relation theory is quite compatible with such an outlook, and is involved in lesser difficulties than any other. But to ontological considerations we shall return in due course.

In conclusion I would call attention to a further consideration of great importance. The fundamental position which I have tried to elaborate in this book, because I regard it as capable of being definitely substantiated, is that of axiological idealism, the view that the universe is systemic in character and that it is oriented with respect to values. It is a position which, as we have seen, rests upon the reality of the self and of universals—including values and disvalues—and which enjoys the advantage of being supported either by the entailment, or by the activity, theory of causality. It is obvious that the soundness of this position remains relatively unaffected by the truth or falsity of *any* theory as to the nature of sense perception. Why, then, have I spent so much time and effort in discussing such theories? In the first place because the problem lay directly in our path. In the second place because many have thought that the solution of this problem carried with it important consequences for cosmology; hence it was desirable to form some estimate of the correctness of this opinion. And, in the third place, the position of axiological idealism will receive some indirect support if it can be shown that the most promising of epistemological theories is compatible with, even if it do not definitely imply the truth of, immaterialism. Such a consideration would certainly be relevant to this philosophy. Yet its significance must not be overestimated. For many philosophies of religion have accepted the reality of matter. It is true that most philosophies of the past which have been unfriendly to religion have done the same. But today the opposition to the religious point of view derives what strength it possesses rather from phenomenalism and from nominalism than from the belief in matter. I think, therefore, that the impression to which I have referred, and which I formerly shared, is a somewhat exaggerated one. Yet the epistemological conclusions we have reached, even if they be of subordinate importance from the point of view of our main interest, are not without significance, inasmuch as they do lend some support to the general position of axiological idealism.

Chapter Eleven

TIME

No sooner does one begin seriously to consider the nature of time than so many questions simultaneously present themselves that one may well feel quite distracted, and utterly at a loss which to take up first. Is time real, we may ask, or is it merely appearance? If it be appearance, of what is it an appearance? What is the relation between time and reality? If time, on the other hand, be real, is everything in time? Or are there some entities which are non-temporal, that is to say, eternal? On the latter assumption, how is the temporal related to the eternal? Does it make sense to speak of the universe as being in time, or ought we to think of time as falling within the universe—and is this, in turn, meaningful? Again, if time be real, are the three dimensions of past, present, and future likewise real? If so, it would seem that events which have already occurred, and events which have not yet occurred, will be quite as real as events which are occurring. Can we admit so much without impugning the reality of time? If our answer be in the negative, shall we seek to save the reality of time by denying that of the future and of the past? How long, then, is the present? If we reduce it to a durationless instant, shall we not have abolished time completely? [1] If, on the contrary, we assert that it has *some* duration, does it not follow that there is a present within the present—which is to say that so-called specious present is illusory? What, then, have we left that is real? Moreover, what becomes of memory if there be no past to remember? To escape such difficulties is it feasible to imitate the example of Lord Russell, and to treat past, present, and future as dependent upon a conscious subject, and to maintain that *in rerum natura* there are only relations of earlier and later? Such are some, though by no means all, of the crucial problems which confront us. Where shall we begin?

Lord Russell's View

Let us begin by considering Lord Russell's position, for if his contention can be made good, the problem of time will, as it were, evapo-

---

1. Thus did the Sautrāntikas lay themselves open to the criticism of the Yogācāras.

rate. We find the gist of his theory, I take it, in section 443 of his *Principles of Mathematics*.

"The notion of change," he writes,

has been much obscured by the doctrine of substance, by the distinction between a thing's nature and its external relations, and by the pre-eminence of subject-predicate propositions. It has been supposed that a thing could, in some way, be different and yet the same: that though predicates define a thing, yet it may have different predicates at different times. Hence the distinction of the essential and the accidental, and a number of other useless distinctions, which were (I hope) employed precisely and consciously by the scholastics, but are used vaguely and unconsciously by the moderns. Change, in this metaphysical sense, I do not at all admit. The so-called predicates of a term are mostly derived from relations to other terms; change is due, ultimately, to the fact that many terms have relations to some parts of time which they do not have to others. But every term is eternal, timeless, and immutable; the relations it may have to parts of time are equally immutable. It is merely the fact that different terms are related to different times that makes the difference between what exists at one time and what exists at another. And though a term may cease to exist, it cannot cease to be; it is still an entity, which can be counted as *one*, and concerning which some propositions are true and others false.

One of Lord Russell's purposes, as he makes quite clear, is to eliminate the notion of an enduring or persisting substance which can lose one characteristic and acquire another and yet remain the same self-identical thing. He has no antipathy, however, to non-temporal particulars, which many would blithely call substances. Kant has told us that only the permanent can change. But if Lord Russell be right, only the eternal can change.

"It will be noticed," observes McTaggart,

that Mr. Russell looks for change, not in the events of the time-series, but in the entity to which those events happen, or of which they are states. If my poker, for example, is hot on a particular Monday, and never before or since, the event of the poker being hot does not change. But the poker changes, because there is a time when this event is happening to it, and a time when it is not happening to it.

But this makes no change in the qualities of the poker. It is always a quality of that poker that it is one which is hot on that particular Monday. And it is always a quality of that poker that it is one which is not hot at any other time. Both these qualities are true of it at any time—the time when it is hot and the time when it is cold. And therefore it seems to be erroneous to say that there is any change in the poker. The fact that it is hot at one point in the series and cold at other points cannot give change, if neither of these facts change—and neither of them does. Nor does any other fact about the poker change, unless its presentness, pastness, or futurity change.[2]

What Lord Russell has done is to apply the word "change" to a relation of discrepancy between propositions which themselves are always true. There can be no doubt about this, for he has told us so himself. "Change," he has written, "is the difference, in respect of truth or falsehood, between a proposition concerning an entity and a time T and a proposition concerning the same entity and another time T', provided that the two propositions differ only by the fact that T occurs in the one where T' occurs in the other." [3]

Thus it is always true, as McTaggart says, that his poker is hot on a certain Monday, and always true that it is cold on any other day; it is always false to say that his poker is cold on that Monday, and always false to say that it is hot on any other day. But to use the word "change" in this sense is to give it a meaning very different from—in fact, diametrically opposed to—that which it bears in common parlance. For in everyday language to speak of change is to talk of an event, a happening, an occurrence (involving alteration of qualities or relations, or both), whereas all that Lord Russell has given us is a set of propositions referring to a series of unalterable states of a non-temporal entity.

"Let us consider," continues McTaggart,

the case of another sort of series. The meridian of Greenwich passes through a series of degrees of latitude. And we can find two points in this series, S and S', such that the proposition "at S the meridian of Greenwich is within the United Kingdom" is true, while the proposition "at S' the meridian of Greenwich is within the United Kingdom" is false. But no one would say

2. *The Nature of Existence*, Vol. II, sec. 315.
3. *Principles of Mathematics* (New York, 1938), sec. 442.

that this gave us change. Why should we say so in the case of the other series? [4]

Why, indeed? One can say, and say truly, that the letter *M* comes before the letter *P* in the alphabet and that the letter *P* comes after the letter *M*, and one can also truly say that the number five comes before the number nine in the series of positive integers and that the number nine comes after the number five; but it is clear to everyone that, in these cases, the relation of before and after is not a temporal relation. There is no time where there is no becoming, and this is as true with respect to the states of McTaggart's poker as it is with respect to the letters of the alphabet or with respect to numbers.

In the course of developing his own theory through a criticism of Lord Russell's, McTaggart has urged that any position in time is either earlier or later than any other position in time and also that every position in time is either past, present, or future. The relations of "earlier than" and "later than," he asserts, are permanent; whereas those of past, present, and future are impermanent. For at any position in time there will, of course, be a plurality of events; but it is possible, for the purpose of our discussion, to treat all coincident events as a single event. All events, then, will be related to one another by permanent relations of "earlier than" and "later than," and the series of events thus interrelated McTaggart calls the B series, whereas the series of past, present, and future events he calls the A series.

Employing this terminology, we may express Lord Russell's contention by the statement that only the B series is objectively real, and that past, present, and future are subjective in character. Yet, as a result of having taken this position he has shown himself unable to account for becoming. Now it is McTaggart's contention that the A series is essential to time. As he points out, it is even more fundamental than the B series, in that while the latter is derived from the former, the former cannot be derived from the latter. The relations of "earlier than" and "later than" are persisting and abiding relations, yet time cannot be constructed out of them. As constituting the B series they presuppose the A series. Moreover, if we appeal to experience, it seems to bear out this contention. "It is clear to begin with," writes McTaggart, "that, in present experience, we never *observe* events in time except as forming both these series. We perceive events in time as being present, and these are the only events which we actually perceive. And all other events which, by memory or by in-

4. *The Nature of Existence*, Vol. II, sec. 316.

ference, we believe to be real, we regard as present, past, or future. Thus the events of time as observed by us form an A series." [5]

As against Lord Russell it is quite clear, I submit, that McTaggart has made out his case. We cannot transform temporal relations into eternal relations. If the relations of "earlier than" and "later than" be enduring relations, there must be time for them to endure through; in other words, they must hold between events which actually occur and not between entities which are timeless.

McTaggart's Theory

If time be real there must, McTaggart maintains, be a real past and a real future as well as a real present. This means that there are events which have occurred, events that are occurring, and events that will occur. If it be objected that an event is an event only while it is occurring, and that, accordingly, it is not permissible to speak of past or future events, McTaggart's position can be restated as follows: there are entities which have occurred, and so were events; there are entities which are occurring, and so are events; and there are entities which will occur, and so will be events. On the assumption that past, present, and future are equally real, this is surely an adequate reply. But inasmuch as the point is purely a terminological one, and, furthermore, inasmuch as it is quite good usage to speak of past and future events, we shall find it more convenient to acquiesce in McTaggart's employment of the term *event*. All events, then, will be coexistent, or at least coreal; those that are future will be approaching us, and those that are past will be receding from us. Does not this mean that there are events which are *now future*, others which are *now past*, and others which are *now occurring*? [6] Certainly it does. And this is the very reason, according to McTaggart, why we must treat time not as real but as appearance.

"It is because the distinctions of past, present, and future seem to me essential for time," declares McTaggart, "that I regard time as unreal." [7] Why does he consider these distinctions as essential? He so considers them, as we have seen,[8] because of the testimony of perception, memory, and inference. And why does he regard this admission

5. *Ibid.*, sec. 307.
6. Obviously there is a real problem here, and one which cannot be exorcised by any linguistic legerdemain, as is attempted, for example, in Professor R. M. Gales, "Is it Now Now?" *Mind*, Vol. LXXVII, No. 289 (Jan., 1964).
7. *The Nature of Existence*, Vol. II, sec. 306.
8. See p. 372–373 above.

as fatal to the reality of time? Because there is no way in which the A series can be derived from the B series. For inasmuch as the relations between its terms are permanent relations, the B series is unable by itself to account for change.

As an instance of three terms thus interrelated let us take the three days of the battle of Gettysburg. And let us take all events in the universe occurring coincidentally with any event which took place during the battle as constituting in company with it a single complex event. We shall thus have three successive cross-sections of the history of the universe. The first day is earlier than the second day, and the second earlier than the third. The third day is later than the second day, and the second later than the first. So it has always been, McTaggart would insist, so it is now, and so it will be forever. At whatever date these statements are made they are true. Yet each day in turn became present. Let us consider the second day. Clearly it was never future, nor did it ever become present, in relation to the first day; for it is later than the first day, and "later than" is a permanent relation, whereas futurity and presentness are impermanent. Neither, of course, was it ever past in relation to the third day; for it is earlier than the third day, and "earlier than" is a permanent relation, whereas pastness is impermanent.

In relation to what, then, did the second day become present? Obviously it could not have become present in relation to any event; for all events are included in the B series, and the relations between them are unchanging. It is clear, moreover, that it could not have become present in relation to some non-temporal entity—an eternal God, for example—since to suppose that such an entity could stand in temporal relations would be to treat it as temporal, and thus implicitly to deny that it is eternal.

The only remaining conceivable hypothesis would seem to be that the second day became present in relation to a present moment.[9] But the moment cannot be permanently present, for this would be a contradiction in terms. It must therefore have become present. Yet it cannot have become present in relation to the moment before it, or to the moment after it, for to these it will stand in the permanent relations of "later than" and "earlier than." Hence it could have be-

9. McTaggart has been accused of hypostatizing moments. It is clear, however, that he referred to them only because Lord Russell had already introduced them (see *Principles of Mathematics*, chap. liv). And I think the first sentence of the last paragraph of section 310 and the first sentence of section 326 of Volume II of *The Nature of Existence* make it plain that McTaggart had no intention, even on the supposition that time is real, of treating moments as metaphysical entities.

come present only in relation to a present moment in another series of moments. And this moment in turn could have become present only in relation to a present moment in yet a third series of moments, and so ad infinitum. We are thus launched upon an infinite regress which is obviously vicious, inasmuch as it requires to be completed if any event is ever to become present.

The status of time, therefore, is that of an appearance. But of what is it an appearance? It will be well for us to scrutinize McTaggart's answer to this question, for even should we find ourselves unable to accept it as it stands, it may yet contain valuable hints from which we can profit. According to McTaggart the A series, together with the B series which is derived from it, are appearances of a real, non-temporal series—in other words, they are this series erroneously perceived.[10] This series McTaggart calls the C series. The terms of the C series are, of course, all coexistent. Whether their number be finite or infinite we cannot be sure, but in either case the series is limited at one end by non-being and at the other by the substance—that is to say, by the self—within which it falls. Each self thus constitutes a C series, the terms of which are all made up of perceptions. Every term, with the exception of the first and last terms, includes the term which is antecedent to it, and is itself included within the term subsequent to it. Not only is each term of the C series a perception, but each, with the exception of the final and all-inclusive term, is a partially erroneous perception. From the point of view of any one of these terms the terms which it includes appear to be earlier and those in which it is included appear to be later in time. Thus temporal appearance is accounted for by a non-temporal series of misperceptions.

A CRITIQUE OF McTAGGART'S THEORY

We have already seen that the multiple relation theory of appearing presupposes on the part of the apprehending subject a confused state

10. Thus McTaggart writes,
It must further be noted that the results at which we have arrived do not give us any reason to suppose that *all* the elements in our experience of time are illusory. We have come to the conclusion that there is no real A series, and that therefore there is no real B series, and no real time-series. But it does not follow that, when we have experience of a time-series, we are not observing a real series. It is possible that, whenever we have an illusory experience of a time-series, we are observing a real series, and that all that is illusory is the appearance that it is a time-series. Such a series as this—a series which is not a time-series, but under certain conditions appears to us to be one—may be called a C series. (*The Nature of Existence*, Vol. II, sec. 347)

of awareness which, whether we pronounce it a misjudgment or a misperception, is ultimate in the sense that it is not derived from any previous judgment. It is plain, therefore, that the epistemological position which we have adopted has certain affinities with that of McTaggart. Nonetheless, the notion of misperception as we find it in McTaggart does involve his theory in considerable difficulty. For he has definitely affirmed that *sub specie temporis* every perception must be correct, subject to the qualification that what falls within the specious present may be apprehended as temporally dislocated.[11] Many, if not most, philosophers would probably agree that this is a very moderate statement. But McTaggart next proceeds, in accordance with his conclusion that time is unreal, to substitute for these largely veridical temporal perceptions eternal perceptions which are erroneous to an extent which is in every case determined by the position of the perception in the C series. And that the amount of error is very considerable becomes quite obvious when we reflect that in McTaggart's theory all reality is spiritual, so that nothing actually possesses any spatial, temporal, or sensible characteristics, although it may appear to do so.

Now it is quite true that I have urged that the multiple relation theory of appearing may prove to be compatible with the position of panpsychism, and that I have also urged that the same can be said of no other theory. Accordingly it may seem that I, of all people, am most constrained to accept McTaggart's doctrine without criticism. And I freely confess that it does seem to me conceivable that those universals which are encountered only in sense experience should all be "non-characterizing characteristics" which only *appear* to characterize particulars. But I have furthermore contended that appearance of this sort involves confusion, and that for confusion to occur there must be real entities which can be confused. There must be a real universal and a real particular, even if the universal do not really characterize the particular. If so much be admitted, I do not, therefore, regard as utterly impossible the view that a relation of inclusion *might* be confused with a relation of temporal priority or posteriority, on the assumption that temporal relations are real universals although devoid of instances.

My difficulty with McTaggart's theory is that it does not account, if I understand it aright, for the experience of passage, of transition from one state to another. I am sitting in a room, let us say. I remember having entered it, and I anticipate leaving it. But on Mc-

11. *Ibid.*, secs. 513–515.

Taggart's view there is no possibility of passing from one state to another. The antecedent state of not being in the room, the state of being in it, and the subsequent state of not being in it are all coexistent, as truly coexistent as are the numbers five, seven, and nine. It is true that the prior state of not being in the room seems to be getting more and more remote, and that the anticipated state of not being in the room seems to be getting nearer and nearer, whereas the state of being in the room seems to be passing; but all this is appearance, and delusive appearance. Eternally I am neither in the room nor out of it, inasmuch as the room itself is only a phenomenon; yet the states of appearing to be in it and appearing to be out of it are eternally coexistent.

It is, of course, quite possible that something should appear to move or change when it is neither moving nor changing. But then something else must be moving or changing; there must be movement or change somewhere, if we are mistakenly to ascribe it to the wrong object. Thus a shooting star passing before a cloud which veils a fixed star may give the mistaken impression that the fixed star is itself in transit.[12] But if there be neither movement nor change anywhere nor anywhen, if no event ever occur, then, so far as I can see, there is no ontological basis for any appearance of passage or transition.

The Theory of Time Expounded in Broad's *Scientific Thought*

Let us next inspect the theory of time elaborated by Professor C. D. Broad in *Scientific Thought*. It is of peculiar interest because he has hoped to escape the difficulty created by McTaggart's viciously infinite regress by denying the reality of the future while conceding the reality both of the present and of the past. For Professor Broad this carries with it the admission that reality is continually expanding in the temporal dimension. Obviously such a view is incompatible with the recognition of the ultimacy of substance; but for Professor Broad this constitutes no deterrent, since, like the Buddhists of the Hīnayāna school, he sees nothing incredible in the notion of absolute becoming.[13] Thus for him the present constitutes, as it were, the knife edge of the past which, like a cosmic glacier, is constantly extending itself into ontological emptiness.

12. I refer here to an actual experience of a relative of mine.
13. Thus we are not astonished to find him later contending that *process* is a more fundamental category than *substance* (see *Examination of McTaggart's Philosophy*, I, 142–166).

A serious difficulty arises, however, from the fact that if there be no future there are no events to which propositions referring to the future can correspond; hence no such propositions can be true. From this it does not follow that they are false; what follows, according to Professor Broad, is that propositions which refer to the future are neither true nor false, that the law of non-contradiction does not apply to them.[14] On the basis of his own presuppositions he is, I think, quite right in this conclusion. For it seems clear that if a proposition which refers to the future be true, there must be a future event to which it corresponds. But according to the theory now before us, there never is, and there never can be, a future event. For every event that ever occurs is present when it occurs, and past after it has occurred. And to say that a proposition referring to the future is made true by its correspondence to a present event seems almost as weird as to say that it is made true by its correspondence to a past event.

McTaggart's Criticism of Broad's View

Against this theory McTaggart has advanced three objections.[15] His first objection is that it is quite certain that propositions referring to the future are either true or false; that it is quite certain, for example, that the proposition, "England will be a republic in 1920," was false in 1919.

The point is so ultimate a one that it is difficult to argue. Does it make sense to say that when we regard ourselves as making assertions with respect to the future what we are really doing is making assertions which describe the present as the kind of present which will issue in such a future? Obviously we can make such assertions. Yet, equally obviously, we can make assertions as to the kind of future that will be produced; and the two sets of assertions must be distinguished from one another. Is it meaningful to affirm that, whereas the former can be true or false, the latter can be neither? If, for instance, I say that the present state of affairs is bound to issue in an economic depression, I seem to be saying something about the present and something also about the future. If what I say about the future be neither true nor false, how can what I say about the present be either true or false? Yet, consider. When I make such a statement

14. Thus McTaggart once remarked to me that Professor Broad was prepared to give up the law of non-contradiction and to keep the reality of time, whereas he, McTaggart, preferred to keep the law of non-contradiction and to give up the reality of time.

15. *The Nature of Existence*, Vol. II, secs. 336–341.

do I mean that there is *now* a *future* event, in some sense coexistent with present events, which is continually approaching in the temporal dimension and which at some definite moment will become present? Can an event be an event before it has occurred, before it has eventuated? Surely it is one thing to say that a foreseen event is occurring now, and quite another thing to say that an event which has not yet occurred is at this moment a genuinely existent entity.

These reflections have brought us to a point where we may profitably consider McTaggart's second objection. It is impossible, he urges, "to deny that the truth of some propositions about the future is implied in the truth of some propositions about the past, and that, therefore, some propositions about the future are true. And we may go further. If no propositions about the past implied propositions about the future, then no propositions about the past could imply propositions about the later past or the present." [16] To concede so much is to concede that past or present events can intrinsically determine the future.[17] To cite McTaggart's own illustration, "If Smith has already died childless, this intrinsically determines that no future event will be a marriage of one of Smith's grandchildren." [18]

It is also true, according to McTaggart, that the future can determine the past. Thus being drunk entails having drunk alcohol, whereas drinking alcohol does not entail being drunk. It may, indeed, be objected that this seeming disparity is due to an incomplete account of the situation. One cannot be intoxicated unless one has previously drunk a certain amount of alcohol, but then one cannot drink that amount of alcohol without subsequently becoming intoxicated. The determination, in this particular case at least, is seen to be reciprocal; [19] the future determines the past, and the past determines the future. Yet this objection is plainly irrelevant. For all that McTaggart's argument requires is the admission that the past determines the future—not necessarily in the case of all past and future events, but at least in the case of some of them—and, if this claim be uncontested, must we not grant that propositions referring to the future can be true, and consequently that there must *presently* be future events to which they correspond?

16. *Ibid.*, sec. 339.
17. *Ibid.*, sec. 338.
18. *Ibid.*
19. That causal determination involves reciprocity McTaggart has emphatically denied. "Beheading a body," he has remarked, "determines its death, but death does not determine beheading. Death may be caused by hanging or poison" (*ibid.*, sec. 219. Cf. Broad, *Examination of McTaggart's Philosophy*, I, 222–223).

At this stage of the controversy Professor Broad intervenes with the accusation that McTaggart has confused the relation of intrinsic determination with that of conveyance.[20] The relation of conveyance holds between two characteristics of the *same thing*—between being colored and being extended, for example. "It is not easy," Professor Broad writes, "to think of any instance of intrinsic determination which is not inferred from conveyance"; [21] and again, more forcefully, "It is not at all clear to me that there are any cases in which we know that ϕ intrinsically determines ψ except by inference from knowledge about the conveyance of one characteristic by another." [22]

Conveyance, accordingly, is a non-temporal relation which holds between characteristics of one and the same entity, and it would seem that Professor Broad believes—although he does not definitely say so— that there are no instances of intrinsic determination which are not inferable from conveyance. But what, then, becomes of the causal connection? We habitually think of the cause as preceding the effect; a temporal relation, therefore, is involved. Moreover we normally assume that the causal connection can hold, not only between an antecedent and a subsequent state of the same particular, but also between antecedent and subsequent states of different particulars. And unless we be willing in Humean fashion to reduce causality to mere contiguity and succession, how can we conceive it otherwise than as a kind of intrinsic determination?

We might of course limit ourselves to asserting that intrinsic determination is present, and yet concede that by actual inspection we can never detect its presence. As critics of the regularity view have pointed out, our contention will then be that we are compelled to posit its presence in order to avoid committing ourselves to the incredible assertion that the so-called laws of nature are mere runs of luck. And this is a position which appears to be intellectually quite respectable. Nevertheless, as Dr. Ewing has urged, it is hard to believe that, in the mental realm at least, we do not actually observe instances of intrinsic determination. His illustration of a state of grief arising out of the awareness of the death of a loved one hits the nail on the head. Here we have the determination of a subsequent state of the self by an antecedent state of the same self. And it may plausibly be urged that it is quite evident that here there is no process of inference involved, that we are as directly aware of the relation of necessitation holding between the two psychic states as we are of

20. *Examination of McTaggart's Philosophy*, I, 197–198.
21. *Ibid.*, p. 198.   22. *Ibid.*, p. 200.

the states themselves. Moreover it can with equal plausibility be maintained that a relation of intrinsic determination may hold between an antecedent state of one self and a subsequent state of another self. Thus the happiness of A may be productive of displeasure in the envious B, an act of self-sacrifice on the part of C may evoke the admiration of D, or an act of deceit on the part of E may awaken the contempt of F. In such cases *both* the psychic states thus connected could not, of course, be observed by the same subject; yet their occurrence and the relation holding between them might with great confidence be inferred.[23]

We conclude, then, as we concluded before in our discussion of causality, that a relation of intrinsic determination is involved in the causal connection; and we agree, therefore, with McTaggart that the past can determine the future. Does this admission involve us in the further concession that the future is objectively real? I think not.

McTaggart's argument, as we have seen, is based upon the contention that it is obvious that propositions referring to the future must be either true or false, and that, if true, there must be facts which include future events to which they correspond. But is there nothing else to which they can correspond? Professor Broad has considered this question and has formulated his answer.

"Every judgment," he declares,

that professes to be about the future would seem then to involve two peculiar and not further analysable kinds of assertion. One of these is about becoming; it asserts that further events will become. The other is about some characteristic; it asserts that this will characterise some of the events which will become. If then we ask: What are judgments which profess to be about future events really about? the answer would seem to be that they are really about some characteristic and about becoming. And if it be asked: What do such judgments assert? the only answer that I can give is that they assert that the sum total of existence will increase through becoming, and that the characteristic in question will characterise some part of what will become. These answers are compatible with the non-existence of the future. The only "constituents" of the judgment, when it is made, are the characteristic —which has the kind of reality which universals possess—and

23. It may be observed that in his discussion of a priori concepts Professor Broad has displayed considerable sympathy for the view that causal relationships are intuitively cognized (*ibid.*, I, 52–53), inconsistent as such an attitude appears to be with his remarks just quoted.

the concept of becoming. About these the judgment makes certain assertions of a quite peculiar and not further analyzable kind. Something called *to-morrow* is not a constituent of judgments which are grammatically about "to-morrow," any more than an individual called *Puck* is a constituent of judgments which profess to be about "Puck." [24]

With the theory thus propounded I am in general sympathy, although—as I have already made clear—I should not be prepared to talk of the sum total of reality increasing, nor yet to speak of the "concept" of becoming. Possibly, also, one might protest that propositions do not "profess" to be about anything, on the ground that the phraseology is anthropomorphic. Probably it would be better to say that propositions may uncritically be taken to be about the future when actually they are about something else. This is the significant point in Professor Broad's reply, and here I wholly concur.

I have already called attention to the fact that an Aristotelian essence may take the form of a pattern according to which a number of characteristics successively manifest themselves in the same particular; the stock example being the process whereby an acorn grows into an oak. The pattern of the process is not itself a particular, nor is it something that occurs. It is rather a timeless complex universal, or, if you like, a universal of the second order constituting a synthesis of universals of the first order. Not every such essence is a pattern of a process of physical growth. We are familiar with many habitual orders of sequence. Thus an economist may say that uncontrolled inflation will produce a depression. Our predictions are often hypothetical—as when a physician asserts that a patient will die if the progress of his disease be not arrested. In such a case the pattern which has begun to manifest itself in a process does not do so completely; the manifestation is cut short by a counter-process—such as a prescribed course of treatment. The convergence of two causal series results in the stultification of one of them. Thus we are led to speak of tendencies and counter-tendencies. And as we contemplate the pattern of a familiar sequence, we think that *this* present state, being of such a nature, necessitates the subsequent presence of *that* state of a certain other nature—whether in the same identical thing or in some other thing. I should therefore say that a proposition which might uncritically be taken to refer to the future is actually about a pattern or essence—which is a timeless reality—and

24. *Scientific Thought* (London, 1923), pp. 76–77.

about a present event—possibly also about certain events in the recent past—wherein that pattern or essence is taken to be manifesting
itself. If this account be accepted, we are freed from the necessity
of assuming that there are *now* events which are not *present* but
future.

McTaggart's third objection is that the contradiction which he believes himself to have found in the notion of a temporal series is
not eliminated. "For," he writes, "although, if Dr. Broad were right, no
moment would have the three incompatible characteristics of past,
present, and future, yet each of them (except the last moment of
time, if there should be a last moment) would have the two incompatible characteristics of past and present. And this would be sufficient
to produce the contradiction." [25]

"The words past and present," he continues,

> clearly indicate different characteristics. And no one, I think,
> would suggest that they are simply compatible, in the way that
> the characteristics red and sweet are. If one man should say,
> "strawberries are red," and another should reply, "that is false, for
> they are sweet," the second man would be talking absolute non-
> sense. But if the first should say "you are eating my strawberries,"
> and the second should reply, "that is false, for I have already
> eaten them," the remark is admittedly not absolute nonsense,
> though its precise relation to the truth would depend on the
> truth about the reality of matter and time.
>
> The terms can only be made compatible by a qualification.
> The proper statement of that qualification seems to me to be, as
> I have said . . . , that, when we say that M is present, we
> mean that it is present at a moment of present time, and will be
> past at some moment of future time, and that, when we say that
> M is past we mean that it has been present at some moment of
> past time, and is past at a moment of present time. Dr. Broad
> will, no doubt, claim to cut out "will be past at some moment of
> future time." But even then it would be true that, when we say
> M is past, we mean that it has been present at some moment
> of past time and is past at a moment of present time, and that,
> when we say M is present, we mean that it is present at a mo-
> ment of present time. As much as this Dr. Broad can say, and
> as much as this he must say, if he admits that each event (except
> a possible last event) is both present and past.

25. *The Nature of Existence*, Vol. II, sec. 341.

Thus we distinguish the presentness and pastness of events by reference to past and present moments. But every moment which is past is also present. And if we attempt to remove this difficulty by saying that it *is* past and *has been* present, then we get an infinite vicious series.[26]

In order to evaluate this criticism aright, it is important to realize that the kernel of McTaggart's argument for the unreality of time is to be found in his assertion that "if anything is to be rightly called past, present, or future, it must be because it is in relation to something else." [27] If this be the case, nothing can be present in itself, or in relation to itself. And from this it follows that nothing can be present at all; for presentness that is due to a relationship to something else will be a derived presentness and, accordingly, presupposes an underived and non-relational presentness.[28] This is the very point that McTaggart is making. Here is the root of the contradiction—or the seeming contradiction. If there be anything wrong with McTaggart's argument, therefore, it will probably be found in his conception of presentness.

According to McTaggart when an event becomes present it does not become later than the event preceding it. It was always later and therefore always existed—on the assumption that time is real—although it was not always present. Now it is clear that on Professor Broad's view, when an event becomes it not only becomes present but also becomes later than the preceding event; for it could not have been later before it became, since before it became it was an absolute nonentity. But McTaggart would still say, I feel sure, that on this assumption, although the becoming event becomes later than the preceding event, it does not become present in relation to the preceding event. For if presentness be a relation, it is not the same relation as "later than." One past event can be later than another but one past event cannot be present in relation to another, although it can be coincident with another past event. For the becoming event to be present, McTaggart would say, it must be present in relation to something outside the series of earlier and later events. What can this something be? What could it be except a present moment? But in relation to what does this moment become present? It cannot become present in relation to the moment before it, for it is later than this moment; nor yet in relation to the moment after

26. *Ibid.*   27. *Ibid.*, sec. 327.
28. We might put the gist of McTaggart's argument in scholastic terms by saying that the notion of presentness involves both *abaliety* and *aseity*, and is, therefore, self-contradictory.

it, for it is earlier than this moment. Clearly, if it is to become present at all, it can do so only in relation to a present moment in another series of moments; and thus we are launched upon an infinite vicious regress.

But how if we deny that presentness is fundamentally relational? I say "fundamentally" because I do not mean to suggest that a present event stands in no relation to past events. What I wish to do is merely to reiterate what I take to be Professor Broad's contention that the presentness of an event *is* its becoming. All events that occur together will be related to one another by the relation of coincidence, but they will not be present in relation to one another; they will be present in themselves, in that they are *eventuating*.

A CRITIQUE OF PROFESSOR BROAD'S VIEW

It may be objected that if we are to deny the reality of the future, we ought to deny that of the past, and to assert that the present alone is real. Shall we, then, say that the future is what will be and the past what has been, and that the present alone is? Clearly this will not do if presentness is to be identified with becoming. We shall have to revise our statement as follows: nothing is or exists, all that is real becomes. Yet is there such a thing as a unit of becoming? How shall we delimit it? Shall we equate the specious present with the real present? But is not this to subjectify time with a vengeance? How do we know, how can we be sure, that all specious presents— human and, presumably, animal—have equivalent durations? Even could we be so assured, we could not presume to deny that within the specious present it is possible to discriminate before and after. Within these sacred limits, therefore, one event can precede another. But that which precedes has ceased to become; hence, on the hypothesis before us, it has ceased to be real. Thus, if time be infinitely divisible, the genuine present, the truly real, is at an infinite remove from us; it is something to which we can never attain. Nor is it feasible to identify the present with an indivisible instant; for by so doing, we should eliminate passage altogether, and thus destroy time very effectually.

Plainly Professor Broad has done well to affirm the reality of the past. But now we shall, of course, have to say that what has become persists. Reality, therefore, as he points out, cannot be reduced to, nor equated with, becoming.

So far I find myself in agreement with Professor Broad. But now I must confess that I am profoundly suspicious of his "event-particle." To speak of absolute becoming, becoming without a subject, is to me as meaningless as to talk of action without an actor or of convexity with out concavity. The point is an ultimate one; and since I have already discussed it, I shall not now dwell upon it; I would only add that the notion of an expanding, growing, or increasing universe—so effectively criticized by Dawes Hicks [29]—I should include under the same condemnation. If the self, as I have maintained, be a substance, it is not something which becomes, but something which *is*. And the same will be true of other simple substances—if such there be.[30]

It will be well, however, to remind ourselves that there are two points of view from which we can envisage substance. In the first place we can think of a substance as a concrete and characterized particular, possessed of qualities and standing in relations. In the second place we can think of substance in abstraction from the characteristics which pertain to it, as an entity which, although it cannot, indeed, exist apart from its characteristics, is not a mere congeries of them, but is other than they. If we contemplate substance from the former point of view, we can justifiably affirm in Kantian language that a substance can change only because it can remain the same, inasmuch as, although its successive states will differ in their respective characteristics, yet they will be states of a common subject.[31] But if we survey it from the second standpoint, we shall envisage substance as a self-identical unit, totally exempt from change. In either case we shall realize that there is no such thing as pure or absolute becoming; it is not becoming, but substance, that is ultimate.

The acceptance of this theory enables us to agree with Professor Broad as to the unreality of the future. The present we shall identify with becoming, the past with that which has become. Or, to put the same contention in other words, what happens is present, what has happened is past. The present will thus be the terminus of the past, but it will not be the terminus of reality. For reality will include not

29. *The Philosophical Bases of Theism*, pp. 185–187.

30. If we apply the term "substance" to combinations of simple substances, we must say that such substances become when they are put together, that they are or exist after they have become, and that, as they are taken apart or disintegrate, they undergo a process which is the reverse of becoming. Perhaps the Middle English *unbe* would be a convenient term to apply to it.

31. With such a point of view Professor Broad would seem to have some sympathy, for he has written, "If time were real, the successive phases in the history of a continuant, such as a bit of matter, would not be parts of *that continuant*. They would be parts of *its history*" (*Examination of McTaggart's Philosophy*, II, Part 1, 249).

only states whose succession constitutes the process of becoming but also the simple substances in which this process goes on, and which themselves do not become, but simply *are*. For the subject of successive states is not itself a state, nor yet a succession of states. Without them it would, indeed, be nothing; but they, without it, would be nothing. They pass; it abides. Or perhaps we should not even say that it abides; for by so saying, we seem to imply that it persists through time. But if time be the series of its successive states, it itself is not in time at all. Of simple substances we may say, therefore, that they are eternal. The process of becoming falls within them, yet they do not become. In this view time, as it were, gets longer. There is more of the past, but there is not any more of reality. For becoming is rooted in being, which neither increases nor diminishes, but only undergoes an alteration of modes.

If I rightly understand Professor Broad, he regards the actual present as a durationless instant, and the specious present as a section of the immediate past viewed from this vantage point. From this it follows that there is a certain amount of illusion and error in all our temporal awareness, since what is just past is perceived as still happening. Professor Broad apparently regards this as a relatively innocent admission as contrasted with McTaggart's frank statement that insofar as anything is perceived to be in time, it is misperceived.[32] I do not myself share this complacency. Doubtless an explanation which would enable us to treat temporal awareness as wholly veridical would be productive of a certain emotional satisfaction. But if the presence of *some* degree of error must be acknowledged, it does not necessarily follow that the theory which admits the smallest amount of error is to be preferred. For our primary concern should be not to defend the pronouncements of common sense but to develop a theory which will be at once coherent and intelligible.

It is therefore with the intelligibility of the notion of an instantaneous present that I am concerned. The conception of a compact series of instants in which there are no next terms may satisfy the requirements of the mathematician, yet are we justified in treating it as an ontological reality?[33] If there be no "next" term, how can one term be the immediate successor of another? And unless there be immediacy of succession, how can there be any succession at all? On the other hand, if we suppose that one durationless instant can immediately succeed another, how can they remain mutually distinct? Will they not all coalesce, as did the ghosts that lay in the grate, and will not our

32. *Ibid.*, pp. 319–323.   33. *Ibid.*, I, 333.

succession have gone aglimmering? Moreover, has not Professor Broad shown himself sympathetic to the Whiteheadian treatment of points and instants by the method of extensive abstraction, with the consequent denial that they are simple particulars? [34] But if an instant be only a converging series of durations, what becomes of the instantaneous present?

There is, moreover, yet another difficulty in regard to this same concept. Is it possible that becoming should occur in a durationless instant? Can it be equated with a mere "event-particle"? Is it not self-evident that becoming is of the nature of process, that it involves passage and transition? Surely, then, even as a line is divisible into shorter and shorter lines but not into extensionless points, so, while a duration can be divided into shorter and shorter durations, it cannot be divided into durationless instants. But, if becoming involve duration, whereas the present is only a durationless instant, the inference seems clearly to be that all becoming is in the past. Yet this would be a most unacceptable conclusion. For the past, we are assuming, is that which *has become*. It is true that past events seem to be getting progressively more remote, yet they are not still going on. They are over and done with. The battle of Hastings is at a further remove from us than it was from Milton, yet the Norman arrows are not now descending upon the English shieldburg.

Must we not agree that the reality of an event is nothing other than its occurring, happening, or becoming; and that, having occurred, it does not in any sense continue or endure? Must we not also agree, however, that the state of being involved in any event on the part of any participating substance, once acquired, does not pass away, but persists; and that the succession of such states constitutes the history of the substance? I think that we must. If so, although the battle of Hastings was a transient event and, once concluded, possessed thereafter no kind of ontological status, yet the simple substances involved therein, be they what they may, are real entities, and the state of being thus involved is part of the history of each of them.

Even though we grant that there are no such ontological entities as instants and points, may we not further agree that the present is the terminus of the past in much the same sense that the edge of a glacier is the terminus of the glacier? If so, that which immediately

34. As Dr. Ewing has well said, "In general we must be very cautious about transferring direct to philosophy statements made in a science. It may well be that statements, though useful scientifically, are only true in a 'Pickwickian' sense, i.e. a sense quite different from the literal one" (*The Fundamental Questions of Philosophy*, p. 146).

precedes the terminus will have become, and will therefore really be past, despite the fact that it falls within what we call the specious present. In other words, we perceive what has just happened as still happening. That this involves misperception is undeniable. And it does not seem farfetched to conclude that such misperception is in some way due to temporal proximity. The blurring of an object held immediately before the eye offers an analogy, although it does not, of course, provide an explanation.

On this view, although there will be new states of a simple substance, this will not mean that there will be more of the substance, only that its history will get longer. For a state or mode of a substance is not, properly speaking, an *ens,* but rather an *ens entis;* and although the states succeed each other, the substance does not temporally elongate itself. It is that in which becoming takes place or *goes on,* but it does not itself *go on.* Simple substance is not a temporal entity, but it is that which makes time possible.

Chapter Twelve

HUMAN DESTINY

On the supposition that the theory of time outlined in the preceding chapter is sound, the question now arises, What is its relevance to the philosophy of religion? What bearing has it upon the problem of human destiny? It is, surely, a highly significant fact that the great religions have all posited some sort of terminus, relative or absolute, to world history, some cumulative and final event which will bring it to a close. Nevertheless, the phrase "relative or absolute" has been introduced in order to bring out a distinction of considerable importance.

Creative Theism and an Absolute Terminus

Zoroastrianism, Judaism, Christianity, and Islam all look forward to a Day of Judgment which will definitely bring to a close the present world order.[1] It is, to say the least, doubtful whether this doctrine should be understood to involve the abolition of time, although so much would seem frequently to be implied by the language of popular piety. Such phrases as "time shall be no more" are familiar to all of us, but it would be uncharitable to inquire precisely what meaning they have for the average believers. When we consult St. Thomas in order to ascertain the point of view of the orthodox Christian theologian, we find that the saved soul will occupy an intermediate position between eternity and time; which is to say that when contemplating the timeless Deity, it will enjoy a "participated eternity," whereas, when communing with its fellow spirits, it will experience succession. In general it would probably be fair to say that for the average adherent of any of these religions, the Last Judgment is thought of as constituting, not the end of time, but the end of world history. The cosmic drama will have been performed, and the curtain will have fallen upon the stage.

The general outlook becomes intelligible when viewed against its background—the doctrine of a creative God. In accordance with this belief, the entire temporal process is conceived as dependent

1. We may conjecture with considerable plausibility that it was the influence of Zoroastrianism upon Judaism which gave rise to this outlook on the part of the latter religion, by which it was transmitted to the two daughter faiths.

upon the divine will. Hence its duration will be what God wills it to be. It might be without beginning or end, it might have both beginning and end, it might begin and never cease, or, lastly, it might never have begun and yet might come to an end. How are we to find out which of these various logically possible alternatives which lie open to his choice has actually been selected by the Deity? As philosophers, so Maimonides tells us (and Aquinas cordially indorses his pronouncement), we cannot find out. Revelation alone can enlighten us.[2]

Leaving aside for the present the topic of revelation, we may nevertheless inquire whether the philosopher's predicament be so utterly hopeless as these eminent thinkers believed, whether rational reflection be wholly incapable of shedding any further light upon the situation as it is envisaged by the believer in a creative God. If the universe be the product of divine creativity, we are surely justified in assuming that it was brought into existence with some definite purpose in view. As to the nature of that purpose it may appear hazardous for the finite intellect to speculate. Yet does it not seem probable that the development and ultimate perfection of the rational creature would constitute a worthy motive, one thoroughly in accordance with the characteristics of benevolence, justice, and wisdom which the theist habitually ascribes to God? If not the sole motive, may we not at least confidently conjecture that it is one of the leading motives which inspired the divine creativity? And will not the thinker who refuses to concede this much find his theism in a very parlous state?

Yet what do we mean, the critic may interject, when we talk so glibly of the "perfection of the rational creature"? Is not the notion of perfection incompatible with that of finitude? "Why callest thou me good?" said Jesus. "There is none good but one, that is God."[3] In the light of this utterance surely nothing more remains to be said.

Now it must at once be conceded that if perfection be defined as the transformation of the finite into the infinite, the notion is nothing other than a contradiction in terms.[4] But this is most certainly not

2. I shall defer discussion of the question of the relation of God to time till we take up the problem of God.

3. Mark 10:18.

4. It is for this reason that I do not propose to discuss in detail the doctrine, so dear to the Advaita and to Sufism, that the goal of the saint's endeavor is to "become God." It seems to me to rest upon an intellectual muddle with a strong emotional coloring. If *per impossibile* the finite self could be transformed into the Deity, it would no longer be what it was; it would have been annihilated. If, on the other hand, we say that it is already identical with God but fails to recognize this identity, we are attributing to the Deity a sort of schizophrenia. It is noteworthy that the similes and metaphors so freely employed by the singularistic

what those thinkers have in mind who tell us that the goal of the religious life is the attainment of perfection. For by a perfect soul they obviously mean a soul which has actualized all its potentialities for good and which has eradicated all its potentialities for evil. And this, for the theists, is to become godlike. When the writer of the first chapter of Genesis spoke of man as made in the image of God he may well have had in mind something of the sort. And so may the son of Sirach when he wrote, "If thou follow after righteousness thou shalt obtain her, and put her on as a long robe of glory." This putting on of the long robe of glory is often referred to in theological language as a process of "deification," or of becoming "deiform."

Are we to conceive of such an attainment as constituting the τέλος of the individual alone, or of humanity as well? Is it possible that the process of evolution is directed to producing a race of wholly deiform beings, and that, once this has been accomplished, the planet which has formed the stage whereon this drama has been performed will have served its purpose? [5] Can we even extend the range of this hypothesis to embrace the entire universe? Is there "some far-off divine event to which the whole creation moves"? There is nothing self-contradictory in such a theory, even though, in our unavoidably narrow perspective, the amount of stage furniture provided by solar systems and galaxies may appear amazingly extended and cumbrous. When viewed from this standpoint, moreover, it would seem natural that the world process should have both a beginning and an end.

On the other hand it would be equally possible to conceive of the creation of new souls as continuously going on in a stable and perpetually enduring physical environment; and it is, I think, to such a hypothesis that the majority of liberal theologians have found themselves attracted. Were this the case, an individual soul, having fairly run its course, might be removed from this "vale of soul-making" and admitted to a purely spiritual environment.

On any of these assumptions the question can still be asked, What happens to the soul when it has attained its τέλος? Does a state of perfection imply a static existence, since whatever happened would in-

---

monist always have to do with the assimilation of one material entity by another —the drop of water by the ocean, for example. I freely recognize that much of the most beautiful religious poetry has been inspired by this doctrine. But that, surely, is because no worthier conception was available to the poets. The lover always *in a sense* identifies himself with his beloved, yet not in the literal sense. Identification, after all, is no more than a metaphor.

5. Professor S. Radhakrishnan and Sri Aurobindo would, I take it, answer this question in the affirmative.

volve an alteration, and therefore a disruption, of the harmony which constitutes perfection? Such a suggestion, temperamentally unattractive as many people will find it, may nevertheless owe its unattractiveness to the limitations of human imaginations which are largely conditioned by sense experience. And it will scarcely be contested that it is precisely with respect to the rarest and most intense experiences of value that we would ask no more than that by being prolonged they continue to be what they are—unless we would add the further petition that by becoming even more intense, they become more truly what they potentially are. That the Beatific Vision of which the mystical theologians speak may be such a static and yet completely satisfying experience is a hypothesis deserving of the most serious consideration. Since such an experience would have a beginning it could not be timeless; yet, inasmuch as it would be devoid of all occurrences or happenings, of all change or alteration, it could be nothing less than a state of pure duration. And yet might it not be something more, something greater? If, as I have argued, becoming depends upon being, and if we admit the possibility that the time-series may have its terminus, beyond that terminus reality would be completely static, there would be no flow or transition or passage, there could not even be duration, nothing would remain but *being*.

To such an altitude mystical speculation has at times ascended. And in such a conception there is a profundity and grandeur to which only the most obtusely this-worldly can be completely blind. Nonetheless, many religious persons, many devout theists, feel impelled to reject it. For them life involves change, the undergoing of fresh experiences, the facing of new situations. Thus A. E. Taylor has sought to vindicate the notion of "progress *in* fruition" as well as that of "progress *to* fruition," and has expatiated upon the possibility of "adventures" and "surprises" in Heaven. For those who take such a position it should logically follow that the time-series is endless, and, hence, that becoming is endless. And from these conclusions it will also follow that perfectibility is a chimera, that no attainment can be ultimate, that no achievement can be final, and that every victory can at most be only the prelude to further conquest. If to live forever have any meaning, we shall be told, it means to be forever active, forever struggling, forever accomplishing. And if we object that the notion of progress is unintelligible unless it involve approximation toward the realization of an ultimate ideal, we shall be informed that the ideal is at an infinite remove from us, that qualitative increase can proceed ad infinitum, so that forever and ever we can continue to become better and better and better and wiser and wiser and wiser, inasmuch as there is no maximum degree either of goodness or of wisdom beyond which we cannot develop.[6] And this very fact, we shall be further informed, should awaken in us, not despair, but exaltation. For attainment in itself is barren; it is the working and planning and striving to attain, together with the tireless resolution and unfaltering courage thus called forth, which give to life all its zest, which make it worth living.

Are we entitled, however, to picture to ourselves the life everlasting as a constant and uninterrupted advance from achievement to achievement? If the struggle be real and meaningful must it not also involve genuine possibilities, not only of success, but also of failure, not only of growth, but also of decay, not only of victory, but also of defeat? Must we not, therefore, look forward to an endless oscillation of experiences, to an interminable sequence of rise and fall, of triumph and of catastrophe?

If we seriously envisage the possibility of such an immortal hurlyburly, we must definitely dismiss the concept of a final deliverance from evil and suffering. The notion of the return of the soul to its fatherland, the glorious anticipation of the *status patriae* with its utterly satisfying *Visio Dei*, must be firmly renounced. There is no homeland of the soul. Even as there can be no fall from which we cannot hope to rise, so there can be no ascent from which we need not fear to fall. If no defeat be irretrievable, no victory will be irreversible.

As we survey the situation in the light of the preceding discussion, we see that the believer in a creative God [7] is faced by a threefold alternative.

1. He may posit a static and changeless existence [8] which is best described in the words of Boethius, *interminabilis vitae tota ac simul perfecta possessio.*

2. He may posit a temporal yet enduring and unending Heaven with limitless possibilities of progressive improvement.

3. He may definitely refuse to admit the possibility of attaining a highest status which, once acquired, cannot be lost, and yet look for-

6. In this connection I may refer the reader to Professor Broad's discussion of the question whether there be qualities which posit their own superlatives (*Examination of McTaggart's Philosophy*, I, 31–45). I am assuming that the religious temporalist would answer in the negative.

7. There are, of course, theists, such as Professor Charles Hartshorne, who do not believe in immortality. For them no such choice lies open.

8. The question will then arise whether the process of becoming cease coincidentally for all selves, or whether the temporal experience of one self can continue after another's has terminated.

ward to an unending future existence with its heights and depths, its joys and sorrows, at times possibly better, at times possibly worse, than this life, at times possibly very much the same sort of thing.

I do not say that these three hypotheses are all equally plausible on the assumption that there is a creative God. I should myself rank them in descending degrees of plausibility in the order in which I have stated them; but at first glance it is not easy to choose between them, and all, I think, deserve to be considered.

RECURRENT CYCLES AND RELATIVE TERMINATIONS

Let us now proceed to inspect the attitudes of the religions and philosophies of India.[9] Here we encounter, despite certain subordinate, yet important, differences, a fundamental unity of outlook very different from that which prevails in the West. Its most distinctive feature, and that to which the unity is largely due, is the absence of the belief in a creative God. Among the Six Systems which constitute the Āstika philosophies we find four which posit a supreme Intelligence —the Nyāya, the Vaiśeṣika, the Yoga, and the Vedānta. But even the various forms of the Vedānta, all of which make the world in some sense dependent upon God, are innocent of any doctrine of creation *ex nihilo*. And for the other systems just referred to, the physical world enjoys an underived existence. Of the three Nāstika philosophies, again, one—that of the Carvākas—is frankly materialistic, while the other two—Jainism and Buddhism—are absolute ontological dualisms.

It is fair to say that in the West, ever since Christianity attained its dominant position, for the popular mind the choice has always seemed to lie between two antithetical points of view—on the one hand a theism which envisaged a creative God, and on the other, materialism or its kindred position, naturalism. In India the situation has been altogether different. As that acute and able interpreter of the Orient to the Occident, the late J. B. Pratt, has pointed out, the one positive conviction which inspires theists and non-theists alike is a belief in the soul—in the soul as an ultimate reality, uncreated, imperishable, everlasting.

This is true, in effect, even of Hīnayāna Buddhism. For although the Hīnayāna will have no traffic with the notion of *dravya* or sub-

9. For our present purpose we need not attempt to discriminate among them, for the religions are all philosophical and the philosophies are all religious. All are primarily concerned with man's ultimate destiny.

stance, although even the concept of *pudgala* or person is pronounced heretical, yet the continuity, and the underived and indestructible character, of the individual consciousness, however illogically, is as strongly emphasized among the Buddhists as among the Jains and among the Āstikas.

Yet the belief in the indestructibility of the soul does not of itself suffice to determine the soul's destiny. It does, indeed, imply a plurality of lives, for, as McTaggart has pointed out, everyone knows of at least one birth and one death, which certifies him of at least three lives; and it seems highly improbable that there should not be many more. A plurality of lives, again, does not necessarily involve reincarnation, yet it renders it highly probable. In general the Hindu view seems to be that rebirth on this planet may be expected to recur at intervals, but it may also recur elsewhere, in *rūpaloka*—the world of form—or in *arūpaloka*—the formless world.

Connected with this belief we encounter the Law of Karma. The universe, both theists and non-theists are agreed, is so ordered that every self is rewarded or punished for all its good or evil deeds committed in previous lives; not necessarily in the *last* life, but in *any* of its lives. Sooner or later justice is done. And here is where the theistic schools enjoy an obvious advantage. For on their view, the Law of Karma cannot enforce itself; there must be a power to enforce it. And this power they locate in a supreme Mind which is exempt from the process of birth and death, and which determines the future lot of any self which is about to be reborn. The atheistic schools are here plainly at a disadvantage, inasmuch as they can point to no guarantor of the Law of Karma. The universe, it may be said, is for them a morally ordered system, and is itself the guarantor of its own law. But for this to be the case, the universe would have to constitute a rationally ordered and axiologically oriented system, which, for these atheistic schools, it emphatically is not. For all of them are absolute dualisms; whether the dualism be as it is for the Jains, between *jīva* and *ajīva*, or, as it is for the Sāṁkhya, between *puruṣa* and *prakṛti*.

A similar advantage is enjoyed by the theists when we encounter the doctrine of world cycles or successive worlds, a doctrine which is accepted by all the schools with the exception of the Jains and the Mīmāṁsakas. According to this theory the entire universe periodically disintegrates into its ultimate constituents, and then, after a period of *pralaya* or world slumber, a fresh universe is organized. Clearly such a view is rendered more plausible if we postulate a controlling Intelligence. It is difficult to see why for the atheist, who is also an absolute dualist, the universe, once disintegrated, should not forever remain so.

Hīnayāna Buddhism, again, labors under a like disadvantage with respect to its doctrine of successive Buddhas, each of whom appears at a time when knowledge of the true religion has been lost, and each of whom initiates a new spiritual renaissance. All this seems clearly to imply both a psychological determinism and a world system whose successive stages are logically interconnected. Yet the Hīnayāna is rootedly opposed to determinism, and is wedded to a dualism, not indeed a dualism of soul and body, but a dualism of psychical and physical events. It is, moreover, unalterably nominalistic, so that every conceivable basis for the doctrine would appear to be repudiated.

Thus those philosophical systems—whether theistic (the Yoga, Nyāya, and Vaiśeṣika), pantheistic (the Advaita), or panentheistic (the Viśiṣṭādvaita)—which posit a supreme Intelligence are more successful in rendering intelligible the notion of a succession of worlds than are the atheistic systems, since these appear totally unable to provide any satisfactory basis, whether a priori or empirical, for the doctrine. But when we come to consider the question of the nature of ultimate deliverance, which is the common concern of all these systems, we encounter a division between positive and negative outlooks which cuts right across that which divides the theistic from the atheistic schools.

Buddhism, indeed, may claim to be above the battle, inasmuch as its founder persistently refused to describe Nirvāṇa in other than negative terms. We are told that it is the end of rebirth and suffering, and that to him who has attained it no predicates whatever can be applied. It seems pretty clear that the Buddha was not an annihilationist, and that those among his followers who have made bold to equate Nirvāṇa with nothingness have spoken without warrant. This leaves open the possibility that Nirvāṇa *may* be an intensely positive state charged with the highest value; yet the Buddha did not say so. Moreover, he enjoined his disciples to leave undetermined what he had left undetermined, which renders any conjectures on our part, to say the least, hazardous.

When we turn to Jainism, however, we discover that the lot of the *jīva* who has attained Nirvāṇa, and has ascended to the "umbrella of the universe," is one of bliss. It is also credited with the possession of limitless knowledge and power. It is hard to see how we can be expected to take the latter attribute literally, for in that case we should be amply justified in blaming the delivered soul for not exerting itself to aid and rescue its fellows still in bondage. Deliverance, it would seem, emancipates the *jīva* forever from the wheel of birth and death so completely that return thereto would be quite inconceivable. The bliss which it enjoys would appear to be connected with the knowledge and power which now pertain to it. But it seems to be a very self-centered and self-absorbed bliss, undisturbed by the suffering and evil in this world, nor does it seem to owe anything to communion with other emancipated souls.[10]

At the other end of the metaphysical spectrum from the Jains, for whom there is no God in the sense of a supreme Self, we find the Advaitins for whom nothing really exists but Brahma, all else being illusion. Yet the Advaitins are quite as convinced as the Jains that deliverance involves entrance into a state of bliss. This state of bliss is supposed to follow upon the realization on the part of the delivered soul of its identity with Brahma. Like all pantheists the Advaitin looks upon the realization of identity, not as involving the annihilation of his own ego, but rather as the expansion of it to the infinite. Since all souls, however, are fundamentally identical with Brahma, all souls are in reality identical with each other. There is only one genuine self, Brahma. Hence deliverance will involve a loneliness and isolation comparable to that which we noted in the case of the Jain. Difficult as it may be for us psychologically to associate positive bliss with such isolation, we must yet acknowledge that both schools, in emphatically affirming its presence, take up an extremely positive attitude.[11]

In contrast to them we find that the Sāṃkhya, Yoga, Nyāya, and Vaiśeṣika philosophies share an extremely negative outlook. This is the more remarkable in that it would seem to be neither emotionally nor theoretically conditioned by any peculiar doctrinal theses sustained by any of these systems; and as a matter of fact, the metaphysical foundations of these various philosophies are sufficiently dissimilar to render this unanimity of outlook all the more noteworthy. We may seek an explanation for it, if we like, in the oft-repeated statement that life in India has always been hard for the great mass of the people; habitual and excessive poverty, frequent pestilences, and chronic misrule and oppression being productive of a general agreement that

10. The Jains agree with the Mīmāṃsakas in rejecting the doctrine of *pralaya*—the temporal gap between successive worlds—but, unlike the Mīmāṃsakas, they believe in the possibility of attaining Nirvāṇa.

11. The position of the Viśiṣādvaita is so like that of Christianity that I shall not here discuss it.

happiness is rare and transitory, whereas sorrow is prevalent and abiding. It is not obvious, however, why this in turn should inspire the conviction that not merely life in this world but life as such is predominantly evil. Nor is it easy, on this hypothesis, to account for the joyous attitude of the Jains and the Vedantins.

The position of the Sāṁkhya and the Yoga is perhaps less extreme than that of the Nyāya and the Vaiśeṣika. For the Sāṁkhya and the Yoga the noumenal self—the *puruṣa*—is not involved in the world process. It is, however, the victim of the mistaken impression that it is so involved, and because of this it is in bondage. When this impression is seen to be erroneous, the self is liberated. Since it is essentially consciousness it cannot cease to be aware, but it can and does cease to be aware of all that goes on in the spatio-temporal world. It is devoid of emotion, of virtue, and of vice. Seemingly it lapses forever into a state of utter self-absorption which resembles that of Aristotle's God.

For the Nyāya and the Vaiśeṣika philosophies, on the other hand, the self is a substance whereof consciousness is only an accident. With deliverance the self loses this accident and passes into an endless state of complete oblivion. This is, indeed, an amazing goal to be striven for; and the conception of it is indicative of a pessimism so profound as to make that of Lord Russell seem like lighthearted optimism. We should not forget, however, that for all these systems there are plenty of heavens and hells, and plenty of opportunities for rebirth in this world; so that the goal, whether it be self-absorbed isolation or oblivion, is for most persons a very remote one.

All the philosophies just mentioned, those which share the negative as well as those which entertain the positive outlook, are, however, agreed that there is a constant trickle of liberated souls from the wheel of birth and death. How is this reconcilable with the doctrine of an unending succession of worlds? The answer is that the number of souls is infinite; hence, however many are liberated, an infinite number always remain in bondage. This view is, certainly, not without its difficulties. In the first place it requires us to conceive of an infinite number of actually coexistent selves. But of any group of coexistent entities, must not the number be definite, and either odd or even? And in the second place, inasmuch as the vast majority of selves, a majority infinite in number, will never be released, the theory rivals in gloom the traditional Christian doctrine of an endless hell to which the major portion of humanity is consigned. Its gloominess, some might urge, is no reflection on its truth. And the observation is doubtless just enough from the standpoint of an absolute dualism.[12] But from the point of view of an axiological idealism the objection is clearly a fatal one.

In contrast to the various opinions thus far presented we discover in the early Mīmāṁsā a philosophy which repudiates both the doctrine of a succession of worlds and that of the possibility of deliverance from the wheel of birth and death. For the Mīmāṁsā, as for all the dualistic philosophies of India, the finite self is uncreated and indestructible. For the self there is therefore no escape by the door of annihilation. Hence, since transcendence of temporal experience is also impossible, the self is condemned to permanent involvement in becoming. This does not mean that it is the victim of fate; for it possesses free will, and the Law of Karma leaves its destiny largely in its own hands. It can rise or fall in the scheme of things, it can ascend to a heaven or sink to a hell. Yet a heaven, however happy, and a hell, however miserable, will come to an end. What does not come to an end but goes on forever is transmigration.

Here we have a point of view markedly similar to that of Plato in the *Phaedrus*. There only the souls of the gods are assured of a blessed and endless life, unbroken by births and deaths. All human souls, on the other hand, even though they obtain admission to the company of the gods, are in perpetual danger of being drawn back into the sense world. The dark horse in the shafts of the soul's chariot proves forever intractable. This clearly means that there is some ineradicable defect in the human soul which renders it perennially susceptible to the appeal of sense experience. It is a conception difficult to reconcile with Plato's habitual outlook; for plainly it is his considered opinion that the soul belongs by nature to the realm of the Forms, in the contemplation whereof it finds its τέλος, and that, when embodied upon this earth, it is in an unnatural state. Yet Plato had a powerful motive for attempting to work out such a conception. For to his characteristically clear Greek mind it seemed plain that whatever is real is definite, with definite limits; hence, whatever the number of souls, it is a finite number. Accordingly he is faced with the obvious question: Why have not all souls already succeeded in escaping from the world of matter and sense, and in returning to their true homeland, the realm of Ideas? Thus, in order to account for the continuance and

12. McTaggart has remarked that Absolute dualism "leaves, indeed, a chance of Immortality, but of an Immortality exposed to so many evils that most people would think it worse than none" (*Philosophical Studies*, p. 195).

perpetuity of generation and corruption,[13] Plato is compelled to posit the recurrent return of souls to this world; and he saw no other way to explain this necessity than by postulating some inherent weakness in the human soul. That he did not feel wholly at ease in so doing we may infer from his resort at this very point to the language of myth.

His employment of this device forces Plato to regard the souls of the gods as permanently and inherently, and not temporarily or accidentally, superior to the souls of men, animals, and plants. To the occidental mind this may seem natural enough, yet it is worthy of remark that it is indicative of an outlook very different from that of India. In general it may be said [14] that in Hindu thought it is the Law of Karma which accounts for the rank of a soul. Every soul is capable of rising to, or falling to, any level within the universe. Yet even at the highest level the gods in the heavens are still attached to the wheel of birth and death, from which, like all other souls, they stand in need of deliverance. It does, indeed, seem somewhat paradoxical that in Greece, where the freedom of the individual was so highly valued, the ontological hierarchy should be classified with such inexorable precision, whereas in India, where absolute monarchy was the normal political structure, the potential equality of all souls should be so definitely affirmed and so widely acknowledged.

When we examine the gods of the *Phaedrus* more closely, however, we observe that, although they are exempt from the danger of falling, they are not wholly self-sufficient. It is through the vision of the Forms, Plato tells us, that they are divine; and this divinity apparently requires regularly to be replenished by the recurrent journey to the vault of the heaven, by the passage through it to a position upon its surface, and by the contemplation of the Forms as they are directly apprehended from thence. If we try to unravel the thought which underlies this mythical presentation, we shall probably not be on the wrong track if we conclude that the status of the individual soul in the universe is determined by two factors: (*a*) its underived and native capacities and (*b*) its recognition of, and conformity to, its relationship to the Forms—by which, in this connection, we are doubtless to understand the Form of Beauty and the Form of the Good.

13. The first argument in the *Phaedo* is based upon the unending nature of this process.

14. True enough, we do find a certain distinction recognized—rather inconsistently it would seem—by Buddhists and Jains, inasmuch as, although every soul can at least hope to attain deliverance, not every soul can aspire to become a Buddha or Tīrthaṁkara.

Both in the case of Plato and in that of the Mīmāṁsakas it is clear that the lot of the soul who has ascended to the company of the gods remains a temporal one, in that it is of a definite duration, having both a beginning and an end. With regard to the liberated soul, as its state is envisaged by other Hindu philosophies, the situation is not so clear. Mokṣa, or deliverance, has a beginning, and in this sense it is plainly temporal; yet it is not clear that it is itself a state of becoming, or even one of purely static persistence. May it not be permissible to say of it that it does not endure, but simply *is?* The answer to this question depends upon our view of time.

STATING THE PROBLEM

I have taken stock of this multiplicity of points of view, both actual and possible, both Western and Eastern, not out of mere idle curiosity, but for the sake of suggestions which we might draw from them. For that there are ideas and conceptions well worth weighing and considering no one whose purview is not lamentably parochial will deny. It is true that if I have been right in my contention that the notion of creation is quite unintelligible, we are compelled to reject the hypothesis of a creative God. But this does not mean that the doctrine of a non-creative God is not worth discussing. Far from it! We shall discuss it, however, from the standpoint of an axiological idealism and on the assumption that the rationality of the universe has already been established. It may be well, therefore, to recapitulate the main points of our previous discussion of this topic.

The cardinal tenets of axiological idealism, as I understand it, are as follows:

1. The underived and ultimate reality of the substantial self.

2. The objective reality of universals: values, disvalues, and neutrals.

3. The linkage of all substances *sub specie temporis* by the internal relation of causality.

4. The direct linkage of selves to values and disvalues by the internal relation of obligation.

We are now concerned with the destiny of the self in the axiologically oriented system of the universe. And the basic question can be put in this way: Is there an ultimate τέλος toward which the self is obligated to strive, and the attainment of which will constitute its perfection, its "deification"? Or is the self bound to the wheel of birth and death, and condemned by its very nature, and by the structure of the universe of which it is a part, to engage forever in an endless battle, a battle for right against wrong, for good against evil, for beauty against ugliness, for virtue against vice? It might appear that on the basis of the general metaphysical position which we have outlined, there will be some grounds for returning seemingly conflicting answers when examining these alternatives.

For we have argued, in the first place, that inasmuch as a substance is not an event or a process, it cannot perish merely by ceasing to become; and that inasmuch as a simple substance has no parts, such a substance cannot perish by being taken to pieces. And we have also contended that for the reason just given, simple substances cannot come into being by being put together. From this it follows that their being is underived, and that they are indestructible. Now, whether or not there be other simple substances, it is quite clear, I submit, that selves are simple substances, and therefore that they are abiding and imperishable entities.

In the Occident this view of the self is the reverse of popular, and when enunciated almost invariably arouses astonishment and incredulity. This, in my judgment, is the joint result of the influence of orthodox Christianity and of the widespread misconception of what is meant by *substance*. In the light of our previous discussion of the nature of the self I shall now assume that the arguments in favor of this view are conclusive. But what follows?

If there have been no time at which the self has not existed, either it is eternal—in the sense of being non-temporal—or else it is sempiternal, in the sense of enduring throughout all time. Let us, for the present, assume that it is the latter.[15] Since, therefore, the self has always existed, the range of possibilities open to it must be clearly defined. Granted that it can rise or fall in the scheme of things, and undergo recurrent good or evil fortune, it is obvious that for it there can be no escape from the wheel of birth and death at any moment within the time-series. A view like that of the Mīmāṁsakas, a view similar to that of Plato when he wrote the *Phaedrus,* would therefore appear to be inescapable.

On the other hand the axiological orientation of the universe is certainly suggestive of a very different conclusion. Since the relation of the self to values is internal in both terms, since values are "there" that they may be instantiated, and since the $\tau\epsilon\lambda\sigma$ of the self is to in-

---

15. This assumption—the soundness of which we shall consider later—would seem a natural one, inasmuch as the self has a history and is capable of action and reaction. With this consideration in mind I have already frequently referred to it as sempiternal.

stantiate them, does not all this point to an ultimacy of attainment? Is the self to "fight as one that beateth the air"? Does not the whole situation become unintelligible unless there be at a finite remove a definite end to be striven for, and unless this end be that "putting on" of the "long robe of glory" which is nothing else than the instantiation of values in a self which is thereby rendered "deiform"? Must there not, then, be a final transition from struggle to attainment, from desire to satisfaction, from anticipation to realization, from expectation to sight, an ultimate and irreversible victory which will set all the bells of the universe aringing?

That these discordant points of view present us with a serious problem is undeniable. Yet it would be premature for us to conclude that our thinking has landed us in a straightforward contradiction.[16] Whether we must pronounce the belief in the eternity—or sempiternity —of the self incompatible with the belief in an "end" or τέλος of the self will depend upon our view of time.

TIME AND ETERNITY

Is it obvious that if becoming be real and not mere appearance, it must be beginningless and endless? Is it obvious that every change must result from a previous change, every motion from a previous motion, every state from a previous state? If the replies to these questions be in the affirmative, and if their truth be self-evident, all controversy is at an end. But is this, indeed, the case? It is of course impossible to argue directly about what is self-evident; for to argue is to attempt to prove, and what can be proved is not self-evident. All that one can do is to inspect as carefully as one can and report what one finds.

It might seem that the notion of time coming to an end is somewhat less paradoxical than that of time beginning. For we are familiar with a state of commotion being followed by one of relative quiescence, with motion going on and then stopping. But a beginning, it might be said, must be initiated by some antecedent event which in its turn follows upon some other; so that the beginning is always relative only, and never absolute. Thus the notion of a primal event would be a contradiction in terms.

16. In any event the choice will not be one between complete optimism and utter pessimism. For in the second view, there will still be evil in the universe; and in the first view, there will still be good, and perhaps a very considerable balance of good over evil and of happiness over unhappiness.

Is the conception, however, of a quiescent universe, of a universe in which no change is occurring anywhere, self-contradictory? Surely not. But a contradiction will arise, it may be said, if we make the further assumption that in such a universe change could ever occur. Once static, always static, once changing always changing—such must be our inevitable conclusion.

Yet may it not be the case that we are uncritically, and perhaps, unwittingly, assuming that even were there no change, there would still be time in the sense of successive moments, and that this succession of moments would constitute duration? Hence, were any change to occur, there would have been time before it occurred; it would not, therefore, be the beginning of time. But the suggestion that moments can constitute in themselves ontological realities is one which will infuriate the exponents of the theory of relativity; and if, to placate them, we dismiss it, our totally quiescent universe will be timeless.

Is it, we may next ask, absolutely inconceivable that time should arise out of the timeless? In other words, is the notion of a primal event, unconditioned by an antecedent event, sheer nonsense? May it not be conditioned by something in the eternal?

The ultimate constituents of reality other than universals, we have agreed, are simple substances. If we accept the panpsychist hypothesis, all these simple substances will be selves. I have urged that this hypothesis is a highly plausible one, but I have not attempted to prove it. I am quite ready to acknowledge the existence of other simple substances if only someone will make their nature intelligible to me and give me some reason for believing in their reality. But the notion of matter seems to be becoming ever vaguer; and the term "energy," which used to be one of measurement, is now frequently employed to designate an activity which appears to be as mysterious as it is ultimate. Let the metaphysician who is drawn to such a concept make the most of it; and let us confine ourselves, for the present at least, to the contemplation of selves, of whose existence we have no doubt and with whose nature we are acquainted by introspection.

A simple substance, as we have already seen is an ultimate and abiding entity which is possessed of characteristics. It is other than the characteristics, and it is that which has them; yet it cannot exist apart from all characteristics. And it does not follow that no characteristics are permanent. Thus a self would not be a self unless it possessed the nature of a self. It must at least be capable of consciousness, feeling, and volition; if it do not have them actually, it must at any rate have them potentially.[17] And if it be true, as I think we must admit, that potentiality is always rooted in actuality, the self can never be devoid of actual possession of some characteristics.

There are other characteristics, however, which the self can acquire and which it can lose. It can be angry, for example, and then cease to be angry; it can be happy, and then cease to be happy. Thus a state of anger may be succeeded by a state of contrition. This succession of states constitutes the history of the self; and if our previous analysis be correct, these states do not pass out of being but are forever retained. A present state moves, as it were, into the past, and from the recent past into the more remote past.

If we view the self as consisting of a substance possessed of certain permanent characteristics, and also as the subject of a series of successive states constituting its history, it is clearly a temporal entity, for it endures throughout the entire time-series. But if we distinguish within this concrete entity the substance, together with its unalterable characteristics, from those characteristics which at one time inhere and at another time do not inhere, and from its states which succeed one another, we are contemplating rather what seems to be the timeless basis of the self.

If, following traditional usage, we call those permanent characteristics which make the self what it is "essential," and those which it can acquire and also lose "accidental," it is obvious that its moral and intellectual status is largely due to the latter. For it is only through effort, progress, and struggle in time that the self can attain its τέλος. May it not be the case, however, that this struggle is necessitated by the changeless and essential nature of the self, and by the changeless and internal relations in which it stands to values and disvalues? In other words, may it not be the eternal axiological orientation of the universe which generates the temporal process? Does not the very character of moral values require us to answer these questions in the affirmative? For the development of morality *is* a struggle, an effort, a growth. Here is where the simile of the "long robe of glory" fails us. For moral character is not something which can be assumed; it is grown. The values must become one's very nature. And they must be freely chosen. A man is not a good man unless he could have been a bad man, or a bad man unless he could have been a good man. Constraint is destructive of genuine virtue and vice; what survives is sham.

17. Probably it always actually possesses consciousness in some degree, however low may be the degree.

I recognize, of course, that the determinist will contest what I have just said; but this consideration leaves me unmoved. For it is precisely at this point that I find his case at its weakest; so weak, indeed, as to be in a state of collapse. I appeal directly to the witness of experience, experience which speaks with so thunderous a voice and in such unambiguous language. When we contemplate our own actions are we not conscious at times of remorse and at other times of self-congratulation; when we contemplate the actions of other men are we not likewise conscious of passing judgments of praise on the one hand and of blame on the other; and is it not quite obvious that these judgments presuppose freedom of choice? There is all the difference in the world between the regret we feel in regard to what we were unable to accomplish and the remorse we feel for not having done what we could have done; between the satisfaction we feel when, despite temptations to yield, we have persevered in the right course, and the very different satisfaction we feel with respect to some natural asset—good eyesight, for example—for which we are not responsible, and for which we cannot assume the credit. And there is all the difference in the world between the praise we bestow upon heroic action requiring the sternest resolution and the admiration we feel for some aesthetic object, such as a beautiful landscape, even as there is between the blame we ascribe to a base act which the circumstances do not seem to have necessitated and the sympathetic grief we feel for a failure which we believe to have been unavoidable.

Yes, I know that the determinist will say that our feelings are deceptive in that they spring from misapprehension; that if we evaluated the situation aright, we should never feel either remorse or self-commendation, nor yet ever permit ourselves to praise or blame. Yet, in making these assertions he, like Pharaoh, King of Egypt, is "but an empty noise." For he can introspect no better than we can; the feelings which, if he be right, no man should ever experience, all men do experience. Moreover, if he be right, all bases for genuine moral judgments are taken away; the words wherein they are stated are the same, but the meaning has been transformed beyond recognition. For where there is no genuine possibility of acting otherwise, there is neither moral value nor disvalue.[18]

The truth of this last statement seems to me self-evident. I make no apology, therefore, for having formulated it. I wish only to make

18. The point of view I have tried to express is practically identical with that so ably presented by Professor C. A. Campbell, *On Selfhood and Godhood*, Lecture IX.

clear that I am not attempting to terminate discussion by any authoritative or dogmatic pronouncement. It is possible to be mistaken about what is self-evident; this we know, for since men have disagreed about what is self-evident, some men must have been mistaken. The determinist thinks that I am mistaken about the above proposition. All that I can do is, in the first place, look again—that is, to introspect and re-examine the proposition—and in the second place, ask him to do the same. If we still disagree, no further rational discussion is possible. Since I do not think I am mistaken, since this proposition does seem to me self-evident, I am content to rest my case upon it.

If, therefore, the exercise of free choice be necessary to the development of moral character, we can see that a temporal process is required by the very structure of the universe, by its axiological orientation. For the universe is so ordered that all is directed to the instantiation of value and to the elimination of disvalue.

Readers of St. Augustine and St. Thomas will recognize the similarity which obtains between the position I have just outlined and that of the scholastics.[19] For them also the time-series is finite in length; for them also time has a beginning and is the product of the eternal. Where we differ obviously and profoundly is in regard to my substitution of the Absolute for the creative God of Christian theism, and also in regard to the manner in which I introduce axiological considerations as explicative. But before we attempt a final evaluation of the hypothesis, let us attempt to work it out yet further in order to test its fruitfulness.

THE FINAL STATE

If the time-series arise out of the eternal, what of the end thereof? The end, we may assume, will be the arrival of the self at its own moral and intellectual maturity, when its capacities for good have been fully developed and its capacities for evil have been utterly eradicated, when it has fully *become,* and so has reached the limit of progress. When it can become no more, it will have reached the end of time. Thus we can see how the axiological structure of the universe involves both the generation and the consummation of time. A state of perfection must clearly be a static state, for if change were possible, it would not be perfect. "A state of intolerable boredom!" the reader

19. I owe, perhaps, a greater debt to J. S. MacKenzie's article, "Eternity" (*Hastings Encyclopedia,* Vol. V), in which, taking McTaggart's position as his point of departure, he undertakes to show that time can be included in eternity.

may ejaculate. But not so fast. As McTaggart has acutely observed, any state short of the highest would be boring and wearisome in the sense that it would be unsatisfying, since there would be something still to be attained, some potentiality yet to be realized. The highest, however, because it was the highest, would be utterly satisfying. Something of what it would be like we can conjecture in the light of those rare experiences in this life when the whole ego is involved in some intense axiological experience. Such a state could not, in the strict sense of the word, be called eternal; for it would have a beginning and would follow upon a preceding state. On the other hand it would not be temporal in the sense of being involved in becoming. It would be wholly static. Perhaps the Thomistic phrase, a "participated eternity," comes close to the mark. But the question what can be the content of such a state raises issues of such importance that it seems advisable to devote to them a separate chapter.

Chapter Thirteen

THE CONTENT OF THE
FINAL STATE

I know when I come to my own immortal I shall find there
In a myriad instant all that the wandering soul found fair,
Empires that never crumbled and thrones all glorious yet,
*And hearts ere they were broken and eyes ere they were wet.**

  'Tis love and the lover that live to all eternity;
  *Set not thy heart on aught else: 'tis only borrowed.***

No question can be of greater importance than the nature of the content of the final state which is the culmination of the whole temporal process, for it is that with respect to which the entire universe is oriented. Unimaginable by us, indeed, it surely is; yet, equally surely, not inconceivable. For it is a state wherein all values are actualized to the greatest degree, and with values we are already empirically acquainted *secundum statum praesentis vitae.* This is assuredly a consideration upon which too great emphasis can scarcely be laid. For some theologians and religious teachers have at times thought to impress their hearers with the incomparable greatness of the state of salvation by dwelling upon its mysterious nature, and by expatiating upon its complete dissimilarity to present experience. But by so doing, they have frustrated their own efforts. To proclaim the ultimate good inconceivable is to destroy our feeling of its reality. That which has charm and attraction for us must have something in common with what we already know. That which responds to the deepest yearnings of the soul must fill a void of which we are already conscious. The worldling is a worldling only because he has forgotten the scent of the fruit upon the tree of life. If Heaven were utterly unlike all that we have experienced it would not be Heaven. It behooves us, then, to discriminate as accurately as we can those elements in our present experience which are capable of being thus transplanted. They are the

* A. E., *Song and Its Fountains* (London, 1932), p. 48.
** Jalālu'ddīn Rumi, *Dīvāni Shamsi Tabrīz,* trans. R. A. Nicholson (Cambridge, 1898), p. 51.

seeds of salvation which, sown in the soil of the temporal, will come to flower in the eternal.

Knowledge in the sense of conscious and intuitive apprehension will certainly be present, but not discursive knowledge which involves transition and growth. Volition, as McTaggart has pointed out,[1] can be present in the form of acquiescence. And what of virtue? Clearly much that we include under that word, and which we highly value in present experience, will have no opportunity to manifest itself where no temptations can assail us. Courage, resolution, integrity, as specific and individual virtues, will not survive the cessation of becoming. Yet they will be, as it were, sublated in the strength and solidity of the integrated personality which will survive.

And what of love? Here, in my judgment, McTaggart has made one of the most important contributions in the history of the philosophy of religion. "It seems to me," he writes, "that, when love reached or passed a certain point, it would be more good than any amount of knowledge, virtue, pleasure, or fulness of life could be. This does not, so far as I am concerned, spring from any belief that I have reached such a point. It is a conclusion which seems to me to follow from contemplating the nature of love, on the one hand, and of the other qualities on the other hand."[2]

Before we assent to this statement it behooves us to inquire what McTaggart meant by love. It is, he tells us, "a species of liking."[3] The contrary of liking is repugnance. "Approval and disapproval," he informs us, "are distinguished from liking and repugnance by the fact that they are for qualities, or for substances in respect of their possession of those qualities, while liking and repugnance are for particular substances as wholes, though they may be *determined* by the qualities of the substances."[4] (There is a rather subtle distinction here, to which we shall shortly return.) Liking, then, is felt for substances. "In confining the name of love," continues McTaggart,

> to an emotion which is only felt toward substances, I think that I am in accordance with usage. It is true that, if a man admires courage or benevolence with a certain intensity, it is not unusual to say that he loves courage or benevolence. But this, I think, would generally be admitted to be a metaphor.

1. "The ideal of volition is rather the experience of perfect harmony between ourselves and our environment which excludes alike action and choice" (*Studies in Hegelian Cosmology*, sec. 270).
2. *The Nature of Existence*, Vol. II, sec. 851.
3. *Ibid.*, sec. 459.   4. *Ibid.*, p. 144, n. 1.

But how is love to be distinguished from other sorts of liking? I propose to confine the word, in the first place, to a liking which is felt toward persons. Here, perhaps, it is more doubtful if common usage supports the restriction. It is not so clear that we are speaking metaphorically when we say that a man loves the Alps, as when we say that he loves justice. Still less is it clear that we are speaking metaphorically when we say that he loves his school or his country. But it is important to have a separate name for the liking which is felt only toward persons, and there is, I think, no question that, however far the common use of the word may extend, the central and typical use of it is for an emotion felt toward persons. And thus, in using it exclusively for that emotion, we shall not depart much from the common use, if we depart at all.

Again, I propose to use the word only of a liking which is intense and passionate. This is in accordance with the general usage of the present, though not of the past.[5]

Having thus fully explained to us what he means by love, McTaggart goes on to emphasize the importance of distinguishing it both from benevolence and from sympathy. "Benevolence is not an emotion at all, but a desire—a desire to do good to some person, or to all persons."[6] Sympathy, on the other hand, "is a different emotion—the emotion which affects us pleasurably in the pleasure of others and painfully in their pain."[7]

McTaggart next proceeds to caution us against exaggerating the closeness of the relation of love to sexual desire. "It is often found in connection with that desire. But it is also found in connection with other bonds of union—kindred, early intimacy, similarity of disposition or of opinions, gratitude, and so forth. And it is also found without any such connection in instances where it can only be said that two people belong to one another—such love as is recorded in the *Vita Nuova* and *In Memoriam*."[8]

I may say at once that I think McTaggart is right in drawing a sharp distinction between an emotion which is felt for persons and an emotion felt for a group or organization composed of persons—for colleges, churches, regiments, or nations, for example. There is undeniably a certain similarity; yet the "feel," if I may so put it, is in each case distinctive and unique. Furthermore I agree that when love has

5. *Ibid.*, sec. 459.   6. *Ibid.*, sec. 460.
7. *Ibid.*   8. *Ibid.*, sec. 461.

"reached or passed a certain point," it constitutes a value greater than any other value, or than any combination of other values. This is a judgment which I take to be ultimate and self-evident; to those who reject it, therefore, I have nothing further to say. But those who, like myself, indorse it, may be interested in some further observations which I shall now offer.

I consider that McTaggart has made a great contribution to clarity by sharply distinguishing between love and benevolence. Unfortunately it is often very difficult to determine whether the word "love" is being employed to designate an emotional or a volitional attitude. In this connection it is very interesting to take cognizance of the parallel drawn by J. B. Pratt between the Buddhist and the Christian points of view.

"It goes without saying, I expect," Pratt remarks,

> that the love which the Buddha urged upon his followers is of the universal and relatively impersonal sort. His expressions in praise of love should be read in connection with passages of another type, such as this verse from the Dhammapada: "Let no man love anything: loss of the beloved is evil. Those who love nothing and hate nothing have no fetters." The Buddha distinguishes clearly three attitudes of mind which, in spite of their obvious difference, get themselves expressed in English by the one word *love*. The first of these is sexual lust. The second is tender personal affection for an individual of a sort so strong and uncontrollable that it tends to occupy one's thoughts and make one's own peace dependent upon the loved one's presence, or at least on his life and welfare. The third meaning of *love* is earnest and even tender good will for all, of a universal and impersonal sort. As is indicated in the words *good will*, this attitude belongs quite as much to the voluntary and conative as to the emotional side of human nature. Now of these three kinds of love the Buddha sternly condemns the first, he regards the second as an unnecessary and avoidable opening to the attacks of sorrow, and he approves thoroughly only the third, the impersonal love which seeks the welfare of all.[9]

Doubtless by some this very impersonal and universal outlook of Buddhism—in other words, its benevolence—will be found appealing; whereas others will exclaim that the attitude commended is essentially self-centered, that the Buddha's counsel is to cultivate an

9. *The Pilgrimage of Buddhism* (New York, 1928), p. 51.

aloofness with respect to the great emotional experiences which give human life its dignity and glory out of a base fear of the suffering which these frequently bring with them. Having made his point, however, Pratt directs his criticism somewhat nearer home:

> I am not sure that the Buddhist doctrine of love is (except for its fear of sorrow) very different from the Christian. Christian discussions of love as a rule are, to be sure, not so explicit in their distinction between personal tender emotion and universal good will as is the Buddha's treatment of the matter; yet when one examines a really typical exposition of love from some authoritative source, the distinction seems implicit, and the love commended is usually of the type the Buddha also would have praised. Take for example the oft-quoted thirteenth chapter of First Corinthians. The Greek ἀγάπη, translated in the King James version *charity* and in the Revised *love*, seems to mean something midway between the two; a universal and impersonal yet tender good will. This surely is not far from the meaning the Buddha put into the word our translators render love (or friendship), in those cases where he praised it and urged its cultivation upon his followers. Nor is there any evidence, as I interpret the Gospels, to show that Jesus advocated the more personal type of emotion.[10]

With the justice of this criticism we are not at present concerned. Once we have recognized that love is emotional and benevolence volitional, the issue before us is that of their relative status. Needless to say, there can be no question as to the excellence of benevolence. The world would be a far better place if there were more of it. Nonetheless, as a volitional activity, it is directed toward the realization of an end which lies beyond itself. It aims at the elimination—or, if this be impossible, at least at the reduction of the amount of—suffering and vice, and at the increase of every kind of good—of virtue, health, and happiness. Could its efforts ever be completely successful, it might be said to have eliminated itself. For a world in which no one needed the help of others, yet in which everyone was persistently trying to help others, would indeed constitute a paradox.

It is because pure benevolence is purely volitional that it is directed upon those who are in need, regardless of what their characters may be. Thus the command to "love" our enemies surely means to be kind to them. To require us to feel an intense emotional attachment to them would be to ask of us what is impossible, and, in many instances at least, would, I suggest, be immoral. It is this volitional character

10. *Ibid.*, p. 52.

of benevolence which so often leads professional altruists to develop, not only a practical efficiency, but with it a certain hardness which is repellent, and which renders "charity" so cold a word. True enough, as Pratt has remarked, benevolence may be blended with a feeling which is "universal and impersonal," but this feeling I take to be what McTaggart has called sympathy. "If we love a person," remarks McTaggart, we shall generally sympathize with him. But we can sympathize with people whom we do not love. It is even possible to sympathize with people whom we hate—at any rate, if the hatred is not very intense." [11]

Like sympathy, benevolence normally accompanies love. If we love people we wish them well, and act with a view to their welfare. Yet love, although it may be said to include them, is more than benevolence and sympathy, for it is inherently and fundamentally personal. Moreover, as McTaggart has pointed out in his essay "On the Further Determination of the Absolute," [12] love neither subordinates the object to the subject, as does volition, nor yet the subject to the object, as does cognition; it involves a more intimate union wherein the subject finds its end in, and realizes itself through, the object. There is thus, as it were, a perfect balance in this relationship between the two relata. Love is therefore peculiarly fitted to constitute the binding element in the universe. For as Hegel has maintained, and as McTaggart agrees, the greater the differentiation of the component terms, the closer must be the unity which includes them.[13]

Hence, inasmuch as persons constitute the *ne plus ultra* of differentiation, the closest of all relationships, namely, that presupposed by the emotion of love, is required to supply the corresponding unity. This is a fact of supreme significance. But before we examine it further, I propose to revert to the distinction mentioned above (p. 412).

Love, according to McTaggart, "is directed to the person, independently of his qualities." [14] This is a contention which we must examine in some detail. We must distinguish, McTaggart tells us, between an emotion which is felt *because* of certain qualities, and an emotion which is felt *in respect* of certain qualities. Thus we may come to love

11. *The Nature of Existence*, Vol. II, sec. 460.
12. This essay has been published *in extenso* in *Philosophical Studies*, and in abridged form it constitutes the ninth chapter of *Studies in Hegelian Cosmology*.
13. Once this principle has been clearly enunciated, it carries with it, to my mind, absolute conviction. As we review the history of philosophy in the light of it, we can see that the chief errors have consisted in deviations from it. Thus pantheism, on the one hand, and extreme pluralism, on the other, are shown to be untenable.
14. *The Nature of Existence*, Vol. II, sec. 466.

a person because of certain qualities which he possesses, or which we believe him to possess, but we do not love him in respect of these qualities. "The determining qualities are not the justification of the emotion, but only the means by which it arises. If this is so, it is natural that their value should sometimes bear no greater relation to the value of the emotion than the intrinsic value of the key of a safe bears to the value of the gold to which it gives us access." [15]

In support of this contention McTaggart appeals to what he takes to be three characteristics of love. In the first place "love is not necessarily proportional to the dignity or adequacy of the qualities which determine it. A trivial cause may determine the direction of intense love." [16] In the second place such determining qualities are, in some cases, not discoverable; yet we do not regard the worth of the emotion as thereby impugned. And in the third place, while it would be absurd to continue to admire a person because of qualities which we once believed him to possess but have now discovered to be lacking, love need not be, and should not be, destroyed by such disillusionment.

"If once the relation has existed," declares McTaggart,

> any disharmony among the qualities need not, and, we feel, ought not, to injure the harmony between the persons. If a person proves irrational or imperfect, this may make us miserable about him. It may make us blame him, or, more probably, make us blame God, or whatever substitute for God our religion may allow us. But it will not make us less interested in him, it will not make us less confident that our relation to him is the meaning of our existence, less compelled to view the universe *sub specie amati*. As well might any imperfection or sin in our own nature render us less interested in our own condition, or convince us that it was unimportant to ourselves.[17]

In accordance with this outlook McTaggart goes so far as to assert that "here we come across a state of spirit in which the value of truth and virtue for us seems to depend on the existence of another person, in the same way as it unquestionably depends for us on our own existence. And this not because the other person is specially interested in truth and virtue, but because all our interest in the universe is conceived as deriving force from his existence." [18]

---

15. *Ibid.*   16. *Ibid.*
17. *Studies in Hegelian Cosmology*, sec. 297. For a less vigorous statement of the same contention see *The Nature of Existence*, Vol. II, sec. 468.
18. *Studies in Hegelian Cosmology*, sec. 296.

Exaggerated as this passage may sound to the unsympathetic ear, we find in McTaggart's last work an even more extreme and explicit statement of the same point of view:

> B may have come to love A because he was virtuous, or he may have come to love him because he was beautiful. But it is possible that B should love C, though he knows him to be ugly, and it is possible that he should love him, though he knows him to be wicked. And, while virtue is more important than beauty, it seems to me that love towards a person known to be wicked is just as truly love (and, for that matter, just as good) as love towards a person known to be virtuous.[19]

I have gone so fully into a discussion of this point because here I find myself compelled to differ from McTaggart. But in doing so, I wish to dissociate myself from what I may call the ultra-moralistic point of view against which, I feel sure, McTaggart was reacting. We frequently encounter the assertion that the strength of love ought to be determined by the worth of its object; and from this premise, taken in conjunction with another, to the effect that God alone is absolutely perfect, theologians, both Christian and Muslim, have concluded that God is the only proper object of whole-souled and all-absorbing devotion, and that to direct such devotion upon any other being is to be guilty of idolatry. We are even told that the only justification for bestowing any degree of love upon a creature is that God loves him. Throughout the centuries this notion has exerted a profound and widespread influence, not only upon the clergy, but also upon the laity both in the Christian and in the Islamic worlds.[20] We find it carried to its logical conclusion in an account which, as its translator, the late

19. *The Nature of Existence*, Vol. II, sec. 463.
20. As an example thereof let me point to Chaucer's admonition to adolescents at the close of *Troilus and Criseyde*:

O yonge, fresshe folkes, he or she,
In which that love up groweth with youre age,
Repeyreth hom from worldly vanyte,
And of youre herte up casteth the visage
To thilke God that after his ymage
Yow made, and thynketh al nis but a faire
This world, that passeth soone as floures faire.

And loveth hym, the which that right for love
Upon a crois, oure soules for to beye,
First starf, and roos, and sit in hevene above;
For he nyl falsen no wight, dar I seys,
That wol his herte al holly on hym leye.
And syn he best to love is, and most make,
What nedeth feynede loves for to seke?

R. A. Nicholson, truly says "would be touching if it were not so edifying." It has to do with the Sūfi saint, Fudayl ibn Iyad.

> One day he had in his lap a child four years old, and chanced to give it a kiss, as is the way of fathers. The child said, "Father, do you love me?" "Yes," said Fudayl. "Do you love God?" "Yes." "How many hearts have you?" "One." "Then," asked the child, "how can you love two with one heart?" Fudayl perceived that the child's words were a divine admonition. In his zeal for God he began to beat his head and repented of his love for the child, and gave his heart wholly to God.[21]

Such an evaluation of love springs from two roots in the history of thought. One is the Hebrew-Christian command to love God with all one's heart and soul and mind and strength.[22] The other is the teaching of Plato's *Symposium* that we should proceed from the love of beautiful bodies to the love of beautiful souls, and from the love of beautiful souls to that of beautiful laws and institutions until we finally ascend to a spiritual altitude at which we are able to contemplate and to love the Form of beauty in its transcendent glory. To this way of thinking McTaggart takes up an attitude of straightforward and uncompromising opposition.

We must remember, furthermore, that McTaggart was a convinced determinist, and that for him moral evil, wherever it be found, constitutes only a stage through which the individual self must inevitably pass in its progress *sub specie temporis* toward ultimate perfection. Reproach, in the sense of a condemnation which implies that the evildoer need not have done the evil, is therefore an illegitimate—indeed, an absurd—attitude. And the same holds true of remorse for one's own conduct. Regret is, of course, permissible; yet with it there should be coupled an acquiescence in what is unavoidable. It is in the light of these considerations, I am convinced, that we must scrutinize McTaggart's position.

Nevertheless, as I have already stated, I find myself unable to accept his view; and this—aside from its determinism—because it seems to me to to presuppose an impossible separation of a substance from its nature. I quite admit, as the reader knows, that the substance is that which *has* the nature, and that the substance is a particular whereas the nature is composed of universals which characterize the substance. But the substance cannot exist apart from its nature. Nor

21. *The Mystics of Islam* (Mystic, Conn., 1966), p. 109.
22. See Deut. 5:1 and Mark 12:30.

can we love it or hate it, any more than we can admire or despise it, apart from its nature. To love a being apart from his characteristics would be equivalent to loving a being with no characteristics at all—in other words, a non-existent entity—which is an impossible supposition.

I quite realize that an opponent might urge that I am using the word "nature" with an unjustifiable looseness. I ought, he might insist, to employ it in one of two senses. On the one hand I might view the substance, as it were, longitudinally; I might identify its nature with all the characteristics which it acquires in the course of its history, that is to say, not only with those which it has *now*, but also with all those which it has ever had and which it will ever have.

Now I fully admit that the word "nature" can legitimately be used in this way, and that it actually has been so used—by so eminent a philosopher as Leibniz, for example. A determinist so using it would say, as Leibniz said, that the history of a substance is merely the progressive manifestation *sub specie temporis* of its nature. And an indeterminist can quite well use the term in the same sense, although he would assert that a man can change his nature by an act of choice.

I also concede that, could we inspect the natures of our fellow-men in this longitudinal dimension, our opinions of them and our emotional reactions toward them might well be profoundly modified. The Christians who knew St. Paul before his conversion as a persecutor who descended upon them "breathing out threatenings and slaughter" would probably have experienced a change of emotion had they been able to see in him the future apostle to the Gentiles and martyr to the faith. But my point is that we do not possess such explicit and detailed knowledge of an eternal individual nature, and of the successive future states in which it will infallibly manifest itself; nor, for the indeterminist, is such knowledge even conceivable. "It is not yet made manifest what we shall be." To assert this is not to deny that we may be aware of an individual's present possession of potentialities whose actualization we may imaginatively forecast; it is only to recognize that his nature is in the process of making.

On the other hand an objector might insist that by the word "nature" I ought to mean *all* the characteristics, and *only* those characteristics, which an individual possesses *now*. Thus, if A be suffering from a toothache at the present moment, this suffering is as truly a part of his nature as it is to be an honest man. I have no right, it may be said, to include the past in my purview any more than the future.

A man's nature is what he is now, and it changes from moment to moment.

This hypothetical criticism I make bold to reject. I quite recognize, of course, that profound alterations may occur in the character of an individual. Probably the most fundamental, and certainly the most dramatic, of these transformations takes place in the case of religious conversion, when the whole focus of the personality changes. And when a man succumbs to a great temptation, his whole character is no doubt basically affected thereby. Yet the transformation is never total. An intelligent villain may become an intelligent saint, but scarcely a stupid one. If Oliver Cromwell, as Baxter believed, from being a genuine patriot became a self-seeking dictator, he nevertheless remained a skilful general and a wise statesman. If Alcibiades were a brilliant politician before he deserted Athens for Sparta, he continued to be so after he deserted Sparta for Athens. Moreover, changes so extensive and so fundamental as to involve a complete reorientation of spiritual outlook do not occur every day or every week. In many lives, probably in most lives, they never occur at all; and rarely do they occur more than once. There are, in other words, qualities which, although not necessarily permanent, are habitual; and it is upon the substance as characterized by them that our emotional response is directed.

I agree, then, with McTaggart when he asserts that "love, as we see it in our present experience, involves a connection between the lover and the beloved which is of peculiar strength and intimacy, and which is stronger and more intimate than any other bond by which two selves may be joined. And we must hold, also, that whenever one of these selves is conscious of this unit, then he loves the other." But I cannot follow him when he continues,

> And this is regardless of the qualities of the two persons, or of the other relations between them. The fact that the union is there, or that the sense of it is there, may depend on the qualities and relations of the two persons. But if there is the union and the sense of it, then there is love, whether the qualities and relations which determine it are known or unknown, vital or trivial. Qualities and relations can only prevent love by preventing the union, or the sense of it, and can only destroy love by destroying the union, or the sense of it. Love is for the person, not for his qualities, nor is it for him in respect of his qualities. It is for him.[23]

23. *The Nature of Existence*, Vol. II, sec. 468.

Now I quite agree that love is for the person; but it is, I contend, for the person as an actual concrete substance with a definite nature, and not for a substance altogether irrespective of its nature—which would be like loving an ontological and axiological zero. I believe that McTaggart has done something extremely important both for religion and for metaphysics in affirming the supreme value of love, but I think that he has weakened his case by overstating it. And now, to press my point, I shall resort to the expedient of citing McTaggart against himself. In *Studies in Hegelian Cosmology* I find the following passage which seems to me clearly expressive of a fundamentally different point of view:

> But what right have we to talk of love coming as a necessary consequence of anything? Is it not the most unreasoning of all things, choosing for itself, often in direct opposition to what would seem the most natural course? I should explain the contradiction as follows. Nothing but perfection could really deserve love. Hence, when it comes in this imperfect world, it only comes in cases in which one is able to disregard the other as he is now— that is, as he really is not—and to care for him as he really is— that is, as he will be. Of course this is only the philosopher's explanation of the matter. To the unphilosophic subject of the explanation it simply takes the form of a wild conviction that the other person, with all his faults, is somehow *in himself* infinitely good—at any rate, infinitely good for his friend. The circumstances which determine in what cases this strange dash into reality can be made are not known to us. And so love is unreasonable. But only because reason is not yet worthy of it. Reason cannot reveal—though in philosophy it may predict—the truth which alone can justify love. When reason is perfected, love will consent to be reasonable.[24]

This passage I believe to be in the main profoundly true. If our view of time be correct, we cannot, indeed, dismiss evil as grounded in appearance. But this is not the point I wish to stress. What does impress me as of great importance is McTaggart's view that in the experience of love, consciousness focuses upon the potential perfection of the beloved as though it were already actualized. If this be true, and if it also be true that potentiality is always rooted in actuality, this means that in the self that is loved there must be present something real and positive upon which love can fasten—the seed, as it were, of an ultimate perfection. And in the light of this assump-

24. *Studies in Hegelian Cosmology*, sec. 273.

tion, we can account for the otherwise perplexing fact that individuals whose characters, to most of their contemporaries, have seemed vicious, and even wicked, have nevertheless been the objects of genuine devotion.[25] Moreover, if love thus involve an intuitive apprehension of an unsubmerged and sound core in the case of a person whose character is on the whole roundly to be condemned, we can understand how it can survive disillusionment with respect to certain qualities which that person was mistakenly believed to possess, whereas admiration could not so survive. For we admire a man, not for what he may become, but for what he is.

Furthermore, it seems to me that by his admission that the presence or absence of certain qualities may "prevent the union," McTaggart has somewhat given away his case. For if these qualities be essential to the establishment of the union, it is difficult to see how they can be totally irrelevant to its continuance; since the admission, surely, goes to support my contention that what is loved is not a shadowy abstraction but a concrete and qualified individual.

I believe, nevertheless, that in his insistence that all that is necessary for love is the closeness of the union, however it may have come about, McTaggart was influenced both by a recognition of the fact that it is at once inevitable and just that admiration should cease when it is found to have been based upon a mistaken evaluation, and by the conviction that to love truly is to love forever. For it might be argued that if love can be destroyed by disillusionment it can be nothing other than intense admiration. Moreover, McTaggart urges, we cannot but regard such cessation as a failure; we feel that love *ought* to have persisted.[26]

If this conviction be sound, it is clearly something worth contending for. And it is a conviction which is thoroughly in accord with McTaggart's whole outlook. For him evil is connected with the manifestation of the eternal in time. As an eternal reality the self is possessed of infinite value.[27] Hence, were we only close enough to any self, the insight springing from this intimacy would enable us, in McTaggart's own words, "to disregard him as he is now—that is, as he really is not—and to care for him as he really is—that is, as he will be." [28] Moreover, since any morally evil state *sub specie temporis* con-

25. As an instance of such a relationship one might point to the friendship of Simon Kenton and Simon Girty.

26. *The Nature of Existence*, Vol. II, sec. 408. Cf. *Studies in Hegelian Cosmology*, sec. 297.

27. *The Nature of Existence*, Vol. II, chap. lxvii.

28. *Studies in Hegelian Cosmology*, sec. 273.

stitutes only a stage though which he must unavoidably pass on his way to the goal of perfection, it would, as I have already remarked, be unjust to think of him—as the indeterminist would undoubtedly think of him—as genuinely accountable for his misdeeds in the sense that he need not have committed them. Thus, were we only close enough to such a man as Stalin, we should, undeterred by his murders of millions of human beings, actually love him. We should see that the poor devil could not have done otherwise; we should even acquiesce in his having done what he did because we should be aware that only by so doing could he progress toward the actualization of the perfection that was potentially present in him. We understand now how it is that for McTaggart love for an evil person can be just as good as love for a good person; for the former is not really evil at all in the indeterminist's sense of the word, any more than a guillotine or a rack is morally evil.

The indeterminist, however, will view things very differently. For him Stalin was really an evil man because he actually chose to do what he need not have done, since he could have chosen otherwise. Nearness to such a man, far from evoking an emotion of love, could generate only loathing and contempt. If anyone had ever loved such a person, could love, any more than admiration, survive the recognition of what he had become? Does it not, then, follow that for a person who, like myself, believes in the reality of time and of free will, the inescapable conclusion must be that love does not involve an eternal relationship, inasmuch as it arises, not only *because of,* but also *in respect of,* characteristics which are acquired in the temporal process, and is bound to perish if these characteristics be lost—as they may be lost—in the temporal process?

We appear to be confronted, accordingly, by the following dilemma: either love for a person who is really evil in the indeterminist's sense of the word is just as possible and just as good as love for a good person, or love, like admiration, in certain circumstances not only *may* cease, but *ought* to cease. Is it possible to escape being impaled upon one or other of the horns of this dilemma?

In reply I would point out that I am not supposing that in present experience love is evoked either by the possession of absolute perfection or of absolute devilishness. I have conceded that in the experience of love we do contemplate as though already actualized all the potentialities the realization of which is requisite for perfection. But I have not supposed that no potentialities for good have as yet been actualized at all.[29] On the contrary, I assume that well-grounded love is evoked by the present possession of qualities which render the loved person lovable.

Could such qualities be wholly lost? The exemplification of them would at least be part of the past and enduring history of the self. It is difficult to see how, except by some abnormal psychic fission, they could ever be totally repudiated. And most psychologists, I believe, would assure us that they could always be reactivated.

I have just spoken of "well-grounded" love. Could genuine love ever be called forth by a complete misapprehension of the nature of the other person involved? Take, for instance, a mother's love for a new-born child. It is extremely improbable that the child will develop into an incarnate devil, utterly unresponsive to the affection it receives. Yet, if we assume that such cases occur, must we not say that what has been loved was a figment of the imagination which was erroneously confused with an actual person, that we are faced, so to speak, with a case of mistaken identity? [30]

Our view of the relation of time to eternity makes it quite possible—indeed, I should say inevitable—that we should acquiesce in McTaggart's view that love involves an eternal relationship. Otherwise we should have to hold that the most intimate of all unions comes about, and that the highest of all values is instantiated, through mere chance. We surely cannot assume that selves are projected higgledy-piggledy into the temporal process. If the universe actually constitutes an axiologically oriented system, there must be an eternal order which is reflected in time. If A, B, C, D, and E have been lifelong acquaintances of F, but if A alone loves F, A must see in F something which B, D, C, and E do not see; and this vision must be due to the fact that A in some way stands nearer to F. Such a relationship may well be called one of *metaphysical nearness;* but I do not think that of itself it suffices to account for love. For love is not a relation but an emotion. It grows out of a relation, but it is a quality, or a state, of A. It is an emotion which sometimes arises very slowly; at other times with astonishing suddenness. But it arises in time. The relation of metaphysical nearness has been implemented by a union which is grounded in the characters of lover and beloved; and these characters, al-

29. A character in which no such qualities were actualized, which was completely devoid of integrity, which was totally self-centered, which was utterly incapable of self-sacrifice, and which succumbed to every temptation, could not, I think, evoke well-grounded love.

30. I recall once seeing a play in which one of the characters remarked, "I loved a woman who never existed."

though based upon a deposit of underived characteristics, have burgeoned in the temporal process.

LOVE IN THE ETERNAL

Is McTaggart right, however, in subordinating to love in the scale of values the emotions felt for groups, institutions, and organizations? "Although such loyalties," he writes, "are trivial by the side of love, yet, by their side most other things are trivial." [31] This I should accept as a true statement. But I should no more think of trying to prove it than I would think of trying to prove that red is other than blue; for each assertion is the expression of a judgment based upon a direct apprehension of the qualities in question.

I would urge, however, that from the point of view of the axiological idealism which has been outlined in the preceding chapters, there is a peculiar fittingness in this state of affairs. For as we have seen, the self is an eternal reality; it is therefore the appropriate object of the most intense of all emotions, an emotion which constitutes the supreme value. On the other hand, every group, every institution, every organization encountered in the temporal process has come into existence and will pass out of existence. But what of the society of perfected persons which, on our present hypothesis, constitutes the goal of the temporal process? Can we feel no emotion for it? Certainly we can. And a strong emotion it will be, yet not so strong as love. For we shall value that society because it includes the persons whom we love; we shall not love them because they are included within it.

In section 201 of his *Studies in Hegelian Cosmology*, after remarking that "the vast majority of the relations which make up our present society" are "relations which have their origin and meaning only with reference to the conditions of our present imperfect existence, and which would be meaningless in the ideal," McTaggart adds, "it is possible that we might find, on further consideration of the nature of Absolute Reality, and of our own lives, some element in the latter which seemed to belong directly to the former—something which did not merely lead to heaven, but *was* heaven."

From our present vantage point we can see what this something is. It is the experience of love which "does not merely lead to heaven, but *is* heaven." This is a doctrine of the highest significance both for religion and for philosophy; let us therefore be at pains to understand it aright. The statement just quoted is not incompatible, al-

31. *The Nature of Existence*, Vol. II, sec. 782.

though at first glance it may appear to be so, with another statement
made by McTaggart in the concluding paragraph of *The Nature of
Existence*. There, speaking of the beatific state when time has faded
into eternity, he tells us that it is a state of love "so direct, so intimate,
and so powerful that even the deepest mystic rapture gives us but
the slightest foretaste of its perfection." From the standpoint which
we have reached as a result of our investigation of the relation of
time to eternity we are fully as much entitled as McTaggart to assume that in Absolute Reality, or in heaven, love will possess an
intensity vastly exceeding, and will involve a union far closer, than any
which our imagination can picture in this life. Yet, if love in this life
provide us only a foretaste, it *is* a foretaste. It has the quality of
heaven. The beatific state will not be a state of some other, and as yet
unfelt, emotion; it will be a state of love. Hence anyone who experiences love here and now is empirically acquainted with the content of the eternal. We shall do well, then, to reject boldly the Buddha's
admonition, "Let no man love anything: loss of the beloved is evil."
This is the counsel of a craven heart. Of course loss of the beloved
is evil. And there are evils even worse than this which love sometimes brings in its train. But they are transient, and they will fade.

In McTaggart's view the eternal relation out of which love arises
fulfils, *sub specie temporis*, the function of the Law of Karma in Hindu-
Buddhist philosophy, in that it determines the *locus* of rebirth. Our
most intimate relations with other selves thus form a matrix which is a
controlling factor throughout the temporal process.[32] This is a highly
novel conception, yet its novelty does not render it less plausible. And

32. "In other words," writes McTaggart,
people who are joined by love cannot be dependent for their proximity to
each other—and consequently for the possibility of their love—on some
chance or mechanical arrangement whose recurrence we would have no
reason to expect. Their love is not the effect of proximity, but its cause. For
their love is the expression of the ultimate fact that each of them is more
closely connected with the other than he is with people in general. And
proximity in a particular life, like everything else, is the effect—or, rather,
the manifestation under particular circumstances—of those relations which
make up the eternal nature of the universe.
    If, therefore, love has joined two people in this life, we have, on the
assumption we have been discussing, good reason for believing that their
existences are bound up with each other, not for one life only, but for ever.
This would not involve their meeting in every life, any more than it would
involve their meeting every day of each life. Love can survive occasional
absences, and is often even stronger for them. And the universe is on a large
scale, which might require long absences. What we are entitled to believe is
that, while time remains, their eternal nearness must continually find its
expression in temporal life. (*Some Dogmas of Religion*, sec. 108)

the acceptance of it follows with logical inevitability from the basic thesis of axiological idealism. For if the destiny of the self be determined by the axiological "set" of the universe, how can we escape the conclusion that the greatest of all values must play the predominant role in the working out of that destiny? [33]

This does not mean that there is no truth in the doctrine of Karma. For the instantiation of all values will be involved in the progressive development of character. Of love, however, not only is it true that it is the supreme value; it is also true that it involves, not merely the relation of individual to value, of particular to universal, but also the relation of individual to individual, of particular to particular. And since the particulars thus related are persons—which, as such, represent the extreme type of differentiation—is it not clear that it is only the closest and most intimate of all relations which can unite them in a world order? Unless our thinking have gone wholly wrong somewhere, this question, I conclude, must be answered in the affirmative.

Free Will and Universal Salvation

It is an extraordinary fact, and one which does not appear to have received sufficient consideration, that, whereas almost all determinists who have been theists have believed in the damnation of the great majority of the human race, almost all those who have believed in universal salvation have been indeterminists. Indeed—with the exception of McTaggart—the only determinists who have been universalists whom I can recall were Makkali Gosāla, the leader of the Ājivakas, and the New England Universalists before they repudiated Calvinism. This does seem an astonishing state of affairs. For it should be just as easy, one would think, for a determinist to believe in universal salvation as to hold the opposing point of view; whereas an indeterminist

33. The desire for future reunion with loved ones lost is one of the profoundest of which humanity has shown itself capable. By saying this I do not, of course, mean to imply that I think that this deep desire accounts for the belief in immortality, that this belief represents nothing more than disguised wishful thinking. Such is not my opinion. As the reader knows, I consider that the arguments in favor of it are quite conclusive. Yet it is rather amazing that relatively little emphasis should have been laid upon reunion in the hymns of the Church and in discussions of the future life. This is doubtless due to the fact that in theistic religions human destiny is conceived to depend upon the will of a "jealous God," and that many theologians and philosophers have persistently endeavored to divert men's devotion from other finite selves, and to direct it toward the Deity. To some extent, then, the belief in God and the belief in a future reunion have rested uneasily together; and McTaggart has been the first eminent thinker to give unqualified expression to the latter belief.

who took such a position might plausibly be accused of inconsistency. For if a man's actions be undetermined, may it not plausibly be maintained that they are also unpredictable? How, then, can one formulate any definite theory as to the fate of the individual?

The belief in free will has indeed helped us hitherto. It has rendered intelligible—so I have urged—the view that the time-series arises out of the very nature of the eternal, in that the relation of obligation in which the self stands to values demands freedom of choice whereby the values can genuinely be adopted by the self and woven into its character. And thus it has helped us to see how the rationality and righteousness of the universe as a whole involves the possibility of irrationality and unrighteousness in its parts. But to the universalist this very same belief might well seem to present an insuperable obstacle.

The believer in a creative God who is prepared to maintain that divine foreknowledge is compatible with the freedom of the human will may, indeed, contend that our assurance that God is good [34] entitles us to affirm that he would not create any self unless he foresaw that that self would ultimately attain perfection. This solution, of course, is not open to those who do not believe in creation. But I would point out that it would involve even those who do so believe in a contradiction. The view that prediction with respect to a man's future acts is, in the majority of instances, compatible with the belief in free will has indeed been explicitly affirmed by that arch-indeterminist, Professor C. A. Campbell, on the gound that in most instances there is no conflict between desire and duty, that it is only relatively infrequently that we are forced to choose. In this connection we must, I think, accept his distinction between the *nature* and the *character* of the self. "The 'nature' of the self," he writes, "and what we commonly call the 'character' of the self are by no means the same thing, and it is utterly vital that they should not be confused. The 'nature' of the self comprehends, but is not without remainder reducible to, its 'character'; it must, if we are to be true to the testimony of our experience of it, be taken as including *also* the authentic creative power of fashioning and re-fashioning 'character.' " [35]

I should demur to the use of the word "creative" in the above passage; but this, I feel sure, is a mere matter of terminology. Most of the self's acts issue from its character. And we may go further and assert

34. Unless he also held that goodness can be predicated univocally of God and man he would not, I should claim, be justified in asserting so much as this.
35. *On Selfhood and Godhood*, p. 177.

that the aim of moral struggle is so to strengthen, develop, and complete the character as to render right action ever more spontaneous, that the ultimate achievement of free will is to eliminate itself.[36] And on our view, when this shall have been accomplished, the process of becoming will have terminated.

For us, however, who are in a state of imperfection it is those relatively infrequent decisions to act not *in accordance with* but *against* the strongest desire which is the expression of our character as so far formed that are of crucial importance for our own development. The situation has been well described by Professor Campbell. "Repeatedly it is urged against the Libertarian, with a great air of triumph, that on his view he can't say *why* I now decide to rise to duty, or now decide to follow my strongest desire in defiance of duty. Of course he can't. If he could he wouldn't be a Libertarian. To account for a free act is a contradiction in terms." [37] In other words, its occurrence is not necessitated by any preceding event. Consequently we cannot *know* that it will occur; and this absence of knowledge is due not to the limitations of our finite intelligences but to the inherent nature of a free act. This does not mean that we can never form any reasonable opinion as to what a man will do. For as Professor Campbell has pointed out, the stronger the desire in opposition to which he chooses to act, the greater will be the moral effort which such an act involves. "It will take a far harder moral effort," he observes, "for the tippler than for the moderate drinker to achieve the same external result of abstention. So much is matter of common agreement. And we are entitled, I think, to take it into account in prediction, on the simple principle that the harder the moral effort required to resist desire the less likely it is to occur." [38] Thus, if we have some knowledge of the formed character of a man and of the circumstances in which he is placed, we can make some sort of judgment as to the probability of his performing a certain act. Yet it is a question only of probability, inasmuch as the act is not necessitated but free. If this conclusion be sound it is clear that even a divine Intelligence, however sagacious its judgments, could not have certain knowledge in advance of what a man may freely will to do. Consequently there is no foundation for the formation of a definite dogma with respect to universal salvation.

Let us therefore assume for the moment that the universalist is

36. Thus Mazzini maintained that the possession of free will is a mark of imperfection, and, consequently, cannot be predicated of God (see the Everyman edition of Mazzini's *Essays,* p. 305).

37. *On Selfhood and Godhood,* p. 175.   38. *Ibid.,* p. 174.

mistaken. This will, surely, involve the further assumption that there
are selves whose native potentialities for good, having never been
actualized, have been finally eradicated, and whose potentialities for
evil have all become actualized. And what will their destiny be? Shall
we suppose that in them the process of becoming never terminates,
that they pass perpetually from one evil life to another? In this connection we may recall Erigena's warning that we must not allow
heretical depravity to seduce us into believing that God sentences
souls to hell.[39] Sinners, he tells us, make their own hell. Readers of
Swedenborg's descriptions of how damned souls torment and perse-
cute one another in the hells will recognize how horrible such a state
might be. Yet does its horribleness render it less plausible to the indeterminist who does not believe in a God who can both create and
annihilate? Perhaps, however, a further assumption is possible. Might
we not legitimately oppose to a state of perfection a state of utter
degradation, to a spiritual zenith a spiritual nadir? Must not the
process of becoming, whether it tend upward or downward, terminate
at last in a static condition? And might not such a state involve a loss
of the consciousness which, in opposition to the "set" of the whole
universe, has given itself over to the irrational and the evil, so that the
final state of such a self would be one of complete oblivion?[40]

Frankly speculative as these suggestions are, it may be worth our
while to contemplate them as alternative possibilities to that envisaged
by the universalist. But this brings us back to a question we have
not yet answered. How does the universalist manage to hold together
the belief in free will and the belief in universal salvation? Clearly it
will not avail him merely to appeal to the power of divine grace; for
if genuine goodness must be the result of free choice, not even divine
grace can force it upon a self. If I mistake not, the more thoughtful
universalist would rest his case upon the assertion that it is quite
incredible that any self should be wholly and irreclaimably given over
to evil. If not in the form of a positive conviction, at least as a hope,
his outlook has been widely shared by humanity. The mystical doctrine of the spark in the soul which never consents to sin even in hell,
and the medieval legend that Judas Iscariot once gave his cloak to a
beggar, bear witness to it.

I am inclined to think that the universalist would state his position
in some such fashion as this. The self, he would say, is fundamentally

39. *Liber de Praedestinatione*, chap. x, II.
40. On this hypothesis the lot of irreclaimably evil souls would be the same as
that of delivered souls in the Nyāya and Vaiśeṣika philosophies.

rational, and evil is essentially irrational. Hence it is inconceivable that evil should ever completely satisfy. Psychoanalysts assure us that we can never at bottom "fool" ourselves. Consequently the self that has succumbed to the attraction of evil at bottom condemns and despises itself; and the more evil it becomes, the more intense will be this deep-seated self-condemnation. Sooner or later, but ultimately and inevitably, therefore, a state of moral nausea will ensue. In a sort of psychic vomit, the self by a tremendous effort will by an act of free will repudiate the evil character which it has formed, and will turn with relief to the rational and the good.

It is difficult to evaluate such an argument as this. It seems to presuppose a profounder knowledge of the psyche than anyone today can claim to possess. I hope that the universalist is right. Yet, like Abu-Sofian in regard to the claims of Muhammad, I confess to a "certain hesitancy." But in the light of our preceding discussion, there is, I firmly believe, one message of consolation which can rightfully command our full assent. It is that which, in Text F of *The Legend of Good Women*, the god of love on his departure communicates to Chaucer: "But er I goo, thus muche I wol the telle: / Ne shal no trewe lover come in helle."

BOOK III

THE PROBLEM OF GOD

CHAPTER ONE

THE CONCEPT OF GOD

Up to this point we have left on one side the whole question of theism. Our concern, in the first place, was with the nature of religion as such; and we saw that religion can be theistic, polytheistic, pantheistic, or atheistic. Our concern, in the second place, was with the metaphysics of religion, and the line of reasoning which we have followed has led us to envisage the universe from the standpoint of a pluralistic axiological idealism which regards ultimate reality as composed of eternal particulars and universals woven together in a cosmic system which is underived and self-existent. Our conclusion, if correct, places the whole problem of theism in a very different perspective from that in which it is usually contemplated by Western thinkers. All through the history of Western philosophy, since the triumph of Christianity, a continual combat has been going on between those committed to the doctrine of a creative God, on the one hand, and the defenders of materialism on the other hand. The same combat is being waged today, although on one side the combatants are arrayed under banners different from those they flaunted in the past. As the defenders of the Roman Empire found themselves assailed, first by Visigoths, next by Ostrogoths, then by Lombards, and finally by Franks, so Christian theists have their materialistic foes replaced by hordes of naturalists, logical positivists, behaviorists, and linguistic analysts. And even as the speech of each and every one of the peoples who invaded Italy was some form of Teutonic, so the thinking of our contemporaries who take these various names is clearly motivated by a common interest, which is to exalt the importance of sense experience and to eliminate, or at least to reduce to the level of complete subordination, the role of spirit.

From our present vantage point we may perhaps permit ourselves to ejaculate, "A plague on both your houses!" For, as we see it, the fundamental issue is being obscured by a mass of verbiage. What was the contention of the Hobbesian materialists? That mind *is* matter. But by this dogmatic pronouncement the distinction between the mental and the physical was not really obliterated. It soon became evident that all that had been accomplished was to enlarge the signification of the word "matter." One could, indeed, now talk, if one wished, of physical matter and mental matter; but by this verbal tactic no problem had been solved, and the ancient issue remained precisely what it had been. Accordingly, the next step was to affirm that although mind was not to be identified with matter, it was nevertheless in some mysterious and inexplicable way derived from, or "secreted" by, matter and was itself without causal efficacy. Like some doctrines of orthodox Christianity this was easier to state than to understand, and to understand than to prove. What was really meant, if anything, by saying that one type of reality produced another so completely different from it? Was it actually any more enlightening than the doctrine of the *Circumincessio?* It scarcely appeared so. Moreover the denial to mind of causal efficacy was a dogma which required a great deal of faith to believe on the part of a man who had ever so much as willed to pick up his pen. Consequently the naturalist, or the "new materialist," found it expedient to repudiate the dogma of the derivation of mind from matter. Instead it was announced that mind had merely "emerged" in the evolutionary process and had "supervened" upon matter. If one inquired out of what it had emerged, one was told that it had emerged from nothing. Nor had it been brought into existence by the agency of some antecedently existing reality. And inasmuch as it was itself antecedently non-existent, it could not have brought itself into being. What, then, was actually meant by the terms "emerge" and "supervene"? It became increasingly clear that they meant nothing at all, that they had reference to no genuine idea, that they were merely verbal stopgaps, ejected in the hope of silencing an opponent. And now what is the latest "dodge" of all? To affirm that consciousness *is* behavior! This is, indeed, a splendid solution, a mere repetition under the most transparent disguise of the original device of classifying mind under the head of matter! It must be a dire need which drives men to such devious courses. And it requires little penetration to see what the need is. It is the desire at all costs to repudiate alike the claims of metaphysics, rationalism, and religion.

Now let us look at the position of the opponent. Not only mind but also matter, asserted the orthodox theist, is the product of creation. And ever since Tertullian's great debate with Praxeas, by creation has been understood creation *ex nihilo.* The importance of this development has, alas, been insufficiently obvious to the non-theological mind. Again and again one finds people talking of the "creativity" of a man of genius who has produced a drama, a symphony, a painting, or a sculpture, in blissful ignorance, seemingly, that the theologian would classify such activity under the heading of "generation." One even hears it said that God has "created creators"! [1]

Let us therefore explicitly recognize that by "creation" must be understood the production of an entity, or entities, *de novo, in toto,* and *ex nihilo.* By the phrase *ex nihilo* it is not meant that nothing is a stuff, a kind of *materia prima* or pure potentiality which already has some kind of being, and which was, or can be, acted upon *ab extra.* What it means is that before creation there was nothing at all other than the Creator. The divine will acts upon no antecedently existing object; the object arises wholly from the will.

How did such a conception—or misconception—ever arise? Through revelation, some may answer. Revelation is a topic to which we have had occasion to refer, but which we have not yet discussed in any thorough manner. But this, at least, may be said in the present connection. If revelation occur, either it is intended to enlighten the understanding or it has some other purpose. In the former case the concept of creation, once imparted, ought to shed much light upon our problems. It may even be contended that it has done so.[2] We have seen how it aids the universalist by inspiring the conviction that God would create no souls not destined to salvation. And in the same way we could account for the increase or decrease of population. Moreover, the sensum theory, which I have made bold to reject because of Dr. Ewing's frank admission that it must employ this very concept, will now be thoroughly rehabilitated. Furthermore, if creation be conceivable, so must its counterpart, annihilation, be; and this consideration might hearten those of us who find it difficult to share the confidence of the universalist by suggesting a way in which a benevolent Providence might deal with the incurably wicked. But do all these considerations afford us any real help? If one could believe in magic, how many scientific problems would cease to perplex us! And does not the notion of creation stand on the same level? Remember the old Scotsman's answer to Livingstone, "When God made the rocks, he made the pebbles in them." If the notion of creation be not intelligible *in se,* its claim to enlighten us is but a vain pretense.

On the other hand, if the dogma of creation be revealed for some other purpose, what can that purpose be? To judge from the way in which traditional theologians treat similar "mysteries," we should have to assume that it is proffered us as a test to try our powers of faith. If

1. As we have seen, Dr. A. C. Ewing would take this statement very seriously.
2. See Tennant, *Philosophical Theology* (Cambridge, 1928), Vol. II, chap. v, for the opinion of a liberal theologian.

the conception of God implied by such an outlook do not appall anyone, I presume that there is nothing that I can say that would disturb
him. But I suggest that those of us who find it nauseating had best
leave the doctrine of revelation for the nonce out of consideration, and
treat the notion of creation as the offspring of human minds.

Viewed from this angle, it seems pretty obviously to have been
derived by illegitimate abstraction from the process of making. In his
formulation of his doctrine of the Four Causes, Aristotle has analyzed
with admirable clarity what is involved in making. There is the maker
—the efficient cause—there is the stuff out of which the thing is made
—the material cause—there is the design imposed upon the stuff—the
formal cause—and there is the end which is the goal of the whole
process, the thing made—the final cause. Thus you make bricks out of
clay, and a house out of bricks. But creation would be like making
bricks without clay, or a house without bricks. For in creation there is
no material cause; there is simply the creative will which is at once
the efficient, formal, and final cause. With the elimination of the material cause has not intelligibility also been eliminated? What is left is
surely as meaningless as the notion of a stick with only one end, or a
board with only one side. And this is the conception which is to function as the substratum of the orthodox theists's universe!

Of course one can see more or less clearly how the formation of this
psychological and metaphysical monstrosity came about. For the notion of making is present in many primitive cosmologies. Before the
world order was established there was some kind of unordered stuff—
a chaos.[3] Upon this the gods acted, and molded it to their design. Or
sometimes a deity was slain, and out of his—or her—body the gods
formed the world. But with the exaltation of the sovereign God in
Hebraic monotheism, the independence of any other reality became
dangerous, inasmuch as it constituted a potential rival. Hence it was
found necessary to suppress all other divinities—either by denying
their existence, or by transforming them into angels (which is to say,
servant-divinities). God must be not only supreme but omnipotent;
consequently all reality must be regarded as the product of his will.
To the establishment of a dogma which interpreted the universe in
terms of divine volition even the requirements of intelligibility must be
sacrificed. Thus a single dominating idea became expanded beyond
the limits of rationality. The doctrine of creation is, in truth, the
reductio ad absurdum of an exaggerated monotheism.

From a psychological standpoint this development becomes more

3. Thus in Genesis we have the earth "without form and void."

comprehensible when we recall that a full-fledged doctrine of the soul either had never arisen or—as is more probable—had passed through a long process of degeneration, among Semitic peoples, as among the Homeric Greeks.[4] By all these peoples the self was conceived of in a very materialistic fashion, the vital principle being identified with the blood or the breath. The notions of Sheol, Aralu, and Hades are closely akin to one another. Survival was not thereby denied, rather it was affirmed; but it was a very anemic survival, the life hereafter being a shadowy replica of life on the earth.

The connection between the development of monotheism and of the belief in a future life among the Hebrews is of interest both from a psychological and a philosophical point of view. The belief in a single supreme God appears to have acquired an impetus somewhat earlier; indeed it has been suspected that faith in an afterlife was actually discouraged by some of the prophets in the interest of monotheism. At first glance it would seem incredible that the phantasmal denizens of the tomblike region of Sheol could ever have been regarded as potential rivals of the heavenly Yahweh, "mighty in battle." Yet there is no getting over the fact that the dead were referred to as *elohim*— gods—and that a certain worship seems to have been accorded them.[5] And the sensitivity of early monotheism appears to have been very great—as is evident from the open repudiation of the ontological and moral dualism of Zoroastrianism, and the explicit declaration that God creates evil.[6] So it would seem quite likely that the belief in a life hereafter did present itself as dangerous to the early monotheists. How strong this opposition originally was we can indeed infer from its ability to propagate itself; for it remained the most distinguishing feature of Saduceeism until the fall of Jerusalem.[7]

When the belief in a future life appeared in a really vital form in Judaism it would seem to have been the joint effect of two causal factors. One of these was doubtless the influence of Zoroastrianism, combined with that of the Persians who had freed Israel from the hated Babylonian yoke and had made possible the return from the captivity. It is, indeed, significant that in the same chapter in which

4. In view of the antiquity and widespread character of the belief, the latter hypothesis would appear to be preferable. Thus Professor Eliade assures us that the anthropologist finds primitive man everywhere regarding himself as in a state of transition **between two worlds.**

5. **Cf.** the language of the witch of Endor (I Sam. 28:13) and the prostration of Saul (*ibid.*, 28:14). Doubtless we have here the survival of an animistic belief once more vigorous.

6. Isa. 45:7.

7. Acts 23:8.

an absolute dualism is repudiated Cyrus should be hailed as the Lord's Messiah.[8] And in the long run the influence of Zoroastrianism proved so irresistible that dualism in a modified form was at last accepted; and Satan, now identified with the champion of evil, was assigned a permanent, although subordinate, position in the cosmos. That the doctrine of the resurrection was imported into Judaic thought from the same source seems to be an inescapable conclusion. Yet the warmth of its welcome must have been due to the fact that it met a growing need in the development of Israel's own religious life.

With the rise of monotheism the desire for an ever closer communion with God became more and more pronounced. To this the Psalms bear witness. Something in the nature of a Bhakti cult was the result, and its growth was doubtless favored by the loss of national independence. The individual had now acquired a new importance. And Yahweh, while still remaining the king of his people, became more and more the personal God of the individual Israelite. Out of the intense consciousness of this connection arose the conviction of its indestructibility. The power of God, now viewed as limitless, extended even to Sheol. Death was now seen to be incapable of dissolving the relationship of love and trust between worshiper and Deity. The might and love of the only true God constituted a guarantee of its permanence. God would certainly redeem his own from "the power of Sheol." This is a fact of great significance; for it is the character of God which, for Jews, Christians, and Moslems, has always constituted the strongest of all arguments for immortality.[9] Thus the belief in a creative God becomes the one and only ground upon which to base the dearest of human hopes.

Why is it that the course of events in India was so markedly dif-

8. Isa. 45:1.

9. It is also significant that the belief was adopted in its crudest and most materialistic form, the resurrection of the body. Sometimes this was combined with the view that the being of the individual totally lapsed between death and the resurrection. But the orthodox view was that the soul, which was originally conceived to be a sort of simulacrum of the body, persisted in the interval in a disembodied state. St. Paul, indeed, appears to have viewed the matter differently, and to have regarded the resurrection as involving the transference of the soul to a numerically different body of a vastly superior kind. But the traditional opinion prevailed, and today the Christian who repeats the Apostles' Creed in Latin professes to believe in the resurrection of *this flesh (huius carnis)*. We are sometimes told today by the "neo-orthodox" that Christianity is the most materialistic of the great religions, as though this were something greatly to its credit, destined, perhaps, to render possible a good understanding with the Moscow of naturalism. Christianity, I should say, is no more materialistic than Judaism, Islam, or Zoroastrianism. But trust the craven insight of the temperamental apologist to detect a potential basis for compromise!

ferent? The reason is a very obvious one—the different status which was accorded to the soul. Very early the belief arose that the soul was an indestructible entity which passed from life to life, being sometimes reborn in another world and sometimes reincarnated upon this earth. The doctrine is similar to, indeed practically identical with, that held by the Orphics and the Pythagoreans. That the same view should be entertained by people so widely separated has suggested a common origin whence, in the prehistoric period, it was derived; but no general agreement upon the subject appears yet to have been reached.[10] This is a concern, however, rather of the anthropologist and the historian than of the philosopher. The theory of a plurality of lives, however, is one which, for philosophical reasons, we have decided to adopt.

From our point of view, therefore, the theistic problem is contemplated under a very different aspect from that which it presents to the average occidental thinker. It is no longer a question of the origin of the universe, for the universe as a whole has no origin. It is self-existent; and of a self-existent reality it is meaningless to ask why it is what it is.[11] All selves are basic and indestructible constituents of the universe. The relevant question to ask is: Are they all potentially equal, or do they differ essentially in capacity? If we assume that there are essential differences between selves, then two possibilities confront us. In either case the universe will be hierarchically organized; but in one case at the apex there will be a single supreme Self, in the other case what we may call a heavenly aristocracy. In the absence of essential differences the universe will be a kind of democracy. All three possibilities are, at first glance at least, quite conceivable; and it is not easy to see upon what grounds we can decide between them.

At this point, however, we must turn aside to answer a stock objection which is sure to be raised. Your conception of God, it will be said, is crude in the extreme. It is vitiated all through by anthropomorphism. You are thinking of God as though he were merely a greater man, or a greater self. How, then, we may reply, are we to think of God? As something "utterly utter"—non-human, indescribable, incomprehensible?

Let us in self-defense appeal to the anthropologist. How did the idea of God originate, and how did it develop? Tyler and the animists advanced an explanation, and one very plausible in its day, one which has become plausible once more now that the theory of the animatists,

10. I suspect that the common origin was the reasonableness of the belief.
11. World orders may conceivably arise and pass away within the universe, but to admit this hypothesis is not to raise any fundamental issue.

which seemed to disqualify it, has been so vigorously blown upon. Man conceived of reality, they maintained, in terms of what he knew best—the self; for after all, he was a self. So he peopled nature with selves. Mountains, rivers, trees were all alive, all conscious, all endowed with feeling and volition. It was dangerous to ford a river without apologizing and asking its permission; for nobody likes to be walked over, and in a resentful mood it might sweep you away. Again it might be possible to frighten away an approaching thunderstorm by brandishing spears, clubs, and bows, and by raising a din of howls and war cries. The conjectural development from animism through polydemonism to polytheism was, in all likelihood, an actual one; the existence of human patriarchs and chieftains suggesting a corresponding state of affairs in the world of spirits. And there can be no doubt that the development of the great monarchies influenced the growth of monotheism. The very title, "king of kings," was reflected in the formula "God of gods." [12] Thus the term "God" is everywhere used to signify an exalted personality. How true this is today is evident from the fact that we think it a perfectly intelligible question to ask, without any preamble or explanation, "Does so-and-so believe in God?" [13] I make bold, therefore, to follow common usage, and to use the word "God" to designate a supreme Self.

To the further possible objection that usage should be so restricted as to apply only to a creative Being, I should reply as follows. Such a restriction would be both arbitrary and inconvenient; for the field of application would thereby be limited to Jewish, Christian, Muslim,

---

12. Cf., for example, Ps. 136:2.

13. It is to be observed that even such forms of pantheism as we find in Sufism and in the Advaita philosophy, while they do not recognize the reality of the individual self, do not deny that God is a Self. McTaggart is, then, fully justified in maintaining that for religion God is a Person. Nevertheless, he points out that some philosophers have employed the term "God" to signify ultimate reality when that reality is regarded as possessing an ordered structure, and not as a mere aggregation of entities. He has urged, however, that it is incumbent upon philosophy to follow the usage of religion for three reasons: (a) If the word "God" is deprived of its religious meaning there is no other word that can take its place, whereas the philosopher can always talk about the Absolute. (b) It is much easier to induce a small number of individuals to alter their usage than to persuade millions of people to do so. (c) The usage of philosophers has not been uniform, inasmuch as some—such as Kant and Lotze—have employed the word in its religious sense. (See *Some Dogmas of Religion* [London, 1906], sec. 153; *Studies in Hegelian Cosmology* [Cambridge, 1901], sec. 96; *The Nature of Existence* [Cambridge, 1927], Vol. II, sec. 153.) With his position I find myself in agreement. Professor Broad's objection to the effect that all Christians would then have to be classified as atheists is quite inadmissible for two reasons: (a) Not all Christians are Trinitarians. (b) Of those that are, in the orthodox sense, it might be correctly said that they are polytheists, but not that they are atheists.

and Zoroastrian theology. Students of comparative religion would then have to adopt and adapt some other term. For while the gods of primitive religion are frequently conceived as the *makers* of the world, the doctrine of creation *ex nihilo* is the product of an advanced stage of theological speculation. Moreover, the gods of polytheism are often represented as coming into being along with the world. Aristotle's God, again, is certainly not creative; yet it would clearly be misleading to classify Aristotle as an atheist. And the same is true of the late Professor Howison. Likewise the Nyāya, Vaiśeṣika, and Yoga philosophies could only with blatant inaccuracy be described as atheistic. Whether or not they be adaquate forms of theism is contestable, but theistic they certainly are.

The additional objection that the terms "atheism" and "atheistic" can be employed only in a pejorative sense, and that, accordingly, the content of the concept signified by the word "God" should be so expanded as to render it applicable to any and every type of religion must also be rejected. For no reproach which genuinely attaches to any school of thought can be removed by a mere verbal device. And if religion be what we take it to be, the contention is sheer nonsense. It may indeed be mistaken to hold that a harmony can obtain between what is highest in our nature and the universe as a whole except upon a basis of theism; yet, to classify those who do so believe as irreligious would be so to narrow the definition of religion as to render it practically useless. For our purposes, in any case, theism is to be equated with the belief in a supreme Self.

The Formulation of the Problem

If the word "creation" stands for no intelligible notion, the same will be true of the word "annihilation." Hence there will be beings that exist independently of God. In the literal sense of the word, therefore, God will not be omnipotent. Yet it is frequently said that the term "omnipotence" ought to be understood to mean only the ability to do whatever is not logically or ontologically impossible.[14] But from the adoption of such a usage, the only important result would be lack of clarity. On this point McTaggart's observation is fully justified:

When popular theology is pressed to reconcile the present exis-

14. If the actual usage of the term by competent theologians be taken into consideration, a strong case can be made out in support of this contention. For most, if not all, theologians have not employed it without qualification. (Cf. *The Nature of Existence*, II, 177, n. 1.)

tence of evil with the goodness of God, then it pleads that omnipotent does not mean omnipotent, but only very powerful. But when the sceptic has been crushed, and what is wanted is a belief in the future extinction of evil, then omnipotence slides back into its strict meaning, and it is triumphantly asserted that the cause which has an omnipotent God on its side must certainly win. The confusion is unintentional, no doubt, but it is dangerous.[15]

For the sake of clarity, therefore, let us recognize that a being whose power is limited in any respect cannot properly be called omnipotent. Consequently, a non-creative God cannot be omnipotent. Nevertheless, it is conceivable that his power might be very great. It is indeed conceivable that he might be able so to control the actions of all other beings as to render them practically his puppets. Yet, as McTaggart has pointed out, once we admit that God's power is limited in any respect and to any degree, we are faced with the question whether we can find any ground for determining how serious these limitations may be.[16] And if we are to account satisfactorily for the presence of evil in the universe, it seems clear that no course is open to us but to stress these limitations. But, then, where are we to stop? If we do not stop somewhere, we shall finally arrive at the concept of a God who is perfectly good yet practically impotent. This would surely be a *reductio ad absurdum* of our whole enterprise. Yet it is worth remembering that Aristotle's God exerts an influence upon the universe only as the final cause of motion, and that, absorbed in self-contemplation, he is altogether oblivious of the entire world. And the God of Averroes very closely resembles him.

Before we take up the intellectual challenge thus presented, let us look for a moment at the conceptions of God which we find in the Yoga, Nyāya, and Vaiśeṣika philosophies of India, for these conceptions are of peculiar interest to us. In the first place they do not play fast and loose with the notion of the self; by which I mean that there is no attempt on their part to reduce finite selves to mere appearances of a single, all-inclusive Self in the manner of the Advaita. Their view is frankly pluralistic; God—Īśvara, the Lord—is one self among other selves. There is no doctrine of creation in these philosophies; all selves are unoriginated and everlasting. Thus the various cosmic perspectives of these systems have much in common with that which has been developed here.

Let us, accordingly, turn our attention in the first place to the con-

15. *Some Dogmas of Religion*, sec. 179.   16. *Ibid.*, secs. 215, 217.

ception of God as we find it in the Yoga philosophy. The world process, as envisaged in this system, goes on practically "on its own." Although stimulated, it is not completely controlled by the divine Intelligence. In this process a multiplicity of souls have become entangled, and from it they seek to escape. Their bondage is due to intellectual confusion, to a failure to comprehend their own eternal status, and to discriminate between it and the realm of nature with its successive cycles of becoming. There is, however, a single, supreme Self whose clear vision is not distorted by error, who has not become entangled in the clutches of external nature, and who is not involved in the process of recurrent birth and death. This Self is Īśvara. Although he acts as a final cause—or part cause—of the evolutionary process, his chief role is a religious one. It is to function as the guide and helper of souls seeking to obtain deliverance from bondage, to escape from the wheel of birth and death. In utterly disinterested and unselfish kindness he extends to them his grace. Here we find, in its purest form, the conception of God as a Saviour.

The belief in such a God, Patañjali tells us, is to be encouraged because it accelerates the process of enlightenment. In fact the accusation has been made that it is intended to possess no more than a pragmatic truth.[17] However this may be, the figure of Īśvara seems well adapted to evoke trust and devotion in the highest sense of these words. While his capacity to help is limited, of his will to do there can be no question. He is the very embodiment of "mercy, pity, peace, and love." One might therefore expect that the beatific vision of Īśvara would form the content, or at least part of the content, of the state of *kaivalya*—i.e., of deliverance or salvation—even as it does for the Christian or Muslim mystic. The astonishing fact is that it does nothing of the sort. The state of liberation is not one of fellowship with Īśvara, nor yet with any other self; [18] it is one of complete psychological and ontological aloofness, as self-absorbed and self-satisfying as that of Aristotle's God.

The communion with his God which the Hebrew prophet or psalmist believed himself to enjoy was originally conceived to be confined to his life in this world; yet, as we have seen, out of its very intensity seems to have developed the conviction that a relationship so precious could not be transitory, but must be permanent, although, had it not been for the impact of Zoroastrianism, this development might not

17. See J. Estlin Carpenter, *Theism in Medieval India* (London, 1921), p. 216, n. 2.
18. *Ibid.*, p. 220, n. 2.

have taken place. In India, however, no such impact occurred, nor was it needed; for the doctrine of the underived existence of the soul was a generally accepted one, and a fundamental tenet of the Sāṁkhya philosophy, of which the Yoga was little more than a theistic deviation. The stage, then, seemed to be fully set for the appearance, against the background of the Yoga philosophy, of a doctrine of the Beatific Vision. Yet no such event occurred. Shall we attempt to explain its failure to occur by attributing a lack of emotional fire to the Indian character? Had we to deal only with the Buddhists, the Jains, the Sāṁkhyas, and the exponents of Jñāna-Yoga, such a hypothesis would by no means be devoid of plausibility. But the wide and enduring appeal of the Bhakti-Yoga shows unquestionably that the Hindu is capable of a strong emotional response; indeed, among the Arvars emotionalism has at times become perfectly maudlin. It may not be amiss to note, however, that Hindus, in common with Christians and Muslims, have tended to look upon emotional attachment to human beings as spiritually worthless—or at least of very subordinate value—and to place all their emphasis upon the love of God alone. Thus we might conclude that the Sāṁkhya, and other forms of the Jñāna-Yoga, appealed to those of a coldly intellectual temperament, while the Bhakti-Yoga attracted all those capable of an emotional enthusiasm, and that the theism of the Yoga philosophy was largely the expression of a pragmatic attitude. For the absence of emotion in the latter is certainly striking. The graciousness of Īśvara is apparently the expression of an altruism as personally uninvolved as was that of the Buddha himself; he is no more concerned to win the love of the souls he saves than a fireman is concerned with his personal relations with the people he rescues from a burning house. And the soul who, through Īśvara's grace, has attained deliverance seems to display neither gratitude nor devotion to its Saviour; quite contentedly it leaves him behind, and passes into eternal isolation.

When we turn to the Nyāya and Vaiśeṣika philosophies—and for our present purpose, these may, as is customary, be treated as one—we find the same attitude, if anything more intensified. Enlightenment is the prelude to complete loss of consciousness; liberation is identified with oblivion. Annihilation might be even more desirable, were that possible; but since the self is a simple and indestructible substance, it is clearly impossible. Consciousness, however, is an accident and can therefore be lost. And since life, even at its best, is more sorrowful than joyful, it is well lost. A delivered soul, then (as the great Advaitin, Saṁkara, scornfully remarks), will on this view have sunk to the same level as an inanimate stool. Were this all that we could find to repay our attention in the Nyāya-Vaiśeṣika philosophy, we need not have concerned ourselves with it.

But there is much more. For here we have the conception of a God who, although not creative, is yet capable of activity upon a cosmic scale; [19] of initiating the formation of an entire universe by bringing together souls, atoms, and universals in an evolutionary process which issues in an ordered world system; and when this system has decayed, and its various constituents have resumed an isolated existence, of once more uniting them—after a suitable period of rest (*pralaya*)—and sweeping them along in another process of world-making. Moreover, Īśvara is the guardian of the Law of Karma. For it is the contention of the Nyāya-Vaiśeṣikas, in opposition to the Buddhists, Jains, Sāṁkhyas, and Mīmāṁsakas, that this law, like other laws, requires an authority to enforce it; and in accordance with this contention, they have worked out a theory which provides one of the most satisfactory answers to the problem of evil which has ever been offered. It is Īśvara who, taking into consideration the merits and demerits which the individual soul has acquired in its previous lives, together with its capacities and incapacities, its strength and weaknesses, determines its rebirth in whatever situation, of those available, is most suited to it. The more one examines the conception of Īśvara in the Nyāya-Vaiśeṣika, the more one becomes impressed by its comprehensiveness and adequacy. The whole outlook is, indeed, amazingly reminiscent of that of Plato in the *Phaedrus*.

Yet the more one considers the three systems we have just scrutinized, the more apparent become both the strength and the weakness of absolute dualism. When contrasted with materialism or naturalism, on the one hand, and with creative theism, on the other, the impression made is a favorable one. There is a straightforward honesty about the position that is very appealing. There is no attempt by any verbal chicanery to disguise the impossibility of deriving life and consciousness from inanimate matter or from a divine fiat. The status of the soul as an ultimate constituent of the universe is frankly recognized and strongly insisted upon.

What disconcerts one is the absence of any recognition of the need for an integrated world view. This will not dismay the pure empiricist, but from the standpoint we have reached, it appears an obvious deficiency. Spirit and matter are ultimate, coexistent, and interactive;

19. In the Nyāya and Vaiśeṣika systems more emphasis is laid upon the cosmic activity of Īśvara than in the Yoga.

yet the existence of neither logically involves that of the other. And—what is of present concern to us—the existence of God is treated as a mere "brute fact." I am not now speaking of the arguments for divine existence; these we shall deal with later. But granted that they are all valid, it cannot but seem strange that a single self should thus be exalted above all others, and above the world process, and that it should be exempt, as no other self is exempt, from birth and death and transmigration. If one can really believe in creation, and convince oneself that both mind and matter enjoy only a derived existence which they owe to the efficacy of a common cause, then a certain systemic character is discernible in the universe; for there is an imparted rationality imposed by the divine volition, and self-existence is attributed to God because it has been denied to everything else, and because it seems obvious that an infinite ontological regress from contingent entity to contingent entity would be vicious. In the systems before us, however, there are so many self-existent entities, all of which are only externally related to each other!

In the Yoga system the conception of God is clearly introduced *ab extra*. It is dragged in "by the head and shoulders." Yet, once there, amazingly little is made of it. In the Nyāya-Vaiśeṣika metaphysics the conception plays a vastly greater role. Īśvara's power is simply enormous. It is true that he can create or destroy neither souls nor atoms, yet he can do almost anything else with them. Whether he can absolutely constrain and override the will of other selves is perhaps a moot point; yet it is clear that he would have no motive for doing so, since he would thereby destroy the free moral life of the individual. But he can bring souls and atoms together and make a universe out of them; and when that universe wears out and disintegrates, he can reassemble them, and so initiate the formation of another universe.

What support can be found for such an hypothesis? It would seem that its sole possible support might be the teleological argument. If we found everywhere evidences of intelligent purpose, we might be justified in inferring the existence of a supreme Mind. But in a universe in which there are innumerable beings which exist independently of Īśvara, how can we be sure just what events are indicative of a divine purpose? After all, there is evil in the universe. Moral evil may be accounted for by an appeal to free will. But what of pain and suffering? These in turn are supposed to be accounted for by the Law of Karma. And from this, we are told, the existence of Īśvara can be inferred, inasmuch as the law requires an authority to enforce it. But how do we know that there is a Law of Karma? We cannot establish its existence by our limited powers of observation. It would seem that it follows from the character of Īśvara. Now it is obvious that we cannot both infer the existence of Īśvara from the Law of Karma and infer the Law of Karma from the character of Īśvara. It would appear, then, that our basic contention must be that the presence of order in the physical universe cannot be accounted for by the random movements of unintelligent atoms, and that we are, therefore, compelled to resort to the theory of the existence of a supreme Mind as a principle of explanation.[20] This does not, however, remove the somewhat bizarre appearance of a universe in which co-existent and only externally related entities—atoms, souls, and Īśvara—are engaged in ceaseless interaction.

I have made this rather extended excursion into Indian philosophy in order to provide a background for the contention that the concept of a non-creative God of limited power cannot stand by itself as the logical *prius* of a whole cosmic system; although it may be possible to show that it requires to be included in any such system. No less earnest a theist than Dawes Hicks has declared that "what philosophers designate the 'Absolute' must include God and other minds, the world of nature and the world of values, not indeed as isolated and disconnected entities, but rather as intimately related to one another and more especially to God, and as thus forming a system or coherent unity." [21] If a successful defense of theism can be developed at all, it must surely be along such a line as this.

It is clear that no other view is open to us if the universe be, as I have argued, an axiologically oriented system. For it is clear that in such a universe, all particulars will be directly or indirectly interrelated by internal relations. Even if we appeal to the activity theory of causality, and work it for all it is worth, we cannot hope to escape this conclusion. For the evidence for the entailment view is too strong to be disregarded. The best we could hope for would be to show that the two could be combined. And then, if we adopted the theistic position, we might try to show that the universe was, so to speak, overbalanced in favor of one of its constituents. But this is the utmost we could reasonably expect to accomplish. And it is at least doubtful

20. That this theory is not devoid of some degree of plausibility, if the existence of matter be conceded, McTaggart himself explicitly admits in *Some Dogmas of Religion*, sec. 201.

21. *The Philosophical Bases of Theism* (London, 1937), p. 262.

whether we could accomplish so much as this. So far as the theistic hypothesis is concerned, the danger is that the systemic character of the universe, and its axiological orientation, may be found to render it otiose.

It may seem that this danger will be less acute if we admit the reality of matter. I have, indeed, urged that the panpsychic hypothesis is preferable, inasmuch as we do know that selves exist, and as, in either case, we have errors in perception to account for. But I do not claim to have demonstrated it. The notion of matter seems to be falling of its own weight; it is becoming daily more and more vague and elusive, and the dynamic element in it is, as it were, getting out of hand.[22] But I have argued that on the supposition that there are material entities, they, like neutral universals, will be included in the axiological "set" of the universe, and that their function will be a subordinate and instrumental one. I do not think, therefore, that theism can derive any valuable support from the belief in matter. It would appear more likely that a better case could be made out for it on the basis of panpsychism.

The issue which confronts us—and this I believe to be the crucial issue—is whether an adequate theory of the nature of the Absolute can be developed without employing the concept of God. And this, so it seems to me, is one which it is very difficult to decide, and which therefore requires to be handled very carefully. If I be right in arguing that the question of the existence of matter is a relatively unimportant one, the issue has so close an affinity to one drawn by McTaggart that it will help to clarify the situation if we consider his account thereof. In the first place, however, I propose to cite his statement of a prior issue—that between two forms of pluralistic idealism.

"We must distinguish," he tells us,

> two varieties of this doctrine. According to the first, the selves, taken separately, are spiritual, but they do not form a spiritual unity. They form a unity, no doubt, for they form the universe, and the universe is certainly more or less of a unity. But the arrangement of that unity is determined by laws of a purely mechanical nature. The relations in which selves find themselves with other selves are determined by laws analogous to those on which, according to the theory which accepts the existence of mat-

22. Its popular successor, its ghostly *simulacrum*, as I should call it, is the notion of *event*. But as I have already tried to show, any attempt to treat this as an ultimate notion is meaningless.

ter, one particle of such matter is brought into relation with other particles.

Having thus outlined one of the two opposing views McTaggart goes on to argue—mistakenly, I think—that it would be less difficult on this theory to avoid postulating the existence of God than it would if we concede the reality of matter, on the ground that the fundamental constituents of the universe would be conscious and active selves, more capable of uniting in an ordered system than lifeless material particles.

"But, while a directing mind," he continues,

> could thus be dispensed with, on this hypothesis, with less improbability than if matter really existed, there would still be the same difficulty in dispensing with it. We perceive traces of order which extend over such large areas of the universe, and which are so minute and exact in their arrangements, that it is impossible to regard them as due to the efforts of a single self no higher than we are. And it seems very difficult to suppose them due to the unconscious co-operation of many such selves, if the relations and juxtapositions of those selves are due to blind forces. On the other hand, if we suppose it to be due to the conscious co-operation of selves, we cannot suppose that those selves are no higher than our own, since the knowledge required in order to plan and carry out such a work would require far more than human capabilities. It is simpler and more probable to fall back on the supposition of a directing person—or possibly a plurality of such persons—of a much higher nature.[23]

In such a view the existence of God would be as much an inexplicable and "brute fact" as that of Īśvara. The theory is one which might conceivably be held by an empirical idealist but which would certainly not impress a rationalist as satisfactory.

McTaggart continues:

> But there is a third hypothesis. We may deny that matter exists, and we may deny that selves are only connected by blind forces. We may also hold that reality consists of a system of selves, and we may hold that the nature of that system can to some extent be determined. We may hold further that what we can determine about that system is such that it shows it to exhibit an order directed towards the production of something of spiritual signifi-

23. *Some Dogmas of Religion*, secs. 202–203.

cance and value—of something which is either completely good, or, at any rate, more good than bad. Such a view as this is the basis of the systems of Fichte, of Hegel, of Lotze.

Now, if we hold this view, it seems to me that the directing mind is not wanted at all to account for the traces of order in the universe. The nature of reality has been seen to be such that it inevitably manifests itself in order directed towards the good. It is a harmonious system—no longer a mere aggregate, whether of atoms or souls—and so it must manifest itself in order. And it is a system of such a nature that it is directed towards some end which is, on the whole, good. And therefore the order in which it manifests itself must be an order directed, to some degree at any rate, towards what is good.[24]

It is quite obvious, of course, that the description given above will apply to an axiologically oriented universe, and that, consequently, we have already definitely committed ourselves to the position thus outlined. Hence this issue between the claims of two conflicting forms of pluralistic idealism—an issue which, in my judgment, is only a preliminary one—is settled with relative ease. But now we come to the fundamental question.

McTaggart says that

the existence of such a harmonious system of selves would not *disprove* the existence of a directing God. It might well be that among those selves was one who, in goodness, wisdom, and power, so much excelled all the others that he might appropriately be called God. And so powerful a being would doubtless have a large share in carrying out the order of the universe. But, although the existence of a harmonious system of selves is not incompatible with the existence of a directing God, it is, as we have seen, incompatible with any possibility of proving his existence by the argument from design.[25] The order in the universe would be there, on this hypothesis, whether there was a God or not, and cannot, therefore, be used to prove his existence.[26]

The fundamental issue involved in our present inquiry, therefore, is simply whether or not the doctrine of an Absolute—which, for us,

24. *Ibid.*, sec. 204.
25. The truth of this statement might be called in question by one who dissented from McTaggart's determinism. As a matter of fact, Dawes Hicks, who definitely believed in a non-creative God, explicitly appeals to the argument from design. (See *The Philosophical Bases of Theism*, chap. vi.)
26. *Some Dogmas of Religion*, sec. 206.

is equivalent to that of an axiologically oriented cosmos—can be satis-factorily developed without including the concept of God. By calling the issue fundamental to our present inquiry I mean to indicate that in my opinion it is in this way that the theistic problem ought to be formulated. I certainly do not consider it the fundamental issue for the philosophy of religion. There the fundamental issue is the status of the self, its relation to the universe as a whole, and the destiny which awaits it. And if the position we have developed be sound, the answer to these questions has already been given, and will remain unaffected by whatever answer be returned to the question whether God exists.

This does not mean, however, that the question is not an important one. As we shall see, it has a very practical importance in present experience. But that the belief in God is not essential to religion is made clear by the fact that there are religions which do not embrace this belief—of such Hīnayāna Buddhism is of course the most im-pressive instance. Neither, unless I have argued in vain, is the belief essential to the metaphysical vindication of the claims of religion. Nonetheless it behooves us to settle the question if we can, and if we cannot, at least to try our hardest.

THE SIGNIFICANCE OF THE PROBLEM

That the problem has a genuine and profound importance both for religion and for philosophy is beyond question. Indeed, if the view of the relation of philosophy to religion which I have defended be sound, it could not be important for one and not be also important for the other. But in addition to this genuine importance, it possesses also, I hold, an illusory importance, an importance which is the result of the conquest of all Europe and of much of Asia and Africa by Christianity and Islam. Both these religions profess to be monotheistic. Islam cer-tainly is so. Orthodox Christianity claims to be so—insincerely, I think—but the result of the claim has been an intellectual muddle from which most orthodox Christians suffer.[27] Leaving this considera-tion aside, however, I would point out that for Christians and Muslims —as well as for Jews who adhere to their religion—the belief in God is beyond all comparison the most vital. All one's standards of right and wrong, all one's hopes of surviving death and of being united with one's loved ones in the life to come, all one's expectations of providen-tial guidance of oneself, one's kindred, one's country, and the human

27. It seems to me that Muslim theologians are fully justified in classifying *orthodox* Christianity, as they do, with the polytheistic religions. What *genuine* Christianity is, of course, is another question.

race depend upon the truth of this one basic tenet. God is the alpha and omega, the beginning and the end, of all one's thoughts and aspirations. For to the average occidental theist, and to the average Muslim as well, the only alternative to theism is materialism or naturalism. From our point of view, however, this is a complete mistake. Our recognition of moral values, our assurance of immortality and of reunion with our beloved, even our hopes of world progress, are independent of our belief in God.

There is indeed a strange and distant resemblance between our position and that of the Yoga philosophy. In the case of the Yoga it is the very absence of any conception of the Absolute, of any coherent and logical structure in the universe, which renders so groundless and arbitrary the introduction of the idea of God; the latter seeming to descend *ab extra* like a metaphysical diving bell lowered into a cosmic ocean. In our case, on the other hand, the apparently groundless and arbitrary character of the theistic hypothesis is due to the closely knit axiological structure of the universe as we envisage it. We have now to ask whether the impression thus produced be the offspring of too hasty a judgment, and whether it need be modified.

There is, moreover, another respect in which the position of the Yoga philosophy may ultimately be seen to resemble our own. For as a theist, the Yogin is concerned with the grace which may be proffered him and the aid which he may receive from Īśvara on his way to deliverance. He is like a drowning man crying for help, and like the drowning man, when he has been rescued, he has no further need of a Saviour. Yet most drowning men, we hope, would be grateful to a rescuer. The indifference of the Yogin impresses us as extraordinary. But we must remember that for him, as for the Sāṁkhya and the Buddhist, every attachment to an embodied self is regarded as a tie which draws one back to reincarnation, and which therefore must be cut. And Īśvara, despite his transcendent status and his exemption from death and rebirth, is treated in this respect like any other self. We may well ask how it is that on what one would suppose to be so fertile a soil, no form of the Bhakti cult ever flourished, but I do not know the answer. It may be that all to whom the Bhakti cult appealed were attracted to a more vigorous form of theism in which the Deity filled a larger role, or it may be that those are right who consider that the concept of God in the Yoga was in the nature of a pragmatic device which was not intended to be taken too seriously.

As we envisage the situation, however, the axiological "set" of the universe and the supreme value of love guarantee the all-satisfying character of the final experience. There is no need to invoke the agency of God. But does it follow that love for God will not form part of the content of that experience?

I shall postpone an attempt to answer this question till a later stage of our discussion. What I wish now to emphasize is the undoubted and obvious fact that trust in a living and benevolent God plays a tremendous part in the daily life of the believer. It played such a part, indeed, even before the rise of monotheism, and long before the concept of "laws of nature" had caused the notion of "miracle" to acquire the definiteness which it had for Locke; and it has continued to play it even to the present day. This is a fact to the significance of which "liberal" thinkers frequently appear strangely blind. To one who reads their writings it often seems that the notion of natural law is invested for them with a strange and awesome majesty, in the light of which the suggestion that the Deity might intervene in particular circumstances and might use his power to deliver the individual involved in overwhelming difficulties is rejected as utterly derogatory to the very idea of God. The believer, it would seem, is expected to acquiesce in whatever may befall him out of reverence for "laws which never can be broken." Yet there is surely something grotesque in the notion that God has thus entangled himself in the laws of which he is the author like a kitten in a ball of string. The natural utterances of piety tell a very different story of the attitude of the believer.

"Some trust in chariots, and some in horses: but we will remember the name of the Lord our God.

They are brought down and fallen; but we are risen, and stand upright." [28]

"Give us help from trouble: for vain is the help of man.

Through God we shall do valiantly: for he it is that shall tread down our enemies." [29]

"With heaven it is all one, to save by many or by few: for victory in battle standeth not in the multitude of a host; but strength is from heaven." [30]

"Except the Lord build the house, they labour in vain that build it: except the Lord keep the city, the watchman waketh but in vain." [31]

These, it may be said, are the expressions of a national, or at least of a communal, consciousness; they reveal only the primitive belief in a God of the nation, the tribe, or the family. But again the language of piety contradicts the objector.

28. Ps. 20:7–8.
30. I Macc. 3:18–19.

29. Ps. 60:11–12.
31. Ps. 127:1.

"The steps of a good man are ordered by the Lord: and he delighteth in his way.

Though he fall, he shall not be utterly cast down: for the Lord upholdeth him with his hand." [32]

"This poor man cried, and the Lord heard him, and saved him out of all his troubles." [33]

"By thee have I run through a troop; and by my God have I leaped over a wall." [34]

"The supplication of a righteous man availeth much in its working. Elijah was a man with like passions with us, and he prayed fervently that it might not rain; and it rained not on the earth for three years and six months. And he prayed again; and the heaven gave rain, and the earth brought forth her fruit." [35]

Citations such as these could be multiplied *ad nauseam*. The Sufi mystics who permitted themselves to starve to death rather than ask for food because to do so would be a breach of trust bear startling witness to the deeply rooted nature of this belief in Providence. I am not now concerned with its truth. What I wish to emphasize is its importance. And in some form it is held by practically all those who believe in a personal God. For even those who consider that it would be "infra dig" for God to infringe for any purpose whatever one of his own natural laws yet would admit that he can strengthen one's spirit and enlighten one's mind. Even the atheistic religions of India do not deny to their adherents the hope of divine aid; for they admit the existence of "gods" in the sense of superhuman beings who, although they themselves stand in need of salvation, are yet not without efficacy in this world.

RELIGIOUS EXPERIENCE AND THE PROBLEM OF GOD

Reflections such as these may well suggest that the proper approach to the question of theism is through religious experience. This, however, may take either of two forms. In the first place we may investigate, as well as we can, the nature of religious experience as reported by those who have enjoyed it, with the object of assembling data upon which to base an argument for the existence of God.[36] Or in the second place, we may turn from the effort to demonstrate to the experience itself. This we may regard as self-authenticating, and even as provid-

32. Ps. 37:23–24. 33. Ps. 33:6.
34. Ps. 18:29. 35. Jas. 5:15–17.
36. The late Dean Inge was an outstanding advocate of this procedure.

ing the only ground of assurance. The two ways are not necessarily mutually exclusive; indeed it is obvious that for the *argumentum ex experientia religiosa* to get under way at all it must presuppose the possibility of direct experience of the divine. Yet one who believes himself to have been granted such an experience may be prepared to regard as worthless all attempts at proof.

We recognize, of course, that a conflict will break out between those who accord to one of these two ways superiority over the other and those who take the precisely opposite view. But both parties will be united in opposition to those who dismiss all religious experience as illusory.

Throughout the history of Christian thought there has been a continuous struggle between adherents of the Platonic-Augustinian tradition, on the one hand, and adherents of the Aristotelian-Thomistic tradition, on the other, the former emphasizing the mystical approach and the latter the logical. The influence of Thomism had gone far to sway the balance in its own favor when, at the beginning of the modern period, the opposing tendency produced two powerful intellectual explosions, one in the Protestant and the other in the Roman Catholic camp. The explosion which took place in the Protestant camp was detonated by John Calvin, that which took place in the Roman Catholic camp by Malebranche. Similar in origin and inspiration as the resultant movements were, their fates have been very different. The tremendous emphasis laid by Calvinism upon religious experience has profoundly affected the entire Protestant world; even the Arminians felt its influence. Ontologism, on the other hand, despite the valiant defense conducted by Malebranche's successors, was slowly overwhelmed by the resurgent tide of Thomism, and was at last formally condemned as a heterodoxy in 1861. Insofar as any crude generalization is ever true, it is true to say that the chief difference between the orthodox Protestant and the Roman Catholic is that the basic appeal of the former is to religious experience and that of the latter to reason.[37]

By saying this I have no intention of suggesting that the Roman Catholic does not attach a high evaluation to religious experience. Quite the contrary is true; the Roman Catholic Church has been a

37. It is true that for the Roman Catholic the domain of reason is limited. When he passes from natural theology to revealed theology his allegiance is no longer to reason but to faith. And faith, for the Roman Catholic, is primarily volitional, whereas for the genuine Calvinist, it is primarily intuitive. Nevertheless, for the Roman Catholic all depends on reason in the sense that reason does demonstrate the existence of God, for as St. Thomas points out, we cannot have faith in God until we know that he exists.

very forcing house of mysticism. The spiritual life has been studied, attempts have been made to discriminate the successive stages of its development, and through the confessional the accumulated wisdom of centuries has been placed at the service of the individual aspirant to divine union; whereas the average Protestant has been left very much to his own devices. Nevertheless, the Thomist emphatically insists that religious experience can be properly evaluated only in the light of a concept of God antecedently arrived at by valid inference from data supplied by sense experience. The idea of God, he contends, is not an article of faith; it is a preamble to the articles. Faith, which is "the assent of the intellect at the command of the will," presupposes knowledge.[38] Hence, even the argument from religious experience, although it admittedly lends itself to rhetorical use by a preacher seeking to quicken the hearts and minds of his congregation, is not deemed conclusive by a Thomistic philosopher or theologian. Unenlightened by reason, we are told, religious experience provides no sufficient criterion for distinguishing between truth and error.

This is clearly a position for which there is much to be said; and which, to the philosopher, has much to commend it. When we turn, however, to examine the attitude of Calvinism, we find ourselves at the opposite extreme. The Calvinist totally repudiates the rationalistic approach.[39] No argument for the existence of God, he observes, has yet convinced everybody. Moreover, even could a conclusive argument be formulated—and if pressed the Calvinist may concede the possibility [40]—such an achievement would be indicative of presumption upon our part, inasmuch as God has already revealed himself, and can rightfully claim our acknowledgment of this fact and our belief in his word.[41] But how can we be sure that God has revealed himself unless we be sure that he exists, and how can we be sure that God exists if it be illegitimate even to attempt to demonstrate his existence? For the Calvinist God is the object of faith. And if faith meant for him what it means to the Roman Catholic, his attitude would be one of the most barefaced and shameless wishful thinking. But such is not the case, since, for the Calvinist, faith is primarily intuitive, not volitional. It involves the direct apprehension of supersensible reality. The very cornerstone upon which Calvin's system is built is the *testimonium Spiritus Sancti internum.*

38. *Sum. Theol.*, I. a. q. 2: a. 2. ad. I^m.
39. The Confession of Rochelle, Art. IX.
40. See August Lecerf, *Introduction à la dogmatique reformée* (Paris, 1931), I, 46.
41. *Ibid.*, pp. 51–52.

This awareness of the divine is not rooted in any native faculty or capacity of human nature; [42] on the contrary, it definitely exceeds the scope of any such power, it is something imparted to man from without. It is a gift of divine grace. To all normal human beings some measure of divine illumination is granted, for it is only as thus enlightened that man can think of God at all. To the elect, however, is given an illumination far more intense and pure. It is an illumination which is axiological in nature, and it enables the elect to discern in the Scriptures the very reflection of the divine glory. The same Spirit, says Calvin, that spoke through the prophets and thereby gave us the Scriptures, supplies through this subjective illumination its authentication of them as the word of God. God thus bears witness to himself.

This fundamental doctrine received further development at the hands of Jonathan Edwards. Making use of Locke's teaching with respect to ideas of the third type, which are the product neither of sensation nor of reflection, but which—if they be real at all—are directly communicated to the mind by the power of God, Edwards insists that the idea thus imparted by the witness of the Spirit is "different from all that can be in the minds of natural men." It is not, he tells us, "notional," by which he seems clearly to mean that it is not of logical import. By means of it no information is imparted to the recipient. Its content is axiological. It is a sense of "the beauty of holiness." About the word "holiness" there still lingers something of the primitive connotation of *taboo;* yet to it now attach the notions of purity and perfection. And to these Edwards has joined the notion of beauty. It would seem that he is thereby reviving for us the Platonic problem of the relation of the Form of the Good to the Form of Beauty. Is one subsumed under the other? If so, which includes which? Is beauty only the lure of goodness? Or is goodness only beauty imperfectly apprehended? Or are both at bottom identical? However we answer these questions, it is clear that the experience Edwards seeks to describe is a tremendous one. Well may he liken it to "opening the blind eyes, raising the dead, and bringing a person into a new world."

It is this basic doctrine which gives to the study of Calvinism its peculiar charm. Here is a religion which dares to found itself upon the mystical experience and—officially at least—upon nothing else. It

---

42. Thus Lecerf assures us that religious feeling, when unenlightened by grace, is one of the most fruitful sources of error (*ibid.*, p. 46), and in the appeal thereto on the part of "Neo-Protestantism," he sees a definite departure from the basic principle of the Reformation (*ibid.*, pp. 38–43).

gives, of course, its own interpretation of that experience; yet it is obviously an interpretation of something real and genuine. And as always when the door is thrown open to mysticism, a wind sweeps in so vital as well nigh to carry us away. Yet this, Calvin assures us, is what every Christian experiences; hence every Christian will know what he is talking about.

How is one to respond to this claim? All the Thomistic arguments seem like so many brown leaves which the living whirlwind sweeps from the floor. Should that whirlwind seize upon us, we are told that it will bear us to a height at which all those capacities ruined by the Fall will be restored to their pristine efficacy, and where we shall become experientially aware of the meaning of the words "adoption" and "sanctification." It is the immense vitality which comes from this appeal to direct experience that renders Calvinism so impressive. And is not all its secret hidden in a single sentence of St. Paul's, "If any man be in Christ he is a new creature"?

When Calvin blows his trumpet and Edwards strikes his lyre one feels very much the same kind of emotional excitement as when one reads Diotima's words to Socrates. As Plato puts it in the *Phaedrus,* "the wings of the soul begin to sprout." Yet this does not absolve the philosopher from his critical task, even though he may feel like a grammarian analyzing a poem. He may begin, however, by modestly pointing out that even if it be true that all genuine Calvinists are mystics, it is also true that there are many so-called Calvinists who are not genuine, and many mystics who are not Calvinists. Why should the Calvinist ask us to accept his interpretation of an experience which, however exalted, is shared by relatively few, and which, for all that we can tell, may be at bottom the same as that of other mystical folk who give it a different interpretation? The Calvinist may answer that he does not ask us to do anything, that if we be of the elect, we will sooner or later share his experience and will then know what to think of it, and if we be not of the elect, there is no use in his talking to us. Undismayed by this rejoinder we may still ask the Calvinist why he is so sure that his insight is veridical. Has he directly apprehended God as he is in himself? The reply is definitely no. In common with St. Thomas—at least with St. Thomas in a certain mood—Calvin denies that the divine Essence can be directly intuited in this life. It is only a kind of reflection thereof that is discerned in the Scriptures by the illumined man. That the Deity is its source is therefore a matter of inference—of inevitable, of utterly convincing evidence, it may be claimed—yet we know that inferences can be mistaken. Why, then, all this talk of certitude? Why is the Calvinist so sure that his vision is not the projection of his own spiritual state? The Thomistic assertion that such an experience can be rightly evaluated only upon the basis of a theistic position established by metaphysical investigation now seems to breathe forth the very spirit of sound good sense.

There is, in truth, an extraordinary similarity between the position of the Calvinist and that of the Advaitin. Why, we ask the Advaitin, are the Vedas to be credited, why should we recognize in them the ultimate religious authority? Because of their antiquity, he replies, because of their beauty, nobility, and majesty. In how very similar language does the Calvinist extol the excellence of his own Scriptures! Why, we again inquire of the Advaitin, should we believe in Brahma? Because the Vedas tell us to do so, he rejoins. And is not the Calvinist logically compelled to give a like answer? For, plainly, he cannot both believe in the inspiration of the Bible because of the attestation of God and believe in God because of the testimony of the Bible. Belief in one must be prior to belief in the other. Moreover, the Calvinist has denied himself any access to God except through the Scriptures. He is fully justified in developing upon the basis of the Scriptures any argument which they are able to support—even as he would be justified in developing upon any other basis any argument which it could support—but there is no getting over the fact that it *is* an argument. His claim to direct intuitive knowledge of the divine is therefore, to say the least, gravely compromised. There is too much "sound and fury" about Calvinism; and when one looks at it closely, too much wishful thinking.

When we turn to ontologism we find an outlook which is somewhat akin to that of Calvinism. The ontologist definitely claims that there is a direct awareness of God; but this awareness—unlike that of the Calvinist—is not supernatural but natural, pertaining to human nature as such. Moreover, it is a confused awareness. On closer examination we discover that ontologism is not all of one piece, that there are no less than three varieties of it. In its most extreme and uncompromising form it is known to neoscholastics as *ontologismus rigidus,* and its outstanding exponent is of course Malebranche. According to this doctrine we are never directly acquainted with physical objects, but only with the archetypal ideas of them in the mind of God; hence, Malebranche maintains, the only justification for believing in a material world is to be found in revelation. A more moderate form of ontologism, termed by neoscholastics *ontologismus mitigatus,* admits direct acquaintance through sensation with physical objects, yet maintains, in opposition to the traditional Thomist view, that it is quite incredible that our knowledge of universals should be acquired by any process of abstraction from sensible particulars—a contention quite in accord with our own position—and, consequently, that they must be known as objects of contemplation to the divine Intelligence, whose experience in this respect we are permitted to share. Third and lastly, there is the *ontologismus idealista* of Rosmini, which holds that the object of direct awareness shared by all men is not the Essence but the concept of God.[43]

As one would expect, we can find in the Protestant world approximations of the same general point of view. Thus we find William Ernest Hocking maintaining that "it is through the knowledge of God that I am able to know men; not first through the knowledge of men that I am able to know or imagine God."[44] Again we discover in Rudolf Otto's *The Idea of the Holy* the doctrine that "the numinous" is a concept not derivable from experience but imposed upon experience, one which forms part of the natural endowment of the human mind, and which is thus innate and a priori. Here we have what appears to be a Protestant counterpart of the *ontologismus idealista* of Rosmini.

At first sight the various forms of ontologism, together with kindred manifestations of the same tendency in Protestant thought, may seem to be highly implausible, and to amount to nothing more than extravagant wishful thinking. But a more careful scrutiny will, I believe, convince us that this is an unfair estimate, and that they are all theories deserving of respectful consideration. By way of analogy let

43. As adherents of traditional orthodoxy the ontologists were confronted by a difficulty arising out of the doctrine that the divine Essence is absolutely simple. It would seem, therefore, that *any* apprehension of God must be complete and adequate. But to admit this would be equivalent to asserting that all men are now in heaven, for the *Visio Dei is* heaven. Moreover, if God be a Trinity, direct awareness of the divine Essence would surely involve a direct awareness of the Trinity; a supposition incompatible with the Thomistic view that the doctrine of the Trinity does not fall within natural theology and cannot be demonstrated by human reason but must be received by faith. Ontologists, however, could appeal to Aquinas' explicit assertion that it is possible for one spirit to apprehend God more perfectly than another (*Con. Gen.*, Book III, chap. lviii). Difficult as it is to reconcile this statement with the doctrine of the divine simplicity, we might interpret it on the analogy of degrees of vividness or brightness. But in any case, it is clear that for St. Thomas a perfect knowledge of God would involve a knowledge of all genera and species (*ibid.*, chap. lix). In disclaiming any such knowledge the ontologist is surely on safe ground. His difficulty is rather to show how there can be partial or imperfect knowledge of a wholly simple Being. But the arguments for and against his position, advanced upon the basis of a Thomistic theology, do not now concern us.

44. *The Meaning of God in Human Experience* (New Haven, 1912), pp. 297–298.

me refer to the realistic theory of universals. I have already ventured to argue that it is the only tenable view; and I do not propose to recapitulate the argument here. But if the supposition that I have been right in so arguing may for the moment be entertained, I would call attention to the fact that on this supposition, not only the man in the street who is utterly ignorant of the meaning of the term "universal," but also the nominalist and the conceptualist, both of whom explicitly deny the subsistence of any such entities *in rerum natura*, must nevertheless in a confused—doubtless in a very confused —way be aware of universals. Otherwise they could not even make use of words, but would be completely tongue-tied. If this actually be the case—and I respectfully submit that it *is* the case—then it is not so astonishing if the ontologist's contention that every atheist is in fact directly, yet confusedly, aware of God, without realizing that he is so, should turn out to be true.

Of the three varieties of ontologism the first two are the more interesting. For Rosmini, like Otto, makes great play with the idea or concept of God; and for both these thinkers it seems clear that this concept is an ontological entity. Such a view is, of course, in complete accordance with the conceptualist doctrine of universals. I have said what I think of this doctrine and shall not repeat my criticism. But if the criticism be just, there is no reason to believe that there is, and every reason to believe that there is not, such an ontological entity as a concept.

Both "rigid" and "mitigated" ontologism reject the Thomistic [45] doctrine that universals are abstracted from sensible particulars, and in so doing they are, I believe, profoundly right. But in company with the Neo-Platonists, the medievals, and many modern thinkers, they are unable or unwilling to conceive of universals as self-subsistent entities, and, accordingly, find a *locus* for them in the divine Intelligence. This involves the assumption that the *being* of universals consists in *being known*, which is, I should maintain, nothing other than the notion of creation under a different name.

This conclusion, however, does not dispose of our problem. For we may still ask whether there be in fact such an experience as direct awareness of God. Yet we see now whither we are drifting. We began by inquiring whether God may be directly apprehended, in which case there would be no need to prove his existence—at least those

---

45. This "moderate realism," as neoscholastics habitually call it, is, so far as I can see, identical with what is usually called "conceptualism." As used by neoscholastics the term "conceptualism" designates rather the position of Kant.

who enjoyed the experience, and recognized it for what it was, would have no need. But now we are asking, or are at least well on the way to asking, what evidence there is for direct experience of the divine. In other words, we are passing from the stage of perception to that of argument. And the argument which, it would seem, we are ready to formulate is the *argumentum ex experientia religiosa.*

It is, of course, conceivable that for the individual his experience may be self-authenticating; although those who do not share it will not know how to appraise it. Nontheless, the individual will do well to recognize that to draw the line between the ultimate data of experience and the process of interpreting these data is a very delicate and difficult business. It behooves him to be neither too self-confident nor too self-distrustful. As Dawes Hicks has well written,

> We have noted that in sense-experience the merely "given" factors, if such there be, constitute a relatively small part of the content experienced, and that taken alone they would constitute no experience. It is essential that the cognitive activity of the individual experiencing subject should come into play, grasping or recognizing the revelations of sense, comparing and combining them, and interpreting them as features of some actual fact. And, if in religious experience there be revelations of a supersensuous kind, we can hardly conceive that *recognition* of them as such is also, along with them, communicated, or imported, so to speak, ready made into the mind without the operation on the individual's part of any process of intellection. Rather are we constrained to acknowledge that such recognition must imply, as recognition in all other cases implies, the exercise of cognitive activity, that what is "given" is only experienced as a revelation through the agency of reflexion, which discriminates its contents and interprets it by notions that are capable of being connected with those which we bring to bear upon our environment generally. However impressive and awe-inspiring an experience may have been, however persuaded the experient may be that what he experienced was a divine manifestation, still the conviction that it was so is *his* conviction; and, like every other conviction of his, not exempt from the possibility of error and illusion.[46]

It is sometimes no easy matter to tell precisely of what we are certain. For certitude may cover, as it were, an area of knowledge,

46. *The Philosophical Bases of Theism*, pp. 46–47.

and yet what falls within that area may be relatively indefinite. I may be quite sure that duty requires me to act and yet be quite uncertain as to which of several possible acts it is that I ought to perform. Or take the case of a general who has to decide whether to bomb a beautiful and historic building which is a nest of enemy sharpshooters. From a military point of view his duty is clear. From an aesthetic point of view it is clear also. Yet the two judgments are in conflict. Most of us, probably, would consider that the Americans were right in shelling Monte Cassino. But would we commend the Venetians for blowing up the Parthenon? Now, even as we may be certain that we ought to do something and yet be uncertain as to what that something is, so we may be certain that a spiritual experience which we have undergone is very meaningful, and yet be uncertain as to what that meaning is. Can we be sure where to draw the line between the data to be interpreted and the interpretation we feel impelled to place upon them? And can we be sure that the interpretation which commends itself to us is the only plausible one, or even the most plausible? With regard to these questions McTaggart has made some very relevant observations.

A man may be confused as to what it is of which he is immediately certain. He may think that his immediate certainty is of the **existence of a personal God**, when, in his case, it may be only that the ultimate reality is spiritual. That an ultimate spiritual reality must necessarily be a personal God may be a proposition which he believes on account of reasons—or which, perhaps, when clearly stated, he is not prepared to accept at all.

Or, again, closer analysis may convince him that the proposition, of which he supposed himself to have an immediate certainty, is really dependent for him upon other propositions. If it can be proved to him that he was not justified in basing it on those other propositions—either because they are false, or because it does not properly follow from them—he will abandon the result which he had previously thought beyond the reach of argument.

So far we have assumed that a belief which is immediate—that is, which does not rest on arguments—cannot be shaken by them. But an immediate belief may rest upon prejudices or tradition. (Of course, if tradition is explicitly accepted as likely to lead to truth, then it is a reason for belief, whether it is a good reason or not, and the conclusion is not immediate. But when a man believes a tradition merely because it has never occurred to him to question it, then the tradition is not a reason for belief, though it is a cause.) Now a belief of this sort, although it does not rest on arguments, may be shaken by them. For it may be shown that it is caused by prejudice or tradition, and this demonstration—though it refutes no arguments for the belief, since there were none to refute—may cause the believer to change his opinion.

The result at which I arrive is that the statement, that any man has an immediate conviction on a matter of religious dogma is one which he ought not to expect to have any relevance for others, and which he ought only to make, even for his own guidance, after careful tests have convinced him, in the first place, of what his belief really is, and in the second place, that it is not based on arguments. Even then, he ought not to consider the matter closed, unless equally careful tests have also convinced him that his immediate conviction is not to be shaken by arguments.[47]

This, of course, is not to be understood to mean that we can never be certain of anything, but only that we have no right to claim certitude unless we have subjected our experience to critical scrutiny. What we have to avoid above all things is intellectual confusion, and this requires a scrupulous vigilance. But if, after we have taken all precautionary measures, certitude remain, there is an end of the matter.[48] Hence, if any man have an immediate certainty of the existence of God, he is dispensed from the necessity of arguing on behalf of the divine existence; yet his neighbor, who has no such immediate certainty, is not so dispensed, but, if he believes, may legitimately be expected to furnish some reason for his belief.

47. *Some Dogmas of Religion*, sec. 36.
48. As McTaggart points out (*ibid.*, sec. 37), we must have some immediate certainties; otherwise every argument would involve us in an infinite regress, and so no knowledge would be possible. But it does not follow, as he also points out, that we must have immediate certainty of the truth of any *religious* belief.

CHAPTER TWO

THE ARGUMENT FROM
RELIGIOUS EXPERIENCE

The preceding discussion has led us to the point of broaching this famous argument, for the transition is easily made from considering the claims of religious experience upon him who has it to the consideration of what claims may rightfully be made in its name upon him who has it not. The argument is, of course, based upon the findings of comparative religion. Everywhere, among all peoples and in all ages, we find individuals who believe themselves to be in contact, or in communication with, the superhuman and the divine. In the case of the great religions this experience seems to have become deepened and intensified. Many of those who partook of it have been outstanding figures in the history of religion and of philosophy; the list of their names constitutes a veritable bead-roll of the most potent personalities in the development of civilizations. Is not the inference that these tremendous individuals were not self-deceived, that they were, as they claimed to be, actually in contact with supreme reality, an inescapable inference?

By way of reinforcement an analogy is often drawn from the arts—from music, painting, sculpture, and poetry. However lamentably deficient our own capacities of performance in these fields may be, or however rudimentary may be our own powers of appreciation, we should be unmitigated vulgarians were we to affect to despise or ridicule the achievements of great men whose contributions constitute the world's cultural treasure. Is not the same true in the field of religion? Must we not acknowledge the prophets and saints as the spiritual pioneers of our race, and be profoundly grateful for the reflected light which they shed upon us who stand in the shadow? And must we not therefore accept their testimony at its face value?

There are several things to be said about this argument. In the first place it is based upon data supplied by the actual practice of religion. And in this there seems a peculiar fittingness. The Thomists' insistence that religious experience is not only not self-authenticating, but that it is also incapable of providing a point of departure for any conclusive argument for the existence of God, is apt to produce an unfavorable impression. It seems expressive of an extremist attitude. The contention that what the theist regards as the very foundation of his whole world view can be established only by arguments based upon data pertaining to other fields than that of religion itself appears to involve an astounding admission. Cannot religion, we may ask, stand on its own feet? Unless it be an illusion, religion must surely be the most vital thing in the world. Shall it, then, go cap in hand to the metaphysician to beg credentials of intellectual respectability? If the Calvinist and the ontologist have overstated their case, still religion ought to be able to provide from its own resources a foundation sufficient for an honest thinker to build thereon a conclusive argument.

This seems to me a not unreasonable expectation on the part of a conventionally minded inquirer. By one who adopts the position we have reached it can indeed be entertained only in a modified form, inasmuch as we do not regard theism as essential to religion. Nonetheless, we may be inclined to argue that if the theist's position be sound, religion itself ought to provide some evidence for it.

When we look at the argument again, however, we see that from the nature of the case, it cannot provide absolute demonstration, that at best it can yield only some degree of probability. But can it yield any significant degree of probability? Granted that a number of individuals profess to have immediate certainty of the divine existence, what are we to make of this? If we avail ourselves of the analogy of art, we shall note that musical composers, painters, and sculptors—in other words, those who are productive—are much fewer in number than the many who are unproductive. If we try to find an analogous distinction in the sphere of religion, it would seem that we must classify as productive the great prophetic figures, those charged with a sense of mission. Yet is such a distinction, however valid, relevant from the point of view of our present interest? For the broader basis which we can give to our argument the better. Now the class of prophets who believe themselves entrusted with a message to deliver to mankind is not only numerically smaller than the class composed of all those who profess to have enjoyed a direct experience of the divine, it is also included within the larger class; and is it not this larger and inclusive class which must furnish the basis for our argument?

Yet can we not develop somewhat further the analogy with aesthetic experience? Were it not the case that the artist exemplifies a capacity which in a far lower degree the many share he would be treated as a harmless eccentric and, instead of admiration and gratitude, would ex-cite only contempt. And is not the world-wide prevalence of religion in like manner indicative of a native capacity, in however rudimentary a degree, of the average human being for spiritual insight; otherwise would not the seers and prophets speak to deaf ears, and would not the saints be treated as madmen? In other words, is not the assumption that the majority take their religion entirely at second hand patently absurd? Must we not assume in every man at least the potential capacity for religious experience?

Put in this way the argument appears to possess considerable force. Granted that at times the influence of religion upon society is seen to wane, such a state of affairs has in the past always been transitory, and has always been followed by a period of renewed vitality.[1] If we can infer anything about the future from our knowledge of the past may we not legitimately expect the same process to continue indefinitely? Could we, indeed, with any plausibility assume that the influence of religion is due to mistaken beliefs about the nature of the physical world, our conviction might well be shaken. But the evidence is all the other way. Not only do we find man religious alike in sorrow and in joy, in disaster and in prosperity, in despair and in triumph; we also observe that religion has kept pace with his intellectual and moral improvement, and that the development of the great world religions has constituted his most outstanding achievement. As far back as we know anything about him man has always been religious, and we can feel quite confident that he always will be. This is indeed a weighty consideration to oppose to the claims of materialists and naturalists, and it is one to which I shall presently return.

Observe, however, the limitations of the argument. Does our assurance that man is inherently and ineradicably religious give us any ground for choosing between various religious perspectives? Is it not plain that it does not? I do not intend to suggest that we might as reasonably revert to human sacrifice, cannibalism, orgiastic festivals, and the worship of trees, rivers, and mountains as embrace Christianity or Islam. The great world religions, however profoundly they differ among themselves, represent a tremendous advance upon the standpoint of primitive man—or even of early civilized man. What I do mean to assert is that our conclusion that human nature is inherently adapted to breathing a spiritual atmosphere can just as easily be exploited by pantheists and by atheistic Buddhists and Hindus as

1. The anxiety of the linguistic analysts to cover their retreat from the extreme position they once so confidently occupied, and to abate their claim to have demolished metaphysics, is indicative of the sort of thing to which I refer.

by theists. It will play equally into the hands of all these. If we want to make out a case for theism—and this is the topic of the present chapter—it is clear that we must do one of two things. Either we must go outside the field of religion and seek in alien territory some foundation adequate to sustain some other argument for the existence of God, or else we must proceed to explore religious experience in its most intense and highly developed form—namely, in mysticism—in the hope of finding there the evidence which has so far eluded us.

If we resolve upon the latter course—and this we must do, or confess ourselves defeated—we must first take cognizance of one of the most perplexing of the questions which face us. Is there such a thing as *the* mystical experience? Were it the case that the mystics of all the great religions, regardless of profound discrepancies in metaphysical and theological outlook, agreed in their accounts of their experiences and in their interpretation thereof, this would certainly be an impressive fact. Yet, as everyone knows, the situation is quite the contrary. The opposite tendencies of theism and pantheism manifest themselves in Buddhism, in Christianity, in Hinduism, and in Islam. The atheistic type of mysticism does, indeed, appear to be largely confined to India where the philosophical background is not unfavorable to it, but the other two types are practically ubiquitous. The relevant question, therefore, would seem to be: Is the experience in itself everywhere and always one and the same, and are the differences in interpretation to be attributed solely to preconceived philosophical and theological ideas which are imposed upon it; or are there several distinct types of mystical experience, and do these divergences in type account in whole or in part for the divergences in interpretation?

Dr. Ewing has made the very interesting suggestion [2] that some of the discrepancies between the reports of mystical experiences might be accounted for on the supposition that there are actually two modes of such experience, each with its own object; in one case the object being the Absolute, in the other a personal God. Of these two hypothetical modes he has written, "Both experiences might be veridical without being incompatible with each other. They would then only seem incompatible because they were conceived wrongly as referring to the same object. And perhaps religion could not attain its full value without both. This suggestion opens up very interesting possibilities for discussion and may by separating the two concepts help to solve some antinomies about God."

Interesting as the suggestion is, its immediate effect is to complicate,

2. "Awareness of God," *Philosophy*, XL, No. 151 (Jan., 1965), 16–17.

rather than to clarify, the situation. Both experiences, as Dr. Ewing truly says, "might be veridical." But there are three other equally relevant hypotheses. In the first place, both experiences might be illusory. In the second place, the experience of the Absolute might be veridical, whereas the experience of a personal God might be illusory. And in the third place, the experience of a personal God might be veridical, and the experience of the Absolute might be illusory. How are we to attempt to decide between these conflicting hypotheses? It might be suggested that as a first step the man who is devoid of any mystical experience should disqualify himself and leave the decision to others. But we have seen that those who do account themselves qualified will certainly disagree among themselves, and who is to adjudicate between them? We can surely agree, I think, that it is not enough for a man to be sure that he actually has undergone a supernormal experience which deserves to be called mystical. A mere reading of Locke's discussion of "enthusiasm" should suffice to disabuse anyone of this idea, for Locke's words are redolent of bitter memories of controversy with just such persons. For a man's opinion to command respect he must be capable of self-analysis, of reflecting upon what he has passed through, and of at least attempting to discriminate between experience and interpretation. And he must be able to sympathize with mystics whose reports of their experiences differ from his own, and to give their opinions respectful consideration. It may be that individuals of this caliber will appear if the time ever come when mutual tolerance and understanding between contemplatives of different traditions will have developed to such a degree that they will be capable of practicing their devotions together and of sharing, at least to some extent, each others' experiences. But at present there seem to be no such outstanding figures, and no consensus of expert opinion to which we may appeal.

And this is precisely why Dr. Ewing's attempt to answer McTaggart's assertion that religious intuition is of value only to the person who has it, and that it is valueless as evidence to the person who has it not, seems to end in failure. "But suppose," writes Dr. Ewing,

this common situation. A man has an intuitive conviction of God. He is aware that what seems to him a veridical intuition might still not be so, and it would be very rash of him to place much confidence in it if he thought himself the only person who had it. But if he finds that the intuitive conviction is very widespread and possessed by a vast number of men who in other respects deserve the titles in a special degree of "good" and "wise," his attitude may well be transformed.[3]

Were the issue really so simple, were it the case that all mystics believed themselves to be in direct contact with a personal God, our choice would be a relatively easy one. We should have only to ask ourselves, Are all mystics deluded or does a personal God exist? But as we well know, and as we have seen that Dr. Ewing himself realizes, the issue is not simple but extremely complicated. If we are to decide between the claims of the theistic, pantheistic, and atheistic mystics we can do so only in the light of our preconceived ontological and cosmological beliefs, which is what St. Thomas says that we ought to do; but by doing that we resign every claim to found a proof of God upon religious experience.

There is, moreover, another, and a very important, aspect of our problem which demands our attention. When we appeal to religious experience as evidential it is natural enough that we should seek to distinguish sharply between beliefs which profess to be based upon it alone and beliefs which are accepted upon authority or which are arrived at by normal inferential processes of human reason.

Dawes Hicks observes:

> The truth is that well-nigh everything which enters into human experience may, under certain circumstances, appear to the experiencing subject to be given in the form of immediacy. Such apprehension may seem to be simply direct and immediate apprehension of a content because at the time nothing of mediate inference is detected in it, although, as we have just seen, that is no guarantee that mediate inference is in fact absent. Taking, then, "immediacy" in this sense, it is important to note that it may evince itself in two quite different ways. There is an immediacy that would seem to be above the level of rational mediation, but there is also an immediacy that is below it.

And he regards it as "the cardinal defect of what is usually called mysticism that it ignores this vital difference." [4]

The subrational kind of immediacy is a confused awareness which is largely devoid of discrimination, comparison, and definiteness. And if I mistake not, it is very much the kind of awareness of God which the ontologist regards as the birthright of every normal man. Supra-

3. *Ibid.*, p. 9.
4. *The Philosophical Bases of Theism,* p. 109.

rational immediacy, on the other hand, comes to men of high intellectual capacity when, after profound and arduous concentration upon some problem, a sudden illumination supervenes, a "synthetic unity of apprehension," we might say, which reduces complexity to order and causes clearness to succeed obscurity. Such states "do not drop from the skies; they come to minds of wide range and profound depth, minds that are saturated with thoughts making for the new ideas and pointing the way towards them. And even then, their claim to be experiences of what is true is entitled to recognition only in so far as they can stand the test of critical scrutiny and rational interpretation." [5]

From this it does not follow that we should rest content with purely inferential knowledge. There is a great difference between inferring that a hole has been dug by human hands and seeing a man digging it. Immediacy of contact is of very great importance, and is rightly highly valued; the danger is that it may so overshadow the mediate inferences involved in perception that the occurrence of these may be unrecognized and unacknowledged. As a result of such oversight, and in an outburst of emotional exuberance, an illegitimate antithesis is sometimes set up between what is asserted to be pure, undiluted, and infallible immediate awareness on the one hand and the laborious and uncertain processes of fallible human reason on the other hand. But such an antithesis cannot stand for a moment in the light of critical scrutiny.

In discussing the very problem we are now considering Dawes Hicks uttered a solemn warning which we shall do well to ponder. "The theories of religious experience which we have just been considering—that it is based upon feeling, or upon immediate intuition, or upon mystic illumination, or upon a non-rational numinous faculty —all presuppose, if I mistake not, a conception of the immanence of the Divine in nature and in the mind of man which would, if consistently adhered to, undermine any attempt to sustain a genuinely theistic view." [6]

The concluding words, I believe, are clearly indicative of the train of thought which inspired this utterance. To Dawes Hicks, as a convinced believer in a personal God, it seemed obvious that there must be some analogy between the communion of the human and the Divine minds and the communion of human minds with one another. Hence to him it appeared preposterous to suppose that God could act upon the human consciousness as a physical force might act upon a physical object, as the sea overwhelms a rock, for example, or as a

5. *Ibid.*, p. 111. 6. *Ibid.*, p. 140.

whirlwind levels a field of corn, that God is capable of bludgeoning or absorbing or consuming us. Let us therefore, he suggests, consider how human minds communicate with one another, and seek to profit from this examination. Hicks writes:

In the first place, whatever be the nature of the mutual *rapport* which is thus assumed to subsist between persons, it certainly cannot be maintained that through its means we are directly apprehensive of the mental states or processes taking place in another mind. If that were the case, the science of psychology would be in a far more advanced stage of completeness than any of the natural sciences! In the second place, whatsoever be the nature of the knowledge we possess of other selves, it is clear that such knowledge is never obtained in isolation, but only through and in connexion with knowledge of the bodily appearances and bodily activities of other persons. And, in the third place, I need scarcely reiterate that we are not justified in taking the terms "direct" or "immediate" to mean, any more in this context than in others, that nothing of the nature of interpretation or reflexion is involved.

In religious experience, it is, I venture to submit, likewise impossible that we can be directly apprehending the actual states or phases of the supreme Mind. However vivid and profound a man's religious experience may be, he can be conscious of God only through the medium of God's manifestations or working in the universe (including therein, of course, finite minds), and through the emotions thus awakened. Or, in more technical phraseology, just as I am aware of my friend's existence through being aware of his essence, so I may be convinced of God's existence through being aware, however imperfectly and inadequately, of what I conceive to be God's essence. Again, I think it true to say that we can never experience the Divine in absolute isolation from everything else; we experience the Divine only through and in correlation with what is other than the Divine. In religious experience the devout soul is conscious of being in communion with the Divine Mind. That communion is acknowledged to be dependent upon nature for its means, and to avail itself of the resources of nature. Nevertheless, while nature is admittedly material for expressing or revealing the presence of the divine life, it is never of itself taken by the experient to be the source of that life or the basis of it.

There is, then, so far as I can see, no insuperable difficulty in recognizing that God may commune with man in a manner analogous to the way in which one finite mind communes with another. Important differences of course there must be. For instance, since we experience other selves only through and in connexion with their bodies, other selves are supposed by us to be more or less confined in their operations to those situations in which their bodies are found. In the case of the supreme Mind, however, we do not suppose that there are any such restrictions. Well-nigh any situation may serve to reveal what we take to be divine, although there is no situation which invariably does so.[7]

These are surely "words of truth and soberness" to anyone who surveys the problem from the theistic point of view. Placing myself for the moment in the same perspective I should feel inclined to observe that, inasmuch as the students of telepathy do not yet appear to have come to any general agreement about whether direct contact of mind with mind may not occur without the intervention of the physical organism, it is presuming too much upon our empirical knowledge to deny dogmatically that the Divine Mind can ever be experienced in "absolute isolation." Nevertheless the point is of small importance. For even if the possibility be granted of direct contact between the human mind and God's Mind without any intervention of a third entity, yet, as we have seen, mediate inference cannot be excluded from such apprehension of the Divine. Awareness not only *that* one perceives something, but that *what* one perceives is other than a state of one's own being, that it is a self, and that it is a self so characterized as to justify one in calling it a Divine Self, all this will inevitably fall under the heading of mediate inference.

I think that Dr. Ewing has in mind an idea very similar to that of Hicks when he writes,

> To say that a cognition is intuitive is not necessarily to deny that it is mediated in some way. Thus the cognition of God might be called "intuitive" because it was not based on argument, and yet might be mediated by certain experiences which could help one to "see God." The apprehension of something may well lead to the realisation of something else without the former being a premise from which the latter is deduced. There is a distinction between seeing some truth as the result of seeing others and inferring it from these others. To say that some being mediates God is to say that a man may by considering that being be put in a state of

7. *Philosophy*, XL, No. 151 (Jan., 1965), 10.

mind in which he can catch a glimpse of God. The awareness of
God is commonly held to be mediated by nature, the goodness in
other people, many kinds of symbols and many specially vivid experiences of life, moral, aesthetic, and practical. For Christians
Christ can in a special degree be said to mediate God, whether
the orthodox doctrine of the incarnation be true or false. The relation of mediation has some analogy to inference and may even
be mistaken for it, but it may carry one beyond what we could
infer. The concept of mediated cognition that is yet not inferential
is not one which has to be specially invented to fit the case of
religion. It may be argued that it is also needed for the solution
of problems such as that of the knowledge of physical objects and
perhaps of other minds, when our cognition is plainly *mediated*
by sense-perceptions and by the bodily behaviour of others but
its objects cannot be either identified with or perhaps satisfactorily inferred from the mediating factor, and it may even turn out
that in a comprehensive epistemology we need to give this concept a place in dealing with every or almost every form of human
cognition.[8]

Inasmuch as Dr. Ewing implies that this theory of mediated, non-
inferential cognition requires to be worked out in detail, I abstain
from any attempt to criticize it beyond remarking that it seems to me
that implicit and unnoticed mediate inference might very easily be
confused with such cognition, if it occur.

In concluding this chapter I wish to state as clearly as I can, and to
accord appropriate emphasis to, two points which appear to me
to comprise the results of our investigation. In the first place, I desire to
stress the significance of the ubiquity and antiquity of the religious
experience of humanity. When we recognize how similar were the
circumstances in which primitive man was placed to those of the animals which surrounded him it is difficult indeed to account for the
fact that he was religious whereas they were not otherwise than by an
appeal to the equally undoubted fact that he was rational whereas
they were not. His cosmic perspective was thus basically conditioned
by two factors, his awareness of himself as a spiritual being and his
assurance that the universe which he inhabited was in some sense also
spiritual.[9] While his outlook was no doubt sufficiently confused, and

8. *Ibid.*

9. Nothing in this connection is more impressive than the widespread custom of
assimilating to death the initiation imposed at adulthood upon all members of a
tribe, with the clear implication that death is an initiation.

sufficiently devoid of precise determination and comparison, to merit the application of Dawes Hicks's phrase "subrational immediacy," it does not for this reason deserve to be totally disregarded. I should therefore feel very disinclined to accept any type of philosophy—such as materialism or naturalism—which does so disregard it, for such an attitude I find expressive of a dogmatic assertiveness unworthy of a philosopher. I do not, be it observed, affirm that the claim that religion originated in delusive, or at least in misunderstood, experiences and fallacious inferences can be positively disproved; I merely point out that the balance of probability is on the other side.

The most fundamental task of philosophy has been by continuous and unremitting effort to dispell and to replace the primitive "subrational immediacy" by clear and constraining mediate inferences, a process which may perchance at times have attained to that state of suprarational immediacy to which Hicks has alluded. But this has involved a very complex process of argumentation, extending to many aspects of human experience, and not to religious experience only. Accordingly I desire in the second place to record my conviction that the study of religious experience, at the level which it has at present reached, does not provide us with sufficient evidence to enable us to adjudicate confidently between the rival claims of theism, pantheism, panentheism, polytheism, and religious atheism.[10] So far I believe that St. Thomas is right. The data which it provides require to be buttressed by material derived from other sources. To the total cosmic perspective religious experience has its own important contribution to make, but it is that total perspective which the philosophy of religion must take as its point of departure.

[*Note*] In a few sentences I propose to carry further the line of argument developed on pages 462–463 and 464–466, and to present a heresy of my own which, whether it prove ultimately sound or not, does seem to me to deserve consideration. We have spoken of the blending of immediacy and mediation in perception; we are familiar with Leibniz'

10. It may be objected that I have myself ventured to pronounce definitely against the claims of pantheism and panentheism. This is correct. But I would point out that I have not done so on the ground that they can find no support in the statements of the mystics and in the reports of religious experiences. Emphatically the contrary is the case. In number such statements are legion, and and pantheists and panentheists have as much right to appeal to them as have theists and atheists to appeal to statements which support their own positions. I have not based my decision upon any evidence derived from religious experience but upon a proposition which rightly or wrongly I accept as self-evident, namely, that one self cannot include another—in the light of which their positions are clearly untenable.

phrase, a "clear-confused perception," and we know that it means an awareness which is definite as to its object yet confused as to the nature of that object. Such, the ontologists tell us, is man's awareness of God. Such, I suggest, is man's awareness of himself. How much of the work of philosophy has been the progressive clarification of this confusion! To realize his direct awareness of himself, to distinguish between himself and his body, to discriminate the vincula, to recognize that he is a substance capable of causal efficacy, unoriginated and indestructible—all this has taken centuries of careful discrimination. But we must not assume that nothing of all this was confusedly grasped before it was definitely and explicitly distinguished. How are we to account for the fact that everywhere and at every time the anthropologist finds man assured of his status as a being in transition between two worlds, convinced that he will live forever in the future as he has always lived in the past? We can account for it only, I would urge, by assuming that man in the very depths of his being is ineradicably conscious of himself as an ultimate and indestructible entity, not accidentally but essentially alive. And here, I believe, we find the germ both of religion and of philosophy.

CHAPTER THREE

THE ONTOLOGICAL ARGUMENT

This famous argument has had a singular history. Whereas throughout the centuries since it was first elaborated by St. Anselm the majority of philosophers have rejected it, a minority of philosophers—and among these some of the most eminent—have regarded it as absolutely conclusive. "Why," asks Dr. Armand Maurer, "do some accept the proof and others deny it? Those who deny it agree that all our knowledge begins with sense experience and that we can know the existence of anything only through the perception of sensible things. On the other hand, those who accept it think that the mind can know real being by turning inward upon itself. But real being is not given to us through sense experience—at least not exclusively—but through our ideas." [1]

This explanation I am unable to accept, if for no other reason than because I myself happen to be one of those people who believe that real being can be known otherwise than through sense experience, and yet reject the argument. Undoubtedly the argument stands at the focus of a number of philosophical issues; hence it is viewed by various thinkers in differing metaphysical perspectives, and some philosophers, I feel sure, are actually uncertain about what the fundamental contention of the argument is.

We must, of course, begin by recognizing that St. Anselm was in some sort a genuine realist in the matter of universals. Here is the philosophical ground of his opposition to Roscellin, whose nominalism seemed to St. Anselm to involve him in pure tritheism. This comes out clearly in his *De Fide Trinitatis* and in his *Monologium*. Let us look for a moment at the opening chapters of the latter work to see how his thought develops.

All good things, he tells us, [2] in thoroughly Platonic fashion, are good through that which is good in itself. And in chapter two he informs us that in the same way there is a supremely great—a *summe magnum*—through participation in which all great things are great. Here we may

---

1. *Medieval Philosophy* (New York, 1962), p. 53.
2. See chap. i.

demur, on the ground that greatness is purely relative, and not an intrinsic quality. St. Anselm, possibly anticipating our hesitancy, explains that he does not mean by greatness superiority in size—*non magnum spatio*. What he does mean is that by which what is good is better, or more worthy, such as wisdom—*quod quanto majus, tanto melius est, aut dignius, ut sapientia.* Nothing can be supremely great which is not supremely good—*non potest esse summe magnum, nisi quod est summus bonus.*

This is an important consideration in the light of what follows; yet we may still ask: Are the terms goodness and greatness genuine synonyms, referring to one and the same reality, or do they stand for two distinct, but inseparably associated, qualities? Is what is good always great, and what is great always good—or can there be something great which is not good? It is perhaps impossible to answer the last question. But St. Anselm definitely tells us [3] that there are degrees of superiority; and my impression is that he holds that to varying degrees of goodness there are corresponding degrees of greatness. That the number of grades should be infinite he regards as an absurd suggestion; [4] there must, then, be a maximum, which is to say that there must be some nature which is superior to others and inferior to none. What is true of goodness and greatness is also true of being. There must be some nature which derives its being from nothing—not even from itself in the sense that it produces itself, but in the sense that it exists of itself.[5]

So far what St. Anselm has said would be quite in accordance with a Platonic realism. But then, in the seventh and eighth chapters, we are informed that all subordinate things were created by the supreme Being *ex nihilo*. Before they were created they may yet be said to have existed in the intelligence of their Creator, somewhat in the manner in which the design of a manufactured article exists in the mind of its maker before he has produced it.[6] This is an important announcement, for we shall find that in the statement of the ontological argument great play is made with the contrasted notions of being *in re* and being *in mente*. In the sixteenth chapter it is affirmed that, whereas a man can be called just if he participate in justice, such language must not be used with respect to the *summa natura*; for this would imply that it is just through something other than itself. The *summa natura is* the highest justice, wisdom, truth, goodness, beauty, etc. To say this, how-

3. Chap. iv.   4. *Ibid.*
5. Chap. iii.   6. Chaps. ix–x.

ever, does not mean that it is a compound or complex of universals; on the contrary, it is absolute unity and absolute simplicity. There is in it no distinction between universal and universal, nor between being and essence. Following thus in the footsteps of Boethius, St. Anselm has arrived at the same goal. We have passed with him beyond Platonic realism. It would not be true to say that his God is a particular, in the sense of being a member of a class, for there is no other like him; yet it is clear that he is, in the language of the medievals, an *individual*. In him the whole plurality of the highest universals collapses into stark unity; the law of identity is no longer applicable.

We now see how inevitable was the passage from Platonic realism to the "moderate realism" of Aquinas, according to which universals are *in re* only in the sense that they can be abstracted from particulars by a mind which is capable of forming concepts. St. Anselm stands at the beginning of this processs; it is even doubtful if he realize how far he has gone along the road. But he has yet in store for us another impressive pronouncement, one which is echoed by later scholastics. In Chapter XVIII he tells us that in a certain sense God alone is, and that compared with him, all other things which seem to be are not.[7] Here we have implied, of course, the doctrine of degrees of being, according to which the highest degree of created being is nearer to nothingness than to absolute being. Thus St. Anselm affirms that "according to this reasoning, therefore, only the Creator-Spirit is, and all created things are not; and yet they are not wholly naught, because by that which absolutely is, they are from nothing made to be something." [8]

How closely does the scholastic theory approximate to the doctrine of the Advaitins that nothing is real except Brahma, and to the teaching of some of the Sufis that God alone exists! We are poised upon the very brink of the abyss of acosmism. It is only the restraining hand of dogma that pulls us back. It is the notion of creation that arrests us. Created entities, far removed as they are from pure being, cannot lapse into nothing, nor yet can they become mere appearance. The metaphysical stage has now been set for the entrance of the ontological argument.

Let us turn, then, to the *Proslogium.* In the second chapter of this

7. "Quadam ratione solus sit: alia vero quaecumque videntur esse, hinc collata, non sint."

8. "Secundum hanc igitur rationem ille solus creator spiritus est: & omnia creata non sunt; nec tamen omnino non sunt, quia per illum, qui solus absolute est de nihilo aliquid facta sunt."

work we find the argument set forth.[9] Without preliminary St. Anselm begins by stating what he takes to be the content of faith, namely, that God is a being than which nothing greater can be conceived. Everyone, even the fool referred to by the psalmist, understands what these words mean; and what he understands is in his understanding. He is convinced, accordingly, that there is in his own understanding something than which nothing greater can be conceived. But to exist *in re* is greater than to exist only in the understanding; hence a being which existed only in the understanding would not be a being than which nothing greater can be conceived. Consequently God, than whom nothing greater can be conceived, must exist *in re*.

The first question to be asked is what is meant by greatness. Our brief glance at the *Monologium* suffices to shed some light thereon, for we have seen that greatness seems to be equated with goodness, or perhaps we should say with "perfections" of all kinds. And we have also seen that the suggestion that there might be an endless number of grades of increasing goodness, being, etc., is repudiated with contempt. We are confronted, then, with the scholastic doctrine of degrees of being, under which all characteristics fall, inasmuch as being is not a genus. And at the apex of this ontological pyramid, and separated from the highest degree that falls beneath it by a wider and deeper gap than that which sunders the said degree from nothingness, is Absolute Being, Absolute Goodness, Wisdom, Beauty, and so forth—I say "is," and not "are," for at this level there is no distinction of quality from quality or of quality from substance, nor of essence from existence.

Whether or not this doctrine be intelligible, I would point out that its truth cannot simply be presupposed, that it requires to be proved. But the ontological argument does in the baldest manner presuppose it. And were it possible to prove the truth of the doctrine, the ontological argument would be otiose.

I have already urged that the doctrine is unintelligible inasmuch as, holding as it does that all "perfections" are actually identical with the Deity and with one another, it flouts the law of identity. I now go further, and contend that the notion of degrees of being is unintelligible. It is self-evident, I maintain, that being admits of degrees no more than does squareness or circularity. If it be objected that it is not a question of more and less, but of levels of being, and if by this

9. In the opinion of Arthur Cushman McGiffert this exposition "remains the best and clearest statement of it that exists" (*A History of Christian Thought* [New York, 1933], II, 193).

be meant that being is a determinable whereof there are many determinants, I should concede the truth of the assertion; nonetheless, I should still maintain that no determinant has more being than any other.

Suppose, however, that we have granted the truth of the doctrine of degrees of being. What follows? Either being must be admitted to be a genus, in which case it will be a universal, or if, in Aristotelian fashion, we reject this suggestion we shall be left with the *summa genera,* each of which will be a universal. But God is not a universal. Thus, even could we know that there is such a universal—whether simple, compound, or complex—as Deity, and even could we know that it could not conceivably have more than one instance, we should still be ignorant as to whether or not there be this one instance.

To talk in this way, it may be urged, is to disregard the scholastic doctrine that God is not a particular but an individual, a unique individual, and that in him there is no distinction between essence and existence. But this doctrine requires to be proved, and the ontological argument does not prove it. From the scholastic point of view, then, St. Thomas' objection holds good. For an angel, who directly apprehends the divine essence, no argument will be necessary. To us, who do not directly apprehend the divine essence, it can be shown that if there be a self-existent Being, in him the dichotomy between universal and particular will be transcended, and that there will be no distinction between essence and existence. But even if all this be true, we still must be shown that there *is* such a Being.

Let us now turn to the distinction upon which so much emphasis is laid between existence *in intellectu* and existence *in re.* What does this really mean? Has it any intelligible meaning? Does everything possess two modes of existence? Does an entity both exist actually, in itself, *in re,* and does it also exist in another entity, namely, in the mind which apprehends it? And if many minds apprehend it, does it enjoy a corresponding plurality of existences? Surely all this is nonsense. What exists in the apprehending mind is nothing apprehended, but an act or state of awareness. To say that a thing exists "only in the mind"—*in intellectu solo*—is equivalent, therefore, to saying that it does not exist at all. Or if we say that what exists in each individual mind is a concept, it will nevertheless be true that a concept of God is not God, and that where the concept exists God does not exist. And to say that it is greater to exist both *in intellectu* and *in re* than *in intellectu solo* is to make a statement which is meaningless and therefore absurd.

Perhaps it will be objected, however, that this sort of criticism is vitiated by the fact that it takes no account of St. Anselm's realism. And indeed, so far as his presentation of the ontological argument is concerned, all that St. Anselm says might have been said by a conceptualist. Still it is proper to remind us that he was a realist, at least so far as his theology permitted him to be, and it is apropos to ask whether in the light of this consideration a different interpretation of what he has said can be offered.

Now it may be pointed out that, whereas for a conceptualist a concept is a mental entity, produced by and contained in the apprehending consciousness for which it constitutes an object of thought, the situation for the realist is very different. To think, the realist will contend, is to think of something. One cannot think of nothing, for to think of nothing is not to think at all. But thought does not create its object. There must be something real to be thought of. When we are aware of particulars, we talk of *perceiving* them; when we are aware of universals, we say that we *conceive* them. This does not necessarily commit us to the assertion that there are two different kinds of entities of which we are aware. Thus, when I think of a fairy, I am quite prepared to admit that so far as I know there is no existent particular to which the description of a fairy applies. But I am not thinking of nothing; I am thinking of something, namely, the nature or essence of a fairy.

Believers in universals frequently attempt to deal with the situation by distinguishing between the reality or being of the essence— that is, the sum total of the universals which constitute the essence— and the existence which pertains to any particular which the essence characterizes.[10] An Aristotelian would say that the essence actually is present both in the object apprehended and in the apprehending mind—in each case, of course, *secundum modum recipientis*—so that the mind really *is* what it *knows*. This is, surely, quite inadmissible. The essence of a fairy is the nature which any fairy would have if there were a fairy, and which would be common to all fairies, if there were fairies. But when I think of a fairy, I am not characterized by fairihood, I do not become a fairy. If by saying that a fairy is in my mind is meant only that fairihood is the object of my thought, the

10. This is a convenient way of speaking, but as I have already said, it seems to me a dangerous one; for it tends to suggest that there are not only two different kinds of entities, but also two ways in which they *are*, or two modes of being, a suggestion which carries with it the implication that to be is not only to be actual but to be active. The use of the Latin *actus* may easily give rise to such a confusion.

expression may be permitted to pass—under protest. Yet it tends to be misleading and confusing.

Now it must be admitted that St. Anselm does talk in this way when he says that what a man understands is in his understanding, and then proceeds to contrast *esse in intellectu solo* with *esse in intellectu et in re*.[11] Does he really mean that when I think of God, God exists in my mind, that I am characterized by Deity, that I become God? Certainly not! What, then, does he mean? If we are to interpret his statement in as Platonic a fashion as possible we must conclude that he means that there is a real nature or essence which, when thought of, must be thought of as the nature of an actually existent Being. While we can think of fairihood and yet disbelieve in the existence of fairies, we cannot think of God without being aware that God must exist. And this means surely, if it mean anything, that in conceiving of God, that is in being aware of his nature, we are also aware that in God essence and existence are identical. But now we see whither we are being carried. We are being carried back to ontologism, to the doctrine that the human mind is naturally endowed with a direct awareness of the divine essence.

"The first kind of existence," writes Professor Richard Taylor,

> was referred to by St. Anselm and the other scholastics as existence *in intellectu*. To say of anything that it exists *in intellectu*—

11. It is worth while observing that in the fifteenth chapter of the *Proslogium* St. Anselm goes so far as to say that God is not only a Being than whom nothing greater can be conceived but also a Being greater than can be conceived—*non solum es quo majus cogitari nequit, es quiddam majus, quam cogitari possit*. If he expects us to take this statement literally, it seems clear that St. Anselm is sawing off the branch he is sitting on. For if we cannot conceive of God, we cannot reason with respect to him. We can talk about the word "God," but to us it will be devoid of meaning. St. Anselm will have hoist his own argument with his own petard. Whatever, therefore, did he intend us to understand, it cannot have been this. What, then, did he mean? The reason which he gives for making the assertion is that, since it is possible to conceive that there is a Being greater than can be conceived, unless God be this Being, it will be possible to conceive that there is a Being greater than God—*quoniam namque valet cogitari esse aliqud huiusmodi; si tu non esse hoc ipsum, potest cogitari aliqud majus te: quod fieri nequit*. It would seem that here we have a confusion between *conceiving of* and *conceiving that*, between thinking of God and thinking of the proposition that there may be a Being so great that he cannot be thought of.

An alternative possibility would be that St. Anselm is using *cogitari* in two different senses—to *think of* and to *comprehend*. If to comprehend be taken to mean "to know all about," St. Anselm might well insist that such a term cannot be applicable to God. In any event the train of reasoning is unfortunately disturbed by this chapter, since, if the ontological argument have any force at all, it clearly depends upon our grasping a definite meaning of the word "God."

roughly in the understanding—is to say nothing more than that a clear idea of it exists, or that someone rightly understands a description that he is given. Thus do winged horses, griffins, unicorns and so on exist, *in intellectu,* together with horses, the sun and the moon, for all these things, whether they actually exist or not, can clearly be described and the descriptions of them conveyed to one's understanding. Such things, moreover, as square circles, colorless bodies and fire that is without heat, can exist *in intellectu,* for these too can be described and accurately defined and the definitions and descriptions of them understood. Indeed, unless one understood what is meant by, say, a square circle— namely, an equal four-sided plane figure all of whose points are equidistant from its center—he could not know with certainty that nothing answering to that description exists anywhere in reality, for he simply would not, under those conditions, understand what it was whose real existence was being denied.[12]

"It should be clear," he adds in a subsequent paragraph,

that these two modes of description are not mutually exclusive. Something might exist in either sense but not the other, or in both senses, or in neither. The sun, for example, exists *in re,* but also *in intellectu,* for we understand what is meant by the sun. The satellites of Mercury, on the other hand, exist *in intellectu* but not *in re,* since Mercury has no satellites. There are, moreover, surely things that exist *in re* but not *in intellectu,* namely, all those real beings as yet undiscovered by men, of which they have formed no conception. Anything, finally, which is unreal and of which no man has ever framed a conception has no existence of either kind. If a man were for the first time to fabricate a description of some unreal and hitherto undreamed of thing, something of which no man had ever before formed a conception, then that thing would thereupon exist in that man's understanding, but until then it would have had no existence at all, even *in intellectu.*[13]

All this, for reasons I have already given, I find impossible to follow. What is an idea or a concept? If an idea or a concept of something be a thought or an awareness of something, then that thought or that awareness occurs, or exists, in the intellect of the thinker; but that of which he thinks or is aware, or which he conceives, does not

12. See his Introduction to *The Ontological Argument,* ed. Professor Alvin Plantinga (New York, 1965), pp. xiii–xiv.
13. *Ibid.,* pp. xiv–xv.

exist in his intellect, unless he be engaged in introspection. And to say that the eternal and self-existent God exists in the mind of the man who thinks of him is surely to use words in a perverted sense. A concept, it may be said, exists in my intellect in the sense that it is an entity which I produce or create. This seems to me quite incredible. If, however, any man can believe it, let him believe it. But it is quite obvious that the concept of God which I produce is not God himself, and that God himself is not produced by, and does not exist in, my intellect. And it is therefore obvious that, since there are not two different modes of existence of the same thing—namely, *esse in intellectu* and *esse in re*—there can be no inference from the one to the other. Nevertheless, Professor Taylor would introduce the following caveat.

As a matter of fact, all men are perfectly accustomed to making this transition when it comes to *denying* the existence *in re* of certain things. Thus, from one's clear understanding of what is meant by a plane four-sided figure, all of whose points are equidistant from the center, one can conclude with certainty that no such being exists. The propriety of doing so is never questioned by anyone, and yet it is a clear instance of drawing a conclusion concerning what does or does not exist in reality solely from the clear conception of something in one's understanding.[14]

"The idea of necessary non-existence or impossible existence," he assures us,

presents little difficulty. We can apply this notion to anything, such as a square circle, which is non-existent by its very nature. It exists *in intellectu*, for anyone can understand a clear definition of such a thing though he cannot, of course, comprehend it. But from one's very understanding of it he can be certain that no such thing exists. It is eternally and ubiquitously non-existent, or cannot exist anywhere or at any time. For the proof of this one need not seek such things and fail to find them anywhere. One need not go beyond the conception of such a thing.[15]

In all this Professor Taylor seems to write like a conceptualist. But I should have thought that even a conceptualist would have shrunk from asserting that one can have a "clear concept," or can frame a "clear definition," of a square circle or of any of its ilk. For even if a concept be a genuine ontological entity produced by the human

14. *Ibid.*, p. xv.   15. *Ibid.*, pp. xvi–xvii.

consciousness and enjoying a mysterious residence *in intellectu*, it must surely have some consistency in its structure, and the elements thereof must be harmoniously conjoined. But it is completely impossible thus to unite in a coherent whole incompatible and utterly antagonistic characteristics. And it is precisely because the conceptualist cannot, on his own principles, actually form a concept of a square circle that he cannot believe in its existence.[16]

Let us turn next to the position of the realist, for whom to conceive is not to produce or to create an entity but to be aware of universals which enjoy objective reality. Is it a tenable assertion to maintain that there actually is such a universal as square-circularity which by its very nature is incapable of characterizing any particular, and of which, therefore, there can be no instance? I should reject the suggestion on two grounds. In the first place such an entity would be a compound universal, and we have already seen sufficient reason to deny that there are compound universals. And in the second place, were we to concede the reality of compound universals, it would still be self-evident that the simple universals thus compounded must be mutually compatible, and capable of coincidentally characterizing a single particular. If these statements be sound, as I believe they are, Professor Taylor's contention that we can argue from existence *in intellectu* to non-existence *in re* must be rejected.

Leaving, however, this consideration aside, I wish now to call attention to the fact that in his *Summa contra Gentiles*,[17] St. Thomas Aquinas explicitly distinguishes two forms of the ontological argument, the first being derived from the second chapter of the *Proslogium*, and the second from the third chapter.[18] In his later work, the *Summa Theologica*, we find, indeed, only the first formulation given.[19] In the *De Veritate* we find only the second,[20] and in his early work, the *Commentary on Peter Lombard's Sentences*, we discover the two woven together, as it were, in a single statement.[21]

Before we proceed to a detailed examination of these various formulations I would call attention to the context in which they are found. In the *Summa contra Gentiles* the chapter in which the two forms are stated as two distinct arguments is entitled "Concerning the opinion of those who say that the existence of God cannot be dem-

16. Gaunilo's objection—*Pro Inspiente*, sec. 5—hits the nail on the head.
17. Book I, chap. x.
18. The same distinction has recently been made by Professor Norman Malcolm. See "Anselm's Ontological Arguments," *Philosophical Review*, LXIX (Jan., 1960), 41–62; cf. *The Ontological Argument*, p. 12.
19. I. a. q. 2.: a. I. 2.   20. Q. 10: a. 12. 2.
21. I. Dist. III. q. I. a. 2. 4.

onstrated because it is self-evident." 22 In the *Summa Theologica* the article wherein the first argument is stated is entitled "Whether God's existence be self-evident." 23 The same title is given to the relevant section in the *Commentary on the Sentences*. In the *De Veritate*, however, the heading reads, "Whether the existence of God be self-evident to the human mind, as are the first principles of demonstration, which cannot be thought not to be." 24

The change of viewpoint is highly significant. The argument is—or the arguments are—directed not to proving the existence of God but to showing why a proof of God's existence is both impossible and needless. A self-evident proposition can neither be proved nor—once it be recognized for what it is—can it be doubted. The question before St. Thomas, then, is whether or not the proposition "God exists" be self-evident. His decision will be in the negative. It will be worth our while, however, to review his various statements of his opponents' case. Let us begin by the two formulations presented in the *Contra Gentiles*.

1. Those things are said to be self-evident which are known as soon as their terms are known. For example, when it is known what is a whole and what is a part, at once it is known that every whole is greater than its part. Of this kind is the assertion that God exists. For by the name "God" we understand something than which something greater cannot be conceived. Moreover, this is formed in the intellect of him who hears and understands the name "God"; so that God must already exist, at least in the intellect. Nor is it possible that he should exist only in the intellect; for that which is both *in intellectu* and *in re* is greater than that which exists in the intellect alone. And nothing can be greater than God, as the meaning of the name makes clear. Whence it follows that it is self-evident that God exists, as is manifest from the signification of the name.[25]

22. "De opinione Dicentium quod Deum esse demonstrari non potest cum sit per se notum."
23. "Utrum Deum esse sit per se notum."
24. "Utrum Deum esse sit per se notum menti humanae, sicut prima principia demonstrationis, quae non possunt cogitari non esse."
25. "Illa enim per se esse nota dicuntur quae statim notis terminis cognoscuntur: sicut cognitio quid est totum et pars, statim cognoscuntur quod omne totum est maius sua parte. Huiusmodi est autem hoc quod dicimus Deum esse. Nam nomine Dei intellegimus aliquid quod maius cogitari non potest. Hoc autem in intellectu formatur ab eo qui audit et intelligit nomen Dei: ut sic saltem in intellectu iam Deum esse oporteat. Nec potest in intellectu solum esse: nam quid in intellectu et re est, maius est eo quod in solo intellectu est; Deo autem nihil esse maius ipsa nominis ration demonstrat. Unde restat quod Deum esse per se notum est, quasi ex ipsa significatione nominis manifestum."

2. Again it is even possible to conceive that something should exist which could not be conceived not to be; which evidently is greater than that which can be conceived not to be. So, therefore, if God himself could be conceived not to be, something greater than God could be conceived, which would contradict the meaning of the name "God." Hence it must be admitted that the existence of God is self-evident.[26]

The statement in the *Summa Theologica* runs as follows:

Furthermore those things are said to be self-evident which are known as soon as their terms are known; which the Philosopher attributes to the first principles of demonstration in the Posterior Analytics; for, if it be known what is a whole and what is a part, at once it is known that every whole is greater than its part. But once it is understood what is meant by the name "God," immediately it is clear that God exists. For by this name is signified that than which nothing greater can be signified. But that which exists *in re* and *in intellectu* is greater than that which exists only in the intellect; hence, since when the name "God" is understood God exists in the intellect, it follows that God exists *in re*. The existence of God is, therefore, self-evident.[27]

We turn now to the *Commentary on the Sentences*. "Furthermore," wrote St. Thomas,

that is self-evident which cannot be thought not to be. But God cannot be thought not to be. That he exists, therefore, is self-evident. The proof of the minor is given by Anselm,[28] God is that than which a greater cannot be thought. But that which cannot be thought not to be is greater than that which can be thought not to be. God, therefore, cannot be thought not to be.

It is possible to advance another proof in support of the same

26. "Item. Cogitari quidem potest quod aliquid sit quod non possit cogitari non esse. Quod maius est evidenter eo quod potest cogitari non esse. Sic ergo Deo aliquid maius cogitari potest, si ipse potest cogitari non esse. Quod est contra rationem nominis. Relinquitur igitur quod Deum esse per se notum est."

27. "Praeterea, illa dicuntur esse per se nota, quae statim, cognitis terminis, cognoscunteu; quod Philosophus attribuit primis demonstrationis principiis, in I Poster.: scito enim quid est totum et quid est pars, statim scitur quod omne totum maius est sua parte. Sed intellecto quid significet hoc nomen Deus, statim habetur quod Deus est. Significatur enim hoc nomine id quo maius significari non potest: maius autem est quod est in re et in intellectu, quam quod est in intellectu tantum; unde cum, intellecto nomine Deus, statim sit in intellectu, sequitur etiam quod sit in re. Ergo Deum esse est per se notum."

28. The reference in the text of the *Vivès* edition is to the fifteenth chapter of the *Proslogium*. This I believe to be a mistake; it is the third chapter which is relevant.

assertion. Nothing can be thought apart from its quiddity. A man, for example, cannot be thought apart from the notion of rational mortal animal. But God's quiddity is his being, as Avicenna says in the *De Intelligentiis,* cap. I. God, therefore, cannot be thought not to be.[29]

Last of all we come to the brief statement in the *De Veritate:*
"Furthermore, God is that than which a greater cannot be conceived, as Anselm says in chapter four of the Proslogium. But that which can be thought not to be is less than that which cannot be thought not to be. God, therefore, cannot be thought not to be." [30]

The Latin phrase which is translated by the English "self-evident" is, of course, *per se notum.* It has the advantage, I consider, of greater definiteness and clarity. Our English phrase means, to be sure, that which is evident *in itself.* Unfortunately, however, it all too readily suggests the meaning that which is evident *to* a self; and it is more difficult than one might antecedently suppose to escape the influence of this regrettable possibility, and to avoid employing the phrase in more than one sense.[31] The Latin *per se notum,* on the other hand, clearly means that which is known in and through itself, and without reference to anything beyond itself. As soon as we grasp the meaning of the terms, we see that the proposition is true.

We must distinguish, St. Thomas tells us, between statements which are *per se nota simpliciter* or *secundum se* or *secundum rem ipsam* and those which are *per se nota quoad nos.* That the proposition should be *per se notum quoad nos*—that is, to us—we must grasp the fact that the predicate is included in the concept of the subject; and some propositions of this kind—that the whole, for example, is greater than its part—are *per se nota* to all men. There are, however, other propositions—such as the proposition that the incorporeal is not in space—

29. "Praeterea, illud est per se notum quod non potest cogitari non esse. Sed Deus non potest cogitari non esse. Ergo ipsum esse est per se notum. Probatio mediae est per Ansemum, *Proslog.,* cap. xv, col. 235.t.i.; Deus est quo majus cogitari non potest. Sed illud quod potest cogitari non esse, est majus eo quod potest cogitari non esse. Ergo Deus non potest cogitari non esse. Potest aliter probari. Nulla res potest cogitari sine sua quidditate, sicut home sine eo quod est animal rationale mortale. Sed Dei quidditas est ipsum esse, ut dicit Avicenna, lib. *De Intelligentiis,* cap. i. Ergo Deus non potest cogitari non esse."

30. Praeterea, Deus est quo majus cogitari non potest, ut Anselmus dicit, in *Proslogio,* cap. iv, Pat. Lat. t. CLVIII, col. 229. Sed illud quod potest cogitari non esse, est minus ille quod non potest cogitari non esse. Ergo Deus non potest cogitari non esse.

31. Thus when Dr. Ewing commits himself to the assertion that there are degrees of self-evidence (see his *Idealism,* pp. 177, 187, n. 1, 260), the reference to an apprehending subject is obvious. I do not accuse so careful a thinker as Dr. Ewing of intellectual confusion, but I think that the use is unfortunate.

which are *per se nota,* not to every man, but only to the more intelligent. Lastly, there are propositions which are *per se nota secundum
se*—that is, in themselves—but which are not *per se nota quoad nos*
because of the limitations of the human intellect. Among these is the
proposition that God exists. It is not *per se notum quoad nos* because
human knowledge rests ultimately upon sense experience; consequently the proposition requires to be proved, and it can be proved
by arguments based upon sense experience.

We are not entitled, according to Aquinas, to make any immediate
inference from what is *in intellectu* to what is *in re.* Granted that we
can conceive of a being than which no greater can be conceived,
or of a being which cannot be conceived not to exist, all that this shows
is that such a concept exists in our intellects; that such a being
actually exists *in rerum natura* is a mere assumption. And from his
own conceptualist standpoint St. Thomas has spoken well.

In what sense, we may now inquire, is it meaningful, on the supposition that God exists, to speak of his existence as necessary? Do
we mean that his existence is ultimate and underived, or do we mean
that to deny his existence would involve us in a contradiction?

A like question may confront the believer in the Absolute. He may
feel inclined to ask, as McTaggart has pointed out, "Why is the universe as a whole what it is, and not something else?" And this
question, McTaggart continues,

> could not be answered. We must not, however, conclude from this
> the existence of any want of rationality in the universe. The truth
> is that the question ought never to have been asked, for it is the
> application of a category, which has meaning only within the uni-
> verse, to the universe as a whole. Of any part we are entitled
> and bound to ask "why," for, by the very fact that it is a part, it
> cannot be self-subsistent, and must depend on other things. But
> when we come to the all embracing totality, then, with the pos-
> sibility of finding a cause, there disappears also the necessity of
> finding one. Self-subsistence is not in itself a contradictory or im-
> possible idea. It *is* contradictory if applied to anything in the
> universe, for whatever is in the universe must be in connection
> with other things. But this can of course be no reason for suspect-
> ing a fallacy when we find ourselves obliged to apply the idea
> to something which has nothing outside it with which it could
> stand in connection.

To put the matter in another light, we must consider that the necessity of finding causes and reasons for phenomena depends on the necessity of showing why they have assumed the particular form which actually exists. The inquiry is thus due to the possibility of things happening otherwise than as they did, which possibility, to gain certain knowledge, must be excluded by assigning definite cause for one event rather than the others. Now every possibility must rest upon some actuality. And the possibility that the whole universe could be different would have no such actuality to rest on, since the possibility extends to all reality. There would be nothing in common between the two associated alterations, and thus the possibility of variation would be unmeaning. And therefore there can be no reason to assign a determining cause.

The necessity which exists for all knowledge to rest on the immediate does not, then, indicate any imperfection which might prove a bar to the development of spirit. For we have seen that the impulse which causes us even here to demand fresh mediation is unjustified, and, indeed, meaningless.[32]

I should, indeed, wish to enter a caveat with respect to the assertion that no part of the universe is self-subsistent; for, while I concede that many groupings of selves into clubs, associations, political parties, tribes, and nations are transient, I hold that all selves are ultimate, uncreated, indestructible and eternal; although I should concede that they are not self-sufficing in that many of their characteristics depend upon mutual interrelationships, and that the working out of their destiny depends upon the axiologically oriented structure of the entire universe. I have not cited the above passage, however, to quarrel with it, but because it brings out so well a point which I wish to emphasize. We can ask with respect to a part why it is precisely what it is, since its nature depends to some extent upon its connections with other parts and with the whole to which it belongs, but it would be meaningless to ask why the all-embracing reality is what it is. In the same way it is legitimate for the believer in a creative God to ask why any creature is what it is, and to refer us for an explanation to the power, wisdom, and will of the Creator; but it would be meaningless to ask why God is what he is, inasmuch as he is ultimate, and his underived nature requires and admits of no explanation.

In the case of St. Thomas' God, however, what I have said will not suffice. His God is not merely ultimate and eternal. There is a

32. *Studies in Hegelian Cosmology*, sec. 269.

logical contradiction in the assertion that his God does not exist, although because of the weakness of our human intellects this contradiction is not immediately evident to us. The contradiction arises inasmuch as in God there is no distinction between essence and existence, whereas in the case of every created being there is such a distinction which renders it possible that it should not have been, so that its existence is imparted to it from without and is dependent upon the divine will. This identity of essence and existence in God is not, according to St. Thomas, an article of faith; it is capable of proof. One proves it by showing that in God there is no composition of matter and form, of actuality and potentiality, of substance and accidents, that God is absolutely simple, and that, therefore, he can admit of no distinction between essence and existence. The proposition that there is and can be no such distinction in God is indeed *per se notum secundum se*, but it is not *per se notum quoad nos*, as is evident from the fact that it does require to be demonstrated to us by conclusive arguments. The fact that it is not *per se notum* to us is due to the limitations of the human intellect for which all knowledge is finally dependent upon sense experience. For an angel, or for one of the saints *in patria*, who can directly perceive the divine essence, it is immediately evident that in God essence and existence are identical, and that consequently it is logically impossible that God should not exist. Hence it is impossible for the angel, or for the beatified saints, to conceive that God does not exist. It is possible for us to do so solely because we cannot directly perceive God *secundum statum praesentis vitae*, unless, in common with Moses and St. Paul, we be favored with a miraculous elevation to a supernatural level.

We now understand why it was that St. Thomas felt himself compelled to reject the ontological argument in whatever form it was presented. What he takes to be its fundamental contention is well expressed in the concluding sentences of his formulation of it in the *Commentary on the Sentences*. This contention is made up of a threefold assertion: (1) that in God essence and existence are identical, (2) that this identity is *per se notum secundum se*, and (3) that it is *per se notum quoad nos*. St. Thomas agrees with the first two assertions, but is compelled by his epistemological outlook to reject the third.

Needless to say, I feel myself compelled to reject all these assertions, inasmuch as the scholastic notion of God does not appear to me to be defensible. A Being in whom there is no distinction between nature and suppositum—that is to say, between universal and particular—and in whom, moreover, every universal is identical with every other universal, would seem to me to be reduced to a mere ontological blank, unthinkable because there is nothing to think, incomprehensible not because of fulness of being but because there is no being at all.

Remembering, however, that St. Thomas was practically a conceptualist,[33] we may still ask how the situation would appear to a realist who believed in the objective reality of universals. It would be meaningful for such a realist to ask with respect to some sensible particular whether it were not possible that it should not have existed, whether its existence were actually necessitated by the general scheme of the universe; but it would be meaningless for him to ask whether any universal, or whether all universals, might not have been, for this would be to ask whether there might not have been a different universe in the stead of the universe which there is.

We know that universals have being because we are directly aware of them. All the universals which would characterize a God, if there were a God, certainly are. And a believer in compound universals could go further than this; for he would doubtless maintain that all such universals together compose a compound universal which we might call "godhead" or "deity." But it would not follow that this compound universal must needs characterize a particular, any more than that every compound universal must do so. For if there be compound universals, and if it be the case that every one of them must characterize at least one particular, all works dealing with mythology will become treatises of natural science. We shall have, not only the universal griffinness, the universal fairiness, the universal ogreness, and a host of similar compound universals; we should also have all the particulars which these perforce characterized. Does the recognition of the reality of a universal, however, entitle us to affirm the existence of an instance thereof? Unless we hold that it is self-evident there cannot be what Professor Broad has called "non-characterizing characteristics," it is clear that we are not so entitled. Of the universal Cook Wilson has well written, "It is what it is not because it is in a plurality; it can be in a plurality because it is what it is." [34]

Reverting now to our examination of the position of St. Thomas let us reconsider what, in every presentation of the argument, he takes to be its fundamental contention. In his eyes it is not directed to

33. He is so, not indeed in scholastic or neoscholastic terminology, but in that of modern non-scholastic philosophers.
34. *Statement and Inference* (Oxford, 1926), II, 711.

demonstrating the existence of God but to showing conclusively that this cannot be done. Why can it not be done? Because the existence of God, so it insists, is *per se notum*. This means that the predicate of the proposition *God exists* is included in the nature of the subject. It means, in other words, that God's existence is included within his nature in the sense that one cannot be distinguished from the other. But for this to be *per se notum quoad nos*, the divine essence must be known by us, and such knowledge exceeds the capacity of human beings whose knowledge is derived from sense experience. It is true that God implants in our minds a knowledge of "the first principles of demonstration," but this only enables us to deal adequately with the data which sense experience presents to us; it does not enable us to rise to a level where we are no longer dependent upon it.

The distinction between what is *per se notum secundum se* and what is *per se notum quoad nos* is thus one of extreme importance. St. Thomas does not doubt that the existence of God is *per se notum secundum se*, nor yet that it is *per se notum quoad angelos et sanctos in patria;* the fact that it is not *per se notum quoad nos* only shows how limited our knowledge really is. What is *per se notum secundum se* requires to be demonstrated to us. And St. Thomas is quite sure that this can be done. It is quite possible to prove the existence of God, and quite possible to show that God is wholly simple, so that there can be in him no distinction between essence and existence. We can know, then, *that* this is true, yet, inasmuch as we cannot become directly aware of the divine essence, we cannot see *how* it is true.

Now, however, another question arises. If the existence of God be *per se notum secundum se*, how is it possible to demonstrate it? How could one prove what is self-evident? All proof rests ultimately upon principles which themselves neither require nor admit of proof, and if the existence of God be included among these, the notion of demonstrating it is surely absurd. The weakness of our human intellects, therefore, would seem definitely to deprive us of all knowledge of God. Only one way of escape from this predicament appears to offer itself. Although we cannot directly prove the truth of what is self-evident, we may do so indirectly by a *reductio ad absurdum* of the contradictory proposition. Does it not follow, accordingly, that all proofs of the existence of God are really *reductiones ad absurdum* of the denial that God exists? Does not, for instance, the cosmological argument show that from the assumption that God does not exist the absurd consequence follows that there is no distinction between the possible and the necessary? Does not the teleological argument show that from the assumption that God does not exist it follows that there is no distinction between accident and design? I think that from St. Thomas' standpoint all the arguments for God's existence must be viewed in this light.

What a transformation of the intellectual situation has taken place! St. Anselm believed that he had developed a completely conclusive proof that God exists. For St. Thomas the argument, were it valid—which it is not—would prove that it is utterly impossible to prove that God exists. Is this the end of the road? Or does a further transformation confront us? Indeed there does. For if the existence of God be *per se notum secundum se,* and if it also be possible for us to know that God exists, must not his existence be *per se notum quoad nos?* Does it not follow, therefore, that what we call the ontological argument is really not an argument at all, but a claim to direct perception? Such is indeed the conclusion of Malebranche, the most eminent of the ontologists.

It is interesting to observe the manner in which Malebranche states his view. His presentation of it is conditioned by the fact that he champions ontologism in its extreme form, namely, the *ontologismus rigidus*—as contemporary neoscholastics call it—which affirms that we are directly, although confusedly, aware of God alone. The archetypes of all finite things of which we are indirectly aware are directly apprehended by us as they exist in the divine Intelligence. Thus it is possible for us to doubt the existence of all physical objects, since these we do not directly perceive. Of the Infinite, however, there can be no archetype nor image; consequently, since we certainly can be aware of the Infinite, we must apprehend it directly. In other words, since we can conceive of God, God must exist.[35]

At first glance Descartes' treatment of the ontological argument would appear to display a high degree of freshness and novelty, inasmuch as he not only lays great emphasis upon the notion of divine perfection, but also seems to regard it as a positive attribute; whereas St. Thomas, in his *Contra Gentiles,* includes it among the negative attributes of God which are established by means of the *via remotionis.*[36] A further examination, however, will convince us, I think, that the divergence of outlook is less than we might have

35. See his *Entretiens sur la metaphysique,* 2.7, 8.1. Cf. Professor Morris Ginsberg's trans., *Dialogues on Metaphysics and on Religion* (London, 1923), pp. 92–93, 203.
36. Book I, chap. xxviii.

supposed. Descartes does indeed follow St. Anselm in presenting the ontological argument as a proof of the existence of God, and not as an attempt to show that a demonstration of the divine existence is impossible. With regard to the divine perfection, however, both writers seem to be fairly in accord. Thus St. Thomas declares, "I call that universally perfect which lacks no excellence of any kind." [37] And in a similar spirit Descartes writes, "That substance which we understand to be the highest perfection, and in which we conceive absolutely nothing which involves any limitation or defect, is called God." [38] And it is clear that both thinkers regard the divine essence as including every kind of supreme excellence. Descartes, again, lays repeated emphasis upon the identity of essence and existence as that which necessitates God's existence.[39] It is interesting, moreover, to observe that, although Descartes' conceptualist way of thinking keeps him from anticipating Malebranche's transformation of the argument into a claim to direct awareness of the divine, he at times comes very close to it.[40] Our investigation of his procedure, however, indicates that Descartes' treatment of the ontological argument raises no issues with which we have not already dealt.[41]

I agree with Professor Hartshorne that the scholastic—or, as he prefers to call it, the "classical"—notion of God is quite indefensible. I agree also that if God be a Being with whom we can enter into personal relations, who can protect, punish, and forgive, he must be involved in the temporal process; that if, even as we, God can form and carry out volitions, he is, even as we are, to some extent involved in con-

37. "Dico universaliter perfectum, cui non deest alicuius generis nobilitas" (ibid.).

38. "Substantia, quam summe perfectam esse intellegimus, & in qua nihil plane concipimus quod aliquem defectem sive perfectionis limitationem involvant, Deus vocatur" (Meditations V, ed. Charles Adam and Paul Tannery [Paris, 1904], VII, 162).

39. See Discourse on Method, Part IV; Meditations V; Principles IV; and Rationes Dei Existentiam, Prop. VIII.

40. Cf. the following passage:
"Et pour ce qui est de Dieu, certes, si mon esprit n'estoit preuenu d'aucuns preiugez, & que ma pensée ne se trouvait point diuertie par la presence continuelle des images des choses sensibles, il n'y auroit aucune chose que ie connusse plutost ny plus facilement que luy. Car y a-t-il rien de foy plus clair & plus manifeste, que de penser qu'il y a un Dieu, c'est à dire un estre souuerain & parfait, en l'idée duquel seul l'existence necessaire ou eternelle est comprise, & par consequent qui existe?" Meditations V, IX, 55.

41. Among contemporary philosophers Professor Charles Hartshorne has probably written more extensively than any other concerning the ontological argument—so extensively that to reply in detail to all that he has written would fill a volume. I must therefore confine myself to a few observations upon what I take to be the most crucial points.

tingency. And I agree further that this affects only his accidents, and not his essential being. But I do not see that this makes the case any better for the ontological argument.

Professor Hartshorne makes great play with the notion of perfection; yet he admits that the argument can be stated, even as St. Anselm stated it, without invoking it. And I do not think that he means by "perfection" anything very different from what Descartes and St. Thomas meant—i.e., fulness of being, lack of deficiency. Hence the fundamental question would seem clearly to be whether God's "nature" or "perfection" be identical with, or inclusive of, his existence. St. Thomas is surely right in asserting that if this be self-evident to us it can be so only because we are directly aware of God's nature, which, on this hypothesis, is to be directly aware of God, in which case perception is substituted for argument; whereas, if it be not self-evident to us, it must be demonstrated by some proof which, if I interpret St. Thomas aright, will amount to a *reductio ad absurdum.*

I should wish, however, to depart from the position of St. Thomas further even than Professor Hartshorne does. For it seems clear to me that if God exist he is a substance in the same sense that other substances are substances, that, as *Primus inter pares,* he is a particular having a nature composed of the universals which characterize him. From this it does not follow that God's existence is contingent in the sense that he might not have been. In the case of God, as in that of the Absolute, such a supposition would be meaningless. What is ultimate simply *is.* But, as McTaggart used to say, the proposition that nothing exists is not self-contradictory; a contradiction arises only when someone asserts it, for then the assertion exists. It is vain to look in the nature of God for some logical implication of his existence.

We come back, then, to the fundamental assertion upon the basic significance of which St. Thomas and Malebranche are agreed—that the so-called ontological argument is in reality no argument at all, but a claim to direct perception. As to the soundness of the claim the two philosophers are in complete disagreement. And to attempt to evaluate its soundness is a difficult business. To a nominalist or a conceptualist who holds that all knowledge is ultimately derivative from sense experience, the issue is a relatively simple one. Either he will dismiss religious experience as illusory, or he will classify it as miraculous—or at least as supernatural. But the epistemological realist finds the situation more complicated. He is quite sure that not all knowledge is finally explicable in terms of the stimulation of sense organs, he is quite convinced that we are aware of some universals—such, for example, as mercy, loyalty, and honesty—which do not characterize any sensible particulars; and this prevents him from dogmatically rejecting the claims of religious experience. Yet it does not help him very effectually to make a definite decision.

Awareness of universals, it may be said, is one thing, and awareness of Other Mind—to use W. E. Hocking's phrase—is another. It is true enough that a universal is one thing and a particular another, yet it is not obvious that awareness of a universal, *as awareness,* is different in character from awareness of a particular. If we follow Plato's lead, we shall, indeed, posit a new power or faculty of knowledge whenever we find a new object of knowledge, or class of objects; yet it is not immediately evident that such a multiplication of psychic powers is necessitated. Awareness, as we introspect, would appear to be in itself a simple thing; and should we accept this conclusion, it will shed little light upon the problem before us, and not render the hypothesis of direct awareness of the divine either more or less probable.

Nevertheless, religious experience, as the theist conceives it, seems clearly to involve the communication of mind with Mind. And if such communication be thought of as direct, will it not obviously be in some respect, or to some degree, similar to what we call telepathy? If it be objected that it would be derogatory to the sacredness of the religious experience to classify it under this heading, the reply can appositely be made that, whatever differences may obtain, there must be *something* in common, and that, accordingly, the genuineness of the telepathic experience will tend to corroborate the claim of the religious. Now the genuineness of telepathic occurrences would appear to be established beyond all cavil. Yet there is the further objection that the directness of telepathic communication, and the possible intervention of the physical, are still subject to debate. A more formidable consideration, however, is the following—that in the case of telepathy we have various means of controlling and testing the experience, whereas in the case of religious experience we have none at all.

In a recent article [42] Dr. Ewing has taken issue with McTaggart's conclusion that religious experience is of value only to the person who has it, and that it is useless as evidence to the person who does not have it. The individual who has such an experience, Dr. Ewing contends, is entitled to conclude that "the situation is totally trans-

42. "Awareness of God," p. 9.

formed by the fact that most people agree with me here, thus confirming my intuitive conviction by theirs." How much importance are we to attach to the word "most"? Have we any means of determining whether a majority of individuals in this or in any other period have actually been, or at least have believed themselves to have been, so favored? I think that it is quite obvious that we have not. We may, indeed, appeal to the universality of religion, and triumphantly point out that no tribe has been discovered to be devoid of it; but does this justify us in any more definite conclusion than that in all lands and at all times—or at least in all lands and at some times—there have been *some* individuals whose religious experience has been at first hand, and who have so influenced their fellows that these have been content to accept it at second hand, and to believe and act in accordance with what their seers have told them? And even could we be sure, as we are not, that most people have at some time enjoyed some degree of firsthand experience, it would seem unpleasantly like counting heads to appeal to this as evidence of the veridical nature of such experience. All that we are sure of is that a large number of persons have believed themselves to have enjoyed direct contact with the divine, that a large number of persons have not had such experiences, and that among those who have had such experiences there has been considerable disagreement as to what it is with which they have been in contact.

We must not, of course, make too much of the unmediated character of such experiences. In any normal perception there is an element of direct awareness, but recognition, comparison, and contrast are also involved,[43] and we have no reason to suppose that these play no part in religious experience.

I find it somewhat difficult to evaluate this suggestion, and Dr. Ewing himself admits that the notion requires to be worked out. Perhaps the conversion from a subjective to an objective view of values, or from a naturalistic theory of the self to a belief in the interaction of mind and body, or again, as Dr. Ewing suggests, the contemplation of natural beauty or of a noble character, might provide the psychological or spiritual stimulus necessarily antecedent to a state of direct awareness of the divine—although the presence of implicit inference would be a possibility which could not be ignored. But we seem to be in-

43. I remember once reading the account of a British trader who on safari arrived at an outpost of civilization where a train was standing at the railroad station. The Negroes with him observed the locomotive with interest, and remarked that it seemed to be very hot and must want a drink. Their error, a natural one, resulted from the employment of normal psychological processes.

evitably driven to the conclusion that the only person competent to evaluate such an experience is the man who has it—and he only if he be at home in the fields of psychology and philosophy.

It may not be amiss, however, to consider certain logical possibilities. (1) It might conceivably be the case, as the Gnostics thought, that there are inherent and ineradicable differences of capacity among men, so that some are endowed by nature with the ability to attain to spiritual insight, whereas others are by a natural deficiency permanently deprived of it. (2) It might be the case that some individuals, although naturally possessed of no greater capacity for spiritual insight than their fellows, are yet arbitrarily chosen, as the Calvinists believe, to be the recipients of divine grace and divine illumination. (3) Or it might be the case that all persons with normal intellectual powers are naturally endowed with a potential ability to attain to direct awareness of the divine. Here we must recognize two subordinate possibilities: (a) It might be that divine co-operation is requisite for such attainment in all, or in some instances, or (b) it might be that success depends entirely upon the effort and resolution of the individual. Between these possibilities I do not believe that we are in a position to decide upon empirical grounds, and one's choice will unavoidably be made in accordance with the general metaphysical view which one has adopted.

Dr. Ewing has made the very interesting suggestion [44] that some of the discrepancies between the reports of mystical experiences may be accounted for on the supposition that there are actually two modes of such experience, each with its own object; in one case the Absolute, in the other a personal God. Of these two hypothetical modes he has written, "Both experiences might be veridical without being incompatible with each other. They would then only seem incompatible because they were conceived wrongly as referring to the same object. And perhaps religion could not attain its full value without both. This suggestion opens up very interesting possibilities for discussion and may by separating the two concepts help to solve some antinomies about God."

This is well said. And in the future, when the mystical experience has been subjected to more intensive study than it has yet received, it is conceivable that some empirical evidence may be provided in support of this hypothesis. At present, however, it is a hypothesis which would seem to complicate, rather than relieve, the situation. With our own point of view it would indeed appear to be more congenial than

44. "Awareness of God," pp. 16–17.

with any other. But how are we to go about demonstrating the truth of such a theory? "If you have the experience," the Calvinist will say, "you will know what to think of it; if you do not have it, you will not know." "If you do not have the experience," the exasperated student of comparative religion might reply, "you will not know what to think of it, and no more will you if you do have it." It is true of course that the experience seems normally to carry conviction with it, yet more to the unreflective than to the reflective mind. Without desiring to depreciate the cognitive element in the experience, I agree with Professor Bertocci [45] in his view that the most impressive thing about it is the spiritual vitality it imparts. Even to read the accounts of the mystics—especially of the philosophical mystics—is an exhilarating experience. And this vitality, which no doubt springs from the conviction of genuine cognition, does strongly suggest an encounter with something objectively real. But suggestion is not demonstration. "First prove the existence of God," says St. Thomas, "and then you will know what to think of it." Though the blast of Calvin's trumpet thrill us to the very depths of our being, must we not acknowledge that as of now St. Thomas has the last word?

45. *The Empirical Argument for God in Late British Thought* (Cambridge, Mass., 1938), pp. 224–225.

CHAPTER FOUR

THE COSMOLOGICAL ARGUMENT

The name which Kant bestowed upon this argument has the advantage of brevity and the disadvantage of vagueness. More definite and more descriptive are the scholastic appellations: "the argument from the contingency of the world" and "the argument from the possible and the necessary." Of the famous *quinque viae* of St. Thomas this constitutes the third.[1] The latter of these two titles recalls the ontological argument, and brings to mind Kant's contention that the cosmological argument presupposes the ontological. The truth of the contention, however, cannot be admitted. For the ontological argument, as we have seen, takes as its starting point either a direct awareness of God or a description of God. In the former case, as Malebranche has pointed out, it is really not an argument at all, but a claim to direct perception. In the latter case it begins with a description or concept of God, and does not even take into consideration the existent world; whereas the third argument can take as its point of departure any concrete reality you please, so long as that reality is recognized as not self-explanatory, and consequently as pointing beyond itself.

The second Kantian objection is that the argument—even if its validity be conceded—leads only to an *ens realissimum*, and gives no ground for identifying this ultimate reality with the God of Christian theology. This objection is no more than a flash in the pan, for St. Thomas would thoroughly agree that no such equation can be

1. In my *Conception of God in the Philosophy of St. Thomas Aquinas* (London, 1933), I expressed the opinion that the first three ways constituted in fact a single argument, and that of the three successive formulations of it by St. Thomas the third is the most adequate. I rather expected to be taken severely to task for making so venturesome an assertion, but my critics received my pronouncement with considerable calmness. On thinking the matter over, however, I have arrived at the conclusion that my statement needs to be qualified. The first of St. Thomas' proofs, the argument from motion, involves the notion of time, and so does the second, the argument from efficient causality—at least if causality be understood to involve the precedence of cause to effect. But the third proof, while it may be said to include the other two, yet has a wider scope, for even in a timeless universe logical dependence might be present. It is the only one of the three arguments, however, with which we need concern ourselves, inasmuch as the other two are in the nature of abstractions from it.

drawn out of hand. He does, indeed, presuppose that all would concede that this ultimate reality may with propriety be called God; yet he is so far from assuming that this admission entitles him to equate it with the God of Christian theology that he at once undertakes to prove his case by working his way through all the multitudinous chapters dealing with the *via remotionis* and the *via affirmativa*, and does not consider his contention made good until the task is completed. Locke, indeed, professes to establish the same conclusion in a few short sentences; yet he realizes, no less than St. Thomas, that it requires to be done. Without expecting one argument, then, to prove everything, let us inspect this argument as it stands, without any prejudgment as to what it *must* prove, or *ought* to prove, with a view only to discovering what, if anything, it does prove.

Before doing so, however, it behooves us to call attention to an important distinction, of which it is to be hoped that all philosophers are by this time aware, but of which many essayists, journalists, and reviewers are obviously unaware, the distinction between the argument before us and the argument for a first cause in the temporal sense of the word "first." The contention of the latter argument is that it is inadmissible to posit in the past an infinite regress of causes and effects, and that, accordingly, there must have occurred at a definite remove from the present an initial causative act from which originated the entire subsequent process, which of course is finite in length. This argument was emphatically rejected by Maimonides and, following him, by St. Thomas.

Like MacKenzie and Dr. Ewing I confess to a dissatisfaction with what appears to me to be so cavalier a treatment of an important problem. For if the series of successive causes and effects have but one end, namely, the present, and if it extend endlessly into the past, we are confronted with a completed infinite. And as Dr. Ewing has pertinently observed, the difficulty is not removed by a redefinition of the term "infinite." This is a mere mathematical "dodge," which may justify itself to the mathematician insofar as he finds it useful, but which, when employed by a metaphysician, constitutes an evasion, and not a solution of the problem. It is not an argument, however, with which we need at the moment to concern ourselves, for even if valid, it leads only to the conclusion which, on axiological grounds, we have already accepted, that the temporal series had a beginning; and acceptance of this conclusion will not help us to decide the question of the existence of God.

The argument we are about to examine is based upon the conten-

tion that an infinite ontological, not a temporal, regress is inconceivable.[2] In other words, it asserts that the dependent implies the
independent, and the contingent the necessary. By the contingent
we are to understand, not that which need not, or might not, have
been—although, if we be indeterminists, we shall hold that there are
contingencies in this sense—but that which is not self-explanatory,
that which does not account for itself but refers us to the scheme of
the universe of which it is a part. And by the necessary we are to
understand, not that whose existence is logically entailed by its essence, not that whose existence cannot be denied without self-
contradiction, but that which is ultimate in the sense that it does
not depend for its existence upon anything else, that which neither
arises nor passes away, which neither comes into being nor ceases
to be, but which *is*.

If we attempt to account for A by the assertion that A is wholly
dependent upon B, our statement will be adequate only if B is entirely
independent, and therefore requires no accounting for. But if B in
turn be dependent upon C, we shall not have accounted for A until
we have brought in C. And if C likewise be dependent upon something other than itself, we shall still not have accounted for A in
a thoroughly satisfactory manner; we shall have accounted for it only
relatively but not absolutely. As metaphysicians we shall be satisfied
only if we have followed the chain of dependence to its ultimate
terminus. For it must terminate somewhere in something which is
completely self-sufficing, and so neither requires nor admits of being
itself accounted for, yet is itself explanatory of the entities dependent
upon it.

Such, as first developed by Avicenna, and subsequently presented
to us by the great scholastics, is the argument from the possible and
the necessary. I may say at once that it appears to me completely
conclusive. But it will not appear conclusive at all to anyone who
accepts what Dr. Ewing has called the regularity view of causality.
Yet we are almost inevitably impelled to ask how anyone can genuinely and confidently accept the regularity view. Presumably some
men can, since so many men profess to do so, and to question their
veracity would be invidious. Yet to do so, as Dr. Ewing has pointed
out, is tantamount to admitting that the so-called laws of nature are
merely "runs of luck." And if this be conceded, my hesitation to throw
my lighted cigar into a wastepaper basket must be put on an intel-

2. Spinoza, indeed, contended that the series might be composed of an infinite
number of particulars provided that it had a first and a final term.

lectual par with some men's unwillingness to walk under a ladder or to sit down with twelve other individuals at a table. In actual daily life no one ever acts in accordance with such a theory. No scientist, for example, would for a moment accept as an adequate explanation of an earthquake the statement that it was a sporadic event in no sense produced, entailed, or necessitated by any preceding event or state of affairs. There must be some very strong urge which can drive men to adopt such a position, for to do so is clearly a last desperate step which must be taken to avoid some excessively unwelcome admission. That there is such an urge, and that it is of a psychological or socio-political rather than of a purely philosophical character I am fully convinced, but this is not the place to discuss the matter. The regularity view of causality we have already discussed at length, and I have no intention of reiterating at this point what I have already said about it.

The fundamental contention that the dependent involves the in-dependent is one which must, and will, be granted by anyone who accepts either the entailment or the activity view of causality, and of course by anyone who maintains that the two theories can be harmonized. We shall have to concede, therefore, that that which arises and passes away cannot be ultimate, that it is manifestly deriva-tive, a consequent which implies a ground, and that it must imme-diately or mediately be dependent upon a reality which is ultimate and which neither begins to be nor ceases to be. In view of our previous examination of the nature of causality the question now before us is not whether the argument be sound, but what it proves. Does it merely lead us, as our examination of the claims of axio-logical idealism has already led us, to an all-inclusive Absolute? Is the mutability of the parts amply accounted for by the stability of the whole? Or does the argument, as most of its proponents have held, at least lay the foundation of a theistic cosmology?

The case for this latter interpretation has been so well stated by A. E. Taylor in his discussion of the argument from motion that I cannot refrain from citing his words:

> The dependence meant in the argument has nothing to do with succession in time. What is really meant is that our knowledge of any event in Nature is not complete until we know the full reason for the event. So long as you only know that A is so because B is so, but cannot tell why B is so, your knowledge is incomplete. It only becomes complete when you are in a position to say that

ultimately A is so because Z is so, Z being something which is its own *raison d'être,* and therefore such that it would be senseless to ask why Z is so. This at once leads to the conclusion that since we always have the right to ask about any event in Nature why that event is so, what are its conditions, the Z which is its own *raison d'être* cannot itself belong to Nature. The point of the reasoning is precisely that it is an argument from the fact that there is a "Nature" to the reality of a "Supernature," and this point is unaffected by the question whether there ever was a beginning of time, or a time when there were no "events." [3]

Before we accord unqualified assent to this argument, we are entitled to ask the precise meanings of the terms "Nature" and "Supernature." And there is no doubt about the answer. "Supernature," for Taylor, is the creative God of orthodox Christian theology, and "Nature" is the created world. If we have been right in rejecting the doctrine of creation as unintelligible, our dissent from this position is a foregone conclusion. Nevertheless we shall do well to examine carefully Taylor's course of reasoning, for a great deal of what he says is profoundly true.

His first point is that if the argument which he has so forcefully stated be rejected, there will be a vast amount of "brute fact" which will remain unaccounted for.

You must have individual variety as well as uniformity, in whatever you choose to take as your postulated original data if you are to get out of the data a world like ours, which, as Mill truly says, is not only uniform but infinitely various. *Ex nihilo, nihil fit,* and equally out of blank uniformity nothing *fit* but a uniformity equally blank. Even if, *per impossibile,* you could exclude all individual variety from the initial data of a system of natural science, you might properly be asked to account for this singular absence of variety, and a naturalistic account of it could only take the form of deriving it from some more ultimate state of things which was not marked by absolute "uniformity." Neither uniformity nor variety is self-explanatory; whichever you start with must simply be taken as brute "fact," for which there is no reason at all, or if there is a reason, it must be found outside Nature in the "supernatural." [4]

3. See his essay, "The Vindication of Religion," in *Essays Catholic and Critical,* ed. E. G. Selwyn (New York, 1926), p. 50.
4. *Ibid.,* pp. 50–51.

Faced with this situation we are obliged, according to Taylor, to choose one of two courses. On the one hand we may make bold to affirm that, whereas the part is contingent and is not self-explanatory, the whole to which it belongs is both necessary and self-explanatory. This is a line of reasoning which has appealed to us, and which we have found on the whole satisfactory. There will, then, Taylor remarks, "be no contrast between Nature and 'supernature,' but only between 'Nature' apprehended as a 'whole' and Nature as we have apprehended her fragmentarily." [5] But, if we take this course, we strike a reef upon which we shall founder; for Nature is not a whole, but merely a "complex of events."

Thus no amount of knowledge of "natural laws" will explain the present actual state of Nature unless we also assume it as a brute fact that the distribution of "matter" and "energy" (or whatever else we take as the ultimates of our system of physics) a hundred millions of years ago was such and such. With the same "laws" and a different "initial" distribution the actual state of the world to-day would be very different. "Collocations," to use Mill's terminology, as well as "laws of causation" have to enter into all our scientific explanations. And though it is true that as our knowledge grows, we are continually learning to assign causes for particular "collocations" originally accepted as bare facts, we only succeed in doing so by falling back on other anterior "collocations" which we have equally to take as unexplained bare facts. As Meyerson puts it, we only get rid of the "inexplicable" at one point at the price of introducing it again somewhere else. Now any attempt to treat the complex of facts we call Nature as something which will be found to be more nearly self-explanatory the more of them we know, and would become quite self-explanatory if we only knew them all, amounts to an attempt to eliminate "bare fact" altogether, and reduce Nature simply to a complex of "laws." In other words, it is an attempt to manufacture particular existents out of mere universals, and therefore must end in failure. And the actual progress of science bears witness to this. The more we advance to the reduction of the visible face of Nature to "law," the more, not the less, complex and baffling become the mass of characters which we have to attribute as bare unexplained fact to our ultimate constituents. An electron is a much stiffer dose of "brute" fact than one of Newton's hard impenetrable corpuscles.[6]

5. *Ibid.*, p. 53.   6. *Ibid.*, pp. 53–54.

If our hearts sink before the difficulties thus presented to us, we shall naturally inquire what is the other alternative which Taylor offers us. It is the frank renunciation of any attempt at ultimate explanation. It is of course possible for a man by an act of will to make this renunciation and to adopt the attitude of the agnostic. Yet by so doing, Taylor points out, he explicitly repudiates the fundamental conviction of the scientist that the attempt at explanation must never be abandoned, that the inexplicable must never be acquiesced in, that "brute fact" must never be accepted at its face value, the conviction to which science owes all the progress it has made in the past and upon which all its hopes of future progress depend.

"Thus," declares Taylor,

> we inevitably reach the conclusion that either the very principles which inspire and guide scientific inquiry itself are an illusion, or Nature itself must be dependent on some reality which is self-explanatory, and therefore not Nature nor any part of Nature, but, in the strict sense of the words, "supernatural" or "transcendent"— transcendent, that is, in the sense that in it there is overcome that duality of "law" and "fact" which is characteristic of Nature and every part of Nature. It is not "brute" fact, and yet it is not an abstract universal law or complex of such laws, but a really existing self-luminous Being, such that you could see, if you only apprehended its true character, that to have that character and to be are the same thing. This is the way in which Nature, as it seems to me, inevitably points beyond itself as the temporal and mutable to an "other" which is eternal and immutable.[7]

It will be observed that although in these passages Taylor makes no great play with the notion of creation, yet it is clearly presupposed. "Nature" is, he tells us, "the complex of events," and "Supernature," as the name implies, is radically to be distinguished from it. Now I quite agree, as I have already repeatedly said, that a series of events cannot be equated with ultimate reality; for events are by their very nature wholly derivative; they are not persisting things or substances; they are essentially transitory. But if we regard the succession of events as suspended, as it were, from a reality which is wholly transcendent and aloof, we shall find ourselves compelled to conceive of physical nature in the light of the Buddhist doctrine of pure momentariness; bereft of being it will consist of mere becoming. But this, I maintain, is utterly incredible. Events are derivative, and not

7. *Ibid.*, p. 55.

ultimate, entities because they involve agents, patients, and inter-relations; and these constitute not a transcendent but an immanent reality which is the abiding ground of becoming.

These considerations in no degree deprive the cosmological argument of its inherent force. For its fundamental contention is that the dependent implies the independent, and the transient the permanent; and to this contention we have heartily acceded. In other words, what the cosmological argument does is to demonstrate the existence of the Absolute. But it does not tell what the Absolute is.

If by "Nature" we are to understand with Taylor "the complex of events," [8] it is clear that it cannot constitute a "true whole" because of the incompleteness necessarily involved in its derivative character. I doubt, however, whether in common usage the meaning of the term be quite so restricted, whether it do not include not only "the complex of events" but also the entities involved in these events; whether, in other words, we be not justified in roughly equating it with the physical world. This last phrase, again, can be taken literally only by men who believe in the reality of matter, and as I have already made clear, I am not one of those; for I have argued that the universe constitutes an intelligible system composed of selves and universals, and that the physical world can best be accounted for as appearance. But I have also maintained that should I be mistaken in this latter contention, and should it prove necessary to concede the genuine and ultimate reality of matter, this will not suffice to disrupt the system. For what gives the system its unity is its axiological orientation. It may be the failure to grasp this aspect of the cosmic situation which has led the Nyāya-Vaiśeṣika philosophy to introduce the notion of a personal God as the ground of world order. By saying this I do not mean to cut short the discussion of the claims of the theistic hypothesis, or to deny in advance that we ourselves may find it necessary—or at least advisable—to postulate the existence of a Being comparable to the Īśvara to Hindu thought and to the God of Howison or Dawes Hicks. We would indeed be presumptuous to do so, for the famous teleological argument has yet to be considered. I am only saying that

8. I do not mean to accuse Taylor of denying the existence of created substances. Yet his argument is stated in terms of events, as though these made up the entire content of nature. Even though the existence of created substances be admitted, however, the situation is not greatly changed. For these substances will be brought into being through the agency of a transcendent and supreme power, and during every moment of their existence they will be sustained by, and their being will be imparted to them by, the same power. Thus, as truly as events, they will "point beyond themselves."

if the universe itself, as I have tried to show, be a coherent and an intelligible system, it is the end to which the cosmological argument leads us.

If we use the term "nature" to signify all that is derivative, contingent, and dependent in the universe, it is clear that there must also be a "supernature" which is composed of that which is underived, ultimate, and abiding. We can say, if we like, that while the whole is necessary, the parts are contingent, if by this we mean that the parts are not isolated entities but are included in the whole and stand in necessary relations to one another. But this should not blind us to the fact that the whole is not a mere aggregate but has a structure of its own. If we prefer, following Erigena and Spinoza, to apply to the whole the term "nature," there will then be no "supernature." But the question of terminology is to be decided by convenience or personal preference; it is relatively insignificant, and the answer to it settles no ultimate issue. Our problem is simply whether within the whole there be included a supreme personal Being.

It is true, nonetheless, that our approach to this problem is in an important respect conditioned by our acceptance of two conclusions taken as previously established—that selves and universals are ultimate and eternal realities and that the notion of creation is unintelligible. Hence we cannot employ this notion after the fashion of Taylor, and of the scholastics before him, to demonstrate the existence of a creative God. As it presents itself to us, therefore, the theistic problem reduces to the question: Is there within the universe, that is to say, within the Absolute, a personal Being whose influence extends to every part of the universe, and who in goodness, wisdom, and power so far surpasses all other beings as to deserve to be called God? This question, it is now plain, the cosmological argument cannot answer. Our only hope of obtaining a positive answer, therefore, lies in the teleological argument. To the teleological argument, then, let us turn.

The Teleological Argument

The argument from design, or—as he renamed it—the physico-theological argument, is subjected, Kant tells us, to the limitation that even if it be sound, it can do no more than prove the existence of an "architect" of the world. An argument which could do this, we may remark in passing, would do a very great deal. And if by "architect" be meant a designer who works with materials which he did not himself produce, we may add that from our point of view it will have done all that any argument on behalf of the theistic hypothesis could do.

It is important for us to notice that unlike the ontological and cosmological arguments the teleological argument, as usually presented, aims at no more than the establishment of a high degree of probability. It is true that if we could point to some event which by general agreement was inexplicable in terms of natural law or of human activity, then, on the principle that every effect requires a cause adequate to produce it, we might argue a priori the existence of a supernatural cause. But such an event would constitute nothing less than a miracle. And now we see why the doctrine of miracles was deemed of so great importance, and was treated with such high respect by such thinkers as Locke and Channing.[9] Their whole outlook on the subject was vastly different from ours, and for three reasons.

In the first place, in their eyes the Four Gospels were documents of unimpeachable authority, all the genuine compositions of the men to whom they are attributed, two of whom were actual apostles, and the other two early disciples of unquestionable integrity, so that all these works included testimony of eyewitnesses with respect to the miracles of Christ. What better evidence could be desired? And the same held true of the miracles recounted in the Old Testament, all of which were supposed to have been recorded by eyewitnesses. How could such testimony be discounted except by employing the hypothesis of deliberate deceit, which seemed too fantastic to be taken seriously. To us, on the other hand, who approach the subject enlightened by the results of modern criticism, and who have some notion of the complex strands which are incorporated in the sacred writings, and of the divergent views of competent critics, the evidence appears highly questionable, and at a far remove from what could be desired.

In the second place, psychologists have made us all to some degree aware of how difficult it is for people of normal intelligence and integrity accurately to recount what they have themselves observed, and how perilous it is to rely confidently upon the testimony of eye-

9. It is interesting to note that the orthodox Jonathan Edwards, whose point of departure is the mystical and aesthetic insight of Calvinism, while he does not dream of denying the occurrence of miracles, treats the whole doctrine very much *de haut en bas,* and attributes to it much less importance than do these heretical thinkers.

witnesses. And in the third place, the study of the history of religion, and of comparative religion, has shown that in an atmosphere of religious excitement the belief in miracles can spring up with ease and may proceed to amazing lengths.

These considerations do not, to my mind, justify us in dismissing offhand the whole question of miracles. The extreme "liberal" has frequently taken up such a position, but in so doing, he becomes a dogmatist. The belief in the *possibility* of miracles would seem to follow logically from the belief in a personal God; for to suppose that the Deity is unable to suspend the functioning of laws which he has himself originated, or which he has at least employed and co-operated with, would appear preposterous. The question for the believer is emphatically one of fact, not of possibility. What is required is evidence, and the evidence is fragile indeed.[10] This is why theologians who still believe in miracles, instead of using them as a basis of proof, are compelled to treat them as occurrences which must be proved, so that the argument *from* miracles has been set aside.

I have referred to the doctrine of miracles only in connection with the question what constitutes evidence of design. For the believer in the regularity view of causality anything can follow from anything, and no event is necessitated. This view we have definitely rejected. For any event we are entitled to seek a reason. Now if a single miraculous event could be definitely authenticated, we should have at once an adequate basis for an argument to the existence of a supernatural cause. In the absence of such an event what other kinds of events are ruled out? What can we take as indicative of purpose? The presence of order, it may be said. But what sort of order? If a blast of wind sweep a pack of cards from a table and scatter them over the floor, they will fall in some sort of order. The order, it may be observed, is not indicative of purpose. Quite so. But what sort of order *is* indicative of purpose? May not chance, or the action of natural laws simulate, so to speak, purpose? Perhaps they may. One might point to the formation of crystals, for example. To find an instance which can plausibly be taken as indicative of purpose must we not be able to point to the adaptation of means to an end such as a rational being would desire, to an end, that is, which is either good in itself

10. The evidence for the appearances of Jesus to his disciples after the crucifixion falls indeed in another category. For here we have the firsthand testimony of Paul as to his own experience, and the testimony of the other disciples transmitted by him. This does not indeed settle the question, for there remains the possibility of illusion. Moreover, it is doubtful whether the appearances, even if genuine, should technically be termed miraculous.

or useful in the sense that it lends itself to the realization of some further end which is good in itself?

Here again, however, we must acknowledge that many events which to the physicist admit of a thoroughly natural explanation have often appeared, and perhaps inevitably appeared, to the religious man as divinely ordained. When, for example, Coligny, fleeing with his household and followers before the Roman Catholics, successfully crossed a river at a ford which was unguarded because the water was at an exceptionally low level, and which therefore was usually impassible, and when thereafter a sudden rainstorm caused the water to rise so as to render passage impracticable for the pursuers, how could the grateful Protestants fail to see the hand of God in these events? True, they were not concerned with evaluating the teleological argument; as good Calvinists they believed in God already, and in the light of this belief they evaluated these events. But we, as philosophers, are trying to evaluate the belief in the light of events. Yet, in disregarding events which have been deemed to be miraculous, and in turning to those of a "natural" order, are we not abandoning quality for quantity? And how are we to determine how many the number of such events must be to satisfy us? And, again, is not the notion of a natural providential event a confusion of incompatible characteristics? Is there any intermediate stage between the completely miraculous and the wholly natural? If the theist be right in holding that all events are dependent upon God, are not all events in an occult sense, as we might say, miraculous? But is the theist right? How are we to classify the events in the light of which his claim is to be evaluated?

What if we turn to the whole material world—on the supposition that there is a material world—and raise the question whether it can be conceived as all-inclusive, self-sustained, and self-explanatory. If we can show that some immaterial principle of order must be admitted, shall we not have vindicated the teleological argument? Here we may derive some assistance from what at first glance might have seemed a most unlikely source, namely, from McTaggart. And there is indeed an apparent inconsistency which I for one do not know how to account for. That every dualistic philosophy if fully developed is bound to transform itself sooner or later into a materialism was an opinion frankly expressed by McTaggart. Nonetheless, in *Some Dogmas of Religion*,[11] we find him arguing that "if we concede the existence of matter, the existence of a finite, non-creative God is highly prob-

11. Secs. 195–201.

able." And this is a contention of great importance for us, since this is the only idea of God compatible with our conception of the Absolute. It is true that, writing in 1906, McTaggart was thinking of matter in terms of the hard indivisible little atoms of the contemporary scientist. Yet this need not deter us from scrutinizing his argument, for it will apply with equal force to the more dynamic, yet more elusive, matter of our own contemporary scientists.

Much of what we observe in experience appears, at any rate, not to be spirit but matter. And the traces of order and goodness are to be observed in this part of our experience as well as in others. Now suppose that this appearance is correct, and that those parts of the universe, which present themselves *prima facie* as matter, really were matter. In that case we should have existent reality which was unconscious, which was not actuated by final causes, since it could desire nothing and judge nothing good, and which was actuated only by causes of a mechanical nature. Moreover, it would either be infinitely divisible, or divided into a great number of very small parts, and its parts would have no intrinsic connexions which should arrange them in order, but would enter into various combinations according to the external forces which actuate them.

If such matter shows an order tending to the good which does not arise from the action of a conscious being with an intention to promote the good, such an order can only arise, as is commonly said, by chance. This does not mean that the events which brought the order had no cause, for every event has a cause. (Even the systems which deny this of human volitions would not deny it of matter.) What then is meant by chance? [12]

To illustrate what he means by chance McTaggart resorts to the supposition that a roulette table, so constructed that letters took the place of numbers, should proceed to spell out the text of *Hamlet*. Let us further assume that the table is an "honest table," so that no chicanery is involved. The result, then, was predetermined, and could have been foreseen by a person equipped with sufficient knowledge of the structure and motion of the table.

There is no contingency in the connexion of the particular cause with the particular effect. We cannot get contingency unless we

12. *Ibid.*, sec. 197.

describe the cause and the effect respectively by some general class to which each of them belongs. And then we get contingency if the nature of the general class to which the cause belongs has no tendency to ensure that the effect shall be of the general class to which, in point of fact, it does belong. Thus it is not contingent that a roulette table of the sort I have described should produce an effect which is a succession of letters. The nature of such roulette tables ensures that they should produce such an effect. It could not, for example, produce a succession of numbers, because the holes are not marked with numbers, but letters. But if we bring the effect under another general class to which it belongs, and call it not merely a succession of letters (which it is) but also a copy of the play of Hamlet (which it also is), then the connexion is contingent. For there is nothing in the nature of such roulette tables as a class which makes it necessary or probable that its effect should come under the general class of copies of Hamlet. Thus we do not say that it is a chance that the table produces a sequence of letters, but we do say that it is a chance that it produces Hamlet.

If then, matter uninfluenced by mind should assume a form which contained ordered means towards a good end, we should say that this was a chance, not meaning that the particular cause could have produced anything but what it did produce, but meaning that there is no necessity or probability that a cause which answers to the description of matter should produce such an effect as answers to the description of ordered means towards a good end.[13]

The advantage of postulating mind as the cause of effects which we deem to be good is that the goodness of the effect provides the mind with a reason for producing it, whereas, if the cause of effects be unintelligent matter, there will be an innumerable number of situations which, so far as we can see, might equally well result, and all of which are equally probable, so that the actual result compared with those not realized will be vastly improbable.

"There is certainly some force in this contention," remarks McTaggart,

but it is not as strong as it is sometimes supposed to be. It is sometimes put as if the antecedent improbability was that of precisely

13. *Ibid.*, sec. 198.

the actual arrangement of the universe occurring among all the possible arrangements which undirected matter might fall into. But this is wrong. For many other arrangements of the universe would have given us as good reason to trace order directed towards good as the present arrangement can. Consequently to account for the present state of the world, we should have, after assuming a directing mind, to assume that it had chanced to produce this particular arrangement, when it might just as well, as far as we can see, have produced any one of many others, and was therefore less likely to have produced the existing one than some one of the others.

Of course, if the present order is produced by a directing mind there must be a sufficient cause why it produced this order rather than another. But then, if the present order were produced by undirected matter, there must be a sufficient cause why it produced this order rather than any other arrangement. The argument was based on the fact that all we know about the nature of undirected matter was equally compatible with an enormous number of other arrangements. And it must accept as relevant the corresponding fact that all we know about the nature of a mind which wills the good would be equally compatible with a number of different orders.

Thus the greater improbability of the hypothesis which excludes a directing mind is not to be expressed, as is sometimes maintained, by the proportion of a large number to unity, but of one large number to another. But the number of arrangements which show some traces of such an order is very small compared with the total number of arrangements of which undirected matter is capable. And thus the argument, if not as strong as has been sometimes supposed, retains considerable strength.[14]

The careful reader will, I assume, be prepared to admit that in these paragraphs McTaggart has given us a very judicial and impartial description of the situation. "But there is another point to be considered," he continues.

The improbability of a result arising by chance depends on the number of times that it does happen compared with the number of times when it might have happened and did not. If I cast a die ten times, and threw a six each time, I should have little

14. *Ibid.*, sec. 200.

doubt that it had been loaded. But if I cast it sixty million times, and got only one run of ten sixes, I should find no difficulty in supposing that it came by chance.

Now it is possible that all the traces of order in the universe are in the position of the run of ten sixes among sixty million throws. Our present decision is based upon the hypothesis that matter does exist, and that its existence is not necessarily connected with spirit. In that case it would be possible that by far the greater amount of the universe at this moment does not exhibit the least traces of order, since it is quite possible that by far the greater amount of the universe is beyond the range of our observation.[15] And it would be possible that by far the greater amount of past time did not exhibit, and that by far the greater amount of future time will not exhibit, any traces of order in any part of the universe. The proportion of the amount of the universe which shows such traces to the amount which does not may be so small as to make the order which we see as explicable by chance as the run of ten sixes in sixty million throws.[16]

Although this consideration to some extent weakens, it does not suffice, McTaggart holds, completely to discredit the argument:

The improbability that the traces of order should be due to chance is thus lessened, but it is not removed. For the existence of vast areas of reality in which no trace of order is to be observed, while certainly possible, is not more than possible.

The conclusion so far seems to be that, if any reality is rightly conceived as matter, then there is a considerable probability— though by no means a certainty—that any traces of order in it are due to a directing person.[17]

15. I do not find that these considerations need be qualified in view of the statements of some contemporary scientists with respect to the spatio-temporal dimensions of the universe. For in the first place we should have to be sure that such views were definitely and finally established, whereas they would appear to be still open to contention. In the second place we should need to be sure that the terms employed by scientists and metaphysicians were employed in a univocal sense. In the third place we should have to be sure that our spatio-temporal universe is inclusive of all reality. And lastly, were we to concede all these points, the result would be merely to reinforce the conclusion which McTaggart proceeds to draw.

16. *Ibid.*, sec. 201.

17. *Ibid.* If faith is, as the scholastics have defined it, "the assent of the intellect at the command of the will," it is pretty obvious that it must take more faith to be a materialist than it does to be a theist.

That the argument thus stated applies, not only to a universe which contains Newtonian matter, but also to one containing any contemporary substitute for the same, is, I think, sufficiently obvious. As we have seen,[18] however, McTaggart holds that, as a matter of fact, the universe contains no matter, that it is composed of spirits, and, moreover, that these spirits constitute a society which possesses a systemic structure, and which is so ordered that *sub specie temporis* it is productive of goodness to an extent which vastly outweighs the amount of evil which it contains. By following a process of reasoning somewhat different from that which he expounds we have reached a very similar conclusion. Accordingly we have now to consider whether he is justified in maintaining that in such a universe no basis can be found for the argument from design.

We must also observe that between McTaggart's system and our own there is an important difference which needs to be emphasized. McTaggart is a confident and complete determinist. For him it is out of the question that any event which occurred should not have occurred, or that any event which did not occur should have occurred. Possibility, therefore, has meaning only in the sense of our own ignorance of actuality. The acts of every self follow inevitably from its own nature and the circumstances in which it is placed; and this is as true of God, if there be a God, as of every other self. If, then, the universe is so ordered as to produce good, the good will assuredly be produced, the process of production being neither hastened nor hindered by any unnecessitated volition.

In our view the situation is very different. Our universe is no less ordered with respect to the production of good than is McTaggart's, but it is our fundamental conviction that moral value can be instantiated only by a genuinely free act. This does not mean, as I have already pointed out, that the act was unmotivated, but that it was unnecessitated, that it was actually possible for the actor to have acted otherwise. The self that acts wrongly acts in opposition to, and in defiance of, the axiological structure of the universe, whereas the self that acts rightly acts in accord therewith. The latter presses on toward the realization of its τέλος, the former recedes from it. Progress toward the ultimate goal may therefore be beneficially or harmfully affected by the free action of the self concerned, and also by the free actions of other selves in a position to influence it. Hence, if there be in the universe a self of superhuman goodness, wisdom, and power, we may rationally expect that its influence will exert a profound ef-

18. *Ibid.*, sec. 206.

fect upon the moral progress and the happiness of subordinate selves. Consequently the question whether such a being exists is of more practical importance to us than it is to McTaggart.

Moreover there is no adequate explanation of the presence of evil in McTaggart's universe. We are told that the evil experiences must unavoidably be passed through so that the good experiences which follow may be attained, but in a deterministic universe this does not appear to be a sufficient explanation, or even an explanation at all. Evil, for McTaggart, is bound up with the temporal process; yet the temporal process is illusory, whereas the evil is real, and is conserved in the eternal. The later stages of the C series are, on the whole, better than the earlier stages; yet why this should be the case, why there should even be a C series, we are not told. It would seem that these are "brute facts" which we are expected to accept "with natural piety," a rather strange state of affairs in a universe as rational as McTaggart's purports to be.

On our view, however, the actualization both of moral good and of moral evil springs from the exercise of free will. The possibility of the one involves that of the other. One of the great advantages of the libertarian's view of the universe is that according to it the rationality of the whole is not only compatible with the actual irrationality of the parts, but also logically involves the possibility of such irrationality. A standing objection to the argument from design has always been the presence of moral evil in the universe. But now we find ourselves in a position to set this objection aside. For if there be a non-creative God, however great his power and however vast his wisdom, he will be compelled to deal with a tremendous number of inferior selves of enormously varying degrees of goodness and evil, of intelligence and of stupidity, each of whom is morally responsible for his individual acts; and even could God constrain all these selves to will and to act as he would wish them to will and to act, he would defeat his own purpose by so doing, for he would thereby transform them from free agents into automata. If this reasoning be sound, the presence of moral evil in the universe is no reflection upon the goodness of God.

The presence of evil in the form of pain and suffering does indeed constitute a much tougher problem, inasmuch as a great deal of it is not due to the agency of human beings. Whether there be any hope of dealing with it satisfactorily, or whether we must finally resign ourselves to accepting it as "brute fact"—that is to say, as "ultimate mystery"—it would certainly be a base evasion on the part of a defender of axiological idealism to take no notice of it. Yet, to attempt to probe it at this stage of our discussion, would involve us in a digression so lengthy as to take us far from the teleological argument. I promise, therefore, to return to it, and to say what I can about it, in the next chapter. For the present I ask no more of the reader than to concede the possibility that the limitations of a finite God may inhibit him from expelling it from the universe. What I desire to do now is to consider more closely the alleged evidence for a directing mind.

The first point I wish to make may not seem to be sufficiently important to be worth stating, yet I think that it deserves our consideration. In the life of any man brought up in the theistic tradition—be he Christian, Jew, or Moslem—who takes his religion seriously and endeavors to practice it, there will in all likelihood have been certain occasions when in great distress and need he has thrown himself upon the divine mercy and has implored deliverance, and subsequent events will have fulfilled his heart's desire as though in direct response to his prayer. And there will have been certain other occasions when his need was as great, or at least appeared to him as great, or even greater, and yet events occurred seemingly in complete disregard of his desire and supplication. The skeptically inclined will say that all these occurrences were equally fortuitous, that when events are what we would wish them to be we regard them as expressions of divine favor, and when they are not as expressions of divine chastisement, but that all such beliefs are merely figments of our imagination. This is one possible explanation. Yet it is not the only possible explanation. If there be a God whose power is finite—and this is the view we have concluded to be the only tenable one—it is quite conceivable that, although always willing and anxious to help us, he might only under some circumstances be able to do so whereas in other circumstances he was unable. Between the two hypotheses, when considered only from the point of view of the individual, we have, I submit, no sufficient basis for decision. We must extend our purview as far as we can if we are to find any evidence which will justify our choice.

I propose, therefore, to take up considerations advanced by Dawes Hicks in his very thorough critique of the teleological argument. His position is one of peculiar interest to us because, unlike the majority of Christian thinkers, he believes in uncreated matter,[19] and it is only

19. See *The Philosophical Bases of Theism*, p. 199. That this was his considered opinion was quite clear to those of his pupils who discussed the subject with him. In his formulation of the teleological, as well as the cosmological, argument Hicks was obviously greatly influenced by Taylor, but in his presentation of the former these two considerations are more definitely distinguished.

the arrangement of that matter that is relevant to his first point.

"It is unquestionable," he writes, "that the conditions of inorganic nature on this planet, at least, are extraordinarily well adapted to the requirements of living organisms in their nurture and growth." [20] He finds it

> surprisingly apparent that the fundamental properties of the three chemical elements—carbon, hydrogen, and oxygen—and of certain of their compounds—water and carbonic acid—as also the wide distribution of these elements and compounds—exhibit a *maximum* of fitness for the needs of precisely such living creatures as we actually find upon this earth. Countless other distributions, countless other conjunctions of properties, would have been no less antecedently possible; and yet we find in nature just *that* distribution, just *that* conjunction of properties, which is the *fittest* for the maintenance of life. Not only so. Each and all of these many unique properties of the three elements are favourable to the process of evolution, and the connexion between them, infinitely improbable as the result of chance, is in truth only fully intelligible, even when mechanically explained, as a *preparation* for the evolutionary process.[21]

It is perhaps not amiss to ask whether, on the assumption that spirit and matter are two co-ordinate and mutually independent realities, their very disparateness would not have rendered it equally possible for life with its marvelous adaptability to utilize with equal facility collocations of very different composition. So far as I can see there is no way of answering this question in the light of our present knowledge. The facts as stated are undoubtedly impressive; and are no less so for a panpsychist than for a believer in matter, inasmuch as they suggest with equal emphasis the activity of spirit.

There is however, another objection which may with some plausibility be advanced, and to which Dawes Hicks has given a very interesting rejoinder:

> It has been maintained, for instance, that the fulfilment of the conditions referred to seem to be very local and temporary; that in all likelihood they are not fulfilled now in the greater part of the universe, that they were certainly not fulfilled in former ages on the earth itself, and that almost certainly they will cease to be fulfilled on the earth itself in the distant future. Consequently, so it has been contended, "it is not antecedently improbable that

20. *Ibid.*, p. 203.   21. *Ibid.*, pp. 203–204.

even very peculiar conditions should be fulfilled for a comparatively small region of a universe which is indefinitely extended
in space and time." [22] But none of these objections seem to me
either strong or convincing. I cannot see, for instance, what the
fact, if it be a fact, that the number of inhabited worlds in space
is comparatively small, has to do with the question. That there
should be no adaptation to living organisms in those portions of
the universe where there are none is scarcely an indication of
thoughtless negligence. The objection would only be of weight if it
were possible to point to a world on which there are living beings
but where there is no such adaptation. Furthermore, if there be
the adaptation, which admittedly there now is, of the environment to life on this planet, then clearly it must have been prepared for in the long geological ages which have preceded this,
and during the still more remote astronomical periods of the formation of the solar system. In short, you cannot cut out our tiny
portion of the universe as a definitely isolated section or region.
On the contrary, it has ramifications which extend indefinitely
far; as, if the adaptation we are considering subsists here and
now, it is certain that its conditions cannot be confined to what
is "very local and temporary," but must have extended over a
vastly wide range, both in space and time.[23]

Dawes Hicks's second point is the difficulty of accounting for the
development of life upon this planet without invoking the conception
of a purposive and directing intelligence:

Admittedly an organism is a complete system of an extremely
intricate kind, consisting of an assembly of delicately adjusted
cell-mechanisms, working co-ordinately in the most unerring manner, a system which is remarkably well adapted to preserve itself
in the presence of varying conditions. An organism is a self-
conserving system, building itself up by appropriating from its
environment suitable material, which it transforms into its own
tissue; responding continuously to changes in its surroundings by
adaptive processes; and, finally, regulating in the minutest fashion
the action of each of its parts in the interest of the whole. Now,
so long as organisms were believed to have originated in their
present forms, and with all their specialized organs "ready made,"
the notion that the adaptation of part to whole, of whole to en-

22. We are here reminded of McTaggart's run of sixes.
23. *The Philosophical Bases of Theism,* pp. 204–205.

vironment, of organ to function, implied special design in each individual case seemed not only plausible but well-nigh inevitable. But a view of that sort was at once seen to be untenable when it became evident that every organic structure has come to be what it is now as a result of a long series of successive and gradual modifications. Yet the theory of evolution has been driving those who have penetrated most profoundly into its meaning to a conception of "design" on a far larger scale than any which was contemplated by Paley. If we survey the course which evolution has taken in our comparatively small region of the cosmos, it becomes apparent that it has been in a significant direction. Through a line of species which had to adapt themselves to their environment, it has led to the emergence of an intelligent and rational being, who *adapts* his environment to himself, who largely *makes*, so to speak, his own environment, and is not wholly made by it.[24] It would seem, then, well-nigh impossible for a reflective mind to look upon this terminus of the process as a mere by-product, as a mere accident of evolution; or, indeed, as anything else than the "end" which has been all along determining the course of development. "Nature," one might almost venture to assert, really does exhibit a "trend" or "bias" to the advent of intelligence. In short, whether we have regard to the structure and functioning of individual organisms, or whether we have regard to the evolutionary process generally, we appear to be driven to the conclusion that in the organic world there is a teleological or purposive principle at work, directing and modifying what would otherwise be mechanically determined elements.[25]

It is indeed difficult, even as Dawes Hicks contends, to see in this long drawn out evolutionary process a succession of purely fortuitous occurrences. If, in the lengthy and complicated setting of the stage throughout the preceding geological periods the presence of intelligence is, as it were, masked, in the course of the development of life it seems to become increasingly apparent until at last we perceive it as genuinely dominant.

When Darwin first propounded his theory, fortified as it was by a tremendous array of evidence, adaptation to environment was loudly trumpeted as the key to the whole process of the evolution of life. Yet, to those who looked deeper, it was evident that there were

24. Here we have an echo of Taylor ("The Vindication of Religion," pp. 55–56).
25. *The Philosophical Bases of Theism*, pp. 206–207.

presuppositions which the theory itself did not account for: (1) the presence of the primal forms of life, (2) the inheritance of acquired characteristics, (3) the presence of variations among the individual members of successive generations which rendered it possible for the test of adaptability to environment to sunder the fit from the unfit, and (4) the capacity to combine in the wonderfully complex organisms of the "higher" and larger animals. In all these there appeared to be no inherent necessity, at least nothing in the nature of inanimate matter that would account for them. And when Wallace, on the basis of empirical investigation, proceeded to introduce the notion of *mutation,* the mystery deepened. Why were not the simplest forms of life content to reproduce their kind with wearisome exactitude, and whence the impetus to the prodigious development of species which seems to have terminated in man? The materialist's explanation was obviously a tour de force which could take in only the scientist blind to metaphysical considerations. And no less so was the view of non-reductive naturalism which appealed to undetermined, unnecessitated, unentailed, fortuitous "emergent" eventualities to solve all problems. Thus the argument from design does seem to be invested with a certain plausibility possessed by no other proffered solution.

Yet, when one surveys the evolutionary process since the first appearance of life on the earth, one has an uncomfortable feeling that the directing mind which is assumed to have envisaged the entire sequence of events, however powerful it may be, is deficient in goodness. When life first began to feed upon life, and the distinction between the vegetable and the animal was thereby established, what we find it hard not to regard as the primal act of immorality was committed from which all subsequent development followed. And what a development! We, supposedly the goal of the whole process, and in our own eyes certainly its supreme achievement, rational beings though we be, can keep ourselves alive only by perpetually devouring other living beings. Let not the vegetarian take to himself too much credit! The vegetables which he consumes are living beings also. How disgusting and revolting does the entire process seem when one looks at it, as it were, from an impartial point of view! Moreover, as the process develops, so does the capacity for pain and suffering. How universally present is pain, how intense the degrees in which it can be experienced, how tenacious its persistence, how brief the duration of even the greatest of physical pleasures, how uncertain our enjoyment of even the higher pleasures of the spirit!

I have presented these considerations with, perhaps, a brutal frankness which nevertheless honesty seems to require. But we must not be content to leave the matter so. While the materialist's hypothesis, as well as that of the naturalist, can definitely be set aside as inadequate to deal with the situation, the argument from design stands upon a different footing. Although it has led us into a maze of questions, we cannot simply dismiss it as an *ignis fatuus*. For it is based upon facts which have implications which cannot be ignored, but require to be clarified.

The line of reasoning which we have followed, and which has been based largely upon an a priori approach, has led us to view the universe as an intelligible and axiologically oriented system, eternal, underived, and self-existent. Shall we now follow the example of McTaggart, and dismiss the hypothesis of a directing mind as a bare possibility which can neither be established nor refuted? To answer this question we need to examine it, together with a number of closely related issues, in the light of the world view which we have adopted. I accordingly invite the interested reader to accompany me in the following chapter, which is frankly speculative, in the scrutiny of certain considerations which I hope will at least widen our perspective.

Chapter Five

A REAPPRAISAL

Let us now attempt to view the whole situation from the standpoint of axiological idealism as we have envisaged it. The word "God," as I have already said, is used in this book to designate a being conceived to be both personal and good.[1] We have also agreed that the notions both of omnipotence and of creativity must be relinquished, and that the only idea of God which may possibly prove to be tenable is that of a non-creative God whose power is limited.[2] Before we proceed further it will be well for us to inquire why the doctrine of monotheism has been regarded by Jews, Christians, and Moslems alike as providing a satisfactory answer to the highest demands of religion.

It was among the Hebrews that the doctrine of a single supreme God gradually developed, and the point of departure of this development was the belief in a God who at a definite moment in history had chosen Israel to be his people, and who had been formally acknowledged by his people as henceforth their national Deity. That he was the most powerful of all gods was at once a natural and comforting assumption, in the light of which national calamities could be interpreted as punishments for national sins and the hope of future recovery from them through divine favor could still be entertained. It is clear that at least among the people at large there was no thought of denying the existence of other gods worshipped by other peoples. The greatest impetus toward the development of a full-fledged monotheism was doubtless the ethical insight of the prophets, from which issues the conception of a holy, just, and merciful God which was vastly superior to the religious ideas of other Semitic peoples. Moreover, among some of the prophets and psalmists there are evi-

1. Believers in the doctrine of analogous predication would not, indeed, hold that God and man can both be good in a univocal sense, but they do hold that God is good *secundum modum altiorem*.

2. Such a view of the Deity is uncommon in the West, yet G. H. Howison and Edgar Sheffield Brightman were both committed to it. Dawes Hicks's theory is more complicated, for his God is the originator both of finite selves and of values, although he is not the creator of matter.

dences of a growing universalism which could only strengthen the tendency toward monotheism. The notion that the origination of the world resulted from the organizing activity of the gods who thereby imposed order upon a pre-existing chaos was an extremely widespread one among primitive man, and was certainly entertained by the Sumerians and Semites. With the expansion of the idea of the national God, it was natural that this function should be definitely ascribed to him alone; and the next step would be either to reduce all other gods to the level of his messengers or "angels," [3] or else to deny their existence altogether. And, lastly, the substitution for the notion of making of the doctrine of creation *ex nihilo* completed the process. In such a manner, if I have recounted it aright, monotheism originated.

What rendered it so highly attractive to such a large section of the human race? The reasons were no doubt manifold; let us endeavor to enumerate some of them. In the first place it imparted what I may call a feeling of "cosmic security." As St. Paul puts it, "If God be for us who can be against us?" A God mighty enough to create and control the universe can certainly aid and deliver those individuals who trust in him. And in the days of great empires the individual was assuming an increasing importance as national units were destroyed and their citizens became amalgamated in a tremendous whole. Moreover, the belief in personal immortality, which in all probability had originally been imported into Judaism from Zoroastrianism, was now associated with monotheism.[4] And this brings in a further consideration. Monotheism was not now simply propagated as a philosophical system. Greek philosophers had so presented it, and had been largely disregarded by the multitude. But in both Judaism and Christianity, as later in Islam, it was based upon a revelation presumed to be infallible and invested with absolute authority. Thus, as Justin Martyr remarks, one is saved from the wearisome task of intellectual investigation and the weighing of arguments, and has only gratefully to

3. This change of terminology tends to conceal the fact that a similar development took place in the thought of many Greek philosophers—an outstanding example being Plato—whereby the many "gods" became subordinated to the supreme Deity.

4. It might be thought that this would tend not only to attract but to repel, for, if enjoyment of an everlasting heaven were a possibility, so was suffering in an everlasting hell. Yet Justin Martyr accounts it an advantage on the part of Christianity that its hell, unlike that of the mystery religions, was unending. Still the individual could hope by leading a moral and pious life to escape hell and to attain to heaven.

accept what one is told to believe. And doubtless Justin Martyr was not alone in welcoming the assurance that intellectual effort could be dispensed with.

On the other hand, many of those who were not averse to mental effort and who were genuinely interested in metaphysical problems, found in monotheism a theory which seemed to provide a satisfactory answer to various pressing questions. The world of contingent and transitory beings was accounted for by showing its dependence upon a self-existent and necessary Being. The universe was rational, not in itself, but as expressive of the purpose of the divine Mind which was the source of the traces of order in the world. On the hypothesis of a plurality of gods, either the existence of these gods must be derived from a common source—such as a primal pair, or the world-egg—or they must be regarded as self-existent and independent entities, the powers of any one of whom were limited by those of his fellows. Monotheism gave to the universe a much closer unity than was compatible with a stark and absolute polytheism. Furthermore, the individual human being did not have to adjust his relationships with a number of supreme beings, each of whom claimed to possess sovereign rights with respect to him; beings who might make upon him irreconcilable demands, and who might fall out with one another and involve him in their mutual hostility. But in whatever circumstances he might find himself, he would always be in direct relation to the supreme power in the universe, could appeal to him for assistance, and could trust in his goodness. "If I ascend up into heaven, thou art there: if I make my bed in hell, behold thou are there. If I take the wings of the morning, and dwell in the utter most parts of the sea; even there shall thy hand lead me, and thy right hand shall hold me." [5]

It is true that if monotheism seemed to fill most wants of the religious man better than any other system antecedently devised, there were some which it did not seem to fill as well. As the conception of God expanded he seemed to become progressively more remote. The local, finite god was a near god; his holy place was perhaps in one's village, or on a neighboring mountain, or possibly a day's journey away. As the master of one's plantation, the mayor of one's town, or the governor of one's province, is more accessible than one's king, so the gods of polytheism seemed more approachable than an all-powerful Deity enthroned in the heavens, whose incomparable greatness rendered him awesome. The worship of angels in Judaism, which

5. Ps. 139:8–10.

required some effort to suppress, and saint-worship both in Christianity and Islam, bear impressive witness to this tendency. The genuine monotheist, of course, regards it as the survival of a primitive way of thinking, and as evincing a misapprehension of his position. He takes pains to assure everyone that the infinity of God renders him not the most remote but the nearest of all beings. Thus Muhammad attributes to God the statement, "We are nearer to a man than the vein in his neck." The supposed disadvantages of monotheism, it is accordingly contended, are illusory; and the acceptance of it is pure gain.

Let us now view the situation from a religious standpoint as far removed as possible from that of monotheism, and this I take to be that of Hīnayāna Buddhism. The gods, or devas, are manifold in number; they are spirits who occupy in the universe a more exalted position than our own. There is surely nothing illogical or fantastic in this conception; indeed it is a very plausible one, and quite compatible with our own world view. That we are not the highest beings in the universe is not a very startling assumption. Let us proceed, however, to contrast the Buddhist position with that of Plato in the *Phaedrus*. For Plato, as for the Buddhist, both gods and human souls are many in number. But the number in each case is, for Plato, not infinite but finite. There appears, moreover, to be a fundamental and ineradicable difference between divine and human nature. The gods indeed owe their divinity to their vision of the Forms; it is axiologically grounded, as we might say. And insofar as men are capable of sharing in this vision, they approximate to divinity. But the vision of the gods is clearer, and their capacity for indulging in it is a permanent and inalienable possession; it is, so to speak, an effortless activity. Human souls, on the other hand, experience great difficulty in attaining to this vision, and, having attained it, are in perpetual danger of losing it, of being dragged downward by the appeal of the sense-world to which they remain continually susceptible. Human nature thus bears the definite stamp of inferiority to the divine; there is a gap between the two which cannot be overpassed. Were it not so a continuous transition of souls from the human to the divine level might leave the earth depopulated of human souls, inasmuch as the number of these is finite, and the process of divinization might thus conceivably come to an end. For the Buddhist, on the contrary, the number of souls is infinite; hence a continuous trickle of souls which return to earth no more presents no difficulty.

For the Buddhist, moreover, all souls are potentially equal. Thus a man can be reborn a god, and a god can be reborn a man. Gods, as well as men, are bound to the wheel of birth and death, and, like men, stand in need of deliverance. Sojourn in one of the heavens is transitory. Heaven therefore offers no permanent refuge. We are even told that life in a heaven involves a certain danger, and that it may tempt one to self-indulgence to such a degree as to result in rebirth in one of the hells.

If anyone object that the word "god" cannot legitimately be applied to a being who himself stands in need of ultimate salvation, I shall not debate the matter with him. As a matter of fact the Buddhists have so applied it—or rather its Pali equivalent. The conception involved is not self-contradictory, nor yet devoid of a certain plausibility. But there are a number of things which can be said about it.

In the first place it might be urged that the function of a god is to benefit his worshippers, and that a being who has not himself attained salvation cannot fulfil this function. But this is to make too strong an assertion. Granted that a being who has not attained salvation cannot bestow it; it does not follow that there is nothing else that he can do. Let us remember that all the benefits which the ancient Babylonians and Israelites hoped to receive from their gods were this-worldly benefits; and while we are in this world, such benefits are not to be despised. Yet there is something more to be added. "For consider," writes Mrs. Rhys Davids, "we have to picture *here* a background, not of Vedic, Olympian almighty ones, but of brave and pious gentlemen who have passed, as 'devas,' to the next world, only to come back one day as men. We see them warding men, and also being spiritually warded by elect men, in a mutual furthering of progress in the long, long way of becoming." [6] There is surely nothing ignoble in the conception of such comradeship between the human and the superhuman.

In the second place it may be objected that any being who is still bound to the wheel of birth and death must be deficient, not only in power, wisdom, and insight, but also in moral goodness, and that to such a being the word "god" can only improperly be applied. Yet what of McTaggart's suggestion that the term may legitimately be applied to a being who is more good than bad? [7] And if the selves whose existence we are postulating have in truth ascended to a super-human level, must we not assume that they exceed in goodness even the best of human beings? This is saying a great deal. If it be the case,

6. *A Manual of Buddhism* (London, 1932), p. 92.
7. *Some Dogmas of Religion*, secs. 152, 194.

as I have suggested, that a self which has fully attained its τέλος has thereby passed beyond the realm of becoming, it is clear that such a self cannot fill the role of a Buddhist deva. Yet this is only a suggestion. We may recall McTaggart's insistence that no self can be perfected unless all selves are perfected. And in this connection it is even more relevant to envisage the Mahāyānist ideal of the Bodhisattva who refuses to enter Nirvāṇa so long as a single soul remains undelivered. The very goodness and unselfishness of such a being chains him to the temporal process. Conjoined with this ideal—and a nobler one has never been formed—is the doctrine that to attain a purely individual salvation is to enter an illusory Nirvāṇa—"the Nirvāṇa of the eye." It is clearly no moral imperfection on the part of such a being that inhibits him from passing into the changeless.

And in the third place, it may be contended that one of the chief faults of polytheism is that it involves the worshipper in a divided allegiance,[8] that it prevents him from concentrating his devotion upon any one deity lest he thereby antagonize some other power or powers. That there is some truth in this objection we must concede, yet we may point out that it applies rather to what we may call the unmitigated or unmodified polytheism of such relatively intellectually primitive peoples as the ancient Greeks, Romans, and Semites—a polytheism which regarded the structure of the universe as entirely dependent upon the fiat of a group of divinities—than to a polytheism which has as its background a world view such as ours which presupposes a self-existent and axiologically oriented Absolute. I am well aware that such a view may appear fanciful to one whose thinking has been nourished exclusively by the Judeo-Christian tradition, but since our thinking has led us rather far afield from this tradition, it will, I believe, be worth our while to push further our examination of the polytheistic hypothesis, which we indeed are logically in a better position to take seriously than are the Hīnayāna Buddhists whose thinking seems obviously to suffer from the lack of such a cosmic background.

Does not Socrates, an objector might continue, advance a very relevant consideration when in the *Euthyphro*[9] he urges that dissensions among the gods may result from conflicting judgments with respect to justice and injustice, the beautiful and the ugly, good and

8. The same objection has been advanced by the Unitarian against the doctrine of the Trinity. See Channing, *Works of William E. Channing* (Boston, 1886), pp. 387–388.

9. (New York, 1953), 7d–8e.

evil? It does not follow that the will of any of these beings should be
at fault, but only that his judgment should be in error. We are quite
familiar with situations in human life where men of the highest
character find themselves in irreconcilable opposition. We have only
to think, for example, of the American and British civil wars. Granted
that in the universe there exist beings at a higher level of development
than ourselves, superior to us in power, wisdom, and goodness yet
still progressing toward perfection, I do not see that the possibility
of such dissensions can be ruled out. Yet I do not see why it should
affect our relations to them, why we should become involved in their
controversies, why they should not extend to us assistance both in
daily life and in moral progress, nor why we should not implore such
help nor be grateful for its bestowal.

In *A Philosophical Scrutiny of Religions,* C. J. Ducasse has ventured upon the following interesting suggestions. He writes,

> If one regards as possible, and assumes as actual, the existence of
> spiritual beings not embodied, or at least not physically embodied,
> then the supposition that some of them are superhuman in a va-
> riety of degrees and of respects becomes exceedingly plausible.
> Even carrying the idea but a little way, it would then be reason-
> able to suppose, for instance, that our earth has a god of its own;
> our solar system, another god, greater in some respects and with
> functions more or less different; our galaxy, a still greater; and
> metagalaxies, if there are such, each a metatheos.[10]

He continues,

> If there are gods, then—to say nothing of devils—their relations
> to one another in the cosmos may be of any one or more kinds.
> For example, feudal, with a common allegiance to a king of the
> gods—such allegiance conditional perhaps on observance of the
> terms of a cosmic *magna charta*. Again, although the gods might
> each have greater power than any beings in his own dominions,
> yet particular gods might be contending for power with one an-
> other, might have relations of friendship or alliance with certain
> other gods, and might have no contact at all with yet others. But
> the relations among the gods could just as easily be those which
> obtain in a democracy; and a democracy among gods might well
> be as messy, even if on a bigger scale and at a higher level, as

10. (New York, 1953), p. 327.

the democracies, or indeed the monarchies, oligarchies, or other polities, which exist among men.[11]

Ducasse now proceeds to call attention to an additional point, that from the Buddhist point of view, godship, like kingship among men, is a rank or title which may be possessed successively by various individuals.[12] Thus a certain self may, in consequence of merit antecedently acquired, occupy the position of Brahma or Indra for a definite period, at the conclusion of which he relinquishes the office to another self morally and intellectually entitled to succeed him; then he is reborn in some other status. This belief is the result of two more fundamental conceptions—the notions of rebirth and of the law of Karma. We have seen that the doctrine of a plurality of lives follows inevitably from the doctrine of the persistence of the self throughout the temporal process. We have also agreed with McTaggart that the relations of love which eternally unite individuals determine the rebirth of these individuals. Yet, although the supreme value of love doubtless renders this the most potent factor, it does not follow that it is the only factor, and that the moral character of each individual is not a contributory factor. In this sense, then, we may recognize the functioning of the law of Karma in an axiologically oriented universe. But the notion of definite ranks, of divine titles or godships, each of which is occupied in turn by a succession of individuals, while compatible with our general position, cannot be deduced from it by a priori reasoning. It is no more than a logical possibility, and the belief in its actuality which is cherished by the Buddhists would seem to repose upon sayings attributed to a teacher credited with a supernormal and infallible insight into the structure of the entire universe. Hence, even should we feel inclined to agree with Ducasse in his conclusion that polytheism is "a *prima facie* more plausible and less vague form of theism than are the current monotheisms," [13] this would not obviate us from the duty of inquiring whether the hypothesis of a supreme, non-creative God may not be defensible.

To deny that God is creative, it may be maintained, commits us to the denial that he is omnipotent. But before we assent we must be clear as to what we mean by omnipotence. Do we mean the ability to perform any action whatever, whether or not the perfor-

11. *Ibid.*, pp. 327–328.
12. *Ibid.*, p. 328. Cf. J. B. Pratt, *The Pilgrimage of Buddhism* (New York, 1928), p. 6, n. 8.
13. *A Philosophical Scrutiny of Religions*, p. 328.

mance thereof involve a violation of the law of contradiction? Such
certainly is the literal sense of the word, yet the notion for which it
stands is as unintelligible as is that of creation. Indeed Professor C. D.
Broad is probably correct in saying that it is "a doctrine which has
never been held by any theologian or philospher of repute." [14] Thus
St. Thomas assures us that by calling God omnipotent we mean only
that he can do all things that are logically possible. If this assertion
be accepted, it seems clear that if we call God's power infinite we
mean no more than when we call it omnipotent. It is subject to
logical limitations. And how far do these extend? Are we in a position
to form any plausible notion of what God *can* do? Thus the libertarian,
for example, if he be a creationist, will hold that it is logically impossible for God both to create men good and to create them free,
since freedom involves the possibility of acting wrongly as well as of
acting rightly. Such a libertarian will no doubt say that God can only
create men potentially good—and, by the same token, potentially
evil. Yet can the libertarian go further, can he plausibly affirm that,
if he willed, God could constrain the wills of all men to function
precisely as he desired, and so reduce them to the status of moral
automata who "dance as he plays"? If such be the case, God will
possess a power which he *could* exercise, but which he refrains from
exercising because he is aware that the exercise thereof would prove
self-defeating. And yet, if we credit God with such a capacity, even
if unexercised, of absolute constraint, do we not thereby involve ourselves in a further difficulty? Concerning this Dawes Hicks, in his
discussion of the mystical experience, has some interesting things
to say.

> For instance, when we are told that in a condition of trance
> the mystic is conscious of being grasped by a higher power, of
> being "possessed" by an agency other than his own, so that his
> faculty of attention is no longer under his voluntary control, we
> at once begin to reflect upon the way in which one soul, one
> spiritual being, can act on or influence another. In the relation
> of mind to mind, is the exercise of force or energy psychologically
> possible? Can we really conceive of an efflux of energy from an-
> other mind operating on our minds, in the presence of which our
> minds are as passive as the wind-swept waves to the force of the
> storm? Or is not a transaction of this kind inherently meaning-

14. Introduction to McTaggart, *Some Dogmas of Religion*, p. xxxviii. For Mc-
Taggart's cogent argument that the term, if used at all, ought to be employed in
the literal sense, see *ibid.*, sec. 179.

less? . . . "To propel by external force," Principal Caird once declared, "is a thing as unintelligible and impossible as to move a stone by argument or melt a metal by affection or love." And he went on to argue that it would not be aught but simply unthinkable and absurd to conceive of God as, by any mysterious application of power, propelling a soul into goodness, or injecting convictions into a thinking mind.[15]

If we regard this passage as constituting a fair statement of the situation, how *are* we to conceive of the power of God? How is he able to perform the functions of God? How is he able to act upon us at all? Through our external environment, it may be said. And if this environment be material, God must be able to act upon matter. I have already urged that if matter be real, the hypothesis of interaction between mind and body, spirit and matter is, from a purely phenomenological point of view, by all odds the most probable one, even as it is unhesitatingly accepted by "the man in the street." And if we can act upon matter, it certainly seems plausible to suppose that God can do so too, even though we have not the least idea of *how* either God or we manage to accomplish it. I have also urged, however, that the notion of matter is progressively becoming more vague and more elusive, that from being a stuff it is becoming transformed into energy, and that the notion of energy will be found to be even more vague and more elusive unless it be identified with volitional activity. It is for this reason that I have suggested that panpsychism presents us with the most plausible theory. If there be anything in this suggestion, then interaction between mind and mind, spirit and spirit, or monad and monad must be posited, however mysterious it may be.

What really goes on behind the screen of appearances? We can all pluck flowers and hurl stones and act upon, and be acted upon by, the bodies of our fellow men. If the reality behind these appearances be psychical in nature, then interaction on the psychical level is possible and actual. Is it going too far to suggest that action directed upon monads or selves possessed of a very low degree of consciousness is more direct and efficacious than that directed upon selves which have attained the level of personality—that is, upon selves endowed with a far greater clarity of awareness both of themselves and of their environment, with a corresponding greatness of capacity for emotion and volition—and thus that our relative independence of

15. *The Philosophical Basis of Theism*, pp. 120–121.

God which Hicks affirms, if it be a fact, is due to our greater spiritual maturity and relative self-sufficiency? This does not seem to me an implausible theory. And it does not follow, surely, that God is totally unable to influence us, but that he cannot reduce us to complete passivity, that our relation to him is one of voluntary co-operation—of persuasion and not of constraint, as Plato and Whitehead would say.

I have warned the reader that this chapter would be frankly speculative, and if he have had the patience to follow me, he will hardly complain that I have misled him. We have been considering hypotheses, their self-consistency, and their implications. And now, continuing in the same vein, I would raise another question. Granted the existence of God, what of his relation to time?

Can we conceive of God as eternal—that is, as timeless? Aquinas and the other great scholastics, together with the majority of Christian theologians, have professed to do so. But how have they gone about it? How has St. Thomas, the most eminent of them all, proceeded? In the first place he assumes that the entire world is composed of contingent entities and argues that all these must depend for their existence upon a necessary being. This dependence he equates with the state of being created by this necessary being. Yet creation involves no change in this being. By a timeless act God brings the world into existence. The notion of a timeless act is, of course, as flat a self-contradiction as anything can be—that is if we take the verbal expression literally. But this would be unfair to St. Thomas. What he clearly means is that by a changeless volitional state God wills the entire world process. Thus we must not suppose, for example, that upon the offering of a particular prayer God decides whether or not to grant it. The offering of the prayer, together with the granting or the refusal of it, are involved in the world process, all the events of which are timelessly willed to occur. This would seem to involve a complete determinism,[16] and, so I think, it really does. Moreover, the fact that the temporal process had a beginning, and does not extend ad infinitum into the past, cannot—according to St. Thomas, who here follows Maimonides—be demonstrated by philosophers, but is known only through revelation.

16. St. Thomas resorts to the following line of defense. From the point of view of time an act which is entailed by an antecedent act is necessitated, whereas an act not so entailed is free. Thus when a man acts freely, his act is not determined by any other event in time. Yet this does not mean that it *might* not have occurred, for all events are what they are because they are willed so to be by God. When a man acts of necessity, he so acts because God so wills; and when he acts freely, again he so acts because God so wills, and he acts precisely as God wills. If this be not determinism, what is it?

If the doctrine of creation *ex nihilo* be rejected, the whole theory falls. And fall, I think, it does. I have already admitted, however, that there is a certain similarity between it and the theory which, under the inspiration of MacKenzie, has been developed in this book, in that both theories regard the temporal process as arising out of the eternal. I would call attention, nonetheless, to the fact that on our view the temporal process is not initiated by any state of divine volition but arises because of the eternal relations of positive and negative obligation between eternal selves and eternal values and disvalues. The history of each self does indeed consist of states which it has acquired by the instantiation of universals which it had not before instantiated—as well as by ceasing to instantiate universals which it had before instantiated—yet in all this there is no coming into existence of anything *ex nihilo*. I believe, therefore, that our theory is free from the difficulties which beset the scholastic doctrine.

On this view, however, if we posit an eternal God, certain untoward consequences will follow. In the first place, although wholly actual, he will be unable to act; for while actuality can be changeless, action involves change, and change temporality. And in the second place, God will be unable to perceive what is occurring in time; for his perception that event *p* is occurring *now* will succeed his previous perception that event *o* is occurring *now*, and this likewise will involve him in temporality. Such a God, accordingly, would be as remote from us as are the Buddhas after they have attained Nirvāṇa. And it seems clear that worship of such a being, who is incapable of response, would express only the emotion of the worshipper, as does the homage offered to Gotama by intelligent Hīnayānists. It may be remarked, moreover, that in the case of Gotama, his state of change-less aloofness is believed to have been attained in consequence of countless lives and countless sufferings in the past, and that this belief makes it possible for the disciple to regard him as an ideal; whereas this will not be true of an eternal God whose aloofness is without beginning.

As a result of these reflections does it not seem plain that if we are to posit a being who can carry out the functions normally ascribed to a God, we must conceive of him, not as a changeless, but as a sempiternal being, as living throughout the entire temporal process? So much, indeed, in our view is true of all selves. Yet may we not assume that God would be exempt from recurrent birth and death? And may we not with equal plausibility ascribe to him omniscience, together with a power which, although subject to limitations, is co-extensive with the universe? Such a doctrine would carry with it

certain advantages, although it would also engender certain difficulties. Let us look first at the advantages.

On this theory the universe, in its temporal manifestation, will be
more closely integrated than on any other view. For such a God will
be approachable everywhere and everywhen. To him Avicenna's
phrase, the "primal administrator" will be thoroughly applicable. As
I have already indicated, the question of the existence of such a God,
from the general point of view which we have adopted, is of greater
importance for the libertarian than for the determinist. Let us glance
at McTaggart's universe which, like our own, is axiologically oriented,
yet, unlike our own, is completely determined. In it no event could be
other than it is, nor could it fail to occur; no free act on the part of
a God could accelerate, even as no free act on the part of any other
intelligence could retard, the inevitable advance of the temporal
process toward its termination in a final state whereof the value will
be infinite. In our universe, on the other hand, although its axiological
orientation constitutes a definite "set" which cannot be altered, progress toward the ultimate goal does not proceed with the same complete inevitability as in McTaggart's world. Contingency enters in,
since we regard the temporal process, although finite in length, as
real, and its origination as connected with the fact that genuine
moral goodness or evil must be freely chosen. We learn from experience that human beings can help or hinder, benefit or harm, one
another. If there exist beings greater and better than ourselves, we
cannot suppose that they regard us with indifference. And if there
exist a supreme Being, excelling all others in goodness and power,
we may confidently assume that his benevolent activity will be exerted wherever and whenever possible. While his ability to help us
will be limited, of his desire do so there can be no question. Such a
being will be worthy of all the admiration that we can bestow upon him
and of all the trust that we can repose in him, and could well be the
object of profound devotion. Theistic philosophers have frequently
treated with contempt the notion of a finite God, yet, as we examine
it, how can we fail to come to the conclusion that it is morally superior to the idea of an almighty and inscrutable Deity, and that it
contains elements of genuine grandeur? [17]

Let us now consider the difficulties which this hypothesis raises.
In the first place, is the assumption that God is involved in the

17. Some of these advantages, although in a lesser degree, would be retained
were we to acquiesce in the hypothesis suggested by Ducasse that there may be a
"god of this planet."

temporal process compatible with our ascription to him of moral perfection? A Bodhisattva may be conceived as voluntarily remaining in the world of time after he has attained perfection and is able to pass into Nirvāṇa, yet his perfection has been acquired in time. But can we conceive of unacquired, native, effortless, and absolute perfection, or is the notion a contradiction in terms? We maintain that the temporal process arises out of moral obligations which require time for their fulfilment. While we regard selves as eternally endowed with certain characteristics, such as spirituality, substantiality, consciousness, we have not included moral goodness or evil among them; these by their very nature, we have contended, must be acquired by free choice. Can we make an exception in the case of God without repudiating our own doctrine? Of course, if our doctrine be erroneous, we ought to repudiate it. Yet it has been developed by a priori arguments resting upon propositions which appeared to us self-evident, whereas the existence of God is as yet, so far as we are concerned, only a hypothesis, and it takes more than a hypothesis to overthrow an argument.

Is there any sense, we must therefore ask, in talking of a moral perfection which is not acquired by effort? Mazzini, a religious thinker of no mean order, believed that there is. "We are free," he writes, "because imperfect; called to ascend, to *deserve*, and therefore, to choose between good and evil; between sacrifice and egotism. Such free will as ours is unknown to God, the perfect Being, whose every act is necessarily identical with the True and the Just; who cannot, without violation of our every conception of His nature, be supposed to break His own law." [18] Moral perfection, therefore, for Mazzini involves absolute determinism and the absence of freedom of choice.

Some of us may find this rather hard to swallow. To realize fully how hard it is, however, we cannot do better than hear what our New England theologian and philosopher, William Ellery Channing, has to say about the perfection of Christ. The presupposition which, Channing assumes, will be granted by all Unitarians, Arians and Humanitarians alike, is the moral perfection of the Christ whose life is recorded in the Gospels; and the argument he brings to bear against the Humanitarians is that, on their view, this perfection is nothing but a sham. He declares,

Make the mind of Jesus a machine—i.e., suppose it placed

18. See his open letter to the Vatican Council of 1870, "From the Council God," trans. L. Martineau and published in *Fortnightly Review*, I (June, 1870). the Everyman edition of his *Essays*, p. 205.

under influences which it could not resist, suppose it to be visited with such continued instruction and suggestion from God as to render its own exertions needless—suppose it to have motives urged upon it by omnipotence, which it could not withstand, and though faultless, he could have no moral worth, no virtue, no greatness.

Christ's peculiar powers, revelations, and connections with God, instead of causing, determining and fixing his character, were on the contrary the effects, results, and recompenses of his character. Instead of making him pure, they were founded on his purity. He was clothed with all his high office, because he was endued with high virtue. He won his glory by his goodness. In saying this, I say of Jesus what I conceive to be true of all beings in all worlds.[19]

Now it is true enough that we do not conceive of divine perfection as due to aid received from a superior power, inasmuch as we conceive of God as superior to all beings, and of his nature as ultimate and self-sufficient. But this is irrelevant to the fundamental question. Is genuine moral perfection compatible with the absence of freedom of choice? If we answer this question in the negative, must we also venture to assert that such faultlessness "could have no moral worth, no virtue, no greatness?" Yet need we return a negative answer? Is the possession of free will compatible with moral perfection? Can we not conceive of a being whose insight is so penetrating, whose emotion is so exalted, and whose volition is so powerful that he will always clearly see and freely choose the right? To this the determinist may well object that we have only restated his position in different language, and that the distinction between his position and ours is purely verbal. Although conceiving is one activity and imagining is another, at this altitude they tend to become confused, and the limitations of our own finitude may well make us hesitant to answer questions the full meaning of which we find it difficult to grasp. But there is a difficulty which is even more obvious.

On our view we find ourselves, as it were, precipitated into time because of the moral obligations laid upon us and the goal which is set for us. But it would be absurd to suppose that a perfect being was precipitated into time. The suggestion that a perfect being should embark upon a struggle to attain perfection is sheer nonsense.

Philosophy of William Ellery Channing (New York, 1952), p. 165. observe how closely Channing's view of Christ approaches the conception of a bodhisattva. In each case struggle in previous lives is necessary antecedent of a state of moral perfection.

If God enter the temporal process, then he must do so voluntarily. Yet this would seem clearly to imply the formation of a definite decision—that is, the performance of a mental act—*before* God has entered into time; and the notion of a non-temporal act is sheer self-contradiction. It is not self-contradictory to suppose that a bodhisattva might voluntarily linger in the realm of time even after he has attained perfection, because he has always been in time, and his perfection has been acquired in time. But it seems clear that a being whose perfection is unacquired must be non-temporal. Thus we find ourselves thrown back upon a position which we have already investigated and found to be, if not untenable, at least very difficult to make any sense of. The Bodhisattva ideal, on the other hand, is quite intelligible, and is also quite compatible with our conception of the systemic structure and axiological "set" of the universe.

Let us now turn to another difficulty in connection with the notion of unacquired and absolute moral perfection. The tradition that God is properly the supreme object of love is, indeed, an ancient one; for it goes back to a period antedating the rise both of Christianity and of Islam. Its origin was, in fact, twofold. On the one hand it is derived from Plato, whose attitude toward human affections appears to have been extraordinarily ambivalent,[20] and on the other hand there is the Old Testament commandment—reiterated by Jesus—that we love the Lord our God with all our heart and soul and strength and mind. Thus Greek philosophy and Semitic theology united to generate the fundamental doctrine of both Christianity and Islam. And by some later theologians this way of thinking was carried so far as to lead to the assertion that the only justification for directing the emotion of love toward creatures is that God so desires, and, consequently, that to do so is to obey the divine will. It is safe to say that such a doctrine could have been developed only within the walls of monasteries and nunneries, and by individuals who had cut themselves off from all human ties. And it is at complete variance with our identification of love as such with the highest value.

It is sometimes urged that such all-absorbing devotion is fittingly directed upon God because God created us, and because the relationship of creature to Creator is closer and stronger than any relationship between creature and creature. But the manly words of Channing—as sincere a believer in creation as ever lived—may lead

20. It is true that it is the good in itself and the beautiful in itself that Plato regards as the proper objects of supreme devotion, but in later thought these became fused with the concept of God.

us, if we hearken to them, to view the matter in a different light. "It is not because He is our Creator merely," he declares, "but because He created us for good and holy purposes; it is not because His will is irresistible, but because his will is the perfection of virtue, that we pay him allegiance. We cannot bow before a being, however great and powerful, who governs tyrannically. We respect nothing but excellence, whether on earth or in heaven. We revere not the loftiness of God's throne, but the equity and goodness in which it is established." [21]

If this be true, if it be because the divine power is totally fused with the divine goodness that God is the appropriate object of whole devotion, cannot the believer in a non-creative God experience this emotion as genuinely as the most convinced creationist? But, if there exist a Being of supreme goodness and beauty, and if it be possible to enter into personal relations with him, and to apprehend in some degree his supernal excellence, is it not inevitable that emotion thus aroused will, as it were, sweep us away, so that all earthly ties will appear relatively insignificant? [22] And will not this hold true, not only of the monk in his monastery or of the theologian in his study, but of every theist who appreciates the genuine significance of what he believes?

Such, in my opinion, was the considered opinion of McTaggart, despite the fact that explicit statement of it is not to be found in his published works. In support of my belief I would cite the following excerpt from one of his letters.

It can't be nice to believe in God I should think. It would be horrible to think that there was anyone who was closer to one than one's friends. I want to feel, and I do feel, that my love for them and the same love that other people have for their friends is the only real thing in the world. I have no room left in my life for God, or rather my life is full of God already. I should say, as the Mahometan girl did in Kipling's story, "I bear witness that there is no God save thee, my beloved." [23]

This outburst reveals very clearly the fundamental incompatibility which McTaggart believed to obtain between his estimate of love as such as the supreme value and the orthodox theist's estimate of love

21. *Works*, p. 376, col. 2.

22. In this respect Channing, at least in certain moods, was prepared to go as far as the majority of theists. "The nearest friend," he writes, "the most loving parent, is but a stranger to us, when contrasted with God" (*Works*, p. 957, col. 2).

23. See G. Lowes Dickinson, *J. McT. E. McTaggart* (Cambridge, 1931), p. 87.

for God as the supreme value. And it presents the philosopher of religion with one of his most basic problems. Yet, it may be asked, has not McTaggart gone too far? The love of a friend, although it takes all there is of one, is not all-absorbing in the sense that it incapacitates one for loving other friends. Do not psychoanalysts tell us that love for any one individual increases our capacity for loving others? Why may not God be loved as a friend? [24] But this raises yet another question. Is it possible to love God as one Person among other persons? Does not his unique position demand a unique devotion? And yet will such unique devotion be love in a univocal sense of the word, or only something resembling it?

Leaving these questions aside for the moment, let us look at the situation from another point of view. If God be a Person possessed of transcendent goodness, will not his love be of an intensity beyond our powers of imagination? And what will be the objects of his love? What can they be except beings vastly inferior to him? We all know how intense the love of "inferior" selves can be. Children can be loved at least as intensely as adults, despite the fact that their strength and intelligence are so markedly inferior. True enough, we know and rejoice in the fact that such inferiority will pass away as they attain maturity. But what of the love of animals? Any genuine lover of pets—especially of "man's oldest friend," the dog—knows how strong and deep such an affection can be, and how fascinating and rewarding it is, when one treats these "lower" selves as persons, to see them respond, and how precious their companionship can be. Is it after this fashion that we must try to conceive of God's love for man? Yet it is surely relevant to question whether such love could be wholly satisfying. Does this consideration point in the direction of a polytheism such as that suggested by Ducasse? At least we may observe that the tendency among Trinitarians, perpetually present although perpetually repressed, to transform their doctrine into some form of tritheism strongly indicates that we have here a real problem.

In this connection it will be relevant to advert to an interesting suggestion of McTaggart's. Although, in accordance with his firm conviction as to the unreality of time, he maintains that it is impossible that any God should actually control the universe, it is, he insists, a genuine possibility that there might be a self who, *sub specie temporis,* appeared to control the universe. I shall let him state the case in his own words.

24. In this connection it may be recalled that one of the favorite Sufi names for God is "the Friend."

We saw that the possibility of any self appearing as a creative God was destroyed by the fact that, *sub specie temporis,* the first moments of the existence of all selves must be taken as simultaneous, and that therefore no self could appear as prior to any other self, and consequently could not appear as his cause. But for a self to appear as a controlling God, it would only be necessary that his volitions should appear as earlier than the events which fulfilled them. And this can happen, and does happen.

From the point of view of our present experience there are persons whose volitions are viewed as being the causes of events. And from this point of view we may say that some of them influence events more than others—that Napoleon, for example, influenced the history of Europe more than one of his grenadiers influenced it. Now it is not impossible that there may be a person of whom, from this standpoint, we might say that his influence was so great that it affected the whole course of the universe, as much as, or more than, Napoleon's influence affected the action of the French army at Austerlitz. And if a person of this sort were also good, he would be a person who, from the standpoint of which we speak, would be regarded as a controlling God.

I see no reason why there should not be such a person—a person who was not a God, but who, *sub specie temporis* and from the standpoint of our present experience, appeared as a controlling God. And such an appearance would be a *phenomenon bene fundatum.* The statement that there was a God would not be true, but it would have as close a relation to the truth as the statements that there are mountains in Switzerland and that thunder follows lightning.[25]

Here we have a curious inversion of the ancient Christian doctrine of deification. Instead of created selves gradually becoming deiform we should have an apparent God gradually becoming reduced to the status of one self among other selves. Of course, we could not accept McTaggart's suggestion without modification, inasmuch as we acknowledge the reality of time. Our temporal process has a real beginning; it is true that all selves enter upon it together, and that, consequently, no self "can appear as prior to any other self." But for us progress in time will be real and not apparent progress; hence the suggestion that one self may so outstrip all others as to rise to a position of unique greatness which may enable it to exercise some degree of control over the whole universe must be taken as stating a genuine

25. *The Nature of Existence,* Vol. II, sec. 496.

possibility. The status of such a being would be not apparent but real; and perhaps it would be appropriate to describe him as a temporal God.

McTaggart does not consider that the belief in such a being as he hypothetically postulates would have much religious value, for he thinks that a "religious emotion" must spring from a belief which is held to be absolutely true, whereas the existence of such a God would be only, as he has said, a *phenomenon bene fundatum*.[26] McTaggart does not tell us explicitly what a religious emotion is, but since he has defined religion as "an emotion resting on a conviction of a harmony between ourselves and the universe at large," [27] it would seem that it must be an emotion suffused with feelings of confidence, peace, and joy, and directed upon an axiologically oriented universe—that is, upon the Absolute. And a like emotion can be generated in our own case, and for the same reason. But the Absolute is not a person. And if the noblest of all emotions be love, there seems no reason why this should not be directed upon McTaggart's apparent God, and with even more justification upon our own temporal God, if such a being exist. It will of course be recognized that in thus modifying McTaggart's hypothesis I have done little more than restate in Western terminology the Bodhisattva ideal.

McTaggart urges that the argument from design, which is so frequently employed in support of the belief in a real God, could equally well be used in defense of the theory of an apparent God. He holds, however, for reasons already familiar to us, that in each case it is devoid of efficacy because (1) the universe is an ordered system and (2) because it is so ordered as to progress *sub specie temporis* toward the realization of very great good. The only question for us to consider is whether the fact that whereas McTaggart denies the reality of time and of free will we concede the reality of both renders the argument more cogent in our case than in his. Our universe, like his, is axiologically oriented; and its general structure no intelligence, however exalted, can alter. Yet in present experience we observe that the actions of individuals can do much, sometimes a great deal, to accelerate or retard the moral progress of their fellows. If there exist beings more powerful than we, the same doubtless holds true of them. And if there exist a being superior to all others, it is quite conceivable that his actions may affect the entire universe. Those who accept the teleological argument as sound believe that they can detect evidences of divine volition.

26. *Ibid.*, sec. 497.   27. *Some Dogmas of Religion*, sec. 3.

Such evidences will appear easier to detect to those who hold that the structure which the universe possesses is not inherent within it but is imposed upon it by a directing Mind. Thus adherents of the Nyāya-Vaiśeṣika philosophy feel justified in positing the existence of Iśvara because they hold that the law of Karma requires an Intelligence to enforce it. And they so believe because their universe is not in itself axiologically oriented. We, however, are not in a position to advance such a hypothesis. If all selves, as we maintain, be uncreated and sempiternal, the doctrine of a plurality of lives seems inevitably to follow. Some principle determinative of rebirth, then, there must be; but this we seem clearly to find in the acquired character of each self and its eternal relationships with other selves. The facts to which Dawes Hicks has pointed in his discussion of the teleological argument are both interesting and impressive. Yet can we feel confident that they reveal the activity of a directing Mind, and that they are not merely involved in the general "set" of the universe toward the actualization of a state of perfection, and are thus included in its progressive development? We have examined with especial interest the witness of religious experience because this seemed to offer the best hope of arriving empirically at some definite conclusion, but the result of our inquiry has been disappointing.

In this chapter we have raised a host of questions, and have considered a number of hypotheses with a view to determining whether they be self-consistent and can claim some degree of plausibility, but there seems to be no way of establishing any one of them empirically. The best that we can do, I think, is to test them by their compatibility with the conception of the Absolute which we developed in Book II. But to do this we need first to raise another question the answer to which, if we can reach an answer, will shed considerable light upon the others.

Are there among selves, as Plato appears to have believed, ultimate and ineradicable differences in respect of intellectual and moral capacity, and are these differences conserved in the final state when the process of becoming has terminated? Does the eternal society of selves thus constitute a hierarchy, whether aristocratic or monarchical? Is the goal which each self can attain relative to its native capacity which can, indeed, from being potential become actual, but which yet falls within definite limits which can never be overpassed? And if this be true of rational selves—or of selves which are more or less rational—do we find below them a spiritual proletariat composed of selves permanently deprived of rationality, and perhaps even of sensibility? Or is there truth in the grand vision of those Mahāyānists who assure us that in every blade of grass there are souls which will attain Nirvāṇa? Are all differences in degrees of capacity gradually eliminated in the temporal process, and does the society of selves in the final state constitute a democracy in which each individual is an aristocrat?

On the former hypothesis the ineradicable differences among selves will constitute so many "brute facts." But "brute facts" are out of place in a rational universe. Shall we then question the rationality of the universe? McTaggart has shown us very clearly what will follow.[28] We must fall back, in the first place, upon the conception of a universe which is partly rational and partly irrational; and we must posit between the rational and irrational principles an eternal equipoise whereof no cause can be discovered and whereof experience vouchsafes no evidence, so that the rational will not gain upon the irrational nor the irrational upon the rational. This is the position of a metaphysical tightrope walker—or rather of a somnambulist who may awaken to his own undoing. From this we must inevitably retreat further; we must boldly assert that the universe is fundamentally irrational, and that such evidences of rationality as it manifests are delusive appearances. We see pretty plainly whither this will carry us—to the position of the nominalist, to that of the denier of objective values, to that of the adherent of the regularity view of causality. Even so, will there not be laws of logic which hold good always and everywhere? These must obviously be explained away as so many empirical generalizations. But by now we shall as nearly as possible have committed intellectual suicide. From the belief that the universe is rational there is, then, no escape except by a refusal to think at all.

If the universe be rational, however, the presence of "brute facts" cannot be admitted. It is quite true that some facts may quite possibly appear "brute" to us only because their underlying rationality has not been detected, but to say this is only to admit that our own understandings are fallible. If we are to think at all, we must try to think rationally. Now there seems to be nothing in the nature of the universe, so far as we have been able to explore it, which would account for the presence of ultimate and ineradicable differences between selves. But we can very well conceive that there might be differences which are transient, and which are due to causes the efficacy of which will finally be exhausted. In present experience we are aware that a powerful intellect may through some mishap, through accident or

28. *Studies in Hegelian Dialectic* (New York, 1922), chap. v.

disease, be reduced practically to an animal or even to a vegetal level, and we are also aware that recoveries from such calamities frequently occur. If all selves enter upon the temporal process endowed with equal capacities, we may confidently anticipate that the lot of each self will be profoundly affected by the manner in which these capacities are employed, that those who fulfil their moral obligations will advance toward their goal, and that those who disregard or rebel against them will recede from it.

I have already several times adverted to the great advantage enjoyed by the position of the libertarian in that it makes clear how the rationality and goodness of the whole is compatible with the presence of irrationality and evil in the parts. But it is absurd, some one may object, to suppose that a subrational self is capable of acknowledging any moral obligations, or ordering its conduct with respect to them. I might point out in passing that the boundary line between rationality and subrationality cannot be defined with a mathematical precision, and that the majority of animals, while they must kill to eat like ourselves, seem to display a general decency which contrasts very favorably with the conduct of a large number of our own species. Yet I should admit that it would be preposterous to suppose that a mosquito, for example, consciously holds before itself the ideal of what a good mosquito should be. But it is not preposterous, I maintain, to hold that those selves which exist at a subrational level do so as a consequence of having antecedently misused their capacities as rational selves. This supposition seems quite in accord with what we might expect in an axiologically oriented universe. And if such be the case, we might reasonably assume that their present condition is only transient, and that in due course of time, having risen again to a rational level, these same selves will find themselves once more invested with the power of free choice.

In the preceding paragraphs I have merely restated in my own way the doctrine of Karma. It is certainly not to the discredit of this doctrine that it has been accepted for more than two millennia by the vast majority of Hindu thinkers, and I venture to affirm that it is a more rational doctrine than the belief in immortality as held by the average Christian or Muslim. And the philosopher who holds it may well look with satisfaction upon his temporal pilgrimage as one in which it is his business, in the words of Kipling, "To learn and discern of his brother, the clod, / Of his brother the brute, and his brother the God." [29] In other words an equalitarian view of the fundamental capacities of all selves is quite compatible with a very inequalitarian

29. "A Song of Kabir" (see *Jungle Book,* Vol. II).

view of their temporal relations to each other. The relations of deity to humanity, of humanity to animality, and of animality to vegetality will, on this hypothesis, be instantiated only within the temporal process, and will find their *relata* in temporal transformations; they will no longer hold when the process has terminated.

We are justified, I would urge, in returning this answer to our question because it is quite compatible with the conception of a rational universe which we have developed, whereas the alternative answer is not. And it is obvious that this conclusion will affect our attitude toward the various questions we have raised in this chapter, for its implications are plainly unfavorable to the conventionally Western point of view. It is clear that the notion of a temporal God or Gods bears a closer relationship to the Bodhisattva ideal than to the theism of Christianity, Judaism, or Islam. I do not see that our position gives us a basis sufficient [30] for deciding the question whether the temporal hierarchy culminates in a single Intelligence better and more powerful than all others, or in a group of beings who have attained perfection, and who thus constitute what we might call a cosmic aristocracy. Our view, however, is quite consistent with our evaluation of love, for it permits us to envisage the final state of "participated eternity" as one in which relations of superiority and inferiority have passed away, and in which all selves are directly or indirectly connected by the relation of love.

[*Note*] In my discussion of theism I have not thought it necessary to enter upon an examination of the scholastic doctrine of analogous predication. (I have gone into the subject at considerable length in *Conception of God in the Philosophy of Aquinas,* chaps. v, viii; *Philosophy of William Ellery Channing,* chap. iii; and *Introduction to the Philosophy of Religion,* chap. viii.) The reason is that it seems to me as evident as anything can well be that a theism which does not maintain that the qualities of God are, in Channing's terminology, *essentially the same* as human qualities, "though differing in degree, in purity, and in extent of operation," is not worth defending.[31] A God whom we can love and trust must himself love in the same sense in

30. Thus the teleological argument might as plausibly be employed to defend Ducasse's hypothesis of a "god of this planet," or his further hypotheses of a "god of our solar system" or a god "of our galaxy," as to sustain that of a "metatheos."

31. Channing has put the whole question in a nutshell: "We know not and we cannot conceive of any other justice or goodness than we learn from our own nature; and if God have not these, He is altogether unknown to us as a moral being; He offers nothing for esteem and love to rest upon; the objection of the infidel is just, that worship is wasted, 'we worship we know not what' " (*Works,* p. 464, col. 1).

which a man loves, and must himself be good in the same sense in which a man can be good. If I had yielded to the temptation to discuss the whole topic afresh this book would have expanded to such proportions that the reader who has had the patience to follow me thus far would probably have given up in despair. I have preferred, therefore, to treat of questions which impress me as of genuine interest and importance, and about which I felt that there was something fresh to be said.

CONCLUSION

At the termination of this extended inquiry let me summarize the principal points which I have tried to make, and the contentions which I have sought to maintain. In Book I we examined the nature of religion and its relation to philosophy. We found that McTaggart's definition of religion was fairly satisfactory, but arrived at the conclusion that it might be improved by extending it to include not only an emotion but also the beliefs which give rise to it and the conduct which follows from it. We also concluded that in religion and philosophy alike man seeks to adjust himself to his universe; consequently, between them there is a fundamental identity whereas their differences are superficial. And we saw that the only way of establishing the truth of religion is by a process of metaphysical inquiry.

This task we undertook in Book II. The position there developed rests upon two pillars: (1) selves as eternal subjects and their temporal sempiternity and (2) the objective reality of universals, including values and disvalues; the two pillars are connected by internal relations of positive and negative obligation between selves and values on the one hand and selves and disvalues on the other, together with the counter-relations of positively obliging between values and selves and negatively obliging between disvalues and selves. Of the various forms of epistemology, that termed by Professor Broad the "multiple relation theory of appearing" we adopted as the most satisfactory. This view is compatible with panpsychism, and I have maintained that of the various ontological theories it is the one which is most in keeping with our general position, although I do not claim to have demonstrated it. Moreover, we developed a doctrine of time as arising out of the relations of selves to values and disvalues, as necessary for the exercise of free will and the consequent instantiation of moral values and disvalues, and as subtended—so to speak—by the eternal, a theory which seemed free from the difficulties besetting other views.

In Book III we undertook to investigate the problem of God. I postponed the treatment of this problem to the conclusion of our inquiry because it is my conviction that the nature of the Absolute must, if possible, first be determined, and that the problem of God can profitably be examined only in the light of conclusions thus reached. How satisfactory my treatment of it has been the reader must judge.

It is obvious that there are important problems connected with religion upon which we have not even touched, or have barely referred to. There is the relation of religion to history, a topic the consideration of which would require an examination of the various philosophies of history in the light of the philosophy of religion. And there is the kindred problem of the relation of the philosophy of religion to the philosophy of politics. These and other inquiries we have been compelled to leave aside, but I hope at some future time to publish my views with regard to them.

INDEX

INDEX

A.E. (quoted), 410
Abraham, 30
Absalom, 7
Absolute, 204–205, 213, 245, 415, 442n, 449, 454, 482, 492, 499, 512, 516; in axiological idealism, 408, 450, 452–453, 507, 533, 554; experience of the, 470–471, 502; nature of, 511, 548
Abu-Sofian, 431
Ācārya, Kunda-kunda, 259n
acosmism, 481
act, 151–153, 154, 178; being as, 361; definition of, 247–248; and free will, 538n
action: abstinence from, 48, 52, 276; right and wrong, 273–275; selfhood and, 403n; *see also* conduct
Adams, John, 255
Advaita Vedānta, 45n, 84, 391n, 395, 397, 398, 442n, 444, 446, 461, 481
aesthetics, 407, 465; religion and, 468–469; value and, 262–264, 266, 269, 273, 290, 293; *see also* art; beauty; pleasure
Africa, 7, 453
afterlife, 439; *see also* Heaven; immortality; postexistence; sempiternity; Sheol
Ahab, king of Israel, 104
Ājivaka sect, 427
Akbar, emperor of Hindustan, 187n
Alcibiades, 420
Alexander, Samuel, 45, 132, 319–320, 323, 335, 347–348, 349
Alexander the Great, 171
Amidism, 67, 80n
Amṛtacandra, 259n
Anabaptism, 59n
analogous predication, doctrine of, 551
Anaxagoras, 316
angels, 87, 181, 438, 483, 494, 529, 530
animatism, 34, 69, 441
animism, 70, 439, 442
Annam, 47
annihilation: creation and, 437, 443;

selfhood and, 35, 37, 38, 40–41, 43, 295–296, 446
Anselm, Saint, 81, 82, 479–482 *passim*, 484–485, 490, 491, 497, 498
anthropology, 20, 21, 439, 441f, 478
anthropomorphism, 14, 26, 103, 104, 156, 277, 281, 382, 441
antinomianism, 53
antinomies, 223, 224, 470
Antisthenes, 255
Apostles' Creed, 440n
appearance, 358; classes of, 325–327; evil and, 421; misperception and, 362; particulars and, 350–351, 357; reality and, 173, 179, 195, 225, 306, 318, 328, 352, 354, 358, 365–366, 481, 537; time as, 375; *see also* multiple inherence; multiple relation
Aquinas, Saint Thomas, 80, 99–100, 408, 460; on divine perfection, 498, 499; on God, 14, 438, 462n, 477, 488–495 *passim*, 497, 503, 504–505, 536, 538, 551; on reason, 145–146; on revelation, 81–82; on time, 390, 391; on truth, 86, 178; on universals, 168, 291, 481
Aralu, 15, 439
Arianism, 541
Aristotelianism, 208, 229, 237, 240, 244, 382, 484
Aristotle, 53, 70, 229; on causation, 438; on evil, 282; on God, 41, 90–91, 399, 443, 444; on species, 250
Armstrong, D. M., 320
art: religion and, 59, 64–65, 467, 468; revelation and, 101
Arvars, 446
Asaṅga, 203, 264
asceticism, 65
aseity, 132, 135, 136, 138, 154, 384n
Assyria, ancient, 15, 43
Āstika philosophies, 395, 396
atheism, 435, 463; Aristotle and, 443; Buddhist, 203, 469; Christianity and, 442n; in Indian religion, 16, 35, 56, 61, 96, 396, 397, 456, 469; Plato on,